The Urbanization

of America

An Historical Anthology

Edited with introductions by
Allen M. Wakstein

Houghton Mifflin Company • Boston
New York • Atlanta • Geneva, Illinois • Dallas • Palo Alto

To Marilyn

Acknowledgments

The impetus for this effort arose from the desire of my undergraduate and graduate students at Boston College to have these readings in a convenient form. Their response to the material and their intellectual demands over the past five years played an important role in making me aware of the kind of book that would contribute to their study of American urban history. I am indebted to the authors and publishers who have granted permission to reprint the material in this volume. I wish also to thank Frank Shelton, Susan Granoff, and Vallance Wickens, of Houghton Mifflin, whose enthusiasm and advice were very helpful. Several of my colleagues at Boston College and its Institute of Human Sciences, particularly Richard C. Bolan, offered helpful suggestions which contributed to the broadening of my approach to urban history. Joseph Doria, my graduate assistant, was industrious in the preparation of the manuscript. Finally, I wish to express a special debt to my wife, Marilyn, who gave invaluable aid and encouragement at every step in the preparation of this book.

A. M. W.

Contents

Introduction

Were we to trace the history of civilization, we would move around the globe from places like Peking to Alexandria, Athens, Rome, Paris, London, and New York—all of them great cities. Paradoxically the city on the one hand reflects some of man's greatest achievements and on the other hand presents one of his greatest dilemmas. Throughout history the city has been the focal point for economic development, cultural achievements, social interaction, and the creation of political institutions. It is in cities that people build and support great medical centers, educational institutions, art galleries, commercial enterprises, and industrial establishments. It is in cities that things happen and man finds the opportunity for his fulfillment. Yet the city falls below our expectations, and in some areas has developed major problems. Contemporary urban centers lack good schools, adequate clinics and hospitals, sufficient recreation facilities, and other sophisticated services which we believe a modern industrial society should have. One finds poverty, slums, racial turmoil, pollution, congestion, alienation, and violence. The simultaneous wonder at and frustration with the city have lured historians toward its study.

The earliest works on the American city, those published in the nineteenth century, were primarily accounts of local events with emphasis on the greatness of the community's physical achievements. Typically written by a member of the community's aristocracy to commemorate an anniversary, these genteel volumes focused on individuals, their roles in community affairs, and their contributions to the nation at large. These provincial historians were motivated not only by local pride, but also by the desire to establish closer ties with a glorious past as compensation for the growing alienation of their class, beset by the problems of urbanization, industrialization, and immigration. Parish documents, town records, reminiscences of old-timers, and the author's own memory provided the material for elaborate accounts, including genealogies, of the first settlers, of those who fought in the various wars, and of the growth of the community's commerce and industry.

In this age when the dominant form of American history was a narrative of political events written by men of letters, it is not surprising that the local historian failed both to bring to his studies more sophistication and to ask meaningful questions about urbanization. Most of the studies do not go beyond the chronicling of events, and in comparison with history as written in this century, they are viewed as "antiquarian." Yet, despite the unpromising connotation sometimes associated with this term,

1

the contributions, in that they are based on the assumption that a community has a personality and a place in history of its own, established a tradition that still has value. Furthermore, these works serve as valuable sources. They provide a framework for nineteenth-century events and thus a place to begin study. A researcher interested in a given community is at a marked advantage if he finds a history written by the local Congregational minister or retired banker.

The growth of professional history in the late nineteenth century and the changing approach to the subject in the twentieth established the foundation for the emergence of a more meaningful urban history. Early in the twentieth century a group of scholars, influenced by Frederick Jackson Turner, James Harvey Robinson, and Charles A. Beard, broke away from the former preoccupation with simply narrating political, diplomatic, and military events. The innovation in their "New History" was its interest in the rise of institutions and the role of economic, social, cultural, and intellectual forces in shaping national history. For the young historians being trained in the 1910's and 1920's this was a period, Arthur M. Schlesinger, Sr., wrote, when history was beginning ". . . to embrace all the agencies and conditions that had influenced man's development." Although not specifically concerned with urban questions, these studies were broader in their scope than anything written previously and indicated interest in subjects, such as industrialization, immigration, and social conditions, that led naturally to the study of the city. The more sophisticated methodology was also important in that it called for more interpretation of historical events, exploration into the causes of social change, and the study of the relationships among the several dimensions of human experience, such as political, economic, and social. The "New History" championed the use of the relevant tools and concepts already developed by the social sciences, particularly anthropology, sociology, psychology, and economics. The purpose of history was no longer to glorify the past but to enable us to understand ourselves and to deal with contemporary problems.

Despite this maturing of the methods and uses of history, the study of the American city was still delayed. Most of the new scholars, under the tutelage of men with quite specific interests, for several decades explored the influence of the frontier, economic interest, and sectional conflict on American institutions, character, and development. Often the research of younger scholars was channeled into topics that would supplement their professors' own interests, and this trend consequently limited the venturing into new areas relevant to a real understanding of America's past. That many historians who came to maturity in the early decades of the twentieth century were from rural or small-town backgrounds, attended isolated, country colleges, and went on to the newer state and private universities located in the corn fields of the Midwest or the foothills of the Appalachian mountains provided further reasons for neglecting the investigation of the city. Growing up in a society which believed in the agrarian myth of emphasizing the virtues of rural individualism and of viewing with suspicion and fear the growing urban centers, these historians naturally drifted into a general anti-urban milieu. When one realizes that background and social conditioning often influence the attitudes and interests of scholars, it is understandable why these historians were attracted to the Turner thesis, which suggested that the frontier was the dominant force influencing America's historical development. They lacked both a general interest in the urban condition and the perception that the city could be a force similar to that of the frontier. Other historians, who do not fall into this category, remained unaware of the urban dimension, simply because of the absence of such media as television and radio, which today involve everyone in urban life.

Although the interpretations by the early modern American historians, particularly Turner and Beard, proved useful and led to a fundamental reappraisal of the forces influencing American development, they were too narrowly conceived to supply a full understanding of the basic questions about America's past. Immigration, ethnic and minority groups, social conditions, entrepreneurship, urbanization, and other topics were either neglected or viewed as negative aspects in the American experience. But, in spite of this failing, the broader concerns and more meaningful approaches of the "New History" did provide the basis for the study of the city. The Turner thesis itself suggested at least implicitly the importance of the city for the twentieth century, since, with the closing of the frontier in 1890, the emerging city seemed to be the likely candidate to replace it as the significant factor in American history. Later Turner openly acknowledged the importance of the city when in 1925 he suggested that for a balanced view of the entire American past we need "an urban reinterpretation of our history."

Finally, by the 1930's, substantial inquiries into urban history had begun. The major historian to stimulate its study was ironically the man who succeeded Turner at Harvard upon his retirement, Arthur M. Schlesinger, Sr. Schlesinger's role in the development of the subject was multiple and decisive. In 1933 he wrote a major work, *The Rise of the City,* in which he saw the growth of the city as the unifying theme of the period 1878 to 1898. Then in 1940 he published a seminal article entitled "The City in American Civilization." The aspect of his influence that has been neglected is that which sprang from his position as teacher and director of graduate students. Unlike most of his contemporaries, Schlesinger encouraged his prospective Ph.D. students to range widely in the selection of their topics, and although he did not personally continue research in urban history, many of his students did. It is indicative of his influence that of the leading urban historians and of those who wrote major urban works during the 1940's and 1950's a substantial majority were his students. (They include Oscar Handlin, Bessie L. Pierce, Blake McKelvey, Carl Bridenbaugh, and Richard C. Wade). It is partly to the credit of Schlesinger's insight and to his free and open direction of young scholars that urban history became an established field.

The growth of interest in urban history coincided with the appearance of criticism of the frontier thesis, and a large number of the studies of the city were written to counteract the prevailing emphasis on the frontier. More important, however, was the emerging awareness that the city had played a significant role in American history. Scholars next sought to demonstrate the magnitude and range of the city's influence in America's development. They discovered not only that the city had an impact on the political, social, and economic life of urban Americans, but that its size and its dynamic nature affected non-urban dwellers and state and national policies as well. This more expansive investigation into the city freed urban history of the provincialism of the nineteenth century. Furthermore, this kind of research provided scholars with a more comprehensive view of America's past, since urban history could be interpolated with national history. Most of the work of urban historians from the 1930's through the 1950's, explored, in the form of urban biographies and period and topical studies, the city's role in the growth of the nation.

Further stimulating this research was the increasing interest in social history and other subjects of an urban orientation. Indeed, much of what we broadly call urban history is not so much the study of urbanization in itself but rather the investigation into a specialized topic, such as immigration, which by its nature has an urban setting. Inquiry into the diverse social and cultural developments naturally led scholars to a study of the urban society, which led in turn to more exploration of the urban social condition. The tenements of Chicago and the slums in New York were the subjects of studies made by Edith Abbott and James Ford in the 1930's. The proliferation of more recent studies of poverty, housing, health, and urban social reform attests to the continued interest in the urban social environment.

One cannot begin to understand the American city as a social entity without recognizing the significance of the immigrant for both the sheer physical growth of the city and its resulting social character. The growing inquiry into immigration history provoked interest in the life of the immigrant in the new world. Most of the immigrants were located in cities; in 1910 one third of the inhabitants of the eight largest cities were foreign born and another third were first generation Americans. As the history of immigrant life in the city was elaborated, and as special studies of the immigrant, in the context of specific groups or of a particular community, were made, more and more scholars found themselves investigating the city. They became aware that the history of immigration and of the city were inextricably entwined. More recently, the focus on black history and the ghetto has made more critical the interest in urbanization. In each case— in the study of social conditions, of the immigrant, and of the black man—the subject obviously transcends urban history. Nevertheless, because of the greater visibility of the subject in the city and the availability and convenience of sources in urban centers, compared with the situation of a more dispersed rural environment, the urban dimension of these problems has received significantly more attention.

The present magnitude of American urban problems has given further impetus to the research and study of urban history. Each generation of historians does not merely rewrite the history it has inherited, but also tends to emphasize particular areas introduced or heightened by its contemporary experience. For example, the interest of economic history during the 1930's in the business cycle, or during the 1950's in economic development, stemmed from public concern with these issues. Likewise, the emergence of the United States in the 1940's as a world leader revived the study of diplomatic relations. International ideological struggles sparked the inquiry into the vitality and validity of our national experience and character, and domestic social upheaval provoked interest in the history of different social classes and minority groups. It is not surprising, therefore, that in the 1960's, an age beset with urban problems, the historian has responded with an examination of our urban experience. Newspapers have been full of articles on such problems. In just one week during the fall of 1968 the *New York Times* reported on the city's school strike, affecting over one million children; welfare recipients "going on the rampage"; proposals for the expansion of the transit system to alleviate clogged streets; the need for more control to clear the air of pollution; and a host of other items, including racial tensions, poor housing, corruption, crime, and violence. National magazines have devoted entire issues to the "Urban Crisis," "The Urban Dilemma," and "The City in Ferment." In addition, the national television networks have developed several series and numerous specials on the subject. As a result, many historians, nurtured on the "New History" and seeing their work as a vehicle for human betterment, have given more attention to the urban past. The researcher has begun to ask such questions as: How did the problems arise? What impact did urban growth have on the economic conditions, social structure, and political institutions of urban dwellers? How did previous periods deal with these problems?

One might wonder why such inquiry did not begin in the late nineteenth and early twentieth century, for then, too, there was an urban crisis. Housing, sanitation, violence, traffic congestion, minority discrimination, and most of the nation's contemporary problems already existed. Public and professional individuals and groups expressed their awareness and concern in newspapers, novels, popular and professional journals, and governmental investigation commissions. This attention, though, was evident in an age before it was commonly accepted in America that history could be an instrument for social reform. When historians, soon after the turn of the century, finally did begin to view history in terms that were broader and more relevant to the contemporary period, further delay ensued, because so many historians still found the frontier thesis compelling, and the profession was preoccupied with other national and sectional issues. Not only did the young scholars look in vain to their older teachers for leadership, but the prospects of a teaching position militated against breaking new ground.

An additional element crucial to the growth of urban history has been the influence of the social sciences. Researchers in the behavioral sciences have pioneered new methods of inquiry and have stimulated thinking about urban history as a subject in itself. That is, they have urged viewing the city as a special environment; although influenced by conditions, events, and movements external to it, it has characteristics that call for the study of the evolution of the city as a separate entity. Drawing primarily on the techniques and questions of the economist, sociologists, political scientist, city planner, and geographer, the historian has begun to examine the formation of the urban environment and the influence of the changing city on urban form and structure, and on social, cultural, economic, and political conditions. In this approach the process of urbanization becomes the important consideration. For the historian interested in social organization and change, the study of the city offers a fruitful opportunity for research. It enables the researcher to look at life in a microcosm. The difficulty in grasping many political, social, and other issues on a national scale may be partially alleviated by reducing them to this smaller dimension. Once one urban structure is understood, it can be used for comparison with others. From here one can work toward a more accurate understanding of the American past, both for itself and for the future, because this microcosmic method, complemented by a judicious exploitation of the social sciences, will provide fresh insights.

The awareness of the important role of the city in the nation's history, the interest in subjects that are urban oriented, the recent urban crisis, and the interest in the city as a way of life have all stimulated historical inquiry. Because scholars wish to share the results of their research with others, because universities desire to play a constructive social role, and because students seek subjects that are relevant to them, there has been a proliferation in recent years of urban-history courses. As late as 1952 Blake McKelvey could name only five historians, each of whom was at a large urban university, teaching courses or seminars directly related to urban history. By 1968, Bayrd Still and Diana Klebanow could identify nearly one hundred and fifty institutions that already had or anticipated courses in urban history. Other colleges probably incorporate a considerable amount of urban material in courses in social, economic, or immigration history. Urban history is clearly a recognized specialty within the discipline, and the prospects for growth are sound. The number of scholars and teachers of urban history will multiply over the next decade, since many of the Ph.D. granting institutions now have faculty qualified to direct training and research in urban subjects. The field is particularly attractive in that it offers considerable new opportunities, that there is little danger of duplication, and that there appears to be a nearly unlimited source of material, since every city presents some possibility for research. The study of urbanization challenges one both to consider the important historical phenomena and to contribute, through the knowledge of the city's development, to a better understanding of critical contemporary problems.

In spite of the efforts of the last four decades, there is as yet no clear structure for the study of American urban history. Probably one will emerge through the thinking and research of this generation of scholars. On one point there is general agreement: Although the history of the city and the nation often are interrelated, the city cannot be viewed simply as a replica of national history; it is also an entity apart from national events. The study of the former should not follow the time periods commonly established for the latter. For this reason, the readings in this volume have been organized by topics relevant to urbanization, and although each has a vaguely defined time period, these periods overlap. Clearly, the study of the city necessitates delving into the full complexity of man and his environment. Therefore, this anthology ranges over a broad variety of subjects embracing the city's physical growth and the conditions that affected that growth, as well as the political, economic, social, cultural, and philosophical changes that have influenced and have been influenced by urbanization. These five categories encompass almost the totality of man's nature and, therefore, the nature of cities. Although individual readings may emphasize one of these elements to the exclusion of others, the reader should consider their interrelationships in order to arrive at a fuller understanding of the totality of the urban experience.

Running throughout this volume are five major themes. The first is the historian's search for a concept of urbanization. Section 1 is devoted primarily to this concern, but many of the remaining selections contribute, at least implicitly, to the concepts discussed. The second is the notion that urbanization is a process, a phenomenon which shows a continuous change over time. To know what happened is not sufficient. We must ask why it happened and what was its impact. In seeking answers to these questions about change in the city, we are often left with a sense that something other than the traditional determinants is relevant. The urban process may be one of these unknown variables that serves as the force or the catalyst for change. This theme is discussed in several of the selections that deal with the concept of the city, but it is specifically dealt with in Sections 2, 4, and 7. The growth of community consciousness is another theme, important because a city is more than a conglomeration of people. The city is composed of people, who, through their interaction, come to an awareness of their interdependence and a willingness to respond to their mutual needs. Several individual readings, primarily those in Sections 2 and 6 elaborate on this phenomenon. The causes of urban growth and development and the social, political, and economic impact of urbanization, the remaining two themes, are discussed in many of the selections throughout the book.

What is necessary in thinking about the urbanization of America is to ask questions: What is a city? What distinguishes one from another? What factors lead to the establishment, growth, and success or failure of a given community? Why do the various types of institutions form? What is the relationship between national movements and urban change? What has been the impact of urbanization on individuals, groups, and institutions? Why and to what extent has man failed to create an urban environment which fulfills his aspirations? If through these selections the reader is able more clearly to formulate these questions, to ask new ones, and to offer some tentative conclusions, then the purpose of this anthology will have been fulfilled.

1 The Study of

Interest in urban history developed as a by-product of interests in other areas. Thus urban history has never been narrowly construed and has always been subject to a wide variety of approaches. Consequently, before embarking upon an examination of the urbanization of America, one should learn something about these approaches and about the types of questions urban historians ask.

The scholars who first became interested in urban history, and those who still compose the largest group of urban historians, have studied the city as a basis for a new synthesis of American history. Arthur M. Schlesinger, Sr., Carl Bridenbaugh, and more recently, Blake McKelvey and Richard C. Wade are some of the leading scholars of this group. Primarily concerned with social change, but also interested in political institutions and economic development, they see the city rather than the frontier as the transforming force in American life. Although interested in urbanization as a subject in itself, they use traditional historical periods, such as the colonial, revolutionary, and progressive eras, and historical themes, such as sectionalism, slavery, industrial development, and reform, to build a framework for the study of

Urbanization

one or several cities. The questions these historians ask are concerned with how the city reflected the period under consideration, and how it altered the larger, more nationally oriented issues. This approach remains important for urban history and should continue to improve our understanding of questions basic to historians. It does, however, possess weaknesses. It fails to define "urban" satisfactorily in either physical, social, economic, political, or demographic terms. These studies either neglect the problem of definition or oversimplify it. Moreover, they tend to relate observed changes solely to the urbanization process. Frequently, however, these changes were equally influenced by broader social and economic trends, such as economic growth, technology, expansion of knowledge, migration, and industrialization. Thus, although poverty exists in cities, it is perhaps an effect more of the industrial revolution or of individuals' socio-economic background than of the urban condition. The difficulty of grasping these complexities is further increased when urbanization is seen to be both cause and effect of most of the changes that have occurred over the past century.

More recently some historians seeking to study the process of urban growth have isolated the subject from national history. Concentrating on city building and its impact on man, they have attempted to define the urban phenomenon and to gain insight into social change. To accomplish these aims, they use questions and techniques drawn from the social sciences, particularly from the ecological school of urban sociology and from economics. A complex conception of the city emerges from their work, one which usually takes into account demographic and physical considerations, as well as economic, political, social, and philosophical ones. The student of urban history must not ignore any of these considerations.

The easiest introduction to the city is to identify its more obvious characteristics, the demographic and physical ones. The demographic approach seeks to establish size and density of an urban population and to determine how these differ from the non-urban. Although it apparently provides the simplest definition, it suggests challenging questions, such as: What are the factors that led to the growth of the population? What is its impact on the individual and institutions? Several readings in Section 2 attempt to explain the workings of social, economic, and cultural forces, as well as the role of individuals in the growth of the cities. Also examined by the demographic method are the broader characteristics of the population, such as age, sex, income level, occupation and other data that can be extrapolated from the census and like reports. This knowledge contributes to an understanding of the differentiation between rural and urban, and it in turn serves as a source of further questions about the nature of urban change. This method is supplemented by a physical one, which borrows techniques from the geographer and urban planner and studies the nature of cities in terms of their visual forms and concrete structures. Here the center of interest is man and the multiple relationships among man, his works, and his environment. Despite the fact that urban historians have begun necessarily to elaborate on the concept of the city beyond the demographic and physical definitions, these two aspects must be delineated and understood in context with the other elements.

One such element is the economic characteristics of a city. Urbanization is thought of as a process that typically involves and is influenced by the concentration of specialized economic activity, a division of labor, technological change, and economic growth. The city embraces a variety of economic activities, and although commerce, industry, and service are all present, one of these categories is usually dominant at a given time. Commerce influenced the growth of urban centers in the pre-industrial age, but, in the last half of the nineteenth century, as Section 4 describes, industry played the significant role. It is not satisfactory merely to describe this changing dominant economic role, and, as Ralph E. Turner indicates in a later selection, one must consider the social consequences of economic change as well.

Furthermore, the city must be recognized as a political entity. It has a government which interacts with its citizens, and the various levels of government relate to one another. These functions and relationships change over time. In the early urban settlements the governing bodies dealt with all facets of the community's life. Later an attitude of laissez-faire prevailed. In the twentieth century, as people have become more aware of urban problems and more willing to accept collective responsibility for them, the body politic has participated more in public affairs. In the growth of cities, increases of size and space, and historical developments, such as immigration and technology, have led to a greater complexity and difficulty in communication, all of which has led to changes in political conditions and forms.

In all of the above means of inquiring into the history of the city, man is the ultimate interest. Urbanization involves changing human relationships and institutions. Consequently, it can be defined as the growth of specialized networks of social relations in which there are complex social patterns of organization, changing family structures, and new social mechanisms. Finally, the city can be defined in normative terms: that is, urbanization as the product and diffusion of a way of life and of a set of collective values.

The readings in this section describe several approaches to the study of the city. The opening selection describes the interests of many of the different academic disciplines that study the city and criticizes the divergences that exist. Although individual efforts should continue, argues Asa Briggs, there should be a fuller exchange of information and techniques as well as group efforts. The need for a multi-disciplinary approach is inherent in the nature of the subject.

The next selection, by Oscar Handlin, describes the differences between the modern city and its predecessors, the forces that have shaped the city, its distinctive characteristics, and the impact it has had on its own environment. His concept of the city embraces more than changes in population, size, or functions. It involves the implementation of new ways of dealing with the expanded city. As the modern technological age advanced, there proceeded the reconstruction of the city plan, its institutions, and the establishment of a rational order dealing with the new complex relationships. Ultimately there emerged a sense of civic consciousness. This characteristic of the modern urban populace has provided the motivation for collective adaptation and development from a rural or pre-industrial society. Handlin's essay calls for a broadening of our thinking about urbanization.

The third selection, by Dwight W. Hoover, summarizes the "diverging paths" that scholars have taken in seeking to deal with American urban history. He points out the strengths and weaknesses of the several approaches and the various assumptions and value systems that each implies. He recommends new lines of inquiry and, although recognizing the value of the social-science approach, explains his preference for thinking along humanistic lines.

Sam Bass Warner, Jr., is the most recent scholar to suggest a systematic way for historians to examine the urban environment. Working from his collection and analysis of data for Philadelphia, he presents a "scaffolding" on which others may build toward a better understanding of urban growth and change. Though addressed primarily to the researcher, his questions and approaches should be of use to the student as well.

The comprehensive approach to the study of urbanization can be used to examine the city over time, within a given time period, for a specific geographic area, and in comparing different cities. No single approach is in itself adequate, and some consideration of each one is necessary. The historians who inquire about the city tend to emphasize, depending on their interest, perspective, and personal background, one approach over the others. The reader will do the same, but should, in the selections that follow, seek to understand the multiplicity of approaches, the kinds of questions that are most meaningful, and the hypotheses that have been advanced

The Multi-discipline Approach to Urban Studies

Asa Briggs*

Many different academic specialisms converge on the study of cities. Geographers have discussed not only the site and situation of cities but problems of internal land use and ecology. Political scientists have examined not only the development of municipal government and administration but the emergence of new political forces in an urban setting, the formulation of new political objectives and the creation of new arts and techniques of leadership. Sociologists have first formulated a branch of sociological study called "urban sociology" and more recently have gone on to scrutinize and to challenge the claims of this sub-subject to be considered a discipline in its own right. Psychologists have investigated "the urban way of life," "the urban personality" and the network of urban "problems" and urban "opportunities." Historians have not only examined the history of particular cities in particular periods of time but have compared one city with another and advanced generalized "urban interpretations" of history to explain features of the national history of particular countries. More recently demographers have suggested that all studies of cities and of urbanization should begin with an analysis of population trends, and so valuable has been that contribution that none of the other specialists have been able to neglect either their methods or their conclusions.

The influence and appeal of particular specialisms as central approaches to the study of cities vary from country to country. In France geographers have always been in a strategic position, in the United States sociologists, in Britain historians. The reasons for these divergences are to be found not only in the history of universities but in the history of societies as a whole. With the growing interest in international academic contacts and with the growing impact of Foundation-sponsored research, some of the old divergences are beginning to be less important than formerly. There is still much overlapping in urban studies, imperfect knowledge of what other specialists are saying and far too little economic division of labor. But teams of workers and a considerable number of urban research societies are now drawing on different disciplines and trying to relate them to each other.

For the first time in history the growth of such organizations is beginning to keep pace with the growth of cities themselves. It is difficult now for any single person to keep abreast with what is being written about cities even in one region of the world, and the inadequacy of earlier works of synthesis is apparent to each kind of specialist. There is need now on the academic front for some measure of agreement about terminology and statistics at least—in the field of national income statistics, a similar need called forth some measure of agreement—and for better exchange of information about what is being done.

TWO

At this point in any discussion of urban research it may be helpful to begin with the obvious: The city is primarily a place in which to live.

*Reprinted with permission from Asa Briggs, "The Study of Cities," *Confluence*, II (Summer, 1958), 107–114. Copyright 1958, by the President and Fellows of Harvard College.

Two consequences follow. First, not only do academic specialisms converge on the study of the city but so do practical, professionalized "subjects" like town planning, subjects concerned with the rules of organization of a city's daily life. Second, no single discipline, either academic or practical, can do more than select certain aspects of the city for detailed treatment, and there are limits to the power of all the disciplines put together to describe or to explain "urban life." The city is always more than a laboratory, although from the work of some of the best-known academic and practical specialists a reader would not always think so.

These two consequences have a bearing on the future development of urban studies. Many of the practical, professionalized studies are still imperfectly grounded in more general urban studies. Architects, for example, despite the fact that they have made imposing contributions to the literature of urban studies, often have little opportunity for studying what other specialists have written about cities. Their sociology stops short at the survey, their history at pat and somewhat superficial accounts of "cities through the ages." In many of the new cities of the world where they have had a relatively free hand—the new administrative city of Chandighar in India, for example—architects' plans proceed on very dubious social pre-suppositions. Town planners too, the more sure they are about routines, frequently tend to forget fundamentals. The fundamentals were stated by a town-planner who was also a sociologist and historian. In his forgotten plan for Colombo (1921) Geddes wrote: "neither the most practical of engineers, nor the most exquisite of aesthetes, neither the best of physicians nor of pedagogues, neither the most spiritual nor the most matter-of-fact of its governing classes can plan for the city alone."

The inability of any single discipline or group of disciplines to "cover" the city comprehensively was also realized by Geddes. He always emphasized the visual as distinct from the abstract. "I very earnestly deprecate the too ordinary legal and administrative habit (in which the literary education has brought us all up) of drawing up regulations or questioning and discussing them without as far as possible basing such too verbal presentments by the fullest possible graphic ones." The point was made just as clearly by the English poet Crabbe in the eighteenth century:

Cities and towns, the various haunts
    of men,
Require the pencil, they defy the
    pen.

Inevitably the pencil directs attention to the subjective element in urban studies. The observer cannot be divorced from what he is observing. Different travellers see the same city in very different ways. The viewpoints of inhabitants differ not only from those of travellers but among themselves: the same city "means" different things to different individuals and groups in its population. In all urban studies there must be a place for full consideration not only of the rules or of the facts of urban concentration and growth but of the image of the city. So far too little attention has been paid to this subject by academic writers on the city, and journalists and creative writers have been far more interesting. The anthology of comments on Chicago collected by Professor Bessie Pierce and that on New York collected by Professor Bayrd Still are extremely illuminating and suggestive. Equally interesting anthologies could be composed for early nineteenth-century Manchester and for twentieth-century Los Angeles. Indeed, Manchester, Chicago and Los Angeles have been alike in their generations in challenging both inhabitants and travellers to translate the shock image of the "new-style" city into words.

It is not only the image of the particular city which is worthy of study or even one image compared and contrasted with another, but the more general images of town and country—which vary considerably from one part of the world to another. In eighteenth-century England, before the rise of the modern industrial city, William Cowper provided the text for much nineteenth-century writing on cities—"God made the country, and man made the town." The anti-urban bias of most British writers on cities has mixed origins, and although it has frequently been noted it has never been fully investigated. In the United States the "country boy" myth has had an important place in American urban culture, it has helped to shape reform movements and it influences literature today. Although it has been investigated more than parallel British myths, the differences between British and American experience remain to be explored. In Australia with its large cities and its own distinctive flavor of urban life, the "bush" retains a special significance in most writing about the country. For at least one school of influential writers on Africa Cowper's comment is more percipient and topical than anything written since.

THREE

The pull of anti-urban writers has been challenged in every generation but it still remains strong. Articles have been published on the subject, symposia have been collected and conferences have been convened to examine it, but there is need for further comparative study and synthesis, touching not only on the different kinds of society in recent times but going back to the very different urban values of Greece and Rome.

In such a study the social historian will be a key specialist. He has within his own specialism three qualifications for making an invaluable contribution to urban studies as a whole. First, he is used to dealing with problems in relation to a long time scale. He will not make the mistake of concentrating on the social phenomena of the contemporary world and using past evidence only for the sake of comparison and underpinning. Second, he is particularly concerned with the relationship between the unique and the general. While recognizing the uniformities of city life—uniformities deriving in the first instance from the mere accumulation of numbers—he will be as sensitive to differences as to common factors, differences within the ranks of what Mumford called "insensate industrial towns" as well as between one kind of city and another. Third, he can appreciate and assess the extent to which the recent development of urban studies has been influenced by general social factors.

The first phase of American urban sociology was intimately bound up with the battle against the slum. The emphasis on urban "problems" was much more marked than in some other parts of the world. In Britain too, until very recently, studies of cities were still strongly influenced by traditions which went back before Booth and Rowntree to the earlier surveys of the nineteenth century. While there is still need for urban studies which follow in this line of development, there is room for very different studies. The recent burst of American writing on the "packaged souls" of suburbia or the ways of living of "ex-urbanites" has so far had no genuine counterpart in Europe. There is scope for the historian to disentangle "science," fashion and social motivation in the mass of twentieth-century writing on urban studies.

Unfortunately, the historian is not always in a position to exploit his special qualifications, for he has hitherto been more confused in purpose than most other specialists who have turned to urban studies. Antiquarianism or local pride have been more compelling influences than the desire to understand or to explain. In writing the history of particular cities he has often not been sure whether he is fitting local history into a stock national framework or whether he is helping to construct a new scaffolding. Other historians may have read his contribution to urban studies, but many other specialists may not have bothered to do so. Although there are some historians of cities who have tried to think out clearly what they are doing and have provided invaluable material and insights, and although there are some historians of *the* city who have advanced stimulating and controversial hypotheses about the role of the city in particular periods or countries, urban history (until recently) has not kept pace with developments in other approaches to urban studies.

The weaknesses of urban sociology, unlike those of history, have not consisted in confusion of purpose so much as in imitation of routines. Techniques which have been applied successfully to the study of one city have been copied indiscriminately in other cities. The same questions have been asked in cities with very different problems. Too little place has been left for originality of approach. For many years in the United States too much attention was paid to the problems of city life and far too little attention to its attractions. In Britain too

much time was devoted to a duplication of surveys. In Asian and African countries the methods used in the West have been followed much too closely. The collection and interpretation of quantitative data were emphasized too exclusively in some of the inquiries, and the conclusions were often written in the premises. A new partnership in the future between historian and sociologist—which is to be hoped for—will be fruitful only if the parents treat each other as equals and together ask new questions as well as old ones.

FOUR

There are four main fields of study which are likely to be cultivated in the next few years. First, and perhaps most popular, is the study of cities outside Europe and the United States. India has recently been visited by as many foreign academic visitors as politicians. Many of them have persuaded the Indians themselves that the study of Indian cities should have high priority in all programs of social research. The differences between American cities as melting pots and Indian cities as centers of group segregation fascinates Americans; the separation of British administrative and residential areas and Indian districts fascinates (and alarms) many Englishmen; the need for greater social control challenges Indians. In Africa too problems of urbanization have captured the interest of politicians and administrators as much as of social scientists; and anthropologists are increasingly switching their attention from tribal to urban communities. One of the byproducts of this study of pre-industrial or early industrial cities may be a more intense study of medieval city life in Europe. To understand the present it may be necessary to go back further into the past.

The second and contrasting area of study is the big "Western" city, seen in relation to a countryside which is itself increasingly urbanized. Changes in the organization of work and of leisure, the growth and distribution of discretionary spending power and the improvement in housing standards are all likely items on the agenda. In this field of research attitudes and aspirations receive as much attention as facts and achievements, and images can never be left out. Relatively little, however, has been written about countries other than the United States, and in all countries there is need for fuller examination of the effect of recent changes on political processes.

The third area—the study of urban population—is more precisely marked out. Available evidence, much of it patchy, unreliable or difficult to interpret, is far from fully sifted. So far, research theses have been contributing a good deal in this field, at any rate in Europe, where the history of local population movements is an increasingly popular topic for postgraduate students to choose.

The fourth area is local urban history, considered narrowly or broadly. Part of the appeal of local history in the middle of the twentieth century is escapist, reflecting a nostalgia for a more manageable, "coherent" and irrecoverable past, and a distaste for uncontrollable international pressures. Properly directed, however, local studies have a place in all programs of research and often produce more revealing results than comprehensive surveys. Some so-called local studies have far more than local implications. There is as yet, for example, no satisfactory history or series of histories of London; if one were to be produced, it would not only be valuable in its own right but would make other histories richer and more complete. If local studies of far less "important"

cities are freed from antiquarianism, they will be increasingly helpful to all students of cities. Civic pride itself is a factor deserving more detailed study; so too is civic rivalry—the innumerable tales of two cities—and the impact of one city on another. Some of these local urban studies may well continue to fulfill the same purpose as similar studies in the past: to serve as signposts to social action, to hold before their readers one of the most dazzling and compelling of all local dreams—the dream of the city beautiful.

In each of the four fields of study there is a place for individual contributions as well as for team work. The drawbacks of relying too heavily on team work in the social studies have recently been stressed by many educational and social critics. In urban studies, in particular, there is much to be gained from individual "encounters," from individual insights and from the jotting down of individual impressions. One of the most acute visitors to Chicago in the 1890's commented that "when you study it in detail, its aspect reveals so little of the personal will, so little caprice and individuality, in its streets and buildings, that it seems like the work of some impersonal power, irresistible, unconscious, like a force of nature, in whose service man was merely a passive instrument." Some urban studies are equally impersonal, or rather they give an equally strong and usually misleading impression of impersonality. In this respect they are less impressive than Chicago, and a little caprice would not only brighten them up but make them more realistic. The place of essays in social studies has never been fully recognized; in the study of cities, in particular, they are at once (along with pictures, photographs and a handful of novels) both evidence and interpretation.

The Modern City as a Field of Historical Study

Oscar Handlin*

Seen from above, the modern city edges imperceptibly out of its setting. There are no clear boundaries. Just now the white trace of the superhighway passed through cultivated fields; now it is lost in an asphalt maze of streets and buildings. As one drives in from the airport or looks out from the train window, clumps of suburban housing, industrial complexes, and occasional green spaces flash by; it is hard to tell where city begins and country ends. Our difficulties with nomenclature reflect the indeterminancy of these limits; we reach for some vague concept of metropolis to describe the release of urban potential from its recognized ambit.

Contrast this visual image with that of the ancient or medieval city. It is still possible, coming up the Rhone, to see Sion in the Valais much as it looked four hundred years ago. From a long way off, one can make out its twin castles jutting into the sky. But the vineyards and orchards, the open fields and clumps of woodland, reach along the roadside to the edge of town. There, we cross a boundary to enter another universe, one which is whole and entire to itself. The record of sieges that lasted for months on end confirms the impression of self-containment. It is much so that Paris must once have been, and Athens.

The cities of the past were, of course, vulnerable to external assault and to disruptive changes that emanated from without. Wars, shifts in patterns of production and trade, and cultural innovations gathered force outside their walls and yet decisively altered their history. But even when they held agricultural lands and even when some residents tilled the soil, those earlier communities possessed an individual life of their own in a sense that their modern successors do not. The ancient world had been a world of cities, but each had been a world unto itself. The towns of the Middle Ages and the Renaissance, even those of the eighteenth century, were self-contained entities walled off from their surroundings, with which they had only precisely defined contacts. They provided a marketplace for the products of rural craftsmen and husbandmen; but the main lines of their trade ran to distant, often overseas, places. They were centers of administration. But the governmental and ecclesiastical functionaries existed apart in detachment. The distance between London and Westminster, between Paris and Versailles, even between Milan and the castle of the Sforzas, was more than symbolic; it measured the genuine isolation of the life of the bourgeois.[1]

On the map today London and Paris and Milan occupy the same sites as did the places which bore those names three hundred years ago; and subtle institutional and cultural ties run across the centuries. But it would be a mistake to regard the later communities as merely, or even primarily, the

[1] Max Weber, *The City* (Translated and edited by Don Martindale and Gertrud Neuwirth; Glencoe, [1958]), 70 ff.; Raffaele d'Ambrosio, *Alle Origini della città le prime esperienze urbane* (Napoli, 1956); A. Temple Patterson, *Radical Leicester* (Leicester, 1954), 3, 165.

descendents of the earlier ones. The modern city is essentially different from its predecessors, and the core of the difference lies in the fact that its life is not that "of an organism, but of an organ." It has become "the heart, the brain, perhaps only the digestive stem, of that great leviathan, the modern state." Its history cannot be understood apart from that of the more comprehensive communities of which it is a part.[2]

The distinctive feature of the great modern city is its unique pattern of relations to the world within which it is situated. Large enough to have a character of its own, the modern city is yet inextricably linked to, dependent upon, the society outside it; and growth in size has increased rather than diminished the force of that dependence. Out of that relationship spring the central problems of urban history— those of the organization of space within the city, of the creation of order among its people, and of the adjustment to its new conditions by the human personality.

It is, of course, perfectly possible to approach the history of these communities in a purely descriptive fashion—to prepare useful accounts of municipalities, markets and cultural centers on an empirical basis. But such efforts will certainly be more rewarding if they are related to large questions of a common and comparative nature. These introductory remarks aim to define some of those questions.

The forces that made the modern city what it is took form outside its own limits. Hence the increases were always unexpected and unanticipated. In the sixteenth and seventeenth centuries London, the first truly modern city, was repeatedly forbidden to

grow; men who knew it as it was could not conceive what it would become. For the same reason, projections of future trends—whether prophetic or scientific—almost without fail fell far short of actuality, even in the most optimistic cultures. It was rare indeed that the facilities of a community anticipated its later needs, as those of Los Angeles did. The direction and rate of expansion were not foreseen because the generative impulses were not contained within the older urban society of merchants, artisans, and functionaries. They sprang from three profound and interrelated changes in the society external to them—the development of the centralized national state, the transformation of the economy from a traditional, household, to a rational, capital-using basis, and the technological destruction of distance.[3]

The political changes were first to show themselves; here the medieval cities were at their weakest. Few of them had ever disposed of substantial military force. Venice and Ragusa were unusual in this respect, perhaps because of their relation to the sea. Most other towns, at best, found protection from a stadtholder, or at worst, remained the victims of *condottieri* or feuding barons. Often they welcomed the security of monarchical authority, but they had no illusions about the extent to which that would increase their own power. In the face of any assertion of royal or national will, they could only acquiesce.[4]

That dependent situation has persisted to this day. Despite their wealth

---

[2] George Unwin, *Studies in Economic History* (London, 1927), 49.

[3] Norman G. Brett-James, *Growth of Stuart London* (London, [1935]), 67 ff., 105 ff., 296 ff.; Walter Besant, *London in the Time of the Tudors* (London, 1904), 83; Boyle Workman, *The City that Grew* (Caroline Walker, ed., Los Angeles, 1935), 266 ff.

[4] William A. Robson, *Great Cities of the World Their Government, Politics and Planning* (New York, [1955]), 78 ff.; Société Jean Bodin, *Recueils*, VI (1954), 265 ff., 367 ff., 434 ff., 541 ff., 612.

and their critical economic position, the great cities do not control themselves; indeed most of them remain underrepresented in their ability to influence state policy. Their subordination in the polity has decisively shaped many aspects of their development.

The economic metamorphosis from which the modern city emerged is conventionally referred to as industrialization—an inappropriate designation because factory production was only slowly, and late, incorporated into the urban economy and was, in any case, only one aspect of a more general development. The eye of the change occurred outside the city rather than within it. First in agriculture and then in industry, old household-oriented modes of production gave way to large-scale rationalized forms, ultimately mechanized, that immensely increased output. The need to distribute the products to territorially wide, rather than to local, markets directly implicated the city.

The influence of technological change upon communications needs little comment. The evidences are all about us; and the development that led from the early roads and canals to the railroad, the telephone, the wireless, and the airplane permitted the speedy concentration of goods, messages, and persons at the focal points of ever wider areas. The simultaneous acceleration in managerial skills that permitted the organized deployment of great numbers of men and materials was equally impressive. The pace of innovation was particularly rapid in the half century after 1875 when the character of the modern city was most precisely defined. Why there should have been so striking an outburst of creativity in those years is as elusive a question as why there should have been so striking a failure of creativity thereafter.

The centralized national state, the new productive system, and vastly improved communications created the modern city. Together they increased its population, they endowed it with novel economic functions, and they imposed upon its way of life a fresh conception of order.

The initial manifestation of the change was a rapid growth in urban population. The centralizing tendencies of the emerging states of the sixteenth and seventeenth centuries brought significant groups of newcomers to the capitals and to regional subcenters. Operations, formerly dispersed in particular units of administration, were now concentrated; and the steady growth of state power created many additional places. Numerous functionaries carried on the expanded volume of government business and brought with them their families and retainers. Moreover many noblemen found it necessary to live close to the focus of authority, either through choice to be near the source of favors as in Bourbon France, or through compulsion to be subject to control as in Tokugawa Japan. Ancillary educational and religious institutions gravitated in the same direction. All the people thus drawn to the city created a market for trade, crafts, and services which swelled the economy of their place of residence.[5]

These developments had subtle, long-term effects. Channels of communication with the rest of the country were established that deepened through use and that conditioned the routes of later railroad and telephone lines. In some places the extensive fiscal transactions of the central government laid a basis for subsequent

[5] See, e.g., Franklin L. Ford, *Strasbourg in Transition 1648–1789* (Cambridge, 1958), 159 ff.; Lewis Mumford, *The City in History. Its Origins, Its Transformations, and Its Prospects* (New York, [1961]), 386 ff.; *Golden Ages of the Great Cities* (London, 1952), 192.

banking developments. As important, the seat of power acquired a symbolic value that later acted as a magnet for other detached elements in the society; and national citizenship facilitated their free entry.

Urban population expanded preponderantly by immigration. Cataclysms of many types outside the city borders precipitously swelled the streams that flowed into it. A stroke of fortune such as the discovery of gold near San Francisco and Johannesburg, or population pressure in the hinterland, or a disaster such as the migrations into Bombay and Calcutta after partition quickly raised the number of residents. Colonial trade contributed to the same effect in London and Amsterdam. Most important of all, structural changes in agriculture and industry involved a total reorganization of the labor force and effectively displaced great numbers of human beings for whom the city was the only refuge.[6]

From these sources was derived the rapid increase in numbers characteristic of the metropolis. Through the nineteenth century the pace accelerated, with the very largest places growing more rapidly than the smaller ones. In 1800 the twenty-one European cities with a population of 100,000 or more held, in all, somewhat more than four and a half million souls, one thirty-fifth of the total. In 1900 there were 147 such places with a population of 40,000,000 or one-tenth of the total; and thirteen and one-fourth million lived within the narrowly defined political limits of the six largest cities. Were there means of estimating the true size of the urban districts involved, the number would be larger still. The same cities in 1960 had a population of about 24,000,000—again a gross underestimation of their genuine numbers. Meanwhile places of comparable dimension had appeared in America and Asia. In 1961 well over 85,000,000 persons lived in the world's twenty largest cities, each of which contained 2,500,000 or more residents. And the process was not yet over.[7]

Mere accretions of population, however, changed the fundamental character of the city but slightly. New people came in, but their presence in itself called for few radical accommodations on the part of the old residents who generally prospered from the increased demand for their services. The city spread through the addition of new areas to its living space. But the organization of life for some time remained much what it had been earlier. Growth to great size was a necessary precondition, but did not in itself bring the modern city into being.

[6] Adna F. Weber, *The Growth of Cities in the Nineteenth Century* (New York, 1899), 230 ff.; Besant, *London in the Time of the Tudors*, 226 ff.; Walter Besant, *London in the Eighteenth Century* (London, 1903), 213 ff.; Percy E. Schramm, ed., *Kaufleute zu Haus und über See Hamburgische Zeugnisse des 17., 18., und 19. Jahrhunderts* (Hamburg, 1949), pt. II; Emile Vandervelde, *L'Exode rural et le retour aux champs* (Paris, 1903), 39 ff.; Robson, *Great Cities*, 112 ff., 141, 683.

[7] *Information Please Almanac, 1961*, 658; Edmund J. James, "The Growth of Great Cities," *Annals of the American Academy of Political and Social Science*, XIII (1899), 1 ff.; Weber, *Growth of Cities*, 20 ff., gives extensive nineteenth-century statistics. See also for more recent data, International Urban Research, *The World's Metropolitan Areas* (Berkeley, 1959); Kingsley Davis, "The Origin and Growth of Urbanization in the World," *American Journal of Sociology*, LX (1955), 429 ff.; Norton S. Ginsburg, "The Great City in Southeast Asia," *ibid.*, LX, 455 ff.; Robert I. Crane, "Urbanism in India," *ibid.*, LX, 463 ff.; Donald J. Bogue, "Urbanism in the United States, 1950," *ibid.*, LX, 471 ff.; Irene B. Taeuber, *Population of Japan* (Princeton, 1958), 25 ff., 45 ff., 96 ff., 126 ff., 148 ff.; Kingsley Davis, *Population of India and Pakistan* (Princeton, 1951), 127 ff.; Vandervelde, *L'Exode rural*, 16 ff.; Edmond Nicolaï, *La Dépopulation des campagnes et l'accroissement de la population des villes* (Bruxelles, 1903); R. Price-Williams, "The Population of London, 1801–81," *Journal of the Statistical Society*, XLVIII (1885), 349 ff.

Edo (Tokyo) in 1868 is said to have had a population of about a million, London in 1660 held more than one-half million people; yet these places were but extended towns which functioned according to patterns set long before. Their nobility, mercantile pursuits, and artisans' handicrafts formed larger aggregates than before, but they were aggregates of units that were essentially unchanged. Characteristically, in such places the building trades occupied a large part of the total labor force, and they altered but little with the passage of time. Other pursuits remained much as they had been earlier. The number of smiths and tailors, of drapers and merchants grew; but the mere multiplication of stalls and shops did not change the character of the bazaar, of the lane or of the exchange.[8]

Nor did the new needs thrust upon the city by the transformation of agriculture and industry after the eighteenth century alone give it its modern identity. Viewed simply on the economic plane, there was nothing inherently novel in the relationship of the city to these changes. It had long been accustomed to receiving the placeless men who sought its shelter and it had always provided a market for the products of the countryside. What was new was the desire, and the ability, to impose a rational order upon the relations created by the new productive system. The evolution of that order not only brought the city into intimate dependence upon the surrounding society; it also entailed a thoroughgoing transformation in the urban way of life.

Earlier markets had been dominated by the characteristics of the fair;

[8] For the population of earlier European cities, see Roger Mols, *Introduction à la démographie historique des villes d'Europe* (Louvain, 1955), II, 502 ff. See also M. Dorothy George, *London Life in the XVIIIth Century* (London, 1925), 155 ff.

buyers and sellers had approached in the expectation that they might meet one another, but the actual encounters had been shot through with chance. Monopolies and other political controls, various systems of correspondence and intelligence, and numerous other devices had aimed to impart some regularity to these transactions, particularly in the exchange of the great staples—wine, wool, and later, spices, tea, tobacco, and sugar. But distance and the vagaries of household production had limited the utility of these efforts. In effect, the movement of goods came to a halt, started and stopped, within the city, and that discontinuity gave the entrepôt a considerable degree of autonomy.

That situation ceased to be tolerable after the eighteenth century. The new techniques resulted in a large and growing capacity for production far beyond local need; they involved heavy capital investments and considerable risk; and they entailed difficult administrative problems. The success of any enterprise hinged upon the ability to anticipate with some precision a favorable relationship between cost of production and selling price. It could only survive by planning, however primitive the means by later standards; and planning required dependability and predictability in access both to markets and to supplies.

The city supplied the essential mechanism: from it radiated the communications network—increasingly more extensive and more rapid—and within it were situated the facilities for transhipping, storing, and processing commodities on their way from producer to consumer. Here, too, was the apparatus of accounting and credit that made the movement of goods possible. The task of the city was that of speedy transmission. The more sensitive communications became, the more thoroughly the city was entangled in a mesh of relations that deprived it of autonomy and integrated it into a larger economic and social whole.[9]

The new role had profound consequences for the internal life of the city. Its effectiveness in the productive system of which it was a part depended upon its ability to create an appropriately functioning order within its own boundaries. The pressures toward doing so were critical in its development.

One can discover premature efforts to create such novel economic relationships in the role of Milan in Lombardy and in the experience of other Renaissance cities with their hinterlands. Such developments were abortive, not only because of their restricted territorial scope and because of technological limitations, but also because the corporate life inherited from the middle ages survived, indeed grew stronger; and that life significantly inhibited further changes. The seventeenth-century syndics who sat for Rembrandt's corporation portraits were custodians of communal organizations which resisted untoward changes. The destruction of their way of life was the necessary preliminary to the creation of a new urban order more in accord with the developing productive system.[10] Where that corporate life was weak or nonexistent to begin with, as in the United States, the process was all the faster.

Destruction of the older way of life was achieved through a convergence of political and economic forces. The national state eroded traditional elements of control and created new loci of power that dominated the city from outside it. The local aristocracy dwindled in importance; the old corporations were drained of influence; privileges were reshuffled; and new people rose to prominence. More generally, the national state undermined all traditional affiliations. It recognized only the indiscriminate relationship of citizenship. In its eyes there were only individuals, not members of clans, guilds, or even of households.

The changes in the productive system redistributed wealth to the advantage of men who could cast aside inherited modes of action to capitalize on fresh opportunities. The new economy encouraged the pursuit of individual profit rather than of status within a defined community; and the city housed a pack of people seeking after gain:

Where every man is for himself
And no man for all.[11]

The result was a new concept of orderly city life, one that no longer rested on a corporate organization of households, but instead depended upon a complex and impersonal arrangement of individuals. The process was already at work in the sixteenth century in England; it was immensely stimulated by the American and the French revolutions and was complete by the end of the nineteenth century.

We shall better be able to understand the character of the inner order of the modern city by regarding some of its specific manifestations.

An entirely new pattern for disposing of space appeared. The layout of the old city was altogether inappro-

[9] Robert M. Fisher, ed., *The Metropolis in Modern Life* (Garden City, 1955), 85 ff.; Weber, *Growth of Cities*, 170 ff. For earlier market relations see, "La Foire," Société Jean Bodin, *Receuils*, V (1953), *passim.*

[10] See Douglas F. Dowd, "Economic Expansion of Lombardy," *Journal of Economic History*, XXI (1961), 143 ff.; *Storia di Milano* (Milan, 1957–1960), VIII, 337 ff., XIV, 835 ff.; Jakob Rosenberg, *Rembrandt* (Cambridge, 1948), I, 70 ff.; Weber, *The City*, 91 ff.; Mumford, *City in History*, 269 ff., 281 ff.; Société Jean Bodin, *Receuils*, VII (1955), 567 ff.; Schramm, *Kaufleute*, 185 ff.

[11] Robert Crowley, quoted in Mumford, *City in History*, 343.

priate. The population had already spread beyond the encircling walls and waters but it was inefficiently organized by a cumbersome and anachronistic plan. Churches, palaces, and other monumental structures occupied central places; squares and plazas pockmarked the limited area; and the streets ran but the short distances between nearby termini.

There was no reason why they should do more, for men had little need to travel since the household was both residence and place of work. Various districts were differentiated by occupational, class, or religious distinctions. But in each case, the basic unit was a self-contained familial entity that had a precisely defined place in the corporate life of the city. An increase in numbers was accommodated by multiplying the units, not by altering their character. In those unusual situations, as in the ghettoes, where space was constricted, the buildings rose upward and expansion was vertical. More frequently, where room was available, new clusters of settlement split off from the old and expansion was lateral. But until well into the nineteenth century growth in most places had simply multiplied the number of clusters; it had not altered their essential character.[12]

Reconstruction of the city plan depended upon the differentiation of living and working quarters. Such specialized use of space, reflecting the growing impersonality of business and its separation from the household, became prevalent everywhere except in professions like medicine, and in the service crafts where a personal relationship survived. Elsewhere, the dispersal of the population went hand

in hand with the destruction of the household and was eased by the engulfment of suburb after suburb. The father and mother and children lived together but their life was detached from work. The categories of experience they shared in the home were unrelated to those of the job. Each individual left after breakfast to take up a separate task in the counting house or the shop or on the scaffold, to return in the evening to his residence some distance away, for each was an integer subject to a separate reckoning in the accounting of the productive system.[13]

The division of function was economical. Every productive or distributive operation became more efficient when it selected the individual employee according to his talents or cost apart from considerations of kin and clan, of family or ethnic grouping. Of course, no society fully realized the ideal of total fluidity that permitted its population to be sorted out in this manner; but the separation of work from residence encouraged an approach in that direction. The fact that single men and women always constituted a large proportion of the migrants into the city stimulated the trend as did related alterations in the behavior of settled families.

As a result space was released from all sorts of traditional expenses. The enterprise no longer had to bear the charge on land of high value, of wasteful drawing rooms and gardens. Precious urban acreage was withdrawn from farming. And the distribution of population by income levels permitted a rational valuation of space in terms of an abstract, calculated, rent. Speculation was the inci-

[12] Gideon Sjoberg, *The Preindustrial City Past and Present* (Glencoe, [1960]), 100 ff.; Martin S. Briggs, "Town-Planning," Charles Singer, *et al.*, eds., *History of Technology* (New York, 1957), III, 269 ff.; *Golden Ages*, 31–34, 67, 230; Mumford, *City in History*, 299 ff.

[13] See Otis D. and Beverly Duncan, "Residential Distribution and Occupational Stratification," *American Journal of Sociology*, LX (1955), 493 ff.; R. P. Dore, *City Life in Japan. A Study of a Tokyo Ward* (Berkeley, 1958), 91 ff.

dental by-product, rather than the cause, of this development.[14]

Specialization required and facilitated the construction of an entirely new urban plant, a good part of which was built with the aid of a remarkable burst of innovation that began shortly after 1820 and which reached its peak between 1875 and 1925. Space was reallocated with an eye toward its most profitable use; and buildings directed toward a single function—trade, industry, or residence—went up with ruthless efficiency. The process of differentiation created demands for services which theretofore had been unneeded or had been supplied within the household, for fresh foods, milk, water, waste disposal, light, transportation, and recreation. In the frenzy of construction, the city was entirely recast and its ties to the past obliterated. Even topography ceased to be an obstacle; hills were razed, marshes and lakes filled in, and shore lines extended to make way for the limitless grid. Goethe could still make out medieval Frankfurt in place names, markets, buildings, fairs, and topography. By 1870, hardly more than a few of these monuments and ceremonies survived.[15]

Now begins the time of travel, at first on foot. Dickens' characters still walk across London, and at about the same time a resident of Tokyo thinks nothing of tramping five miles to and five miles from his destination every day. Even in twentieth century Rio or Tokyo an inefficient transport system compels workers to spend six hours a day between home and job.[16] But in cost-conscious societies speed is an important consideration; in its interest new streets are driven through the city, straight and wide to carry an ever heavier stream of vehicles—at first horse drawn, later, motor propelled. The wheels roll above and below as well as on the ground and inconvenient rivers are bridged over and tunneled under. The critical breakthrough comes with the appearance of the common carrier. At the beginning of the nineteenth century, every conveyance still bears the appearance of the personal or family carriage or litter—even the long distance stages that take fare-paying passengers. It is not at all clear, when the first railroads are built, that they will follow a different line of development. But the carriages are thrown open for all to enter; mass travel becomes possible; and the meanest laborer moves on wheels.

The pace and ingenuity of this work were impressive by any standard. That the subways of London, Paris, New York, and Boston were built faster than those of Moscow, Stockholm, or Rome fifty years later must mean something, although it would be hazardous to try to make the meaning precise. Any such comparison is to some degree arbitrary and perhaps far-fetched. Yet the standard of achievement certainly was not lower a half century ago than now, if we take into account the presumed improvement in technology since then. Travelers to New York today are aware that it will take seven years (1957–1964) to reconstruct La Guardia Airport and that Idlewild has been more than a decade in the building. Their predecessors fifty years ago were likely to reach the city through one of the largest buildings ever theretofore constructed at one time, one covering eight acres of ground, with exterior walls of one half a mile. They could enter through two tunnels under the Hudson River and four under the

[14] Mumford, *City in History*, 421 ff.; Fisher, *Metropolis in Modern Life*, 125 ff.; Weber, *Growth of Cities*, 322 ff.

[15] *The Auto-Biography of Goethe. Truth and Poetry: From My Own Life* (John Oxenford, transl., London, 1948), 3, 4, 7–10, 12 ff.

[16] Fukuzawa Yukichi, *Autobiography* (transl. by Eiichi Kiyooka, Tokyo, [1948]); Robson, *Great Cities*, 510; Brett-James, *Stuart London*, 420 ff.

East River extending more than eighteen miles from Harrison, New Jersey, to Jamaica, Long Island. Work on this project began in June 1903; the Hudson tunnels were finished in three years, the East River tunnels in less than five and the Pennsylvania station in less than six. In September, 1910, the whole complex was in operation.[17]

The modern city demanded an immense number and variety of new buildings. Already in the eighteenth century architects like Claude-Nicholas Ledoux were compelled to devise new shapes for warehouses, for banks, for other commercial structures, and for dwellings appropriate to various classes of residents. Considerations of cost compelled them to adhere to the rule of geometry, and to stress functionalism and the rational organization of materials and space. In doing so they struggled against counterpressures toward tradition and individualism, against counterpulls toward exoticism and a romanticized view of nature. By the second half of the nineteenth century, they had begun to work out the styles that accommodated the life of the modern city.[18]

Certainly the New York tenement block of 1900 was an unlovely object. Having dispensed with the old central court, it could pile its residents up in suffocating density. The reformers of the period were altogether right to attack overcrowding there and elsewhere and to complain that the cities had not adequately met their housing needs. Only, one must remember that overcrowding and need are relative concepts; and few later efforts have

been notably more successful.[19] Comparison with the experience of Moscow in the 1930's, to say nothing of Calcutta in the 1950's, puts the achievements of a half-century ago in better perspective.[20]

The altered situation of the city called also for a new conception of time. In the rural past, years, months, days, and hours had been less meaningful than seasons, than the related succession of religious occasions, than the rising and setting of the sun. Small communities had their own flexible conceptions of chronology. Such habits had extended to the city as well. Each household had a large margin within which to set its own pace, for the tempo of all activities was leisurely. An analysis of the course of an eighteenth-century merchant's day, for instance, revealed long disposable intervals so that even when he was busy, it was upon terms he could shape for himself.[21]

The complex interrelationships of life in the modern city, however, called for unprecedented precision. The arrival of all those integers who worked together, from whatever part of the city they inhabited, had to be coordinated to the moment. There was no natural span for such labor; arbitrary beginnings and ends had to be set, made uniform and adhered to. The dictatorship of the clock and the schedule became absolute.[22]

[17] Pennsylvania Railroad Company, *The New York Improvement and Tunnel Extension of the Pennsylvania Railroad* (Philadelphia, 1910).

[18] Emil Kaufmann, "Three Revolutionary Architects," *Transactions of the American Philosophical Society*, XLII (1952), 494 ff.; Helen Rosenau, *The Ideal City in Its Architectural Evolution* (London, [1959]), 79 ff.

[19] Mumford, *City in History*, 465 ff.; Dore, *City Life in Japan*, 40 ff.; Reinhard E. Petermann, *Wien im Zeitalter Kaiser Franz Joseph I* (Vienna, 1908), 128 ff.

[20] Alec Nove, ed., *The Soviet Seven Year Plan* (London, [1960]), 75 ff.; Harry Schwartz, *Russia's Soviet Economy* (2 ed., New York, 1954), 453 ff.; Robson, *Great Cities*, 384 ff.

[21] Arthur H. Cole, "The Tempo of Mercantile Life in Colonial America," *Business History Review*, XXXIII (1959), 277 ff.; *Golden Ages*, 44, 45.

[22] On the problem of time, see Pitirim A. Sorokin and Robert K. Merton, "Social Time: A Methodological and Functional Analysis," *American Journal of Sociology*, XLII (1937), 615 ff.

No earlier human experience had made such demands. The army camp, plantation, labor, and the ship's crew which came closest to it were coherent, closed societies, the members of which lived close together and in isolation from outsiders; the tasks involved had a rhythm of their own that regulated their budgets of time. But the modern city could not function except under the rule of a precise and arbitrary chronological order which alone could coordinate the activities of thousands of individuals whose necessary encounters with one another were totally impersonal. By the same token, literacy or some alternative code of signals was essential to the coexistence of people who did not know one another.

The new uses of space and time were indicative of what order meant in the modern city. Its complex life demanded myriad daily contacts of such sensitivity that it could not depend, as earlier, upon well-established and static connections among the stable households and the fixed corporate groups in which its population had been distributed. Instead it required its residents to behave individually and impersonally in terms of their function, and it assured regularity of contacts by rigid allocations of space and time.

That order made it possible to bring manufacturing, like other large-scale activities, into the cities. The planners of the early great factories thought of the only models of disciplined activity familiar to them, the barrack and the army camp; their sites—visionary or actual—were therefore invariably in the countryside, where the tolling bell from the clock tower of the mill replaced that of the village church. The similarity in design of factories and prisons was by no means coincidental.[23]

The urban factory was conceivable only well in the nineteenth century when it was possible to imagine that a labor force would come to work regularly and dependably. The process of transition in actuality took a number of forms. Some factory centers, like Manchester, grew into cities. In other cases, as in Pittsburgh or Zurich, a commercial center expanded to engulf nearby industrial communities. Elsewhere industry was drawn in by the attractions of superior transportation facilities, or by the presence of an abundant labor supply, as in Berlin, or Chicago; or the shift was a product of conscious government decisions as in Moscow after 1928. But whatever the immediate impulse, the necessary condition was the order that permitted the factory to function.[24]

The way of life of the modern city created grave social and personal problems. Any increase of size had always complicated the police of the community. But so long as the family, the clan, or the guild remained accountable for the behavior of its members, so long as the normal ambit of activities was restricted to a familiar quarter, the primary danger of deviant behavior came from strangers. When the decay of the household weakened the sense of collective security, the initial response was to control or exclude outsiders, to arrive at some accommodation with violent elements, and to maintain the isolation of the district within which its residents felt safe. At the end of the eighteenth century, as large a place as London had not moved beyond this point.

But these expedients were not long useful. The modern city was no *colluvies gentium*—a fortuitous accumulation of unfused populaces—as were ancient Rome, or Alexandria. Ex-

[23] Kaufmann, "Three Revolutionary Architects," 509 ff.; Rosenau, *Ideal City*, 121, 133.

[24] See, e.g., Catherine E. Reiser, *Pittsburgh's Commercial Development 1800–1850* (Harrisburg, 1951), 28, 191 ff.

tended travel and promiscuous contacts were essential to it; and the frequent mingling of men unknown to each other generated the need for holding each individual responsible for his behavior. The ultimate goal was some sort of total index that would precisely identify and infallibly locate each person so that he could be called to account for his obligations and punished for his delinquencies. The steady development of governmental power, the contrivance of numerous devices for registration, and the appearance of a professional corps of administrators were steps toward an approximation of that goal.

More was involved than the containment of criminality. The urban resident had positive as well as negative responsibilities. He had not merely to refrain from such actions as were injurious to others; he was expected, in ways that were difficult to define explicitly, also to contribute to the total well-being of the community by civic actions. The collective tasks of the old household and guild could not be left in abeyance. Someone had to provide care for dependent persons, education for children, facilities for worship, media for cultural and sociable expression, and commemorative monuments and objects of awe and beauty. The police of a city thus included a wide range of functions connected with its health and security. The state assumed some of these obligations, but the scope of its activity varied widely from country to country. Although we cannot yet explain convincingly the differences in the depth of its involvement, it is clear that it nowhere preempted the field entirely. Much remained to be done through other forms.[25]

It was not possible, although men often longed to do so, to revive the old corporate institutions or the solidary rural communities from which so many residents had migrated. The modern city contained too many disparate elements, too often thrown together, and in too fluid a pattern of relations to permit such regressions. Instead, where abstinence by the state left a vacuum, the characteristic device of a voluntary association, directed toward the specific function, met the need. The rapid proliferation of such organizations drew together memberships united by common interests, common antecedents, or common point of view. The wide expanse of the city and the continuing migration which peopled it, shaped such groupings. In some places the effective modes of organization fell within territorial, neighborhood lines; the *quartier,* ward, *ku,* or *favela* was the matrix within which associations formed. Elsewhere cultural or ethnic affiliations supplied the determining limits of cooperative action.[26]

For a long time, the cost of this adjustment was recurrent, overt conflict. Leadership was effective only within limited circles, and there were few means of resolving the frequent crises that led easily into outbreaks of violence. Bread riots in the West and rice riots in the East expressed the desperation of the uncared-for elements in the community; and racial or social antipathies, smoldering beneath the

---

[25] Louis Wirth, "Urbanism as a Way of Life," *American Journal of Sociology,* XLIV (1938), 20 ff.; Patterson, *Radical Leicester,* 222 ff.; Dore, *City Life in Japan,* 71 ff.

[26] See, in general, Lloyd Rodwin, ed., *The Future Metropolis* (New York, 1961), 23 ff. For specific illustrations see Louis Chevalier, "La Formation de la population parisienne au XIXe Siècle," Institut National d'Etudes Démographiques, *Travaux et Documents,* X (1950); Alphonse Daudet, *Numa Roumestan— Moeurs parisiennes* (Paris, 1881), ch. iii; Dore, *City Life in Japan,* 255 f.; Alexander Campbell, *The Heart of Japan* (New York, 1961), 3 ff.; William A. Jenks, *Vienna and the Young Hitler* (New York, 1960), 4.

surface, erupted at the least disturbance.[27]

By the end of the nineteenth century, the instruments for controlling such dangerous disorders were at least available, if not always effectively used. The reconstruction of the great cities permitted a strategic disposition of power to contain the mob. The maintenance of an armed police force deterred overt lawbreakers. Moreover, by then a complex of philanthropic, religious, educational, and cultural institutions had begun to elicit the acquiescence of the urban masses through persuasion. Thereafter conflicts took more negotiable forms, in the bargaining of labor unions and employers, and in politics which was less a partisan contest for power than an instrument of group accommodation. Disputes were increasingly subject to conciliable resolution through the mediating efforts of recognized leaders. However, the issues which could be confronted on the municipal level were limited and concrete; and the deeper economic and emotional grievances of the population were likely to be displaced into other channels.[28]

The life of the modern city created subtle personal problems. Here were distilled many of the general effects of change in the past two centuries: the break with tradition and the dissolution of inherited beliefs, the impact of science and technology, and the transformation of the family and of the productive system. In the city, as elsewhere, such decisive innovations were a source of both release and tension in the human spirit. Only, concentrated as they were in their urban form, these new impulses were far more volatile than elsewhere. Furthermore, the man of the city passed through experiences unique to his setting. The number and variety and speed of his contacts, the products of an original conception of space and time, the separation from nature, the impersonality and individuality of work all were novel to the human situation.

Evidence of the negative consequences was painfully abundant. On the Bowery or in Brigittenau drifted the uprooted masses who had lost personality, identity, and norms and who now were trapped in every form of disorder. The deterioration of man to bum was all too familiar in every modern city. Even the less desperate were heedless of the restraints of church and family; in London, Berlin, and New York of the third quarter of the nineteenth century, a majority of marriages and burials were unsolemnized by the clergy. The most prosperous tore at each other in vicious competition except when they indulged in fierce and expensive debauchery. High rates of mortality, suicide, alcoholism, insanity, and other forms of delinquency showed that men reared in one environment could not simply shift to another without substantial damage to themselves.[29]

At the high point of change, in the half century after 1875, there were two distinct, although not contradictory, interpretations of the effects of the modern city upon the human personality. Those who focused their attention upon institutional develop-

---

[27] Société Jean Bodin, *Receuils*, VII (1955), 398 ff.; J.B. Sansom, *The Western World and Japan* (New York, 1958), 242; J. D. Chambers, *Nottinghamshire in the Eighteenth Century* (London, 1932), 40 ff.; Besant, *London in the Eighteenth Century*, 475 ff.; George Rudé, *The Crowd in the French Revolution* (Oxford, 1959), 232 ff.

[28] Robson, *Great Cities*, 210 ff.

[29] See Petermann, *Wien*, 331 ff.; Jenks, *Vienna and the Young Hitler*, 11; George, *London Life*, 21 ff.; Besant, *London in the Eighteenth Century*, 140 ff., 263 ff.; Fisher, *Metropolis in Modern Life*, 18 ff.

ments, like Georg Simmel, Emile Durkheim, and, to some extent, Max Weber, took particular note of the decay of old forms which left the individual unsheltered, unprotected, and isolated, and therefore prone to deterioration. The later exaggerations of Spengler and Mumford distend these insights into a vision of imminent catastrophe.[30]

Exaggeration was easy because personal disorders were more visible in the city than in the country. But these observers were also limited by a fixed preference for what the city had been, a total systematic unit comprehending a defined order of institutions that no longer existed. It is significant that their views mirrored somber predictions, made long before. Rousseau and others had already warned of the inevitable results of urban detachment from nature before the process had even taken form. "Of all animals man is least capable of living in flocks. Penned up like sheep, men soon lose all. The breath of man is fatal to his fellows. . . . Cities are the burial pit of the human species."[31]

The personal hardships of adjustment to city life were genuine but they were distorted when examined in the perspective of the corporate, rural past. Other observers, whose gaze was fastened on the residents as human beings, made out a somewhat different pattern. "What can ever be more stately and admirable to me," asked Whitman, "than mast-hemm'd Manhattan?" Observing the curious procession of the ferry riders leaving work behind for their thousands of homes, he felt and expressed the wonder of their each being a person.[32] This was often the response of compassionate onlookers. At first regard, the city was totally inhuman; jungle, wilderness, hive, machine—these were the terms of the metaphors that sprang spontaneously to mind. But those sensitive enough to look more deeply found marvelous assertions of the human spirit even under these unpropitious circumstances. Here life was real and hard, and tested the human heart and mind so that emotions were deeper and reason more acute than elsewhere. Social scientists influenced by Darwinian conception of the survival of the fittest readily assumed that the city was the new environment within which a new, superior man would develop. And some who began half to understand the character of that life were tempted to idealize and romanticize even its least lovely aspects, the slums, the ruthless competition, and the grinding order.[33]

The two responses were not irreconcilable; indeed, in retrospect, they seem almost complementary, or perhaps, they were but different ways of describing the identical process. The decay of familiar institutions was another way of saying the release from traditional restraints; the unsheltered individual was also the liberated individual. The breakdown of the household and the attenuation of all the relationships formerly centered in it were the conditions of the liberation of modern man to all his painful

[30] Georg Simmel, "Die Grosstädte und das Geistesleben," *Jahrbuch der Gehe-Stiftung zu Dresden*, IX (1903), 187 ff.; Kurt H. Wolff, ed., *Georg Simmel, 1858–1918*, (Columbus, Ohio, [1959]), 100 ff., 221 ff.; Emile Durkheim, *De la Division du travail social* (5 ed., Paris, 1926), *passim*, but especially the preface to the second edition; Oswald Spengler, *The Decline of the West* (New York, 1950), II, 92 ff.; Mumford, *City in History, passim*. See also Wirth, "Urbanism as a Way of Life," *loc. cit.*, 20 ff.

[31] J[ean]. J[acques]. Rousseau, *Emile ou de l'éducation* (Paris, 1854), Book I, p. 36; Robert A. Kann, *A Study in Austrian Intellectual History* (New York, 1960), 63; see also the point of view implicit in such novels as E. M. Forster, *Howard's End* (London, 1910).

[32] Walt Whitman, *Complete Writings* (New York, 1902), I, 196.

[33] See also Weber, *Growth of Cities*, 368 ff., 441 ff.

tensions, all his creative opportunities. The hard stone of the city streets provided the stage for this drama; and it is the task of historical scholarship to explain its triumphs, its defeats, and its conflicts.

The modern city provided the scene for great outbursts of cultural creativity. Georgian London, Paris in the first decades of the Third Republic, Vienna toward the end of the reign of Franz Joseph, and Berlin of the 1920's were the settings of great achievements of the human spirit, in literature, in art, in music, and in science. Yet these were also, and at the same time, the scenes of bitter struggles for existence, of acute hardships suffered by hundreds of thousands of ill-prepared newcomers beaten down by insoluble problems. John Gay and William Hogarth, Anatole France and Honoré Daumier, Robert Musil and Berthold Brecht, and Charlie Chaplin and René Clair compiled a record of personal disasters, of moral disintegration, of human costs so high it could only be contemplated under the palliative gloss of humor. The laughter of their audiences did not conceal, it recognized the harsh truth. Yet the withering away of traditional guides to life, so debilitating in many ways, also set the individual free, left room for spontaneity and discovery, brought together selective new combinations of people, ideas, and forms, that permitted man to catch unsuspected glimpses of an unknown universe and an unfamiliar self.

Every aspect of the development of the modern city generated conflicts not resolvable within its own boundaries; that was a condition of its intimate relations with the society beyond its borders. The urban residents were divided among themselves, and they had to reckon with outsiders in their midst and beyond the walls, whose interests were intimately bound up with their own. Disputes of great importance were the result.

The city plan was therefore never simply the realization of an abstract design. Even in places created entirely afresh, as in Washington or St. Petersburg, it was the product of inescapable compromises. Within the city, the primary interest of the entrepreneurial groups and of the laboring population was to economize on the use of space. They wanted low rents, an efficient, functional allocation of the resources, and speedy interior transportation.

Such people met the determined, and sometimes effective, resistance of other elements, whose conceptions were still dominated by the static images of the rural landscape. The aristocracy—genuine and putative— wished to bring with them the commodious features of their landed estates. They expected the city to provide them with elegant squares to set off their homes, with picturesque monuments, and with parks and boulevards that would supply a back drop for the May Corso, for the Spring Parade, for the *ausflug* or Sunday excursion, for the gentleman on horseback and the lady in her carriage. Public transportation concerned them not at all.[34]

Immigrants who prospered to a lesser degree clung to the rural village as the model of home; they built wasteful villas in the sprawling suburbs and sought a restricted transport system that would take them conveniently to their desks and counters, yet prevent the city from engulfing them. Often their dogged struggles for autonomy hopelessly complicated any effort at urban reorganization, a problem as troublesome in Vienna, Leipzig, Man-

[34] See Percy E. Schramm, *Hamburg, Deutschland und die Welt* (Hamburg, [1952]), 350 ff.; Mumford, *City in History*, 395 ff.

chester, and Liverpool in 1890 as in Boston and Nashville in 1960.[35]

The persistence of the rural model prevented these people from thinking of the city as a whole and as it was. From Robert Owen, Fourier, and the utopian socialists, to Ebenezer Howard, Frank Lloyd Wright, and Lewis Mumford, a good-hearted but illusory plea went forth for the re-building of urban life in garden cities or multiplied suburbs, where adults would not be tempted to squander their resources in the pub or music hall, nor children theirs in the sweet-shop; and all would have access to the salubrious and moral air of the coun-tryside.[36]

To such pressures were added those of agriculturists and industrialists in the hinterland concerned only with lowering the cost of transshipment, and of the state, increasingly preoccu-pied with security against insurrection or lesser threats to order. The great planners, like Baron Haussmann in Paris, found room for maneuver in the play of these forces against one an-other. But rarely did they find the city material they could mold into a unified and coherent whole.[37]

Urban elements were at a disadvan-tage in the determination of both mu-nicipal and national policies. The level of tariffs in the 1880's and 1890's, the routes of canals and railroads, and the character of the banking system vi-tally affected all cities. Yet their in-fluence was perilously weak, under-represented in the councils of state

and divided, while the rural interests were monolithic and well entrenched. Paris, Rio, Rome did not govern them-selves; and voices from the Platteland or Upstate were more likely to com-mand than those from Johannesburg or New York. The political power of the country generally outweighed the economic power of the city.[38]

The clash of interests took its most subtle and most significant form in the contact of the diverse cultures that converged on the modern city. The folk traditions of the old bourgeois did not survive the disintegration of the corporate bodies in which it had been embedded; it was totally dis-rupted by the pressure from both above and below of alien elements.

The aristocracy surrendered its iso-lation and shifted some of its activi-ties to the city. Still stabilized by its landed estates, it also drew support from new wealth and, in the nine-teenth century, began the quest for a uniform, hierarchical culture at the peak of which it could stand. It wished more than indulgence in a lavish style of life; it wished also gen-eral acquiescence in its position. In-deed, to some extent it flouted the con-ventions of inferiors precisely in order to demonstrate its superiority. Legally recognized rank as in England and Prussia, the pretense of ancient lineage as in Austria and France, or arbitrary registers of inclusion as in the United States, asserted its claims to pre-emi-nence. In addition, it transformed the theater, the opera and the museum into institutions to display its domi-nance. The aristocracy turned music into classics, art into old masters, and literature into rare books, possessions symbolic of its status.[39]

---

[35] Robson, *Great Cities*, 30 ff., 60 ff., 75 ff.; Sam B. Warner, *Street Car Suburbs* (Cambridge, 1962); Weber, *Growth of Cities*, 469 ff.; H. J. Dyos, *Victorian Suburbs* (Leicester, 1961).

[36] Rosenau, *Ideal City*, 130 ff.; Robert Owen, *Book of the New Moral World* (London, 1842), II 16; Ralph Neville, *Garden Cities* (Manchester, 1904); G. Montague Harris, *The Garden City Movement* (London, 1906); Mumford, *City in History*, 514 ff.

[37] David H. Pinkney, *Napoleon III and the Rebuilding of Paris* (Princeton, 1958), 25 ff.

[38] Robson, *Great Cities*, 685; Schramm, *Hamburg*, 187 ff.

[39] Oscar Handlin, *John Dewey's Challenge to Education* (New York, [1959]), 33 ff., George D. Painter, *Proust; the Early Years* (Boston, 1959), Robert Musil, *The Man*

The problems of other migrants into the city were of quite another order. The mass of displaced peasants were eager to transplant their inherited culture but the soil was inhospitable. Folk wisdom, inappropriate to the new conditions, took on the appearance of superstition; and folk art, detached from its communal setting, lost much of its authenticity. However these people fared, they were driven by anxiety—to retain the rewards of success, to avoid the penalties of failure. Some escaped through alcohol; others found moments of relief in the excitement of the yellow press, the music hall, and the popular theater.[40]

Above all, they needed to interpret their lives by seeing themselves as actors in a meaningful drama, and since it was inconceivable that they should be conquering heroes, they most readily visualized themselves as victims.

Of whom? Rarely of the aristocrat. Peasant and gentleman had a long history of accommodation; and their roles in city life engendered few direct conflicts. The lowly felt no compulsion to ape the high born, and gaped at the splendor of the carriages on the way to the opera without envy.

More often the villains were the capitalists, big business, whose wealth was abstract, was located in no communal context, and was attached to no responsibilities of position. Or sometimes, the enemy was the stranger—the Slav or the Jew or the Catholic or the Protestant Masons or the barbaric foreigner—who could be blamed for the ills of the city. Inhuman materialism, disregard of traditional faith, sensuality and obscenity were crimes against man; and for crimes, criminals were responsible; and they who came were guilty so that we who left home were but the innocent victims.[41]

The factory workers and craftsmen who held places in disciplined organizations found belief in socialism; the class struggle explained their present situation and offered them the hope of an acceptable future. But millions of placeless men could not so readily tear themselves away from the past. The shopkeepers and clerks, the casual laborers, the chaotic mass of men without function did not want the future; they wanted the security of the homes and families and blood communities they had never had or had lost in migration. That is, they wanted a miracle; and in their eagerness they became the gullible victims of nationalistic, racist, religious and quasi-religious fantasies of every sort. There is a particular interest, in Europe, in the ease with which these people allied themselves with some sectors of the aristocracy under the banner of a universal faith—Ultramontane Catholicism, pan-Germanism, pan-Slavism. Drumont and the royalist officer corps in France, Luëger and Prince Alois Liechtenstein in Austria, illustrated the attractiveness of tradition and authority for the demagogue and his mob. Perhaps analogous elements were involved in the revival of Shinto in Japan after 1868; they were certainly present in the history of fascism.[42]

The true miracle, however, was the emergence of a sense of civic consciousness connected with the old burgher traditions but responsive to

---

Without Qualities (London, 1953); Hans Rosenberg, *Bureaucracy, Aristocracy and Autocracy* (Cambridge, 1958), 182 ff.; Hannah Arendt, *The Origins of Totalitarianism* (New York, [1951]), 54 ff.; Norman Jacobs, ed., *Culture for the Millions?* (Princeton, 1961), 43 ff.; Kann, *Austrian Intellectual History*, 146 ff.

[40] Jacobs, *Culture for Millions?* 64 ff.

[41] Oscar Handlin, *Adventure in Freedom* (New York, 1954), 174 ff.; Kann, *Austrian Intellectual History*, 50 ff., 109 ff.

[42] Dore, *City Life in Japan*, 291 ff.; Arendt, *Origins of Totalitarianism*, 301 ff.; Jenks, *Vienna and the Young Hitler*, 40 ff., 74 ff., 126 ff.

the new character of the modern city. Its characteristics were tolerance to the point of latitudinarianism, rationalism, cosmopolitanism, pragmatism, and receptivity to change. It attracted the settled middle-class elements of the city, the leaders of organized labor and even demagogues suddenly charged with responsibility, as Luëger was in Vienna and La Guardia in New York; its essence was a creative reaction to the problems of the place; its achievement was the monumental building of the city to which I earlier referred.

Some decades ago—and I am deliberately vague about the date—a significant change appeared. The immediate local causes seemed to be the two wars, the depression, and new shifts in technology and population. However, these may be but manifestations of some larger turning in the history of the society of which the modern city is a part.

The differences between city and country have been attenuated almost to the vanishing point. The movement of people, goods, and messages has become so rapid and has extended over such a long period as to create a new situation. To put it bluntly, the urbanization of the whole society may be in process of destroying the distinctive role of the modern city. It is symptomatic of this change that, in western societies, most migrations now originate, as well as terminate, in the modern metropolis.

This change may be related to a general slackening of urban spirit. The worldwide movement to the suburbs is not in itself new; this was always one of the ways in which the city expanded. What is new is the effective motivation—the insistence upon constructing small, uniform, coherent communities, and the surrender of the adventure of life in the larger units with all the hazards and opportunities of unpredictable contacts. Increasingly the men who now people the metropolis long for the security of isolation from the life about them. They strive to locate their families in space, with a minimum of connections to the hazards of the external world.[43]

Finally, there has been a perceptible decline in urban creativity. The regression to private transportation is indicative of what has been happening in other spheres as well. Despite other advances in technology and despite refinements in methods, the last thirty or forty years have witnessed no innovations to match those of the thirty or forty years earlier. We have done little more than elaborate upon the inherited plant; nowhere has there been an adequate response to the challenge of new conditions.

We console ourselves with the calculation that if the modern city has ceased to grow, the metropolitan region continues to expand. What difference that will make remains to be seen. In any case, it seems likely that we stand at the beginnings of a transformation as consequential as that which, two hundred years ago, brought the modern city into being.

Therein lies the historian's opportunity to throw light on the problems of those involved with today's city, either as practitioners or as participants. His task is not to predict, but to order the past from which the present grows in a comprehensible manner. He can illuminate the growth of the modern city from the eighteenth to the twentieth centuries to make clear what was permanent and what transient, what essential and what incidental, in its development.

Such an account as this essay has

---

[43] Mumford, *City in History*, 511 ff.; Louis Wirth, *Community Life and Social Policy* (Chicago, [1956]), 206 ff.

presented has perforce touched upon a few themes abstracted from a large number of cases. Yet the historian must deal with particulars, not with generalities. Certainly the stress, laid here upon the connections between the modern city and the surrounding society points to the decisive role of political, cultural, and economic variants, widely different from place to place.

Comparisons crowd immediately to mind. Did the differences between Washington and St. Petersburg in 1900, new capitals of expanding nations, emanate from the hundred-year disparity in their ages or from discernible differences between the United States and Russia? Did Shanghai and Singapore become what they did because they were perched on the edge of Oriental societies or because they were colonial enclaves? Did a tropical situation set the experiences of Rio and Havana apart from those of cities in the temperate zone; did their European population distinguish them from other tropical cities? Why did some cities fail to grow as others did, why were some more successful than others in resolving their problems?

No amount of theorizing about the nature of the city will answer questions such as these. We need fewer studies of the city in history than of the history of cities. However useful a general theory of the city may be, only the detailed tracing of an immense range of variables, in context, will illuminate the dynamics of the processes here outlined.[44] We can readily enough associate such gross phenomena as the growth of population and the rise of the centralized state, as technological change and the development of modern industry, as the disruption of the traditional household and the decline of corporate life. But *how* these developments unfolded, what was the causal nexus among them, we shall only learn when we make out the interplay among them by focusing upon *a* city specifically in all its uniqueness.

In the modern city, the contest between the human will and nature assumed a special form. Here man, crowded in upon himself and yet alone, discovered his potentialities for good and evil, for weakness and strength. Compelled to act within a framework of impersonal institutions, he was forced to probe the meaning of his own personality.

In the balance for two centuries now has lain the issue of whether he will master, or be mastered by, the awesome instruments he has created. The record of that issue deserves the best energies of the historian.

[44] Weber, *The City*, 11 ff.; Wirth, "Urbanism," 8 ff.; Sjoberg, *Preindustrial City*, 4 ff., 321 ff.

The Diverging Paths of American Urban History

Dwight W. Hoover*

The years following World War II have been characterized by an increased interest in urban themes. As succeeding census reports show growing metropolitan areas and as urban problems attract America's attention, the city looms larger and larger. Historians share in the increased awareness of the city; in the years since 1945 the number of urban histories has increased and the number of historians specializing in urban history has grown commensurately.[1] The trend at the present seems irreversible; more not less effort will be devoted to the history of the American city.

However, urban historians have not yet agreed upon an all embracing theory, one that would provide an organizing principle upon which the history of the city could be based. Several approaches have been suggested; each approach has had its disciples. No single theory has gained the universal approbation of urban historians. Each is based upon different assumptions and value systems; each has its drawbacks and its virtues. The purpose of this essay is to explore the paths that are now most heavily used by scholars of the city.

Part of the dilemma of the urban historian is the dilemma of the recent historian, whether to remain a humanist or become a social scientist, whether to turn to aesthetics or to sociology. More specifically, the problem of the urban historian begins with the subject to be studied. Is the historian to study the city or urban civilization?[2] Is urban history to attempt the formulation of a general law or urbanization, or is it to essay a comparative study of persisting institutions? Is the city itself the source of social change or is it only part of a larger source? What element in the cities is crucial to development? As scholars search for answers, the projection of Kenneth Boulding concerning the future ought to haunt us all. When 90% of the population becomes urban, Boulding says, the city will have no separate meaning. An Iowa farmer at present is an exurbanite who is part of an occupational subculture.[3] If urban culture becomes the only standard, will urban history become the only history? Perhaps the historical future belongs to the urban historian and urban interpretations.

Any consideration of a theory of urban history must start with A. M. Schlesinger. Channing's fifth volume[4] in his *A History of the United States* had hinted at the importance of the city, but the bold claims of an urban historian were initially made by Schle-

[1] For bibliographical data see Allen F. Davis, "The American Historian vs. the City," *Social Studies*, LVI (Mar.-Apr. 1965), 91–96, 127–35; and Charles N. Glaab, "The Historian and the American City: A Bibliographical Survey," in Philip M. Hauser and Leo F. Schnore, eds., *The Study of Urbanization* (New York, 1965).

*Reprinted with permission from Dwight W. Hoover, "The Diverging Paths of American Urban History," *American Quarterly*, XX (Summer II 1968), 296–317, published by the University of Pennsylvania. Copyright, 1968, Trustees of the University of Pennsylvania.

[2] John Burchard, "Some Afterthoughts," in Oscar Handlin and John Burchard, eds., *The Historian and the City* (Cambridge, 1963), p. 254.

[3] *Ibid.*, "The Death of the City," p. 143.

[4] W. Stull Holt in his article, "Some Consequences of the Urban Movement in American History," *Pacific Historical Review*, XXII (Nov. 1953), 337–51, vividly recounts how he discovered that what he thought was an original idea had been anticipated by Channing.

singer. In 1933 he wrote *The Rise of the City* in which he attempted to place the American city in its proper perspective; and in the *Mississippi Valley Historical Review* (June 1940), his article "The City in American History" blazed a trail which many urban historians have followed. Schlesinger claimed to have found the key to social change in America in the city. For him, the city was the frontier where new ideas, revolutionary in impact, were originated, and where social practices, under pressure by problems generated by people living in close proximity, changed to fit new experiences. Innovation, hence change, in both social and intellectual spheres was a product of city life. On the basis of this assumption, Schlesinger proposed a program for historians. From colonial times to the present, the city should be the prime object of study. The major elements within the city to be investigated should be the characteristic economic institutions and social practices of the citizens. Thus, Schlesinger wished to change both the locus and the focus of American historians.

The claims of Schlesinger for an urban centered history did not go unchallenged. William Diamond the following year commented devastatingly upon some of the weaknesses of the Schlesinger thesis. His criticisms are still apropos for urban historians today. Schlesinger failed, according to Diamond, to define either the city or urbanization clearly, to take cognizance of Mumford's work which showed the city to be more than one entity, to distinguish between the cultural traits that were permanent in the city and those that were merely transitional, and to demonstrate that an urban-rural division of history was more significant than others in explaining behavior. Above all, Diamond insisted that Schlesinger's concept of the

city was ambiguous, just as the Turnerian concept of the frontier had been. All Schlesinger had done was to substitute one broad generalization for another.[5] Since neither the city nor the frontier was rigorously enough defined, no light was shed on the problem of cause in history.

Diamond's criticisms, appropriate and convincing as they appear to be, did not dim the hopes of urban historians who found the concept of the city as originator of social change appealing. Indeed, the analogy of the city with the frontier proved too compelling to discard. A decade later, W. Stull Holt explicitly thought of the city in these terms while reviewing studies done of individual cities: Bessie Pierce's *A History of Chicago,* Bayrd Still's *Milwaukee,* and Constance McLaughlin Green's *Holyoke, Massachusetts.* The histories of these specific cities, Holt said, "are like the various histories of sections of the frontier such as Roosevelt's *Winning of the West* before Turner in his famous essay saw the forest as well as the trees."[6] (One might wonder whether the comparison with Roosevelt would be considered complimentary by these historians.) Holt, however, was not completely satisfied with the generalizations of Schlesinger and tried to add to the description of the urban experience. Several consequences of living in cities were significant to Holt. These included an older population, a lowered birth rate, more freedom for women and a change in the conception of the function of the state from a negative to a positive one, necessitated by problems of public health,

[5] "On the Danger of an Urban Interpretation of History," in Eric J. Goldman, ed., *Historiography and Urbanization* (Baltimore, 1941), pp. 67–108.
[6] "Some Consequences of the Urban Movement in American History," p. 339.
[7] Diamond had pointed to a lower birth rate in the city twelve years before.

education and sanitation.[7] These characteristics of an urban population, both demographic and ideological, were the ones that had made the city the innovator in the American past. The quality of city populations and the necessity to regulate the environment in order to survive had produced the welfare state which is most characteristic of American life.

Two comments are in order here. Using Diamond's insight that there are trends in the city that are short rather than long range, two of Holt's city population characteristics, an older population and a lower birth rate, are temporary. Again much depends upon the definition of the city. Does the city include the suburbs? If so, the population is not noticeably older than the aging rural population. If only the inner city is used, the Negro migration to and the white flight from the center still tends to weaken the generalization. The population age is more a function of socio-economic class than residence, and the demographic features of the city reflect the social make-up of the times. Secondly, the change in political theory attributable to urban condition discounts the cries for federal regulation by farmers in the nineteenth century and the considerable federal aid to rural interests in the twentieth. One could well argue that farmers, although retaining a Jeffersonian anti-governmental ideology, were among the first to enter a planned society; and city dwellers, although not averse to aid, among the last.

Despite the demurrers, the Schlesinger thesis has persisted. Carl Bridenbaugh in *Cities in Revolt* (1955) and *Cities in the Wilderness* (1938) traced the role of cities in the American Revolution and in frontier settlement, attributing to the cities considerable credit for both these movements. Richard C. Wade has also continued the tradition in *The Urban Frontier:*

The Rise of Western Cities (1959) and *Slavery in the Cities: The Antebellum South* (1964). Despite the rural nature of both the trans-Appalachian West and the South in the pre-Civil War period, Wade portrayed cities as important transforming forces. In the South the rural institution of slavery underwent a noticeable transformation into a kind of urban segregation under the liberalizing influence of urban living conditions. In the West Wade concludes that "Cities represented the most aggressive and dynamic forces."[8] Both Bridenbaugh and Wade center the city in the middle of political, intellectual and social developments from the beginning of the Republic.

In addition to specific studies of American cities Wade has, perhaps, made the best summation of the claims for urban innovation. Among the contributions made by cities to American life Wade lists are the origin of settlement, particularly in the West; the responsibility for triggering the revolution, especially in Boston; the promotion of economic growth through city rivalry in the nineteenth century; the coming together of North and West in the Civil War because of Chicago's triumph over St. Louis as a railroad center; the degeneration of slavery in the South; the development of techniques of political manipulation such as boss rule; and the reactions to this manipulation such as progressive reform.[9] With Wade, as with Schlesinger, the cities are where social change originated.

Another urban historian, Blake McKelvey, studying the period after the Civil War, 1865–1915, made as great claims for the role of the city.

[8] *The Urban Frontier* (Chicago, 1964), pp. 341–42.

[9] "The City in History—Some American Perspectives," in Werner Z. Hirsch, ed., *Urban Life and Form* (New York, 1963), pp. 59–77.

McKelvey explicitly tied the city to the frontier, stating that the unexploited potential of older established cities or of hamlets near them provided a substitute for the closing of the frontier in 1890.[10] That McKelvey's book is in the Schlesinger tradition is evident in the topics he considered; economic growth, especially in banking and credit facilities; the development of regional centers with outlying tributaries; the expansion of transport facilities; and technological change. These all are cited as having been advanced by urbanization. A corollary theme was the interaction between social forces and the city, especially in education, public health, recreation and the arts. McKelvey gave much credit to the urban atmosphere for the changing of American attitudes in the social realm and economic institutions in the economic sphere.

Perhaps the most prolific woman urban historian in America is Constance McLaughlin Green, who, like McKelvey, came to consider the broader theme of the city in American development through the biography of individual cities.[11] Green's two volumes on American urban history, *American Cities in the Growth of the Nation* (1957) and *The Rise of Urban America* (1965) viewed the city as an important factor in the development of an American way of life.[12] In the earlier book Green had a series of vignettes, four involving cities of a particular type—seaboard cities of the nineteenth century, river cities, New England manufacturing cities and

cities of the great plains—and four individual cities—Chicago, Seattle, Detroit and Washington. As can be seen, this division was socio-economic, reflecting an interest in unique social and economic development of particular cities. In *American Cities in the Growth of the Nation,* there was not the concerted attempt to tie city growth in the United States together as in the later book, *The Rise of Urban America,* but Mrs. Green's second effort at a larger urban history is quite inferior to her first. *American Cities in the Growth of the Nation* has many valuable insights in it while *The Rise of Urban America* seems slim by comparison. It is essentially a conventional social and economic history placed in an urban setting, and suffers from the lack of any overall conceptual framework. While Mrs. Green assumes that cities have shaped American life, she is never as explicit as Schlesinger or Wade, making her synthesis disjointed and weak.

The kind of urban history that Wade, McKelvey and Green write is obvious. Taking the themes already extant in American history—sectionalism, the growth of public education, reform and reaction—these historians search for the roots in movements in the city. With varying degrees of sophistication, they switch the locale of historical change from the frontier to the city. Unlike Schlesinger, they are modest and less willing to make sweeping claims for the place of the city in American history, although implicitly they believe that place has been severely undervalued by earlier historians. For this group of urban historians, urban history is social history drawn from the city.

Urban history following this path does reveal a number of possibilities for further research, particularly in recent history. The role of city in civil rights movement, as Green suggests,

[10] *The Urbanization of America*, 1865–1915 (New Brunswick, 1963), p. 32.

[11] McKelvey studied Rochester while Green has written histories of Holyoke, Naugatuck and Washington, D.C.

[12] McKelvey in his review of *The Rise of Urban America* in the *American Historical Review*, LXXI (Jan. 1966), 680, criticized Green for not emphasizing the importance of the city enough.

the attraction of McCarthyism in the city, the city origins of the New Deal, isolationism in the cities, modern Republicanism in the cities, all could be studied in depth. However, the substitution of the city for the frontier as an organizing principle has pernicious as well as fruitful results. By explaining too much, the city as a cause of social change blocks other, better explanations.

Still, the use of the Schlesinger thesis gave some differentiation to urban history which biographies of individual cities or collective biographies seemed to lack. But all of the histories considered so far suffer, as Roy Lubove says, from the same difficulty: "The main point is that all the publications in this category deal with cities, or life in cities, but rarely with urban history as distinguished from social, economic or political history in the context of the city."[13] The need for a unique framework for urban history remains unmet in this approach.

Possibilities other than social history became evident in the post-World War II period. Earlier definitions of urban history by historians proved too gross and the need to be more precise was obvious. In addition, the work being done by social scientists seemed to offer a theoretical basis for a study of the city as a process of urbanization. Urban historians, like other historians, were not unaware of the prestige attached to scientific enterprises. The discipline that offered the most promising insights was sociology,

which had had a continuing interest in community studies, and not political science, which had become involved elsewhere.[14]

For years the center for urban sociology was located at the University of Chicago from which sociologists fanned out to study the city. The most productive theory also came from Chicago. Robert Park, one of the pioneers of urban sociology, had derived an ecological model from biology and seemed to regard human ecology like plant and animal ecology with "social equivalents."[15] Park proposed to study population movements and land values in the aggregate and to deny the possibility of the planned urban environment. The city environment, rather, was a natural, unplanned one which determined interdependence between individuals. Park's associate, Burgess, developed an ecological map of Chicago in the 1920s which was composed of five concentric circles, each representing a different environment or natural area. The crude ecology of Park and Burgess soon came under attack as being inadequate. In the 1930s the retreat from the original ecological presumption began and the strict determinism softened, as Louis Wirth, Park's student, shifted Park's ecological emphasis somewhat in order to meet the criticisms. Starting with

[13] "The Urbanization Process: An Approach to Historical Research," *Journal of the American Institute of Planners*, XXXIII (Jan. 1967), 33. Lubove sees three categories in urban history: social, cultural, economic and political studies; the formation of the urban environment studies, or urban history as the process of city building over time; and urbanization as a broad societal process. Lubove believes the second category is the most promising one, since it focuses on city building and makes possible a connection between technology and social organization.

[14] R. T. Daland's "Political Science and the Study of Urbanism: A Bibliographical Essay," *American Political Science Review*, LI (June 1957), 491–509, reports on the dearth of interest in urban studies in political science in the 1950s.

[15] Leonard Reissman, *The Urban Process: Cities in Industrial Society* (Glencoe, Ill., 1964), p. 98. Reissman's book contains an excellent, short description of various urban sociologists with a corresponding typology into which each is placed. Park and Burgess are called ecological empiricists, Wirth and Redfield theoreticians. This should be compared to Gideon Sjoberg's chapter, "Theory and Research in Urban Sociology," in *The Study of Urbanization* where Park and Burgess are identified as the Chicago school and Wirth and Redfield as the urbanization school.

ideal types of cultures, urban-industrial and rural-folk, similar to the distinction between *Geminschaft* and *Gesellschaft* and to the urban-rural dichotomy of Schlesinger, Wirth attributed the difference between the two types to urbanization. Urbanism was:

> that cumulative accentuation of the characteristics distinctive of the mode of life which is associated with the growth of cities, and finally to the changes in the direction of modes of life among people, wherever they may be, who have come under the spell of influences which the city exerts by virtue of the power of its institutions and personalities operating through the means of communication and transportation.[16]

From Wirth's statement it is apparent that while ecological considerations are still important, other influences on the creation of an urban type also must be taken into account. A theory of urbanization followed with three necessary factors: physical structure (population, technology, ecology); social organization (status groups, institutions); and collective behavior (group attitudes, ideologies). Wirth's theory has been quite fruitful; but, like many other seminal ideas, has rarely been taken whole. The diverging paths of urban history lead out from Wirth.[17] The first category, physical structure, has appealed

primarily to sociologists who have emphasized ecology and population aggregates and to historians who have visualized communications as the key to the cities in naturalistic, reductionist fashion. Still others have concentrated upon the second category and traced the evolution and influence of social stratification and institutions in the growth of the city. Still others see the third as most meaningful and have written about the mutual interaction of ideas and the city. Finally, there are those historians who attempt to use all three categories in an explanation of the process of urbanization, which for these individuals, is urban history.

The first group, the ecologists, are still physically located in Chicago. The death blow to the original ecology of Park seemingly was struck by a book written by Walter Firey, *Land Use in Central Boston* (1946), which showed that community and society were inseparable and that urban land value was a function of cultural demands set by community sentiment as well as by location. Yet old ideas are hard to kill. The same year in Chicago the Chicago Community Inventory was created by a grant from the Wiebolt Foundation. In 1951, Philip M. Hauser, a sociologist interested both in studies of population and comparative urbanization, became director. Hauser has collaborated with Leo F. Schnore, a Wisconsin sociologist, also interested in population theory. Schnore and another sociologist, Otis D. Duncan, have attempted to revive ecology as a respectable explanation for the structure of cities, and hence are in a direct line from Robert Park. Using Amos H. Hawley's *Human Ecology* (1950) as a base, these sociologists continue to insist that population aggregates are the most important element in the study of the city and that statistical manipulation is the necessary tool. A typical

[16] "Urbanism As a Way of Life," *American Journal of Sociology*, XLIV (July 1938), 1–24. Wirth's article is a landmark in the field of urbanization. Perhaps Wirth's greatest strength lay in his ability to project into the future. Reissman characterizes Wirth as a deductive theorist, a characterization that is basically sound.

[17] This is not to argue that present day urban historians, or sociologists for that matter, recognize their debt to Wirth or call themselves disciples of Wirth. While his framework is a suggestive one, the fitting of individuals into that framework is an arbitrary act. Nor is the framework to be considered as a completely satisfactory one.

ecological statement by Duncan and Schnore is contained in a 1959 issue of *American Journal of Sociology,* published by the University of Chicago. Duncan and Schnore argue that ecology offered the best insights into the perennial problems of sociologists emanating from social organization—bureaucracy and stratification. In addition the ecological approach provided a theory of social change which the cultural and behavioral schools could not do. Finally, ecology was the best base for interdisciplinary cooperation. After presenting a case for ecology, Duncan and Schnore then constructed a modified ecological complex consisting of population, environment, technology and organization.[18] The relationship between men and their environment combined with social organization and technology made up all of the necessary ingredients for urbanization. Wirth's third division was ignored and the first expanded to occupy almost the whole of urban studies.

The ecological approach has not converted a great number of sociologists. Duncan and Schnore were immediately challenged for distortion of the cultural and behavioral assumptions of sociologists and for attempting to include all of sociological endeavor under one great imperial network.[19] In addition, their belief that more orthodox methodologies were inadequate for studying social organization was not matched by a completely convincing methodology of their own. Duncan and Schnore opted for a quantitative method, deliberately incomplete (an abstract model), and

for comparative analysis of aggregates.[20] For Duncan and Schnore, the greatest asset was the statistical manipulation of increased sophistication possible in the ecological approach.[21]

More recently the assumptions of the ecologists have been specifically attacked. While admitting that ecology is the "closest we have come to a systematic theory of the city,"[22] Reissman argues that ecologists are still biological determinists. The study of population aggregates and the principles that keep these aggregates operative is undertaken as analogous to animal ecology. Thus, the environment in ecological discussions assumes the causative function; adaption to the environment by man includes culture, social stratification and institutions. In finding this cause for social change the ecologists have returned to a Spencerian figure of a social organism.[23]

The rehabilitation of ecology by sociologists like Duncan and Schnore came during the 1950s when urban historians were casting about for an organizing theory. One individual in particular, Eric Lampard, has tried to promote the ecological principle as the framework for urban history.

Lampard explicitly uses the ecological ideas of Duncan and Schnore in his framework for the study of urbanization.[24] For Lampard, as for the ecologists, community structure is the

[18] "Cultural, Behavioral and Ecological Perspectives in the Study of Social Organization," *American Journal of Sociology,* LXV (Sept. 1959), 132–46. Schnore has elaborated on this thesis in *The Urban Scene: Human Ecology and Demography* (New York, 1965).

[19] Peter H. Rossi, "Comment," *American Journal of Sociology,* LXV (Sept. 1959), 146–49.

[20] "Rejoinder," *American Journal of Sociology,* LXV (Sept. 1959), 149–53.

[21] Otis Dudley Duncan does recognize inherent statistical problems in the theory of ecological correlations as seen in his article written with Beverly Davis, "An Alternative to Ecological Correlation," *American Sociological Review,* XVIII (Dec. 1953), 665–66.

[22] *The Urban Process,* p. 93. Reissman uses the term neo-ecologists for these sociologists.

[23] Roy Lubove has the same criticism in "The Urbanization Process: An Approach to Historical Research." Ecologists err in ignoring the role of values, small groups, interpersonal relations and cultural traits in shaping the city.

[24] "American Historians and the Study of Urbanization," *American Historical Review,* LXVII (Oct. 1961), 49–61.

result of a changing equilibrium between population and environment mediated by technology and organization. Lampard urges the adoption of the ecological complex of Amos Hawley, Otis Duncan and Leo Schnore, as well as the study of urbanization as a societal process without committing the past errors of confusing the pathological aspects of the process with the normal.

Lampard not only urges historians to be ecologists; he also dissects the failures of urban history.[25] Tracing the backgrounds of urban history, Lampard finds the difficulty in this past. Coming out of social history, urban history concentrated on social problems rather than social change, on conflicts of interest and ideas rather than social organization and social structure.[26] Because of these preoccupations, urban history lacks both a general, theoretical framework and relevant data to that framework.[27] Lampard proposes to remedy both deficiencies. "At stake in a broader view of urban history is the possibility of making the societal process of urbanization central to the study of social change. Efforts should be made to conceptualize urbanization in ways that actually *represent* social change."[28] Basic to social change is ecology—population, its changing composition and its distribution in space and time.[29] The theoretical framework for the urban historian, then, should be the study of population change. The necessary social data is to be found in migration and social mobility, which includes both occupational shifts and changes in social status.[30] Of the salient ways to advance on the city—

structural, behavioral and demographical—the demographic is best, according to Lampard.[31]

Lampard represents a bridge between the neo-ecological sociologists and the urban historian. At a time when the study of population movements and ecology are out of favor with the majority of sociologists, Lampard attempts to make ecological assumptions palatable to historians and to convince historians that they must study population change. While no historian has become an avowed ecologist, certainly there is a noticeable tendency to make population studies on a quantified basis.[32]

That the study of population mobility can be instructive is illustrated by a pioneer work of Stephen Thernstrom. Thernstrom was connected with another center for studying urban and regional affairs, the Joint Center for Urban Studies of Harvard University and Massachusetts Institute of Technology. Begun in 1959, the Joint Center has been interested in basic research in a variety of disciplines including aesthetics, architectural history and urban planning. Its basic orientation was not sociological, as was Chicago's, so its studies have ranged more widely. Indeed, the ecological tradition was never strong at the Joint Center because of the considerable impact of *Land Use in Central Boston*.

Thernstrom's book, *Poverty and Progress,* did utilize criteria for studying Newburyport similar to those proposed by Lampard. Using manuscript census schedules and local records of the 1850–1880 period, Thernstrom analyzed occupational, geographic and inter-generational mobility among laborers and their sons, as well as prop-

[25] "Urbanization and Social Change," *The Historian and the City.*
[26] *Ibid.,* pp. 226–27.
[27] *Ibid.,* p. 232.
[28] *Ibid.,* p. 233.
[29] *Ibid.,* p. 236.
[30] *Ibid.,* p. 235.
[31] *Ibid.,* p. 238.
[32] For bibliographical material see "The Historian and the American City: A Bibliographical Survey."

erty accumulations and other evidence of increased affluence. All of this was designed to discover social mobility in mid-nineteenth century Newburyport. Thernstrom's conclusions were that social mobility was minimal, that occupational shifts upward were slight, and that property accumulations seldom amounted to more than a house. On the basis of these conclusions, Thernstrom hazarded an opinion that the open class system of the nineteenth century was largely mythical. As he put it, "The findings of the present study, however, when coupled with scattered evidence concerning social mobility in several twentieth-century American cities, permit a more definite verdict: to rise from the bottom of the social scale has not become increasingly difficult in modern America: If anything it appears to have become somewhat less difficult."[33]

Thernstrom's work cut in several directions. On the one hand, it opened the door for other urban historians to study further social mobility in other American cities to see if Thernstrom's results obtain. (Curiously enough, Thernstrom indicates that his findings are not too divergent from Curti's study of Trempealeau County.) In particular, those communities that had been already studied without much consideration of the time dimension by sociologists or anthropologists provide a base from which to work. Not only Yankee City, but Middletown and Elmtown, could be examined; and since some of the census data is now being programmed for computers, the possibility of machine assisted research also obtains. Thernstrom presently is engaged in just such a study of Boston under a grant from the American Council of Learned Societies. Furthermore, the study of mobility could be extended to other than

the laborer category; studies of middle and upper class mobility might well be assayed. Perhaps Thernstrom, more than any other urban historian, has shown the way for further statistical attacks on the city.

On the other hand, Thernstrom's work is a devastating criticism of the ahistorical social scientist, and of W. Lloyd Warner, in particular. After giving Warner due credit for the magnitude of his efforts, Thernstrom listed his major failures: not coming to grips with social mobility, not seeing changes in population composition or in the character of institutions, and unwillingness to use objective criteria for classes. From these failures Thernstrom derives an unequivocal theorem: "The distortions of the Yankee City volumes should suggest that the student of modern society is not free to take his history or leave it alone. Interpretation of the present requires assumptions about the past."[34] The choice is between an assumed past and a studied one. Warner had been guilty of holding romantic assumptions about Newburyport's past; he had not bothered to examine that past, and, as a result, had produced a distorted study. Equally important with the critique of Warner was Thernstrom's insistence that a community study be done over a span of time. The urban historian becomes an indispensable part of a community study, not an unnecessary luxury. Because of its opening of new areas of investigation and reassertion of the value of historical methods, Thernstrom's book is a landmark in urban history.[35] But Thernstrom's posi-

[33] *Poverty and Progress* (Cambridge, 1964), p. 216.

[34] *Ibid.*, p. 239.
[35] *Poverty and Progress* has aroused much opposition as might be expected from its temerity in attacking a giant like Warner. Reviewers of the book had a number of qualifications both about Thernstrom's methods and conclusions.
The necessity of history in community studies is not a position solely held by historians, however, as several sociologists testify.

tion is not an ecological one; it does not operate with aggregates or mathematical models.

Another approach is to use one particular category in the study of communities as Seymour Mandlebaum has done with communications in New York in the era of Boss Tweed.[36] Rather than study popula-

---

These sociologists—John R. Seeley, Morris S. Schwartz, Kurt H. Wolff and Maurice Stein—have opted for the older tradition of humanistic, historical sociology instead of the middle range theories of Merton and the structural-functional bifurcation of the majority of sociologists of the day. For representative essays see Maurice Stein and Arthur J. Vidich, eds., *Sociology On Trial* (1963), and Arthur J. Vidich, Joseph Bensman and Maurice Stein, eds., *Reflections on Community Studies* (1964). Perhaps the most vocal and impressive individual in this group, to the author, is Maurice Stein. As early as 1960, Stein's *The Eclipse of Community* traced the history of twentieth-century sociology, focusing upon the reasons for the switch of interest from community to small groups studies. His major conclusion was that the change from the study of cities to a study of peer groups was a reflection of new attitudes and tensions in sociologists themselves. Stein even spoke kindly of Park and the Lynds, at a time when such praise was quite out of fashion. To further his heresy, Stein recommended the use of some of Collingwood's insights by sociologists. (Indeed, the burden of Stein and his ilk is that the participant-observer must attain a kind of empathy with the community he is studying.) Stein, in relating how he came to a position of appreciating "how much was lost when historical contexts were abandoned in favor of historical generalizations whether these took the form of structural-functional propositions or survey reports," shows some of the characteristics of an urban historian. After learning middle range theories at Columbia from Merton, Stein had to teach urban sociology and sociology of community. In order to accomplish this Stein returned to Park, Warner and the Lynds and from them arrived at a working theory of urbanization. For Stein, sociology in the western tradition combines history, system and drama. Orthodox sociology has become interested only in system, neglecting both history and drama. To return to a wider, more vital sociology, it is necessary to turn back to history and to poetic metaphors. The polemic nature of Stein's argument from the left has stimulated much reaction, but may also serve as a corrective to sociological orthodoxy.

[36] *Boss Tweed's New York* (New York, 1965).

---

tion characteristics as Thernstrom did, Mandlebaum studied technology in the form of communications networks in Tweed's New York. Mandlebaum has returned to Park, who held that the key to the city is communication. However, the theoretical basis here is much more sophisticated. While Mandlebaum has not become involved in the mathematical methods of Karl W. Deutsch in *The Nerves of Government* (1963) or Richard L. Meier in *A Communications Theory of Urban Growth* (1962), he does suggest that these have promise for the future. The central theme of Mandlebaum's book is the primitive state of communication networks in New York City in Tweed's time. Basic to Tweed's ascendancy was the failure of information to be exchanged in any kind of adequate manner. Mandlebaum does effect a limited rehabilitation of Tweed, arguing that he was a product of a system of decentralized decision making and narrow, insufficient communication between decision centers. In a sense Mandlebaum suggests a theory of social change; when the price of ignorance becomes too high, citizens demand better information. When better information is had, political organizations change. When more sophistication in communications is desired, social evolution results.

There is an obvious difficulty in using communications theory as a basis for urban history. Once again a kind of naturalistic determinism permeates this theory. Communications theory shares the same real problem of neo-ecology, the use of organic analogy. Deutsch's book uses a figure that is singularly Spencerian, nerves of government; and the conception of a city hampered in social development by channels of communication can easily become the city as a biological organism. Despite this demurrer, the use of the model may be expected to increase.

Another possibility emerging from Wirth's third category this time is the study of group attitudes and ideologies regarding the city. The organizing principle in this approach might well be called, as several scholars have already done, the image of the city. The image of the city involves, not necessarily simultaneously, intellectual history, a theory of aesthetics, history of planning, perception theory and social psychology. In all cases the interest of the historian is in the concept of the city, whether that concept be a rational construct, an aesthetic reaction or a trained perception. Moreover, this approach has the virtue of being humanistic and nondeterministic.

Perhaps the most traditional way to undertake urban history in this fashion is through intellectual history, the study of the concept of urbanism and anti-urbanism. The antagonisms between rural and urban ways of life and thought have long been noted by historians as well as by those involved in popular culture. Almost every student of Jefferson has mentioned his anti-urban sentiments, and the reaction to the urbanization in the last half of the nineteenth century has been well documented.[37] However, the generalization was crude; urbanization and industrialization were sometimes used synonymously and the assumptions that anti-urbanism was a single, unchanging strand in American thought remained relatively unexamined.

An attempt to analyze some of the ideas of leading American theorists concerning the city was made, not by intellectual historians, but by a phi-

losopher and a social worker, Morton and Lucia White. Operating from the institutional impetus of the Joint Center for Urban Studies, as well as the Center for Advanced Study in the Behavioral Sciences, the Whites gleaned selective attitudes toward the city and published them in *The Intellectual Versus the City* (1962).[38] The title gives away the plot; the opinions of the city considered are largely negative. In the individuals whose ideas were presented, from Benjamin Franklin to Frank Lloyd Wright, from the early republic to the twentieth century, anti-urbanism was a constant theme. However, the Whites were able to distinguish two varieties of anti-urbanism, one romantic and the other nonromantic. The earliest critique of the city, the romantic ones, shared by Jefferson and Emerson, held that the city was overcivilized and distorted nature. Since nature was the repository of virtue, the city was evil. The romantic view of the city is most often the one cited in anti-urban views, but it is not the most recent or persistent. Commencing after the Civil War, the second critique of the city, one shared by Robert Park and Henry James, made an opposing point, the city is undercivilized. The city had failed to achieve the kind of community necessary for human development, whether that development be intellectual as it was for Henry Adams and Henry James, or emotional as Robert Park and Jane Addams envisaged in their hopes for improved small group relationships. The Whites professed to find anti-urbanism even in persons most intimately connected with the city in a time when the city was becoming the dominant form of American life; the

[37] From Schlesinger's *The Rise of the City* (1933) to McKelvey's *The Urbanization of America* (1963) the theme persists. Thirty years is only a short time and the step is small.

[38] The thesis of *The Intellectual Versus the City* is contained in an essay by Morton White entitled "Two Stages in the Critique of the American City" in *The Historian and the City*.

concept of sophisticated anti-urbanism is perhaps their most original contribution.

While *The Intellectual Versus the City* is a compelling book, it is at the same time unsatisfactory. On the one hand, anti-urbanism is demonstrated; but, on the other, the nagging question persists as to whether the two views (or, for that matter, the many views in the book) belong in the same category, springing as they do from different premises. The romantic view could not countenance the city; the nonromantic could and did. The romantic would wish to destroy the city; the nonromantic to transform it. In addition, the growth of American cities in the period after the Civil War, the period that the Whites treat most extensively, poses the question of how this was possible without considerable intellectual energy behind it.[39] Furthermore, the twofold division of anti-urbanism is admittedly too simple; even the Whites suggest this. Hence, the investigation of anti-urban themes in American thought has continuing possibilities.

Not only could such a study be made of intellectuals, but also of leaders of popular culture. A case can be made that there is and was considerable uneasiness about urban life on the level of popular culture. One recent example of the possibility is Robert H. Walker's study of popular verse published between 1876 and 1905. After studying six thousand volumes of verse (one wonders at Walker's strength and persistence after scanning some of the poems), Walker concludes that the poetical images of the city were negative, portraying the city as an ugly place where economic inequities were the rule, where crime, drunkenness, sexual excesses, amorality prevailed, where existence was characterized by craftiness, overcompetitiveness and artificiality.[40] The view of the city as immoral and threatening on a less rarefied level of abstraction does seem to support the Whites' thesis, although the poetical critique of the city is a romantic one in the nonromantic era. This, of course, does not demolish the Whites' categories; one might suppose that a poetic image would always be romantic.

A much broader approach toward the images of the city comes from Anselm Strauss, a sociologist. Recognizing Park's dictum that the city is a state of mind, Strauss tried to identify the many minds that have conceived of the city and the many cities that have been seen.[41] Strauss' book, *Images of the American City*, shows some of the possibilities in the conceptualization of the city. For richness of suggestions for further study this book must rate high in the historiography of urban studies. Strauss is impressed with the symbolic imagery of the city and treats aesthetic dimensions left out by quantifying sociologists.

Strauss began with a premise that

[39] I am indebted to Charles N. Glaab for this insight. He has proposed to do a study of pro-urban thought which is badly needed. See his "The Historian and the American Urban Tradition," *Wisconsin Magazine of History*, LXVII (Autumn 1963), 12–25, reprinted in A. S. Eisenstadt, *The Craft of American History* (Harper Torchbook, 1966), which elaborates some pro-urban sentiment. Also in opposition to the Whites is Frank Freidel, whose chapter, "Boosters, Intellectuals, and the American City," in *The Historian and The City* suggests many nonintellectuals and even some intellectuals, Benjamin Franklin for one, were pro-city. Boorstin's *The Americans: The National Experience* (New York, 1965), is supportive of Freidel.

[40] "The Poet and the Rise of the City," *Mississippi Valley Historical Review*, XLIX (June 1962), 85–99.
[41] *Images of the American City* (New York, 1961). However, Strauss' work has serious flaws in it primarily because of the lack of historical perspective. Had Strauss been more familiar with historical method, the book would have been sounder.

multiplies the images of the city. He argued that the city cannot be comprehended as a whole; that, at best, only parts can be visualized. Therefore, symbolic representation of the city is necessary and such symbolism is a function of physical, social and perceptual factors. As Strauss put it:

> The city, I am suggesting, can be viewed as a complex related set of symbolized areas. Any given population will be cognizant of only a small number of these areas: most areas will lie outside of effective perception; others will be conceived in such ways that will hardly ever be visited, and will indeed be avoided.[42]

For each group in each area in every age there is a city. Strauss only begins to show the possible images of the city inherent in this approach. Among those he does treat are those views of the city found in ethnic groups, in urban novels, in visiting tourists, in city boosters, in mediators between towns and cities, in planners and in suburbanites. Not that these are by any means all new views of the city; some of them were used by the Whites, Park and Wirth. The accomplishment of Strauss is to collect all of the views together as examples of the multifaceted nature of the city, to suggest the barrenness of a single image of the city, and to use literature in an imaginative way.

Strauss in the case of Chicago shows how varying images of the city, over a period of time, can coalesce into one image. However, the thrust of his work is in two other directions. One is the direction of the positive image of the city. The negative concept of the city must certainly be qualified in order to meet Strauss' suggestions. Particularly intriguing is Strauss' discussion of the

image of the city held by ethnic groups and the image of the city as the country. Strauss shows how it is possible for the city to be an urban village, which leads to the question of why the city could not be also an extension of Europe or of the countryside.[43] In the second place, the insistence upon the human necessity of symbolically representing the city is thought provoking. Projected into the past, several areas for investigation become obvious. In addition to studying the city in literature, the novel and the poem, why not study the city in painting? Or why not combine the two as Leo Marx did in *The Machine in the Garden* (1964), detailing the impact of technology on American imaginations? Indeed some form of middle landscape might be as typical of views of the city as views of industrialization. Or symbolic representation of a particular section of a city might be studied as Allan Trachtenberg has done for the Brooklyn Bridge, *The Brooklyn Bridge* (1965).

Basic to the theoretical underpinning of the visual concept of the city is a book from the Joint Center for Urban Studies. That book is Kevin Lynch's *The Image of the City* (1960). In *The Image of the City* Lynch holds that cities must provide an image for their inhabitants. While some are more manageable than others, having parts more easily recognized and organized into a coherent pattern, all cities are represented symbolically by their citizens.[44] To prove this thesis Lynch analyzed three rather disparate cities—Boston, Jersey City

[42] *Ibid.*, p. 59.

[43] Herbert Gans, another sociologist, in his study of Italian-Americans in Boston, *The Urban Villagers* (1962), concludes that the populace did live in a symbolically bounded village. There is no logical reason why the city, contrary to Tönnies and Redfield, could not be an extension of village or folk culture. Oscar Lewis has shown that this is possible in Mexico and New York City.

[44] (Cambridge, 1960), pp. 2–3.

and Los Angeles—using interviews as well as field reconaissance.

In each city a form emerged; each city had the requisite identity, structure and meaning.[45] To be sure, Lynch has a message; in order to enhance the ability of Americans to learn the images of their cities a concerted attempt to operate directly on the external physical shapes of the cities must be made.[46] Lynch's book is a plea for a new kind of urban design to create the kind of a city that can be easily managed into an image. As Lynch sees the problem, the question is not whether a city has an image; it is how can designers aid the image-making process? In support of his major thesis of environmental images Lynch cites material from psychology and anthropology. Using data gathered from studies of perception and from studies of primitive tribes, Lynch holds symbolic representation of environment is found everywhere in man. At M.I.T., Lynch is striving to improve visual education through training perception for city planners.[47] Much of the image of the city approach to urban history lies in the area of design of American cities and Lynch has outlined both a method and a philosophy to come to terms with urban design.

The history of the design of American cities considered in a holistic way has been the province of Christopher Tunnard. Predating Strauss and Lynch, and yet anticipating them both, Tunnard is an ardent proponent of the city as an aesthetic whole and of city planning as a humanistic experience. Like Lynch's, Tunnard's

books[48] are pleas for better civic design and for a recognition that cities do have some basic image. Tunnard asserts that American townscapes in the past, as in the present, reflect American values. As values have changed, the purposes for which cities of the past were built have become foggy or even lost. Tunnard suggests in *American Skyline* a kind of topology for American city architecture. In America there have been seven eras of city development. There are: 1609–1775, colonial; 1775–1825, young republic; 1825–1850, romantic; 1850–1880, the age of steam and iron; 1880–1910, expanding city (the city as a way of life, the city beautiful); 1910–1933, city of towers; 1933—the regional city. Each of these eras had distinctive city designs, reflecting changing values. This periodization is as satisfactory, it seems to me, as more conventional political ones; and the study of cities as architectural entities is as viable as the study of images expressed by poets.

The impressionistic studies of Tunnard were followed by two others which were pioneering in their own ways. John Burchard and Albert Bush-Brown produced *The Architecture of America: A Social and Cultural History* (1961). Although including more than city architecture, Burchard and Bush-Brown do consider the city as occupying a central role in American art forms. Another approach to urban history through aesthetics is John W. Reps' *The Making of Urban America: A History of City Planning in the United States.*[49] In the first full-scale study of planning, Reps ranges from European back-

---

[45] *Ibid.*, p. 8.
[46] *Ibid.*, p. 12.
[47] Jerome Bruner in "Education as Social Invention," *Saturday Review* (Feb. 19, 1966), mentions Lynch's project with favor. Of course, the idea of underlying structure is one of Bruner's favorites, so the praise is not unexpected.

[48] *The City of Man* (New York, 1953) and with Henry H. Reed, *American Skyline* (Cambridge, 1953). The first is more general, treating both European and American cities; the second is specifically oriented to the design history of American cities.
[49] (Princeton, 1965).

grounds to 1910 when two-dimensional concern of width of street and spatial patterns gives way to a three-dimensional interest in design, location and mass of buildings.[50] Voluminously illustrated, *The Making of Urban America* dispels the myth that American city planning was unimaginative and undeviatingly based upon a gridiron pattern. In this, Reps and Tunnard agree. They also agree on the historic importance of the Chicago World's Fair of 1893 as a watershed for the image of the city. The arrangement of the fair made possible a visualization of architectural arrangement that was most significant in stimulating the imagination of the American public.[51] Perhaps the aesthetic history of the city could be periodized thusly, before the Chicago World's Fair and after.

The image of the city approach to urban history offers many possibilities. A history of the American concept of the city in painting, by city boosters, in immigrant letters, in school textbooks, in expositions and fairs, in popular magazines, requires more detailed exploration. The idea of community in American cities has yet to be done. These are only a few of the avenues that branch off the main path of the image of the city. However, just as the urban historians of the neo-ecological approach lean toward sociology, the core of the image of the city seems to be aesthetics, particularly city design.

Not that this approach is free of danger. Attempts to derive images must necessarily be tenuous, unless concrete plans are used, as in Reps,

and the deviation could be highly subjective. The emphasis upon quantification is unlikely to intrude (although this cannot be dismissed as a possibility). Rather the necessary qualifications seem to be artistic training and sensibility, plus an ability to go behind the obvious. Urban history as a history of the images of the city will also entice another clientele, those persuaded that history is art.

Beyond those scholars who can be subsumed under one or two Wirthian categories are those who attempt a synthesis of physical structure, social organization and collective behavior. Among such urban historians are individuals such as A. Theodore Brown, Charles N. Glaab and Roy Lubove. Brown and Glaab were influenced by R. Richard Wohl who collaborated with the sociologist Anselm Strauss, and who, while teaching at the University of Chicago, was also assisting in the study of the community of Kansas City. Wohl, who had a wide-ranging mind and competencies in history, economics and sociology, did stimulate Glaab and Brown at Kansas City.[52] Another individual prominent in the attempt to fit these categories together has been Roy Lubove. Lubove, who has done some theoretical work, prefers to call this attempt a study of "the formation of the urban environment."[53] Such a title reflects the volitional aspects of city building, which is an important part of Lubove's theory.

All three of these historians share certain assumptions. They emphasize city building as interaction between decision-making individuals and groups

---

[50] *Ibid.*, p. 524.

[51] The earlier views of the fair as an artistic disaster seem to be disappearing, perhaps as the proponents of Sullivan and Wright lose some of their popularity. One suspects that the denial of design that Reps, Tunnard and Lynch attack is in part a product of the rejection of nineteenth-century art and artistic values. If Victorian furniture becomes more popular (as it seems to be), this may herald further change.

[52] For an article reflecting the conjunction, see R. Richard Wohl and A. Theodore Brown, "The Usable Past: A Study of Historical Traditions in Kansas City," *Huntington Library Quarterly*, XXIII (May 1960), 237–59.

[53] "The Urbanization Process: An Approach to Historical Research," p. 33.

—holding certain ideological views and under social and economic pressures— and technological and population change. They focus attention on city planning and city promotion.[54] While these historians are sympathetic with social science and behavioral approaches, they object to the determinism of the ecological sociologists which leaves out elements of value. The human and accidental aspects of city building are emphasized, the study of rational as well as nonrational forces operating upon men and communities:

for the history of many American cities, if closely examined, demonstrates a decidedly undeterministic pattern of false starts, fundamental changes in the direction of community policy, and discernible turning points.[55]

The kind of urban studies these historians view as most promising centers upon areas and periods where technological innovation occurs, where social change is obvious and where decision-making can be found. Two works that illustrate the possibilities of this approach are Julius Rubin's *Canal or Railroad? Imitation and Innovation in the Response to the Erie Canal in Philadelphia, Baltimore, and Boston* (1961), and Sam B. Warner Jr.'s *Streetcar Suburbs: The Process of Growth in Boston, 1870–1900* (1962). In the first book, Rubin, an economist, argued that the response of three communities, Philadelphia, Baltimore and Boston to the Erie Canal was quite different and that the different responses were products not of differences in physical characteristics, nor in economic development, but rather of attitudinal differences. As Rubin put it:

If so, the differences in behavior are to be explained by attitudinal rather than situational factors; by divergencies in the history and traditions of the three regions which produced differences in the attitudes that the decision-making groups brought to the common problem rather than by differences in the problem itself.[56]

In the second book, published by the Joint Center for Urban Studies, Warner studied suburban growth in Roxbury, West Roxbury and Dorchester, Massachusetts, through the examination of 23,000 building permits issued from 1870 to 1900. He was able to derive from this examination a process of growth which included technological change, the introduction of the streetcar; decisional factors, where to locate the lines; social mobility, the rise in occupational status of those moving to the suburbs; and an attitudinal factor, the view of the suburbs. Warner's work tied all of the Wirthian categories together into one neat package; and, since his effort was quantitative, Warner could claim to be as scientific as any ecologist. It is no surprise than that Lubove calls Warner's study one of the most satisfactory of the environmental analyses.[57]

The urban historians who operate with the definition of urbanization as the creation of a city through time stress both planning and technology, both social organization and change.

[54] *Ibid.;* A. Theodore Brown and Charles N. Glaab, "Nature and Enterprise: Two Studies in the Culture of 19th Century Midwestern City Growth," *Bulletin of the Central Mississippi Valley American Studies Association,* II (Fall 1958), 1–19; Charles N. Glaab, "Visions of Metropolis: William Gilpin and Theories of City Growth in the American West," *Wisconsin Journal of History,* LXV (Autumn 1961), 21–31.
[55] "Visions of Metropolis: William Gilpin and Theories of City Growth in the American West," p. 31.
[56] (New York, 1961), p. 9.
[57] "The Urbanization Process: An Approach to Historical Research," p. 38.

Two of Lubove's books, *The Progressives and the Slums: Tenement House Reform in New York City, 1890–1917* (1962), and *Community Planning in the 1920's: The Regional Planning Association of America* (1963), reflect his connection of the image of the city with environmental change and social reform, as does his book of readings, *The Urban Community: Housing and Planning in the Progressive Era* (1967). Lubove also emphasizes the changes in ideas from regarding the city as a product of natural forces to the view of the city as a creation of man. Lubove does not ignore technology either; his volumes add this consideration also.

Perhaps more than Lubove, A. Theodore Brown and Charles N. Glaab emphasize the connection between technology and decision-making. Brown's *Frontier Community: Kansas City to 1870* (1963) and Glaab's *Kansas City and the Railroads: Community Policy in the Growth of a Regional Metropolis* (1962) attempt to answer the question as to how Kansas City was able to become a successful regional center despite challenges from more promising sites. In both cases the answers are complex, involving city promoters, railroad and bridge development and theories of city growth. Moreover, the answers are not deterministic. Glaab and Brown also collaborated to write a general history, *A History of Urban America* (1967). In it, the authors attempt to apply the same conceptual structure which they used in their monographic studies of Kansas City. They concentrate on the process of urbanization and on the factors, physical, social and ideological, that bear on this process. They do not regard the city as a fixed environment initiating social change but treat the city as Lubove says it should be treated, as an "artifact."

While *A History of Urban America* has some weaknesses, among them a tendency to overstate the role of the city in America, it is, I think, the most satisfactory urban history to date.

The younger generation of urban historians represented by Brown, Glaab and Lubove are characterized by considerable sophistication, energy and reach. They are not content to concentrate upon one part of urbanization but instead opt for a more comprehensive approach. Neither are they sympathetic with a deterministic, mechanical explanation of urbanization; they prefer humanistic explanations of city development. Because of these qualities, they are the true heirs of Louis Wirth.

For the purpose of this essay, a number of approaches to urban history have been delineated and historians have been arbitrarily placed in one or another category. The author recognizes the injustices done and admits that some urban historians belong in more than one category. McKelvey includes images of the city, Stein is very interested in the symbolic representation of communities. However, the concern has been for the major thrust of each person's ideas.

Urban history will certainly become increasingly important as people concentrate more and more in cities. The paths already laid out will be traveled, improved, widened and made more or less beautiful, but perhaps the really significant organizing principle for urban history has yet to be found. Perhaps it will come from a center for urban or behavioral studies; perhaps it will come from another discipline; or perhaps some historian, out of his past experience or present inspiration, will hit upon a more satisfactory way of depicting the impact of the city upon American life.

A Scaffolding for Urban History

Sam Bass Warner, Jr.*

From the moment American historians began writing self-conscious urban history they assumed the city was a particular kind of place, an environment, or set of environments, that called for special historical investigation. In his pioneering *Rise of the City, 1878–1898* (New York, 1933), Arthur M. Schlesinger, Sr., took the common-sense view that the crowding in slums, the intense social and economic interactions of the downtown, and the diurnal rhythms of the suburbs, all forced men to learn new styles of life if they were to prosper, indeed if they were to survive. Subsequent urban historians, whether their subject was immigrants, industrial cities, or colonial towns, repeatedly asserted that the city, either as a whole or by its parts, bore uniquely upon the lives of the men and women whose stories they told. Thus far, however, historians have failed to study the sources of this uniqueness in any systematic way.

Perhaps because the idea of a city as a special place, or a cluster of special places, seemed such a truism, it appeared not to be worthy of investigation in its own right. Perhaps because the demands for environmental history forced historians to labor so long to master the detail of a locale, few of them would contemplate a comparative study or a survey of a long time period. Or, perhaps the tradition of local history that has long stressed the distinctiveness of each urban portrait has prevented historians from considering the comparative and sequential aspects of urban environments. Whatever the cause of the lack of system, now thirty-five years after Schlesinger began the specialty, urban history still lacks a study of the succession of urban environments for any major city and the custom of research that would allow a reader to compare the history of one city to the history of any other.

This failure to examine the environment of cities in any systematic way has had serious consequences for the specialty. Teachers of urban history courses in American colleges must patch together chronological series out of books that do not treat comparable events, although the entire selection purports to deal with urbanization. A common sequence touching some of the important areas in American urban history might leap, for example, from Carl Bridenbaugh's description of colonial towns, to Oscar Handlin's analysis of Boston from 1830 to 1880, to Jacob Riis' account of New York's Lower East Side, to Lincoln Steffens' survey of municipal corruption, to Gilbert Osofsky's history of Harlem.[1] There is analysis of urban environments in Handlin, Riis, and Osofsky, although the data presented do not allow strict comparison without much outside knowledge.

[1] Carl Bridenbaugh, *Cities in the Wilderness: The First Century of Urban Life in America, 1625–1742* (New York, 1938), and *Cities in Revolt: Urban Life in America, 1743–1776* (New York, 1955); Oscar Handlin, *Boston's Immigrants: A Study in Acculturation* (Cambridge, Mass., 1941); Jacob Riis, *How the Other Half Lives: Studies among the Tenements of New York* (New York, 1890); Lincoln Steffens, *The Shame of the Cities* (New York, 1904); Gilbert Osofsky, *Harlem: The Making of a Ghetto. Negro New York, 1890–1930* (New York, 1966).

*Reprinted with permission from Sam Bass Warner, Jr., "If All the World Were Philadelphia: A Scaffolding for Urban History, 1774–1930," *American Historical Review*, LXXIV (October, 1968), 26–43.

There is no concept of environment in Bridenbaugh and Steffens. The latter's argument rests on an interpretation of the structure of urban industry in the early twentieth century, but none of the other books give information on the earlier or later industrial structure. There are immigrants in Bridenbaugh's towns, but no information on acculturation. Just as frustrating to teacher and student as this lack of consistent information from book to book is the fact that no outline of the process of urbanization can be elicited from a chronological reading of our major urban histories. Except to the most imaginative reader, the usual shelf of urban history books looks like a line of disconnected local histories.

From time to time more systematic methods of viewing change in urban environments have been proposed. Soon after Schlesinger's work appeared, Lewis Mumford wrote his wide-ranging urban history of Europe and America, *The Culture of Cities* (New York, 1938). In it he divided urban history according to technological periods, arguing that urban environments responded to a regular sequence of technological events.[2] Economic historians have also worked with the concept of a process of development, and their periods complement the technological periods that Mumford derived intuitively. The economists have related the size of cities to economic functions and thereby tied urban history directly to the history of industrialization.[3] By

extension of their reasoning, it is possible to relate internal environments to general economic change by regarding these environments as products of the developing scale and complexity of local, national, and international markets. Thus, the colonial American town becomes a product of an Atlantic system for the exchange of staples and manufactured goods; the big city to which the immigrants came in the early nineteenth century becomes a product of increased interregional commerce; the modern metropolis becomes a product of highly specialized regional and interregional exchanges in which services of all kinds have grown to supplant in significance older manufacturing and commercial functions. The idea of such urban sequences is as old as the concept of industrialization. What is new is the growing ability of economic historians to specify the relationships that determine urban growth and change.

Today it is possible to arrange the kind of basic facts that urban historians tend to gather in the course of their studies in such a way as to reveal the sequences suggested by Mumford and the economic historians. Such an arrangement gives the writer, and later his readers, a measure by which to judge the typicality of the subject; it also enables the writer and his readers to get some idea of where the particular events under discussion fit within the process of Atlantic urbanization. An orderly presentation of a few facts can, in short, provide a kind of intellectual scaffolding for urban history.

This article will demonstrate a systematic arrangement of a few facts

---

[2] In this work and its predecessor, *Technics and Civilization* (New York, 1934), Mumford elaborated a scheme first proposed by the Scottish biologist and city planner, Patrick Geddes, in his *Cities in Evolution* (London, 1915).

[3] Eric E. Lampard, "History of Cities in Economically Advanced Areas," *Economic Development and Cultural Change*, III (Jan. 1955), 81–136; Eugene Smolensky and Donald Ratajczak, "The Conception of Cities,"

Explorations in Entrepreneurial History, 2d Ser., II (Winter 1965), 90–131; and a useful survey of various systematic methods of urban study, Philip M. Hauser and Leo F. Schnore, *The Study of Urbanization* (New York, 1965).

about the population of Philadelphia during the years 1774, 1860, and 1930. It will discuss, in order, the growth of the population, the course of industrialization, the changing locations of workplaces and homes, the shifting intensity of residential clusters, and the group organization of work. Philadelphia has special merit for such a demonstration because it became a big city early in our history and because it industrialized early.

By the best current estimate the population of urban Philadelphia in 1775 (Philadelphia, Northern Liberties, and Southwark) was 24,000[4] Such a size did not make it the rival of Edinburgh and Dublin, as it has often been described,[5] but rather an ordinary provincial town comparable to many towns throughout Europe and Latin America. Though a new town, its physical, social, and economic environments must have been long familiar to the European world. This very typicality of Philadelphia suggests that comparative studies of contemporary European and Latin American provincial cities would reveal important dimensions of the pre-industrial world.

In 1860 the consolidated city of Philadelphia (consolidated in 1854 to include all of Philadelphia County) held a population of 566,000, second only to New York in numbers of inhabitants.[6] So rapid had been its growth that it had become one of the great cities of the world, about the same size as the old cities of Vienna and Moscow or the new city of Liverpool. As in the case of Liverpool, industrialization, immigration, and boomtown conditions were its hallmarks.

In 1930 Philadelphia's population (within the same boundaries as in 1860) had risen to 1,951,000. It was then, as it has remained, one of the nation's "big five," grouped with New York, Chicago, Los Angeles, and Detroit. In comparison to other cities of the world it ranked twelfth, behind Osaka, Paris, Leningrad, and Buenos Aires.[7] In this period the key social issue was the manner in which a city of such unprecedented size structured its masses of people and its heavy volume of economic activities.

It is impossible to classify with precision the occupations of city dwellers over a century and a half of modern history. Crude listings can, nevertheless, give useful perspectives on the nature of urban economic life. The statistics for Philadelphia suggest two quite different perspectives: a view of continuity and a view of change.

In terms of continuity, differences of a few percentage points may be read both to suggest the stability of urban life and to point to fundamental change. Note, for example, in Table I the move in the Manufacturing category from 52.4 per cent to 45.3 per cent, in the professions from 3.1 per cent to 6.3 per cent, or in the building trades from 7.6 per cent to 8.1 per cent. Although the span from 1774 to 1930 is generally treated by historians

[4] This figure is calculated from manuscript tax lists and constables' returns. Other colonial statistics in this paper are from 1774. This size of population is of the same magnitude as that used by Everett S. Lee, "Population," in *The Growth of Seaport Cities, 1790–1825*, ed. David T. Gilchrist (Charlottesville, Va., 1967), 28.

[5] Bridenbaugh, *Cities in Revolt*, 217.

[6] New York's population was 805,651, Brooklyn's 266,661, giving a combined urban population of 1,072,312. (*U. S. Eighth Census: 1860, Population*, I, xxxi–xxxii.) Baltimore was third with 212,418.

[7] The 1860 and 1930 world population data are from Vladimir S. Woytinsky and Emma S. Woytinsky, *World Population and Production* (New York, 1953), 120–22. The population of all cities is according to their political boundaries, not their metropolitan regions.

TABLE I

A COMPARISON OF SOME ELEMENTS OF THE WORK STRUCTURE
OF PHILADELPHIA, 1774–1930[8]

	1774	1860	1930
Occupation:			
Laborers, all industrial categories	13.3	8.1	8.7
Clerks of all kinds, office, and sales	0.8	3.4	13.9
All other occupations	85.9	88.5	77.4
	100.0%	100.0%	100.0%
Workers by industrial categories:			
Manufacturing and mechanical industries	52.4	54.9	45.3
Building	7.6	8.3	8.1
Clothing	7.6	11.7	4.5
Bakeries	3.3	0.9	1.2
Iron, steel, and shipbuilding except autos and blast furnaces	6.2	4.5	4.7
Metalworking except iron and steel	2.0	2.4	0.6
Paper and printing	0.8	3.2	2.9
Miscellaneous textiles except wool and knitting	1.8	4.8	3.8
Balance of manufacturing	23.1	19.1	19.5
Nonmanufacturing	47.6	45.1	54.7
Wholesale and retail except autos	21.1	11.2	15.3
Transportation except railroads and transit	12.3	3.6	2.6
Professional and semiprofessional except entertainment	3.1	4.3	6.3
Hotels, laundries, and domestic service except slaves and indentured servants	5.9	21.8	12.8
Other nonmanufacturing industries	5.2	4.2	17.7
	100.0%	100.0%	100.0%
Total Classified	3,654	3,012	864,926

[8] The classification of the Philadelphia work force of this table is that of the 1930 US Census, *Fifteenth Census, Classified Index of Occupations* (Washington, D.C., 1930), and *Alphabetical Index of Occupations* (Washington, D.C., 1930). One exception only has been made: wooden shipbuilding trades have been placed with the iron, steel, and shipbuilding categories for 1774 and 1860. The categories chosen for this table are those showing some specificity and continuity through all three periods and did not, like banking, contain so many unspecified clerks, or, like cotton mills, contain so many unspecified operatives as to defy 1774 or 1860 restoration. Occupations that could not be distributed by industry like gentleman, widow, clerk, agent, operative, laborer, foreman, and helper, have been omitted from the industrial categorization of 1774 and 1860 and therefore do not enter into the percentage distributions of those years. These variations in classification between 1774, 1860, and 1930 probably account for small fluctuations in the Index of Dissimilarity of Table III. In a few cases the census names of some industrial categories have been altered for clarity. The census' Other Iron and Steel category appears in the table as Iron, steel, and shipbuilding except autos and blast furnaces; the census' Other Textiles appears as Miscellaneous textiles except wool and knitting; the census' Other Professional appears as Professional and semi-professional except entertainment. The table's category Hotels, laundries, and domestic service except slaves and indentured servants is a grouping of three census categories: Hotels, Restaurants, and Boarding Houses; Laundries and Cleaning Shops; Other Domestic Services. The 1774 list of occupations was drawn up from a careful comparison of names given on the 1774 Provincial Property Tax List for Philadelphia County with the 1775 Constable's Return for Philadelphia. The tax list is deposited in the Pennsylvania Historical and Museum Commission, Harrisburg; the Constable's Return is in the Archives of the City of Philadelphia, City Hall, Philadelphia. The 1860 material was drawn from a random sample of 3,666 persons taken from the original Eighth Census schedules for Philadelphia County now deposited in the National Archives. The 1930 data were transcribed from unpublished schedules of the Fifteenth Census now in my possession.

as a time of major revolutions, over the entire 150 years the city fulfilled a basic set of functions: it provided clothing, food, and housing for its residents, and professional services, markets, and manufactures for its residents and its trading region. From such a placid viewpoint, even a sharp decline, such as that of the transport-workers, or an equally sharp rise, such as that of the clerks, can be regarded as merely a shift in the nature of the city's commerce, not a departure from its historic functions. This perspective of continuity is especially useful to political history since it helps to explain the enduring power of urban businessmen, the commercialism of urban leadership, and the perseverance of business ideology at all levels of city politics.

The grouping of occupational statistics can also be used to place a city's history in a perspective of change. One can, for instance, interpret the shifts in the percentage of persons engaged in manufacturing and mechanical industries in the three years we are using (1774, 52.4 per cent; 1860, 54.9 per cent; 1930, 45.3 per cent) to suggest a steady decline in the proportions of Philadelphians engaged in manufactures from a peak in 1774. This interpretation seems proper because the 1774 percentage radically understates manufacturing activity. Colonial tax lists did not report the contribution of female domestic labor although such labor constituted an important fraction of the city's output. Indeed, one economic historian has estimated that on the eve of the Revolution four thousand Philadelphia women were spinning and weaving.[9] If this interpretation is correct, then the course of urban industrialization takes on a special character. Not only

did successive changes in industrial organization and machine processes free men and women from manufacturing for other occupations, but urban industrialization was a progressive sequence, ever lessening the commitment of the urban work force to manufacturing. Such a long trend differs from our common-sense impression that manufacturing occupied more and more city workers from President Jackson's time to the Hoover era.

More detailed comparisons of occupational and industrial groupings can also be made. Such groupings reflect changes in the structure of Philadelphia's economy that accompanied changes in the city's role in the Atlantic and American economy. During the first wave of industrialization, from 1774 to 1860, the proportions of unskilled laborers fell rapidly while the numbers of office and sales clerks multiplied. General wholesaling and retailing, however, declined with the differentiation of the old importing merchant's and general storekeeper's functions into distinct specialties. The labor force tied to marine transport and drayage declined sharply, while new industries like clothing, paper, and printing and some lines of textiles rose to great importance.

In the second wave of industrialization, during the interval 1860–1930, office and sales clerks again multiplied, but unskilled laborers remained a more or less steady proportion of the working population. Clothing, printing, baking, and textiles declined in relative importance, though they remained heavy users of Philadelphia's labor force. New industries, especially electrical machinery and auto parts, surged into prominence.[10] Such changes in manufacturing went

[9] Anne Bezanson, *Prices and Inflation during the American Revolution: Pennsylvania, 1770–1790* (Philadelphia, 1951), 129.

[10] See Table IV; and Gladys L. Palmer, *Philadelphia Workers in a Changing Economy* (Philadelphia, 1956), 20–52.

forward within the context of a general decline in the proportion of Philadelphians engaged in manufactures and a strong rise in professions, government, commerce, and some services.

In sum, even such a crude table (Table IV) shows that Philadelphia, despite its unique historical mixture of manufacturing, banking, and transportation, participated in the general trend of American and European industrialization suggested by Colin Clark.[11] Philadelphians' economic effort shifted steadily from an early concentration on manufactures and commerce toward a modern emphasis on services, education, and government.

As in the case of all large American cities, Philadelphia's growth was propelled by heavy in-migrations of rural native and foreign immigrants. The successive waves of foreign migration have been well documented, and now recent internal migrations have been estimated in state-by-state detail.[12] Today's practical concern with the social and political problems of black core cities and white metropolitan rings has obscured some of the history of urban settlement. The modern core of poverty and ring of affluence date from the late nineteenth century and were not characteristic of the first wave of urban growth.[13]

A kind of core and ring distribution of city dwellers manifested itself from the beginning, but it was much weaker and the reverse of the later distribution. In 1774 the poor seemed to have been pushed to the fringes of the city by the high cost of land near the Delaware River wharves. Then, during the early nineteenth century, Philadelphia grew so rapidly, and from such small beginnings, that no large stock of old housing existed to absorb or to ghettoize the waves of poor people flooding into the city.

Like inhabitants of a booming Latin American city today, Philadelphians of all income levels had to locate in new construction. Shanties, shacks, backyard houses, and alley tenements, as well as the monstrous conversions of the early nineteenth century, all so movingly reported by the nation's first sanitary inspectors, testify to the unpleasant clash of low incomes with the costs of new construction.[14] Under these conditions the poor tended to settle in backyards everywhere, in any old, decaying street that was not being seized by business, and especially at the outer edge of the city where land was cheapest, or could be squatted on.

If laborers are taken as proxies for low-income families, then Table II shows the tendency of poverty to concentrate at the ring of the city in 1860, not at the core; clerks concentrated next to the downtown. Such commonplace occupations as carpenters, machinists, shoemakers, and tailors settled in reasonably even proportions in both parts of the city. By 1930 the large stocks of old, cheap housing in the core of the city had completely reversed this pattern; low rents concentrated in the core, homeowners and middle-income rentpayers ($50.00–$99.00) at the ring.

[11] Colin Clark, *The Conditions of Economic Progress* (2d ed., London, 1951), Chap. ix.

[12] Conrad Taeuber and Irene B. Taeuber, *The Changing Population of the United States* (New York, 1958); Simon Kuznets et al., *Population Redistribution and Economic Growth, United States, 1870–1950* (3 vols., Philadelphia, 1957–64).

[13] Sam Bass Warner, Jr., *Streetcar Suburbs: The Process of Growth in Boston, 1870–1900* (Cambridge, Mass., 1962), gives a detailed account of the development of this core and ring pattern in Boston; Leo F. Schnore, *The Urban Scene, Human Ecology and Demography* (New York, 1965), demonstrates three quite different patterns for race, education, and income in large American metropolitan regions, 1950–1960.

[14] *Transactions of the American Medical Association*, II (1849); John H. Griscom, *The Sanitary Condition of the Laboring Population of New York* (New York, 1845).

TABLE II

LOCATION OF FOREIGN-BORN, NEGROES, AND SELECTED OCCUPATIONS, TENURES, AND RENTS, BY PER CENT IN CORE OR RING, 1860, 1930[15]

1860

	Negro	Foreign-Born	Britain	Germany	Ireland	Total Population
Ring	34.9	62.1	73.7	60.4	60.8	61.9
Core	65.1	37.9	26.3	39.6	39.2	38.1
Total Number	22,185	168,556	22,398	43,833	94,989	565,529

	Laborer	Clerk	Carpenter	Machinist	Shoemaker	Tailor	Sample
Ring	75.5	40.6	61.7	69.5	66.9	68.9	58.9
Core	24.5	59.4	38.3	30.5	33.1	31.1	41.1
Number in Sample	442	283	149	82	181	122	4,740

1930

	Negro	Britain	Germany	Ireland	Italy	Poland	Russia	Total Population
Ring	19.7	52.6	43.8	52.0	29.5	27.4	30.0	70.4
Core	80.3	47.4	56.2	48.0	70.5	72.6	70.0	29.6
Total Number	222,504	36,593	38,066	31,359	68,156	30,582	80,959	1,950,961

	Own Their Home	Rent at under $15	Rent $15–$29	Rent $30–$49	Rent $50–$99	Rent $100+	Total Families
Ring	52.4	10.9	16.8	40.3	60.5	44.2	44.2
Core	47.6	89.1	83.2	59.7	29.5	55.8	55.8
Number of Families	232,591	10,142	63,432	96,026	36,427	6,538	448,653

[15] The core is the original municipality of Philadelphia, 1860, Wards 5–10; the ring is the eighteen outer wards. The location of the Negroes was given in U.S. *Ninth Census: 1870*, I, *Population*, 254; the location of the foreign-born was determined by transcribing the original eighth census schedules at the National Archives. The error in the transcription was less than 1.0 per cent. The location of the occupations was determined from a sample of *McElroy's Street Directory* for 1860. The ring wards are northeast 23, 35, 41; south 48; west 34, 46, 40; northwest 38, 21, 22, 42; the core is the thirty-seven inner wards of the city. All figures calculated from unpublished tract statistics of the fifteenth census, 1930. The owning families plus the renting families do not quite add to 100 per cent because there were 3,497 families who were listed as renting, but did not specify their rental group. (*U.S. Fifteenth Census: 1930, Population, Families*, IV, 1162–63.)

Complementary patterns can be observed in the location of immigrants. In 1860, except for the British who clustered in the ring to be near the city's outer textile mills, immigrants were rather evenly distributed between core and ring. In 1930 the major immigrant groups, the Italians, Poles, and Russians, and the incoming Negroes concentrated in the cheap housing in the core. By the twentieth century, income, ethnic, and racial segregation had become as characteristic of the giant industrial metropolis as jumble and huggermugger had characterized the earlier big city.

As significant to the social geography and social history of the city as the general placement of income, ethnic, and racial groups by core and ring is the question of the intensity of residential clustering. For example, are the shops and houses of the printers so tightly clustered together in one neighborhood that they encourage the establishment of benevolent societies and unions somewhat in the manner of the medieval city with its guilds? Or are the printers' homes so dispersed that only the conditions in the shops themselves contribute to association? Are the immigrants of a given period so tightly clustered that they experience American culture only through the strong filter of an ethnic ghetto? Or are the immigrants mixed in with large proportions of other poor people so that their assimilation is a process of adapting to some more general culture of the American poor? Variations in the intensity of clustering will also affect the historian's evaluation of the functions of political bosses and their ward machines and of the services of city institutions like hospitals, schools, theaters, and saloons. By noting the ward location of the workers classified according to their industrial groups for Table I, and by adding information on the for-

eign-born and on rents, as it became available, one can compare the intensity of residential clustering in 1774, 1860, and 1930.

In the history of Philadelphia, the general trend in concentrations of settlement was striking. Between 1774 and 1860 necessity and convenience caused the members of some industries to cluster their homes. Then, with the improvement in intracity transportation and the creation of large business organizations, the necessity to hive faded away. As this industrial cause of clustering lapsed, intense segregation based on income, race, foreign birth, and class rose to prominence as the organizing principle of the metropolis. (See Table III.)

A value of twenty-five on the accompanying Index of Dissimilarity (Table III) makes a convenient boundary between strong and weak clustering.[16] Some groupings of industry like the building trades, wholesaling, and retailing never established strong residential clusters. In 1774 the laborers' homes clustered most intensely at the outer fringe of town; the other strong gatherings were the printers; the shipbuilders near the port; blacksmiths, tinsmiths, and coppersmiths (these occupations are included within the US census categories of Table III, namely, Metalworking except iron and steel; Iron, steel, and shipbuilding; Paper and printing).

The big city of 1860 continued some of these tendencies toward industrial concentration: professionals such as lawyers and doctors lived and practiced near the downtown; bakers lived and worked there, too, and also clustered near the city's eleven public markets. The strongest industrial cluster of this era, and remaining so in 1930, was the textileworkers. Another

[16] Karl E. Taeuber and Alma F. Taeuber, *Negroes in Cities: Residential Segregation and Neighborhood Change* (Chicago, 1965), 43–62.

TABLE III

INDEX OF DISSIMILARITY, PHILADELPHIA, SOUTHWARK, AND NORTHERN LIBERTIES, 1774; PHILADELPHIA, 1860; 1930[17]

1774	Index No.	1860	Index No.	1930	Index No.
				Rental under $15 per month	56.0
				Italy, foreign-born	50.7
				Negro, native and foreign	50.7
				Rental $100+	50.2
		Negro, free, native-born	47.3	Russia, foreign-born	44.4
				Poland, foreign-born	44.0
				Miscellaneous textiles	42.3
Laborers	37.2	Miscellaneous textiles	40.3	Rental $15–$29	35.3
Metalworking except iron and steel	32.5	Germany, foreign-born	34.1	Germany, foreign-born	32.4
				Rental $50–$99	31.5
		Bakeries	30.7	Hotels, laundries, and domestics	30.8
Iron, steel, and shipbuilding	29.4	Iron, steel, and shipbuilding	29.0		
Paper and printing	29.4			Clothing	27.7
				Transportation except railroads and transit	27.2
		Hotels, laundries, and domestics	25.9	Britain, except Northern Ireland, foreign-born	26.6
		Metalworking except iron and steel	25.6		
		Professional except entertainment	25.4		
Transportation except railroads and transit	24.7				
Miscellaneous textiles	24.3				

63

TABLE III (CONTINUED)

1774	Index No.	1860	Index No.	1930	Index No.
Clothing	22.3			Professional except entertainment	23.1
				Owned occupied home	22.6
Building trades	21.2	Laborers	21.9	Ireland, Northern and Southern, foreign-born	21.5
		Clothing	21.8		
Wholesale and retail	20.5	Ireland, Northern and Southern, foreign-born	19.8	Iron, steel, and shipbuilding	20.8
German patronyms	19.7	Transportation except railroads and transit	19.6	Rental $30–$49 (the median)	17.7
Professional except entertainment	19.7	Paper and printing	19.0		
Bakeries	16.7	Building trades	16.4	Metalworking except iron and steel	16.4
				Bakeries	15.2
Hotels, laundries, and domestics	15.1			Paper and printing	11.4
		Pennsylvania, native-born	10.1	Building	10.4
		Wholesale and retail	9.6		
Homeowners	6.1			Wholesale and retail	5.3

[17] This Index of Dissimilarity should give the reader some measure by which he can compare the intensity of residential clustering in Philadelphia in 1774 to clustering in 1860 and clustering in 1930. The index has been frequently used by sociologists to discuss segregation in modern American cities. The values of the index in this table are lower than for modern studies because all the tabulations had to be based upon ward data, the ward being the only subdivision of the city for which material was available in all three periods. To construct the index, proportions of each group (laborers, foreign-born Irish, and so forth) to the total population of each ward

sign of the future, visible from the tabulation for 1860, was the concentration of the hotel, laundry, and domestic workers. In this case their stronghold lay on the south side of the downtown, the site in 1930 of Philadelphia's sin and slum district. The evidence of the free Negroes also tells of the longstanding caste rules against that race. Theirs was the most intense segregation. The foreign-born Germans had created a strong cluster on the north side of town, but the largest immigrant group of all, the Irish, were evenly distributed throughout the city. They lived in basements, alleys, and attics on every block.[18]

In 1930, except for the textile group, well-paid skilled workers were scattered through the city's wards without much regard as to their in-

dustries. The new clusters of industry groupings shown in Table III were those who lacked skills and were not well paid: truckers, expressmen, sailors, clothing-workers, and workers in hotels, laundries, and domestic service. These were also the trades of the Negroes and the new immigrants. The index for 1930, then, shows the modern metropolitan pattern: high concentration of low skills and low rents. All the disfavored groups did not live in the same place, to be sure, but these groups divided up what was available wherever cheap old housing prevailed. In Philadelphia in the 1920's these conditions could be found especially in the core and in the old industrial sections of the north side. The rich, of course, huddled together, as segregated in their way as the poorest Negro.

These trends nicely match the general trend in the building of the American metropolis and the aging of its structures. They also reflect the strong early twentieth-century prejudice against foreigners and the intense caste feeling against Negroes. In this sense, the history of Philadelphia seems to conform to the general national history of urban growth, immigration, and industrialization.[19]

Because most of our social historians who are interested in big cities have been concerned with immigrants,

were calculated. Next the proportion of the group to the total population of the city was calculated. Then the index was computed. The index measures the degree to which the group in question clustered in some wards in higher proportions than its proportion to the total population of the city. It is a measure of the variation of the ward-by-ward distribution of one group as compared to all others in the city. If the index number were 0, then in each ward of the city the group in question would be distributed in precisely its proportion to the entire city's population. If the index number were 100, the group would be entirely concentrated in its ward, or wards, and present in no others. A full explanation of the index and other methods of measuring clustering appears in Taeuber and Taeuber, *Negroes in Cities*, 203–204, 223–38. The sources for the occupations and origins of this table were the same as those mentioned in the note to Table I. For a more complete description of the archival research behind the data for 1774, see Sam Bass Warner, Jr., *The Private City: Philadelphia in Three Periods of Its Growth* (Philadelphia, 1968), 225–28.

[18] I have compared these Philadelphia Index of Dissimilarity values for foreign-born in 1860 with those of Boston at about the same period. The results are similar: they indicate that the Irish assimilation in Boston also took place in mixed poor neighborhoods of both foreign-born and native poor as well as in heterogeneous wards of all classes and backgrounds. The Index of Dissimilarity values for Boston (twelve wards, 1855) were: foreign-born Irish, 8.0; foreign-born Canadians, 13.9; foreign-born Germans and Dutch, 33.8. (*Census of Massachusetts: 1855* [Boston, 1856], 124–27.)

[19] Students in my seminar at Washington University did some computations of the Index of Dissimilarity for 1910 and 1950 and arrived at values consistent with those given here for Philadelphia in 1930 for Baltimore, Boston, Chicago, Cincinnati, Houston, Kansas City, Los Angeles, Louisville, Manhattan and Brooklyn, St. Louis, and San Francisco. Stanley Lieberson did a careful study of ethnic group patterns in Boston, Buffalo, Chicago, Cincinnati, Cleveland, Columbus, Philadelphia, Pittsburgh, St. Louis, and Syracuse, using similar methods. His results also fit with my values for Philadelphia. (Stanley Lieberson, *Ethnic Patterns in American Cities* [New York, 1963], 209–18.)

and because our labor historians have not been concerned with cities, American history has failed to deal with the interaction between urban environments and the social organization of work. The simplest statistical computation shows that we have ignored a series of events of wide implication and enormous magnitude. The arrangement of most of the economic activities of a city into work groups is as much of a revolution in the environments of cities as the introduction of the automobile or electricity. In this important dimension of social structure, the town of 1774, the big city of 1860, and the industrial metropolis of 1930 all differed markedly from each other.

In eighteenth-century Philadelphia, with but very few exceptions, most people labored alone, with their family, or with a partner or a helper

or two.[20] The first wave of industrialization brought a large fraction of the city's manufacturing workers into a group organization of work. (See Table IV.) The technique of rationalizing tasks so that they could be performed by groups of men and women working within one shop, rather than as individuals laboring in a neighborhood of households, was to my mind the largest component in the first wave of urban industrialization. The early increases in productivity in most lines of urban manufacture came from the work of groups, not from the new machines. The violent strikes and the

[20] The exceptions were shipyards, ropewalks, and distilleries in the city. In the country the plantation for manufacture or agriculture was the setting for group work. The only other common cases were ships and the army. (Richard B. Morris, *Government and Labor in Early America* [New York, 1946], 38–40; Carl Bridenbaugh, *The Colonial Craftsman* [New York, 1950], 126–29, 136–39, 141–43.)

TABLE IV

AVERAGE SIZE OF ESTABLISHMENTS IN MAJOR LINES
OF MANUFACTURE, PHILADELPHIA, 1860, 1930[21]

Total Persons Employed	1860	Average No. Persons Per Establishment
98,397	All lines of manufacture	15.6
1,255	Locomotives	627.5
4,793	Cotton goods	94.0
1,131	Gas fixtures	75.4
3,258	Cotton and woolen goods	63.9
1,021	Umbrellas and parasols	48.6
3,290	Shirts, collars, etc.	45.7
14,387	Clothing, men's and boys'	40.9
1,219	Silk fringes and trimmings	39.3
1,876	Bricks	38.3
2,285	Hosiery, woolen	32.2
1,613	Machinery, general, of iron	26.4
2,680	Carpets	21.6
1,190	Bookbinders	20.0
1,038	Carriages and coaches	20.0
1,326	Leather	15.8
8,434	Boots and shoes	12.0
1,627	Furniture and cabinetmakers' wares	10.1
1,290	Cigars	5.6
1,138	Millinery, laces, etc.	4.9
54,851		

TABLE IV (CONTINUED)

Total Persons Employed	1930	Average No. Persons Per Establishment
292,616	All lines of manufacture	52.6
1,986	Sugar refining	662.0
3,103	Iron and steel mills	443.3
20,280	Electrical machinery	375.6
1,535	Paper	307.0
5,105	Leather	204.2
8,321	Worsted goods	180.9
8,564	Cigars and cigarettes	161.6
26,693	Knit goods	134.1
1,861	Chemicals	124.1
1,245	Dental goods and equipment	113.2
13,806	Printing and publishing, newspaper and magazine	99.3
3,479	Silk and rayon manufacture	94.0
2,219	Cotton, small wares	92.5
1,829	Druggists' preparations	91.5
5,692	Cotton goods	79.1
3,002	Woolen goods	73.2
3,327	Shirts	72.3
1,840	Meat packing, wholesale	59.4
13,083	Foundry and machine-shop production	59.2
3,227	Boxes, paper	50.4
4,056	Dyeing and finishing textiles	41.4
4,676	Furniture, including store fixtures	41.0
11,680	Clothing, men's and boys'	39.6
3,884	Confectionery	39.2
2,070	Paints and varnishes	37.6
1,432	Ice cream	36.7
1,114	Structural and ornamental iron	35.9
9,304	Clothing, women's	31.3
1,464	Fancy and miscellaneous articles	30.5
1,463	Planing mill products	28.7
1,513	Nonferrous metals	28.0
1,293	Copper, tin, sheet ironwork	21.9
8,413	Bread and bakery products	16.5
7,319	Printing and publishing, book and job	15.2
189,878		

[21] A major line of manufacturing is one that employed one thousand or more persons in the city of Philadelphia. Office help is included with the mill hands, supervisors, owners, and employers. Many children are omitted in 1860 in those lines, like cigar making, that were dominated by small shops. (Philadelphia Board of Trade, *Manufactures of Philadelphia* [Philadelphia, 1861], 5–18; *U.S. Fifteenth Census: 1930, Manufactures*, III, 466–67.)

anti-Catholic and anti-Negro riots of the 1830's and 1840's testify to the painful and revolutionary effect of this social change.[22] By 1930 three-quarters of Philadelphia's work force —in office, factory, store, and government—labored in groups.[23]

In the simplest sense this transformation of the organization of work had the effect of creating a new lattice of loyalties and social relationships in the city. If factory workers may be taken as indicative of the behavior of clerical and retail help, then the University of Pennsylvania's Wharton School studies show that most city dwellers in the 1920's settled down to more or less permanent jobs after four or five years of shopping around.[24] It seems fair to reason that in time the men and women of his work group must have become important members of a worker's social life and that the group must have become a source of discipline, loyalty, and culture in its own right. These were some of the positive results of removing a large fraction of the city's work force from entrepreneurial roles.[25]

Research on the historical interactions between the group organization of work and urban residential environments is not yet fairly begun, yet such research seems to hold great promise for extending our comprehension of the processes of urban history. In my own study of Philadelphia I have found that even such simple information as the average size of establishment by industry adds significantly to the understanding of such important events as the rise and decline of unions and strikes, epidemics of street violence, and the development of an isolated mill-town culture in one quarter of Philadelphia as opposed to the suburban-downtown white-collar culture of another quarter.[26]

To sum up, what in the way of intellectual scaffolding for urban history does this survey of Philadelphia offer? It provides a descriptive framework relating changes in scale to changes in structure.

First, at each period of Philadelphia's history (1774, 1860, 1930) the city had grown to a radically different size, from 24,000 to 566,000 to 1,951,000. The proportions of the social elements of the city were thoroughly altered by such shifts, as were all the city's environments. The basic distribution of the city's jobs and houses according to core and ring varied with each period, and the variations depended directly upon rapid urban growth. The implications of such changes in social geography for political institutions, communications within the city, municipal institutions, and informal associations have yet to be explored with any thoroughness.

[22] *History of Labour in the United States*, ed. John R. Commons (4 vols., New York, 1918–35), I, 185–230.
[23] It seems reasonable to estimate that conditions of work in groups prevailed in all lines of activity where the average size of the establishment was fifteen or more. (William M. Hench, *Trends in the Size of Industrial Companies in Philadelphia for 1915–1930* [Philadelphia, 1948], 7–8, 21–23; *U.S. Fourteenth Census: 1920*, IX, *Manufactures*, 1277; *U.S. Fifteenth Census: 1930, Manufactures*, III, 444, *Wholesale Distribution*, II, 1262–67; Pennsylvania Department of Labor and Industry, "Employment Fluctuations in Pennsylvania 1921–1927," *Special Bulletin 24* [Harrisburg, 1928], 30.)
[24] Anne Bezanson *et al., Four Years of Labor Mobility: A Study of Labor Turnover from a Group of Selected Plants in Philadelphia, 1921–1924* (Philadelphia, 1925), 70–96.
[25] A good way to get some feeling for the issues of urban work groups would be to look at the data in *The Pittsburgh Survey*, ed. Paul U. Kellogg (6 vols., New York, 1909–14), in the light of the suggestions of Robert Blauner *Alienation and Freedom: The Factory Worker and His Industry* (Chicago, 1964); and Marc

Fried, "The Role of Work in a Mobile Society," *Planning for a Nation of Cities*, ed. Sam Bass Warner, Jr. (Cambridge, Mass., 1966), 81–104.
[26] *Id., The Private City.*

Here is a great opportunity for studies of small areas that would reinterpret the materials of local history.

Second, the occupational history of the city changes according to the sequences suggested by current generalizations of economic history. The very conformity of Philadelphia to these generalizations suggests that the city responded to advances in transportation, business organization, and technology as a member of a large Atlantic economy and society.

Third, the social geography of industrialization appears to have been one of complex changes. The interaction of the events of industrialization with those of rapid growth seems to have shifted residential segregation away from clustering by occupations toward clustering by classes, ethnicity, and race. Studies of these events are just beginning.[27]

Fourth, industrialization populated the city with a new set of social units: work groups. The nature of these groups, their number, and their impact upon other events in the history of large cities changed significantly over time. Again, the subject is unexplored and calls for research that combines local and institutional history.

Altogether the Philadelphia data confirm the utility of Mumford's descriptive sociotechnical categories and the economic historians' developmental sequences as a useful basis for analysis of the history of any large modern city, or for the comparison of different cities. The unities of scale, social structure, economic institutions, and technology at various stages in the modern process of industrialization and urbanization are inescapable.

This article is offered as the first attempt to discover and arrange the data for one large modern city in such a way that historians may find evidence of the processes they have long speculated upon. It is hoped, further, that the data concerning Philadelphia will give urban historians a scaffolding on which to build the studies of small areas that are required for the history of changing urban environments. Since the data are simple, moreover, their systematic arrangement should encourage historians of other cities to make comparisons that will enable us to say if all the world really was Philadelphia.

[27] There is a suggestive study of Manhattan in 1840 that unfortunately suffers from the incompleteness of street directory data: Allan R. Pred, *Annals of the Association of American Geographers*, LVI (June 1966), 307–38.

2 The Establishment and Growth

Early American cities grew up reflecting the cultural heritage and mercantilist policies of the Old World. The location, character, form, and growth of these cities, however, were influenced by specific features of the New World, in terms of its physical environment, human needs and influences, cultural and philosophical outlook, and technological state.

A prerequisite for the emergence of a city is, in the language of the sociologist, a favorable ecological base. Without it the aspirations of the settlers cannot be fulfilled. The first site of Charleston was abandoned when the inhabitants associated the marshy location with the fever that was plaguing them. Similar disadvantages accompanied their second choice, but these were compensated by the presence of a large, fertile hinterland. Climate, topography, and natural resources played varying roles in the locating of colonial settlements and in their future development. Different periods in time present different needs, and the criteria that loom largest in one period may later be displaced by others. The commerce and industry of eighteenth-century cities required that these cities be located at a seaport or at the fall line of a river.

# of Urban Centers

In the nineteenth century, the emergence of the railroad for transportation and of electrical power for energy made these stipulations less important, and proximity to a hinterland and deposits of natural resources became necessary. In the twentieth century, the emphasis on leisure time has placed a premium on a favorable outdoor climate.

The success of one city relative to another is never solely determined by environment. Man interacts with his environment and shapes the character and form of the city through his needs and actions. That cities are founded and that they develop in the distinctive ways that they do depends on deliberate decisions by individuals and groups of individuals. Fundamental to a city's origin in colonial America was the need for security from hostile enemies and strange surroundings, for religious community, and for the establishment of administrative units. The location of Boston, which originally was an island joined to the mainland by a narrow strip of land, served as a source of protection. Providence and New Haven were settled by dissatisfied Puritans who desired to establish their own religious community. Norfolk, Balitmore, and New York were founded as a result of the mercantilist need to establish administrative outposts.

In time, military, religious, and political considerations in urban development gave way to economic considerations. The increased agricultural productivity of a region, which promoted the need for market places as sources of exchange of goods, was fundamental to the initial growth of most early cities. The development of commerce and transportation, in the colonial period and for the first half of the nineteenth century, generated the consonant growth of the cities, which not only provided selling, docking, and storage facilities, but also supplied the supporting population for the commercial activity. Later the growth and concentration of manufacturing industries became more significant. The rise of one city and the decline of another were often determined by a city's capacity for satisfying the economic needs of the region. Urban growth is an integral part of the history of promotional efforts by entrepreneurs and the economic rivalries between cities for economic expansion and domination.

Another determinant in urban growth was the need for social and cultural interaction. The gregarious nature of man, his desire for education and recreation, his ambition to acquire conveniences and luxuries, and his search for distinction in business, politics, and scholarship led to his concentration in cities. The quantitative development and qualitative evaluation of the city were influenced by the extent to which it fulfilled these needs. A concentrated population called for new social and political institutions, and the city's ability to respond progressively to these demands influenced its capacity for growth. This, in turn, coupled with a city's social and cultural characteristics, provides a new basis for judging the quality of urban life.

Each of these controlling conditions was constrained or aided by the state of technology. The development of more effective weapons made the city less dependent on walls and allowed for the dispersion of population. The advancement of medical knowledge eliminated some fears and enabled the population to deal with real health threats. The streetcar encouraged horizontal expansion, while the skyscraper permitted vertical expansion. Communication and transportation influenced size and location. Availability of power, like steam or electricity, influenced the economic growth and the social structure. Although there are many examples which illuminate the relationship between technology and urbanization, it is arguable as to which is cause and which is effect. This problem will be further explored in Section 4.

To a large extent the character of inquiries into the establishment and growth of urban centers is determined by the definition of urbanization. The readings in the previous section suggested several ways of looking at the urban process; the following five readings vary in their views and should be considered in light of their assumptions. The first, by Carl Bridenbaugh, assumes a broad sweep of the beginning one-hundred years of urban life in the American colonies and discusses several of its characteristics. The second, by Julius Rubin, explores the notion of city growth and considers the conditions which influenced it. The next two elaborate on the role of urban rivalry and internal improvements. Finally, Charles Glaab's selection brings back into focus the importance of man's decisions in urban growth.

The period covered by this section brings us just into the post-Civil War era, and although it discusses many aspects of the city, it is not all-inclusive. Readings in later sections, such as those in "Urbanization and Industrialization" and several in "Metropolitanization," give the reader a fuller understanding of those elements that contribute to the development of urban centers. Factors which were relevant in the early years of urban growth in a pre-industrial society became less important later; they were replaced with the ascendancy of industrialization, service-oriented activities, government policy, immigration, and recreation.

The Foundations of American Urban Society

Carl Bridenbaugh*

The first hundred years of town history on the American continent witnessed the foundation and gradual development of a truly urban society. The story of American life is customarily regarded as a compound of sectional histories, and in the early colonial period two sections are commonly considered,—the tidewater and the frontier. Yet the tidewater was itself divided, and if we consider the sections as social and psychological rather than as purely geographical entities, it is possible to distinguish three of them,—the rural, agricultural society of the countryside; the restless, advancing society of the frontier; and the urban, commercial society of the larger seaports. Beginning as small specks in the wilderness, the five communities grew from tiny villages into towns, and finally attained the status of small cities. With other village communities of similar interests and outlook which multiplied and grew in the eighteenth century, they emerged as a social and economic "section" extending the length of the Atlantic seaboard, and exhibiting definite urban characteristics in striking contrast to rural farming districts and wilder regions of the frontier. Life in urban areas produced its own peculiar problems to be faced, and the urban viewpoint, based upon continuous close contacts with Europe, derived less from agriculture than from trade. Commercially minded town society looked to the East rather than the West, and was destined from the first to serve as the connecting link between colonial America and its Old World parents.

The future of the colonial towns became immediately evident from the conditions surrounding their birth. Designed as trading communities, they were established on sites most favorable for the pursuit of commerce. They were the western outposts of European commercial expansion in the seventeenth century. City-dwellers from the Old World formed the larger proportion of early town populations, and from the start commercial relations with England or Holland were maintained. Most significantly, the founding process occurred at a time when western Europe, under Dutch and English leadership, was gradually outgrowing and casting off the limitations of medieval feudal economy. Colonial towns grew to maturity in the era of world expansion attending the emergence of modern capitalism, and being new communities, with few irrevocably established customs or traditions, they frequently adapted themselves to the economic drift with more ease and readiness than did the older cities of England. Moreover, the colonizing movement was itself an expression of early capitalistic activity. It called forth organized rather than individual efforts and resources, created new and wider markets for economic development, and opened up seemingly unlimited territories for imperialistic exploitation. It thus produced a marked effect upon Old World economy, accelerating the breakdown of local units of business, and facilitating the formation of larger and more complex organizations of commerce and finance.

*From *Cities in the Wilderness,* by Carl Bridenbaugh. Copyright 1938 and renewed 1966 by Carl Bridenbaugh. Reprinted by permission of Alfred A. Knopf, Inc.

The problems which confronted town-dwellers in America were not only those of urban communities, but of a pioneer society as well. Urban development depends largely upon community wealth, and upon the willingness of the group to devote portions of it to projects for civic betterment, or to consent to taxation for this purpose. To a considerable extent the nature of town governments and the extent of authority vested in them conditioned the expenditure of town wealth for community enterprises. Here the colonists were hampered by the traditional nature of the charters of medieval English municipal corporations, whose limitations ill accorded with circumstances in seventeenth and eighteenth century America, especially with the imperious demands for expansion and immediate activity in the New World. In New England towns a new political organization, the town meeting, developed, which exhibited considerable efficiency in the handling of urban problems. This institution was more immediately susceptible to social wants and requirements than were the aristocratic, self-perpetuating corporations founded in America after the example of English municipal governments. Its greater powers of local taxation, and the fact that it placed the spending of public moneys and the enactment of civic ordinances in the hands of those directly affected by these operations, made it a far more effective form of government for dealing with community problems. These problems were the greater, because in the first century of their history the five colonial seaports enjoyed a much more rapid physical growth than did the cities of contemporary Europe. The individual enterprise of American towndwellers, and the commercial expansion and prosperity they achieved, aided in the solution of these problems of town living, but much of the efficiency and success which attended their efforts may be attributed to the emergence in the New World of a relatively high sense of civic responsibility in the early eighteenth century, at a time when public consciousness in Europe had receded to an extremely low ebb.

The towns were primarily commercial communities seeking treasure by foreign trade, and their economic vitality and commercial demands led to their early breaking the narrow bonds of medieval economic practice to forge ahead on uncharted but highly profitable commercial adventures. All five, during their first century, developed from simple manorial organizations, completely dependent upon European connections, into full-fledged commercial centers, only partially tied to England, and in many cases competing with British cities for a share of imperial traffic. Boston entered early into the West Indian provision trade, thereby setting an example for other American commercial communities. Soon Massachusetts mariners were seeking to monopolize the colonial carrying traffic in ships of their own building, and the profits of carrier and middleman became the basis of the Bay town's prosperity. Her priority in this field gave her an advantage which other seaports did not begin to overcome until the fourth decade of the eighteenth century. A further foundation for urban economic prosperity lay in the existence of an expanding frontier society with its great need for manufactured products. This made possible an earlier development of the towns as distributing centers for a wide hinterland than was the case with English cities like Bristol, Norwich and Exeter, and became in this first century as important a factor in the economic growth of New York, Philadelphia and Charles Town as in that of the New England metropolis. As a producer of staple goods for exchange in trade, Boston, with its limited back country was at a disadvantage. More fortunate were New York with its flour and furs, Philadelphia, with its great staples of wheat, meat and lumber, and Charles Town, which after 1710 found prosperity in the important South Carolina crops of rice and indigo. Eventually the communities enjoying this sound economic backing rose to threaten the supremacy of Boston in colonial trade, while Newport and Philadelphia cut heavily into the Bay town's West India commerce. In the eighteenth century also Newport attained importance in shipbuilding and the slave trade. By 1742 Boston merchants were facing a period of relative decline, while their competitors in other colonial towns found the volume and profits of their traffic steadily mounting.

Continual increase in the volume of colonial trade and enlargement of the territory served by the towns led to greater complexity in commercial relations. In the early years merchants performed all types of business, but toward 1700 their functions began to be more specialized. Retail merchandising having definitely emerged by 1700, the great merchant now dealt chiefly with larger operations of exporting, importing and wholesaling, leaving much of the small trade to the shopkeeper. Demands of trade had by 1710 necessitated the issuance of paper currency in most of the colonies, and the establishment of the colonial post office to serve intercolonial communication. Growing business further led to the creation of insurance offices and some extension of credit facilities. Profits from trade, originally completely absorbed in shipbuilding ventures and industries subsidiary to shipping, now began to create a surplus which sought investment in land, or,

in some communities, in the development of certain forms of manufacturing.

Economic prosperity thus made possible the rise of colonial cities. It led to physical expansion of town boundaries, and facilitated dealing with urban problems by corporate effort. Wealth wrung from trade, more than any other single factor, determined the growth of a town society, in which urban amusements and a colonial culture might thrive. This is not, however, to force the history of urban America within the narrow bounds of an exclusively economic interpretation. Social and intellectual development are dependent upon and conditioned by economic progress, but they are not its necessary and inevitable result. They are altered, encouraged or stifled by the action and influence of material forces, but they are not necessarily caused or even initiated solely by economic factors.

When we consider American urban society, apart from its economic aspects, we find it characterized by certain problems affecting it as a unit, and with which as a unit it had to deal. Such problems in general, or collective attempts for their control and regulation, are either absent from or unimportant in rural or frontier societies, but in the case of our urban section they are present, in rudimentary form at least, from its inception. They persist and grow with the maturing of that section, and the means taken for dealing with them further differentiate the urban from other types of society.

Logically, the first of these problems to appear are the physical, and of these the most immediate was housing. As in rural regions this remained for the most part an individual problem, and there are only a few cases on record where even indirectly, by sale or subdivision of land or by encouragement of artisans, the community stepped in to relieve a housing shortage. On the other hand, the laying out and maintaining of a highway system constituted a problem, perhaps the first, which transcended private initiative. Not that the community at any time scorned the assistance of private enterprise; a favorite device, at Boston and elsewhere, throughout the colonial era, was by remission of taxes or grant of other privileges to encourage individuals to open up streets and undertake paving operations for public use at their own charge. But from the beginning public authorities indicated the location of roads, supervised the opening up of new ones, ordered their clearing or partial paving by abutters, and strove to prevent encroachments upon them. At Philadelphia and Charles Town, where some prior power had surveyed and planned the thoroughfares, the first task of local authorities was light; it was more arduous in other communities, where there was no preliminary plan, and where the design had constantly to be expanded and altered to keep pace with town growth. The problems accompanying the mere existence of a highway system,—paving, cleaning and upkeep,—called for full exercise of municipal authority. Sometimes the community exacted from each inhabitant a yearly amount of labor on the streets; in other cases it hired this labor and paid for it outright. In either case it had to levy special taxes, for materials or labor or both. To insure some cleanliness in the streets, it passed mandatory ordinances restricting the conduct of townsmen, impressed the services of carters, and employed public funds for the hire of scavengers. Further to protect the public ways, it restricted and regulated the traffic upon them, especially the weight of cart loads and the width of their wheels. Less necessary but de-

sirable improvements in the highways, like the construction of drains, first came about through private demand and initiative, but as the civic power matured and public funds became available, these too became public functions and responsibilities. In either the municipal or the individual approach to highway problems the towns had good precedent in the Mother Country. In actual execution, especially with regard to refinements like paving and drainage, they seem in some cases to have gone beyond contemporary English cities. With a few exceptions, this generalization does not apply to the corporation governed towns, or to the unfortunately ungoverned metropolis of South Carolina.

Highways may be said to constitute the most rudimentary of public utilities, but there were others,—bridges, wharves, and engineering projects,— of which colonial townsfolk almost immediately felt the need. In the beginning, while municipal authority was politically and financially feeble, these were almost solely the product of private enterprise, but with the gradual tendency of town development they became increasingly matters of public concern. Following Old World precedent, bridges were conceived as parts of the highway system, and hence undoubtedly under public control, but they were usually constructed and operated by private persons or companies, under grant from local or provincial authorities. As the century progressed, in a few cases, notably at Philadelphia and Boston, town governments directly managed the operation and upkeep of bridges. Land reclamation projects, and harbor facilities like lighthouses, pursued a similar history. In the case of wharves, they were either a municipal or a private concern. Most towns maintained a minimum of public docking facilities, while more ambitious wharf projects, like the Long Wharves of Boston and Newport, were only within the capacity of private capital. At Philadelphia public docking facilities were so excellent as to discourage employment of private capital in their erection; at New York, so poor as to require it. Toward the end of the era, when the demands of trade began to make regular transportation between communities desirable, stage and freight routes, too, were operated by private capital, under license, usually from the provincial government.

Fire constitutes a threat especially dangerous to urban communities, and as buildings in colonial towns were from the beginning placed close together, its imminence was immediately felt. The combatting and prevention of fire called forth more than individual efforts from the start. Municipal ordinances required the keeping of fire fighting equipment by all townsmen, regulated their chimneys, forbade bonfires, fireworks, and the housing of explosives in crowded areas. Public authorities had also to make direct outlays for fire fighting equipment of their own, and hire companies for its care and operation. In Boston, Philadelphia and Newport private societies for the protection of property during fires were organized to supplement public agencies. Similarly, water supply for fire uses was a matter of public concern and regulation. Boston, with its crowded streets and buildings of inflammable construction, and its willingness to spend public money and energy for public welfare, was in general far in the forefront with regard to its fire defenses, but by the end of the first century all towns possessed fire engines of the latest European model, and fire fighting regulations equal or superior to those of the average English town.

A distinctive urban function grew

in part out of the fire hazards of crowded sections,—the enactment of building regulations. Only public authority could specify the nature of legal building materials as did Boston after the fire of 1679 and the South Carolina Assembly after the Charles Town fire of 1740. Exercise of municipal powers was also necessary to prevent imperfect construction and dangerous neglect of town chimneys and hearths. In addition, conditions of urban congestion led to party-wall regulations like those of Boston and Philadelphia.

Another, more subtle class of problems, those which involved the personal relationships of inhabitants, affected town society from its inception. Intensified by the peculiar conditions of urban life, they required collective rather than individual efforts and powers for their control. Old World experience had taught town-dwellers the immediate need for means of preserving the public peace in settled communities, and the early appearance of constables in all towns supplied the traditional response to that need. For their security after nightfall the towns appointed bellmen or watchmen of varying degrees of efficiency. New York, after developing a highly effective nocturnal police in the seventeenth century, allowed this institution to languish from unwillingness to devote the necessary public funds thereto; other towns were slower in supplying the need, though somewhat more successful by the end of the first century. Efficiency of the watch was in direct ratio to the availability of public funds for its support,—impressment of a citizen's watch having revealed its inadequacy by the turn of the century,—and here the New England towns, with their powers of local taxation, were at a distinct advantage. There are numerous instances, during periods of unusual danger or disturbance like wars or epidemics, when the towns entirely failed in their efforts to preserve nocturnal peace, and their functions had to be taken over by the military arm of the provincial government.

Existence of crime and disorder early became a community concern in urban settlements. Here invitations to lawbreaking existed in the inequalities of wealth and opportunity, and materials for its perpetration in the diverse and unruly elements of town and seaport society. The concentration of people, many of them hardworked and underprivileged, also made for mob disorders, which increased in violence and frequency with the growth of the towns. Presence of sailors, blacks, foreigners, paupers, unpopular religious sects, interlopers in trade, profiteers, and rival political factions, all provided increasing incentives for disorder and violence as the period progressed. Town society clearly soon passed beyond the stage where individual efforts or the force of public opinion could deal with this problem; rather it required the sanctions of the law. Provincial governments passed legislation, and municipal authorities enacted ordinances outlawing offenses against society. Riot acts were drawn up by colonial assemblies, and the local constabulary did its best to round up and confine the perpetrators of disorder and violence. In general, the towns could do little to remove the causes of criminality, and the solution of this peculiarly vexing problem of city life remained as remote in the seventeenth and eighteenth centuries as today.

For punishments, colonial authorities followed a number of Old World precedents, favoring especially the speediest and least expensive methods, —fines, floggings, public humiliation, restitution of stolen goods, and, occasionally, mutilation. In general, their criminal codes were less brutal than those of contemporary Europe. Efforts to make the whole community a partner in the work of law enforcement appeared in the division with informers of the proceeds from fines. Prisons were still generally places of detention for those awaiting trial, though imprisonment as punishment for crime seems to have become more widespread as the period advanced, and save in the case of debtors was probably somewhat more in use in the colonies than in the Old World. The frequency of jail breaks indicates the inefficiency of all colonial prisons, and their inadequacy suggests the absence of more vicious criminal types that troubled older societies. Yet colonial prisons were probably no more inadequate than those of contemporary England, and certainly far less squalid and brutal. Save in the case of Philadelphia in the eighteenth century, the rudimentary penology of the times made no distinction between various classes of offenders, and absence of prison facilities led to frequent misuse of alms and workhouses, wherein pauper and lawbreaker were housed together.

Offenses against the moral and ethical standards which society imposes appear more flagrant in the comparative populousness and congestion of urban environments, and early forced themselves upon the attention of colonial communities. In addition, the psychology of the times made many aspects of the regulation of conduct, manners and dress a legitimate province for the public authority. Early appearance of prostitution in the towns shocked authorities into decreeing harsh penalties for it and similar offenses. With its increasing prevalence in a society which included growingly diverse and uncontrollable elements, they seem everywhere to have become less concerned with the actual offense than with the fear lest the illegitimate offspring become charges to the community. Drunkenness was a prevailing vice, and in all towns the authorities and the better elements fought to eradicate it. Excellent tavern legislation in several of the towns reduced this offense to a minimum, but illegal sale of liquor, and misuse of the legitimate product, continued to baffle municipal authority throughout the period. Sabbath legislation in every town,—as strict in the Anglican South as in Puritan New England,—attempted to insure the sacred character of the Lord's Day. Gambling, card-playing, loitering, idleness, extravagance in dress and behavior, and evidence of frivolity came under the ban of public regulation, either through colony or municipal authority, or as at Philadelphia through the dominant religious group. Especially at Boston and Philadelphia many seemingly innocent amusements suffered from the disapproval of a stern and narrow religion, which served as a powerful and useful supplement to the civic power.

The existence and effects of crime and immorality are intensified in urban communities; so, too, the problem of pauperism. Reports of travelers as to the absence of poverty from colonial towns can only be regarded as comparatively true, for in each town numbers of those unable to care for themselves soon constituted a problem of which the community had to take cognizance. The generally excellent methods with which the towns met this problem indicate a considerable sense of civic maturity and responsibility. New York and Charles Town favored the out-relief method through most of the period, but Boston and Philadelphia had by the end of the century well-regulated and practically self-supporting workhouses, and Newport maintained an adequate almshouse. Considerable direct relief had to be granted, especially at Boston, and in all towns save New York private or religious organizations supplemented the public work of poor relief. Methods to forestall the growth of poverty were devised, such as compulsory apprenticeship of poor children, exclusion of strangers without obvious means of livelihood, and, especially in the New England towns, restriction of immigration. In times of particular stress special devices had to be resorted to, as the distribution of corn or firewood, or a temporary embargo on export of necessary commodities. At Boston, where the problem of poverty became acute in the 1670's and was never thereafter absent, careful registration of all aliens and dependents prevailed, and a public granary was maintained.

The general health, which in rural regions may be privately cared for, early became in urban communities a matter for public concern, and municipal ordinances soon restricted the conduct of inhabitants in matters which might affect the general well-being. Location of wells and privies, and of slaughterhouses and tan pits which might become public nuisances, removal of dumps and disposal of refuse were all subjects of municipal regulation. Similarly, public authorities directed inhabitants in their behavior during epidemics, and enacted quarantine regulations in an attempt to prevent visitations of infectious disease. Toward the end of the century excellent isolation hospitals appeared in several of the towns, erected and operated by the municipality. Despite failure in this period of all attempts to regulate the practice of medicine by town or colony, the medical profession in the towns attained a relatively high development for the times.

In their approach to the physical and social problems of urban life the towns were imitators, not originators. The townsmen came to America with a fund of European experience from which they seldom deviated, and new methods as they employed them had usually first to cross the Atlantic. Poor relief and tavern legislation were directly imported from Great Britain, and the towns might conceivably have done better with their police problem had not Old World precedent served them so exclusively as a guide. Yet it may be said that in several cases there are distinct improvements in the thoroughness with which old methods were employed, and which may usually be traced to the individual civic pride of townsmen, reflected in their municipal governments. This is especially true of communities which enjoyed the town meeting form of government, where, as we have seen, the direct demands of townspeople could effect greater thoroughness and efficiency in dealing with town business, but even in the corporation governments of America there is less indifference to the public welfare than may be noted in contemporary England or Europe. Visitors were impressed with the excellence of poor relief at Boston and Philadelphia, and with Philadelphia's model prison. Fire defences in the towns were a combination of English and Dutch examples, and, especially at Boston, probably unsurpassed for their time. Solution of urban problems in colonial towns was continually hampered by lack of public funds or of necessary authority for obtaining them, —the sad decline of New York's excellent watch is an illustration,—but it was assisted, where public power failed, either politically or financially, by an encouraging growth of civic consciousness among private individuals and non-political organizations. Establishment of private agencies for charity, education, fire protection, improvement of morals, and the like, and the appearance of individual benefactors to the public welfare of the community, in an age not distinguished for civic virtue or interest, is a remarkable and significant accomplishment of town society in colonial America.

Having as they all did a common model and experience, colonial towns exhibit a remarkable similarity in the solution of their urban problems. There are many instances of the failure of a community to provide the usual and accepted necessary solution, but, with the possible exception of Philadelphia's eighteenth century prison, hardly a single example of the development by one town of a unique institution. By the time that local divergences from the original plan might have been expected to appear, communication had sufficiently improved to permit of one town's borrowing from the successful experience of another. The same holds true for privately initiated supplements of municipal endeavor. The Scot's Charitable Society and the Fire Society appeared in Boston, copied from European models, and at a later date are further copied by other American towns. In the eighteenth century, because of its long experience in dealing with urban problems, the greater efficiency of its form of government, and its willingness to spend public money for the public good, Boston became the great example, with respect to municipal institutions, for other towns on the continent, but it enjoyed no monopoly of this function. New Yorkers had the fire defences of Philadelphia held up to them as a model, Bostonians were shamed by the excellence of Philadelphia's market, while Charlestonians tried to fashion their city government after the example of the corporation of New York. By the end of the period under review this inter-city exchange of experience had resulted in a striking similarity in municipal institutions, as well as a fairly uniform level of their development. Boston, for the reasons enumerated above, was probably still somewhat in advance in matters of social and material concern, though with its humanitarian agencies Philadelphia was running a close second. Charles Town, within the limits of its governmental incapacity, dealt in fairly efficient fashion with its problems; at Newport, a lesser development of these problems had not yet necessitated any great display of urban consciousness. Even at New York, where political factionalism, a selfish corporation, and the difficulty of amalgamating two languages and nationalities prevented a consistent and devoted attempt to solve the problems of urban living, a comparison of its municipal life with that of older provincial cities of the British Empire would not have resulted in discredit to the former.

The accumulation of economic resources and their concentration in urban units, their direction in commercial ventures which attracted and supported large populations within these units, and the problems of providing for the physical and social well-being of those who thus became city-dwellers, all these aspects of urban development succeeded in bringing forth in America a distinctive society. In constitution, spiritual life, recreational activities, and intellectual pursuits it differed from types of society to be found in other sections of the continent. In respect neither to national origins nor to economic status of their inhabitants did the towns long remain homogeneous. Settled originally by people of the same nation, usually of the same locality, they soon came to include children of other European countries and of another race. Early in their history there could be found small groups of Scots in Boston, French Huguenots in Boston, New

York and Charles Town, Welsh in Philadelphia, and a few Jews in every town. Many Germans settled in the 1680's in the environs of Philadelphia, and New York from the time of the first English occupation presented the problem of two peoples, each with their own language, schools and churches, living side by side under government by the numerically weaker group. This incipient cosmopolitanism flowered with the renewed immigration of the early eighteenth century, when all towns received numbers of Scotch-Irish, and the middle and southern cities, especially Philadelphia, large accessions of German exiles. For the most part these strangers were allowed to settle peaceably in colonial towns, whose economic expansion enabled them easily to absorb the newcomers, and though recent arrivals seldom attained social recognition or overcame the barrier of language where it existed, still there was little nativism and small emphasis on the superior advantages of Anglo-Saxon nativity. Such bountiful immigration did, however, lead to many restrictions, especially in the north, where the labor market was well supplied and the poor rates over-burdened, to establishment of special churches and social organizations, and in Philadelphia, at least, to common use of the German language in business transactions. By far the greater problem was created by the presence of African Negroes in all towns. In Boston and Newport, where they were used mainly as house servants, and where many of them were free, the problem was negligible. They were subect to various discriminatory rules, such as those which required them to work out their obligations to the community in menial labor rather than by watch or militia duty. But at New York and Charles Town their greater numbers kept constantly present the fear of servile insurrection. At the former town they were the unfortunate objects of such waves of hysteria as the Negro Conspiracy of 1741, and at Charles Town, where they at times equalled the white population in numbers, a severe slave code kept them in subjection.

Social stratification further differentiated urban society from the easy democracy of the back country, where any man might own land and all must work with their hands. Distinctions between the well-to-do and the not-so-rich were perhaps relatively unimportant in the beginning, when society was still so fluid that luck or diligence might elevate a man above his fellows in a short time, but with the accumulation of wealth and economic power in the hands of a few, and the coming in of numbers of artisans, indentured servants and immigrant laborers, class lines tightened and society crystallized into easily recognizable categories of better, middling, and poorer sorts. In all towns native aristocracies were commercial in origin, even at Charles Town where they later sought land as a basis for social distinction. They consolidated their position by means of wealth from successful trading ventures, collecting thereby social prestige and political influence. They lived grandly, dressed gaily, kept horses and coaches, and employed the labor of the less fortunate. The commercial, political and social leadership of the towns was in their hands. Later, as urban life became more sophisticated, they contributed to the development of secular amusements and to the relaxation of earlier strict moral codes. They gained further brilliance by alliance with representatives of British officialdom in America. Below them the middle class, professional people, tradesmen and artisans, lived comfortably but more plainly, enjoying in prosperous times many of

the good things of life, but in hard times feeling the pinch far more than did their wealthy neighbors. Steady laborers might know periods of prosperity, but many of them could be squeezed out by the vicissitudes of the economic cycle. They performed the menial labor of the towns, enlisted as common seamen, and constituted a group from which much urban poverty and disorder were recruited. Negro and Indian slaves, mere unprivileged pieces of property, rounded out the caste system as it developed itself in metropolitan America.

Save Newport, each of the towns had originally been dedicated to a dominant Protestant religious organization, but after a century of growth diversity, indifference and actual unbelief came to characterize the religious scene. The complexities of town society were in large measure responsible for this development, for different national or social groups soon evolved their favored sects and denominations. When the ministry could no longer speak with one voice to all elements of town populations, it lost much of its influence, both social and clerical, and the appearance of agnosticism and irreverence was rapid. In general, at the end of the first century, Anglicanism was in all towns the religion of officials and aristocrats; Quakerism and Congregationalism, which had once in their own localities enjoyed this favored position, had joined the ranks of middle class religions, which further included Baptists and Presbyterians; while for the common man a religious refuge was just appearing in the enthusiastic, emotional revivalism of Whitefield. Absence of devotion penetrated all classes; the poorer sort were largely indifferent to the attractions of religion, freethinking characterized such middle class groups as Franklin's Junto, and aristocrats indulged a fashionable Deism. In contrast, a stern and uniform religious fundamentalism for a much longer time characterized the rural communities of the countryside.

Much of their power the quasi-established churches had attained in an age when religious concerns so dominated men's thoughts as to exclude many other aspects of life. But the commercial success of colonial towns altered this singleness of outlook by acquainting townsmen with the delights of secular grandeurs and providing money for their enjoyment. As the age advanced the church step by step gave way before the institution of more attractive secular recreations. Most successful of these, appearing very early and appealing to all classes, was the tavern. Instituted originally as a necessary convenience for strangers and travelers, it soon showed itself to be the resort of all classes of townsmen, the place where they conducted much of their business and where much of their social life was passed. In the eighteenth century coffee houses became as in England the rendezvous of business men and the scene of many commercial transactions. Taverns served not only as places of casual conviviality, but as headquarters for the multifarious clubs into which town social life gradually organized itself. They also offered opportunities for cards, billiards and games of chance, and housed the many traveling shows and exhibitions which the better transportation of the eighteenth century made possible.

Games, contests, tavern recreations, and public celebration of holidays constituted the entertainment of the common man, but for the aristocrats mounting wealth and sophistication were creating more elaborate forms of amusement. To the hearty private dinners and occasional excursions of early days succeeded great public banquets, dances and balls, musical entertainments, and finally, in two of the towns, dramatic presentations. Gradually the commercial aristocracy of the towns, combining with royal officials, evolved a society whose entertainments were artificial, costly, sophisticated and exclusive. But for aristocrat or common man, the vicarious amusements that money could buy, and their variety and attractiveness, differentiated town society from that of the countryside with its simpler, spontaneous pleasures, and tended to draw town-dwellers away from a strict and narrow conception of life as a duty and a task. Copied as they were from the recreations of English society, they also tended to make social life in the towns more like that of the metropolis.

A final characteristic of town society was that it offered to its members a wider intellectual opportunity and challenge than was possible to the man whose life was bounded by his fields or by the hard necessity of clearing away the forest. From earliest childhood opportunities for education, free or otherwise, were open to the town-dweller. Especially was this true of the poor, whose educational needs were largely cared for by religious societies, charity schools, or compulsory apprenticeship. This last system enabled youth of the poorer classes to equip themselves for a trade. In other strata of society young men might fit themselves for business at private vocational schools, for a place in society with private masters, or for higher education for a learned profession at public or private Latin schools or with a private tutor. Young women, too, in the towns might purchase instruction in various fields of learning or merely in the polite arts of feminine society. Also, in the northern English towns, Boston, Newport and Philadelphia, there was from the start a tradition of scholarliness and of respect for intellectual achievement. It followed that a society so trained, constantly in contact by ship with Europe, was alive and ready to adopt the intellectual fashions of the age. Hence, in this first century of American life, most of the intellectual activity, in science, literature and the arts, and what intellectual progress there was, took place in the towns. Only there were there material and opportunity for such activity. And rather than regard the results of that progress with condescension, we should, with James Franklin's subscriber, wonder at the contrary. In comparison with the Augustan Age of eighteenth century London, intellectual and social life in the colonies may seem bare and sterile, but in comparison with intellectual barrenness of provincial life in England itself, its cultivation and sophistication appear revealed. Urban culture in the eighteenth century was provincial culture at its best, nourished during this period of faltering imitation, which had to precede that of native accomplishment, by constant contact with the vital intellectual currents of England and Europe.

In these various ways the developments of a hundred years of life under relatively urban conditions created a society at once distinct from that of rural regions, whether tidewater or back country, and even further removed from that of the westward reaching frontier. The communal attitude toward the solution of the physical and social problems of diversified populations dwelling together in close propinquity, and the constantly widening outlook which material progress, commercial expansion, and contact with the larger world of affairs made possible, were its distinguishing characteristics. In general, this society was more cooperative and social, less individualistic in its outlook toward problems of daily life, far more susceptible to outside influences and examples, less aggressively independent than the society of frontier America. At the same time it was more polished, urbane, and sophisticated, more aware of fashion and change, more sure of itself and proud of its achievements, more able to meet representatives from the outside world as equals without bluster or apology than the rural society of the colonial back country. Because its outlook was eastward rather than westward, it was more nearly a European society in an American setting. It had appropriated various points on the American continent and transformed them as nearly as possible into likenesses of what it had known at home. It was itself less transformed in the process than might have been expected, because the contact with the homeland never ceased, but rather increased with the passage of years. Its importance to American life as a whole was therefore great. Here were centers of the transit of civilization from Old World to New,—five points at the least through which currents of world thought and endeavor might enter, to be like other commodities assimilated and redistributed throughout the countryside. It was well for the future of national America that its society should not remain completely rural and agricultural, isolated and self-sufficient, ignorant of outside developments and distrustful of new ideas from abroad, as it might well have done had there been no cities. Instead, the five towns provided the nucleus for a wider and more gracious living in the New World.

Growth and Expansion of Urban Centers

Julius Rubin*

The study of city growth as an aspect of the process of economic development has engaged the attention of economic historians and sociologists in Europe for many decades; and more recently it has aroused considerable interest among social scientists working on the problems of the underdeveloped countries. For economic historians of the United States, however, it has rarely been a central theme. While such subjects as the role of cities as demanders and organizers of large-scale transportation systems have received careful attention, the conditions which give rise to cities have only recently begun to come into focus.

This neglect seems all the more curious when we consider the longstanding interest in urban topics within other disciplines in this country. We know a good deal from political historians about internal urban organization; from sociologists about urban disorganization and rural-urban differences; from geographers about the physical settings of cities and the structural relations among them. But there has been little work here either on the agricultural conditions for urban growth or on the crucial subject of the character and timing of city growth within the development process.

The difference in focus between European and American economic historians reflects, of course, differences in the conditions of city growth. Historians tend to study the dramatic, or at least that which has dramatic possibilities, but from the point of view of the economic historian the rise of the American city is a most undramatic event. Except for parts of the South in certain phases, the American town was not at all in the European sense the herald of a new society; nor was it forced to establish its right to exist in the hostile environment of a tradition-bound society. Instead it appeared simultaneously with agricultural settlement and from the beginning profoundly affected the development of the countryside. The keynote has been mutual influence and adaptation rather than conflict.

I hasten to add that this is a relative statement; that urban-rural conflict is one of the enduring themes of American history. But it is significant that American sociologists have so often tied themselves into terminological knots by first defining some aspect of behavior as characteristic of the city and then finding that it is distributed widely across the countryside.[1] Rural-urban differences exist of course, but they should not obscure the fact that the cultural gap between peasant and townsman so prominent in the history of continental Europe was from the beginning a minor affair in North America. This relative cultural homogeneity is one of those background factors which tend to be taken for

---

*Reprinted with permission from David T. Gilchrist, ed., *The Growth of Seaport Cities, 1790–1825*, published for the Eleutherian Mills-Hagley Foundation by the University Press of Virginia, Charlottesville, 1967, 3–21.

[1] Two recent discussions are Richard Dewey, "The Rural-Urban Continuum: Real but Relatively Unimportant," *American Journal of Sociology*, 66 (July 1960), 60–66; and Charles T. Stewart, Jr., "The Urban-Rural Dichotomy: Concepts and Uses," *ibid.*, 64 (Sept. 1958), 152–58. Cf. William Diamond, "On the Dangers of an Urban Interpretation of History," in Eric F. Goldman, ed., *Historiography and Urbanization* (Baltimore, 1941), 107–8.

granted. But it had a profound influence on urban development in this country and deserves some analysis.

To an important degree it was a question of immigrant origins. In the meager literature on comparative urban growth in the Americas there is one study, by St. Julien Childs, which throws some light on this factor. It is a comparison of the short-lived sixteenth-century Spanish settlement of Santa Elena and the seventeenth-century English settlement of Charles Town, both on the coast of present-day South Carolina.[2] Though the physical environment and Indian problem that confronted the two settlements were almost identical, there were striking differences in institutions and policies. Childs is persuasive in ascribing these differences to a difference in origins, origins which he terms "rural" for the Spaniards and "urban" for the English. In his usage, the terms refer not to residence or occupation but to a world view and a set of attitudes and skills which were the result of generations of particular kinds of experiences.

In both settlements the leader was a country squire. But Pedro Menéndez de Avilés was a cavalier impoverished by inflation who found in military service the one possible road to fortune, while Sir Anthony Ashley Cooper was a squire whose ancestors, by enclosures and by shrewd investments, had left him large income-bearing rural estates as well as important interests in the City. Menéndez sought, besides the rehabilitation of his family's fortunes, only the aggrandizement of the Spanish church and state. Ashley Cooper, hostile to the clergy and skeptical toward his government, framed for the autonomous province of Carolina a written constitution creating a deistic

republic such as he wished to see in England.

The mass of settlers displayed corresponding characteristics. While the elite of the Spanish colony consisted of professional soldiers and the agriculturalists were peasants transplanted from rural villages at the crown's expense, the English colony attracted Whigs and Nonconformists, merchants and sea captains, men who paid their own way and brought enough capital to set themselves up in trade and as planters. The poorer settlers made their way to the new country under the arduous conditions of indentures.

These contrasting origins produced corresponding differences in institutions: in Santa Elena, a concentrated settlement dominated by professional soldiers, with an agriculture almost entirely oriented toward community subsistence; in Charles Town, an unpaid militia, a scattered settlement in defiance of the wishes of the leadership, and agriculturalists so immediately and intensely devoted to the finding of a money crop that the leader of the settlement had to plead with them to "provide for ye belly."

Such a comparison of course indicates nothing about the direction of change. Presumably Spanish settlements of this type would have evolved in the direction of their English counterparts under the influence of the geography and the economic opportunities of the region. But it seems just as clear that the pace of development of the eastern seaboard was determined in large part by the fact that so large a proportion of the immigrants came from long-commercialized areas—from cities and towns and from villages with a highly commercialized agriculture and domestic industry. Colonial America, though certainly 90 per cent agricultural in an occupational sense, may also be de-

---

[2] "Cavaliers and Burghers in the Carolina Low Country," in Goldman, *op. cit.*, 1–20.

scribed as 90 percent urban in a cultural sense.

Up to perhaps the 1780's this cultural homogeneity is easily explained, for the immigrants came from the most commercially developed coastal strips, islands, and river valleys of Europe rather than from the intensely rural interior. And with the exception of parts of the South, they established here a coastal economy very much like the economies from which they came, one in which the bulk of the agriculturalists could establish easy and intimate commercial connections for their crops, crops which were so diverse and suitable for so many widely scattered home and foreign markets that they could be distributed only through the agency of domestic ports.[3] The unique character of the American port cities in the eighteenth-century colonial world—in size and diversity of trade they ranked among the largest ports of coastal and island Europe— may be attributed to the fact that only in America were the behavioral and environmental conditions of the northern European coastal economies so faithfully reproduced.[4]

But if we adhere to the central point, that of the cultural similarity of townsman and farmer, then an interesting question arises concerning the further development of this economy. It was easy enough for a commercial people to retain their commercial outlook while settling a fertile and indented coastal strip on the edge of an expanding Atlantic economy. But what would happen when the great interior was settled? Would it be possible for agriculturalists in the interior

of a continent to maintain their commercial viewpoint and skills? In part this would depend on the pace of technological innovation in the transport field. Canals and railroads turn continents into islands. During the Revolution, Gouverneur Morris remarked that though Americans were still crawling on the edge of the continent, they would soon conquer it with the aid of a great New York canal. But as it turned out, this was far too optimistic a view. Steamships affected the interior only after the War of 1812, the great canal only in the 1820's. The long-range railroads were not completed for still another generation. Large-scale settlement of the interior preceded all the great transport innovations by a generation or more.

Under these circumstances, that cultural gap between town and country dweller, so typical of the interior of Europe, might have appeared here as well. Toynbee refers to the barbarization invariably produced by the isolation of life on frontiers. It is conceivable that a rapid loss of literacy and an intensely conservative set of rural values could have developed in the interior while the coast continued a commercial development based upon its old ties with the Atlantic world. That commercial development would have had rather narrow limits; presumably the development of the northern ports would have approximated more closely the actual fate of the ports below Baltimore. This is of course extremely "iffy" history, but elements of such a dual economy did appear in comparable areas of Spanish settlement such as Argentina; and there was in the long run a considerable regression to an essentially rural culture in large parts of the American South. At any rate, an analysis of the development of the Atlantic ports must take into account the problem that was posed when for the first time large

[3] See George Rogers Taylor, "American Growth before 1840: An Exploratory Essay," *Journal of Economic History*, 24 (Dec. 1964), 435–36.

[4] On the uniqueness of the American port city, see Carl Bridenbaugh, *Cities in Revolt: Urban Life in America, 1743–1776* (New York, 1955), 216–17; and Taylor, *op. cit.*

numbers of these colonists from coastal civilizations were confronted with
the isolation of a continental interior.

The problem is of course far from
new and received its classic analysis
from Guy S. Callender in 1903. Callender began by criticizing Adam
Smith's opinion that because of the
plenitude of fertile lands the sparsely
settled colony of a civilized nation
"advances more rapidly to wealth and
greatness than any other human society." The statement is misleading,
Callender claimed, because it does not
take into account the need for a nonagricultural market. Such a market
will not appear easily or quickly in a
new country because the availability
of cheap unoccupied land prevents the
creation of a laboring class for manufacturing industries. This does not prevent the small-scale production of
necessities which cannot be obtained
by trade, but manufacturing cannot go
much beyond this. In such new countries, it is easy to attain a condition of
rude comfort, but, Callender concluded, "the community cannot advance rapidly in the production of
wealth and the accumulation of capital; division of labor and development
of skill do not take place; town life
does not arise; and social and economic progress is slow. It may even
happen that a community suffers a decline in both its economic efficiency
and social life if compelled to remain
for several generations under such
conditions."[5] We are all familiar with
Callender's brilliant analysis of the
conditions which finally removed these
limitations on the growth of the trans-
Appalachian West. After the War of
1812 the extension of cotton cultivation into the Southwest combined with
the use of steamboats on the western
waters provided the region with the
first great market for its agricultural
surpluses.[6] Later the Erie Canal and
the great railroad lines provided a
more efficient solution to the problem.

The analysis requires reexamina-
tion. Callender made his whole argument depend on a particular combination of events which occurred outside
the communities of the Northwest.
The process is viewed as discontinu-
ous: first, settlement and stasis, then
a great breakthrough. I believe it can
be demonstrated, however, that most
interior regions, on either side of the
mountains, went through a process of
urban-industrial development despite
their relative isolation and that this
advance preparation explains a good
deal about the pace and direction of
development when that isolation was
destroyed by transport innovations.
Furthermore, it is evident that the rate
of growth of the seaports before the
appearance of the canal and railroad
was dependent not only on the physical size, population, and fertility of
their hinterlands but also on the extent
to which those hinterlands were commercialized, industrialized, and linked
to the ports. This would suggest that
an examination of port-hinterland relations from the vantage point of the
interior town may be more useful than
the traditional emphasis on the opposition of a commercialized East to an
agricultural West.

Callender referred to the towns of
the Ohio Valley before the steamship,
but by comparing their size with the
size of those which became common
in a later period, he minimized their
effect.[7] Though these towns were undoubtedly small, they were neverthe-

[5] "The Early Transportation and Banking
Enterprises of the States in Relation to the
Growth of Corporations," *Quarterly Journal
of Economics*, 17 (1903), as reprinted in Joseph
T. Lambie and Richard V. Clemence, eds.,
Economic Change in America (Harrisburg, Pa.,
1954), 526–27.

[6] *Ibid.*, 532–35. See also Louis B. Schmidt,
"Internal Commerce and the Development of
the National Economy before 1860," *Journal
of Political Economy*, 47 (Dec. 1939), 798–822.

[7] *Op. cit.*, 529–30.

less important centers of industry, commerce, and an entrepreneurial spirit. Consider the case of Rochester. The first families to settle in the village came in 1812. A gristmill and a cotton factory appeared in 1815. When the settlement was incorporated in 1817 it had 700 people and a weekly newspaper. In 1821, before the arrival of the canal, there were twenty-eight flour and sawmills in the city and its immediate vicinity; farmers throughout the region were cutting staves for coopers to assemble into barrels for millers and distillers; bark and hides were collected from up the valley for the city's tannery and for the saddlers and shoemakers whose products were in demand on the expanding frontiers; there was a paper mill in town as well as a cotton and wool textile factory; and there were the usual triphammer shops and blacksmith forges. This was only one of a dozen villages in the region.[8] We can take it for granted that the maintenance of the rapid pace of development of that first decade would soon require a radical improvement in long-range transportation. Nevertheless, the level of urban-industrial activity achieved without canal or railroad is impressive. That this kind of town could appear in an interior with primitive means of transport may be attributed to three factors: the highly commercialized background of the interior population, expressed as an intense desire for goods above the subsistence level; the relative—not absolute—isolation produced by a geography which permitted limited but significant relations with the coast; and the constant stream of migrants which in some respects took the place of a movement of goods.

With regard to the first factor mentioned—the strength of the farmer's drive toward markets—the issue has been confused by the tendency to use the same word, "subsistence," to refer to both attitudes and actual behavior. The authors of the classic histories of American agriculture evidently refer to behavior: they designate as "subsistence" any farmer who lives principally on goods and services produced by himself and his family; that is, subsistence involves general-purpose farming with only a marginal cash crop.[9] This use of the term leaves open the question of motivation. The subsistence farmer in the motivational sense does not want, or at least does not expect, any increase in commercial ties. He trades only for necessities and for this purpose produces a marginal cash crop. But the hope of obtaining a wider range of goods from the outside world is foreign to him. With such an agricultural population, urban development is of an entirely different character than that which occurred in the United States. The towns are principally administrative centers and their trade is heavily weighted on the side of luxuries for an elite. In such an economy, as one geographer has put it, "the towns face one another" and have little effect on the bulk of the population.[10]

With the exception of the migratory frontiersman, this kind of farmer

[8] Blake McKelvey, *Rochester, the Water-Power City, 1812–1854* (Cambridge, Mass., 1945), 87–88; Whitney R. Cross, "Creating a City: Rochester, 1824–1834" (unpublished Master's essay, Rochester, 1936), 32–33. For detailed data on the rise of towns in another inland region, see James S. Matthews, *Expressions of Urbanism in the Sequent Occupance of Northeastern Ohio*, University of Chicago, Department of Geography, *Research Papers*, No. 5 (1945).

[9] Lewis C. Gray, *History of Agriculture in Southern United States to 1860* (Washington, D.C., 1933), I, 451–53; Percy W. Bidwell and John I. Falconer, *History of Agriculture in Northern United States, 1620–1860* (Washington, D.C., 1925), 126–27, 129–31.

[10] Charles T. Stewart, Jr., "The Size and Spacing of Cities," *Geographic Review*, 48 (April 1958), as reprinted in Harold M. Mayer and Clyde F. Kohn, eds., *Readings in Urban Geography* (Chicago, 1959), 248.

has not been significant in American history. As Douglass C. North has put it, farmers here have remained close to a subsistence level only "because means of transportation were lacking rather than because of a non-market orientation. In Europe a subsistence or village economy with local markets was built into the social and economic structure for centuries. In America subsistence was only a frontier condition to be overcome as rapidly as means of transport could be built up."[11] It may be added that in few interior areas was there ever anything like a subsistence economy. Settlement was generally along valleys with at least one important commercial outlet permitting significant though limited amounts of exports. It is true that with increasing density of settlement there could be found in every region numbers of isolated farmers, far even from the obstructed rivers and the primitive roads, but I doubt if they were the majority in most northern regions. Areas like the New England hill country have received entirely too much emphasis. As the historian of that region has remarked, the characteristics of the farmer there have determined to a remarkable degree the popular image of the American farmer, yet they had little in common with those of agriculturalists farther west.[12] However in New England too the population had, in Child's terminology, an urbanized tradition, which expressed itself as an out-migration of men in-

stead of a movement of goods. They thereby avoided the extreme of a stagnant economy combined with overpopulation which is so often found among motivationally subsistent farmers.[13]

This brings me to the second factor that may account for inland urban-industrial development, that of relative isolation. While the transport barriers did not prevent a long-distance connection, they limited it sufficiently to provide the equivalent of a tariff barrier for locally produced manufactures. The historian of the industries of Lancaster County pointed out that while the inland situation of the county protected its artisans from wares produced in the port cities and overseas, at the same time the ports played an important role in supplying to the county's manufacturers such commodities as millstones and even foreign hides when the local tanneries needed an increased supply.[14] There is a paucity of data on this point, but it may be possible to investigate the extent to which the industries of the interior depended upon the port cities at the same time they were protected from them.

The third factor to consider is the character of local markets. The interior town is often pictured as primarily a collection point for the long-range export of crops and a distribution point for imported manufactures. Though this function undoubtedly provided the indispensable nucleus, the wide range of local manufactures indicates that other factors were at work. In part this range reflected the characteristics of the processing industries, which required the production of salt, casks, boats, and so on,

---

[11] "Locational Theory and Regional Economic Growth," *Journal of Political Economy*, 63 (June 1955), as reprinted in John Friedmann and William Alonso, eds., *Regional Development and Planning: A Reader* (Cambridge, Mass., 1964), 253.

[12] Harold F. Wilson, *The Hill Country of Northern New England* (New York, 1936), 4; see also Malcolm Keir, "Some Responses to Environment in Massachusetts," Geographical Society of Philadelphia, *Bulletin* (July–Aug. 1917), 121–22; Jackson Turner Main, *The Social Structure of Revolutionary America* (Princeton, N.J., 1965), 18, 23–24, 33.

[13] Wilson, *op. cit.*, 24–25.

[14] Carlton O. Wittlinger, "Early Manufacturing in Lancaster County, Pennsylvania, 1710–1840" (unpublished Ph.D. dissertation, Pennsylvania, 1953), 199.

and whose by-products, particularly those of meat packing, became the raw materials of a number of industries. But these industries, important as they were, do not fully account for town creation. Many of them were often rural in location and some used very little nonagricultural labor. Flour milling, the great export industry of Rochester, involved a labor cost of less than two cents a barrel and could have directly supported perhaps 5 per cent of the town's population.[15]

The emphasis upon the export industries and their linkages is based upon the assumption that commodity exports were the sole source of an interior region's foreign exchange. For long periods of time, however, most inland regions possessed in addition a nineteenth-century financial equivalent of the modern mass tourist industry. I refer to the market provided by migrants newly settling in an area as well as by those passing through to settle farther west. "A stream of consumers," declared Lewis D. Stilwell with regard to Vermont, "flows past the producer's own doorstep," and these demanded a wide variety of industrial as well as agricultural goods.[16]

The process repeated itself behind every frontier. In 1794 there were only thirty-six artisans in Pittsburgh, but so great was the stimulus of the immigrant trade that by 1803 the numerous shops of the city were producing $350,000 in manufactures, according to one observer, and were able to provide transients with almost all the articles they needed to begin life in their new homes. Once on the farms, the settlers continued to provide a large market for locally and regionally produced manufactures. Six factories at Pittsburgh were producing annually

an estimated $200,000 worth of glass by 1814, and while ironmaking was still mainly a rural industry, there was extensive fabrication in the city of household wares and farm implements as well as a number of nail factories.[17]

The basis for this remarkable industrial development was a demand by new settlers and transients which was far above the requirements of a subsistence level of living. Only the original settlers, the migratory frontiersmen, lived at anything like a subsistence level. These men bartered their products for a rigidly limited set of necessities: tea, coffee, powder, shot. Their cabins used no nails or glass and they were true jacks of all trades. The agriculturalists who succeeded them came in with liquid resources and a far higher customary standard of living. Local businessmen were keenly aware of the fact that settlers brought considerable amounts of cash into their areas and indeed Isaac Lippincott remarked that "it was the falling off of this trade which caused the interior sections to feel the pressure of hard times from 1819 to 1822."[18]

In accounting for town creation in interior regions, then, we return to that crucial factor, the highly commercialized background of so much of the American population of the period, a background which had accustomed them to a relatively high standard of living and which had given them the resources partially to maintain that standard in the crucial early period of settlement. This factor may explain as well the origins of the labor force in the towns. Callender

[15] Cross, *op. cit.*, 77–78.
[16] *Migration from Vermont, 1776–1860* (Montpelier, Vt., 1948), 103; Wittlinger, *op. cit.*, 199.

[17] Isaac Lippincott, *A History of Manufactures in the Ohio Valley to the Year 1860* (New York, 1914), 52–55, 63, 82–89, 104–5, 112–14; Wittlinger, *op. cit.*, 197–98; Richard C. Wade, *The Urban Frontier: The Rise of the Western Cities, 1700–1830* (Cambridge, Mass., 1959), 12, 20, 41, 46–47.
[18] *Op. cit.*, 63.

stressed the difficulties of finding laborers in an area of cheap and easily available land. But the problem is unnecessarily exaggerated if we think in terms of large-scale industry, unskilled work, and unpleasant industrial conditions. This may be heresy, but it is not really surprising that a proportion of the migrants preferred urban life. Richard Wade has suggested that "many settlers came across the mountains in search of promising towns as well as good land," that "their inducements were not so much fertile soil as opportunities in infant cities." Wade quoted Daniel Drake's comment that proprietors competed for those migrants who came from "those portions of the Union which cherish and build up cities" and he pointed out that in 1787 Lexington petitioned the Virginia legislature for incorporation, to "be an inducement to well-disposed persons, artisans and mechanics who from motives of convenience do prefer a Town life."[19] Similarly, Blake McKelvey, in his discussion of the rapid settlement of the lower Genesee, remarked that many "settlers trooped in not as farmers but as artisans and mechanics eager to locate in a thriving village."[20]

The term "village" raises the question of size. Most of these towns had populations in the hundreds, certainly not large enough to be included in the usual urban-size classifications. The largest town in the Ohio Valley region in 1805, Lexington, had a population of 2,800, though, as one observer put it, with some exaggeration, "Perhaps there is no manufacture in this country which is not found there."[21] Central places of this size today are far more specialized. A narrow range of activities carried on in a very slowly changing agricultural environment produces our image of the static village. But the same number of people in an early western river town could reproduce in microcosm some of the characteristics of the port cities of the period.

One way of gauging the effects of interior urbanization on hinterland and port is to compare the northern regions in which the towns flourished with the areas of the South in which they were stunted in their growth or actually destroyed by the appearance of the plantation. In his history of southern agriculture, Lewis C. Gray stressed the fact that all the interior areas of the eighteenth-century South with fertile soil and favorable topography were characterized by considerable diversification, which he attributed to the remoteness of markets and to the prevalence in the population of men who had been artisans by training. In all such areas from Maryland to Georgia he found weaving shops, flour mills, sawmills, oil mills, brickyards, ropewalks, ironworks, furnaces, forges, and rolling and slitting mills. As in the North, traveling journeymen and small shop manufacturers were numerous and diverse. These activities, for which George S. Gibb coined the striking and significant term, "pre-industrial revolution," tended to concentrate in the towns which appeared throughout the back country. Gray added that "correlative with the development of community industries, the farm economy lost some of its self-sufficiency, and took on a greater degree of comfort and an improved mode of living. Farming itself became more systematic and less slipshod and primitive."[22]

Regions dominated by the plantation took an entirely different course.

[19] Op. cit., 34–35.
[20] Op. cit., 49.
[21] Lippincott, op. cit., 110.

[22] Gray, op. cit., I, 123, 442–43; Gibb, "The Pre-industrial Revolution in America," Business Historical Society, Bulletin, 20 (Oct. 1946), 103–16.

In the tidewater areas, the tobacco plantation combined with the excellent river system inhibited for a while even the development of ports as staple-collection points. Later the spread of the cotton plantation into the upland regions actually destroyed the interior urban-industrial economy. It is not that industrial activity was given up. Some of it was: with the shift to cotton, processing activities became less important. But it should be kept in mind that diversified farmers always constituted the great majority of the white population in most cotton and tobacco areas. More important than the reduced scale of industry was its dispersion. Instead of centering in towns it became to a significant extent the activity of slaves on plantations.[23] At the same time the commercial basis of local towns was weakened by the planter's proclivity for long-distance trading with the factors of the port cities and by his consequent ability to supply surrounding farmers and small planters from his own store. As in industry, commerce was not destroyed, but the basis for agglomeration was weakened.[24] The farmers in plantation areas were thereby deprived of the northern type of variegated and enterprising industrial town and had to rely instead on a country store with a narrow range of goods operating in the economically passive environment of the county courthouse town.[25] These

circumstances, operating for a generation, seem to have reduced considerably the commercial attachments and expectations otherwise so prevalent on the American scene. To a degree, a motivationally subsistent agricultural class appeared. A common practice of farmers in the plantation areas was to raise the minimal amount of cash crop needed to buy a narrow and rigid range of necessities: tobacco, lead, powder, and sugar.[26]

These differences between northern and southern interior development were increased by the transport innovations. In the North and in parts of the upper South, the railroad and canal produced no break in the industrial tradition. With the end of relative isolation, some industries fell, but others with greater locational advantages increased their markets. The pool of industrial skills, the experience with larger industrial units, and the entrepreneurial environment of the northern towns all helped to produce an adaptation rather than a destruction of industry.[27] In the South, the advent of the railroad and cheap northern manufactures in the interior marked the end of a good deal of plantation industrial activity and of the towns.[28] This situation is often summed up with the statement that by the 1840's and 1850's investment in industry in the plantation South was

---

[23] See Lewis E. Atherton, *The Southern Country Store, 1800–1860* (Baton Rouge, La., 1949), 29–30.

[24] *Ibid.*

[25] Charles H. Ambler, *Sectionalism in Virginia from 1776 to 1861* (Chicago, 1910), 11; Atherton, *op. cit.*, 34–36, 41–42; Arthur P. Middleton, *Tobacco Coast: A Maritime History of the Chesapeake Bay in the Colonial Era* (Newport News, Va., 1953), 109–10, 157–62; Rosser H. Taylor, *Ante-Bellum South Carolina* (Chapel Hill, N.C., 1942), 23–24. On the difference between Northwest and Southwest in number of interior towns, see Stanley Elkins and Eric McKittrick, "A Meaning for Turner's Frontier," *Political Science Quarterly*, 69 (Sept. 1954), 341–42 (esp. *n.* 42), 352. On the

"dreamy idleness" of the southern town, see William Garrett Brown, *The Lower South in American History* (New York, 1930), 38–39.

[26] Clement Eaton, *The Growth of Southern Civilization, 1790–1860* (New York, 1961), 156; Robert R. Russel, "The Effects of Slavery upon Nonslave-holders in the Antebellum South," *Agricultural History*, 15 (April 1941), 113.

[27] Cross, *op. cit.*, 78–86, 89; Harvey S. Perloff *et al.*, *Regions, Resources and Economic Growth* (Baltimore, 1960), 118–19; Victor S. Clark, *History of Manufactures in the United States* (New York, 1929), I, 338–60.

[28] Thomas J. Wertenbaker, *The Old South* (New York, 1942), 137–42; Gray, *op. cit.*, I, 453–55, II, 685.

far less profitable than investment in agriculture. For the historical economist interested in the static relationships that validate economic theory, it is sufficient to note this end result. But for the economic historian who tries to trace the development of the factors determining relative profitability, the fate of interior town life is crucial.

The most striking consequences of the differences between northern and southern development appeared when a major transformation of agricultural methods was required. In both regions, soil exhaustion and western competition forced upon eastern agriculturalists a shift to more intensive cultivation. Such a shift is always painful and costly. But it is less so wherever towns and industry are close by. Throughout the North it was the towns and the port cities which demanded the industrial raw materials and the dairy, meat, and vegetable products of intensive agriculture at the same time that they provided the press and the organizational basis for the local agricultural improvement societies; and it was largely the towns which absorbed marginal farmers into local industry on a part- or full-time basis while improving the condition of the remaining farmers by supplying them with agricultural implements and seeds, by direct investment in improved agriculture and by organizing the movements for local turnpikes and canals.[29]

These examples illustrate the great difference in the effects of local as against long-distance markets. The distant market may be crucial to begin with, but in the long run the farmer's

flexibility and adaptability is largely determined by the local town and local industry.[30] In the tobacco South, where the shift to intensive farming took place largely in relation to the European market and to markets provided at a distance by Philadelphia and Baltimore, the process was more difficult and lengthy. One important consequence was that southern ports were often surrounded by belts of ravaged lands containing a sparse and poverty-stricken population.[31]

Thus far, everything has been viewed from the vantage point of the inland town. But this emphasis, justified though it may be as a corrective, is inadequate as a description of the urban development process in America. Quite properly, these single-cause explanations produce in historians the response that we are told nature always has to a vacuum. I should like to end by suggesting the value of a more complex approach, one developed by geographers of the human ecology school for the analysis of modern urban relationships. This approach has been based in part upon certain concepts advanced by Norman S. B. Gras in a volume misnamed *An Introduction to Economic History*.[32]

The book seems to have had little influence among economic historians, perhaps because Gras presented a stages theory of growth of a type which had previously been taken altogether too seriously by some members of the German Historical School. In his view, there is a progression from a "settled village economy" to a "town economy" and then finally to a "metropolitan economy." The crucial point is the discussion of metropolitan de-

[29] David M. Ellis, *Landlords and Farmers in the Hudson-Mohawk Region, 1790–1850* (Ithaca, N.Y., 1946), 90–94, 98–99, 118, 126–27, 146, 155–57; Bidwell and Falconer, *op. cit.*, 202–3, 242–43; Vivian D. Wiser, "The Movement for Agricultural Improvement in Maryland, 1785–1865" (unpublished Ph.D. dissertation, Maryland, 1963), 82–85.

[30] See Perloff *et al.*, *op. cit.*, 83–85, on the importance of "nodality"; and Theodore W. Schultz, *The Economic Organization of Agriculture* (New York, 1953), Chapter IX.

[31] Gray, *op. cit.*, I, 445, II, 613–14, 908–17; Wertenbaker, *op. cit.*, 349–50.

[32] New York, 1922.

velopment in terms not merely of the rise of cities, but of the development of metropolitan areas in which the metropolis as focal point exercises important political and social as well as economic influences on the hinterland and the hinterland in turn profoundly affects the metropolis.[33]

The town economy appears when a village develops specialized full-time traders and extends its trading network from a local to a multivillage basis. The town then becomes the trading nucleus where villagers of the region dispose of their surplus products and buy manufactures which the town both produces and imports. Gras stressed the fact that those who settled America came from the parts of Europe where a town economy prevailed and added the following remarks about the interior regions here:

> While at first blush we may think of those who settled beyond the Alleghenies as establishing independent domestic economy, we discern on second thought that their independence was in nearly all cases short-lived or really non-existent, for somewhere near the settler there grew up a town on which his dependence was great and lasting. And these towns on examination prove to bear a strong resemblance not only in their general economic functions but in their market regulations to the towns of the Old World.[34]

The "town economy" is succeeded by the "metropolitan economy" when one of the towns expands the area of its commercial and financial influence. This metropolis is often a port located on the boundary of its hinterland and serves as a link between the hinterland trade and the so-called "extended

trade" with other metropolitan economies and developing areas overseas. A manufacturing center such as early twentieth-century Pittsburgh was not a metropolis, according to Gras, because it was relatively insignificant as a market and financial center for its region.[35]

The central concept is that of metropolitan dominance, in which the metropolis is the center of the trade and transportation of the region and the provider of a host of specialized goods and services to the region. To Gras, the metropolitan economy represented an extension of the spatial division of labor. An alternative, a system of coordinate towns on a checkerboard pattern, is conceivable. But the cost of storing a great variety of wares in all such towns would be enormous. Similar considerations apply to transport, the capital market, and other types of specialized services. Consequently the spider web with the metropolis at the center replaces the checkerboard and permits a great increase in the quantity, quality, and variety of goods and services throughout the hinterland.[36]

In recent years urban geographers under the influence of biological analogies have extended the concept of metropolitan dominance in such a way as to highlight the existence of cumulative interactions between metropolis and hinterland. Donald J. Bogue, in his *Structure of the Metropolitan Community*, explained this use of the term "dominance" by presenting the following analogy from the field of plant ecology:

> A single hardwood tree standing alone in a field has very little control over the number and types of plants which grow in the field. Its presence changes the field very

---

[33] See D. C. Masters, *The Rise of Toronto, 1850–1890* (Toronto, 1947), vii–viii.

[34] *Op. cit.*, 155.

[35] *Ibid.*, 181–85, 187–91, 194–95, 294.

[36] *Ibid.*, 204–5.

little except in its immediate vicinity. The situation would be very different if the field were populated with many hardwood trees. Whereas the leaves which fall from a single tree are quickly blown away by the wind, a forest of trees breaks the wind, permitting the leaves to fall to the ground at the base of the trees. Humus is produced; the soil is thereby enriched, and the water-holding capacity of the soil is increased. The combined shade of the trees controls the amount of sunlight and modifies the temperature of the soil. . . . This forest has reacted upon the habitat. . . . Only those species which are adapted to the conditions imposed by the forest can thrive within it. . . . The smaller species are dependent upon the dominant species for maintaining certain environmental conditions necessary for their survival. The dominant species may be dependent upon the lesser species for other functions, such as preventing erosion. . . . Thus, a genuine community of interdependent units emerges, based upon the hardwood trees as dominants.[37]

This is only an analogy: I intend no reduction of human cultures to trees. The major point is that under certain conditions, which it is important to specify, a culture can change its habitat in such a way as to produce the conditions for the culture's survival and growth. These terms may seem strange because, under the influence of economics, we have not been accustomed to specifying cultural characteristics. Nevertheless, it may be useful at times to consider economic history from the viewpoint of cultural ecology, that is, as the product of a series of interchanges between those cultural characteristics of a group which are closely related to economic activities and those aspects of the environment which are significant for economic adaptation.[38]

An outline review of the interior development of the United States may suggest the value of this point of view. In the economies that grew up on the coasts of the Atlantic, geographic conditions favored the development of a dense trade and communications network which produced commercial and urban characteristics in rural and urban dwellers alike. It is in this sense that the term "town economy" can be justified. The migrants from these town economies found that conditions in the interior stood in the way of the dense communications networks required to maintain their particular culture, but two factors permitted a rapid modification of these conditions. The first was the commercial character of the settlers themselves; the second was the rapid secretion by the port cities of primitive transportation lines and long-range commercial networks. These made possible the ubiquitous interior towns.

In the South, where a particular combination of geographic and institutional factors inhibited interior urbanization, the population remained in relative isolation and its urban characteristics gradually eroded. But in the North the interior towns quickly became, in some crucial ways, small-scale reproductions of the port cities. These towns increased the regional influence of the ports by becoming centers of enterprise themselves, producing in their turn roads and commercial networks on a local level. Gradually,

[37] *The Structure of the Metropolitan Community: A Study of Dominance and Subdominance* (Ann Arbor, Mich., 1949), 10–11.

[38] See the review of ecological theory in Clifford Geertz's brilliant economic history, *Agricultural Involution: The Process of Ecological Change in Indonesia* (Berkeley, Calif., 1963), 1–11.

between the port and the hinterland cities a metropolitan division of labor was established, which made possible an increase in the quantity and variety of goods and services available in the hinterland, and this in turn facilitated industrial development throughout the region. On this basis, the interior towns could exert those many and diverse influences upon the surrounding agriculturalists, influences which maintained their attachment to markets, increased their skills, and eased the transition to intensive farming. In turn, the successful development of the town-organized hinterlands affected the growth rate of the ports by providing larger markets for port goods and services, by supplying larger quantities and higher qualities of industrial raw materials and produce, and by affecting the skills and the outlook of those who were to migrate to the factories. The consequent rapid development of interacting port and hinterland reinforced that regional cultural homogeneity, that similarity of town and country dweller, that had all along provided the indispensable basis for what became a regional system of "metropolitan dominance."

In the succeeding period, the long-range canal and railroad lines were promoted by coalitions of eastern and western interests which are often referred to as "urban" and "rural" respectively. But very little work has been done on the western components of these movements. Such work may validate the suggestion that these coalitions were based upon a fundamental similarity in the partners; that in fact the ability of the cities to attain their regional goals in the 1820's and after was a result of a previous condition of metropolitan dominance. But it is necessary to add that all of the relationships suggested in this paper require far more research than anyone has yet given them. Investigation in detail would test their accuracy and would provide a basis for comparisons of the growth curves of the various port-hinterland complexes. In the meantime, they deserve only the status of working hypotheses.

Competition Between Western Cities

Richard C. Wade*

Part of Philadelphia's appeal to town-dwellers was its leadership among the nation's cities, for nearly every young metropolis in the valley coveted a similar primacy in the West. Indeed, one of the most striking characteristics of this period was the development of an urban imperialism which saw rising young giants seek to spread their power and influence over the entire new country. The drive for supremacy, furthermore, was quite conscious, infusing an extraordinary dynamic into city growth, but also breeding bitter rivalries among the claimants. In the ensuing struggles, the economically strongest survived and flourished, while the less successful fell behind. Smaller places were trampled in the process, some being swallowed up by ambitious neighbors, others being overwhelmed before they could attain a challenging position. The contest, however, produced no final victor. In fact, the lead changed three times, and though Cincinnati commanded the field in 1830, Pittsburgh, Louisville, and St. Louis were still in the running. The rivalries developed very early.

*Reprinted by permission of the publishers from Richard C. Wade *The Urban Frontier: The Rise of Western Cities, 1790–1830*, Cambridge, Mass.: Harvard University Press, Copyright, 1959, by the President and Fellows of Harvard College, pp. 322–336.

Lexington jumped off to a quick start, but by 1810 Pittsburgh, enjoying a commercial and manufacturing boom, forged ahead. The postwar depression undermined its leadership, however, and Cincinnati moved forward to take its place. The fierce competition led to widespread speculation about the outcome. Most of the prophecy was wishful, stemming from the hopes of boosters and involving doubtful calculations. In 1816, for instance, a Pittsburger summed up many of the elements of this competition in [the] chart [below] (with ratings presumably on a scale of excellence from one to ten) designed to illustrate the inevitability of the Iron City's supremacy. Not only did the author work out the estimates in scientific detail, but he also predicted that the totals represented the population (in thousands) which each would reach in 1830.

Before a city could hope to enter the urban sweepstake for the largest prize, it had to eliminate whatever rivals arose in its own area. In many instances the odds in these battles were so uneven that smaller places gave in quickly. In others, a decision came only after a bitter and prolonged struggle. Edwardsville, Illinois, fell easily before St. Louis, but Wheeling's submission to Pittsburgh followed a decade of acrimony. Sometimes defeat

	Pittsburgh	Lexington	Cincinnati
Situation for inland trade and navigation	9	2	6
Adaptness for manufactures . . .	9	3	5
Fertility of surrounding soil . . .	2	7	4
Salubrity	9	7	5
Pleasantness and beauty	.3	1	.6
Elegance of scite [sic] and environs	1	.3	.6
	30.3	20.3	21.2

meant the end of independence for a town. Louisville, for example, ultimately annexed Shippingport and Portland, while Pittsburgh reached across the river to take in Allegheny. In other cases, the penalty for failure was the lessening of power and prestige. Steubenville and Wheeling, unable to sustain their position against Pittsburgh in the Upper Ohio, had to settle for a much reduced pace of development. The same fate befell Ste. Genevieve, an early challenger of St. Louis's domination of the Mississippi and Missouri. Occasionally a victor reduced its competitor to a mere economic appendage. This is what happened to Jeffersonville and New Albany, Indiana, after Louisville captured the trade of the Falls.

Though struggles for regional primacy characterized the urban growth of the entire West, the most celebrated was Pittsburgh's duel with Wheeling. Both were situated on the Ohio and both hoped to capture its flourishing commerce. Wheeling's great advantage lay in its down-river position, where it outflanked the shoals and rapids which dominated the approach to Pittsburgh. During the late summer, low water made navigation difficult and at times impossible, inducing some merchants to use the Virginia town as a transshipment point to the East. This fact alone made Wheeling a competitor, for in no other department could it match the Iron City. Pittsburgh's detractors saw this situation as early as 1793, when the Army considered establishing a post at Wheeling. Isaac Craig complained that "this new arrangement, . . . has Originated in the Brain of the Gentlemen in Washington who envy Pittsburgh, and . . . have represented to General Knox, that Navigation is practicable from Wheeling in the dry season." The same consideration made Wheeling a stop in the mail route to

the West and the Ohio River terminus of the National Road.

Despite these advantages, Wheeling's population barely reached 1,000 by 1815, while Pittsburgh had become the new country's leading metropolis. A serious rivalry seemed almost ridiculous. But the postwar depression, felling the Iron City, gave its smaller neighbor the hope of rising on the ruins. This prospect brightened in 1816, when, after many abortive attempts to change the terminus, the National Road was completed to Wheeling. Optimism about the town's future abounded throughout the valley. A Steubenville editor caught the spirit in verse:

Wheeling has secured her roads,
Come waggoners, come and bring
    your loads.
Emigrants, come hither, and build a
    town,
And make Wheeling a place of renown.

By 1822, 5,000 wagons were arriving annually in the booming settlement. "Wheeling is a thriving place," a traveler observed; "it bids fair to rival Pittsburgh in the trade of the Western country."

The Iron City, troubled by a stagnant economy and worried about its future, warily watched the progress of this upstart. Actually, Wheeling's challenge was only a small part of Pittsburgh's total problem, but its very ludicrousness made the situation all the more intolerable. "A miserable Virginia country town, which can never be more than two hundred yards wide, having the mere advantage of a free turnpike road and a warehouse or two, to become rivals of this *Emporium* of the West!" exclaimed the incredulous editor of the *Statesman*. As Wheeling continued to prosper, Pittsburgh accused its competitor of unfair practices, particularly of circulating the rumor that ships could not go up the river to "the Point." "They have taken to lying," the *Statesman* snapped. "We cannot believe this report," the *Gazette* asserted with more charity; "the citizens with whom we are acquainted in that place, are too honorable to countenance such childish, hurtless falsehood," especially since "everybody acquainted with the river knows that the water is as good if not better above than for 100 miles below."

Civic leaders in Wheeling, feeling their oats and certain that the National Road provided a secure base for unlimited growth, continually goaded the stricken giant. "Strange that a 'miserable Virginia Country Town,' a 'mere village,' should have attracted so much attention at the 'emporium of the West,' " the *Northwestern Gazette* observed. Moreover, it asserted that the difficulty of navigation on the Upper Ohio was not mere rumor. "During the drier part of the season the greater part of the Western Merchants order their goods to Wheeling and *not* to Pittsburgh. This fact is a stubborn and decisive one. It speaks volumes. It is a demonstration." A patronizing condescension expressed an increasing confidence. "Pittsburgh may, if she will, be a large and respectable manufacturing town. She may also retain a portion of the carrying trade," the same source graciously conceded. There seemed no limit to Wheeling's assurance. Travelers reported that its residents were "actually doing nothing but walking about on stilts, and stroking their chins with utmost self-complacency. Every man who is so fortunate as to own about 60 feet front and 120 feet back, considers himself . . . snug."

The next few years demonstrated, however, that history was only teasing. Wheeling's hopes for greatness were soon dashed. The National Road proved disappointing as a freight carrier, and Pittsburgh recovered from its depression, once again becoming the urban focus of the Upper Ohio. Though the Virginia town could boast over 5,000 inhabitants in 1830, its rate of growth lagged and its future prospects dimmed. To some shrewd observers the outcome was not unexpected. A Steubenville editor, consoling his readers in 1816 after their efforts to get the National Road had failed, asserted that cities could not be reared on mere highway traffic. "Rely on agriculture and manufactures," he counseled, "and you will do well without the mail or the turnpike bubble—it is not the sound of the coachman's horn that will make a town flourish."

Though Pittsburgh beat back Wheeling's challenge, it could not maintain its Western leadership. Cincinnati, less affected by the postwar collapse, surged by the Iron City and established its primacy throughout the new country. It was not content, however, to win its supremacy by another's injury. Rather it developed its own positive program to widen its commercial opportunities and spread its influence. In fact, the city was so alive with ideas that one visitor referred to it as "that hot bed of projects," and another observed "great plans on foot; whenever two or three meet at a corner nothing is heard but schemes." In broad terms the object of Cincinnati's statesmanship was threefold: to tap the growing trade on the Great Lakes by water links to the Ohio, to facilitate traffic on the river by a canal around the Falls, and to reach into the hinterland with improved roads. Later another canal—this time down the Licking "into the heart of Kentucky"—a bridge across the Ohio, and a railway to Lexington were added. Success would have made the entire valley dependent upon this urban center, and given the Ohio metropolis command of the strategic routes of trade and travel.

This ambitious program caused great concern in Pittsburgh. "We honestly confess," the *Gazette* admitted, that "a canal from the lakes either into the Ohio or the Great Miami . . . adds another item to the amount of our present uneasiness." By tipping the commerce of the valley northward, Cincinnati would substantially reduce the Iron City's importance as the central station between East and West. "Without this trade," the *Statesman* warned, "what can Philadelphia and Pittsburgh become but deserted villages, compared with their great rivals?" Pennsylvania responded to this threat by improving the turnpike between its urban centers and ultimately constructing an elaborate canal across the mountains. In addition, Pittsburgh proposed to head off Cincinnati by building a water route to Lake Erie or tying into the Ohio system below Cleveland.

The challenge to Cincinnati's supremacy, however, came not only from a resurgent Pittsburgh, but also from a booming downriver neighbor, Louisville. As early as 1819 a visitor noted this two-front war. "I discovered two ruling passions in Cincinnati; enmity against Pittsburgh and jealousy of Louisville." In one regard the Falls City was the more serious rival, because as a commercial center it competed directly with the Ohio emporium. In fact, guerilla warfare between the two towns for advantage in the rural market began early in the century. But the great object of contention was the control and traffic on the river—the West's central commercial artery.

In this contest Louisville held one key advantage. Its strategic position at the Falls gave it command of both parts of the Ohio. All passengers and

goods had to pass through the town, except during the few months of high water when even large vessels could move safely over the rapids. It was a clumsy system, and from the earliest days many people envisaged a canal around the chutes. Nothing came of these plans until the coming of the steamboat immensely expanded traffic and made the interruption seem intolerable. Though nearly every shipper favored a canal, it was not until Cincinnati, anxious both to loosen river commerce and weaken a rival city, put its weight behind the improvement that any real activity developed.

Cincinnati had a deep stake in this project. A canal would not only aid the town generally but also advance the interests of some powerful groups. The mercantile community was anxious to get freer trade, and many residents had large investments in companies which hoped to dig on either the Kentucky or Indiana side of the Falls. Others owned real estate in the area. William Lytle, for example, had large holdings around Portland of an estimated value of between $100,000 and $500,000. Moreover, ordinary Cincinnatians had come to the conclusion that a canal would serve a broad public purpose. Hence in 1817 a town meeting was called to discuss the issue. An editor provided the backdrop: "No question was ever agitated here that involved more important consequences to this town." And from the beginning Louisville was cast as the villain of the piece. *Liberty Hall* referred to it as "a little town" trying to make "all the upper country tributary to it, by compelling us to deposit our goods in its warehouses and pay extravagant prices for transportation around or over the Falls."

Since the Falls City could frustrate any project on Kentucky soil, Cincinnati's first move was to build on the opposite side. The Indiana legislature incorporated the Jeffersonville Ohio Canal Company in 1817, empowering it to sell 20,000 shares of stock at $50 apiece, and authorizing a lottery for $100,000 more. From the outset it was clear that the scheme stemmed from the Queen City. Not only did that town provide more than half the concern's directors, but also the campaign for funds emphasized its role. "The public may be assured that the wealth, influence, enterprise and talents of Cincinnati are at the head of this measure," *Liberty Hall* declared in 1818. Moreover, advocates underlined the stake of the Ohio metropolis, warning residents that if they did not support the drive they "deserved to be hewers of wood and drawers of water" for Louisville. In May 1819 a prominent Cincinnatian gave the ceremonial address as digging began on the Indiana side.

Louisville hesitated to support any canal. The city had flourished on the transportation break, and many inhabitants felt that facilitating travel over the rapids would destroy the very *raison d'être* of the place. That view was probably extreme, but in the short run no one could deny that certain interests were jeopardized. "It must be admitted that the business of a portion of our population would be affected," the *Public Advertiser* confessed. "The storage and forwarding business would probably be diminished—and there might be less use for hacks and drays." Tavern and hotel owners shared this anxiety, while the pilots who guided the ships through the chutes faced almost certain unemployment.

Unwilling to sacrifice these interests and uneasy about the town's future, Louisville leaders tried to deflect the mounting enthusiasm for a canal. Their first strategy was to suggest a small cut around the Falls which would accommodate keelboats and lesser craft. This expedient found few supporters, and Louisville next tried to reduce the pressure by paving the road to Portland and Shippingport, thus, facilitating the transshipment process. But this, too, was inadequate, and within a few years the clamor for a canal became irresistible.

Yet the city still hoped to salvage something out of defeat, to find some compensation for the loss of its strategic position. In 1824 a local editor laid down the conditions. "It is true that we could feel but little interest in opening a canal merely for the purpose of navigation," he conceded. "A canal to be useful . . . should be constructed to give us ample water power, for various and extensive manufacturing establishments; and a sufficient number of dry docks for the building and . . . repair of nearly all the steamboats employed on western waters, should be constructed as necessary appendages." If the project included these items, he declared, then "the citizens of Louisville will be found among its most zealous advocates."

The Falls City could afford to take its pound of flesh, because building on the Indiana side was much less feasible than the Kentucky route. The engineering problems were immensely more complicated, and the cost was nearly three times as great. In 1819 an official committee, comprised of delegates from Virginia, Pennsylvania, Ohio, and Kentucky, estimated the expense of the northern plan at $1,100,000 and the southern one at $350,000. Hence few people acquainted with the situation took seriously the Jeffersonville Ohio Canal Company's enterprise. Yet the disadvantages of the Indiana route were not insurmountable, and Louisvillians realized that in the long run the Falls would be skirted on one side or the other. If they dragged their feet too much, their opponents would press for action regardless of the cost or difficulty. This possibility ultimately brought the Kentucky emporium to its knees.

While Louisville reluctantly yielded at the Falls, Cincinnati pursued the rest of its expansion program. By 1822 the Miami Canal to Dayton was open, and work had begun on the state system which ultimately connected the Great Lakes with the Ohio River. Though the Queen City could claim less success in the Kentucky area, its economic supremacy in the West was not questioned. The new country's largest urban center, it had corralled the bulk of the region's mounting commerce and become the nexus of trade lines that reached from the Atlantic Ocean to the Gulf of Mexico.

Cincinnati's economic primacy, however, did not yet carry with it cultural leadership. This honor still belonged to Lexington, whose polish and sophistication were the envy of every transmontane town. "Cincinnati may be the Tyre, but Lexington is unquestionably the Athens of the West," *Liberty Hall* conceded in 1820. This admission reflected a sense of inadequacy which constantly shadowed the Queen City and compromised its claim to total supremacy. One resident suggested an ambitious lecture program to overcome the deficiency and "convince those persons at a distance who pronounce us as a *Commercial* people alone, that we have here, both the *Tyre* and the *Athens* of the West." Another observer, though not armed with a remedy, made the same point. "It may be well for us," he counseled, "when we can catch a moment from the grovelling pursuits of commercial operations, to cull and admire the varied sweets of those literary and scientific effusions, which have stamped Lexington as the headquarters of *Science and Letters* in the Western country."

The establishment and success of Transylvania University aggravated this inferiority complex. Not only did it lend prestige to another place, but it also lured local youths to its classrooms. The *Western Spy* admitted that it was "particularly mortifying to see the College of a neighboring state attract both Students and Professors" from the Ohio metropolis. In the early twenties Cincinnati countered with a medical school which it hoped would become a "powerful rival" and "ultimately go beyond" the Kentucky institution. But it was not until financial difficulties and fire brought down Transylvania that the Queen City could claim cultural parity with its Blue Grass rival.

Lexington's position also bred jealousy in Louisville. Though the larger and more prosperous of the two by 1825, the Falls City had to concede that intellectual primacy rested with its Kentucky neighbor. This admission was not easy to make, because the two towns had been bitter foes for many years. They contended for political leadership in the state; earlier, in fact, each had hoped to become its capital. Moreover, their economic interests often collided, with Lexington depending upon manufacturing and protection and Louisville emphasizing commerce and wanting freer trade. Neither yielded readily to the other on any issue. Yet the cultural leadership of the Blue Grass town was too obvious to be denied, and, from the Falls City viewpoint, it was certainly too important to be permanently surrendered.

There was, however, something of a family quarrel about this rivalry. Despite their differences, both professed love for mother Kentucky, and occasionally one deferred to the other out of filial pride. In 1820, for example, Louisville's *Public Advertiser* supported state aid to Transylvania, explaining that "distinguished institutions of learning in our own state, where education from its cheapness, shall be within the reach of the poor, is the *pivot* on which the grandeur of the state depends." In addition, the Falls City stood to gain by its success. "Louisville cannot be jealous of Lexington," the same newspaper declared; "her future interest is measurably blended with that of Transylvania University; for as that flourishes Lexington will become a more extensive and important customer to her in a commercial point of view." Likewise, when Lexington tried to get money for a hospital, its old foe offered support, but for perhaps less elevated reasons. If the Blue Grass got such an institution, "one of the same kind at this place cannot, consistently, be refused," the editor observed.

And nothing forced the two to discover common interests more quickly than the appearance of a hostile outsider. When Cincinnati planned a medical school to compete with Transylvania, Louisville stood behind the testimony of the university, whose spokesman urged the state to give additional money to the institution. Otherwise, he warned, "in the struggle that must ensue, we of Transylvania will be compelled to enter the lists naked and defenceless, our opponents of Cincinnati being . . . armed. The issue of such a conflict cannot be doubted. We shall certainly be vanquished and your young men will . . . repair to the eastern schools for medical education, or Kentucky must become tributary to the state of Ohio." Lexington reciprocated when the Queen City threatened a canal on the Indiana side of the river.

Kind words were few, however, and mutual aid sporadic. Usually the two communities did little to conceal their animosity. In fact, Louisville had no sooner supported Transylvania's expansion than it began again its vicious barrage on the school and its town. The attack stemmed from a mixture of political, economic, and urban motives, but it centered on the university because it was at once the symbol of Lexington's importance and its most vulnerable spot. The city's economy never recovered from the postwar depression and only its cultural renaissance kept stores and shops open. If the college failed, all failed. This was understood in the Falls City. Indeed, the *Public Advertiser* noted that the "ablest and best citizens" of the Blue Grass metropolis had tried to give a "new impetus" to the place by the encouragement of its "literary establishments." Knowingly, then, Louisville struck at Lexington where it would hurt most.

Nor was there anything gentle about the tactics. In 1816, during the first debate over state assistance to Transylvania, John Rowan from the Falls City argued that the institution ought to be moved elsewhere to keep it from "improper influence" and the "many means of corrupting the morals of youth," which existed in the town. Four years later the criticism had become more barbed. "If you wish to jeopardize every amiable trait in the private character of your son, send him to Lexington," the *Public Advertiser* contended, linking the college to radical politics. "If you wish him to become a Robespierre or a Murat, send him to Lexington to learn the rudiments of Jacobinism and disorganization." By 1829 a Louisville editor was warning parents that at the university their children would be "surrounded by political desperadoes" and that "the very atmosphere of the place has been calculated to pollute the morals and principles of the youth attending it."

Lexington, though an old veteran of urban rivalries, had not anticipated this bitterness. "We thought of all our institutions, it was the pride and boast of the town; and the least calculated to excite the envy, and stir up the opposition of any individual or section of the country." But the assault threatened the city's very life, and it fought back. The defense was generally constructive, detailing the achievements of Transylvania and extolling its influence on students and the new country. Graduates wrote testimonials and local citizens publicized the healthfulness and "literary atmosphere" of the community, while officials dispelled rumors about the snobbery of the college.

The case was good, but Lexington strategists bungled in several respects. In 1829 not a single Jacksonian was appointed to the Board of Trustees, and not enough was done to quiet the uneasiness of either the farmers or the highly religious. As a result, when Transylvania needed support most, it was almost friendless. By 1830 the campaign instituted by Louisville had destroyed Kentucky's brightest ornament and pulled the most substantial prop from Lexington's economy.

Even before Transylvania's demise Lexington felt itself slipping economically, and it tried to steady itself by better connections with the trade of the Ohio River. Canals and roads proved either impractical or inadequate, and in 1829 civic leaders planned a railroad. The act of incorporation in the next year left the northern terminus undecided, with the understanding that it would be either Louisville or Cincinnati. The uncertainty set off a curious kind of competition between those two cities. Neither could foresee the impact that a railroad might have on its own importance, yet they equally feared that it would give their rival a substantial advantage.

Louisville was especially wary. This looked like the canal issue in another form, and many people thought it wise to wait for the results of the first project. Moreover, some of the same local interests seemed to be threatened. The hack and dray owners protested that their $125,000 business would be jeopardized. And since the railroad would pass through the city and continue on to Portland, others feared the growth of a "rival town" on the Western end of the Falls. The city council, walking gingerly because of this opposition, appointed a committee to look into the question, and called a public hearing to sound out local opinion. The meeting attracted over three hundred people, and after a lively debate, it voted to keep the tracks out of Louisville.

Very quickly, however, civic leaders realized that any alternative terminus was more perilous to the Falls City than the possible dislocations occasioned by accepting the railroad. Thus "S" wrote that if "we are to have a rival town, the nearer to us the less dangerous," and a "Gentleman in Lexington" warned that its "great rival, Cincinnati" was "straining every nerve" to induce the company to build in that direction. By December 1830 the tide had turned, and the council invited the Lexington and Ohio Railroad to come to Louisville.

Cincinnati, despite its official policy, had many qualms about a railroad from Lexington. "Why should the citizens of Cincinnati be so anxious to create a rival town across the river?" asked the editor of the *Advertiser*. Yet the same logic which drove Louisville to change its mind sustained the Queen City's original decision. On December 7, 1830, a public meeting declared that the project "would conduce to the prosperity of this city, in an eminent degree," and a committee of prominent civic leaders invited the company's directors to come to

Cincinnati to discuss details. These events, coupled with Louisville's acceptance, brought great rejoicing to Lexington, for it now looked as though the railroad would bring it a share of the Ohio's commerce and arrest at last the economic decay which had brought the "Athens of the West" to the very brink of disaster.

The struggle for primacy and power —and occasionally survival—was one of the most persistent and striking characteristics of the early urban history of the West. Like imperial states, cities carved out extensive dependencies, extended their influence over the economic and political life of the hinterland, and fought with contending places over strategic trade routes. Nor was the contest limited to the young giants, for smaller towns joined the scramble. Cleveland and Sandusky, for example, clashed over the location of the northern terminus of the Ohio canal, the stakes being nothing less than the burgeoning commerce between the river and the lakes. And

their instinct to fight was sound, for the outcome shaped the future of both.

Like most imperialisms, the struggle among Western cities left a record of damage and achievement. It trampled new villages, smothered promising towns, and even brought down established metropolises. Conflicting ambitions infused increasing bitterness into the intercourse of rivals, and made suspicion, jealousy, and vindictiveness a normal part of urban relationships. Yet competition also brought rapid expansion. The fear of failure was a dynamic force, pushing civic leaders into improvements long before they thought them necessary. The constant search for new markets furnished an invaluable stimulus to commercial and industrial enterprise. And, at its best, urban imperialism bred a strong pride in community accomplishment. As one resident put it, "there exists in our city a spirit . . . which may render any man proud of being called a Cincinnatian."

Man and Environment in the Growth of a City
Charles N. Glaab*

Today, Kansas City, Missouri, is an American metropolis and a national transportation center. Theories of city location and growth often make an individual city seem the creation of complex economic and geographic forces that focus in a time-space dimension; in terms of this type of analysis, the rise of Kansas City appears logical and perhaps even inevitable. But men have also played a part in making cities. Local historians of American cities emphasize this point—sometimes to the exclusion of any other—and, to explain a city's existence and its development, single out heroic actions by community leaders in times of crisis. The recorded history of Kansas City embodies this kind of interpretation of the city's formative years.

In an introduction to the most recent formal history of Kansas City, Roy A. Roberts, publisher of the *Kansas City Star* and a leading contemporary spokesman for the community, asserted that a distinct lesson could be learned from reading about the city's past. Why had Kansas City become a magnificent metropolis? "Enterprise, daring, above all faith pushed Kansas City ahead. Men, not chance did it." Specifically, he pointed to the battle for railroads, in which vigorous and wise leadership had won the struggle with rival communities for regional supremacy. To Roberts, the work of early city-builders in gaining railroads symbolized "what became known, and is still known as the

'Kansas City spirit'—not just a Chamber of Commerce slogan, but a living, meaningful thing."[1]

Scholarly analysis suggests that a complex of economic, social, and ecological relationships shape the nature of a city. But significant also in determining the "personality" and quality of life in any city are the legends, impressions, and evaluations that it uses to interpret its past. These stored social memories, when sharply focused, serve as a useful urban myth, which city leaders can invoke when making community decisions. In Kansas City, the principal community legend—complete with heroes, villains, a traitor, frantic journeys, and a dramatic confrontation of the enemy—concerns the coming of the railroads. The Hannibal and St. Joseph bridge, the first railroad bridge constructed across the Missouri River, has served as the city's special symbol. The winning of this bridge became, in Kansas City's self-evaluation, the key to its success and a tribute to the bold resourcefulness of a small group of inspired city fathers.

The significance that local chroniclers of the legend have assigned to the Hannibal and St. Joseph bridge reflects a generally accurate historical judgment. Railroads did make Kansas City a leading American city. In the 1850's the future metropolis was one of several small trading towns on the western edge of settlement. The Civil War nearly destroyed the community. But the 1867 decision of the Hannibal and St. Joseph–Chicago, Burlington and Quincy railroad system to support

*Charles N. Glaab, reprinted with permission from *Kansas City and the Railroads: Community Policy in the Growth of a Regional Metropolis*, Madison: The State Historical Society of Wisconsin, 1962, 1–9.

[1] Henry C. Haskell, Jr., and Richard B. Fowler, *City of the Future* (Kansas City, 1950), 5.

the building of a line from Cameron, Missouri, to Kansas City, and to bridge the Missouri River at the latter point, caused an immediate boom in the town and fixed the pattern of regional railroad connections permanently in its favor. Within a few years, Kansas City became the regional metropolis and began its rise as a major American meat-packing and transportation center. In the life of a city great events demand great legends. The winning of the bridge was of such consequence to Kansas City that the heroic legend began to take shape at a very early date.

On July 3, 1869, the Hannibal and St. Joseph bridge was opened to traffic. Because the powerful current of the Missouri and the shifting nature of the river's channel had created formidable engineering problems, two-and-a half years had been required to build it. Twice the chief engineer, Octave Chanute, failed to establish a firm footing under the bridge's fourth pier. He eventually had to introduce new construction techniques from Germany to finish the work. But at last it was done, and Kansas City celebrated.[2]

A newspaper reporter from neighboring St. Joseph attended the July 3 festivities. Considering the years of intense rivalry between the two communities he should have been less enthusiastic than local reporters. But he too was exuberant; the occasion, he wrote, was "without parallel in western celebrations." Forty thousand people were present. To the accompaniment of bands and artillery salvos, railroad employees drove a lavishly decorated train across the bridge. Ten thousand people marched to a grove south of town to hear the major address of the day. As more cannons boomed, a man named Holman made a successful balloon ascension from the public square. A mammoth barbecue followed in the late afternoon. In the evening, town leaders and visiting dignitaries attended a grand banquet at the Broadway Hotel, where in a series of toasts and responses, speakers commemorated the significance of the event. It was "such a spectacle," the St. Joseph writer observed, "as is not likely to be witnessed more than once in a lifetime."[3]

The occasion demanded full and enthusiastic treatment by the local press. "Today will live forever in the annals of Kansas City as the greatest event in her history," declared the *Kansas City Times*. The bridge was "truly the bridge of destiny," one of the paper's writers asserted. "Circumstances created it, and for a time fortune coquetted with it, and wafted it hither as a prophetic wand, now pointed towards Leavenworth, then towards Kansas City. . . ." Everything had depended upon obtaining the bridge. Had Kansas City lost out, it would have surrendered to Leavenworth and would have become a town of secondary importance. "Truly the present and future greatness of Kansas City turned on that day's work." The moral was plain. The victory demonstrated on "how slender a thread sometimes hang the fortunes of cities as well as men and nations."[4]

Although details differed, the newspaper accounts presented a common story of dramatic, vigorous local action in the achievement of the victory. From 1856 on, Kansas City leaders had realized the importance of building a connection northward to the Hannibal and St. Joseph Railroad— the first railroad completed into western Missouri. They had chosen Cam-

[2] For a detailed account of the method of construction of the bridge, see Octave Chanute and George Morison, *The Kansas City Bridge* (New York, 1870).

[3] *Weekly Gazette* (St. Joseph), July 8, 1869.
[4] *Kansas City Weekly Times*, July 8, 1869.

eron, Missouri, thirty-five miles east of St. Joseph, as the terminus for a local project. Their Kansas City–Cameron company, organized in 1859, had made little progress when the Civil War stopped railroad building in the region. Right after the war, they resumed their efforts to raise money and to get the co-operation of the Hannibal and St. Joseph owners in Boston. But interests in the nearby Kansas town of Leavenworth, which had made tremendous gains during the war, also had organized a Cameron project. Quite by chance the news leaked out in 1866 that the Leavenworth promoters were about to close a contract with the Hannibal and St. Jo.—in fact, that they were already in Boston ready to sign. Immediately, Kansas City leaders called a meeting, and Charles E. Kearney, president of the Kansas City and Cameron, dispatched three powerful representatives of the local business community, Kersey L. Coates, John W. Reid, and Theodore S. Case, to Boston to try to delay these proceedings. The Hannibal and St. Jo owners were astonished to learn of the interest of the Kansas Citians in building a Cameron connection. They favored the Leavenworth group, but Kansas City's superior geographical position, eloquently argued by the three Kansas Citians, persuaded them to delay the negotiations. Finally, the Boston people sent James Joy, the western representative of the Hannibal and St. Jo., to look over the situation firsthand. Joy had "studied the map" and recognized Kansas City's superior natural advantages. He ordered Kearney to go ahead with the Cameron road and the bridge. Because of this decision and the subsequent support by Joy of the city's interests, Kansas City would become the "metropolis of the Middle Missouri Valley."[5]

These initial newspaper accounts established two elements essential to the legend. First, there was the quality of sudden decision: Leavenworth was about to steal the prize; only at the last possible instance did the people of Kansas City act. Secondly, the bridge decision was crucial in Kansas City's history: if the plan of Leavenworth had not been thwarted, all would have been lost to the rival town.

The first and in many ways the ablest of Kansas City's historians, William H. Miller, who as secretary of the board of trade in the 1870's and 1880's reflected the views of the local business community, added the remaining vital aspects of the bridge legend. First, he supplied the traitor. Before the war, Miller wrote, the Kansas City company had negotiated a contract with the Hannibal and St. Jo. promising its aid in building the Cameron line. John T. K. Hayward, a Hannibal and St. Jo. official who had been assisting the Kansas Citians in their effort, signed this contract for the Boston company. Then at some point between 1860 and 1866, Hayward had lost his position with the Hannibal and St. Jo. and had sold out to Leavenworth interests. He continued to represent himself to Kansas Citians as a Hannibal and St. Jo. man; at the same time he furthered Leavenworth's quest for its Cameron connection. His machinations accounted for the presence of Leavenworth negotiators in Boston and also accounted for their near success. For among the pre-Civil War officers of the Hannibal and St. Jo., only Hayward and John W. Brooks knew of the old contract. And Brooks, in 1866, was away in Europe![6]

Miller also described some adroit Congressional maneuvering by local figures that helped make the eventual favorable decision possible. James Joy,

[5] *Ibid.; Daily Journal of Commerce* (Kansas City), July 3, 1869.

[6] William H. Miller, *History of Kansas City* (Kansas City, 1881), 116–117.

in analyzing Kansas City's proposition, agreed to resurrect the old contract provided local leaders could get Congressional authorization for a bridge across the Missouri River. Upon receiving this news, Kearney immediately telegraphed Robert T. Van Horn, an editor of Kansas City's leading newspaper who was then serving as United States Representative, to push the required bill through Congress. Van Horn managed to get the Kansas City bridge authorization tacked on as an amendment to an omnibus bridge bill. The House voted to accept the amendment. Just then, Kansas Congressman Sidney Clarke rushed onto the floor with an amendment to authorize a bridge at Leavenworth. But the previous question had been moved and seconded. Clarke was too late by minutes. Van Horn had turned the tide in Kansas City's favor.

Miller had obviously improved the dramatic quality of the legend. There was now a personal villain, John Hayward, instead of the more abstract enemy, "Leavenworth." The Van Horn episode in Congress strengthened the climax. The foiling of Leavenworth's dupe, the unresourceful Sidney Clarke, even added a bit of comic relief.

Later historians and journalists in recounting the bridge victory relied largely on Miller's account. But in rewriting the story, they often portrayed the events as high melodrama. The "dirty work" in hated Leavenworth, the treachery of Hayward, the frantic trip to Boston, the "fast political footwork" and "lightning-like" procedures in Congress all received exaggeratedly colorful and often inaccurate treatment. Moreover, there were fundamental shifts in emphasis in these later accounts. Many early versions of the legend had Kansas City's natural advantages determining the bridge decision; later writers hinged the outcome on the prewar contract. By the 1880's the doctrine of natural advan-

tages, fundamental in Midwestern urban rationales in the ante-bellum period, had begun to pass out of fashion. The prior-contract story harmonized with the triumph of local enterprise, a theme consistently celebrated in local historiography of the late nineteenth century. Also important was the tendency for James Joy to disappear completely from later presentations. If a writer paid tribute to the "Kansas City spirit," he naturally found it inconvenient to have the future of the city dependent on the whim of an Eastern railroad builder.[7]

During the years after 1869, the story of the bridge victory was also absorbed into local folklore, and suffered the usual alterations of historical fact involved in community assimilation of the knowledge of significant events. This sort of material—available in quantity—adversely influenced any later writer's effort to reconstruct the events that led to the bridge victory. For example, one early Kansas Citian recalled a version of the episode that seemed to bear virtually no relation to the written accounts. "On wintry nights in 1867," he reminisced, "a few old chums would frequently meet in the back room of the little rented Postoffice to laugh and joke over the contest for the bridge in other cities. . . . As the pleasantries subsided, one of those present cried out: 'What about Kansas City's getting into the fight?' A guffaw laugh followed. Then an interchange of hospitality. Then the question was renewed. The fun in the question gradually abated. Kansas City's contempt for its northern rivals seemed to grow in the little

[7] For versions of the bridge victory in city histories, see William Griffith, *History of Kansas City* (Kansas City, 1900), 48–49; Carrie W. Whitney, *Kansas City: Its History and Its People, 1808–1908* (3 vols., Chicago, 1908), I, 252; Roy Ellis, *A Civic History of Kansas City* (Springfield, Mo., 1930), 33; Darrell Garwood, *Crossroads of America* (New York, 1948), 121–122; Haskell and Fowler, *City of the Future*, 46–47.

gathering. No arguments followed. . . . 'We can get all the money needed; we are not poor. Our banks will back up their customers. Let us get going.' Checks were drawn out. Everyone present was a committee to arouse the bankers. Horses were mounted, and every man with money within a radius of ten miles was ordered out of bed. When the second morning cast its light, reports were nearly all handed in at the rendezvous. The bankers accepted the checks and drew up orders on their eastern correspondents. The amount demanded to insure the bridge was at hand. Before noon four of Kansas City's enterprising citizens had started for the nearest railroad, miles east. When they presented themselves in the general office of the railroad interest way off in Boston they handed their certified checks from Kansas City to the capitalists who owned the North Missouri Railroad, now the Wabash Railroad. Those checks were large enough to justify bringing the railroad from Cameron junction to what is now North Kansas City . . . and to meet the bonus for the bridge. . . ."[8] Every fact in the account is wrong. The year is wrong, the wrong railway company is involved, and the origin of the idea of trying to obtain a bridge is altogether fanciful. But the presentation is true to the spirit of the legend, for it emphasizes spontaneous community decision and inspired, vigorous local action. And these qualities are fundamental in all versions of the episode.

During the 1870's the legend of the bridge became part of the city's history. By this time, Kansas City was on its way to becoming the metropolis of the lower Missouri River valley. Railroad rivalry had been settled in

[8] William J. Dalton, *The Life of Father Bernard Donnelly* (Kansas City, 1921), 89–90. This work collects the oral reminiscences of Donnelly.

her favor. The arguments that town promoters had used in prewar days, strategic location and natural advantages, had little utility in advancing the interests of an established city facing problems other than the attraction of outside attention and investment. The bridge victory offered a new basis for appeals to action: reassert the spirit of the Cameron railroad builders; continue the monumental work that they had started; show the same type of enterprise, aggressiveness and daring that they had shown. If this were done, all would be well, and Kansas City would continue on its path to greatness. In subsequent years, the bridge legend became, as Roberts made clear, the main buttress of a more comprehensive urban myth, "the Kansas City spirit," which emphasized the community's superior leadership, energy, and willingness to support projects to advance the city.

The bridge legend, at least in some of its presentations, supplies reasonably accurate history. Some facts are misinterpreted: the prior contract and Van Horn's Congressional coup did not have the importance that has been assigned to them. But the actual chronicling of events is sometimes reasonably close to the truth.

Nevertheless, there are serious weaknesses in all presentations of the legend. Even considered just as an account of one narrow aspect of community policy during the period—the building of the Cameron road and the winning of the bridge—it is far from adequate. In all the versions, time is compressed. By implication at least, events extending over several months are treated as if they had occurred in a day or two. Moreover, the legend is extremely selective. It ignores a complex of regional railroad developments during the period that affected the decision to bridge the Missouri River at Kansas City. The whole story hinges on one brilliant stroke of local effort—the successful persuasion of the Hannibal and St. Jo. railroad to support the Kansas City project. All that came before or after is ignored. The Boston journey may well have been a rather spectacular affair, but it was preceded by months of fruitless negotiations. Even after the Hannibal and St. Jo. decision, the local promoters experienced many trials before they were able to complete their railroad. The legend of the bridge isolates for consideration only one achievement in a succession of failures.

The early history of Kansas City does not sustain the view that local leaders through heroic action created a city. Nor does it reveal the unfolding of a design whereby a wilderness community steadily and surely emerges as railroad center and metropolis. It shows instead a pattern of false starts, obvious turning points, and fortuitous combinations of circumstance. The scope, character, and direction of community policy—conditioned by a complex framework of ideological, geographic, and economic influences —had profound effects on the rise of a leading American city and on the pattern of the American railroad system. But Roberts' proposition that "men, not chance did it" posed false opposites. In this case, as perhaps in all cases, the two were inseparable.

3 The Growth and Development

The dramatic urban concentration which occurred during the eighteen hundreds, after centuries of relatively static population growth, presented new demands. Rural society had always needed facilities, such as water and sanitation, and protection against natural and social forces, like fire and hostile enemies. Most of these needs, however, had been provided for on an individual or ad hoc group basis. The urban environment began to make some of these functions difficult to fulfill, to add complexity to simple problems, and to present new contingencies which demanded attention.

As population concentrated, the need and opportunity to perform these functions collectively and formally became obvious. As increased density increased use, water supplies became inadequate or polluted. There were no docking and market facilities for securing and selling goods from Europe and the countryside. Urban streets, through heavier traffic, became quickly rutted, or after a rain, seas of mud. The city dweller, unable to use his rubbish to feed his pig or to replenish the soil, watched refuse and garbage begin to clog the streets. Knowing little of the nature of disease,

# of Urban Services

he helplessly witnessed increased incidents of sickness and epidemics. He had no protection from fire or security of his person and property. All of these problems presented the city with new challenges to which in its inception it had provided no solutions.

One way of defining a city is: A group of people who have the ability to respond to their collective needs. This concept, discussed in Section 1, implies the existence of a sense of community and the ability to impose a rational order on new complex relationships. Urbanism in the early American population centers can be measured, as Carl Bridenbaugh suggested, by the willingness of its members to initiate community services and the degree to which they succeeded. More and better services were provided by cities competing to attract people and outside investment. Problems which were the most threatening, such as fire or hostile enemies, or the solution to which offered the most immediate returns, such as transportation and market facilities, quickly received attention. Newer problems, or those which directly affected only a small or uninfluential segment of the population, were often ignored and proved more difficult to remedy.

The establishment of urban services posed three problems: First, the community had to become aware of a need. Coming from a rural background where clear water was readily available and where isolation lessened the danger of communicable disease, the urbanite had to recognize the problems created by his new environment. Second, the community had to develop an adequate technology. Before transit systems could be planned, appropriate mechanical devices had to be invented. Before effective public health measures could be initiated, knowledge of the source and prevention of disease had to be discovered. Third, the community had to be willing to accept corporate responsibility. In an age dominated by individualism and a laissez-faire philosophy, each effort to implement a community service was long debated and delayed. At the heart of the controversy was the question of whether to provide these services through public or private agencies, and further complications arose because decisions were made frequently by political leaders concerned less with community than with personal welfare.

The selections in this chapter illuminate these problems through the specific discussion of the establishment of a water supply, a professional police force, and an urban transportation system. In each case the community responded to the physical and social changes that are concomitant with urban growth. The establishment of these services manifests urbanization and contributes to its continued development. Instead of the decentralizing process, the move to suburbia, that took place in the twentieth century, the development of urban services in the nineteenth century contributed to centralization and specialized functioning. This centralization, as exemplified by Milwaukee's establishment of a full range of urban services, can be seen as the touchstone for the growth of the cosmopolitan city.

While this section deals with only some problems of urban services, it treats those problems extensively. Admittedly many other difficulties existed. Poverty, although not unique to the urban condition, was present in a new guise, in that the poor lacked even the means to provide their own food. The provision of open-air spaces, streets, waste removal, lighting, and market and commercial facilities, as well as other needs, demanded the community's attention. By the twentieth century many of these questions of urban services had been given attention, but with few exceptions they were far from resolved. Indeed, the failure to deal with them effectively in the past has been at the root of contemporary problems. The debate continues as to which needs are the individual's responsibility and which are the community's. Should society provide a minimum standard of housing and health for every person? What level of education is it the responsibility of the community to provide? Should the city use public funds to build a transit system to unclog the street, a sports stadium to provide entertainment, or new port facilities for trade? Even in those areas which are accepted as the responsibility of the community, there is dispute as to the degree of involvement and the methods and procedures to follow.

The Need for an Urban Water Supply

Nelson M. Blake*

In an anxious age when civil defense workers practice caring for the victims of an imagined atomic attack and science fiction magazines speculate on the horrid possibilities of an invasion from outer space, the suggestion of still another conceivable disaster will hardly be welcome, but—

Just suppose that through an act of sabotage or a sudden assault New York City or any other great city were to be deprived of its entire water supply. The results would not be as instantly horrifying as the explosion of a hydrogen bomb, but over a short period of time the disaster would be almost as demoralizing to urban life.

The first affliction to be dreaded by a waterless city would obviously be thirst. The fretful child would cry out in vain for a drink. The feverish sick would toss in thirsty anguish. The office water cooler would stand empty. The glass of water which the hungry had always taken for granted with their meals would be unavailable. Without water, coffee and tea would also disappear from the menu, together with locally manufactured beer and soft drinks.

With the water supply knocked out, city dwellers would discover that their choice of foods was shockingly limited. Whatever was usually cooked in water—vegetables, soups, stewed meats, and the like—could not be prepared. The baker and the housewife would have no water to make their breadstuffs and pastries.

To add to the discomfort of bever-

ageless and monotonous meals, the fastidious diner would recoil from unwashed dishes and tableware. Indeed, the water famine would completely upset the whole pattern of habits by which modern man keeps himself clean. Workers would have to go to and from their jobs unbathed; clothes would get dirtier and dirtier; floors would remain unscrubbed. Defenses against man's most deadly enemies, the disease-causing germs, would be dangerously lowered. And the fact that not a toilet in the whole city would flush would open up another fatal breach in the walls of public health. Without water the whole sewerage system by which a great city rids itself of human and industrial wastes would fail.

Thirst, malnutrition, and disease would not be the only dangers menacing the population. The fire department would be left without weapons to fight any but the most minor conflagrations. Automatic sprinkler systems would no longer function. Millions of dollars worth of property would be exposed to grave jeopardy.

The purpose of suggesting the complete confusion and fear into which a modern city would be plunged by the loss of its water supply is not to create alarm about an imaginary and improbable disaster. Rather, this desolate picture has been described to emphasize the fact that urban life, and this is now the life of a majority of Americans, is peculiarly dependent upon water. Without it, cities simply could not exist.

If this be true, the indispensable precondition to the great growth of American cities during the nineteenth century was a recognition of the vital importance of water supply and the

*Reprinted with permission from Nelson M. Blake, *Water for the Cities: A History of the Urban Water Supply Problem in the United States*, pp. 1–2, 4, 5–8, 9–11, 12–17. Copyright © 1956 by Syracuse University Press, Syracuse, New York. All rights reserved.

taking of adequate steps to meet this need. In 1790 American cities drew their water almost exclusively from springs, wells, and cisterns, sources became steadily more inadequate in quantity and quality as the population grew. By 1860, after resorting to many unsatisfactory makeshifts, most cities had learned a great lesson. No longer could they depend upon internal sources of supply; at whatever expense or difficulty they must impound the waters of outlying lakes and rivers and bring this lifegiving stream through aqueducts and pipes into the very homes of their citizens.

. . .

By twentieth-century standards Philadelphia in 1790 was little more than an overgrown town. Within the boundaries of the old city some 28,522 inhabitants lived; in the adjoining districts of the Northern Liberties and the Southwark there were 13,998 more, making a total of 42,520 persons, the largest concentration of population in the new nation. Philadelphia's principal rivals were New York with 33,131 inhabitants and Boston with 18,038. Other busy ports were Charleston and Baltimore with populations of 16,359 and 13,503 respectively.

. . .

City life in the 1790's was not all profit and pleasure. Life and property in the urban communities were none too safe. Although the cities were growing rapidly, their institutions of local government were still those of villages. Constables and marshals by day and watchmen by night provided little protection against crime. Thefts and assaults were frequent, and occasional riots threw the cities into an uproar and resulted in much damage to property.

Even more serious was the danger of fire in the closely-built streets and alleys. The great Boston fire of 1711

left a hundred families homeless; the New York fire of 1776 destroyed 493 houses, about one-quarter of all those in the city. Serious conflagrations that gutted five or six buildings broke out again and again. To combat these, volunteer fire companies had been organized, but their activities with buckets and primitive hand pump engines were often ineffective. Sometimes, especially during summer droughts or winter freezes, the firemen were badly handicapped by a shortage of water in the wells and rivers. In 1791, Philadelphia was thrown into a panic by a report that arsonists were at work. Rewards totalling one thousand dollars were posted for the arrest of the criminals, and special patrols were organized to guard the city day and night.

The greatest threat of all to the lives of the city dwellers came from disease. Long before 1790, American towns, like those of the Old World, had been periodically scourged by epidemics of smallpox, yellow fever, and other fatal maladies. But all previous American experience was overshadowed by the great yellow fever epidemic of 1793 which terrified Philadelphia for three months. Over four thousand deaths, amounting to almost ten per cent of the population, were charged to the deadly pestilence. The shocking mortality was only one part of the story. Business in the nation's leading port, then serving as both the capital of the United States and of Pennsylvania, came to a standstill as twenty-three thousand inhabitants, almost one-half of the population, fled the city to find whatever accommodations they could in the surrounding countryside. Most of those who remained in the city avoided all contact with their neighbors, hoping somehow to save themselves from the prevailing malady. Only a heroic few risked their lives in such desperately needed services as attending the sick, moving them to an emergency hospital on the city's outskirts, burying the dead, and providing food and shelter for the orphans and other destitute victims of the great disaster.

Philadelphia's tragic ordeal attracted the horrified interest of her sister cities. To protect themselves from infection they improvised strict quarantine measures against travelers from Philadelphia, but they demonstrated their humanity by raising funds and sending shiploads of emergency supplies to the stricken capital. Most of the other cities gained their own first-hand acquaintance with yellow fever before the decade was over. In 1794, the pestilence attacked Baltimore and New Haven, while appearing in less serious degree in Philadelphia again. In 1795, the rapidly growing port of New York was attacked, together with Baltimore and Norfolk; in 1796, the afflicted cities included Newburyport, Boston, and Charleston.

Philadelphia suffered a third visitation of the fever in 1797, a year in which Norfolk, Baltimore, Bristol, and Providence were also infected. The agony of the decade reached a terrifying peak in 1798. In Philadelphia the devastation approached that of 1793; thirty-five hundred victims died, and forty thousand persons, three-quarters of the population, fled the city. The situation in New York, where over two thousand deaths were recorded, was almost as bad, while the disease also invaded Boston and seven of the smaller port cities. In 1799, yellow fever continued its ravages with visitations to Philadelphia, New York, and Charleston, as well as other places.

The epidemics of these years provoked bitter controversy. On the matter of proper treatment the doctors were divided between the disciples of Philadelphia's famous Dr. Benjamin Rush, who believed in attacking yellow fever through a ferocious counter-offensive of bleedings and purgings, and the anti-Rushites, like Dr. William Currie of Philadelphia, who advocated milder remedies.

More significant than the dispute over treatment was the difference of opinion over the cause of the disease. Currie and others insisted that yellow fever was a distinct and special disease, brought into American ports periodically through ships from the West Indies and other disease-ridden foreign areas. The Rushites hotly denied this, pronouncing that the malady "commonly called the yellow fever" was only "the bilious, remitting fever of warm climates excited to a higher degree of malignity." The cause was "putrid exhalations from the gutters, streets, ponds and marshy grounds in the neighborhood of the city." In Charles Brockden Brown's *Arthur Mervyn,* one of the earliest American novels, one character refers to another thus: "He combatted an opinion I had casually formed respecting the origin of this epidemic, and imputed it, not to infectious substances imported from the East or West, but to a morbid constitution of the atmosphere, owing wholly or in part to filthy streets, airless habitations, and squalid persons."

So deep did the division between the two professional factions run that the doctors of Philadelphia grouped themselves in separate societies. Those who believed that yellow fever was imported from foreign sources associated with the College of Physicians, while their rivals who insisted upon the domestic origin of the fever joined the Academy of Medicine.

When harassed public officials appealed to the doctors for advice on practical measures to prevent a return of the pestilence, the answers that they received inevitably mirrored the rival theories. The College of Physicians placed its emphasis on strict inspection of incoming ships and quarantine for all sailors and passengers who had been exposed to disease. The Academy of Medicine recommended energetic steps to purge the city of refuse and filth.

Today we may smile at the pundits' quarrel, complacent in our knowledge that both parties were wrong. Few episodes in the history of science are more familiar than the experiments in which Dr. Walter Reed and his heroic colleagues demonstrated that yellow fever is transmitted by the female mosquito of the species *Stegomyia fasciata*. Gorging itself on the blood of a person ill with the fever, the insect carries within its tiny body the virus of the fatal disease and injects it into the blood stream of the next person whom it bites.

Indeed, much of the fascination of reading the yellow fever literature of the 1790's derives from the fact that we find frequent allusions to the unrecognized villain lurking upon the scene of her crimes. Thus, we read in Dr. E. H. Smith's description of the New York epidemic of 1795 that there were "clouds of musketoes, incredibly large and distressing: and these continued to afflict us, long after the time when they commonly depart. . . . The irritation, restlessness, and consequent watchfulness and fatigue, occasioned by these animals, no doubt predisposed the well to be affected by the fever; while they extremely harassed the sick, and retarded their recovery."

How close observers might come to a major truth without drawing the essential inference is suggested by the words of Dr. Valentine Seaman, who wrote in 1796: "It has been observed by Dr. Rush, in Vol. 1 of his Med. Observations, as well as by Dr. Lind, that musquetoes generally attend a sickly season—the same was observed here during the last summer: the cause is very clear, for circumstances favoring the rise of putrid miasmata, equally favor the generation of these insects."

But if both medical factions missed the truth about the transmission of yellow fever, both correctly apprehended some of the secondary causes. Those who believed that the disease was to be attributed to foreign sources were partly right, since the initial cases from which the mosquitos carried on their deadly propagation were probably brought into the port cities on ships from foreign ports. Those who believed in the domestic origin of the fever had also grasped a portion of the truth, since the fetid marshes and the stagnant pools to which they so much objected must have provided breeding places for the disease-carrying insects.

Fortunately, the municipal authorities, unwilling to choose between the rival theorists, decided to take the advice of both. Out of the yellow fever horrors of the 1790's emerged clearer concepts of public health. State legislatures passed stringent quarantine laws to regulate the ports, and Boards of Health were created to deal with these and other matters. Of equal importance was the new determination to cleanse the cities of their dangerous accumulations of filth. Many citizens, shocked out of indifference by the great terror, began to look at —and smell of—the neighborhoods in which they were living.

• • •

If filth vitiated the air and caused disease, the obvious counter-measure was to remove the filth. "All the large towns," observed *Claypoole's American Daily Advertiser* in 1798, "are turning their most serious attention to maintaining CLEANLINESS in their houses, yards and streets. Their suffering experience has not been learned in vain." Even the anti-Rushites who believed that the most effective preventative measure was to quarantine incoming ships conceded that civic cleanliness would help. In 1799, Dr. Currie gave this advice:

My observations however incline me to believe, that although the yellow fever is never generated in this country, it is communicated from one to another more readily and certainly when the atmosphere is replete with putrid exhalations, than when it is more pure or free from such exhalations. Prudence, therefore, dictates the propriety of removing from the city and its vicinity all putrifiable substances, and to promote coolness and ventilation during the hot season, as far as practicable. . . .

Moralists were particularly zealous in urging their fellow-citizens to clean themselves up. Noah Webster stated the matter thus:

I am persuaded that the Americans may be convinced by *facts*, that even in our climate, Epidemic and Pestilential Maladies may be generated by local causes. If they can be convinced of this, that sources of disease and death may be found among themselves created by their own negligence, it is a great point gained; for until they learn this, they will never attend to the means of preserving life and health. They will still wallow in filth, croud their cities with low dirty houses and narrow streets; neglect the use of bathing and washing; and live like savages, devouring, in hot seasons, undue quantities of animal food at their tables, and reeling home after midnight debauches.

The new passion for civic cleanliness obviously demanded a liberal use of water. One of the earliest suggestions for combatting the Philadelphia epidemic of 1793 was that the fire companies should flush the streets daily. In January, 1794, the City Council ordered that five water carts be provided for the regular watering and cleaning of the streets, particularly during hot weather. In an unsuccessful attempt to guard Philadelphia against yellow fever in July, 1798, the City Commissioners issued orders to wash the gutters and to wet the streets three times a week. Nor was Philadelphia alone in this new ambition to use water freely in cleaning the streets. Similar exhortations appeared in the newspapers of New York and Baltimore. Noah Webster advised:

Water is perhaps the best purifyer of the houses and streets of cities, as well as of infected clothes. The use of water cannot be too liberal; but care must be taken that none of it remains to stagnate about or near buildings.

Not content to preach cleanliness as a virtue in itself, some venturers in science attempted more elaborate explanations of the relationship between water and health. Dr. Joseph Browne of New York believed that putrefying animal and vegetable matter decreased the amount of "animal vital air" in the atmosphere and increased the proneness that animals had to contract diseases of a putrid nature. "If this theory be just, it is of utmost importance to remove from the houses, streets, and docks, every species of animal and vegetable matter when in a putrefactive state, to which nothing so effectually contributes as a plentiful supply of water." Dr. Browne also believed that less animal vital air was present in the atmosphere when the city pavements were overheated during the summer months. Sprinkling the streets would cool the air and render it more healthful. "I do not presume to say that the introduction of a large quantity of water into the City, would alone prevent the rise and spreading of putrid diseases, but I am well warranted in saying that, under providence, it would more than all other things, contribute to this most desirable end."

A similar line of reasoning led John Sevier, once a famous Tennessee frontiersman, to suggest the possibility of what in the twentieth century would be called air-conditioning. Noting that yellow fever regularly abated under the influence of autumn's cool and refreshing breezes, Sevier wrote to Dr. Benjamin Rush that could some substitute as near in effect as possible be constructed, it would be the most sure and likely means to eradicate the dreadful disorder.

I now beg leave to suppose for a moment constructing what we call in Tennessee a water blast, such as we now blow our Furnaces and Forges with. . . . A machine of this kind, I am induced to believe, would sufficiently ventilate the largest Hospital, or building erected for the Reception of the sick. . . .

I have conjectured that could the water . . . be elevated high enough for to afford strong blasts of the kind I have mentioned, that you might then have as many erected in different and suitable stations as might be a ventilation sufficient to disperse great parts of the floating contaminated mists and vapours; also purify, cool and refresh the vicinity in which they might be placed.

Less ambitious were frequent suggestions that the air might be cooled and rendered more healthful by public fountains.

Although primary importance was placed in increasing the quantity of water so that it might be more freely used, men of intelligence began to insist that the water supply should be pure as well as copious. In his will Franklin had pointed out the danger that Philadelphia's wells might ultimately become contaminated as had those of the cities of the Old World. As yellow fever scourged the city again and again, it was only natural to suspect that this had already happened. In October, 1798, the Board of Managers of the Marine and City Hospitals recommended that the city commissioners "have the pumps frequently and copiously worked, as the water is extremely offensive and unwholesome."

The proximity of Philadelphia's wells to graveyards and privies began to arouse concern. The writer of a letter to one of the newspapers complained that Philadelphia had more church yards than any city he had ever known. Drainage from these, added to "the local putrefaction of the necessaries," would breed pestilence forever if not removed or altered. "The pumps of the city are deprived of air; the necessaries are dug above the depth of the pumps. Therefore the situation of the poisons the above things contain are communicated to the water, and poison is drank as well as breathed. . . ."

The suspicion grew that most of the water of the city was no longer safe. Visiting Philadelphia in 1798, the brilliant young engineer, Benjamin Henry Latrobe, speculated on the terrible ravages of yellow fewer. The city's streets were mostly wide and straight, so the cause of disease could not be lack of ventilation. There were, to be sure, very filthy alleys, while the backyards of most of the houses were littered with refuse. But, he reasoned, some cause, more powerful and specific, must be at work.

Each house had its privy and its drain which discharged its contents into a boghole sunk into the ground. In every street close to the footpath was a range of pumps from which all the water used for drinking or cooking was drawn. The water of each of these pumps, Latrobe concluded, must be contaminated by the sewage. Dramatic evidence that such was the case appeared to be provided when a number of persons were reported to have fallen dead in the streets, immediately after drinking from the pumps. Some doctors explained these sudden deaths as the result of gulping down excessively cold water while the body was overheated from exercise; others thought that they were simply cases of apoplexy brought on by the summer heat.

But Latrobe had his own characteristically ingenious explanation. Above the water in the pump, he believed, there was confined a quantity of noxious gas. When the innocent water drinker put his mouth to the spout and raised the pump handle, he took this fatal effluvium into his system. This theory seemed to Latrobe to be confirmed by the fact that no further deaths were reported after the pumps were provided with iron ladles chained to the stocks so that drinkers no longer had to put their mouths to the spouts. (It was left, of course, for our own germ-conscious generation to speculate on how much disease was now communicated by this common drinking vessel!)

. . .

Rising demand for a pure and plentiful water supply drew attention to the inadequate sources upon which the American cities were dependent. For the most part, these were still the familiar resources of rural communities: springs, wells, and cisterns. Townsmen living close to some spot where water bubbled to the surface of the earth considered themselves fortunate and filled their buckets regularly from these favorite springs. In Baltimore, for example, a familiar landmark as early as 1752 was Cool Spring, situated near the western bank of the harbor. Here water was drawn for both townspeople and ships; here, too, was a natural meeting place for housewives, servants, and youthful lovers.

Water from mineral springs was sometimes enthusiastically offered for sale. In 1787, an advertisement in the *Pennsylvania Gazette* described three different kinds of medicinal water available at Harrowgate, four miles from Philadelphia:

> The subscriber submits it to the judgment of the physicians of Philadelphia, when, in what diseases, and in what quantity, to recommend the use of these mineral waters. He will only observe that the Harrowgate waters have rendered essential service to persons afflicted with diseases and obstructions of the stomach, bowels, and kidneys. It has also removed worms, and relieved the irregular gout and chronic rheumatism. Externally applied, these waters in many cases cured ulcers and other eruptions of the skin.

The most common means by which town dwellers obtained a supply of water were through wells and pumps. Although many inhabitants provided for their own supply in this way, provision for water was not exclusively left to individual enterprise. Public wells and pumps were institutions of long standing. In 1658, the Dutch of New Amsterdam dug a public well in front of the old fort, situated just south of New York's present-day Bowling Green. After the English conquest of the colony, six more wells were ordered "for the public good of the city." Boston's famous town pump had its origin in 1774 when a town meeting resolved that a well should be dug in Dock Square as a project to give work relief to the poor who were suffering unemployment through the operation of the Boston Port Bill.

By the end of the eighteenth century it had become a common occurrence for the inhabitants on a certain street or in a special locality to join in petitioning the municipal authorities that a public well should be dug and a pump erected at some convenient place. If the petition was granted, the cost of the improvement was assessed against the residents who would benefit. In Baltimore, for example, the records of the Special Commissioners for 1789 reveal that to pay for a new pump at the corner of Gay and Second Streets nine property holders were assessed sums ranging from eight shillings to £6 5s. The total cost of the well and pump was £12 19s 5d.

Public pumps were particularly characteristic of Philadelphia. In 1796, an investigating committee reported that there were in the city about three hundred public pumps and wells. The City Commissioners were authorized to sink as many new wells as might, in their opinion, contribute to the convenience of the citizens. About fifteen new wells were dug and pumps fixed therein each year. The purity of the well water had once been a matter of civic pride. The Swedish traveler, Peter Kalm, visiting the city in 1748, had written: "The good and clear water in Philadelphia is likewise one of its advantages. For although there are no fountains in the town, there is a well in every house and several in the streets, all of which furnish excellent water for boiling, drinking, washing and other uses." But in 1794, the reputation of the wells was quite different. The French colonial lawyer, Moreau de St. Mery, reported that none of the water was

particularly good; some of the pumps had a better reputation than others, but this was only relative. In rainy weather, seepage from the cemeteries drained into the water.

New York also provided an increasing number of public pumps. By 1809 there were 249 of these. But the New York well water was notoriously bad. As early as 1748 Peter Kalm remarked that even the horses balked at drinking it. The only good water, he noted, was obtained from a large spring a short distance from town, which the inhabitants used for their tea and kitchen purposes. So much in demand was the water from this source that shortly before the Revolution a pump was placed over the spring and ornamental grounds were laid out. The Tea Water Pump Garden became a popular resort, where tea and other beverages could be purchased. Still later, sale of the Tea Water developed into a thriving private enterprise. Jedediah Morse's *American Gazeteer* of 1797 thus described it:

> Most of the people are supplied every day with fresh water, conveyed to their doors in casks, from a pump near the head of Queen street, which receives it from a spring almost a mile from the centre of the city. This well is about 20 feet deep and four feet diameter. The average quantity drawn daily from this remarkable well, is 110 hogsheads of 130 gallons each. In some hot summer days 216 hogsheads have been drawn from it; and what is very singular, there is never more or less than about 3 feet water in the well. The water is sold commonly at three pence a hogshead at the pump.

Two horses driven by a boy operated the pump, and the distribution of the water to individual householders was in the hands of some twenty-four carters, whose margin of profit was ample since they purchased the water by the barrel at a price of about six cents for 130 gallons and sold it by the bucketful at about one cent a gallon.

Even the purity of the famous Tea Water, however, was not above suspicion. It was located dangerously near the filthy body of water known as the Collect or the Fresh Water Pond. However appropriate the latter name may have been in earlier days, by the 1780's the Collect was notorious as "a very sink and common sewer," where housewives did their washing and threw their slop buckets, and other people threw dead dogs and cats. A competing New Tea Water Pump on Magazine Street was available, but this was even closer to the Collect.

Many households obtained their water for bathing, washing dishes, scrubbing floors, and laundering by collecting rain water from the roofs in cisterns. Water from this source was perfectly soft and was easily worked into lather. But cistern water, like well water, tended to deteriorate with the growth of the towns. Housewives complained that dust and cinders often spoiled the water for washing clothes.

Growing discontent with the water situation would have developed in any case, and the yellow fever panic only hastened and dramatized this development. Gentlemen, well-read in the Latin classics, were keenly aware that men had not always and everywhere been dependent on the local supplies of water that springs, wells, and cisterns could provide. They knew that one of the essential foundations for the urban civilization of the Roman Empire had been a bold system of aqueducts conveying pure water from distant sources into the great metropolis.

A detailed description of these was available in *De Aquis Urbis Romae,* written by Frontinus, appointed superintendent of the aqueducts at Rome in 97 A.D. By this time the Roman water system had been in the process of development for over four hundred years; nine aqueducts had been built, some of them more than fifty miles long; the total length of the aqueducts exceeded 255 miles and the average daily supply of the city was probably about thirty-eight million gallons. Built of stone and lined with cement, these structures demonstrated extraordinary engineering skill. Sometimes they ran beneath the surface of the earth; sometimes they were supported on structures of solid masonry; sometimes they were carried across valleys on magnificent arched bridges. Within the city, water was distributed, in part through lead pipes, to public baths and fountains, to the shops of artisans, and to the private houses of the wealthier citizens. Even more remarkable were some of the aqeducts which had been built to supply the cities of the Roman provinces. Many of these still stood, sturdy and firm, sixteen hundred years later in countries like France and Spain.

The Romans had not been the only aqueduct builders. Before Roman times, people like the Phoenicians and the Greeks had often shown boldness and imagination in providing for their water needs. In later years Constantinople was supplied with water by aqueduct, while the Renaissance Popes recognized the needs of the city of Rome and took steps to restore some of the ancient works. To provide water for the gay fountains of Versailles, Louis XIV spent vast sums of money on machinery to raise the water of the Seine by water wheels and convey it to his palace grounds by canals and conduits.

With much of this previous experience eighteenth-century Americans had little contact, but the example of London was more familiar. In 1609, Hugh Middleton began the work of supplying London with water from sources some thirty-eight miles to the north by means of an open canal, the so-called New River. Management of this system was vested in a private corporation, the New River Company. A second private concern, the Chelsea Water Company, began operations in 1721; a third, the Lambeth Water Works, entered the field in 1783. Between 1805 and 1822, five more water companies were organized. The total daily supply from these sources was over twenty-eight million gallons. Of this, about thirteen million gallons was drawn from the River Lea and other distant sources through the New River Canal; the rest was pumped by water wheels and steam engines from the Thames close to the city.

Even in colonial America a few attempts had been made to improve the water supply. One of the earliest incorporations in the colonies was that of the Water Works Company by the Massachusetts General Court in 1652. The proprietors of this Boston enterprise constructed the so-called Conduit, a reservoir some twelve feet square into which water was conveyed through bored logs from nearby wells and springs. This supply served the convenience of neighboring families and was valuable in time of fire. But it never fulfilled the expectations of its promoters and eventually fell into disuse.

In 1754, Hans Christopher Christiansen began the construction of a system of water works for the Moravian colonists at Bethlehem, Pennsylvania. An English traveler in 1796 reported:

Every house in the town is supplied with an abundance of excellent water from a spring, which is forced through pipes by means of

an hydraulic machine worked by water, and which is situated on the banks of the creek. Some of the houses are supplied with water in every room. The machine is very simple, and would easily raise the water, if necessary, several hundred feet.

When a group of Moravians moved to Salem, North Carolina, they apparently carried their interest in water works with them, because a visitor to that town in 1786 noted that every house was supplied with water, brought a mile and a half in conduits.

In 1772, two private water companies, the Providence Water Company and Rawson's Fountain Society, were organized to supply the inhabitants of Providence, Rhode Island. Each of them drew water from springs about a mile from town and conveyed it through bored wooden logs.

The most ambitious project of colonial days was that of Christopher Colles, an Irish-born engineer, whom the Common Council of New York commissioned in 1774 to construct a system of water works. To finance the enterprise the municipality issued bonds and paper money to the amount of £11,400. By April, 1776, the project had been carried far enough to amaze a young Yankee officer in Washington's army. Although a Harvard graduate, Lieutenant Isaac Bangs had obviously never heard of steam engines before:

The work already accomplished is to convey water from the side of a hill, nigh a pond, to the top of the hill, from which, being higher than any part of the city, the water is to be conveyed in pipes. The well is 40 feet in diameter and 30 feet down to the surface of the water. In this well is an engine which forces the water almost to the top, and from thence through a wooden tube up to the top of the hill, which is a distance of about five rods. At the top of the hill is a pond covering one quarter of an acre, and being about from 8 to 11 feet deep. Thus far I could easily comprehend the operation of the works; but now the mystery was, how the machine in the well was first actuated and kept in motion. This (as I at length discovered with surprise,) was done by the power of boiling water. I found that, by means of a large copper boiler, the steam or vapor of the water is conveyed from thence into a strong copper tube of 18 inches diameter and 10 feet long, which stands in a perpendicular position. The lower part or end of this tube is light, but the upper end has in it a movable stopper which may move upwards or downwards with as much ease as possible, and at the same time keep the air without from entering into the tube. In order to keep it tight, another part of the works constantly supplies the top of the tube, above the stopper with a small jet of water. The steam of the hot water (as I take it) entering into the tube, rarifies the air therein to a great degree, when the stopper is let loose and flies upward with rapidity to the upper end of the tube, and immediately is thrown back by the pressure of the air from without. When it gets to the bottom, it is again driven upwards by the same cause as before, and repelled downward in like manner by the air, causing a constant motion. To this stopper a stout lever is fastened in the middle upon an axis. This lever is moved up and down in the tube, and thus works the engine in the well, forcing the water up to the top of the hill.

Lieutenant Bangs' description is clearly that of a steam engine of the New-comen, or atmospheric type, like those which had been used for pumping water from English mines since about 1711. Before Colles could complete his system by laying wooden distributing pipes through the streets, the whole project was brought to a halt by the British occupation of New York and other vicissitudes of the Revolutionary War. After the long conflict was over, little was left of the water works except the well and numerous unpaid bills embarrassing both to the city and to Colles.

American city dwellers, shocked by the yellow fever epidemics into taking steps to improve their water supply, could therefore draw upon the earlier experience of other peoples and even to some extent on their own experiments. What was perhaps more important, they could call upon the technical knowledge of a growing number of engineers who had learned to make surveys, take levels, construct watertight masonry, fashion steam engines, and build embankments, bridges, and tunnels. Many of these men had learned the lessons of practical engineering by working on the turnpikes and canals of England; others were gaining the same information during the first considerable construction of similar works in the United States during these very years of the 1790's.

The technical knowledge for the building of water works was thus available. What was now required was for citizens long accustomed to rural institutions to accept the necessity of making the more complicated provisions required by urban life. And when the city dwellers had finally accepted the fact that great water works were necessary, the question must then be answered: should these large investments be made by the municipalities themselves or by private corporations? Should the example of Rome or that of London be followed?

Building an Intra-urban Transportation System

George Rogers Taylor*

The need to develop means for facilitating the mass movement of people in the largest American cities first became insistent in the late 1820s. Two circumstances helped create pressure for improved urban transportation of persons: First, the closely built-up sections of the most populous cities began to extend beyond an area in which people could conveniently walk to and from work. Second, economic changes began to affect long-established relationships between the places where men worked and where they lived and to encourage the growth of specialized subcenters within the business districts. To provide increased mobility within the central city and its metropolitan area, omnibuses, steam commuter trains, and horsecars were introduced during the three pre-Civil War decades. Each of these innovations served to encourage urban growth and to further ecological developments, many of which were already under way.

URBAN POPULATION EXPANSION, 1820-1860

Three of the five most populous American cities, New York, Philadelphia, and Boston, have been selected for this study. Both Brooklyn and Baltimore were larger than Boston in 1860. However, Brooklyn is treated as part of New York's suburban area. Boston, while smaller than Baltimore in 1860, grew more rapidly between

---

*Reprinted with permission from George Rogers Taylor, "The Beginnings of Mass Transportation in Urban America," *Smithsonian Journal of History*, I (Summer and Autumn, 1966), 35–41, 43–48, 31, 33–35, 38–39, 43, 46–47, 49–52.

1820 and 1860 and earlier provided for mass transportation.

The almost continuously increasing importance of large cities in American history is an old story, but the rate of urban expansion from 1820 to 1860 and especially during the two decades preceding the Civil War merits more attention than it has received. The rate of urban growth (cities of 2,500 or more) remained extraordinarily high from 1820 to 1860 with the increase in the urban population reaching an all-time peak of 92.1 per cent over the decade of the 1840s. The decennial rate of increase in the 1850s exceeded 75 per cent and was close to 63 per cent during both the 1820s and the 1830s. And the larger cities registered the most rapid growth for, while all cities over 2,500 increased in population by nine times between 1820 and 1860, the population of places of over 50,000 in 1820 rose more than twelve times.

Detailed statistics of population growth for the three cities studied appear in Table I. Most striking is the absolute increase in total (central city plus suburbs) population for each metropolis. New York, numbering about 150,000 in 1820, rose by over 1,000,000 between that date and 1860. Philadelphia, with only 138,000 at the earlier date, increased by more than 400,000 during the following forty years. Boston, with a total of 63,000 in 1820, added 225,000 by 1860. The percentage rates of population growth in the four decades preceding the Civil War maintained a remarkably high level, with 1840–1850 registering the highest growth rates for both the central cities and the suburbs in each of the three cities. In that banner dec-

TABLE I

POPULATION AND DECENNIAL RATES OF INCREASE FOR NEW YORK, BOSTON, AND PHILADELPHIA AND THEIR SUBURBS, 1810–1860

	Boston			New York			Philadelphia		
	City	Suburbs	Total	City	Suburbs	Total	City	Suburbs	Total
Population 1810	33,787	15,867	49,654	96,373	23,361	119,734	53,722	58,488	112,210
Population 1820	43,298	19,949	63,247	123,706	28,350	152,056	63,802	73,295	137,097
Percentage increase 1810–1820	28.1	25.7	27.4	28.4	21.4	27.0	18.8	25.3	22.2
Population 1830	61,392	26,962	88,354	202,589	39,689	242,278	80,462	108,335	188,797
Percentage increase 1820–1830	41.8	35.2	39.7	63.8	40.0	59.3	26.1	47.8	37.7
Population 1840	85,000	39,037	124,037	312,710	78,404	391,114	93,665	164,372	258,037
Percentage increase 1830–1840	38.5	44.8	40.4	54.4	97.5	61.4	16.4	51.7	36.7
Population 1850	136,881	72,091	208,972	515,547	180,568	696,115	121,376	287,386	408,762
Percentage increase 1840–1850	61.0	84.7	68.5	64.9	130.3	78.0	29.6	74.8	58.4
Population 1860	177,840	110,895	288,735	813,669	361,110	1,174,779	137,756	427,773	565,529
Percentage increase 1850–1860	29.9	53.8	38.2	57.8	100.0	68.8	11.0	48.8	38.4

ade New York's suburban population increased 130 per cent, Boston's 85 per cent, and Philadelphia's 75 per cent.

Over the time period covered in Table I the respective areas of each central city and its suburbs have been held constant. This permits a meaningful comparison of the decennial growth of population in each central city and its metropolitan area unaffected by changes in the boundary of either. But comparisons *among* the cities must be made with caution not only because of the wide variations in the size and expansion possibilities of the central cities but also because the size of the suburban areas varies significantly from city to city.

As the table indicates, a large part of the constantly growing numbers of urban dwellers crowded into the older sections of the great cities. Even in the America of open spaces and cheap, abundant land where city walls never set limits to expansion, city people lived for the most part huddled close together in row houses and solid blocks as was common in the great cities of Europe. So it was that foreign visitors to New York, Boston, and Philadelphia in the early 19th century took note of the restless energy of the inhabitants and often complained of filthy streets, even less well cared for than those in European centers. But significantly, they seldom commented upon the crowded compactness of American cities, for in this respect cities in the new country closely resembled those in the old. In the years of accelerated population growth following 1830, older portions of American cities often became even more crowded than the congested areas of London and Paris. By 1850 New York had reached in its "fully settled area" a population density of 135.6 persons to the acre; the comparable figure for Boston was 82.7, for Phila-

delphia 80.0 and for London 116.9. In an age when most residences in American cities were two- or three-story wooden or brick structures, such densities meant that living conditions in the poorer districts became intolerably congested. Of course, had it been possible for the cities to spread out uniformly in all directions, the excessive crowding as well as the onset of the urban transportation crisis might have been at least temporarily postponed. But for each of the cities under consideration, rivers, mud flats, or arms of the sea imposed a constricted pattern of settlement, with the growing edge increasingly distant from the commercial center.

The towns and cities clustered about each of the central cities constituted the suburbs. Most of these, including even settlements as closely adjacent to Philadelphia as the Northern Liberties, had their own economic focus. They did not serve, at least until the 1840s and 1850s, as places of residence for any considerable number of persons employed in the central city. But increasing population pressures developing in the forties made the suburbs more attractive as places in which to live. The unprecedented rate of suburban growth as shown in Table I at least partially reflects this development.

Year after year New York City spread northward on Manhattan Island between its two "rivers." Until about 1820 the built-up area of the city reached to a little below Fourteenth Street on the west side of the island and a good half mile lower on the east side. As a result, no part of the thickly settled area was more than about one and three-quarters miles from the City Hall or Canal Street. Population spread slowly northward in the 1820s and 1830s, actually pushing out less than one-half mile in most neighborhoods. Then in the next two decades the densely settled area expanded rapidly, though unevenly, northward across the width of the island. By 1860 the heavily settled district reached Forty-second Street and passed it in one sector to extend as far north as Fiftieth Street. Distances of three and four miles now lay between City Hall and the heavily populated sections of the city.

As the closely built-up area of New York shifted northward with increasing acceleration during the forties and the fifties, nearby suburban areas accessible by water became attractive as places of residence for those employed in lower Manhattan. Ferry service from Long Island and the New Jersey shore remained too slow and undependable to encourage large numbers to commute to New York City, at least until well into the forties. But this service improved in the late forties, and the number of commuters rose rapidly. The population of suburban New York increased at a rate unexampled at the time. The number of inhabitants in the four boroughs outside Manhattan Island doubled in the fifties, came close to doing so in the thirties, and rose by 130 per cent in the forties. Brooklyn, closest borough to downtown New York and by far the largest of the four, increased in population from a mere 21,000 in 1820 to 279,000 in 1860. With improved ferry service, two nearby New Jersey cities, Newark and Jersey City, became, in fact, a part of suburban New York City. Between 1840 and 1860 the size of the first rose from 17,000 to 72,000 and that of the second from 3,000 to 29,000.

Boston, like New York, was surrounded by water, except for a narrow neck of land connecting with Roxbury. But its area was so limited that as early as 1820, when its population totaled only 43,000, it had already begun to seem crowded. However, by building bridges, filling in mud flats and shallow bays, and by leveling down hills Boston continuously added to its habitable limits. With the opening of a direct bridge to South Boston in 1828 population began flowing into that sparsely settled area bringing its population to 17,000 by 1855. Noodle's Island, East Boston, practically uninhabited in 1831, achieved a population of 16,000 twenty-five years later. Despite some expansion, Boston's area measured only about two square miles by 1840, or less than one-tenth that of Manhattan Island.

As Boston became more crowded, the adjacant and nearby towns provided room for expansion. Of the seven contiguous towns none was more than five miles from the center of Boston, and though routes to some were necessarily roundabout, others were conveniently direct. From Roxbury a direct overland route led to Boston on the neck of the peninsula. Charlestown, only one mile distant, and Cambridge, three miles, were easily reached by bridges and ferries. Each one of the nearby towns had its own local, commercial, or manufacturing focus, but increasingly in the prewar decades each also provided a haven for those who, while working in the city, sought to live in the suburbs.

The area of the city of Philadelphia, until its limits were enlarged in 1854 to correspond with those of the county of the same name, slightly exceeded two square miles, as did that of Boston in 1840. Bounded by Vine Street on the north and Cedar Street (South Street) on the south, it extended for about a mile along the Schuylkill River on the west and the Delaware on the east. The eastern half became solidly built up by 1830, the whole rectangle by 1850. Adjoining areas like the Northern Liberties and Southwark had become densely populated before 1830. In the immediate prewar decades suburbs and satellite cities spread rapidly northward and even westward across the Schuylkill. When in 1854 the boundaries of the city became identical with those of the county the total area rose from about two to one hundred twenty square miles. As a result, except for a small section across the Delaware River at Camden, the city limits then included the whole suburban or commuting area. So, although the Delaware River to the east and mud flats to the south limited growth, wide, thinly settled, adjacent areas to the north and west invited expansion.

CHANGING URBAN PATTERNS

As late as the 1820s the ecology of the leading American cities still closely resembled that of the pre-industrial cities of western Europe. At the center of the metropolis clustered the churches, the public buildings, and the homes of the most prominent and well-to-do citizens. Nearby lived lesser merchants and leading craftsmen, their residences frequently intermingled with commercial buildings. Often their stores or workshops were on the first floor of their houses, their living quarters on the second. Junior partners, journeymen, or apprentices might "live in" as part of the employer's family. Where a combination of home, shop, and living quarters no longer served, or where a considerable number of employees was required, as in shipyards, ropewalks, distilleries, and sugar refineries, the workers lived close to their employment, necessarily within walking distance. The chief business of the great seaports was commerce; the location of the wharves determined the focus of activity. Warehouses and countinghouses, the establishments of great merchants and the retail outlets of petty tradesmen,

the taverns and grogshops all crowded close to the waterfront, and the longshoremen, hustlers, clerks, ship chandlers, sailmakers, and coopers lived nearby.

Revolutionary developments in manufacturing, transportation, and communications during the three pre-Civil War decades, an increasing specialization of economic institutions, and the phenomenal surge in city population already described combined to effect important changes in the pattern of urban living. In each seaport commerce and industry expanded as never before. In the area adjacent to the water front a greatly increased work force lived under intolerably crowded conditions; beyond the densely settled part of the central city and in the suburbs, thanks to new transportation facilities, many merchants, professional men, and members of a growing middle class established their homes.

The tendency, continuing from colonial times, for business activity to focus on or near the waterfront of the leading seaport cities intensified as foreign trade expanded, exceeding all previous growth records, and the American merchant marine reached its most glorious age. At the same time industries long established in the harbor areas grew prodigiously: not only establishments catering to the merchant marine like shipbuilding and the manufacture of ship's supplies such as sails, rope, and bread, but also plants dependent upon sea-borne raw materials like distilling, sugar refining, and tobacco processing.

As long as the new system of factory production introduced into the United States early in the 19th century required water power to operate heavy machinery, inland cities located on favorable river sites like Lowell and Chicopee became the chief centers of manufacturing development. But the situation changed when, beginning in the 1840s, abundant supplies of cheap coal became available along the Atlantic seaboard. Stimulated by this cheap fuel, improvements in the construction and operation of steam engines, and a growing demand for manufactured products, factory production expanded phenomenally in the chief seaport cities. Clusters of manufacturing plants, especially those devoted to the production of metal products such as castings, machines, engines, and transportation equipment, grew out from older locations or formed new focuses of population growth along the edges of the central city, commonly where railroad lines terminated. Such expansion not infrequently accompanied the boom in shipbuilding already under way along the East River of New York City, the Delaware River at Philadelphia, and in East Boston at the New England port.

The growing volume of business combined with an increasing differentiation of function, as specialists continued to take over the manifold activities of the great merchants of an earlier day, led to the rapid enlargement of the business section in each of the three cities. Banks, countinghouses, markets, exchanges, factories, warehouses, lumber yards, coffee houses, and taverns crowded into the old residential areas near the water front. More workers were needed in the business district, but fewer could make their homes there. As a result, living conditions became ever more congested in adjacent neighborhoods. Thus, the wards bordering on the old harbor area of lower Manhattan actually lost inhabitants. The population of the Second Ward, having crested close to 9,000 in 1825, declined to about 2,500 in 1860. The Third Ward, with nearly 12,000 in 1845, mustered only about 4,000 at the later date. As

the population was pushed out of these areas, displaced persons crowded into the nearby neighborhoods to the north contributing to the notorious slum conditions in wards Six, Eleven, and Thirteen, where by 1860 population density reached more than 300 to the acre. Boston's Fourth Ward, the business and financial center of the city, lost more than half its residents between 1850 and 1860. During the same decade the population of the adjoining Seventh Ward to the south tripled as Irish immigrants continued to press into that already congested area. A similar situation arose in Philadelphia where, during the same decade, the central city showed a relatively small population increase (see Table I).

The city workers, their numbers growing more rapidly than ever before, partly by natural increase but largely from an unprecedented inflow from the countryside and from foreign countries, pressed into the older residential areas of the central city, turning them into slums notorious even for that day. Whole families often lived packed into single rooms or damp cellars, and social and sanitary conditions became intolerably bad. A study of living conditions in New York City in 1864 found nearly a half million people living in tenement houses and over fifteen thousand living in cellars. In these crowded areas household industry or take-home work commonly played an important role. In the suburbs just north of Philadelphia male weavers worked hand looms under their own roofs. In all three cities seamstresses found employment in these congested areas doing piecework at home. Especially in New York and Boston, slum sections became havens for hordes of recently arrived immigrants. There, unaccustomed to city living and with low wages and irregular employment, they often formed ethnic islands. Sharing their poverty and their squalor with their own countrymen, they remained within walking distance of the waterfront where the great majority found employment as unskilled laborers. Some of the most impoverished of the recently arrived German and Irish immigrants to New York City lived as squatters in shanties erected on unoccupied rocky or hilly ground within the city or on open land beyond the settled area. They secured a precarious living as ragpickers, cinder gatherers, or day laborers engaged in the building of new streets and sewers.

For the great majority of low-income workers, improved mass transportation failed, as this study will show, to provide an opportunity to escape from the congestion of the central city at least before 1860. Riding to work continued to be prohibitively expensive for most city dwellers. So, as the metropolis grew and its thickly settled area spread out, the distance between the places where men lived and where they found employment lengthened. Most workmen continued, as they had from time immemorial, to walk to work. Some may have gone considerable distances on foot—perhaps as much as three or even four miles night and morning. But this must have been most exceptional. We do know from an official count on September 6, 1851, that 14,310 persons entered Boston on foot. But it seems unlikely that many of these walked farther than about two miles —a distance which would normally require at least thirty minutes. One authority observes that ". . . few workingmen can afford to spend more than half an hour in going to their work. . . ." The case of the employees of a gas company in the Northern Liberties (Philadelphia), as indicated by the payroll for December 3, 1852,

may be fairly typical. Of twenty-one workers none lived more than one and two-thirds miles from the gas plant and all but five lived within one mile.

In the years of rapid urban growth following the twenties, the great merchants and professional men (some of whom already had "country" homes) were not alone in fleeing from the noise and confusion of the water front, the dirt, the stench, and the intolerably crowded conditions of the old central city. They were joined by many businessmen of intermediate means, retailers, managers, contractors, speculators, and junior partners. Even some better-paid clerks, accountants, and specially skilled craftsmen fled from the noise and confusion. Thus, in New York City, those financially able to do so moved ever northward on the island as business establishments and slums pressed in behind them. Describing the situation in Manhattan, an editorial in the *American Railroad Journal* stated, "The gradual appropriation of the whole lower part of the Island to places of business, compel the greater part of our business men to reside from two to four miles 'up town'."

As late as the 1840s, some merchants in Boston still had their fine residences on Summer Street, only a few minutes walk from the wharves, but most had already moved on to Beacon Hill or Roxbury and others had homes in nearby suburbs such as Cambridge. Of course, some wealthy individuals and even those in a few exclusive neighborhoods held out against the tide, forcing the city to surge around and beyond them. This was notably true in conservative Philadelphia where until after the Civil War some of the élite clung to the area south of Washington Square along Second, Third, and Fourth Streets, only a short distance from the busy wharves on the Delaware. But most of the rising business and professional men there as elsewhere pushed outward, in this case toward the north in the vicinity of Broad Street, farther northwest to suburban areas, and westward across the Schuylkill River.

The growth in population of the suburban areas resulted only in part, and doubtless in rather small part before the latter 1840s, from an increase in the number of those who worked in the central city but lived in nearby towns. Many of the suburban towns and cities were of about the same age as the central city itself. Like Brooklyn, Cambridge, and Kensington, they originally developed as, and, in fact, continued in some degree to be, relatively autonomous commercial and manufacturing centers. Nevertheless, strong centralizing influences which tended to bind the great city together as one economic unit predominated. One of these was certainly improved urban transportation by which the limits of the walking city were enlarged, chiefly for those of moderately high incomes before the Civil War, and more generally for those with lower incomes thereafter. A Philadelphian wrote with rare insight in 1859, ". . . already the great mass of our population 'lives along the line' of a [horse] railway; and before the next decade shall have far advanced, every rural vicinage within our corporate limits will be 'grappled with hooks of steel' to the steps of the Exchange." Without effective mass transportation it is difficult to see how the great, highly centralized cities of the late 19th century could have emerged. In any case, the growth in the size of the cities and their suburbs and the accompanying differentiation in the economic services performed led to major developments in urban transportation. Or, stating the matter the other way around, improvements in

urban transportation made possible the expansion of the great city and increased functional specialization.

THE ERA OF THE OMNIBUS

The omnibus was the earliest important innovation introduced to promote urban mobility. Of French origin, the term "omnibus" came into common American use in the early 1830s. Usually drawn by two horses, the omnibus carried about twelve passengers, operated over a fixed route on city streets, and picked up and dropped passengers at frequent intervals. Fares charged were ordinarily a fixed amount seldom varying with the distance traveled.

Before the introduction of the omnibuses and the transition vehicles immediately preceding them, hacks or hackney coaches, the forerunners of modern taxis, provided rapid transportation within the city. But coach fees were so high that their use was commonly restricted to the very well-to-do. The rate charged in New York City for a single passenger varied from twenty-five cents to thirty-seven and a half cents for any distance not exceeding a mile, for more than one mile and less than two the rate was fifty cents. Of course many of the relatively affluent owned their own carriages, but for the great mass of city dwellers movement within the urban area required walking.

The need for a public system of mass transportation appeared earliest in New York City where, as in Boston and Philadelphia, the true omnibus evolved as a compromise between the long distance stagecoach and the hackney coach. As early as 1811, a few stagecoaches operated on infrequent schedules from lower Manhattan to Greenwich. In 1816 they ran every two hours, charging a fare of one shilling. The service appears to have developed slowly at first, but by the closing years of the 1820s numerous lines had begun operation. Hackney coaches also came into use over regular routes. They began to operate "from a certain place or places to any other certain place or places," stopping to let down or take up passengers on the way. Most important, however, were stagecoaches whose operation to Greenwich and up and down Broadway was already presenting New York's Common Council with problems concerning license fees and regulation.

In Boston the evolution from stagecoach to omnibus came rapidly during the 1820s. The great Back Bay area had not yet been reclaimed, and the small peninsula on which the city stood began to be closely built up. So Roxbury across the neck and the nearby villages connected with Boston by bridges and ferries became increasingly attractive as places of residence. Short stage lines were operating once a day at least as early as 1823 between Boston and such towns as Dedham, Waltham, and Dorchester and twice daily to Cambridge. Though such lines soon spread to other nearby communities, stagecoach service remained infrequent and fares high. In 1825 the rate by stagecoach to such nearby towns as Medford (five miles) and Milton (seven miles) was thirty-seven and a half cents, and to Lexington (ten miles) fifty cents. Then, early in 1826, an hourly stage established within the city itself began operating from Roxbury to Boston with a fare of nine cents. In a single week late in April it was reported that ". . . about eleven hundred passengers passed *to and fro* by this conveyance. . . ." The success of this experiment apparently encouraged the development of other similar short stagecoach or "omnibus" lines. The July 4, 1826, issue of *Badger & Porter's Stage Register* listed

not only the service between Roxbury and Boston but also an hourly stage between Charlestown and Boston, and less frequent service on lines from Cambridge to Boston and from Dorchester and South Boston into the city. Moreover, as in New York, the hackney coach was pressed into service as an omnibus. A hack is reported to have operated every other hour between Cambridgeport and Boston as early as 1826, and three years later a similar conveyance ran on a regular schedule between South Boston and Boston.

In Philadelphia the evolutionary process from stagecoach to omnibus came more slowly but developed much as in New York and Boston. Apparently one of the first omnibus-like coaches in Philadelphia began operation in December, 1831. It ran hourly from the Merchants' Coffee House on Second Street to Schuylkill Seventh (now Sixteenth) and Chestnut Streets with fares at ten cents or twelve tickets for one dollar. It soon proved a failure, but two years later two omnibus lines were in regular operation within the city and numerous short stagecoach lines gave service, mostly only twice a day, to such nearby places as Germantown, Frankford, Darby, and Fairmount.

In urban United States history the years from about 1830 to the early 1850s may well be termed the Era of the Omnibus. During this period of unprecedented city growth, the omnibus facilitated and helped to make possible the urban expansion. As early as 1830, "upwards of seventy unwieldy omnibus coaches" were operating in New York City, and William Dunlap recorded in his diary on July 4, 1833, that he waited on Broadway but "after long standing was obliged to walk home, all the stages numerous as they are being throng'd." At about this time the term "omnibus" began to come into common use and the shape and construction of the vehicle became more or less standardized. Somewhat larger than the usual long-distance stagecoach, the omnibus normally seated twelve persons, though more might be crowded in when traffic was heavy. A coachman mounted on an elevated seat at the front of the vehicle collected the fares and drove a span of horses. At times these vehicles were larger and more elaborate. At least some omnibuses were luxuriously upholstered, were drawn by four to six horses, and carried a boy attendant to collect the fares. In the winter they provided a smooth and quiet ride on the snow-packed streets when, as was usual at least in New York, runners replaced the wheels.

By 1833 the age of the omnibus had arrived in New York City. In that year eighty of these vehicles, still referred to by some as "city stages," were licensed to operate on the streets. Of these only sixteen went beyond the city proper to Harlem, Manhattanville, and Yorkville. The license fee which had been one dollar per annum became twenty dollars for four-horse and ten dollars for two-horse vehicles in 1834. Yet the number of omnibuses rose to ninety-seven in that year and stood at one hundred eight in 1837. Commenting on the "noise and bustle" contributed by these vehicles, the New York *Gazette and General Advertiser* for August 5, 1834, said New York might well be termed "The City of Omnibuses." In 1839, sixty-seven omnibuses were counted passing a point on Broadway during one-half

hour at a "comparatively dull hour in the afternoon."

The number of these vehicles increased at a much more rapid rate than the population of the city. A visitor to New York City in 1846, commenting on the constant increase in the number of omnibuses, reported that 12 of them could be seen at one time. The licenses granted by New York City for omnibuses numbered 260 in 1847, rose to 425 in 1850, and reached a high point, 683, in 1853. A committee of the New York Board of Aldermen reporting in 1850 found the facilities quite inadequate for public needs. "During certain periods of the day and evening," their report stated, "and always during inclement weather, passengers are packed into these vehicles, without regard to comfort or even decency, sometimes, and many are utterly unable to secure seats, even after waiting for hours." A guidebook published in 1853 reported omnibuses were daily averaging 13,420 trips and collecting 120,000 fares from passengers. But the competition of the newly introduced horsecars soon made itself felt. Annual declines in the number of omnibus licenses issued reduced the total by 1858 to the level attained at the beginning of the decade. The number then rose for a few years, but had fallen to 231 by 1865. (See Table II.)

In Boston, too, the number of omnibuses rose rapidly. Greatly increased travel to Roxbury was reported by 1840. In that year *The Boston Almanac* listed eighteen lines, some operating to points within the city, and others to more than a dozen nearby

TABLE II

NUMBER OF OMNIBUS LICENSES ISSUED BY NEW YORK CITY, 1846–1865

1846	255	1851	568	1856	588	1861	589
1847	260	1852	561	1857	489	1862	574
1848	327	1853	683	1858	424	1863	565
1849	370	1854	622	1859	439	1864	397
1850	425	1855	593	1860	536	1865	231

suburban communities. But the traffic within Boston was confined to a very large extent (nearly 50 per cent in 1848) to the Roxbury route and outside the city to Cambridge and Charlestown (close to 40 per cent). The total number of omnibuses and stages operating was reported as two hundred fifty in 1847.

In Philadelphia, as in Boston, the omnibus was well established during the 1830s and became essential to city transportation during the 1840s. Heavy coaches drawn by four horses served suburban areas such as Germantown and Chestnut Hill. One company operated eight of these daily between Philadelphia and Chestnut Hill. *Disturnell's Guide* for June, 1847, lists fourteen omnibus routes leaving from the Merchants' Exchange, some of them at five-minute intervals. By the end of 1848, omnibuses numbering one hundred thirty-eight and operated by eighteen different lines departed from the Exchange. The congestion became so great at that place in 1849 that the City Council required some omnibuses to change their starting point. In 1857 when horsecars were being introduced, Philadelphia had three hundred twenty-two omnibuses in operation.

In most other American cities of appreciable size, omnibus lines began regular operation well before 1860. Washington, reported to have had service between Georgetown and the Navy Yard as early as 1830, was by 1850 imposing fines for reckless driving and limiting the occupancy of each vehicle to twelve passengers. In the middle forties omnibuses operated regularly in Baltimore and Pittsburgh, and by the opening of the next decade they provided mass transportation in such rapidly growing centers as Chicago and Toronto.

Within all three cities to which this study is directed the usual omnibus fare during the 1830s was twelve and a half cents, although rates on very short lines were often less. Thus the charge to the South Street ferry in Philadelphia was only five cents in 1838. For those who could afford to buy small blocks of tickets or to purchase season tickets the cost was considerably lower. At least by 1837 a price reduction of one-third was made in New York when six or twelve tickets were purchased, and in Philadelphia an annual subscription permitted persons who used the omnibuses four time a day to reduce the cost to one cent for each ride. By the late forties omnibus fares for single tickets had generally fallen to six and a quarter cents—a reduction roughly equivalent to the decline in the general level of prices. In the early fifties six cents appears to have been the usual fare in New York and six and a quarter cents in Boston. In 1852 severe competition among omnibus lines forced fares in Philadelphia as low as three cents over most routes, and by 1860 fares in New York varied from four to six cents.

Who rode in the omnibuses? A New Yorker reported in 1849 that it depended upon the time of day: "In the early morning . . . the omnibus is chiefly occupied by junior clerks with big iron keys in their hands, or laborers with tin kettles between their feet, on their way to their downtown avocations." Later in the morning come the "sleek and rotund burghers of above Bleecker . . ." And not long after them "Gotham's fair wives and daughters" on their way to shop, to see the dentist, or to visit the milliner or dressmaker. The same author also notes the patronage of omnibuses by young gentlemen on the way to the theater who "thus preserve their patent leather pumps." It seems most unlikely, however, that many ordinary wage earners customarily patronized the omnibuses. In the forties and fifties, when common laborers ordinarily received wages of less than one dollar a day and skilled craftsmen seldom earned more than two, very few could afford to spend twelve or even six cents a day for omnibus fare. Certainly budgets for workers' families printed in the early fifties made no provision for such expenditures. The shocking living conditions associated with overcrowding spread throughout the central portion of all of these cities during the omnibus era and grew worse with the increased flow of immigrants after 1846, and this congestion arose, in no small degree, because most common laborers were forced by brute necessity to live within walking distance of their work.

But for the relatively well-to-do and a growing middle class, the omnibus proved a great convenience. Omnibuses, wrote a New Yorker in 1837 ". . . are particularly convenient for merchants and others doing business in the lower part of the city, and living in the upper part. After staying till three o'clock to settle their money affairs in Wall Street, they would be late to dinner, were they obliged to foot it a mile or two; and most of them would not like to pay from three to four shillings for coach hire." So the overcrowding of downtown areas led many of those who could afford it to move outward from the business districts, and the omnibus made this change of residence feasible for merchants, traders, professional men, and possibly some skilled workers. The situation is well described by Sir Charles Lyell, who, on his visit to New York City in May, 1846, wrote that since he had been in the city five months earlier ". . . whole streets had been built, and several squares finished in the northern or fashionable end of town, to which the merchants are now resorting, leaving the business end, near the Battery, where they formerly lived. Hence there is a con-

stant increase of omnibuses passing through Broadway, and other streets running north and south." And conditions appear to have been similar in Philadelphia where, as in New York, the bulk of the population was compressed in the area between two "rivers." In Boston proper, distances were short and omnibuses proved a convenience for the well-to-do, especially those who lived in the suburbs and entered the city by suburban train, for among the most popular omnibus lines were those running from the railroad stations into the central city. Omnibuses also operated between nearby suburbs and Boston, but the service was too limited and the fares much too high to attract many common laborers.

Several other factors help to explain the heavy patronage of the omnibus lines. Most businessmen still followed the practice of going home for their midday meal and then returning to their offices around three or four in the afternoon. For many this entailed added use of public transportation. Also, the spreading out of the business area and the accompanying differentiation of function necessitated an increased amount of travel within the city. Couriers sent with messages or documents made use of the omnibus lines and merchants and other businessmen, no longer located close to the exchange or the financial district, found the use of the horse-drawn vehicles a great convenience. Finally, when the weather was cold or wet, few who could afford to do so failed to seek the shelter of the omnibuses even though the distance to be traveled might be only a few blocks.

THE COMMUTER RAILROADS

The first crude railroads reached out from the leading seaport cities during the 1830s, the same decade which saw the rise of the omnibus.

Not originally designed to facilitate travel between the suburbs and the central city, the railroads had, by the end of the decade, developed substantial commuter services. In the forties and fifties, commuter trains played a most important role in metropolitan Boston, a less important one in Philadelphia and New York.

By 1838 four railroad lines branched out from Boston: the Boston & Lowell, the Boston & Worcester, the Boston & Providence, and the Eastern. The total was raised to seven by 1845, with the addition of the Fitchburg, the Boston & Maine, and the Old Colony. Except for the Eastern, which used a ferry from East Boston until its railroad bridge was completed in 1854, each one of these railroads entered into the city proper. The railroad stations were so located as to make even the most distant not more than about a half hour's walk from the business district. Omnibuses operating at frequent intervals into the central city from each of the railroad stations served those who did not wish to walk and could afford the six and a fourth cents fare.

Railroad fares from nearby towns into Boston were at first so expensive as to be beyond the reach of workingmen and most middle-class persons. Nor did early attempts to provide a somewhat cheaper service in second-class coaches attract many patrons. Season tickets by the full, half, or quarter year were first offered in 1838 and 1839. Prices of these tickets, though high at first, fell rapidly during the early and middle forties and remained at a uniquely low level later in that decade and during the early fifties. Thus, three-month [season] tickets between Malden and Boston (five miles) on the Boston & Maine cost $10.00 in 1846, fell to $6.87 in 1848, and were priced at $8.25 during the early 1850s. On the Boston &

Worcester the three-month ticket from Brighton (five miles) had been $15.00 in 1846 and fell to $10.00 in 1850. The rate to Dedham, almost twice as far (nine and a half miles), held at $12.00 in the early fifties. Charges as low as these compared favorably with the fare charged by omnibuses within the city: six and a fourth cents in the late forties and five cents in the fifties. Commutation tickets at $12.00 a quarter came to a little over eight cents a ride and at $6.87 to less than five cents a ride. If Roxbury commuters purchased season tickets in 1850, they paid only about three and a half cents on the railroad, while each omnibus ride cost six cents.

Low as were these commutation fares, they were beyond the reach of most ordinary workmen. But, for a considerable number of small merchants and tradesmen and perhaps a few skilled mechanics and better-paid clerks, living in the nearby suburbs now became feasible. Contemporary evidence indicates that, at least by the early 1850s, commuter railroad service permitted "by far the larger part of her [Boston's] business men [to] reside out of the city." A writer in *Hunt's Merchants' Magazine* reports, somewhat ambiguously, that old Boston residents, giving way before foreign workers, have moved to the suburbs where, "availing themselves of the frequent omnibuses, or of special trains run almost hourly, and commuting for passage at $20.00 to $40.00 a year; they reach their stores and offices in the morning; and at night sleep with their wives and children in the suburbs."

The number of commuters increased rapidly after the late 1840s. A stockholders' committee of the Boston & Providence Railroad reported that commuters between Boston and Dedham numbered only 320 in 1848–49, but that a great increase had come about by 1854. The average number of passengers entering Boston daily by railroad train apparently increased from about 20 to 50 per cent between 1848 and 1851. By 1850 the passenger trains entering or leaving Boston numbered 240. Almost all of these carried commuters and more than half were strictly commuter trains going no more than fifteen miles from the Boston station. In his book published in 1856, E. B. Grant estimates the number of season tickets sold annually to have been 6500.

Why did railroads prove much less important for commuters in New York and Philadelphia than in the Boston area? Partly because in the extensive, solidly built-up areas of New York and Philadelphia, omnibuses provided convenient service over the short distances involved. The stretches of water surrounding the Boston isthmus and the relatively few bridges necessitated roundabout and expensive omnibus trips from suburban areas into that city. Also, since the steam railroads entering Boston across waterways or tidal flats penetrated only a short distance into the city, they aroused less opposition from those who deplored the operation of locomotives on city streets. But, in New York and Philadelphia, railroads utilized the city streets for considerable distances through the central city. When operated by steam locomotives, they were disliked because of their noise and smoke, and feared because of the danger to persons and property. Consequently, regulations in both cities required passenger coaches to be detached from the locomotive at the entrance to the more thickly settled areas and pulled into the central city by horses or mules. The inconvenience and delay caused by these regulations, as well as the slower time possible under animal power, somewhat reduced the attractiveness of dis-

tant suburban living in the vicinity of these two cities.

Two railroads served New York City before 1860: the Hudson River Railroad Company and the New York & Harlem Railroad Company. The former, chartered in 1846, entered the city on the west side along the Hudson River. Steam engines provided power as far as the depot at Tenth Avenue and 31st Street, and horses provided it from there to the terminal in lower New York City at Chambers and Hudson Streets. This railroad provided neither a local nor a commuter service for New Yorkers. The New York & Harlem Railroad, however, played an important role in urban transportation. Chartered by a special act of the state legislature in 1831, it began operations from Pine to 14th Streets late in 1832. The railroad extended its tracks both to the north and south in the next few years so that, by 1839, passenger cars operated between the City Hall and Harlem. The original charter permitted the use of steam locomotives but the company relied chiefly on horses and mules. In 1838 the Harlem Railroad owned four locomotives, forty cars, and one hundred horses. The New York City Council prohibited the use of steam locomotives in 1845 below 32nd Street and in 1856 below 42nd Street. The railroad companies seem to have evaded strict compliance with this regulation. In 1850 the editor of the *American Railroad Journal* noted that the Hudson River Railroad was quietly operating a locomotive which ate its own smoke. He urged that New York City should not, like Boston, restrict the use of steam within the city. Nevertheless, prohibition against steam continued and became effective below 42nd Street at least by the late fifties.

The phrase "ate its own smoke" refers to a Dummy locomotive operated by the Hudson River Railroad in 1850. The entire locomotive was enclosed in a box to disguise the mechanism, and the engine condensed its steam instead of emitting an exhaust. These features were designed to make the machine as silent and inoffensive as possible when it was used within New York's city limits. The Dummy locomotive, devised by Henry Waterman, a mechanic of the railroad, was created to replace the horses formerly used for this service. It was expected to result in a great operating economy, but mechanical deficiencies and public alarm against the use of steam locomotives on city streets temporarily ended the Dummy's operation. Several years later, however, the idea was revived with considerable success.

Traffic on the Harlem Railroad grew rapidly over the years. For the year ending August 1840 the road carried over one million passengers. This total rose to three and a half million by 1859. The Harlem appears to have been unique in that it both carried large numbers of local passengers within the central city and also provided important commutation services to the more remote northern end of the island. Over relatively short distances within the city where horses were used, from the City Hall to 27th Street or 32nd Street, and after 1854 as far as 42nd Street, the Harlem Railroad competed effectively with the omnibuses. Fares (six cents in 1853) were about the same as the omnibus fares, and the service was frequent: about every five or six minutes during the day. At the same time, traffic from the suburban and country areas expanded as business and professional men sought homes away from crowded lower Manhattan. The fare from City Hall beyond 42nd Street to Yorkville (five and a half miles) was usually about twelve cents. To Harlem (eight miles) the charge for single tickets in

1838 was twenty-five cents. The fare remained twelve cents in the late forties and early fifties, and went up to fifteen cents by 1855. Season tickets were also expensive: $25.00 for six months or about twenty-three cents for each round trip. The annual number of commuters as reported early in 1853 was 804, a sum apparently between one-fourth and one-fifth of the total number of commuters in the Boston area. Though few, if any, city workers could afford to expend such sums to go to and from work, they could and did crowd the Harlem cars to get into the country for a Sunday holiday.

Steam ferries operating in the waters about Manhattan also brought an increasing number of commuters into New York City. Fifteen regular ferry lines served New York City from nearby places in 1853, a number which rose to 26 by 1860. In 1853, the popular Fulton Street ferry from Brooklyn left every five minutes during the day, that from Jersey City every ten minutes. The fare on the former was one cent, on the latter three or four cents. Most Brooklyn residences were actually nearer the New York business district than were those in the upper part of New York City. Convenient and cheap transportation, therefore, as well as what the guidebook describes as the "pure air and delightful prospects of Brooklyn," led many who worked in New York to live in that suburb.

A growing number of businessmen lived in more distant areas and depended upon steam trains to bring them into the ferry terminals. Thus, as early as 1849, between eighty and one hundred commuters made the trip to New York by means of the Flushing, North Shore & Central Railroad and the connecting ferry. As the one-way through fare, including the ferry charge, varied from ten to twenty cents, these commuters clearly had relatively high incomes. The New Jersey Railroad and Transportation Company, reported in the *American Railway Times* to be the first commuter railroad in the United States, ran 58 trains in 1849 and 144 in 1859 between New Brunswick and Jersey City. By the later date, yearly commutation tickets were priced at $50.00, about sixteen cents a round trip. This must have been one of the busiest commuter lines in the country. It seems likely that many of the commuters continued to ferry across New York harbor to Manhattan, but it is again obvious that they must have been chiefly businessmen rather than workmen.

Only one of the railroads diverging from Philadelphia in the pre-Civil War years became an important commuter line, the Philadelphia, Germantown & Norristown Railroad Company. Serving a pleasantly rolling residential area northwest of the original city limits, this railroad had two branches. One led seven miles to Germantown, where after the middle fifties it connected with the Chestnut Hill Railroad, which continued four miles beyond to Chestnut Hill. The other, more southern branch ran along the Schuylkill River through Manayunk to Norristown. The railroad's passenger station located at Ninth and Green Streets provided a convenient terminal in the congested Spring Garden area. From there to the centrally located Merchant's Exchange was about fifteen blocks: a rather long walk, but omnibuses were available for those wishing to ride.

Primarily a passenger railroad, the Philadelphia, Germantown & Norristown received nearly three-fourths of its revenue (in 1850) from the transportation of passengers. Beginning in the late forties, commuter business expanded rapidly, especially on the Germantown branch. The number of trains to and from Germantown, which had varied from three to six in the late forties, rose to 40 by 1859. Between 1850 and 1860, the annual number of passengers on the Germantown branch increased over sevenfold. A considerable portion of the increased traffic resulted from the growing number of daily commuters. The directors of the railroad reported in 1859 that more than six hundred yearly tickets were issued to residents of Germantown, ". . . whose business requires their daily attendance in the city [Philadelphia]." In 1860 they observed that "hundreds have gone from the densely settled portions of the city to those places [Germantown, Roxborough, and Manayunk] with the intention of permanently remaining. . . ."

In Philadelphia, as in Boston and New York, however, commuting by railroad trains (even to nearby suburbs) was limited largely to the relatively affluent. Quarterly commutation tickets from Germantown cost $10.00 and yearly tickets $30.00 during the fifties, and even this price was raised in 1860. Such rates were apparently not too expensive for the Philadelphia businessmen of whom a contemporary wrote, "Many . . . have summer residences in the vicinity of the road, while others permanently reside in the country."

None of the other railroads entering Philadelphia could match the Philadelphia, Germantown & Norristown in speed and convenience for commuters. It alone brought its steam trains directly into the densely settled area. Three New Jersey Railroads, the Camden & Amboy, the Camden & Atlantic, and the short West Jersey, terminated at Camden across the Delaware from Philadelphia. The five lines entering Philadelphia from the west across the Schuylkill depended upon horses to bring their coaches into the central city. None of these lines operated suburban trains. Apparently horse-drawn cars were utilized only to a limited extent for local passenger transportation within the city. On two roads which led northward, passengers encountered similar difficulties or delays. The tracks of the Philadelphia and Trenton Railroad terminated at Tacony on the Delaware River, whence passengers were transported seven miles by steamboat to Philadelphia. The North Pennsylvania Railroad, not in full operation until 1855, ran almost directly north from its terminal at Front and Willow Streets only two blocks from the Delaware River. Horses or mules drew the passenger cars one mile northward from this terminal to Master Street where a steam locomotive took over. Neither of these two railroads provided important commuter services before the Civil War.

BEGINNINGS OF THE HORSECARS

The era of the omnibus and the beginnings of the commuter railroads extended into the early 1850s. Their important contribution has often been overlooked because the sensational success of the horse railways revolutionized the urban transportation of persons in the years immediately preceding the Civil War. The moving of railroad cars by means of animal power had been common since the early 1830s. Yet between 1852 and 1860 construction of street railways proceeded so rapidly and their popularity became so great that contemporaries hailed them as the "improvement of the age." Summarizing the extent of this change, a student of urban transportation states:

In 1840 omnibuses in the Boston area carried about 1,000,000 passengers. In 1857, the Boston and Worcester Railroad carried about

500,000 to the neighboring cities. But in 1860 the Metropolitan Railroad Corporation, the largest horse-drawn railroad in Boston, alone carried 6,410,850, and the various horse railroads in the city carried a total of 13,695,193.

Powered by horses, cables, and finally electric motors, the streetcar dominated urban transport during the latter half of the 19th century. In this study, our attention centers on the horsecar's beginnings in New York, Boston, and Philadelphia, its advantages over established methods of local transportation, and its contribution to early city growth.

The first horsecars were little more than omnibuses operating on rails laid in city streets. The cars in operation during the late 1850s were ordinarily drawn by two horses and easily accommodated about 40 persons. A contemporary reported that "the cars will hold sitting and standing, from 60 to 65 passengers, and will, at a pinch, hold 74." A light, open, one-horse car suitable for warm-weather use carried almost as many passengers. Larger and heavier passenger cars, such as those in common use on steam railroads, required as many as four or six horses to move them through the streets.

A wave of enthusiasm for horse-railway construction struck first in New York City, where a special committee of the Board of Aldermen recommended the chartering of horse-railway companies in 1850. The Common Council granted charters to the Sixth and Eighth Avenue lines in 1852 and to the Second and Third Avenue lines in the following year. Quickly constructed through city streets, these pioneer horse railways enjoyed a tremendous patronage.

The horsecar lines proved profitable investments despite huge bribes to politicians and the purchase of the existing omnibus companies at inflated prices. The Third Avenue line reportedly paid about $400,000 to buy out five omnibus companies. By September 30, 1857, horse railways in New York City including Brooklyn extended for 44 miles, by 1860 for 142 miles. In the earlier year the streetcars of metropolitan New York carried 32,000,000 passengers, and by 1860 the number was close to 45,000,000.

The street-railway building boom in Boston followed that in New York by about two years. The state legislature approved two lines in 1853: the Cambridge Railroad Company, to be built from Cambridge to Boston, and the Metropolitan Railroad Company to connect Boston and Roxbury. By 1856, when these pioneer lines had gone into operation, many similar projects were under way. Fifty-seven miles of horse-railway lines were in operation by November 30, 1860, and 13.7 million passengers had been transported during the year then ending. The passenger total exceeded the number of passengers carried on steam trains in the whole state during the same twelve-month period.

Last of the three cities to accept the street railway, Philadelphia made up for the delay by rushing construction so enthusiastically that a local publication referred to "its epidemic character." Progress had been slow at first. A special committee of the city council reported favorably in 1855; a company was chartered to operate a line on Fifth and Sixth Streets in 1857, and the first cars ran in January 1858. Then, as opposition collapsed, eighteen companies secured charters by the end of 1859. By the close of 1860, eighteen street railways were operating 155 miles of line in Philadelphia, a total slightly greater than that for metropolitan New York and more than twice that for the city of Boston.

As the omnibuses seemed to become indispensable for urban transportation and their numbers increased, they gave rise to increasing complaints. Often dirty, crowded, and ill-ventilated, they surged from side to side of the street, picking up and putting down passengers on signal without plan or system. They cluttered up busy streets, caused traffic jams, invited accidents endangering life and damaging property, and made a terrific din' as they clattered over the cobblestones. An editorial writer called the omnibus "a perfect Bedlam on wheels" and declared that "Modern martyrdom may be succinctly defined as riding in a New York omnibus." Another report stated: ". . . the omnibuses are . . . a constant source of peril to both pedestrians and vehicles, everywhere threatening with opposite and confusing dangers, requiring a constant vigilance to avoid them, and often impossible to be avoided, as is attested by so many serious, and sometimes fatal, accidents."

Although horsecars might also become stuffy, dirty, and overcrowded, they possessed marked advantages over the omnibuses. The rails provided a relatively smooth, quiet, and accident-free ride in cars with a capacity two to four times that of an ordinary omnibus. The average speed of the streetcars, six to eight miles an hour, exceeded that of the omnibuses by about one-third. Pulling wheeled vehicles over smooth rails proved more efficient and cheaper than dragging them over the rutted and uneven cobblestones of the city streets. One horse, pulling over rails, it was held, could do the work of three or four on a common road. Furthermore, as the cars moved down the middle of the street, they caused a minimum of interference with other traffic. Drivers of wagons and carriages often found it advantageous to keep the wheels on one side of their vehicles rolling on a streetcar rail. In Philadelphia both wheels could be engaged, for the city required the tracks to be laid with the usual wagon gauge of five feet two and a half inches. These matters were important, since major streets in the central city were becoming seriously choked with traffic by the early fifties.

Why, despite the obvious advantages of the streetcar, was its general adoption postponed until the 1850s? Before the development of the steam railroads and the coming of the omnibus car around 1830, Americans were familiar with the tramway. All of the early American tramways, including the "railroad" operated in 1826 at Quincy, Massachusetts, depended upon horse power. And the use of rails laid through city streets to transport horse-drawn passenger and freight cars was as old as the railroad itself in New York, Philadelphia, and elsewhere.

The delay in the building of street railroads in New York seems especially surprising. At the same time that the Harlem Railroad developed its long-distance and commuter business, its local horse-drawn streetcars had become increasingly important for short distance city transportation. It may well be that the success of the Harlem line helps to account for New York's priority in building horse railroads, but the question remains as to why the building of other horsecar lines did not come about until after the Harlem Railroad had been in operation for nearly twenty years. In Boston, where the steam railways entered the central city, no important experiment with street railways seems to have been made prior to the 1850s. The first genuine horse-railway service in Philadelphia appears to have originated, as in New York, on the lower end of a steam-railroad line. The North Pennsylvania Railroad having

extended its tracks from its terminal at the corner of Washington and Cherry Streets about one and a half miles to the corner of Front and Willow Streets, there began on January 3, 1855, the operation of so-called "passenger (Omnibus) cars." This, the Philadelphia *Evening Argus* reported, marked "the commencement of Railroad omnibuses in this city."

On the city portions of the early steam railroads in New York and Philadelphia, horses were engaged in pulling not only the relatively light cars serving local traffic but also the heavier commuter and long-distance passenger coaches, as well as freight cars of every description. Under such circumstances, perhaps it is not surprising that the advantages of specialized, horse-drawn street passenger railways were not more quickly recognized. An anonymous writer said regarding Philadelphia: ". . . burden-cars are drawn by animal power through Market and Broad Streets and the obstruction of these thoroughfares by the continuous transit of coal, lime and freight cars, is a serious detriment to the streets. . . ." Another commentator referred to the delays caused by "long strings of mules, of a dozen each, constantly passing and repassing with a single car." Steam engines were prohibited on the tracks laid through the city streets connecting the Philadelphia railway lines with each other and with the docks along the Delaware River. The use of these railways for local passenger transportation appears to have been limited and sporadic.

Arguments advanced against the construction of street railways lost most of their persuasiveness as experimentation progressed. Owners of retail stores, especially those dependent on the "carriage trade," discovered location on a horsecar line to be a positive advantage. Traffic was clearly expedited instead of being slowed down as some had feared. And the interference of the track with other vehicles decreased as builders learned to lay the tracks more nearly flush with the surface of the streets. Nevertheless the rails did make ". . . the streets inconvenient for all other vehicles. . . ."

Such considerations as those noted above, along with a not unusual amount of popular prejudice and inertia, helped to delay the building of street railways. Also, in all three cities, vested interests, especially those of the omnibus companies, and the cupidity of politicians strongly reinforced conservative influences. In New York the Board of Aldermen had, in 1850, accused the omnibus interests of standing in the way of the construction of needed streetcar lines. A year later the Aldermen granted street railway company charters to political favorites who, in buying out the omnibus companies at inflated prices, enriched themselves as owners of the companies purchased. It will be remembered that these were the years when the Tammany Hall boss, Fernando Wood, enlivened New York City politics. The editor of the *American Railway Times,* noting the extremely high cost of building the New York street railways—$213,988 per mile for the Sixth Avenue line as against an average per-mile outlay of $43,000 for all United States steam railroads—commented that the costs of "Common Councils and Aldermen are included in the right of way."

In Boston, where political corruption was only slightly less notorious than in New York, the editor of the *American Railway Times* asserted that the "Metropolitan Company today rules the city with a rod of iron" and said there had been a "dishonest doubling and octupling of the cost by those who are building and control the roads." Conditions in Philadelphia differed from those in the other two

cities chiefly in that the political influences appear to have been more effective in delaying approval of charters for street railways. The Pennsylvania legislature finally granted its first street railway franchise in 1857. A rash of special acts granting charters followed in the next two years, accompanied by the usual charges of illegal rewards to members of the legislature and the Common Council.

Other large American cities, including Baltimore, Chicago, Cincinnati, Pittsburgh, and St. Louis, acquired their first horse railways in 1859 or 1860. Horsecars began operating in Paris in 1853, but an experiment in London with horsecar lines (tramways) in 1861–1862 failed dismally. Not until 1870 did they operate successfully on London streets. The original failure in London, surprising in view of the widespread success elsewhere, warrants brief comment. George Francis Train, an American whose exuberance and sensational promotional methods antagonized at least a part of the British public, finally obtained official authority and built three short tramways in . London in 1861. Their failure and removal the next year appears to have resulted from their location in fashionable neighborhoods where neither much support nor much patronage could be expected; their rails which, especially when not properly seated, seriously interfered with other traffic; and their misfortune in being overshadowed in public interest by the great railways building boom then attracting the enthusiastic attention of investors in the London area.

Steam trains moved in limited degree on the rails in the three cities under study. But steam power was nowhere regularly used for local, short-distance transportation. In Boston, where railroads penetrated at most only a short distance into the city, the issue did not become important. In New York, and especially in Philadelphia, strong opposition arose to the use of steam engines within the city. This opposition stemmed in part from the supposed danger threatened by the steam engine, not entirely an imaginary one, since two early Harlem engines had blown up within the city limits. Also, at least on the earliest trains, the crude braking system did not permit quick stops. Small efficiency units with the engine located at one end of the car proved unpopular with passengers who feared to ride in them even when the engine was concealed. By 1850 such objections had lost much of their validity, but the prejudice remained.

Vested interests in Philadelphia playing on popular fears prevented steam railroads from making connections through the central city until after the Civil War. A handbill circulated by Philadelphia interests shows a child being run over by a railroad engine and warns mothers of being "hurried home to mourn a Dreadful Casualty!" The real opposition appears to have come from Philadelphia commercial interests which opposed through railroad connections in the city in the belief that their business would suffer and Philadelphia would become, as the handbill claimed, a mere "SUBURB OF NEW YORK!"

Cheaper, more convenient, and faster than the omnibuses, the horsecars proved tremendously popular as soon as they were introduced. Fares within the central city were ordinarily five cents. This was a reduction of only one cent below the usual omnibus charge of six cents, but the streetcar lines were ordinarily considerably longer than omnibus routes, and transfers to other streetcar lines were often available at a small additional charge. So, wherever streetcars operated, they soon took away most of the omnibus

trade. But, where the demand was great and horsecars were not permitted, as on Broadway in New York City, the omnibuses continued to do a thriving business.

As pointed out earlier, the railroads entering Boston built up a very substantial commuter business by charging low prices to those who purchased yearly, half-yearly, or quarterly tickets. In the early fifties the railroad managements found that, with growing expenses, the commuter passengers did not cover their added cost at the low season ticket rates. Despite vigorous public protests, the railroad substantially increased commuter fares. When the Fitchburg Railroad raised its charges, angry commuters burned the president in effigy, and traffic fell off as some people returned to patronizing the slower, less convenient omnibuses. The situation was ripe for the introduction of the horsecars. When in 1856 a streetcar line began operating on the Cambridge-Boston route, travel on the main line of the Fitchburg fell off drastically, and the following year the Harvard Branch Railroad, operated between Cambridge and Watertown by the Fitchburg Railroad, suspended operation as a result of horsecar competition.

The commuter trains were faster than the horsecars, and they continued to serve the more distant suburbs, but the streetcars drew a larger and larger share of the total traffic. They offered greater convenience because they ran more often and made more frequent stops. It is true that, in some cases, seasonal commutation fares on the steam roads were as low as and occasionally even lower than single fares on the horsecars. But this was only rarely the case, and prices of single tickets on the railroads were always considerably higher. In fact, the low commuter fares charged by the steam railroads could be maintained only when they led to increased single-fare purchases by commuters' families and others.

At the same time that the relatively cheap single fares of the street railways hurt the suburban railroads, they benefited the professional men and skilled workers who sought to live out of the central city. Many of these people who could manage to pay the necessary single streetcar fares would have found it difficult, even impossible, to advance the considerable sums necessary to invest in season commutation tickets. In Philadelphia the only important commuter railroad, the Philadelphia, Germantown & Norristown Railroad, was forced to reduce its single-ticket fares in 1859 when it had to meet competition from a horse railroad. By 1860 the horse railroads had established their leading position in urban transportation. A contributor to the *American Railway Times* wrote: "They are steadily drawing the settlement of new population to their lines, and a large proportion of the persons who are now going into the country to build homes, prefer the location on the line of the Horse rather than on the Steam Railways; that is, everywhere within eight or ten miles of the cities."

As the area of the city expanded, the inhabitants, whether bent on business or pleasure, felt an increasing need for expeditious transportation. This demand developed more and more from those who sought to move to the outskirts from their residences in the older and increasingly crowded part of the city. In 1850, the year before the first horsecar lines were chartered in New York City, a report to the Aldermen declared that as crowding grew in the central city and high rents were charged for ". . . undesirable, crowded, and unwholesome tenements in the lower part of the city . . . ," all who could sought homes ". . . in the upper portions and suburbs

of the city. . . ." The streetcar apparently facilitated this trend. Thus a newspaper comment in 1860 refers to the horse railways as ". . . spreading . . . the laboring population to the suburbs. . . ." A report of 1866 concerning New York stated that, "In the morning, between six and seven, and the same hours at night, the cars are filled with mechanical labourers, clerks, factory girls, while later in the morning, and the earlier eve, our more wealthy business men favor these roads." Oscar Handlin indicates that the extension of horsecar lines to the nearby Boston suburb of Roxbury before 1860 led a considerable number of immigrant workers to make their homes there.

So the horsecars appear to have made possible some migration from the congested central city, although contemporaries' reports appear to be based as much on expectation as realization. At any rate, so far as can be judged for the years before the Civil War, the chief benefits of the horsecars were less for the unskilled workers than for the middle- and upper-income receivers who had patronized the omnibuses. The speed of the horsecars was too slow (about eight miles an hour) and their fares too high to make them very useful to the great mass of the poorest workers. Men who labored ten hours a day (or even two or three hours longer) could not spend unlimited time going to and from work. And even though the horse railway fare was only five cents each way, the cost came to a considerable sum for men who earned between one and two dollars a day. Under these circumstances, the facilities for rapid transit did not meet the needs of the tenement dwellers in the most crowded districts, and the density of population in the slums of the great cities grew rapidly despite the spread of horse railways. In 1860 more than half of the inhabitants of New York City still lived below 14th Street, an area about one-tenth the size of the whole island, and the crowding was almost as excessive in Boston and Philadelphia.

The development of new methods of urban transportation between 1830 and 1860 thus encouraged a centralized pattern of metropolitan growth which retained the focus of commerce and communications in the business district of the old walking city. This resulted as much from the effectiveness of the innovations in urban transportation as from their defects. The improved means of transportation provided mobility for high- and middle-income groups, thus facilitating the emergence of specialized business and residential districts and promoting the division of the business districts into separate sections for the performance of particular functions. But half or more of the persons inhabiting the great cities lived in the slums of the walking city, typically crowded between the business district on one side and desirable residential suburbs on the other. By facilitating this differentiation, the innovations in urban transportation contributed to the profound social and economic changes of the 19th century and no doubt played a part in making possible the phenomenally high level of per capita economic growth which characterized that epoch. On the other hand, it should not be overlooked that the innovations in urban transportation brought with them concealed costs of considerable significance. Against increases in workers' income must be counted the necessary outlays for transportation. And, offsetting other advantages, including the decreased hours of labor which became substantial only much later, should be placed the time necessarily consumed in going to and from work. It must also be emphasized that the failure to provide really cheap and rapid mass transport condemned hundreds of thousands of the poorer workers to live in the crowded, unsanitary slums of the central city. The beginnings of mass urban transportation in New York, Boston, and Philadelphia brought significant technological progress, as this paper has shown, but increased urban mobility also brought economic and social developments whose impact merits much further study and whose end is not yet.

The Expansion of Police Functions

Roger Lane*

The inaugural address of Mayor John Prescott Bigelow in 1849 gave the ultimate expression to the mercantile optimism of contemporary Boston: "The long winter of New England Isolation is broken,—she warms and flourishes in friendly and thrifty intercourse with the luxuriant West; and it is not too much to anticipate that the day will come, when there will be no greater or more prosperous city upon the American continent than the City of the Pilgrims."

Bigelow was speaking especially of the possibilities opened by the new railroads. Business was excellent. The city was still growing at the high rate, between 40 and 50 per cent a decade, which had been maintained since incorporation. And its citizens were still supremely confident in the future, in the vitality of progress and reform.

Governmental expansion between 1845 and 1853 kept pace with commercial growth. Between 1845 and 1847 the budget tripled, leaping from $974,102.14 to $3,293,579.92. In 1846 ground was broken for the public water system, the largest and most dramatic of capital projects. Handsome school buildings were completed in the next few years, as the educational system expanded. Several parks were established, and the Public Library opened in 1852. As ordinary departmental expenses continued to mount, in the years after 1845 "the expenditures of Boston were on a municipal basis."

But confidence in size was in the same period beginning to be clouded by social and political doubts. During 1845–46, as the waterworks was brought to Boston, the potato famine came to Ireland. Irish immigration reached a peak during the late 1840's and early 1850's. The newcomers brought problems more obvious than their gifts; increase in drink and poverty strained the institutions of charity and police. Their coming also helped to exacerbate a tense political atmosphere. As the Free-Soil and Know-Nothing movements grew and the older parties splintered and regrouped, men's hopes for the material future were balanced by fear for the political. Humanitarian reform in the city, no longer new, was in some ways accepted. In others the movement was discouraged, brought to a peak and then frustrated.

In an atmosphere of expansion, many of these developments created demands for more vigorous police activity. The local authorities, still unused to the possession of force, were called upon or tempted to use it in a variety of new ways, some of which provoked popular excitement. In the process of experiment, both the government and the citizens began, often painfully, to discover the limits necessary to a politic use of the police force.

In December of 1845, the doubts had not yet begun to temper the optimism. The results of the municipal election that month were interpreted with especial enthusiasm in the press. The regular Whig candidate, overwhelmingly elected, was Josiah Quincy, Jr., in many ways the ideal choice. Quincy was a reformer, and

*Reprinted by permission of the publishers from Roger Lane *Policing the City, Boston, 1822-1885,* Cambridge, Mass.: Harvard University Press, Copyright, 1967, by the President and Fellows of Harvard College, pp. 59–84.

by heredity and in his own right exemplified the tradition of aristocratic involvement in local affairs. As treasurer of the popularly subscribed Worcester Railroad, he was a forceful spokesman of public improvement. His belief in progress was measured by his willingness to multiply dramatically the city's spending and debt. And his program for dealing with the attendant problems was equally uncompromising. Crime and disorder, disease, drink, and poverty would all be met by a vigorous police, expanded for the purpose.

To assure this vigor the mayor chose Francis Tukey, a personal friend, to head the department. Only thirty-two years old in 1846, the new marshal had originally come to Boston from Maine, as a mechanic. But he had shown his ambition by working his way through law school in two years, and his enormous gusto made him well suited to take on responsibility for the most rapidly growing department in the city. The regular force was more than doubled at the time of his appointment, as eighteen new men were chosen with him, raising the total to thirty. Eight were detailed as a special night force. And three more, within months, were added to serve as detectives, the first on the public payroll.

During and after Quincy's administration the regular police expenses continued to climb. The $12,232.14 spent in 1845–46 mounted to $49,-251.27 in 1851–52, exclusive of the money spent on internal health. By 1851 there were twenty-two night men, usually detailed to patrol the business district as a supplement to the watch and often used as a flying squad of raiders. Most of the forty-four day men did ordinary patrol service, covering beats of three to four miles each. The detectives were assigned to the central office, together with several headquarters officials, the marshal himself, and the two deputies.

This great growth in the marshal's office overshadowed the more modest gains of the watch, which, moving from 150 men in 1840 to 190 in 1851, roughly kept pace with the population. The effect was felt more severely by the constables, whose numbers were cut back, in 1848, from forty-four to thirty men. The reduction in number reflected a change in duty. The constables like Derastus Clapp and William Eaton who had shown a talent for thief-catching were transferred to the police, as detectives. The rest, in practice, virtually ceased to operate independently of the courts. While occasionally serving criminal warrants, they were increasingly confined to civil business. The new model police could handle the rest.

Respect for the reorganized police department, and the number of men available, enabled the city to expand their activities. Some of the new duties were merely odd jobs, as when members of the force were used as messengers to deliver official reports. Others were extensions of existing practice. The men had always helped to provide emergency aid to the unfortunate, for example, and during the later 1840's this service was made official. Budgets for the police and watch included fifty or a hundred dollars a year to cover medical treatment for the victims of accident or sudden illness, and a similar amount made up "cash disbursement for the immediate relief of sufferers in various ways."

Still other responsibilities were entirely new, reflections of growth in both the department and the city. One resulted from the need to regulate the city's thriving "intelligence offices." These were employment bureaus, open to "domestics, servants, or . . . other laborers except seamen." Pregnant with possibilities for the cruelest kind of fraud, they were subjected to license and control in 1848, under the charge of a special officer who joined the superintendent of second-hand shops at headquarters. His inspection of the books of these companies provided information about that growing pool of transients and immigrants which was in many ways a subject of concern.

More important still was the city's first systematic attempt at traffic regulation. Since 1797 the commonwealth had had a statute regarding hacks and trucks, which required both rate regulation and the prominent display of a license number. But despite an occasional petition this had not been enforced between the incorporation and 1846. In that year the marshal was ordered to keep the licenses on record, collect the fees, and check on the conditions. A third special officer was employed to do this work full time, and to answer complaints about lost articles, high rates, or conduct in violation of a series of strengthened traffic ordinances.

A fourth special officer joined the force in 1850, in response to a long-continued agitation. Nothing was more obviously essential to progress than the instruction of youth, one of the major concerns of the younger Quincy. The increasing emphasis on universal education demanded that as many as possible be reached. A special committee of the city council reported in 1846 that "the mischief caused by habits of truancy, which prevail in many of our schools can hardly be overrated. No valuable or permanent reform will ever be carried into full effect until this obstacle is removed." Existing law required only that "the resident ministers of the gospel, the selectmen, and the school committees, in the several towns . . . exert their best endeavors that . . . youth shall regularly attend the schools provided."

But like so much of the legislation of the commonwealth, this did not fit conditions in the mid-century city. In 1850 educational reformers accordingly secured an act which set penalties for truant children, and especially for those parents who profited from "their wretched gains or . . . dishonest pursuits." The law also enabled Boston to detail a policeman to enforce it. The whole force made arrests for truancy, and the special officer, Theodore Parker's "moral missionary," offered counsel to several hundred delinquents and their families. His work, in company with that of the other new officers, demonstrated again the flexibility of the police department and its usefulness in dealing with the emergent problems of the municipality.

But for Mayor Quincy and many who supported him in three successful campaigns, the most important function of the police was dramatized in the city's first major campaign against vice. The growth of reform sentiment had been reflected earlier in city politics, but the more uncompromising reformers had never won a majority in the city council, and between the two Quincys the mayors had generally been moderates. Before 1846, the government had neither the force nor the purpose required for a concerted attack on immorality.

Because police estimates and statistics were not published before 1850, it is difficult to measure the city's efforts to deal with vice. But the temperance campaign did have some effect. It is clear that between the early 1830's and the middle of the 1840's the number of places selling liquor in Boston declined, possibly in absolute terms and certainly in proportion to population. It is more difficult to estimate the extent of gambling and prostitution. The latter problem probably increased, at least absolutely, with the number of unskilled and homeless girls seeking work in the city. The existence of numerous houses of prostitution was acknowledged openly and lightly in the popular press. Disorderly houses were sometimes prosecuted, and individual nightwalkers arrested when complained against. Arrests on the initiative of police officers themselves were probably made only when aggravated by circumstances. The elder Quincy had seen the problem as insoluble, capable at best of being hidden away. And despite increasing intolerance toward this and other moral offenses, nothing more ambitious had been done.

But the younger Quincy abandoned this fatalistic attitude. Although more moderate than some of his supporters, the new mayor was definitely a reformer. He supported Horace Mann's program for the schools; his brother was an abolitionist; and he was the only firm prohibitionist ever elected to head the city. He was willing to use the law and the police to enforce his ideals, and his election tipped the balance in the city government.

Since 1842 the aldermen had cited legal uncertainty as the official reason for failure to grant liquor licenses. But in 1847, the decisions of the United States Supreme Court in the License Cases made it impossible any longer to avoid the issue, and the policy was reviewed. When the board split, four to four, over the wisdom of granting liquor permits, the mayor cast his deciding vote against them. His reasons were not based on caution, or like those of Mayor Chapman, earlier, on a professed abhorrence of monopoly. Instead he firmly stated his belief in both the benefits and the possibility of prohibition. Marshal Tukey's views, if nonideological were equally stark. When the aldermen later asked him how best to check the increase in crime, "he contented himself with the simple statement—'execute the law.'"

This process was begun in the easiest manner, in the fall of 1846, through the Sunday laws, where proof was required only of the fact of doing business and not of its nature. But after the official decision in 1847, the license law itself was used to justify arrests and raids by the night police. The business of executing the law, urged on by organized groups, developed a momentum of its own under Tukey, which survived Quincy's three years in office. The continual harassment of sellers increased even during the administration of the conservative Mayor Bigelow, elected in 1848. Bigelow's opposition to prohibition was overridden by a unanimous vote of the alderman. In 1850 the police made 417 arrests for violations of the license laws, and over 41 for keeping noisy and disorderly houses. In 1851, the figure for license violations reached 718, the largest single cause of arrest other than simple drunkenness itself.

At the same time, the police under both the Quincy and Bigelow administrations intensified their efforts against other kinds of vice. Gaming arrests increased. The numbers of those taken in for drunkenness continued to climb. And for the first time action was taken to curb prostitution.

Quincy ordered the first move against prostitutes as a class, to end the ancient connection between vice and the stage. Many of Boston's theaters hired special policemen to eject trouble-makers, but they made no effort to limit their use as places of assignation. It was notorious that the drama often only raised the curtain on the evening, and in some places a special section, the "third row," was set aside for prostitutes. The aldermen in 1847 voted to clean up this situation through the use of the licensing power. All theater owners were required to hire regular officers from the city, who were ordered to keep liquor and prostitutes out of the premises. The wages, while charged to the police appropriation, comprised the license fee.

More dramatic was the "descent," or raid. Begun under Quincy, the practice was extended by Marshal Tukey and reached its height during the late winter and spring of 1851. By that time it covered not one place but several and attacked gambling and other offenses as well as illegal liquor selling. On Saturday night, March 8, eighty-six people were arrested for "shaking props" in a gaming resort, to the especial delight of the penny press. Afterwards the marshal invited the public to the police office, to inspect the captured gambling instruments. Twenty-seven more arrests were made the next Friday, and were followed by a similar exhibition. A month later, on April 23, Tukey staged "the Celebrated Ann Street Descent," aimed partly at gamblers but largely at prostitution.

Nothing before had been organized on the scale of the Ann Street venture, which originated either with private reformers or the police themselves. The whole street was raided, and the one night's work netted sixty men and ninety women. Thirty-five were sentenced as "keepers of brothels, noisy and disorderly houses, violaters of the license and Sunday laws, etc." The remaining men were prosecuted as "tipplers, vagabonds, pipe players, etc.," and the women as prostitutes. Most significant was the advantage taken of the pioneering of John Augustus: many of the women, by arrangement with the courts, were given suspended sentences and hired out as domestics to private families.

All of this was fascinating for the press, but the exploits of the marshal's detective bureau were the subject of an even greater and more continuous interest. The detectives, when first organized, were formally distinguished from the other day police only by their function. But they were beginning, in the later 1840's, to acquire a special glamour. In part this was a reflection of interest in their antagonists. The police court news introduced in the 1830's had concentrated sometimes on misery, sometimes on humor, but almost always on the violence and petty offenses of a class that was more perishing than dangerous. But in the 1840's and 1850's, this was supplemented by news of professional roguery of a different kind. The detectives were now engaged with "noted" or "notable" thieves, often from out of town. And the papers assumed a readership which needed no help in identifying men like "Bristol Bill" and similar characters.

The three full-time detectives were selected in this period largely for "their knowledge of rogues and their schemes." Two were former constables, who continued to work as they had before being brought under public direction—with one important exception. Late in 1845, after a watchman claimed $2,000 offered for the arrest of an incendiary, the government had objected. In the case of *Poole* v. *Boston,* the city solicitor argued that persons performing paid duty should not be eligible for rewards from the treasury. Although none of his precedents involved peace officers or criminal rewards, the Supreme Judicial Court upheld his view. And in 1846, when the detectives were organized, the aldermen ruled that public rewards would be granted policemen only by special vote. More important, it voted to forbid both witness fees and later private rewards under the same condition.

In practice, these rules could be evaded; one way was to make semi-official the arrangements which had before been private. Those requesting detective work were often asked to contribute to a "discretionary fund" kept by the marshal for use in procuring evidence and witnesses, and sometimes the city was billed in small amounts under the same heads.

Many of the applicants were sailors and others victimized by "panel thieves," who specialized in robbing loose clothing in bawdy houses, and the detectives were often occupied in policing these places and restricting them to their primary functions. At other times they simply circulated in crowds in order to spot pickpockets. But there was higher work to do as well. Marshal Tukey was once authorized to pursue offenders all the way to Canada, on behalf of the New England Association Against Counterfeiting. As detective service became less a private and more a public responsibility, the city on at least one occasion furnished half the salary of a Boston-based agent of the bankers' organization. At other times, since it employed the only regular detectives in New England, the city lent them out to pursue safe robbers in such places as Provincetown and Lynn.

Tukey basked in his reputation as "Our Vidocq," after the famous French inspector, and his talent for publicity magnified the intrinsic interest that these operations held for the press and public. In January 1848, the police drew a crowd by mysteriously digging into Boston Common to uncover a cache of allegedly stolen money. And in 1851 the marshal introduced, as a regular institution, a weekly "show-up of rogues," designed to identify suspicious persons for the benefit of both police and public. At the first of these spectacles, "Seventy-six pickpockets, burglars, panel thieves, etc."—among them twelve women—were "shown up to the whole of the police force." None were legally under arrest, and all, upon leaving the office, were forced to run a gauntlet of crowing citizens who tore

their clothing and marked their backs with crosses in chalk.

The "show-up" was an almost totalitarian display of power, fully appropriate for a man who had become the most important local officer in Boston. The marshal was still superintendent of the department of internal health, although most of the work was delegated to Deputy Hezekiah Earle. The department's two large yards employed a number of full-time artisans, blacksmiths, and painters, in addition to the casual labor required in sweeping the streets. The marshal was responsible for the vaccination program. And he possessed all the old power of the board of health to institute proceedings of eviction, condemnation, and transportation to the South Boston institutions for the contagious. By 1851–52, the various expenses of the internal health department, including the cost of buying horses and grain, fuel, paint, and lime, reached $79,573.87. Tukey's other job as head of the police was strengthened by the fact that he was able successfully to demand the right of approving appointments. His salary had been raised in 1847, at Mayor Quincy's suggestion, to $1,800, a figure exceeded only by the mayor, the treasurer, and the city solicitor. This put him on a level above the municipal judges; and his deputies, at $1,100 each, earned more than many department heads.

But his official position did not fully explain Tukey's remarkable hold on the public. He had arrived in Boston just as the always latent excitement in police work was beginning to emerge, and he was well equipped to exploit it. Unlike earlier men who had dominated the local scene, he had no aristocratic pretensions and no family connections. Once, when he was fined for his persistently reckless driving, the *Daily Mail* observed that "the spirit of the b'hoy" had triumphed over "the dignity of the officer." But for most readers of the penny press, the marshal's frankly coarse behavior had an appeal of its own. And few papers treated him so lightly; he was hard, and rude, rather than familiar. A big man, with curly hair and an impressive, heavy face—one editor called him "beautiful"—he kept his own men at some distance, and most of them were afraid to speak to him unasked. The fact that he was a popular hero, admired by temperance men and bankers as well as reporters, made his elective superiors equally hesitant to interfere with him. He was obviously ambitious, and it was said that Mayor Seaver, elected in 1851, owed Tukey his election.

But despite the marshal's commanding position, his power rested on an uncertain base. The same activity that made him newsworthy to all and praiseworthy to some made him offensive to others. He was always in controversy, "a terror to evildoers and to some who were not evildoers." And as remarked in the *Bunker Hill Aurora,* the maxim that "it is easier to get than to retain popularity" was especially applicable to officers of police.

The same methods which excited admiration when applied to gamblers were not so acceptable when used against other citizens. The drive to enforce the traffic ordinances goaded the owners of omnibus lines into carrying the issue all the way to the Supreme Judicial Court. And the technique of mass arrests was used as frequently in connection with the bylaws as with moral offenses. On February 2, 1848, 91 people were arrested for failure to clean up icy sidewalks. On two occasions in the same year, 50 more were brought in for keeping unlicensed dogs. On April 21, 1851, 101 were arrested for dog law violations, and on December 23, 112 for neglecting icy sidewalks. Some 83 more sidewalk offenders were brought in on February 5, 1852, 65 dog law violators on March 9. The gentle tactics of Marshal Pollard were exploded for "a policy to have as many cases of this kind before the court, at the same time, as possible, giving the defendants but little opportunity to complain of partiality, and plenty of time to wait in court." There was no provision until late in the century for issuing summonses in minor criminal cases, and no means of transportation for those brought in. An arrest in the 1850's meant a long walk through the streets with a policeman, accompanied by howls in disreputable areas and stares in the respectable.

The activities of the marshal's detective bureau also opened up an area of vulnerability, this one of more long-term importance. Official detective work was still a novelty, and its publicity brought it close attention. The men had no scientific aids, no files or photographs, only a few handbills. But since the proposal of Washington's Mayor Gates, in 1829, the invention of the telegraph was beginning to make it possible for detectives in various cities to communicate. Some states, New York and Pennsylvania the most important, made public announcement of the release of convicts from prison. Descriptions were relayed to the marshal's office, and if it appeared that an ex-convict or suspected thief might head for Boston, his agents stood watch at the railroad terminals. The keepers of pawnshops were useful in local cases. And the detectives had skills of their own; the term "shadow" was already used, and many men developed extraordinary memories for the faces and habits of criminals. But with all of these aids, criminals themselves were the most essential to detective work. It was necessary to overlook some offenses to concentrate on others, as in panel thievery, or to overlook the crime to concentrate on recovery.

One ex-detective who had worked in New York during the middle of the century explained, "There are but two great classes in civilization—the oppressed and the oppressors, the trampled upon and the detective. He is dishonest, crafty, unscrupulous, when necessary to be so. He tells black lies when he cannot avoid it, and white lying, at least, is his chief stock in trade. He is the outgrowth of a diseased and corrupted state of things, and is, consequently, morally diseased himself." The same authority concluded that there was no alternative; the detective was useful, even necessary. So long as there was a demand, the business of bribery and extortion, the harassing of ex-convicts, and the compounding of felony were inevitable.

But since this inevitability was not widely recognized or accepted, so far at least as it concerned public officers, the detective system was a weak spot in the reputation of any police force. The first attack on detective procedures came soon after the agents were officially connected with the force; critics remarked that while Tukey was proud of the amount of stolen goods his men recovered, a total worth $16,121 in 1850, he never talked about the means of recovery. For those who knew, the information was potential ammunition, all the more valuable since the marshal's popularity with several groups was beginning to wane.

One new complaint centered on Tukey's published attitude toward juvenile delinquency. The marshal, together with many other citizens, was disturbed by the number of neglected children in the city, estimating that some fifteen hundred, between the ages of six and sixteen, were beyond the reach of parental or other discipline. But he saw the problem not as an educational reformer but as a policeman, concerned only with keeping children off the streets, where, drifting into petty crime and vicious habits, they made trouble for his men. The courts, Tukey believed, were too easy on young offenders under the new truant law. His recommendation was that guilty juveniles be bound out as apprentices or domestics until their majority, a proposal denounced as reactionary by the friends of Horace Mann.

This attack, while minor in itself, reminded reformers that while the marshal was sometimes with them he was not of them, and it came at a time when many of them were disillusioned with his performance for other reasons. The more ardent spirits in the temperance movement had from the beginning called for vigorous enforcement of the no-license policy. Drink was regarded as the primary agent of all of the evils of contemporary society, the most widely recognized cause of poverty, crime, and disease, of seduction, broken families, prostitution, irreligion, and corruption. The temperance ideal was part of a wider vision of the progress of civilization, and specifically of Boston. And while in some respects this vision reached a height during the late 1840's, in others it was beginning to fade.

The decline was in part a natural reaction to exaggerated hopes. In part it was related to increasing concern for the Union and absorption in the national problem of slavery. But for many it was precipitated by the evidence that there had been no social progress in Boston, a problem aggravated by the irony that the decade of reform overlapped the decade of the Irish coming.

The tensions that the Irish presence created had occasionally erupted before 1845. But the immigration following the Great Famine was unprecedented. The number of arrivals shot up until by 1850 thirty-five thousand of the one hundred thirty-six thousand residents of the city were Irish by birth. More revealing of their impact are the statistics of misery. The wretched economic and physical condition of the newcomers was partly reflected in the amount annually spent on institutional poor relief, which rose from $43,700 in 1845 to $136,217 in 1852. Smallpox became a problem again after 1845. Cholera struck in 1849. And the death rate, boosted by dirt and overcrowding in the Irish districts, averaged 29.4 per thousand in the five-year period before 1850, a record for the century.

The coming of the Irish was an enormous shock to the police of the city. As superintendent of internal health, the marshal was the official most concerned with rapidly deteriorating sanitary conditions. The increase in minor criminality was equally troublesome. Irish mores and misery made the prohibitory liquor policy, especially, impossible to enforce. The friends of temperance later recalled the early 1840's as the period when the movement in Boston had reached its peak. Whether or not the voluntarism of the Washingtonians and their imitators was more effective than the harassing tactics of Marshal Tukey, it was clear by the later 1840's that the policy inaugurated by Mayor Quincy was not achieving its ends.

The mayor, and more especially the marshal, blamed the failure of their crusade upon the courts. In fact, the vice laws themselves were the result of compromise. They recorded official condemnation of immoral behavior, to the satisfaction of puritans and reformers. But in a large city, where thousands of inhabitants were habitual violators, prosecution was necessarily partial. And when the police brought in large numbers whose conduct was not considered extreme, and who had not prompted private complaints, the courts were often lenient. Judges had considerable latitude in fixing penalties, and were dependent both upon political favor and the willingness of juries to convict. Tukey complained that liquor dealers were fined an average of only twenty-four dollars each; the victims of the great gambling raids in 1851 were assessed at three dollars apiece, as first offenders.

But these complaints, reflecting an increasingly intransigent majority opinion, only emphasized that police action in itself was insufficient. Mayor Bigelow's plea, in 1849, for a careful return to the license system, did not move the aldermen, who had a variety of reasons for supporting the existing policy. But it did express a widespread disillusion. Quincy's "experiment," he noted, had had a fair trial, "aided by an efficient police, and backed by . . . a large and influential body of his fellow citizens. What has been the result?" The answer was more than disappointing. An appalling increase in intemperance and attendant crimes made it seem "as if the saturnalia of Bacchus, or some more malignant of the heathen deities, took date from the vote which was to overthrow his altars, and confound his votaries.

The marshal's own figures bore out this complaint. In 1851, Tukey estimated, there were 227 houses of ill fame operating in the city, and 26 gambling places. An even 1,500 shops sold liquors, 900 run by Irishmen. These were not taverns, or even groceries; 1,031 of them sold nothing else.

Almost in proportion as critics were discouraged with these returns on their hopes for a better city, they turned to the most distant problem of slavery. In this battle there were fewer daily reminders of failure, and less frustration. Here was no apparent victory lost but a movement still gathering force. Under the administration of Mayor Quincy there were no local incidents involving mob violence. But active antislavery sentiment was still minority opinion, and conflict again developed during the tenure of Mayor Bigelow. While reformers had urged a more vigilant professional police force for other reasons, they discovered in this context that the marshal was not merely a disappointing ally but actually an opponent.

The problem had become more acute since the Latimer case in 1843. The Mexican War and its aftermath, including Webster's Seventh of March Speech, the Compromise of 1850, and the evident Southern determination to enforce the new fugitive slave law, had all contributed to political fragmentation in Massachusetts. To Mayor Bigelow, for many years an intimate associate of Governor Everett, the disintegration of the long dominant Whig party was especially painful. But despite its usual caution, the city government was unable to avoid involvement in controversy beyond its limits. Marshal Tukey, stationed at Faneuil Hall in November of 1850, failed to take action when a great abolitionist meeting to denounce the apostate Webster was broken up by a disorderly invasion. Edmund Quincy, brother of the former mayor, demanded that the city council rebuke the marshal for neglect of duty. While Tukey was absolved, the point was made. In future, both abolitionists and Webster Whigs were denied the use of Faneuil Hall,

a move which satisfied neither group.

The city government also took a vacillating attitude toward the fugitive slave act in actual operation. Since the Latimer affair, the city had successfully avoided involvement in any of the infrequent incidents involving fugitives in Boston. But in the first case which tested the new personal liberty law, the antislavery men abandoned their usual peaceful tactics. The change was precipitated on February 15, 1851. Fully nine Deputy United States Marshals arrested the escaped slave Shadrach in a Cornhill coffee shop, in full view of the patrons. Deputy Patrick Riley, fearing trouble, notified both Bigelow and Tukey, neither of whom took official notice. With Boston's jail facilities legally unavailable, Shadrach was confined in the federal courtroom, a place without bars or means of defense. When a writ of *de homine replegniando* and a petition of *habeas corpus* were both denied, a crowd of free Negroes stormed the courtroom and carried Shadrach to safety. For those who believed in the recent national compromise, the rescue was a clear breach of faith, an outrage against law and property. The conservative press was furious. In New York, the affair was branded "a deep stain upon the city of Boston," and it was remarked that no member of the marshal's office, down the hall from the courtroom, had taken any note of the mob and its action.

Both Bigelow and Tukey were sensitive to these criticisms, one as a Whig politician, the other as a professional policeman. Both got a chance at redemption a month later, when a search was begun for seventeen-year-old Thomas Sims, from Savannah, who had stowed away on a brig and slipped off into Boston Harbor. While the law forbade any overt aid either in catching or holding a fugitive, the mayor and the marshal could still take such steps judged necessary to prevent a public disturbance.

When United States Marshal Devens received a warrant for Sims, he asked for help from Tukey, who commanded an experienced group of officers fully familiar with the city. Tukey in turn passed the warrant on to two of the police, who were then deputized by Devens. The city marshal later explained that he would not ordinarily help the arrest of a fugitive, but that riot and bloodshed had to be avoided. It had been shown that the federal officers, in contrast to his own, had "neither courage, shrewdness, or strength to do it." And it was the two deputized policemen who finally did overtake Sims, on the night of April 3. As in the Latimer case, the fugitive was first told that he was being arrested for theft. When he became suspicious and resisted, he managed to stab Officer Butman seriously with his knife. But despite this scuffle, the affair was consummated swiftly, and Sims locked up on the third floor of the courthouse.

The circumstances of the arrest were of doubtful legality, and the conduct of the individual policemen was further obnoxious. Asa O. Butman, especially, became notorious for his "generous" refusal to press assault charges, an action which might have rescued the fugitive from federal jurisdiction and would certainly have helped the argument that the police were only doing their duty. Once again the Boston Vigilance Committee distributed placards denouncing police officers as "Slave Catchers" and "Kidnappers."

More maddening than the arrest itself was the scene at the courthouse. By the time Sim's friends got in to see him the building was surrounded by a guard consisting of every patrolman on the force, day and night men both. The sight left no doubt about the position of official Boston. When United States Commissioner Curtis asked for help, Bigelow had given Tukey a generalized order to preserve the peace about the courthouse, leaving the details to him. In the nine days of Sims's incarceration the marshal's men not only held guard but were otherwise obtrusive. Tukey himself often slipped into the surrounding crowd, warning off countrymen with pitchforks and feeling for weapons in pockets; at one point he was arrested by a deputy sheriff when a Negro, roughly searched, pressed a suit for false detention. In preparation for the final march to return Sims to the harbor, the police were drilled with borrowed United States sabers, their first official experience with weapons other than the customary short club. Borrowing an idea he had developed during the famous Parkman-Webster murder trial, Tukey had the courthouse surrounded by a heavy chain, waist high, to hold back the crowd. Only those on legitimate business, and with passes signed by the federal marshal, were allowed to go through. The symbolism was not lost on the abolitionists and others. There were no openings in the chain, and no gate; some insisted that they be let in by unfastening the corners, and Sims's attorney generally vaulted over. Chief Justice Lemuel Shaw, however, the man who had turned down the writ and petition in the Shadrach case, was observed habitually to duck or stoop under. "This was the hour of the deepest humiliation in Massachusetts."

After a rescue plot was aborted and all legal counters failed, Sims was marched off on April 12 with a police and militia escort, the first fugitive ever successfully returned from the city. While the whole affair helped the Boston force to win a reputation in some quarters as the most efficient in the country, it also made bitter enemies for the officers in general and the marshal in particular. When questioned by abolitionist T. W. Higginson, Tukey averred that he was only doing a painful duty: "I know I am violating the state law . . . but I am acting under orders, and it is the mayor and the aldermen who are responsible." But while this was ultimately true, it was clear that Tukey had acted with excessive zeal. An investigation was carried out by the state Senate, then in control of a reform coalition of Free-Soil men and Democrats. The mayor was obviously a weakling, and no testimony implicated him either in the original arrest, in Butman's refusal to press charges, or in the offer of fifteen hundred volunteers, "Marshal Tukey's gentlemen," to help keep the peace. Tukey's remark to Higginson, publicly relayed to the investigators, did not save his reputation with reformers and simply inflamed his relations with the mayor and other members of Boston's conservative Whig machine.

The marshal was a confident and outspoken man, and a bold actor, at a time when caution was the rule in local politics. Some kind of conflict was inevitable, and whether or not the Sims case began it, it had fully arrived later in the year with the fight over the appointment of Barney McGinniskin to the police force.

The Whig ascendancy in Massachusetts had been broken in the state election of 1850, which resulted in a controlling coalition between Democrats and Free-Soilers in the legislature. The Sims affair had contributed further to that Whig division exacerbated by Webster's Seventh of March position. In Boston, the center and strength of regular Whiggery, there was no real hope of winning back the reformers in number. But there was a chance that the conservative Irish Democrats, themselves unhappy with the reform coalition, might be persuaded to join an opposing alliance. Evidently as part of this intended *rapprochement,* it was proposed, in June of 1851, to add an Irishman to the police.

Custom dictated that this or any political use of the department had to be carried out within narrow limits. None of the seven city marshals had been a political chieftain, and in fact none had held elective office before or after appointment. The fragmentation of local politics made it impossible that watchmen or police be subjected to any rigid political test. The blatant political use of appointments was inhibited also by the fact that police and watchmen did not serve annual terms, like constables, but during good behavior. In order to remove one man to make way for another, it was necessary not merely that he fail of reappointment at a given date, along with a number of his fellows, but that he be fired individually. This was a drastic course, which often stirred up petitions for a hearing. Usually the annual turnover was low. But occasionally a list with a few additions and subtractions was drawn up and voted "in place of all those now serving." And with applications running between two and three times the number of jobs available, prospective members did seek to exercise influence. Many presented the aldermen with petitions signed by merchants and other citizens. Others, in place of these extended references, undoubtedly had individual sponsors on the board.

The movement to appoint McGinniskin was calculated not to violate any of the customary procedures. A number of businessmen signed a petition in his behalf, and Marshal Tukey reported on June 9 the results of the usual investigation; the candidate was temperate, a taxpayer, forty-two years old, twenty-two years a resident of the United States. With his eligibility assured, the board of aldermen on September 19 confirmed his nomination, although he did not immediately report for duty.

The subsequent controversy built up all during the state campaign season. Only one alderman at first opposed McGinniskin, and he received a ringing rebuff from the mayor. In a speech delivered on October 8, and later reported as far away as London, Bigelow noted that the principal objection offered was "that it is a dangerous precedent to appoint a foreigner to stations of such trust." But he had himself served with two respectable Irish members of the legislature. The city crier, David Hill, a veteran of the Mexican War, had been appointed without reference to his Irish birth, and so had the late constable Michael Riley. Nativist intolerance was not ground for objection, and McGinniskin's personal qualifications could not be challenged when "he stands the scrutiny of our lynx-eyed city marshal."

But in the months following, the marshal himself became the leader in the fight against McGinniskin, in defiance of the mayor and apparently as spokesman for the force. Although it was true that Irishmen had served the city earlier, the men were convinced that their own department was something different. The police were no more prejudiced than other groups; given the fact that the Irish, during the 1850's, comprised the vast majority of those arrested for all crimes, it is notable that the force did not develop a more fearsome reputation as an engine of nativism. Marshal Tukey's first annual report, written in 1851, directed its bitterness not at the immigrants but at their poverty and plight. His men customarily aided the residents of the Irish districts with gifts of firewood and other necessities in emergencies, and organized a regular charity for the benefit of the poor, principally Irish. But there were instances of discrimination and violence. And the gap between a rough compassion and acceptance onto the force was not easily bridged.

Unlike the constables, the police acted not solely as individuals but as members of a group, with a developing professional pride. Their two dollars a day was about twice the pay of common labor. And the attractiveness of the job was measured above all by its year-round security and the prospects of permanence. The men were drawn from the class of apprentices, artisans, and mechanics, and the number of working days in the year raised their annual income well above that of the typical master mason.

In an open letter to the press, published on the day of the state elections, Marshal Tukey objected above all to McGinniskin's imperfect credentials, a threat to the status of every other member of the force. Not a respectable worker, he was a "common cabman," from Ann Street, the most notorious in the city. Ten years earlier he had been convicted of a criminal offense, as a participant in a riot at St. Mary's Church. And although the marshal disclaimed any prejudice, the candidate's behavior as well as his name was outrageously Irish: he had arrived at work, for the first time, on the afternoon of November 3, announcing himself to the night force as "Barney McGinniskin, fresh from the bogs of Ireland!"

The marshal refused to assign him duty, and the mayor took no action. Bigelow and the incumbent aldermen had won considerable unpopularity, partly because of the Sims affair. With a major turnover in the city government expected, the impasse was left to the next administration. Since things looked "a little squally" to the marshal and his men, they decided to "dabble a little in politics." The first December election resulted in no choice, and John H. Wilkins, the regular Whig nominee, was forced to follow tradition and withdraw. The police were then instructed to vote for Chairman Benjamin Seaver of the common council, who replaced him, and Seaver was able with their help to win the needed majority.

But united political action by the police was a novelty in Boston, and not appreciated. Mayor Seaver, once inaugurated with a sympathetic Whig council, felt no obligation. He ordered McGinniskin kept. And he followed this by firing the whole night police force, which had most conspicuously marched to the polls in a body; its duties were abolished, and the night left entirely to the watch.

The abolition of the night force was another blow at Tukey. His only previous defeat had come in 1850, when the total number of night men was cut from twenty-two to seven, and much of his 1851 report was devoted to an argument for their restoration. They had been, he argued, a fine lot of men, all young, all married, full-time workers serving a probationary period before appointment to the day force. And through the several years of their existence they had captured more criminals than the entire rival body of over two hundred watchmen.

Their activities as night raiders accounted for their favor with the marshal, but also for their unpopularity with regular politicians and much of the public. And their services as the especial guardians of mercantile property were outweighed by their roughness, and by hints of venality confirmed when at least one ex-member was indicted for burglary. Neither the cutback in 1850 nor the total abolition of 1852 was seriously protested in the press, which was showing other signs of impatience with Tukey's methods.

The weekly "show-up" was becoming notorious, as its novelty declined and its abuses were more apparent. Many were indignant at the showing up of a young woman transvestite from New York, obviously displayed as entertainment. By 1852, even the *Mail*, ordinarily inclined to the marshal's support, was calling for the abolition of the practice, unique to Boston.

In April of 1852, the mayor and aldermen cut further into the marshal's authority by voting to limit the tenure of policemen to one year. It was argued that this procedure would help in firing incompetents, by subjecting them to a close annual review. Tukey had in fact suggested a similar change earlier, in order to get rid of some whom he considered "unfit to be policemen." But he had since been satisfied by a promise, obtained from earlier administrations, that all new applicants must be cleared through him. With the exception of McGinniskin, the force by 1852 was largely composed of his men. The timing of the new rule made it clear that Seaver was determined to choose policemen more sympathetic to his own views.

At the same time, the administration was showing its intention to abandon prohibition, the policy which had originally inspired the marshal's appointment and activities. As the reform legislature prepared a new liquor law, more drastic than the original Fifteen-Gallon Act of 1838, the board of aldermen reversed its ten-year-old no-license policy. During the winter and spring, the city granted a total of 612 liquor licenses. The move was not made in open defiance of the friends of temperance; as Mayor Seaver suggested, the licenses were no more than existing law allowed, and less than a majority of applications. Their issuance would allow discrimination, making enforcement easier by enabling a drive against those remaining unlicensed. In fact the board voted to stop issuing permits on May 17, the day that the new prohibitory bill was vetoed by Governor Boutwell. But when five days later the bill was re-passed, it became clear that whatever the city's intention with respect to the license law, it was not going to cooperate in the enforcement of prohibition.

This showdown had been approaching for several years. Even before the 1850 election of the Free-Soil–Democratic coalition, the state had tightened its liquor legislation. Chapter 232 of the Acts of 1850, which in a few words substituted the term "intoxicating" for "spirituous" in the basic license law, brought wines, beer, and even the countryman's cider under regulation for the first time. But the new statute, Chapter 322 of the Acts of 1852, was still more drastic than anything passed before. The private sale of liquor was forbidden entirely; state agents alone could sell for medicinal and scientific purposes. Far-reaching search and seizure provisions were designed to help enforcement. And violation, for the first time in the history of the commonwealth's liquor legislation, was made a jailable offense, upon the third conviction.

Most important for local politics was section seven, which decreed that "It shall be the duty of mayors and aldermen to prosecute" violations upon complaint. Outright defiance of the whole law, by an open policy of granting yet more liquor licenses, was defeated in the board of aldermen by a five to two vote. But with the aid of the city solicitor, the Seaver administration did find legal means of evading the spirit of section seven. Among these was a reform of the police department, the agency through which any prosecutions would have to be instituted.

In June, the council passed a new police ordinance. In most respects this simply summed up existing rules and legislation. Following the order of April, police appointments were to be made annually. The title of the "City Marshal" was changed to "Chief of Police," although the chief was specifically given the same duties that the marshal had had. He was to post a $2,000 bond with the city treasurer, to appoint his own deputies, and to have "precedence and control over constables and police officers when engaged in the same service." To this end he was entitled to make departmental rules and regulations. His office was to be open at stated hours for the reception of complaints, and he was to attend to the prosecution and trial of those acted upon. He was to be a full-time officer, in charge of the "peace, order and cleanliness of the city," charged especially with the removal of nuisances and obstructions in the streets. The only thing omitted was mention of the law, as distinct from the ordinances, and the stipulation, as had been the case with the marshal, that the chief be sworn as a constable. Constables and sheriffs, as officers of the state, were charged with carrying out the search and seizure provisions of the new liquor act; "chiefs of police" were not mentioned. As Mayor Seaver explained, the services of the chief were highly important, and "these services could not be had if that officer is employed in searching for and removing property."

When the new ordinance was followed by no announcement appointing a chief, it was clear that Marshal Tukey was in trouble. The newspapers chose up sides with spirit; the Whig *Mail* commented, "There is a great deal of feeling existing in this community in regard to the selection of a chief of police." The *Congregationalist* was outraged; linking Tukey's firing with a proliquor policy, it estimated that three-quarters of the city's businessmen and voters were for him. The *Mercantile Journal* made this "four-fifths of business men and legal voters," and the *Mail* put it at 90 per cent. When the job was finally given to Gilbert Nurse, a former councilman then serving as assistant clerk of the Faneuil Hall Market, even the *Bunker Hill Aurora* was disturbed. That paper had complained in June that "the city marshal was in a fair way to become the entire government," but it wondered in July whether any new man could match Tukey's achievements in office. And while most other journals were noncommittal, and some hostile, few could defend the administration's refusal to explain. The aldermen, on July 15, unanimously tabled Tukey's request for a public hearing.

With local candidates, still bent on ignoring more distant issues, it was natural that the Tukey affair should dominate the fall campaign. The regular or "partisan" Whigs renominated Seaver in December. The Democrats, with no more hope than usual, put up one of their own. And the combined opposition, organizing as the Citizens Union Party, chose Dr. J. C. V. Smith, three years earlier fired as physician of the Port of Boston and ever since an opponent of the dominant Whig faction. Smith had earlier found common cause with the Native Americans, but it was possible to claim him on several sides of the wider reform issues which troubled many of his supporters. The regular Whig newspapers regarded him as a puppet, and reserved their fire for ex-Marshal Tukey, "the Warwick of the Citizens' Movement."

A committee of aldermen, officially appointed to consider further reforms in the police department, was active throughout the campaign season. Although it did not formally report until the day after election, pro-administration papers did not wait to print their own versions of its findings. "The Great Caesar fell for his ambition," wrote the editor of the *Atlas,* "The Great Tukey, because, like the Sons of Levi, he took too much upon himself." The accompanying story condemned the marshal's questionable accounting methods and his secret auctions of unclaimed stolen property; it reminded readers of his frequent lawsuits and of the doubtful character of his night police. The editorial was especially outraged at his lust for power, his defiance in the McGinniskin case, his political use of the force, his evident intention to "run the city."

Direct accusations of this kind went far beyond the decorum which the papers ordinarily maintained in covering local elections. Together with an even more heated campaign of rumor, and the natural excitement surrounding the liquor issue, they made the canvass in 1852 the largest in the history of the city. The outcome was a triumph for the Whig strategy. Mayor Seaver, with the help of many Democrats, won a total of 6,018 votes, Dr. Smith 5,021, the regular Democrat 899.

The formal report of the aldermanic investigating committee, when released the next day, proved less personal and more significant than the newspaper accounts. It was couched as an argument against the then current proposal for a union of the watch and police. In warning against an undue concentration of power in the hands of a single man, it did mention that "the previous head of the department" had once interfered in local politics and had been heard to use profanity. But the bulk of the report was an impersonal defense of changes already made, of decreased expenses, annual appointments, and the abolition of the night force. Its central criticism of the earlier regime concerned not Tukey's integrity but his purpose and methods.

An undue and overpublicized emphasis on criminal law enforcement tended, in the opinion of the committee, to create a morbidly excitable public opinion. The amount of crime in the city could easily be exaggerated, damaging its reputation. Large numbers of those arrested were visitors seeking excitement. The police had earlier been overzealous, pursuing offenders beyond the city and even out of the country, while the watch had in recent months without theatrics quietly reduced the incidence of burglary. The main business of the chief and his men, the report concluded, was the enforcement of the city's own rules and ordinances, and they should concentrate less on roguery and more on the removal of obstructions from the streets. "The police, while it should be argus-eyed, seing all things, should be itself unseen and unobserved."

On the day this report was delivered, the former marshal also appeared before the board with a formal claim of election fraud. While this was rejected, he was given a final chance to redeem his reputation. An alderman's death created a vacancy on the board, and it was necessary to call a special election on February 1. The Whigs nominated Sampson Reed, a member of the outgoing board and principal author of the report on the police. The Citizens, in January, countered with Tukey himself. With both men running at large, the anti-Tukey campaign lost none of its fervor. And this time it was aimed at the most sensitive aspect of the police business. The marshal had been accused before of dictatorial ends and methods; now he was accused of personal and professional immorality, of compounding felonies, possible bribery, and "abetting with rogues."

To answer his critics, the Citizens' candidate on the Friday night before the election held a mass meeting in the historic forum at Faneuil Hall. Ushered in to a "perfect storm of applause, mingled with hisses, catcalls, unearthly yells and sounds infernal," he maintained a cool command of the packed house despite constant interruptions, "great merriment," "laughter," cries of "pickpockets!" and "Barney!" And he proceeded, with occasional difficulties, to make his case.

Tukey disposed of the older charges in the familiar way. He had never denied his role in the 1851 elections or his hostility to Barney McGinniskin. He only regretted in both cases that he had been betrayed. In one he had been battling political partisanship, in the other the appointment of a convicted rioter. His audience had heard it all before. What they had come for, knowing the marshal's gift for invective, was his arraignment of the clique of aldermen who ran the ruling Whig machine.

The talk lived up to expectations. He had been accused, Tukey noted, of living rent free in the house of a gambler. In fact he owned his own home—but certain members of the city council lived in a West End bawdy house, and there were others "whose family relations have been to this city, and tried to bargain with burglars to break open the bank in the towns where they live." There had been talk of the "misuse of obscene books and prints—when they or some of their supporters were always the first callers for any such . . . as were taken by the police." "They" had accused him of profanity, whereas "they can go into a house of ill-fame in the city of New York, and set in it with a prostitute on one knee, with one arm around her waist, and the other holding a glass of champagne at the expense of the City of Boston. (Laughter and shouts)." "These things are facts and I know it, for I was in New York City with them. (Great merriment)." His opponent was "an honest old fogy," the marshal concluded, but it was time for a change: "Some members of the city government had been in city hall so long that their seats stank. (Laughter and shouts)."

It was a grand performance, but largely irrelevant to the main charge, that of malfeasance in office, first by misappropriating money and second by "abetting with rogues." Tukey's defense here was more reasoned and careful than his flamboyant countercharges. As to the first, the mayor had authorized the auction of stolen goods unclaimed after a year. He had kept books, and the money had gone to a charity administered by the police. The second charge the marshal freely admitted. He was proud in some cases to have saved reputations by failure to prosecute for panel thieving. In others he was ordered not to. And in more important cases, this was simply the system; he mentioned several in which the district attorney, the sheriff, or some other official had interfered on behalf of a victim seeking to recover his property. "Such bargaining is right and cannot be helped."

The voters next Monday had a unique chance to pass judgment upon this defense and the whole system of police administration under Tukey. And the judgment was unmistakable. The December election had been close; the special election resulted in 4,936 votes for Reed, 2,354 for Tukey, and 620 for the Democrat. The defeated candidate, in humiliation, quit the city to try his energies in the bold new State of California.

Between 1846 and 1853 the city had had its first experience with a tough cop. And after the initial period of hope and excitement it had clearly rejected that experience. The February vote signaled more than a personal repudiation of Marshal Tukey. The duties of police in general and of the marshal in particular had been growing steadily. While the emphasis had shifted from the original concern for internal health, only the superintendence of sewers had been subtracted from the marshal's responsibilities, and a host had been added. Neither the legislature nor the courts had intervened in the process. The citizens and their local representatives had voluntarily used the police to the utmost, raising their expenditures in every year between 1838 and Seaver's election in 1852. But by mid-century there was an apparent desire for a check.

A number of administrative reforms were needed. Equally important, the police had to be confined within limits which would not antagonize any substantial sections of the community. There had been little trouble in an earlier period, under a system of popular administration. In the 1820's and early 1830's the peace officers of the city had dealt only with those who had injured a specific complainant, or with a voiceless class of unfortunates. But the growth of the city had made the system of private complaints by itself obsolescent, so that it was necessary for the police to take the initiative. At the same time new duties brought them into contact with a larger proportion of citizens. A continuing revolution in politics and social attitudes, added to the older one in publishing, was beginning to give voice to the class which filled the watchhouses and jails.

The new organization of police made it possible for the first time in generations to attempt a wide enforcement of the criminal code, especially the vice laws. But while the earlier lack of execution was largely the result of weakness, it had served a useful function also, as part of the system of compromise which made the law tolerable. Even the ordinances were often resented where applied. And especially in a time of severe political tension, there was need for caution in enforcement.

By 1853 the city had had fifteen years of experience with the new police. The government during that time had been controlled by both reformers and conservatives. And both groups had found that a vigorous police was in itself no solution to their problems. The force employed in raiding a barroom might be used again in guarding fugitives. The department needed strength in order to maintain the peace, protect property, and alleviate misery in a city still swelling with immigration. But it also needed discretion, in order to serve as a buffer between the literal demands of the law and the desires of the citizens.

Establishing a Full Range of Urban Services
Bayrd Still*

At the outset of cityhood, Milwaukee, like most of her sister cities of the Great Lakes area, was in what might be called the "subscription stage" of her municipal career. Just as the cultural opportunities available in the city were made possible by the subscriptions of interested citizens, so most of its urban services resulted from the sense of individual responsibility that also had prompted widespread local investment in the railroads and factories that were expected to advance the city's growth. Two or three days' work on the streets, a duty which now could be commuted at the rate of 75 cents a day, was expected of all able-bodied men. Street and sidewalk improvements as well as the eradication of nuisances were to be taken care of individually or charged against the property benefited. The average home had its own provisions for water supply and waste disposal. A city marshal and ward constables, elected by the people, were available to enforce the law; but many citizens undertook to guard their own persons and possessions. Some property owners employed private watchmen, and as late as 1855, when an ordinance was passed compelling all citizens to aid the police if called upon to do so, many residents still resorted to carrying their own weapons. Fire protection was left to companies of volunteers who, on occasion, turned policemen and helped maintain the peace when riot or disorder went beyond the capacity of the mayor or marshal to suppress. By the close of the first generation of city-

hood, however, this tradition of municipal "self-help" was giving way to a specialization in urban administration which developments in science and increased wealth encouraged and which the growth of population and its attendant problems made inevitable. Moreover, by that time the suspicions which had long existed between the wards and the nationalities had begun to wane; and the public had less fear that city-wide municipal institutions would come under "political" or "foreign" control. As a result, by 1870, regularized police protection, a semiprofessional fire department, systematic relief organizations, corporate-owned urban transit, and the creation of a city-wide board of public works charged with the development of streets and sewers were but a few indications that corporate enterprise or the municipality itself were beginning to accept a responsibility to do for the community as a whole what hitherto had been accomplished with increasing difficulty by the voluntary efforts and subscriptions of its public-minded citizenry.

Fear of fire as well as of the burglaries and disorders common to lake shore cities prompted pressure for improved police facilities by the turn of the fifties. In April 1850 the *Sentinel* called attention to the inadequacy of a police that consisted of only the marshal, ward constables, and two or three watchmen employed in as many wards. "The watch should be a matter of general city regulation," the editor wrote; "and their number should be increased." On the occasion of riots in the early fifties, the mayor had to call upon the volunteer firemen to guarantee order. Finally, an ordinance, passed

*Reprinted with permission from Bayrd Still, *Milwaukee: The History of a City*, Madison: The State Historical Society of Wisconsin, 1948, 230–253.

in January 1852 and effective only until the following April, provided for fifteen night watchmen to be paid out of the general city fund. In addition to arresting violators of the peace, they were to watch for fires and wake the occupants of a burning house, their cry of fire and the number of the ward to be repeated by the other watchmen. A series of thefts, murders, and incendiary fires in 1855 led the newspapers, the board of trade, and the principal property owners and merchants to urge the establishment of police facilities that would provide more continuous protection than was afforded by ward constables or a paid night watch. As a result, a police department was formally established on September 10, 1855. Five Germans, three Irishmen, and four Americans constituted the force—one patrolman for every 3,000 inhabitants. Its first chief was William Beck, a farmer from the neighboring town of Granville who, after migrating from Germany, had become a member of the New York constabulary. The chief, to be appointed by the mayor and council, was to receive $800, later $1,500, a year. Compensation of the policemen, who were appointed by the mayor and chief, rose from $30 a month, at the outset, to $50 a month in the following year. Beck, who contended that it was necessary "to whip a man in a fair fight before you could arrest him," imposed strict standards of discipline on the young patrol; and it speedily brought order to what had been an increasingly unruly community. As early as 1856, when the police were urged to wear their badges conspicuously, there was an attempt to differentiate the representatives of law and order from the other members of the community; but although uniform dress was prescribed as early as 1859, it was apparently not achieved until 1874.

Retrenchment after the panic of 1857 caused a reduction in the department; and, as a result, the inadequacy of police protection was criticized throughout the ensuing decade. In 1865 the *Sentinel* complained that charter limitations accounted for a situation which restricted Milwaukee to one patrolman for every 3,000 inhabitants, whereas the ratio "in nearly every other city of the Union" was one to 1,000. A metropolitan police bill, proposed in 1864, might have given impulse to reform; but it was opposed by the party then in control of the city. Relief came in 1866 when the municipality was authorized to double salaries and increase personnel. By the close of the decade the number of patrolmen was twice what it had been in 1861. The forty-two men on the force represented one to every 1,700 citizens and were such a guarantee of order that Mayor O'Neill could boast in 1869 that Milwaukee was the "most orderly city on the continent."

City growth also brought the substitution of professional fire fighting in the sixties for the volunteer methods that had prevailed in the first years of cityhood. The charter of 1846 had provided for democratically organized fire companies formed of volunteers who should be exempted from highway labor and military duty; but every householder was to have two buckets ready in case of emergency; and during fires, the mayor, aldermen, and citizens in general were expected to lend a hand. The prevalence of the fire hazard kept the question of protection constantly before the council; and the forties and fifties saw repeated criticism of its failure to supply the companies with adequate equipment and to allow them freedom to choose their officers. Destructive fires in the business district led to the ruling that "no *wooden* buildings should be permitted to be erected again in that part of the city" and later to prohibitions upon the deposit of ashes, carrying of fire in the streets, setting off fireworks near buildings, and using unenclosed candles in livery stables. At the same time, regulations were enacted to prevent chimneys, hearths, ovens, boilers, and the like from causing fire.

Throughout the fifties the city's leading businessmen continued to participate actively in the fire-fighting function and the volunteer fire companies to be supported by civic subscription as well as public funds. The roster of a sack company, organized in September 1851, constituted a list of the city's most "solid citizens." On it were Lynde, Prentiss, Mitchell, Blossom, Kilbourn, H. and J. Ludington, Sweet, Rogers, Sexton, Holton, White, Bielfeld, Walker, Lapham, Noonan, James Kneeland, and many others. The members of the company, each vested with the powers of a special constable, were to act as special police at all fires, carrying white canvas sacks and staves and taking charge of exposed property. In 1853, a Chicagoan contrasted the fire departments of the cities in the East with that of Milwaukee where "the best citizens and most respectable business men are members." Through benefit concerts and dances, funds were raised to supplement the city's support of the Ocean, Neptune, and Cataract companies and their disabled members. The report of the department's treasurer for 1851 revealed that the year's donations from individuals and business houses had totaled $1,955, a benefit concert had netted $483.56, initiation fees had brought in $58, and $25 had been paid out for relief. In 1852 the city's contribution to fire protection was $4,409.48; the department paid out about $225 of its funds, retaining the rest to be loaned at interest.

A lack of volunteers in 1852 made it look as if the pay system, to which the city of St. Louis had resorted in 1851, might have to be adopted, and only a campaign for volunteers and the the the council's promise to act more speedily than in the past upon the department's bills for equipment postponed this development. Somewhat later, however, the press was regretting the misplaced liberality of citizens who offered money and distributed brandy and beer by the pailful to the firemen during fires, a generosity which paralyzed the efforts of half of the department at a destructive fire in 1854. But modern invention, as well as the expansion of the city and the lack of zealous recruits, was shortly to bring the volunteer system to an end. The example of other large cities of the West, whose officials were investigating the use of steam fire engines in the late fifties, and the destruction caused by serious fires on the turn of the sixties prompted the purchase of a steam fire engine, costing $3,500, which arrived on November 6, 1861. Christened the "Solomon Juneau," it was escorted to the Newhall House by members of the fire department and a brass band; and there its ability to throw a stream of water 25 feet above the building was soon demonstrated. Since the new engine prevented competition with companies lacking such equipment and required more mechanical training to operate than the average businessman could boast, the advent of the "Solomon Juneau" marked the decline of volunteer fire fighting, a trend which the manpower demands of the Civil War and the increasing size of the city had already begun to bring about. Engine Company No. 1 held its last meeting on April 3, 1863; firemen giving half-time service had been receiving wages since November 1861; and when they were put on full time and full pay in the early seventies the day of the self-governing volunteer department, composed of men of means and influence, was over. Municipal expenditures for fire protection increased from $9,388.-69 in 1861 to $45,272.59 in 1870.

Apart from a meager and inadequate tax to support almshouses and furnish medical care for the sick poor, urban relief in this period of the city's history was supplied through subscription and personal benevolence. Especially during the cessation of navigation there were insistent pleas for community aid, and according to Mayor Upham private enterprise was best equipped to meet the demand. The Ladies' Benevolent Society, headed in 1849 by Mrs. A. D. Smith and Mrs. W. P. Lynde, solicited gifts and organized benefit concerts and donation parties. Late in 1855, the Milwaukee Relief Society, patterned after similar institutions in certain other large cities, was organized to systematize collections. During 1856 its receipts were $1,052.33, of which $1,046.10 was disbursed. The "hard times" following 1857 brought increased demands for relief. Soup-kitchens were subsidized by private gifts, and meal tickets were sold to residents who might wish to offer them to the poor. The managers of the society trusted "to the benevolence of our citizens for the food to be supplied." In January 1858, they were taking care of about 720 individuals; and applicants to the soup house numbered from 200 to 220 daily. An association for the relief of the German poor in the city had been organized in November 1857.

During the sixties, the relief problems normally attending the cessation of navigation were complicated by the destitution of the families of soldiers participating in the Civil War. Each winter saw the organization of a relief society, variously called the Milwau-kee Relief Society or the Provident Association. Headed by C. A. Staples, it was designed to do away with street begging and to systematize the collection of funds and the investigation of needy cases through the services of ward committees and two paid agents. Provisions, wood, and small amounts of tea, sugar, soap, and candles were distributed to the poor. Subscriptions, drawn from the Chamber of Commerce and from a canvass of merchants and citizens, netted from $6,000 to $8,000 yearly; and from 350 to 750 families a season were given aid. In addition to this systematic but voluntary city-wide charity, upon which the community as a whole put the responsibility of dispensing its benevolence, other enterprises depended upon subscriptions from the charitable. Among these were the Milwaukee Hospital, founded by Dr. W. A. Passavant in 1863, St. Mary's Hospital, St. Rose's Orphan Asylum, the Milwaukee Orphan Asylum, established by the Ladies' Benevolent Society and partly subsidized by the council, the Home of the Friendless, opened in 1867, the Hebrew Relief Society, founded in the same year, and the Union Bethel Mission societies.

While many community responsibilities were at the outset left to the initiative of volunteers, the municipality did assume some obligations with respect to the physical appearance of the city and the health and welfare of its citizens. In the main, however, this was confined to authorizing action which the citizens were forced to carry out. In this the council was only imitating the practice of the other cities of the Great Lakes area. A major problem during the first generation of cityhood was the grading and construction of the streets and sidewalks needed in a community hewn from the wilderness. Although ward taxes were levied for this work, from two-thirds to three-fourths of the cost was borne by the owners of the property benefited. Planks and bricks were the customary materials for sidewalk construction in the forties, but by the fifties there was agitation for the use of stone rather than wood. By the close of 1852, disillusionment with the continued graveling of East Water Street, the city's "principal business thoroughfare," brought the suggestion that the street be planked, a method of street improvement that had been "thoroughly tested in Chicago and Cleveland," and was then "undergoing a most successful trial on Third Street" in Milwaukee. The flagstone pavement laid by Guido Pfister and the firm of Sexton and Wing in front of their stores in 1853 provided an example which the press hoped other merchants would emulate. Shortly thereafter, and over the protests of many of the property holders, the council ordered the construction of a costly limestone pavement on East Water Street which promised to be "the most comfortable and durable piece of pavement in the West." A marked increase in projects for street improvement coincided with the aldermen's assumption of the office of street commissioner under the charter of 1852, and in spite of Mayor Cross's counsel of economy, the expenditure of nearly $900,000 for highway purposes was authorized in the expansive middle fifties. This concern for street improvement out of all proportion to other urban services may be explained by the personal interest of members of the council in the contracts, a situation which led to accusations that the aldermen and councilors were improving streets to the advantage of their own property, ordering work done where it was not needed in order to make jobs, and letting contracts on adjoining streets at prices varying

from 50 cents to $1.70 per yard. The collapse of 1857 brought street and bridge construction to a halt. Relatively little new work was done in the sixties and then only when the property owners petitioned to have it. Nicholson pavement was laid on East Water Street in the summer of 1863, and shortly thereafter the press began to suggest that the city at large, rather than the lot owners, should bear the expense of improving the principal thoroughfares, since "the city at large" was "benefitted by all this traffic and travel." In 1869 the responsibility for street improvement was transferred from the council to the board of public works. The Gas Company held the concession for street lighting in the sixties.

Concern for the cleanliness of the streets was a major consideration behind the proposals for types of pavement which would be durable, clean, less destructive of the health of horses, and at the same time free of the "clattering, banging noise" that, according to the editor, "shocks our nerves during the day and robs us of sleep during the night." Street sprinkling was done on a subscription basis in the early fifties; by the late sixties the primitive methods, wherein the streets were moistened by swinging a huge tin watering pot from side to side, had given way to the barrel on wheels; and the improved rotary sprinkler, in use in Philadelphia, was being suggested. As early as 1856 the council had attempted to prevent citizens from throwing garbage in the streets, but it took police regulations in 1866, requiring householders to keep their cellars and lots clean, to achieve the desired results; and even then it was deemed impossible to compel every housekeeper to keep a waste barrel as was done in some cities of the Union.

Cleanliness of the streets was related less to aesthetic considerations than to a problem which gave the civic officials great concern in the mid-century, and that was the question of public health. For community health was regarded not only as of importance to the individual but also as a major factor in inducing the flow of immigration and business to the city. Hence the city fathers did their best both to protect the citizens against diseases that immigrants might bring and, what was almost more important, to minimize rumors of sickness that would affect the city's reputation abroad. Thus the press was accused of advertising Milwaukee as "a plague-stricken city" when it reported the existence of smallpox in 1846. From the point of view of the citizens, the regulations in the interest of the public health were reluctantly accepted encroachments upon the traditional liberty of the individual. Compulsory vaccination against smallpox in 1847 prompted charges that the measure violated natural rights. According to one of the unsuccessful opponents of the measure in the city council, "A Nero might pass such a law, but it would disgrace a body of freemen to do so." In the years of the dread cholera epidemic, prohibitions were placed on the accumulation of "garbage or filth . . . to poison the atmosphere," a precaution prompted by the theory that cholera was not a contagious but an atmospheric disease, produced by impure air. An elaborate ordinance, passed in September 1846, and substantially repeated in 1855, created a board of health, empowered to investigate the cause of disease, order the removal of nuisances, and provide a pesthouse. Steamship captains and stage drivers were to be fined $50 for bringing into the city passengers who had been sick at the outset of a voyage. Harbor masters were to inspect migrants for contagious diseases; and bystanders were obliged, on pain of fine, to prevent such passengers from landing.

Despite the precaution of cleaning the streets and purifying the gutters with lime, undertaken both by the city and by the citizenry, as an individual responsibility, in the years of heavy migration—1849, 1850, and to some extent in 1854—cholera took a heavy toll. The press was concerned that honest figures be given lest rumor magnify the numbers. It took Chicago newspapers to task in 1850 for "shameful" misrepresentation. In 1852 the *Sentinel* was at pains to point out that, slander of eastern editors to the contrary, the city was "distressingly healthy (for the doctors)." The fear of cholera, and later of smallpox, continued during the sixties to be the major motivation for measures enforcing clean-up campaigns and the removal of slaughter houses beyond the city limits. In general, the mayor and council constituted the board of health until the late sixties; but in 1867 the State legislature authorized the appointment of a separate board of health, and Dr. James Johnson became the city's first health officer. This board went systematically to work to abate nuisances and regulate slaughter houses with the result that sanitary improvement was speedily achieved.

By the middle fifties the concern for city health had given rise to agitation for a "thorough system of sewerage for the city." This became imperative with the developing congestion of the business district, where the primitive methods of waste disposal, used in less populous parts of the city, could not be followed. Large sums of money had been expended for wooden sewers in the various wards before adequate consideration was given to the need of a city-wide system. In 1858, a correspondent to the *Sentinel,* apprising Milwaukee of "the results obtained in other cities," came to the conclusion that sewers should be of brick and pottery; that the cost should be assessed against the lots; and that the work could be better done by three commissioners than by the street commissioners of the several wards. In 1863 Mayor O'Neill called attention to the need of sewers, and construction was begun in the Second and Fifth wards; but from complaints made of "the streams of liquid filth" detected on Wisconsin Street in 1865 it appears that reform was slow to be accomplished. By the late sixties most of the citizens were convinced that a "complete and harmonious system" of sewerage "throughout the whole city" was needed. In 1866 the legislature created a short-lived sewerage commission; but since this became involved in a political quarrel between the State legislature and the city authorities, the board of public works, created in 1869, was left to develop an adequate disposal system in succeeding years.

In the early years of cityhood, the corporation assumed little responsibility for the aesthetic or recreational side of urban life. The ornamental value of shade trees was recognized as early as 1847, but it was expected that every lot owner would see his duty and plant some. As for parks, although a park or public promenade was suggested as early as 1848, the commercial public gardens of Lackner, Bielfeld, and others and the many unenclosed spaces within the limits of the community were thought sufficient to the need. By the middle sixties, however, less open space for recreation was available, and few grounds within the city remained unoccupied. A proposal for ward parks in 1859 came to nothing; but by the late sixties, the citizens, stimulated by park construction in New York, Cleveland, and Detroit, began to look favorably upon the development of a lake park,

"so located as to be accessible to those who cannot afford to go into the country for their recreation." Legislative permission was granted in 1868, and the park was constructed from Division to Biddle streets. Mayor O'Neill's inaugural admonition in 1869 to assume the "duties . . . of a metropolitan city" stressed the need of public parks which would "afford our citizens a place of healthy and innocent recreation." He recommended the acquisition of a rural park and the improvement of single squares within the wards.

Inspired in part by concern for an adequate food and fuel supply and in part by the traditional behavior of older urban communities, the city government early attempted to regulate the local economy in ways similar to those which had been employed since colonial times, and indeed even since the Middle Ages, to insure the self-sufficiency of the urban unit. Kilbourn donated land for a public market— thought essential to guarantee a sufficient supply of food, fodder, and firewood for a community in which potential scarcity might breed monopolistic, unsanitary, or fraudulent practices; and the construction of a market house, decided upon by 1847, was completed in 1850 after months of wrangling among the wards. The example of the older cities was followed in the enactment of ordinances compelling vendors of fresh meat, poultry, eggs, butter, lard, fruit, and vegetables to sell their goods at the public market during market hours unless licensed to do otherwise; prohibiting the pitching of quoits, the presence of dogs, and the use of obscene language in the market place; and forbidding the purchase of goods at the market for resale or the forestalling of country producers to buy their goods for the same purpose. Apparently these regulations were not strictly enforced, for by the late sixties there was renewed agitation for more systematic market legislation. A correspondent to the *Sentinel* cited the experience of other large cities where vendors of produce were compelled to observe market restrictions and contended that regulations which appeared to be violations of freedom of trade were necessary to preserve the public from fraud and extortion. It was "an important matter that . . . large cities should be supplied with fresh and wholesome provisions and vegetables," he wrote. Leniency in this respect might breed "disease and ravaging plague." A market ordinance, enacted in October 1869, applied to all markets in the city and authorized thoroughgoing regulation and inspection.

A corollary regulation of urban merchandising led to ordinances enacted in the late forties and early fifties for the supervision of weights and measures in the purchase of boards, bricks, coal, casks, hay, flour, tobacco, potash, and salted provisions such as fish—restrictions which in some quarters were opposed as unsound in principle, "whatever the regulations of other cities 'down East' or 'out West.'" In 1859 the farmers in the vicinity opposed as an inequitable tax the weighing charge of 5 cents per load of wood and 25 cents per load of hay—a concession sold by the city to the highest bidder. According to the assize of bread, decreed by ordinance in 1846, the weight of the loaf and the initials of the baker were to be indicated on each loaf of bread.

An attempt to deal with the confusions attending the increase in population led to laws against undue noise, street obstructions, and "speeding." Ordinances were passed in 1846 and 1852 prohibiting the use of bells, cries, drums, and fifes at auctions and disturbances of the peace by runners and solicitors for boats, railroads, or public houses. The citizens were forbidden to clutter the sidewalks with rubbish, lumber, or merchandise or to leave horses unfastened in the streets. One of the first acts of the city council was to ban all "signs, boxes, barrels, barber poles, big pitchers, big hats, big boots, etc." from the curbstones of the sidewalks. Ten years later, in an effort to regulate traffic, it was decreed that horses were not to be driven faster than at a "moderate trot" in the streets or at more than a "walk" at crossings, on penalty of $5.00 for every offense. Apparently the traffic regulations were enforced, for in April 1854, Thomas Dunn was fined $5.00 for driving his horse faster than at a walk on the Spring Street bridge. After the fashion of traffic violators, he asserted: "Well, it's a pretty good way to get a bridge built anyhow, . . . but it's all a poor man can do now to earn oats for his horse." John Bowers, fined a similar sum for reckless driving in 1858, claimed that his horse was a "high-blood English animal" and "no man under the sun" could make him go slow unless he had a mind to. The first appearance of the velocipede or bicycle—hailed in 1869 as heralding a new era in Milwaukee history—brought an additional traffic hazard; but for the time being the new device was given the fredom of the sidewalk.

In spite of prohibitions passed during the village period, the running at large of swine, cattle, and other stray animals and fowls was a continuing reminder of the erstwhile agrarianism of the community. Ordinances were enacted from the year of cityhood forward, but stray animals remained a destructive urban nuisance. Disregarding the complaints of a citizen whose daughter had barely escaped injury from a savage old sow on the corners of Main and Division streets, many Irish residents, supported by Tim O'Brien, the city marshal, demanded the liberty of the streets for their animals. A mass meeting held at the Albany Hall on July 13, 1859, was the first real blast against the cows and hogs; and it was followed by a one-man crusade in which Caleb Wall, city auctioneer, finally shamed the council into correction of the nuisance.

Certain pursuits related to the public welfare were regulated, especially if in the practice of them the reputation of the city were involved. The operation of hackney coaches was controlled as to licenses and rates; and interest in attracting immigrants prompted an ordinance of May 3, 1849, which fixed a maximum charge of 10 cents an article on the goods of passengers landed on the piers of the city. The regulations and restrictions in the interest of urban order were probably variously enforced and did not work as great an interference with the liberty of the individual as their existence on the statute books would imply. Indeed, as has already been suggested, some of the ordinances were undoubtedly enacted more in compliance with charter provisions copied from the constitutional framework of other cities than out of immediate concern for the reform. From the middle fifties forward, however, as the growth of the city made necessary an adjustment to increased population and commercial specialization, there was undoubtedly greater interest in enforcing the restrictions that promised to promote a more orderly community life. Proof of this is found in the statistics of arrests under such headings: for 1854, 238; 1860, 211; 1861, 119; and 1864, 236.

As the community matured, and science and industry offered solutions to its problems which the results of voluntary association could not match, private corporate enterprise began to replace individual subscription in meeting urban needs. This was true in connection with the improvement of facilities for street lighting, a city water supply, and urban transit. By the fall of 1849, George F. Lee of Philadelphia, soliciting stock subscriptions for a proposed local gas works, had convinced Milwaukeeans of the "superior cheapness, convenience, and brilliancy of Gas Lights to all other means of lighting Streets, Stores, and Dwellings"; and the *Sentinel* lent its support by refuting all claims that gas light was "too costly a luxury for so young a city as Milwaukee." Lee's plan gained the approval of the council, but delays forced it to lapse; and it was not until two years later that the work was undertaken by John Lockwood on behalf of the Milwaukee Gas Light Company, chartered on January 3, 1852. Two of the trustees of the new company—James H. Rogers and William P. Lynde—had been members of the council while Lee's plan was subject to "delay." Alexander Mitchell became one of the directors and Rogers, president. The company was to build the works and fixtures at its own expense; in return the city was to guarantee it the exclusive right to supply the city with gas illumination for fifteen years at a cost of not more than $2.50 a thousand feet.

Lockwood, who was to figure significantly in the development of Milwaukee's public works, was well equipped to direct the enterprise. He had spent the preceding six years building similar plants in Ohio, Kentucky, and Indiana. A preliminary mishap blew out one side of the gas works, but when the city was lighted for the first time on November 23, 1852, Young's Hall was reported to be a "blaze of light" and there was "brilliant illumination in the streets." By February 1857, seven miles of pipe had been laid, and five more were promised for the ensuing year. Already, the stock, owned principally in Troy, New York, was paying excellent dividends. The complaints of George Dyer in May of 1856 led to the decision that the company, "though a private corporation," was affected with a public interest and must supply gas on demand. Attempts to incorporate a competitive enterprise were quashed in 1857, but in 1858 there was agitation to see that the city and its citizens were getting their money's worth. In 1859 publicity was given to the fact that the city of Philadelphia owned its gas works.

Less successful were the persistent efforts to achieve an adequate water supply by constructing a pumping works that would make drinking water available from the lake. Public cisterns provided no security in case of fire, and both public and private wells were contaminated by sewage. In the business district one had to walk half a mile to find a pump and then risk his health in drinking the water. On the turn of the sixties many families were resorting to the use of rain water filtered from their cisterns. Private capital, organized as the Lake Michigan Hydraulic Company, stood ready to build a pumping plant, if either the citizens or the city would subscribe to a share of the stock. In 1851, Lockwood, acting for the company, negotiated a contract with the city; but since the popular imagination was obsessed at the moment with railroad promotion, the required subsidy of $75,000 failed to materialize. The *Sentinel,* charged by the *Free Democrat* with having a pecuniary interest in the enterprise, continued to agitate, stressing especially the importance of waterworks in time of fire. A second organization, the Milwaukee Hydraulic Company, of which J. H. Rogers was one of the incorporators, carried negotiations to the point where bonds were issued by the council in 1857; but this plan, too, miscarried. During the decade between 1857 and 1867, a number of proposals were put forward in public meetings, but nothing came of them. By 1867, New York, Philadelphia, and Cincinnati capitalists were canvassing the situation; and in the following year the council authorized E. S. Chesbrough, city engineer of Chicago, to make preliminary plans. By 1871, the city's financial situation warranted its undertaking the work, and a board of water commissioners, headed by Alexander Mitchell, began to supervise construction at public expense. City water was available in November 1873.

In the decade of the sixties Milwaukee had its first experience with horse railroads—"as much a necessity for busy and growing cities," according to the editor of the *Sentinel,* "as is a Fire Department, or Gas, or Water Works." Agitation for the new mode of urban transit began in the summer of 1859, when George H. Walker, Dr. L. W. Weeks, W. S. Johnson, F. S. Blodgett, and G. D. Davis petitioned the council for permission to lay tracks and operate the River and Lake Shore City Railway Company through the streets of the First, Third, and Seventh wards. Opponents of the proposal objected to such a use of the public thoroughfares without exacting a license fee or consulting the owners of adjoining property; but its advocates won their point by asserting that the citizens of Chicago, St. Louis, and Cincinnati were already enjoying this mode of travel, that in Cleveland construction was under way, and that any city without it would be "regarded by travelers as . . . decidedly behind the age." As a result, on May 30, 1860, crowds lined the streets as two blue and buff vehicles, each drawn by four horses, made their first trip from what is now the North Water Street bridge to East Juneau Avenue. Within the year, new rails were added, and the rolling stock was increased.

The plan for the West Side Passenger Railway Company, incorporated in November 1859 for operation in the Second, Fourth, Fifth, Sixth, Eighth, and Ninth wards, collapsed in ward politics; but the success of the original horse-car enterprise led to a wave of petitions for additional companies. Among them were the West Water Street Horse Railway Company and the Cold Spring City Railway Company, whose incorporators included Alexander Mitchell, Hans Crocker, C. D. Davis, E. B. Wolcott, and O. Alexander. The advent of the Civil War prevented these lines from being built. At its close, the council was open-handed in the privileges it granted to John Plankinton, Frederick Layton, Samuel Marshall, and Charles F. Ilsley, when they organized the Milwaukee City Railway Company in 1865; but the enterprise was never financially very successful. In 1866 an increase in fares from 5 to 6 cents was under criticism, and the press was making the practical suggestion that the cars be marked to indicate their destination. A decline in profits in the late sixties led both the Lake Shore and the Milwaukee City companies to sell out their franchises, rights, and properties to Isaac Ellsworth, who ultimately restored the business to a paying basis.

It was the problems presented by the desire for large-scale public works that led, as has already been indicated, to the substitution of an appointed administrative board for the untrained, politically chosen, and easily corruptible ward officers who hitherto had managed the development of municipal improvements. The creation of a public debt commission in 1861 began

a practice which prompted agitation throughout the ensuing decade to extend the use of administrative boards to other urban problems. The metropolitan police bill, proposed in 1864 but defeated through the play of politics, would have given control of all matters relating to police, fire, and health to a board including the mayor and three other persons appointed by the governor and senate. A short-lived sewerage commission, appointed in 1866, and a separate, mayor-appointed board of health, authorized in 1867, preceded the creation of the board of public works in 1869. This board, to be appointed by the mayor, with the consent of a majority of the council, was given general control over streets, sewers, bridges, sidewalks, wharves, and public buildings in all parts of the city. The replacement of interested ward councilors by presumed specialists marked some advance in municipal administration but it did not do much to overcome the disintegration of the city's administrative organization or to enhance the executive strength of the mayor, the weakness of whose position was to be a continuing characteristic of the city's constitutional structure.

While the realization of a city-wide board of public works was most significant for its promise of an increasingly professionalized and less self-interested approach in the administration of the problems of the emerging metropolis, it was not without meaning as a sign of the long-awaited triumph of the "city" over the "ward" point of view. And there were smaller, but no less suggestive indications of the city's impending metropolitan stature. One was the "never ceasing and ever increasing influx . . . of families from the rural districts," which according to the *Sentinel,* swelled the great mass of young men and women "flocking to learn the tricks and trades of city life." Another was the resort to apartment and boarding house living until the "number of boarders" who could be "stowed away on a given area of floor room and the amount of food required to supply a given number of stomachs" were reported to be "cyphered down to the smallest possible point by the genius of boarding house proprietors." And finally, there was evidence that Milwaukee was beginning to feel her age and sense her history. An Old Settlers' Club was founded on July 5, 1869; and late December of that year saw the first annual supper of the Milwaukee Pioneer Club. A toast proposed on this occasion revealed the community's awareness of the accomplishments of the short generation which had brought the metropolis into view:

> Milwaukee City: Here she is. Look at her—her capacious harbor, her yellow brick, her stately elevators, warehouses and stores, and her palatial private residences; the emporium of the state; the greatest wheat market of the continent; the home of industry, social refinement, public order and peace; and all the solid growth of thirty-five years.

The generation from 1846 to the turn of the seventies was a period of transition in Milwaukee's urban life, a period in which a village was accommodating itself to city ways. The community was a bifurcated society throughout the period, in the sense that the populous and self-assertive *Deutsch-Athen,* with its German theater, schools, newspapers, fire and military companies, relief societies, and baseball team, paralleling those of the English-speaking residents, existed coordinately beside the American community within the frame of the developing city. It was a time in which personal promotion was largely responsible for the city's development, and voluntary association and subscription the means of meeting the community's needs. In a sense, this generation was the age of Mitchell, Kilbourn, Rogers, Holton, Huebschmann, and the other vigorous individuals who took a personal responsibility for nurturing and cultivating the city's growth. Alexander Mitchell pushed to corporate magnitude the railroad enterprise whose promotion had been the climax of Kilbourn's speculative career; and his business acumen, together with that of men like Rogers and Holton, fostered the commercial and corporate wealth of the community. Huebschmann represented the participation and contribution of transplanted Europeanism at its best, and Rufus King had a hand in every scheme for cultural, industrial, or municipal improvement, using the columns of the *Sentinel* to goad the citizenry to achieve their metropolitan destiny. Men of self-made wealth, the "solid citizens" of this period played an active role in the political and economic life of the expanding city, conscious of their obligation to promote its good as well as aware of the profits to be gained from encouraging its growth.

Fluctuations of the business cycle had significant effect upon the developing community; hence, the boom years of the middle fifties permitted an expansion and accomplishment along all lines, which, together with the timely completion of harbor improvement and railroad connections to the Mississippi, gave Milwaukee an impetus to cityhood which later depression could not check and which only because of its more advantageous geographical position Chicago could surpass. At last, the expansion of both the population and the physical limits of the city resulted in an inevitable trend toward city ways. In the things of the spirit as well as in the management of municipal problems the amateur was beginning to give way to the professional. In the early part of the period the existence of truly professional services was a matter of chance. The artist Vianden, the musician Balatka, the educator Engelmann, and Chief Beck of the police department all had hoped to become farmers; but the growing urban community provided a more congenial outlet for their abilities, and they in turn made a "chance" contribution to the specialization of its society. By the close of the period, the opportunity to gratify the higher tastes was less haphazard than at the outset, and disillusionment with management by the "average man" was prompting a resort to somewhat more specialized and professional administration of municipal government. The need of city-wide improvements and the magnitude of the municipal undertakings of the seventies did much to destroy the ward separatism of the Middle Period. But more important was the fact that a new generation was beginning to identify itself with the city as a whole rather than with one of its formerly "provincial" parts. The "lure of the city" was in the air; the drift to the metropolis was the innovation of the age; and Milwaukee, already benefiting from the advantage of her geographical position, the development of her hinterland, and the ingenuity of her citizenry, was ready to profit from the trend.

4 Urbanization and

The transformation of the United States from an agricultural to a predominantly industrial nation was directly accompanied by accelerated urbanization. These changes are interrelated and nearly inseparable. Which came first, the mounting industrial strength or the increasing urban dominance, may be arguable, but the fact of the profound concomitant changes is not.

The evolution of the modern industrial city in the United States is a phenomenon of the last two centuries. The major thrust began in the early eighteen hundreds, and by the 1910's the dominant urban form was the city as we know it now. This development is borne out by the changes in the composition of employment and by the increased productivity of workers between 1860 and 1890 in some of the country's most important cities. St. Louis had only 5.8 per cent of its population engaged in manufacturing in 1860, and by 1890 the percentage rose to 20.8. In Detroit, productivity per worker rose during the same years from $685 to $1,055. Equally dramatic increases in employment and productivity in manufacturing occurred in such cities as New York, Chicago, and San Francisco, and less dramatic but,

Industrialization 185

nevertheless, significant changes occurred in other major cities. The impetus that manufacturing gave to urban growth between 1860 and 1910 is also manifested by the fact that manufacturing output increased more than did the national and urban populations. The important industrial metropolises of today experienced their largest absolute gains in population and wealth during the post-Civil War era, and their growth at that time made up a substantial part of the total urban increase of the period.

The expansion of most urban centers prior to 1820 was primarily a result of commercial and service activity. As was suggested in Section 2, the development of a commercialized agriculture, accompanied by expanded transportation systems, facilitated the exchange of products between the city and its hinterland and stimulated urban growth. Furthermore, some people who had accumulated capital from agriculture and commerce sought new opportunities for investment in the rising urban industries. After the Civil War, financiers of the principal Eastern cities were no longer interested primarily in foreign commerce but had turned instead to manufacturing. Urban expansion for the rest of the nineteenth century depended more and more on industrial development.

Although the precise relationship between industrialization and urbanization has not been established, several economic and socio-cultural theories have been advanced to describe it. One suggests that the growth of commercial agriculture and of transportation links to the city provided the impetus for the establishment of processing plants. Many American cities, such as Rochester and Minneapolis, began industrialization in this fashion. Their growth, in this respect, was dependent on their relationship to the hinterland. Another hypothesis derives from the same ideas that constitute the theory of economic development. The emphasis of the theory is on the factors of production which influence economic change, that is, on land, labor, capital, and business skill. The theory holds that the effective combination and exploitation of these factors in the nineteenth century was the basis for industrial growth. The concentration of population in cities supplied the necessary labor force, accumulation of capital, and competitive spirit. But unless there is sufficient demand, these factors lie idle. The expansion of the urban population provided its own internal market for the sale of industrial products, and transportation links to regional markets opened up new sources of demand. Section 2 showed the important role played by the proliferation of canal and rail transportation systems in the growth of cities, but, without the demand for exchange of goods, transportation would have served little function.

Very important in the growth of the modern industrial city was the development of specialization. Understanding why a division of labor occurs within the city requires a knowledge of the relationship between economic factors and socio-cultural elements. The city provided a vigorous environment where expertise, initiative, and achievement were valued along with the tendency to seek material advancement. These values were the inducement to specialize, for specialization provided the means for more efficient production, which in turn brought about more success and security. Specialization could have occurred almost anywhere, but only in the city did various specialized economic activities find the opportunity to be integrated and utilized so that benefits could be realized. Because its success made it self-stimulating, specialization was a dynamic and spiraling process, conducive to a city's constantly reaching for a higher plateau of economic activity.

Although it is clear that urbanization in some instances influenced industrialization, the converse is also true. Each aided the development of the other. For example, while concentration of population provided a ready-made labor force (urbanization affecting industrialization), industrial opportunity attracted labor and further increased the size of cities (industrialization affecting urbanization). Industrialization both had an economic impact on the growth of cities and produced specific social consequences.

While economic expansion created new opportunities for personal wealth, it also disrupted traditional patterns of living and created widespread dislocation and deprivation. Oscar Handlin, in his selection in Section 1, identified some of the general social changes that accompanied industrialization: a restructured family life, the reallocation of land use, a new concept of time, and grave social and personal problems. Industrialization also transformed the relationships between owners and employees and between men and their work. It further intensified old problems of cities and raised critical new questions regarding public health, housing, utilities, public services, law and order, and the like. The inability of the old forms to deal with these problems called for the creation of new institutions and techniques.

The material in this section is centered on the rise of the industrial city, the relationship between industrialization and urbanization, and the impact of the one on the other. The first selection describes the growth of two New England industrial cities, Holyoke, Massachusetts, and Naugatuck, Connecticut, both representative of scores of communities which cumulatively contributed to the transformation of America's economy. The next selection, by Blake McKelvey, emphasizes the impetus given to the rise of the city by economic and human elements and discusses the important contributions to national life of the industrial cities. Edward C. Kirkland's work deals with the influence that the building of American cities had on the general economy. The previous section showed how urban services were introduced and how their growth related to the creation of a community; Kirkland suggests the economic importance of this growth. The last essay, by Ralph E. Turner, explores the effect of the industrial city on social and cultural development, particularly the circumstances of life and the behavior and thought of the masses.

These themes recur in subsequent sections. The specific problems of the late nineteenth century, the new political forms, efforts at social planning, the philosophical attitudes in response to the material conditions, the metropolitanization of the twentieth century, and contemporary urban problems are all partially rooted in the industrialization process described in this section. Although new economic directions arose by the twentieth century, industrialization continued to contribute to the building of the city and to its physical, political, and social conditions and institutions.

Establishing Manufacturing Cities

Constance McLaughlin Green*

While South Carolina planters were dedicating Charleston to King Cotton and while the river cities of the West were widening their spheres of commercial influence in the country's interior, New England began shaping a new economic pattern for herself. The upper Mississippi valley and the shores of Lake Michigan were still Indian country when New Englanders, led by Boston capitalists, first turned from the sea to look inland. Their gaze for a generation after 1830 would be divided between the sea and the backcountry; but they saw that New England's ocean-going commerce would profit as much from native exports as from a carrying trade dependent on the whims of foreign governments or of rival states in the Union. Merchants with contacts in distant ports, and shipbuilders too, saw the wisdom of developing a hinterland on which to draw. To draw from a remote backcountry meant developing transport facilities, canals, roads hard enough to be passable at every season and wagon trains to traverse them, or, best of all, railroads and steam-powered cars. Eventually New England railroads could reach out into the rich farmlands of western New York and beyond, but until then something more than New England forests and the meagre surpluses of New England farms would be needed to feed the steam roads with freight. Manufactured goods would supply exports, and the feasibility of cotton manufacture using New England streams to provide water power to run machinery had

been proved well before 1820. New England's first mills had been located near the seaboard. To supply freight for roads running into Boston from the west would necessitate building factories inland. Thus it came about that the spread of manufacturing through all the interior of New England and the development of New England railroads were inextricably intertwined.

Manifestly conversion to an industrial economy could be neither immediate nor universal. The canny Boston merchant who observed the success of Francis Lowell's Waltham Company could plan to invest money in imitative ventures, on the principle that diversification was a hedge against losses in trading voyages. Building a factory, however, constructing machinery, and recruiting hands to run it might still look risky, even after the tariff of 1828 gave substantial protection to infant industry. That mercantile capital nevertheless flowed in to multiply cotton mills in New England bears testimony to the adventurousness and self-confidence of the New England merchant. Other goods besides cottons were needed by the expanding young nation, but in the 1830's and 1840's textile manufacture was the one essential industry in which mechanization had gone far and hence in which large-scale production was possible. Though makers of firearms and clocks were already using a few machine tools which enabled them to produce interchangeable parts, neither muskets nor time-pieces could command the wide market waiting for sturdy cotton cloth. Plantations owners needed it in quantity for field hands, and every housewife in America welcomed a

*Reprinted with permission from Constance McLaughlin Green, *American Cities in the Growth of the Nation*, Tuckahoe, New York: John De Graff, Inc., 1957, 79–85, 87–93, 95–99.

chance to buy cheap fabrics instead of having to spin and weave at home. Boston capitalists, once won over to industrial investment, therefore concentrated their resources upon cotton mills and the machine shops to equip them.

HOLYOKE

In 1833 Boston enterprisers, anticipating the day when railroads from the city would reach across Massachusetts, built a dam and cotton mills at the falls of the Chicopee river tributary to the Connecticut. Chicopee prospered so remarkably that her promoters began looking for other mill sites in western Massachusetts. New England's mightiest potential waterpower lay mid-way between Springfield, just below Chicopee, and Northampton, eighteen miles north, where the Connecticut river dropped sixty feet over rapids and falls within the space of a mile. Easy access to the locality was provided by the Western Railroad, which by 1845 stretched from Boston a hundred miles to Springfield and on to the New York State border. But tracks from New York City also ran into Springfield, meeting there with a line from Northampton. Consequently, New Englanders reasoned, if Boston, not New York, was to control the Connecticut valley, Boston money must develop the region. If Boston capitalists could acquire the site at the Great Falls of the Connecticut and harness its power, they could build and direct the fortunes of the greatest cotton-manufacturing city in the world. That was their hope.

In the summer of 1847 the scheme began to materialize when landowners on the right bank sold their farms to a newly incorporated company, the Hadley Falls Company. The power rights were assumed to be appurtenant to the land. As nearly every important man or business firm in Boston bought shares in the venture, the list of stockholders read like a Boston *Social Register,* the local equivalent of Debrett. Directors immediately engaged an experienced engineer to plan the layout of the company town and direct the building of a dam and canal system. Two and a half years later their 'New City' came into being, with a score of mill sites available for sale. Eventually, the directors believed, there would be space and power for forty-eight huge factories; England's Manchester would take second place to this manufacturing mammoth. Directors named the place Holyoke, in honor of a seventeenth-century Puritan pioneer of the Connecticut valley. Everything necessary for a booming mill town seemed to be in readiness—rail connections, vast power, the financial backing of successful Bostonians. Possibly even the charm of the natural setting would prove an asset.

Above the dam and the great bend of the river, wooded hillsides came down to the railroad along the river's edge, while, on the other shore, farm and pasture lands rolled off to the east. A few miles north rose the wooded shoulders of Mt Tom and the pine-clad sweep of the Mt Holyoke range, between which the river cut. In the nearby towns of Amherst and South Hadley Center stood two institutions of learning, already famous, Amherst College founded in 1821 by Congregationalists opposed to Unitarian rationalism, and Mt Holyoke Seminary where young women trained as missionaries and from which, a generation later, would come some of the foremost women scholars of America. Dignified Springfield and Northampton, with two centuries of New England town life behind them, were Holyoke's downstream and upstream neighbors. New England tradition pervaded the countryside. The mills built up in Chicopee, to be sure, were foreshadowing a little of what sudden industrial development might bring. Stockholders of the Hadley Falls Company, however, saw no reason to doubt that they were about to reap fat dividends and simultaneously to shed prosperity and other urban benefits upon the Connecticut valley.

But something went wrong. Not only were Holyoke's founders doomed to disappointment; succeeding generations of ambitious men also failed to infuse into the community the civic consciousness and unity that characterize a vigorous city. Holyoke is not decayed; on the contrary, she may in time find her way out of her confusions to take a distinguished place among the smaller cities of the United States where life is the richer for being simpler than it can be in a great metropolis. But Holyoke, now over a century old, has never flowered. For a brief period, perhaps from about 1878 to 1893, she gave signs of sturdy growth. Then a slow paralysis set in, and the promise was not fulfilled. Today she has far more to recommend her than a dozen other New England manufacturing cities—Manchester, New Hampshire, where abandonment of half the cotton mills has crippled the community; Fall River, Massachusetts, where one-time busy textile mills today house a series of virtual sweatshops; or Gardner, where furniture manufacture, once flourishing, has petered out with the exhaustion of New England's lumber supply. Nevertheless, if Holyoke is not one of New England's dreary mill towns, she is still far from realizing the hopes her founders and later comers alike had for her.

The first troubles of Holyoke grew out of the Boston stockholders' basic concept: from this community they planned to derive profit—profit from cotton manufacture, from sale of power and real estate, and from freight fed to their railroads; but they planned to make the profits as absentee owners. Since flimsy structures would be a poor investment, company directors were determined to have nothing shoddy in the 'New City'. The company tenements were models for their day. The harmonious proportions of the brick rows and the pine panelling in the foremen's houses were unusually fine. Mills built for sale or company use were solid in construction. But no stockholder had the remotest intention of personally concerning himself with life in the town. Build well, sell property at good prices, and hire agents to live on the spot to watch over the investment and manage the cotton mills. Boston investors would live in Boston and occasionally, from handsome offices in Milk Street, issue orders that might leave mill hands in Holyoke jobless and hungry or bring hordes of new workers to crowd into the tenements. Company policy was to discourage small enterprise. By holding its property for high prices, the company hampered the growth of a solid middle class. Because in 1847 the locality had been farmland, there were no roots for a community other than what the company planted; and the planting was shallow. The absentee owners intended to control Holyoke's economic life, but wanted no responsibility for her social or spiritual wellbeing. Men who in Boston still shared in civic affairs were unwilling to extend their civil obligations to their own distant creation.

The second difficulty was closely related to the first. Into the New City, with its lack of indigenous social patterns, the Hadley Falls Company poured immigrants fresh from Europe to serve as mill hands and unskilled labor. Before native Americans who arrived on the scene could lay the foundations of a New England community, they were inundated by a flood of Irish, mostly County Cork and County Kerry men, hardworking, but completely alien. The system that Lowell had inaugurated and other Boston millowners had followed was to employ in their factories farmers' daughters from the neighborhood. By housing them under careful chaperonage in company boarding houses, companies had stilled parental objections. Until about 1850 this plan had worked well. Harriet Martineau had described with admiration the arrangements provided in Lowell where young women of education served as mill operatives and spent their leisure in high-minded discussion and in publishing their own magazine, the *Lowell Offering.* As the 1850's wore on, this system ceased to function, partly because farm girls were no longer tempted by the long hours and low pay, and partly because uneducated immigrants seeping in as fellow employees stripped factory work of its one-time dignity. In Holyoke native mill hands were nearly unobtainable almost as soon as the factories opened. The incoming Irish families were ignorant of American ways, were largely illiterate, spoke a brogue often so broad as to be scarcely understandable, were usually penniless, and, worst of all in the Protestant Yankee view, were staunchly Roman Catholic. Before the 1850's were out, a number of French Canadians came from Quebec Province to add another foreign element and another brand of Catholicism. By 1860 most New England mill towns had a sizeable admixture of foreign-born in their population, but none was so lacking as Holyoke in an established social order on which to build.

That adjustments between native Americans and foreign-born were not made readily and permanently can probably be attributed to the economic ills that beset the village in its early years. Some of those misfortunes can again be laid at the door of the Hadley Falls Company. Miscalculation of the demand for manufacturing property in the United States of the 1850's left the company in straitened circumstances, its capital tied up in power rights and real estate which did not sell. Furthermore, though directors were obliged in 1854 to deviate from their policy of holding mill sites for cotton manufacture and sold two sites for paper mills, they clung to their original scheme long after events showed it unsound. For a decade the town scarcely grew at all. Depression in the cotton industry caused occasional layoffs of the work force in the two cotton mills that had been built, and general doubts about the future of the community prevailed well before the panic of 1857 struck the country. The panic was not the fault of the Hadley Falls Company, but the effects upon both company and town were disastrous. The company was eventually forced to sell out at auction at a small fraction of its original investment, and meanwhile Holyoke all but fell apart. Although the paper mills and a small wire factory started in 1857 managed to operate, unemployment spread. Householders with means to take themselves elsewhere moved away, leaving behind only the poverty-stricken and those who could not quickly get rid of their commitments. Gloom, anger, and hunger stalked the streets. It was not an atmosphere in which to build cordial community feeling.

Thus when a group of Hartford, Connecticut, men bought the Hadley Falls property in 1859, the new Holyoke Water Power Company acquired overlordship of a discouraged town along with possession of valuable industrial potentials. The canals were skilfully laid out and well built, mill sites were ready for factories, and a machine shop existed equipped to make the water wheels and machinery for any new enterprise. Dirt roads as well as the railroad connected Holyoke with Springfield and Northampton, while a swing ferry served for crossing the river below the great dam to the South Hadley shore. Beyond the shanties of the Irish immigrants on the outskirts of the town stretched the fields and hills of the enchanting New England countryside. Along the alternately muddy and dusty streets within the village stood several rows of mill tenements, frame boarding houses, scattered private dwellings, a few stores, and a bank. Three Protestant churches had built places of worship in the course of the ten years since the town had been organized, and Roman Catholics, urged on by a resident priest, had somehow found money to build St Jerome's church. A district schoolhouse not far from the dam and several schools in the outlying areas of the township supplied the legal minimum of education for future citizens of the Commonwealth. But uncertainty about what lay ahead long cast shadows over the village.

The Holyoke Water Power Company made perfectly clear its intention of letting the town run its own civic affairs. As for industrial promotion, the new resident agent decided to make haste slowly. The new company could afford to wait, for it had purchased what had cost the Hadley Falls Company over $2,000,000 for only $350,-000. On the other hand, the locality with its abundant cheap power was unusually well situated to manufacturing enterprise, and in the months before the outbreak of the Civil War hope for the future stirred. The cotton mills were running full time, machine-shop orders increased, and the two paper companies, once despised by Hadley Falls directors as too insignifi-

cant to bother about, were making money. Unemployment disappeared, and a few newcomers moved into the town. Still, troubles were not yet over. The Civil War cut off the supply of southern cotton and in the summer of 1862 shut down the chief cotton mill in Holyoke altogether. The Union army took off the younger men, and prices of necessities shot up.

The turning point came in 1863. Demand for clothing for the Union armies, together with passage of a high war tariff, gave new incentives, and the agent of the Holyoke Water Power Company, seizing the opportunity to attract new enterprise to Holyoke, persuaded company directors to build a mill for lease and to adopt a policy of lending money to men to launch new ventures. In this way a machine shop and two woolen mills were started. At the end of the war suddenly the town began to grow.

Most Massachusetts manufacturing towns concentrated upon a particular type of article—to begin with, cotton, woolen goods next, and then, in one town or another, boots and shoes, tools, furniture, or small wooden wares; before the end of the nineteenth century few communities developed diversified manufacturing. Contrary to the expectations of her founders, Holyoke became, not a cotton, but a paper city. For paper-making she had the all-important advantages of abundant cheap power and chemically pure, soft water. Ample power was essential because paper machines, once started, had to be kept running until the batch of halfstuff was run through; interrupting the run meant costly breaks in the paper. Operating the heavy machines required great, as well as steady, power. Furthermore, washing the rags for the preliminary processes needed not only gallons and gallons of water but water of special chemical properties. These the Connecticut river had. In spite of the earlier troubles of the town, the paper mills established in the 1850's had flourished, and men who had been clerks and salesmen in these concerns now saw the chance to use their experience for themselves. The Holyoke Water Power Company's new policy of advancing credit enabled men to organize paper companies with very little initial capital, to pay off indebtedness from profits, and then to expand. Between 1865 and September 1873, eleven paper mills began operation in Holyoke. And these were largely locally owned and locally managed. Absenteeism all but disappeared.

Nothing succeeds like success. Though paper-making was Holyoke's speciality, as the town began to boom, new textile mills and new machine shops also appeared—a thread mill, factories for manufacturing heavy overcoatings and dress goods, shops for making machinery and water wheels, and job shops for repair and maintenance work. As new mills required more mill hands and more housing, brick kilns and lumber yards sprang up to supply building contractors. One cheerful promoter described the scene in the summer of 1873 in typical American style: 'The spirit of hustle and bustle pervaded the busy town.'

The rapid growth brought its penalties. Tenements had to be located near the mills because workpeople had only shanks's mares for transportation. Mill whistles sounded at six in the morning and at six at night, and walking through heavy snow in winter or mud in spring meant that people must live within a mile or two of their work. People crowded into tenements, sometimes ten to twelve families in a house built for two or three. The charming spot just above the dam with a beautiful view of the river and hills became a slum. The newcomers were usually ignorant of the most elementary rules of health and sanitation, and, had they been educated, poverty and lack of facilities would still have made their quarters uncomfortable at best, foul at worst. By the mid-seventies Holyoke's death rate was higher than that of any town or city in Massachusetts, save Fall River, and as late as 1890, when doctors and householders knew more of preventive measures than in the 1870's, Holyoke's infant mortality was 312 per thousand of the population under one year of age. In 1873 the town was prospering, confident, expanding; it was also filled with poverty, disease, and human wretchedness. Contrasts were sharpened, where they were not actually created, by the swiftness with which a rural countryside had been turned into a mill city.

One may at moments be tempted to curse the Boston capitalists whose greed, or ambitions, or notions of material progress converted lovely country into industrial hideousness. On the other hand, having created the havoc, many of these same Bostonians joined with men of conscience in other parts of the Commonwealth to force enactment of state laws creating a Bureau of Labor Statistics to investigate conditions in Massachusetts mill towns. The first annual reports of the Massachusetts Bureau of Labor Statistics, published yearly after 1870, were based upon facts collected by state inspectors who saw with their own eyes. In the section on Holyoke the report of 1875 gave details too precise to be challenged:

Holyoke has more and worse large tenement houses than any manufacturing town of textile fabrics in the state. . . . The sanitary arrangements are very imperfect, and in many cases, there is no provision for carrying the slops from the sinks, but they are allowed to run wherever they can make their way. Portions of yards are covered with filth and green slime, and within twenty feet, people are living in basements three feet below the level of the yard.

With specific details such as these in print, Massachusetts citizens of the 1870's and 1880's could know what industrialism was imposing upon the Commonwealth and could struggle to mitigate its ills. The resulting social legislation made the Massachusetts Labor Code a model for other enlightened states.

In 1873 Holyoke became an incorporated city. Selectmen paid by the day for occasional services could not cope, men believed, with civic problems as well as could Mayor, Aldermen, Boards of Public Works and Health, and all the formal officialdom of a city government. Unfortunately, new machinery of government did not remake the community, and during the 1870's citizens chose city officials from the Yankee Protestant group who had dominated the town during the years when Holyoke's immigrants were too new to know their way about amid the mazes of American municipal politics. Then, because the Irish learned quickly and were eager for office, after 1880 naturalized Irish officials invaded the betowered granite City Hall in full force. Native Americans were not only in an overwhelmed minority, but the difficulty of making Holyoke a decent place to live in made holding public office a thankless task. Competent Yankees, grown reluctant to run for office or to campaign vigorously for election, were, by implication, now ready to let the foreign-born take a try. Problems remained. Probably the Irish politicians did very little worse than native-born could have done, though the Irish saloon

keeper and the liquor interests in general had undue power in the city administration.

The inroads on local politics, made with steadily mounting vigor by the erstwhile immigrants, intensified Yankee hostility to the foreign-born. Resentments focused on the Irish because they were the most numerous and the most aggressive. They seemed to New Englanders to be a different breed of human, superstitious at times, always emotional, lacking in discipline, not perhaps of spirit but of behavior, disconcertingly prone to assert themselves to be as good as the next fellow. Brawny, generally good-humored, occasionally stirred to violent anger, they were a force to reckon with. Their growing numbers stirred nameless apprehensions in Protestant native Americans. In proportion as the Irish rose in the economic scale and outgrew any one of their original colonies, the 'Patch' or the 'Flats' or 'Tigertown', native Americans disliked them the more. As the power of the Roman Catholic church grew in the community with the increase of Catholic immigrants, Protestant apprehensions mounted still higher. French-Canadian and German Catholics came to be regarded by the more rigid native New Englanders as lesser and almost innocuous evils. In fact, native Americans nourished faint and vain hopes that differences between the French-speaking Catholics and the English-speaking Irish would cancel out each other's influence.

The prolonged perpetuation of this feud stemmed partly from Yankee guilt. The ignorance and poverty of the immigrants put upon property-holders—and they were predominantly Protestants—a heavy burden of taxation to provide schools. The alternative of acquiescing in Catholic parochial schools hurt New Englanders' conscience, for it meant abandoning the New England ideal of free, public, non-sectarian schools where all received the same education. The emotional conflict set up by this choice was real, even if unacknowledged. Yet the increasing number of Holyoke children who attended parochial schools as time went on heightened the sense of difference between Protestant and Catholic. Furthermore, the determination of both Protestant leaders and Catholic priests to prevent intermarriages between young people of the two faiths entailed the restriction of social contacts. Yankees, seeking to protect themselves from the discomforts of rubbing elbows with people bred in a different world, educated in different schools, and steeped in a religion that was anathema to the Puritan, took refuge in an air of superiority that incensed the people they excluded. Irish and, to a lesser extent, French-Canadians retaliated by sneering at the 'uppity Yankee'. The insecurity of each group contributed to the widening and deepening rather than the gradual disappearance of the cleft.

The panic of 1873 and the five-year business depression that followed curtailed Holyoke's prosperity until at the end of the seventies the city was rescued by another boom. A silk manufacturer and an alpaca company built mills, prospered, and became employers of large numbers of operators. Paper-making resumed at a quickened pace. New companies emerged, some coming from outside, more of them offshoots of existing local enterprises. Like the earlier paper companies, the new were owned and run by men who made their homes in the city. By 1890 about 80 per cent of the country's fine writing and bond paper was made here. The fifteen years preceding the panic of 1893 marked Holyoke's heyday. The Paper City's business activities expanded, employment and population mounted steadily, and, in spite of social cleavages and political wrangling, the community began to see herself as overshadowing in wealth and importance her older neighbor, Springfield. A successful paper manufacturer built an Opera House in Holyoke which far surpassed anything rival cities in the valley could boast. Fine carriages drawn by thorough-breds raced along the city streets, and elegant clothes and European tours came to be part of the scheme of things for the prospering mill owners.

But Holyoke's distinction was tied to paper-making, and by the mid-nineties her career as a paper city was doomed by the increasing use of wood pulp. Since 1880 sulphite papers had been encroaching upon rag, and by 1900 for most purposes sulphite had wholly supplanted rag papers. Despite rail connections with Quebec Province and Maine, Holyoke was now too far from the pulp-wood supply to compete easily. Where spruce chips were available, there pulp-mills went up; paper mills followed. Most of New England's spruce forests were gone. Maine and Canada supplied the East, Wisconsin and the Pacific Northwest the rest of the country. With her natural advantages for paper-making thus lost, Holyoke ceased to be America's leading paper city. Well before men comprehended the full force of this technological change, the panic of the 1890's began to take heavy toll. And then at the end of the depression a group of New York stock manipulators hit upon the plan of consolidating Holyoke's paper companies together with a few located elsewhere. The promoters argued that economies in purchasing materials and in marketing the product, plus elimination of competition between separate companies, would make more money for all. They slid over the obvious fact that their plan spelled monopoly if it worked. All but three of the local paper manufacturers were seduced, and what was to have been the great writing-paper trust was formed. The attempt at monopoly failed, and the 'combine' was soon operating at such a loss that it was forced to close several of its mills in order to avoid bankruptcy. Today, as for fifty years past, Holyoke's most successful paper companies are those that refused to sell out to the combine and maintained their independence.

The community never entirely recovered. The local textile companies for a time fared better, and down through World War I men dared hope that the setback in the local paper industry need not blight the city's growth. Then textiles also suffered reverses. The zest and confidence that gave Holyoke promise in the era when she ruled the paper world were gone. The South, having found in the 1920's that her cheap labor offered an industrial advantage and that cotton manufacture need no longer be a New England preserve, captured the coarse cotton trade entirely, made inroads upon the fine cotton market and, with the introduction of synthetic fibres, was able to compete with northern mills on an equal footing. Changes in fashion and the increasing use of heated automobiles wiped out the market for Holyoke's woolens and worsteds; by 1950 only one woolen mill remained. Meanwhile, the introduction of automatic looms reduced employment at the silk mills. The machinery and machine-tool plants, universally sensitive to industrial fluctuations, here suspended operations during most of the thirties until the war clouds in Europe in 1939 rained sudden new business upon American firms. After the war, demand again dropped. Fortunately, toward the end of the decade several enterprises new to the city appeared. Establishing themselves in buildings left empty after the demise of local companies,

these concerns, though none of them large, between them dispelled fears of widespread unemployment or a general exodus of workmen. Yet citizens today, in so far as they remember the grave economic and social problems of Holyoke's recent past, dare not believe in an untroubled future.

NAUGATUCK

Naugatuck, named for an Indian tribe of the region, is a very much simpler community to understand. One of several score small Connecticut manufacturing towns and cities, Naugatuck today is distinguished for the uninterrupted success of her most important industries and, perhaps a corollary, the relatively peaceful course of community development. Unlike most Massachusetts mill towns, she has had some diversification of manufacture from the early nineteenth century onward. Located in western Connecticut some twenty miles north of Long Island Sound, she never fell within Boston's orbit but was linked by river and Sound, and later by rail, to New York City. Naugatuck's history is one of gradual evolution from a one-hundred-and-fifty-year old agrarianism through intermediate steps of small-scale manufacturing to full industrialism in the twentieth century. Where Holyoke was created by a sudden artificial imposition upon a nearly empty countryside, Naugatuck grew slowly through each stage, feeling her way as she went. In 1950 Naugatuck's population was 18,000; Holyoke's was 55,000. In the smaller place adjustments to an industrial society came little by little, whereas the Bostonians' New City had to struggle with a revolutionizing new order at once. It should therefore not be surprising to find the lesser place the less troubled and possessed of the more immediately promising future.

Naugatuck was an offshoot of the very much older, wealthier town and city of Waterbury, Connecticut. Waterbury had been settled in the 1680's, at about the same time as Charleston, South Carolina. Toward the end of the eighteenth century the settlers of the southernmost stretch of Waterbury had requested and were granted the privilege of setting up a 'winter parish', in order to be relieved of the necessity of weekly attendance at meeting in the town center. For Waterbury, like other eighteenth-century Connecticut towns, was an orthodox Congregational community in which churchgoing was obligatory. The winter privilege, so-called, eventually became a year-round privilege, dependent on settlers' supporting their own separate ministry and their own place of worship. Fifty years later, in 1844, Salem parish of Waterbury was separated from the mother town to become the independent town of Naugatuck.

The Naugatuck valley is a slit in the high hills of western Connecticut. Five miles from Long Island Sound the Naugatuck river flows into the Housatonic, the chief river between the mighty Connecticut and the Hudson. At Naugatuck's site the valley widens slightly, leaving between the steep hills to the east and the west enough level land to attract eighteenth-century farmers. And the eighteenth-century village, six miles downstream from the Waterbury town center, had been primarily a farming community. But save at the 'intervales', formed by the river where slowing of the current permitted alluvial deposits to collect, the soil was thin and far less suited to agriculture than the fertile country beyond the mountains in New York State and the Ohio valley. Hence early in the nineteenth century, as news of the rich lands to be bought in the West spread through the Naugatuck valley, dozens of farmers sold their holdings and trekked westward, leaving behind them the men whose interests lay less in tillage than in using other resources of the region. The main resource was the water power of the mountain brooks tumbling down the wooded hillsides into the Naugatuck river. Men had set up water wheels along these streams early in the eighteenth century to saw wood or grind meal or full cloth, and in time they discovered that they could turn out various farm and household wares to sell to their neighbors. The upshot was a kind of natural selection: farmers moved west, the tinkerers remained.

The objects men could make profitably in this hillbound locality were few. Because of the lack or roughness of roads in the early nineteenth century, saleable goods had to be small wares that pedlars could pack on their backs—'Yankee notions'—pins, needles, wooden bowls, mousetraps, buttons, clocks, knives, Britannia-ware forks and spoons. The pedlar of Yankee notions was preeminently a Connecticut product. He was accused by people of other states of peddling wooden nutmegs, so that Connecticut is often called derisively the 'Nutmeg State'. Naugatuck, decades before the town was separated from Waterbury, was producing her full share of Yankee notions. As turnpikes and railroads began to thread through Connecticut and peddling as a method of marketing vanished, reason would suggest that the village producing these wares on so small a scale would shrivel away for want of links with the world outside the narrow valley. That this did not happen was due to luck and perspicacity combined.

In 1843 chance in the person of Charles Goodyear brought unique opportunity to Naugatuck. Though Goodyear had discovered in 1839 how to harden rubber by vulcanizing, he had failed to find anyone to put faith in his invention until he returned to Naugatuck, his boyhood home, to demonstrate the process to his two brothers-in-law. Both were shrewd business men, William DeForest, owner and manager of a small woolen mill, Milo Lewis of a cotton-warp mill. Goodyear brought with him several strips of raw rubber, two shoe lasts, and his oldest daughter. In the tiny office of DeForest's mill, the seventeen-year-old Eleanor showed her uncles how to shape the soft rubber over the forms. Her father then vulcanized the rubber still on the lasts. When DeForest and Lewis saw the result, a pair of durable rubber overshoes, both men were sufficiently impressed to put up money to organize the Goodyear's Metallic Rubber Shoe Company. Thus the enterprise began that first made Naugatuck famous. The adage that the world beats a path to the door of the man who makes a better mousetrap held true for the village. Even before a railroad, built up the valley in 1849, solved the transportation problem, the home of the product unobtainable elsewhere was becoming a manufacturing center of some importance.

Just as new paper companies sprang up in Holyoke once paper-making was well launched there, so, following in the wake of the shoe company, other rubber companies appeared in Naugatuck. Here was a new industry and only here were people to be found with any experience in making rubber goods. A rubber glove factory, opened in 1847, was soon producing surgeons' gloves, ponchos for the army, and other rubber wearing apparel. Later companies made rubber balls and tennis shoes. But always most important of all were rubber 'arctics' or galoshes. Indeed so successful were the Goodyear plants that both the original investors, DeForest and Lewis,

eventually abandoned woolen and cotton manufacture to concentrate upon rubber. The DeForest woolen mill continued under new ownership, but when in 1869 the cotton-warp mill burned, Lewis did not bother to rebuild it.

For a generation after 1844 the new rubber factories, the small textile mills, and the old Yankee notions shops alike used the water of the river or its tributary brooks for power. But, as the village turned into a factory town and new workers' families arrived, need of housing led builders to strip the hillsides barer and barer of trees, until the brooks dried to mere trickles and the 'raging Naugatuck' to a shallow stream. Then only the shops that converted to steam power could survive. For the individual owner of a shop 'up the brook' the cost of carting coal up the hillsides or of moving to a site along the river was usually ruinous. Still the safety-pin maker and several cutlery firms carried on to the end of the century, and the woolen mill ran, though at a steadily slackening rate, till after the first World War.

The survival of these small enterprises could not alone have saved Naugatuck from becoming, like most Massachusetts mill towns, dependent upon a single industry. It was the malleable iron foundry established by Bronson Tuttle in 1858 that provided the redeeming balance. Tuttle, starting at the age of twenty-two with his father's blessing and some of the profits of his father's hoe shop, formed a partnership with John Whittemore, the penniless twenty-year-old son of a Congregational minister in a neighboring town. The partners made an ideal team. Whittemore early displayed a genius for finance, and Tuttle, despite his inexperience, showed unusual abilities as a 'production man'. Malleable iron castings in the days before Americans had learned to make steel were in great demand for a variety of purposes. Malleable iron was cheaper than imported steel and far stronger and more easily worked than ordinary iron. The foundry's first big order, placed in the early months of the Civil War, was for wagon hub-caps for the Union army. When domestic steel manufacture began to relegate wrought and cast iron wares to the background, Tuttle and Whittemore skilfully shifted their production to new articles for which steel was unsuited. The 'fish plates' that tie together the rails on a railroad, brackets to hold the insulators to telegraph poles, and a host of other items individually small and inexpensive but, ordered in quantity, highly profitable to make, kept the foundry busy and brought a fortune to its owners.

Operatives to man the rubber shops and the malleable iron foundry soon had to be recruited from outside the town limits. As elsewhere in New England, the immigrants at first came largely from Ireland. Some Scottish families followed and, slightly later, Germans and a few Swedes. By the end of the 1880's the town was distinctly polyglot. Towards the end of the century Poles and other Slavs came in some numbers. Crowding and unwholesome living quarters appeared in Naugatuck, as in all industrializing American communities, but since her growth was never rapid, social adjustments were relatively easy. Naugatuck took fifty years from the beginning of her career as a factory town in 1844 to reach a population of 9,000, and fifty years more did not double that number. Townspeople made the religious adjustment well, partly because the influx of aliens was gradual and partly because the men guiding the town's religious life were exceptionally wise. Under the aegis of intelligent and humane Congregational and Episcopal pastors and Catholic priests, Protestants and Catholics arrived almost at once at a *modus vivendi* as wholesome as it was rare. A larger mutual tolerance of different faiths still obtains in Naugatuck than is usually to be found in New England cities where the proportion of Catholics to Protestants is high. In fact, though most people in Naugatuck attend church every week, religion is not a divisive element in the city's social structure.

Other adjustments were less successful. Connecticut leaders of the nineteenth century blandly assumed that their first men of industry could do no wrong. There were none of the careful factory inspections that Massachusetts insisted on, no Connecticut laws limiting hours or stipulating safety devices. In the absence of state or local records, the historian must guess at conditions in Naugatuck's mills. The golden picture old residents like to paint of mill-owners and mill hands as all one happy family looks suspect. Hours were long and, thanks to the seasonal character of work in the rubber shoe shops, annual earnings for employees of the town's chief enterprise were low. During shutdowns wage-earners eked out a livelihood by farm work in the neighborhood or by domestic labor. At the foundry a contracting system, common in many metal-working shops in nineteenth-century New England, put workmen at the mercy of the foremen who, having entered into contract with the company-owners to perform certain jobs for a flat yearly sum, hired their own help at the lowest wages men would accept. Choices of occupation for semi-skilled workmen were too few to encourage protest. Before the first World War no unions emerged, save a few feeble organizations among carpenters and bricklayers. Indeed, Naugatuck industrialists prided themselves on having no unionization—proof, they contended, that everybody was supremely satisfied with things as they were. Employers clung to this view in the face of a ten-week strike in the rubber shops in 1919. Yet in the mid-1930's when the Congress of Industrial Organization began its campaign for members, even in this paradise agitation for unionization appeared. Upon the passage of the National Labor Relations Act, Naugatuck's rubber workers organized and, forcing union recognition, won a satisfactory contract. Thus it was twenty years after collective bargaining had been accepted in most of New England before Naugatuck employers succumbed.

Town government, meanwhile, had given way to borough government. The reasons that impelled townspeople in 1892 to petition the Connecticut legislature for a borough charter, if nowhere officially recorded, are nevertheless easy to surmise. Were Naugatuck, under the influence of rapidly expanding industry, suddenly to grow greatly, the system of administering town affairs through selectmen who gave to their public duties only a few days a year would no longer suffice. Local newspapers, moreover, obliquely hinted at gross mismanagement of town business in the years immediately preceding when petty political bosses appeared to be running the selectmen. The town needed a new broom; a borough charter might supply it. A chartered borough, in the United States a form of municipality peculiar to Connecticut, has an elected Warden and advisory Board of Burgesses who have more responsibility and authority than town selectmen but less power than a city mayor and councilmen. As under the town system, citizens in town meeting yearly approve a detailed budget of proposed public expenditures, and money voted for one purpose cannot be spent for another. Hence, although the Warden is empowered to disburse funds, control of the purse strings remains with the citizens themselves. In Naugatuck the chief advantage of borough government derived from the concentration of authority in the hands of a single official. This arrangement, in contrast to the diffusion of responsibility among three Selectmen, a Superintendent of Roads, a Fence Viewer, a Hay-Warden, and a dozen other town officials, enabled the Warden to direct municipal planning effectively.

Shortly before the inauguration of borough government, a change occurred that ultimately was to have more far-reaching consequences for the community than new political forms. In 1892 the rubber companies of Naugatuck and several elsewhere combined to form the United States Rubber Company. The consolidation came as no surprise, for as early as 1853 rubber manufacturers had toyed with the idea. The new company had no immediate effect upon Naugatuck. Indeed for the next thirty years each local superintendent ran his own shop as if it were an independent mill. Then, as technology called for specially educated chemists and engineers to revolutionize methods of production, significant changes began: the autonomy of the local superintendent vanished, automatic machinery wiped out the distinction between the skilled craftsmen and the semi-skilled, and the special consideration formerly accorded to old employees disappeared. The depression at the end of the 1920's, requiring of manufacturers greater efficiency and more careful financial management in order to compete and survive, emphasized these changes. The culmination of this local revolution was reached about 1930 when the United States Rubber Company embarked upon a regime of switching its key men from one plant to another, a practice now standard in many big American corporations with branches in a dozen cities. After 1930 few important executives in Naugatuck's rubber plants remained there more than four years. In nineteenth-century Naugatuck such shifting about as occurred was among the wage-earners, who moved on if jobs looked better elsewhere; the white-collar and employer group stayed put. In mid-twentieth century it is the top level that most frequently moves and the working people who are rooted. Thus the men who a generation ago would have been community leaders, the men of most education, experience, and vision, now have no sense of being part of the community and take little responsibility for it. Naugatuck is just one way-station on the course of their industrial and business careers.

The policy of deliberate detachment from local affairs which the United States Rubber Company developed and maintained after the late twenties may have been partly the result of determination to escape the charge of making the borough a company town, where company patronage controlled major decisions and company interests received first attention, but where, when anything went wrong, blame fell upon the corporation. Naugatuck was small enough and sufficiently dependent upon the rubber shops to have given such accusations plausibility. The official explanation was even simpler. In the 1920's, as the company opened new plants in a number of cities, directors reportedly decreed that all must be treated alike. The easiest way to act upon that resolution was to remain rigidly aloof from every community. Certainly during the depression responsibility for any town or city was a heavy burden to bear. Yet a company decision saved Naugatuck in the thirties from the unemployment and suffering that most of New England, and indeed most of the

country, faced. Company directors chose to keep Naugatuck's mills running and to concentrate here work formerly done elsewhere. Thus the borough's chief industry, so far from curtailing operations, brought in new people, thereby giving merchants new customers and causing a small building boom. Old residents who growl at the Rubber Company's impersonal behavior concede that its action, though taken without special thought for the borough, benefited the community as nothing else then could.

While United States Rubber Company officials rank themselves as temporary residents and accordingly tend to be indifferent to community concerns, among other citizens local pride runs high. Artificial social barriers and unwarranted discriminations are rare, and this virtue redeems any lingering complacency. Furthermore, the constant coming and going of industrial executives has combined with the family automobile and the steady rise in the general level of prosperity to dispel Naugatuck's provincialism. Physically the borough is unlikely to grow very much more; the hills and surrounding townships hem her in geographically, and nothing points to any large increase in population within these boundaries. Scant space remains for new industrial plants and increasing mechanization in existing factories makes creation of more jobs improbable. But as rising pay scales promise people already employed in Naugatuck a steadily improving material standard of living, bigness ceases to be a borough goal.

Holyoke, deliberately conceived and unloved offspring of Boston, and Naugatuck, spontaneous product of the Connecticut hills, represent two facets of New England's industrial growth. The story of other cities would reveal still other forces at work—New Bedford, for example, whaling port converted to cotton manufacture; Meriden, rural village become a silversmithing center; or Bridgeport, grown powerful through the transformation of tiny shops into mighty machine-tool and machinery plants. Yet these and other New England mill towns, turned into cities, were ancillary rather than essential to the sweep of urbanization across the continent. The course of events in the rest of the country would have been no different had any particular New England manufacturing city never arisen. Nevertheless, the cumulative effect of the rise of this congeries of industrial cities was considerable. While capital for new settlement rarely stemmed direct from these sources, and while the westward movement drew its strength less from mill hands than from other elements of the population of the East, the growth of these small industrial centers enlarged the markets in the West and, in turn, created new stores of manufactured goods to supply western towns. Furthermore, by feeding the railroads of New England and the New York area, individually unimportant cities of New England tightened the unity of the country and contributed to the shift from an agrarian to an industrial economy.

The Age of the Industrial City

Blake McKelvey*

So many ambitious towns sprang up in the early days on each frontier that many were threatened with atrophy when the railroads enabled a few to stake out broad hinterlands at the expense of their neighbors. Only through industrial enterprise could most cities hope to prosper. Some enjoyed special opportunities as a result of the timely discovery of mineral resources nearby or at points easily reached by cheap water transport. A few achieved industrial leadership through the exploitation of local water power or by the invention of machinery to process regional products more efficiently. Others escaped a way-station fate because a steady flow of immigrants spurred residents to develop new industries based in part on cheap labor and to produce for a national market. Still others prospered through the manufacture of patented or specialty articles. Several combined these tactics, and all labored to produce a marketable surplus.

The rise or decline of an individual town was of major concern only to its promoters and its more settled residents; others could and did move elsewhere without loss. But the widespread survival of many threatened communities by means of industrial enterprise was of primary significance. A few such towns became the prototypes of the industrial city and endowed it with special characteristics. Several others pressed the advantages their manufacturing activities brought and did so with such vigor that they achieved metropolitan status; a few of these,

notably Minneapolis, acquired regional hegemony. Moreover the emphasis they gave to industry forced their commercial rivals also to accord it increased attention. To promote these efforts, the business leaders of most communities reorganized old boards of trade or established new associations. By the turn of the century the industrial output of American cities had so outstripped that of any foreign country that the character of international trade was transformed, and with it the services performed by the great ports.

The industrialization of America is a separate story, but the impetus given to that development by the rise of the city cannot be overlooked. The impetus given to industrialism by the rapid discovery and exploitation of the country's natural resources is more fully documented and understood, and so also is the effect of the great influx of immigrant workmen in this period. Here, however, we are interested in the converse side of these historic movements—the contributions that new sources of energy and raw materials, new supplies of labor and industrial skills, new machines and techniques of production made to urban growth.

Because of their glamour, the successive gold rushes have long had a place in American history, yet their product never compared in value with that of the silver and copper mines and appeared insignificant when measured against the output of the iron and coal fields. Similar contrasts marked their respective towns. Gold-mining towns such as Virginia City were more

*Reprinted with permission from Blake McKelvey, *The Urbanization of America, 1860–1915*, New Brunswick, N.J.: Rutgers University Press, 1963, 35–46, © 1963 by Rutgers, the State University.

pretentious than those based on silver and copper, but their permanence depended on the discovery nearby of "baser" metals. Not even the iron- and copper-mining camps became major cities (Butte, Montana, was a possible exception). Only where abundant supplies of coal or other fuels were found was manufacturing encouraged and urban growth maintained.

Even in the coal fields, few mining towns became major cities. In the hard-coal region of Pennsylvania, where the ore deposits extended over several counties, numerous settlements or "patches" sprang up about many colliery shafts, creating a density of as much as 1300 persons per square mile without achieving the integration essential for urban status. By 1900 only Scranton and Wilkes-Barre had exceeded 100,000 and 50,000 respectively, and this chiefly because they were not as exclusively occupied with mining as, for example, neighboring Hazelton, which barely numbered 25,-000 a decade later. In fact Scranton, at the turn of the century, had more industrial workers than either miners or tradesmen.

Generally a nearby commercial or industrial city supplied the marketing, banking, and other urban services for mining districts, thus strengthening its claim to regional leadership. Sometimes a mining town developed a new industry to convert the products of neighboring collieries, as in the coke district around Uniontown and Brownville, only to see its control absorbed in time by a regional capital, in this case Pittsburgh. Most mining communities, victims of absentee ownership and constricted by their specialty, failed to develop the internal leadership necessary to attract competing transport arteries or to tap new sources of credit.

Other fuel strikes brought dubious benefits to communities at their sites, but presented great opportunities to the commercial marts that acquired control. The oil towns of northwestern Pennsylvania, which displayed great vitality during the seventies, were soon checked as monopoly control over refining and marketing siphoned the profits of the industry into the hands of Rockefeller and his colleagues in Cleveland and other processing centers. Natural gas brought a sudden boom to several communities, notably Findlay and Toledo, Ohio, but their fortunes ebbed with the arrival of outside control. Toledo, already an important railroad hub and advantageously situated for lake trade, remained primarily a regional market until civic leaders, reasserting the town's rights to its power resources, enabled industry finally to pull ahead of commerce and boost the city into the 100,000 bracket by the close of the period.

Some cities prospered as processors of regional farm products. Minneapolis, a small neighbor of St. Paul in the seventies, captured leadership in the wheat belt of the Northwest during the eighties by developing mills able to produce a better flour from the spring wheat of that area than St. Louis or other rivals could mill from winter wheat. Kansas City won its independence from St. Louis and Chicago by building up its meat-packing industry. Milwaukee ventured with less success into each of these fields but achieved its greatest triumph in the brewing industry, likewise based on products of the area. Memphis competed with many other places in lumber milling but excelled in the production of cotton-seed oil. Each of these and several like them strengthened their positions by developing accessory industries and by extending urban economic services to a hinterland which they constantly endeavored to expand. All attained metropolitan status chiefly because of their manufacturing services.

Many cities, even when overshadowed by near neighbors, prospered through the employment of cheap immigrant labor. The shoe industry, in which the introduction of machinery after the mid-century tended to supersede old craft skills, lent itself to this use. Lynn and Haverhill had developed a reputation for shoes in earlier decades, and after the Civil War Cincinnati and Rochester, among others, began to specialize in this field. New York and Philadelphia, because of their large markets and abundant supply of newcomers, became shoe producers, although not as important as the older New England centers, where the earlier craftsmen supervised a new work force of immigrants.

But cheap labor, even when supplied from abroad, did not long remain content in America, and the shoe industry produced some of the most determined union-organizing drives of these decades. Unfortunately, from the viewpoint of the cities involved, when union demands mounted in one town, many firms (except those engaged in quality production) sought new sites, such as Milwaukee, Chicago, or Manchester, New Hampshire, where the organizers had not yet penetrated. The migration of shoe companies, facilitated by the practice of leasing rather than purchasing the machinery, presented a constant threat to cities in this field. It also provided an extreme example of the industrial mobility that contributed to both the diffusion and the fluidity of America's urban development.

The textile industry, too, displayed an intense interest in cheap labor, but the range of its migrations was limited.

Originally established at water-power sites in New England, where textiles nurtured several of the country's first factory towns, notably Lowell and Manchester, this industry quickly replaced its early native-born labor from the first influx of Irish and other immigrant groups, thus speeding the urbanization as well as the cosmopolitan transformation of the Yankee homeland. During the post–Civil War expansion, when steam began to supplement water power, Fall River pulled into the lead among textile centers because of its easy access to water-borne coal and its cheap immigrant labor, including that of women and children. Some textile towns added other specialties; Chicopee developed tool shops and began to produce bicycles; Holyoke became a paper city; Lowell ventured into woolens, carpets, knitted products, and other enterprises. Successive waves of new immigrants—Polish, French, Canadian, and Portuguese—enabled management to fight off many union demands; yet pressure from the workers and the restraints of labor legislation in America's second most urbanized commonwealth presented Massachusetts textile firms with an increasing disadvantage in competition with the new cotton mills of the South.

The development of the textile industry in the South had a substantial economic basis. The slow spread of cotton factories in North and South Carolina and Georgia during post–Civil War years uncovered a new supply of cheap labor in the poor whites of the Piedmont area and began in the eighties to attract northern capital, some of it from the New England firms themselves. Advances in technology—the Northrop automatic loom and the ring spindle, which eliminated the skilled mule spinners who had formed the backbone of textile unions in the North—enabled the southern mills to employ unskilled labor and to defeat the first effort at organization around 1900. Since many northern firms hesitated to make the fresh investments that new machinery required, New England textile cities saw the greater part of the expanding market after 1890 pass by default to new towns in the South.

A major reason for the embarrassment of some of the New England towns was the defection of their absentee enterpreneurs and the failure to replace their talents from among the immigrant workers. On the other hand, some cities prospered because of the enterprise and skills that waves of newcomers brought. British and Dutch glassmakers strengthened the economy of Pittsburgh and Toledo and gave economic vitality to Corning, New York, La Salle, Illinois, and many other towns. German brewers helped to build up Cincinnati, St. Louis, Rochester, Chicago, and especially Milwaukee; despite some opposition from local temperance forces, they ultimately won acceptance and influence in each place. Skilled mechanics and technicians from England, Germany, and elsewhere received a more immediate welcome and financial support in developing enterprises ranging in one town from buttons to optical instruments; the classic example of immigrant enterprise, however, was the clothing industry, and many cities fattened upon it.

When the ready-to-wear clothing trade appeared at mid-century its most enterprising leaders were German Jews. Many who had gained a footing as tailors or peddlers or retail merchants now expanded their operations by employing some of their more recently arrived fellow countrymen. Several of these firms, which sprang up in the more populous centers and engaged the talents of vigorous salesmen, installed the newly invented sewing machines, employing women and girls to operate them. As cutting machines were perfected and the specialization of tasks increased, some of the shops blossomed into factories. Others, particularly in New York and Chicago, where the largest influx of a new wave of Eastern European Jews occurred, developed a contract system that enabled the recent comers to work under men of their own group and in neighborhood lofts where they could speak their native tongue.

This activity spread widely and unobtrusively, helping to sustain sizable colonies of Eastern Jews in Boston and Baltimore, in Cleveland, Cincinnati, Rochester, and a dozen smaller places. Every member of the family lent a hand, but it soon became evident that only the contract bosses were prospering. Again a union movement developed and brought long years of bitter strife, with both the owners and the organizers seeking to gain an advantage by playing one city against another in regional lockouts and boycotts. Nevertheless the industry, responding to the rapid urban growth, continued to expand, and the companies, closely dependent on their labor supply, could not migrate freely. Wages remained low, and the wide use of sweatshops helped to foster living standards that were among the worst in America—so wretched, in fact, that the public conscience was pricked. Soon local, state, and federal investigations began to study the problem. New pressure for governmental supervision developed, and a resurgence of union effort occurred among the workers as the period closed.

If the classic example of immigrant enterprise was the clothing industry, that of the native was the commercial bank, though foreign-born bankers increased in number after the seventies. Each new settlement boasted one or more of these institutions, which quickly multiplied as the towns grew. By 1880, 6532 banks with national, state, or private charters—one to every 2000 urban residents—served a variety of functions, among them the promotion of city growth. Although the accumulation and use of private savings was still a minor feature, as was investment banking, the facility these establishments brought to commercial transactions, and the concentration they effected of fluid capital in the sixteen cities designated as redemption centers under the National Banking Act of 1863–64, strengthened the leading marts within their respective regions and tied their economy to the great central reserve capital in New York.

It was not the banks, however, but enterprising men who determined the direction of a city's industrial development. Sometimes an influx of newcomers with special skills transformed a town's activity. Thus at Rochester after the mid-century, when flour milling and canalling had passed their apogee, a host of immigrant craftsmen created the clothing, shoe, nursery, brewing, and woodworking industries that gave it a new burst of growth, placing it in the 100,000 bracket by 1885. The lack of convenient coal, iron, and other natural resources had threatened to blight the "Flower City's" manufacturing prospects, but the new industries depended less on raw materials than on human skills and on the excellence of their products. Such varied and specialized instruments were designed and built that they again transformed Rochester, within three decades, into a center of technical industry. A young bank clerk, George Eastman, discovered that the

photographic laboratory he set up in his mother's kitchen held more fascination than a teller's cage, and the city soon shared his rewards.

Enterprise in abundance characterized most cities throughout these decades. Growth itself created a rich market, not only for food and apparel and building materials but also for a variety of new articles that promised urban convenience. Ingenious men perfected the telephone, the elevator, the trolley car, the bicycle, and the automobile—to name only a few that contributed to the ease and speed of communications in cities, thus increasing the momentum of their growth. Energetic promoters extended the use of these products widely through the towns of America and at the same time greatly benefited those where the factories were located.

The widespread technological advance frequently prompted independent inventors to work on similar problems at the same time. Occasionally a city assembled so many skilled craftsmen in a particular industry that it generated innovations and attracted experts from distant places. The Edison shops at Harrison, New Jersey, the Brush Electric Company at Cleveland, and the Thomson-Houston works at Lynn drew proficient electrical workers to these centers; Eastman attracted to Rochester rival photographic and optical companies eager to share its concentration of specialized skills. Although many manufacturers, impelled to acquire patent rights that might obstruct the development of their products, hastened to absorb competitors, the formation of new firms almost in the shadow of the expanding companies often continued unabated. Some of the new concerns developed subsidiary articles which they produced for the major distributors—speed shutters for cameras in Rochester, lamp stems for incandescent globes at Harrison—thus contributing to the integration of major community industries while retaining the enterprise many restless but talented craftsmen desired.

The upsurge of inventiveness flooded the patent office with applications as the 120,000 registered before 1870 mounted by 1910 to well over a million. Promoters who helped to develop the new mechanical devices generally enlisted support from local capitalists. The limited-dividend corporation, freely available under the general laws of most states, proved especially attractive, and such incorporations, almost nonexistent in manufacturing in 1860, numbered over 40,000 at the close of the century. Although they comprised barely a tenth of all establishments, they produced 60 per cent of the value, and almost completely dominated the metal and technical branches. The flexibility of these economic "persons"—their capacity for expansion or consolidation, for a shift in leadership or a change in product—fitted admirably for growing cities faced with problems of economic integration.

The most rapid increase among giant corporations occurred at the turn of the century, as they mushroomed from twelve in 1896, each valued at $10 million or more, to fifty that exceeded $50 million by 1903. Even after the move for consolidation began and strong, often monopolistic groups took hold, a rapidly expanding market and more effective sales promotion frequently enabled the trust to keep all its affiliated plants in operation, at least for a time. Sometimes a new factory site was selected, as in the case of the General Electric Company, a consolidation of Edison and rival concerns, but the new beginning it made

at Schenectady in 1886 could not absorb all the work in process at Harrison, Lynn, and Cleveland, among other places. Several of the old centers prospered, while Schenectady became an industrial city of high quality.

Numerous towns, though not the majority, enjoyed similar benefits. The typewriter brought life to Ilion, New York, and new vigor to Syracuse; telephone factories clustered for a time at Boston and Chicago, but soon spread out; the cash register placed Dayton on the industrial map. A score of cities manufactured elevators, and many more contributed to the production of trolley cars and their equipment. Bicycle companies sprang up in a host of towns during the early nineties, but shortly after 1899, when the American Bicycle Company absorbed forty-eight of them, production was centered in ten plants at Springfield, Massachusetts, and Hartford, Connecticut, each of which suffered a severe blow when the trust collapsed a few seasons later. Several former cycle factories had meanwhile shifted to the manufacture of automobiles, in which Detroit quickly took the lead. Its surplus of capital from an expiring lumber trade, together with an overabundance of skilled marine-engine mechanics, welcomed the new industry.

So many cities suffered from the migration of old companies and other effects of consolidation that the antitrust forces won general approval. The long battle for the regulation of railroads had spread anti-monopoly doctrines, nurturing a strong faith in competition, and prepared the way for the speedy adoption of the Sherman Anti-Trust Act in 1890. Yet its vague provisions left many issues undecided. In the courts, where the rising trusts had much more effective representation than in the legislatures, the legal curbs atrophied and almost disappeared. Protests against government interference with "free enterprise," on which the welfare, particularly of industrial cities, seemed to depend, enlisted support from most business groups and discouraged efforts to half consolidations. Only the more flagrant invasions of local community interests aroused effective action, such as the Standard Oil Company's stranglehold over the fortunes of Toledo and other Ohio towns in the early nineties, or the Trans-Missouri Freight Association's attempt to control the traffic of the Southwest a few years later. Champions of the efficiency of large-scale enterprise multiplied, and in 1889 New Jersey provided a corporate form for the holding companies that widely superseded the old trusts.

In most cities new firms quickly replaced those absorbed or otherwise lost, and many small market towns grew into promising industrial centers. The number reporting at least 10,000 factory workers increased from thirty to fifty-four during the last two decades of the century; those listing 5000 or more rose from forty-five to eighty-one. After 1900 many factories migrated to the suburbs, and this presented the parent city with new problems of economic integration. All growing towns felt an increasing need for local leadership.

Boards of trade and chambers of commerce sprang up in city after city as rallying points for their businessmen. Only a few of the thirty or more such organizations formed before the Civil War had survived, notably those of Chicago, Buffalo, Pittsburgh, and New York. Now the extension of the telegraph and the laying of the Atlantic cable in 1866 opened new possibilities for long-distance trade negotiations and stimulated the formation of organizations to conduct local exchanges and disseminate trade information.

Most of the new crop of business clubs were, like their predecessors, chiefly concerned with commerce, but in 1869 the Milwaukee Chamber of Commerce raised a fund of $860 "to promote the city's industrial growth." Its list of the town's advantages for trade and industry, published in 1871 and widely circulated, heralded a new, more industrial approach. A few years later, the same body initiated an industrial exposition patterned after the Centennial in Philadelphia. Its building, erected at a cost of $300,000 and opened in 1881, supplied facilities for annual exhibitions during the next two decades and inspired businessmen in St. Louis, Chicago, and Minneapolis to similar efforts.

The most forthright move in this direction occurred at Philadelphia in 1894, when the city council organized a Commercial Museum and provided it with a building and equipment to display local industrial products and to promote foreign trade. San Francisco, St. Louis, and Boston established similar museums. Not to be outdone, an Association for the Advancement of Milwaukee urged real-estate men to grant free sites or free rent to new industrial ventures and collected subscriptions from capitalists to back them. The association, which also proposed tax concessions, boasted after two years that its efforts had attracted a score of new industries to the city, helping it to reach fifteenth place by 1900.

Some of the post–Civil War boards of trade declined after a few seasons, but new organizations generally appeared in response to urgent business needs. Several midwestern towns formed promotional bodies similar to Milwaukee's. In 1892 the Cleveland Board of Trade created a committee for the promotion of industry, which led in turn to the reorganization of the board as a Chamber of Commerce a year later, when a full-time secretary was engaged to handle such activities and to develop new civic and welfare functions. Other chambers, too, were seeking competent secretaries, and in 1913 as their activities became standardized the newly established Harvard Business School organized a course for them.

The effort to provide free sites or other subsidies for new industries lost favor in some chambers after concerns of questionable merit accepted such benefits only to move on when a higher bid arrived. But the promotional value of numerous trade conventions, industrial exhibitions, and publications that featured local advantages gained wide acceptance among the several hundred boards and chambers of the early 1900's. If the annual reports often sounded a bit boastful, even to local observers, such growing industrial cities as Milwaukee, Cleveland, Pittsburgh, Detroit, Buffalo, Columbus, and Rochester—not to mention several of the new towns of the West—all gladly supported active groups.

Although the basic philosophy of most of these chambers involved unfaltering support for "free enterprise," especially after events in the nineties sharpened the issue, some of their committees did try to establish voluntary standards of production and fair dealing. Their resolutions generally opposed state and federal regulations, but many were quick to appeal to the I. C. C. or to an appropriate state authority when a long-haul railroad rate schedule or some other monopoly practice seemed prejudicial to the locality. Their concern for the city's welfare often aligned them against freebooting utility combines and highhanded industrial giants. Leadership in the continuing attack on trusts and corporate monopolies generally came from other sources, but the chambers were exponents of community business interests.

Most growing towns had, of course, developed a sense of the community's interest long before organizations to promote it emerged. An informal leadership, which later sociologists would call the power structure, generally directed important aspects of the development of each city. The promoters of town sites and urban subdivisions, who frequently joined the merchants to support and direct the expansive projects of the commercial centers, seldom gave effective leadership to the industrial cities. There the initiative more frequently came from ambitious craftsmen, often men with inventive talents, whose struggle to produce and market new products transformed them into captains of industry. They were the most alert developers of each town's external economy. Newcomers from abroad, and others from small towns nearby, rose in this fashion to positions of influence.

Many industrial cities developed specialties based on the skills of their workers or the inventive talents of their technicians. On the other hand the mining towns and some others largely dependent on one industry frequently lost control to absentee owners who opposed the development of independent enterprise. The widespread reaction to, or fear of, that fate strengthened the antimonopoly forces of the commercial centers, plagued by railroad pools, and hastened the triumph of the progressive movement.

The most important contribution of the industrial cities was the mounting output of their factories. Statistics show that the value added by manufacturing doubled between 1859 and 1879 and more than doubled again in the prosperous eighties, and yet again, despite two depressions, by 1909. The value added by manufacturing increased tenfold in the half-century, almost trebling the increased value of farm products. Moreover the portion of the national income derived from manufacturing mounted from 16.6 to 20.8 per cent during the last three decades, while that derived from agriculture held steady and the contributions of both trade and transportation declined.

In this period, at least, industry rather than commerce was the chief source of urban growth. Over nine-tenths of the industrial production occurred in urban factories, and as their output increased a surplus for export developed in some fields. Shipments abroad of manufactured foodstuffs and of finished industrial products mounted steadily after 1876 until, by 1898, even the latter exceeded comparable imports. As American factories progressively crowded European products out of the domestic consumer trade, the American farm was relieved of the burden of balancing foreign payments. The export of foodstuffs, both raw and manufactured, declined after the turn of the century, but the exports of other manufactured products more than took up the slack, maintaining a sufficiently favorable balance of trade to liquidate some of the foreign investments. Thus urban industrial growth freed the national economy not only from dependence on European factories, but also from reliance on foreign banks for new capital. That, however, was only a minor aspect of the industrial city's accomplishment, for the value added to its products exceeded the total value of all imports almost seven to one by 1899, as contrasted with a ratio of five to two, four decades earlier. As foreign trade diminished in relative importance, domestic trade mounted, and the industrial worker produced material goods in sufficient volume to raise the standards of consumption throughout the country.

Urban Growth and Industrial Development

Edward C. Kirkland*

URBAN GROWTH AND THE WELFARE OF THE ECONOMY

To those who believed that the welfare of the American economy depended upon the production of capital goods, the decade of the eighties brought forebodings. The most obvious support for this theory had been the construction of the railroad network. Its constantly extending mileage had given employment and business directly to thousands; it had also stimulated auxiliary activities such as the iron and steel industry and the engineering trades. Now railroad expansion was slowing down. What was to take its place? What power was now to pull the economy forward?

Though the answer was by no means obvious, the new generative factor was the growth of American cities. There had been cities, of course, in the colonial era, and in the first half of the nineteenth century population had gone cityward as well as westward. But after the Civil War the railroads and the industrialization of the economy compelled urbanization at rapid speed. In 1860 the number of places in the United States with a population of 8,000 or over was 141; in 1900, it was 545. At the same time there was a progressive increase in the absolute totals of urban dwellers. Whereas in 1860 just over 5,000,000 people lived in cities, in 1900 the urban population was just under 25,000,000. The eighties was the decade *par excellence*

of urban growth: for those ten years the Federal Census reported "A very large increase in urban population."

The startling accessions of population to cities came from two migrations: one from the country to the city and the other from abroad. On the whole the former, at least in quantitative terms, was probably the more important. Since the country-city migration was merely a population displacement within the national boundaries, it is hard to estimate its net effects. In 1891 the *Commercial and Financial Chronicle,* brooding over the decline of New Hampshire and Massachusetts small towns, expressed distress at this "decay" and "the melancholy story of the farming towns" but added that so long as Massachusetts "as a whole, is showing such vigor, there is no room for lamentations over the drift of population away from the barren hillsides." On the other hand, immigrants from abroad represented an addition to the economy. These were producers and consumers the United States had not had before. And they came fast and numerously in the late nineteenth century. In 1882 their number, 788,992, set a record up to that time and one not to be surpassed until 1903.

Though not all immigrants went to cities, and the enlarging population, wherever located, was a stimulus to the economy, there were differences between cities and rural regions which were of profound importance. The compacting and concentration of population stimulated economic activities, for example urban transportation and the provision of electricity from a central station, which a dispersed pop-

*Reprinted with permission from Edward C. Kirkland, *Industry Comes of Age: Business, Labor, and Public Policy, 1860–1897,* New York: Holt, Rinehart and Winston, Inc., 1961, 237–246, 255–261, copyright in the possession of the author.

ulation in those days could neither have called into being nor supported. Where people were gathered in communities, standards of taste, convenience, and economic necessity compelled other improvements. For instance, officials of Augusta, Maine, complained in 1880: "The method of keeping . . . the main street in condition, is to haul on gravel in the summer and grade up in places where needed. In the fall and spring this makes a road-bed of 6 or 8 inches of mud. . . . Then in the spring our streets are scraped and the gravel that was hauled in is again carted out." This was a road condition to which dwellers had become, perforce, reconciled. It was humiliating to an aspiring city if "not a single paved street exists."

Furthermore, in the country the building of houses and barns was apt to be assimilated to the partially self-sufficing regime of the farm; in the urban communities it was set apart and organized into commercial construction, the building industry. In 1900, 63 per cent of the establishments in the building trade were located in the country's 209 cities and construction expenditures on farms constituted less than 10 per cent of the nation's total. Finally, in the city considerations of the relation between sanitation and health, to mention no other factors, raised problems that had to be met by community rather than individual or familial action. The provision of pure water and the disposal of waste meant that in the city reliance upon public policy in social and economic matters came earlier and went deeper than elsewhere in the United States.

The problems and challenges inherent in these figures and circumstances induced in some a state of ecstasy. As F. C. Howe of Cleveland was to write: "The possibility of a free, orderly, and beautiful city became to me an absorbing passion. . . . I had an architectonic vision of what a city might be. I saw it as a picture. It was not economy, efficiency, and business methods that interested me so much as a city planned, built, and conducted as a community enterprise. . . . The city was the enthusiasm of my life. And I saw cities as social agencies that would make life easier for people, full of pleasure, beauty, and opportunity." Whatever Howe might dream, the city wore a very material aspect. It had to be built. To some extent the increase in municipal debt mirrored this necessity. Though such debts might occasionally represent operational costs they were primarily capital expenditures. In 1860 net municipal indebtedness in the country was estimated at $200,000,000; in 1880 it was $725,000,000, and in 1902 $1,433,000,000. Whereas early in the period these sums were fed into the economy via city subscriptions to railroad securities or other forms of railroad subsidy, the revulsion against the railroad-aid policy in the hard times after 1873 meant that municipal expenditures for other purposes became more important.

Unhappily for purposes of historically measuring and tracing such expenditures, statistical data cannot be pushed very far back into the nineteenth century. But the investment in municipal water works in 1905 was estimated at "considerably more than a billion dollars"; in gas works, plants and distributing systems, the sum in 1900 was $567,000,506, about twenty times what it had been in 1860. In 1860 neither central electric power stations nor electric railways existed. In 1902 the issued capitalization and funded debt of electric stations selling power in the commercial market was $627,515,875. At the same date for street railways the capitalization and funded debt was $2,308,282,099.

THE CHOICE OF PUBLIC OR PRIVATE ENTERPRISE

Cities could turn over the provision of municipal services to private enterprise or furnish them at first hand through municipal ownership and operation. Though state legislatures restricted the capacity of cities to go into debt and otherwise limited their functions, cities remained public corporations chartered for public purposes. In favorable circumstances the legal hindrances to activity were not excessive. In 1897 the appellate division of the New York Supreme Court, validating New York City's issue of bonds for the construction and ownership of a subway, asserted that it was a principle of our nation's policy "to foster and protect private enterprise." Nonetheless the municipal ownership of a subway system was neither "socialism nor paternalism." There were other purposes cities could fulfill by their energy and expenditure. It was futile to formulate "a complete definition of 'a city purpose' . . . in view of the fact that reasons may arise which we are unable to foresee or now consider." In the same decade the justices of the Massachusetts Supreme Court unanimously approved a wide area for the municipal provision of public services.

If the city chose to fulfill its functions through the agency of a private corporation, the transfer of responsibility was usually effected by the grant of a franchise, either from the state or city government depending upon the date and jurisdiction. Such contractual documents permitted a private corporation to acquire property through eminent domain and to use the streets to lay pipes, install conduits, put down rails, or string wires. "The political science of the street is of fundamental importance in most municipal problems," commented one expert. Since the streets were generally not wide enough to accommodate competitors, a franchise was usually equivalent to a monopoly grant. The franchise grant might or might not contain time limitations, rate and service regulations, provisions for recapture, or provide for payments by the grantee. In other words, it roughly resembled the earliest railroad charters.

THE IMPROVEMENT OF STREETS

Even the most confirmed advocate of private enterprise admitted that streets were a legitimate responsibility of government. Expenditures for this purpose were, of course, not large so long as the making of streets did not depart widely from that of country roads. Cities graveled their streets or, as in Philadelphia, used an abundant supply of local materials for cobblestones. Though these methods had the advantage of cheapness, such streets were dirty, rough, noisy, uneven, damaging to traffic and uncomfortable for riders. The rationale for innovation was not long in coming. "Smooth and clean highways are a wise investment from every point of view, and that so long as the work is done in a thorough and scientific manner, the result is worth having, regardless of cost. No city should think itself rich enough to prosper without them, and no city is so poor that it can not afford them if it has any reason whatever for continued existence. Good roadways are cheap at any cost, and bad ones are so disastrously expensive that only a very rich country, like the United States, can afford them."

Apparently about the time of the Civil War, eastern cities became aware of the possibilities and advantages of paving their streets with small granite blocks. Soon quarries in Massachusetts and Maine, along the coast or accessible to it, became interested in the paving-stone industry. A specialized craft of stone cutters recruited from Yankees and immigrants from the British Isles began hammering out the "New York block" eight to twelve inches long, seven to eight inches deep, and three-and-one-half to four-and-one-half inches wide. Coastal sailing vessels distributed the product to cities up and down the Atlantic and there were even some shipments to the interior. On the whole cities without easy access to quarries relied upon other materials. After the mid-seventies pioneer communities in the Midwest were laying down brick pavements, a material far superior to wooden blocks, which in spite of their tendency to decay and heave, were also a contemporary fashion. Chicago was noted for its "floating pavements" of cedar block, "which are said to rise with the floods of water filling the roadways after heavy rainfalls." Finally, taking a cue from the experiences of Paris and London, American cities about 1870 began the use of asphalt. At first the raw material came from the great Pitch Lake deposit in Trinidad; by the end of the century the refining of American crude oils was producing a domestic supply.

Though cities owned the streets and could improve them through their own officials and employees, the task could also, without a franchise, be turned over to private contractors. Like all jobs, these contracts were much sought after and there frequently grew up a political alliance between the city government and favored contractors. The latter provided a labor force, frequently Irish or Italian, and the labor force provided voters at election time.

WATER AND SEWERAGE

Cities had also to face the problem of providing abundant supplies of water for their own use, for fire fighting, for industrial purposes, and for their own populations. After research during the closing decades of the nineteenth century had validated the germ theory of disease, the water had to be pure. Building dams and aqueducts, installing pumping apparatus to raise the water to standpipes or high basins, laying out an elaborate distribution system of water mains was an expensive business. Generally speaking, whether the municipality should build and own the works or turn the job over to a private corporation depended upon the empirical consideration of what was the less painful way of raising the money. On the one hand municipal officials and citizens were loath to increase city debt; on the other, private capitalists, though they were sometimes granted subsidies and a monopoly of providing water service, hesitated to invest in enterprises in the determination of whose rates social and sanitary considerations were more important than the law of supply and demand. Though ancient Rome had undertaken the task of water supply and classical precedents meant a great deal to Americans, more influential in the United States was the example of its two leading cities. In Philadelphia the Fairmount works opened in 1799–1801, and in New York, where the original Croton system was opened in 1842, water works were municipal undertakings. Since New York had earlier experimented with private enterprise, its eventual choice of public ownership and operation was all the more influential.

Interlocked with the water problem was the provision of improved sewage facilities. In some instances, as in Chicago and Milwaukee, the sewers emptied into the lakes from which the cities drew their water supplies; everywhere the wider employment of water closets raised problems of disposal.

Slowly and quarrelsomely, most municipalities brought themselves to provide facilities through the sale of bonds and the levy of assessments upon abutting property owners. In Chicago the heroic measure of reversing the flow of the Chicago River, into which most waste was dumped, away from Lake Michigan and into the Mississippi was completed in 1871 at the cost of $3,000,000.

LIGHTING

The provision of modern lighting facilities had, of course, to wait upon the course of invention. In 1816 Baltimore, the first American city to do so, introduced illuminating gas made from coal. In the seventies a dual transformation affected the gas industry. The Standard Oil group became definitely interested in piping and selling natural gas, used primarily for industrial and heating purposes, and also in the production of gas oil, a derivative from petroleum, which was used to produce water gas, a product with superior illuminating qualities. These changes, of course, soon confronted the competition of electric lighting. Frank Brush's invention of an improved arc light devised a source of illumination peculiarly fitted for the outdoors. The Edison incandescent light early in the eighties was designed for interior use, and it was not until a later date that it competed with the arc light for street illumination. In any case, the advent of electrical lighting slowed the expansion of gas as an illuminant. In many ways the problems connected with lighting were like those of providing water. There was a dual market for the product—a private one, homes and businesses, and a public one, street lighting. Both gas and electricity had to use the streets, the one for mains, the other for wires or conduits.

URBAN TRANSPORTATION

As cities grew in population and enlarged in area, a new problem emerged —urban transportation. Before the Civil War the omnibus and the horse-car furnished public conveyances. Horse-car lines were often adjuncts to speculation in suburban real estate. But these methods were hazardous, uncomfortable, and inefficient. They so heightened street congestion, already intense enough, that a person could proceed on foot more quickly to his destination. More rapid means of locomotion had been introduced into the city incidental to the search by steam railroads for convenient urban terminals. Though railroads secured franchises permitting them to lay rails along the streets, such documents were usually foresighted enough to prohibit locomotives from traveling along city thoroughfares and to insist that there steam should give way to mule or horse-power.

One obvious solution for the dilemma was to construct roadways at different levels and to permit locomotives and cars to travel the elevated one. Still there were real business uncertainties in such undertakings. In view of the proclivity of steam trains to jump the track or to run off bridges, elevated railroads threatened dangers. There was also considerable doubt whether people would take the trouble to walk upstairs for improved transport. Whatever the attitude of passengers, abutting property owners were quickly aware that an iron elevated structure along the street and the frequent passage of noisy trains was likely to diminish rather than enhance the value of their property. Nevertheless the need was so great that a Rapid Transit Commission appointed by the Mayor of New York recommended in the early seventies for two of the north and south avenues in the city an elevated system capable of carrying 15,000 passengers a day. By the next decade elevated roads had demonstrated their success. Eastern cities imitated New York, and in the early nineties Chicago, destined to become the city of "El's," already had its lines.

Eventually the elevateds were electrified. So were the surface lines. Cities, unless in special circumstances like San Francisco's discarded the use of an endless cable beneath the pavement to tow cars and relied, particularly after Sprague's demonstration in Richmond, upon an overhead electric wire or an underground one with which a shoe from the car made contact. By the nineties there "was an active 'boom' in electric railway building" and speculation. "It is stimulated by the apparent cheapness of electricity as compared with horse power, by the expectation of large profits, and in some cases probably by the hope of successful deals in the securities of the company."

Private capitalists solicited and secured the franchises for these networks of urban transportation and operated the completed enterprises. Whereas local capital had once undertaken this task, capitalists without local ties moved into the enterprise. A hope of steady dividends prosaically earned from operations was hardly their aim. Instead they applied to urban transportation the most dubious devices of speculation and personal enrichment developed in the railroad world: the construction company, the lease, consolidation, stock-watering and Wall Street speculation. In some cases those practicing these arts in the new area were railroad men; for instance, in the eighties Jay Gould applied his unquestioned talents to the New York elevated system. He transferred its complicated affairs to the arena of Wall Street, journalistic rumors, and the courts. Eventually the growing returns from the consolidations he put together placed the stock on a dividend basis and made it one of the "blue chips" in the Gould estate.

In street railways a national "syndicate" appeared, originating in Philadelphia. Its leaders, Peter A. B. Widener and William L. Elkins, started their business careers, as had John D. Rockefeller, in the provision trades. Clearly this occupation as a training ground and reservoir of capital possessed a magic of its own. Dabbling in politics, Widener, Elkins, and others had by 1884 gathered within their Philadelphia Traction Company at least half the street car lines of the city. Elkins, who had invested in oil and had sold out to the Standard, once remarked, "Give me the Broadway franchise and the coal-oil trade of Philadelphia and I will retire." Actually this was a rather limited objective. In 1886 the Philadelphia group, with the alliance of broker Charles T. Yerkes, invaded Chicago. In the resulting process of consolidation and leasing, the capitalization of the various enterprises roughly doubled and cable cars superseded the horse-drawn ones.

In New York City William Collins Whitney, a graduate of Yale and a reform anti-Tweed Democrat who had married a Standard Oil fortune, formed an alliance with T. F. Ryan, a Virginia farm boy now a broker. Whitney once remarked of his associate, "If Ryan lives long enough, he'll have all the money in the world." Whitney and Ryan called to their assistance the Philadelphians Widener and Elkins and were also fortunate enough to retain as counsel Elihu Root to plot a path through the intricacies of New York law and politics, though in the latter area Whitney himself was adroit enough. These capitalists went ahead to consolidate all the surface lines of New York City. The first instrument was the Metropolitan Traction Company, a holding company incorporated in New Jersey. Like holding companies elsewhere, it exchanged its stock for the concerns it acquired; it also leased enterprises. In 1893 their corporate means of expansion became the Metropolitan Street Railway Company of New York. Whatever the legal form, the battle for consolidation was waged in the city and state governments and with frequent recourse to the counts. A trail of injunctions and receiverships marked this continual litigation. Nor were the vacillations of securities on Wall Street forgotten.

Though Whitney's brother became the urban transportation magnate of Boston through his own efforts, the Widener-Elkins-Whitney-Ryan syndicate at the end of the century were reputed to have built up the street railway systems in New York, Chicago, Philadelphia, and Pittsburgh and in at least one hundred cities and towns from Maine to Pennsylvania. In addition they had become influential in gas and electric-lighting companies as far west as Omaha and as far south as St. Augustine. The united capitalization of their street railways was a billion dollars and of their lighting companies $300,000,000.

URBAN BUILDING

Private expenditures for residential and business purposes were the most important contribution American cities made to the economy. An index of the dollar value of building permits in terms of 1913 dollars reveals how important this stimulus was. The index reached a peak in 1890 which was not approached again until 1925. Such figures, as usual, obliterate distinctions. But so can the impressionistic, qualitative observations of travelers.

In an oft-quoted sentence Lord Bryce, after excepting a few historic American cities, remarked, "American cities differ from one another only herein, that some of them are built more with brick than with wood, and others more with wood than brick." Actually, building followed a straight-line evolution from wood to brick to stone. For stone was the prestige building material, granite enjoying the highest favor. Governmental buildings—customs houses, post-offices, courthouses, and jails—were built of it, as were buildings having a public aspect— banks, hotels, churches, markets, and railroad stations. Since granite was hard to work and therefore expensive, those with lesser means turned to softer stones, and brownstone fitted the prescription perfectly. Since its chief deposits lay along the lower Connecticut River, it could be shipped cheaply by water; the large blocks, straight from the quarry, were easily worked up and fitted near the spot of construction. Brownstone fronts dominated the domestic architecture of Boston's Back Bay and flowed like a chocolate tide along the avenues and cross streets of New York. The birthplace of Theodore Roosevelt had a brownstone front; Commodore Vanderbilt gave the material a certain cachet when he built his palace on Fifth Avenue of it. To the Commodore, granite, like the law, was "too slow," and he wanted the building done before he died. Of the stone buildings in New York, over three-quarters had brownstone fronts, and its use penetrated even to Chicago. The slate quarries, which furnished fire-proof roofing, and the lime quarries, whose product was processed in kilns to make interior finish plaster, were associated industries. All in all, the number of building stone quarries in the United States increased from 1,444 in 1850 to 5,764 in 1902.

Houses with brownstone fronts usually had side and rear walls of brick. In some communities, for example Philadelphia, brick had been the traditional material for super-structures of the more pretentious early buildings. By century's end, even the slums of Philadelphia were brick single-family houses. Since the costs of transportation increased rapidly with the distance such heavy materials were carried, nearly every city was rimmed with clay pits from which its buildings had been dug. Every state in the Union, except two in the Far West, reported brickyards. Nonetheless there was a tendency for the industry to gravitate to deposits of superior clay and to utilize at these locations brick-making machinery.

In the United States even the interior structure of stone and brick edifices—flooring, beams, roofs—was generally of wood. Furthermore there were factors which made it the preferred material for the whole building. Forests were abundant. Moreover a revolutionary new technique for building houses and working wood kept prices down. In the 1830's an ingenious migrant from New England to Chicago invented the balloon frame. Previously a frame house had been composed of heavy timbers fitted together; the balloon frame used a multitude of lighter pieces and relied upon the exterior boarding to give the structure rigidity and strength. The house utilized the principle of the box. Later, multiplication and refinement of woodworking machinery released workers from making blinds, sash, doors, and mouldings by hand in a shop during the winter and transferred this task to a shop using machinery all the year round, thus doing the work more cheaply and in some instances performing prodigies hand workers could not attempt.

The census of 1880 observed that, "Having a larger and more rapidly-increasing population than any other country that is noted for its consumption of iron, we are consequently the largest consumers of nails and spikes in the construction of dwellings and public buildings, stores, warehouses, offices and similar structures." So pronounced were the advantages of wooden construction that great American cities clung to it even after the Chicago fire of 1871 demonstrated its danger.

Whatever the building façade, the interior was mechanized. The American stove, "works of real art," "handsome, bright, cheerful, healthful, and clean," and one of the early triumphs of American mass production, gave way to an industry of steamfitting and heating apparatus. The same domestic mechanization created the indoor bathroom and toilet, thus benefiting the porcelain industry.

American construction now began to utilize new materials of the industrial age. In New York City Peter Cooper, the ironmaster, decided to support the floors of his Cooper Union on horizontal rolled iron beams. By 1859 his plant was rolling beams 4 feet long and 9 inches deep. Somewhat earlier Harpers rebuilt their burned down publishing plant with one seven stories high, using iron beams supported by iron columns; instead of brick or stone, it had a cast-iron front. By the eighties architects were considering the feasibility of a building whose support was a metal frame or cage and whose walls were simply filler between the beams and columns. In 1885 the plans of a Chicago engineer, W. LeBaron Jenney, materialized in the ten stories of the Home Insurance Company building, the "first skyscraper." Of course steel had now superseded iron. Whereas the census of 1880 had mentioned neither iron nor steel for buildings, the census of

1900 noted the production of 856,983 tons of structural shapes of iron and steel. Unhappily it did not specify what proportion went into buildings.

The construction industry stimulated the economy directly. Materials had to be manufactured and put together or installed. Occupations ranging from sophisticated manufacturing such as wood working to the handicrafts of carpenter, mason, painter, plumber, and plasterer boomed. In 1900, expenditures on construction turned out an annual product valued at $1,946,-000,000. In the sixties an American calculator had surmised by extrapolation from data then available that there was "a vast annual demand for 130,000 new houses" and foresaw that the better construction and luxuries of a "modern house" with "modern improvements" constantly increased the expenditure per house. For the decade as a whole he put their total cost at $1,300,000,000. This was quite unlike the course of affairs in the "old and stationary countries of Europe," where "old cities" were already built and there was consequently "no active and continued demand for labor and capital to provide new dwellings to accommodate swelling numbers."

The American ideal of owning one's home was deep-seated. Home ownership conferred prestige, showed others that the owner was getting ahead and reassured him that he was "Americanized." In farming the dream was widely realized; in urban living, much less so. In New York City in 1900, rented homes constituted 87.9 per cent of the total; in Chicago 74.9. Since urban population was notably on the wing, it relied on rented properties. Builders of all sorts relied in large part on borrowed money. The owner did not issue stock, he encumbered the property with a mortgage. Though most figures for construction in the

late nineteenth century contain a good deal of surmise, it seems reasonably accurate to say that the non-farm mortgage debt rose from $3,811,000,-000 in 1890 to $4,661,000,000 in 1900. While the major share of this mortgage debt was held by individuals, savings banks and insurance companies under legal restrictions were also large holders.

Such arrangements facilitated home ownership without funds; they also aided speculative tenement building. Builders who went into this operation generally bought the land from an owner, borrowing money from him for the purchase; the latter frequently lent a portion of the funds for the purchase of material. When the building was done, the builder tried to sell it as soon as possible to an investor who would put in some money of his own and purchase the mortgages accumulated along the way. Land owners and builder hoped to make their gains by marking up the value of the property in the course of these transactions.

By the mere fact of its existence, the city regulated the kind of edifices it had. Even with minimum planning, the city had to lay out the pattern of the streets. In Philadelphia the rectangular system or gridiron went back to its founder, William Penn. Between 1808 and 1811, three commissioners appointed by the New York state legislature laid out the gridiron plan of north and south avenues and cross streets for New York City and applied it from the old town of crooked streets on lower Manhattan to 155th Street. Chicago also had the gridiron. While this design had the advantage of fixing precise boundaries for property and thus facilitating its conveyance, it necessarily determined the size of the conventional lot: in New York, 25 feet frontage and 100 feet in depth, and in Chicago "the shoe-string lot," also with a 25 foot frontage but often

125 feet deep. Both sizes were ill-adapted for tenement construction, a tenement being a house occupied by three or more families. When multi-family houses were built with higher standards they came to be called apartment houses and furnished abode for the well-to-do and middle classes.

Although tenements appeared in New York as early as the 1830's, it was in the seventies, as congestion deepened, that the typical brick tenement, five or six stories high, appeared, occupying most of the front part of the narrow lot. Since Chicago lots were a little deeper and the city could spread out over the prairie, tenements there became wooden houses two or three stories high. There was one on the front of the lot, one in the rear on an alley, and sometimes one between.

Families were crowded into these dwellings until the density of population per square mile became record-making. In 1893 well over half the population of New York City lived in tenements; in thirty-two acres of the eleventh ward, there were 986.4 persons per acre, a density which only parts of Bombay approached. The crowded urban regions by their filth and lack of ventilation bred more than their share of mortality and illness; to them also were ascribed prostitution, drunkenness, crime, poverty, and the break-down of family life. The more conservative feared they were seed beds of social discontent and revolution.

Charity societies, settlement houses staffed by professors, divines, and social service workers, and individual reformers such as Jacob Riis protested the growth of slums. The particularities of their indictment and proposed remedies would seem to fall within the "public purpose," the responsibility for which in other matters majority opinion had often assigned to city governments. Some European prece-dents, to which American reformers were usually attune, pointed in the same direction. But though there were many who asserted that private philanthropy and the self-denial of rich men would remove the slum, rare was the proposal to do so through municipally owned housing. For local authorities to spend public money "competing with private enterprise in housing the masses is bad principle and worse policy." Since housing was not a "natural monopoly," public housing lacked that justification.

The answer was regulatory legislation. In New York after years of investigation and report, the legislature passed the first tenement house law in 1867. Successive years saw amendments or new acts until the passage of a general tenement house act in 1901, "the most significant regulatory act in America's history of housing." It was widely copied elsewhere. This act "would not have been possible except for the vogue of restrictive legislation that so largely dominated American thought at the opening of the twentieth century." Whereas in 1867 it had been thought sufficient to give each sleeping room ventilation by transom to another room or hall and to prescribe one toilet or privy for each twenty occupants, by 1901 the law restricted tenement houses to 70 per cent of the lot, required for every room a window opening upon street, yard, or court, compelled the installation of running water and a private toilet in each apartment, and prescribed a certain minimum of cubic feet of space for each occupant. The evolution of these requirements had been accompanied by a tightening of administration through the Board of Health or Building Department and had culminated in a Tenement House Department in 1901. Some provisions of the act were to govern only future construction; others were to compel the alteration of "old-law tenements."

As in other aspects of the economy, the regulatory movement headed into a dilemma. If pushed far enough to accomplish the sanitary and social objectives sought for, it might so increase expenses of construction and hence rents as to defeat its purposes. For a while housing reformers were able to console themselves with the reflection that alterations in "old-law tenements" benefited the landlords by decreasing vacancies and increasing the rents which the occupants ought to be willing to pay. But as congestion continued and new-law tenements were not constructed fast enough, and as apartments in old-law tenements continued in use into the twentieth century, regrets that regulation had not started earlier and chiding landlords for greed hardly seemed an adequate clarification of the situation. What the reformers wanted was expansion under standards which the community could approve. But one employer had noted in the eighties, "Capitalists consider tenement houses a poor investment, paying poor returns."

The Industrial City and Cultural Change
Ralph E. Turner*

In 1832 the *Manchester Guardian,* commenting on an exposure of bad living conditions among the factory population, offered as an apology for their existence the following observation: "The manufacturing system as it exists in Great Britain, and the inconceivably immense towns under it, are without previous parallel in the history of the world." This recognition of the industrial city as an unprecedented phenomenon was developed, not as an apology for bad living conditions, but as an explanation of the general changes under way in society, by two English observers of early industrialism, namely, William Cooke Taylor and Robert Vaughan, both of whom, it is worth noting, were historians. Taylor wrote a general history of civilization under the title *The Natural History of Society* (1841), besides many textbooks; and Vaughan, before he became president of the Lancashire Independent College at Manchester, was professor of history at the University of London. In a sense, therefore, it may be said that the view of the industrial city as a center of cultural change belongs peculiarly to historians.

Taylor held that the industrial town was a "new element" in society, which could not develop without deranging old institutions and relationships. It exhibited, he said, "a system of social life constructed on a wholly new principle, a principle yet vague and indefinite but developing itself by its own spontaneous force, and daily producing effects which no human foresight

had anticipated." Above all, he was impressed by the formation of the urban masses who, developing new habits of thought without external aid or guidance, would ultimately, like the slow rising and gradual swelling of the ocean, "bear all elements of society aloft upon its bosom." But, although these masses lacked guidance, they were, in his opinion, no worse off than their superiors who, however educated, found little in past human experience of use in understanding the unforeseen innovations of the factory towns. The Greek verse, said Taylor, meant nothing in Manchester, and philosophy knew no circumstances like those which prevailed there.

Vaughan, who pointed out the fact, none too well recognized even today, that rural and urban populations have played different roles in the growth of civilization, argued that in the "unavoidable intercourse" of the new towns there was occurring an education of the people that would stimulate science, advance self-government, improve the arts and literature, and raise the general level of popular life. "Such, indeed, is often the astuteness acquired in the exercise of this greatest of free schools," he said, "that the smith of Sheffield, or the weaver of Manchester, would frequently prove, on any common ground, more than a match for a college graduate." Vaughan saw the new industrial towns as centers of "vast experiments" like those which had occurred in the cities of other lands and ages.

For us who live today in the midst of what is a chaos understood badly if at all, the views of Taylor and Vaughan may provide a point of departure for a consideration of the pre-

---

*Reprinted with permission from Caroline F. Ware, ed., *The Cultural Approach to History*, New York: Columbia University Press, 1940, 228–242.

vailing confusion. At least, it is clear that, if the English industrial city of the 1840's was a scene of "vast experiments," today, with similar cities having become the dominant type of community in all industrial nations, "vast experiments" have probably been carried further than they had gone in the early nineteenth century. Similarly, if, as Taylor said, the urban masses will ultimately bear all society aloft, it is probable that the tendency of this bearing is more clear today than when he noted it.

An examination of the industrial city as a center of cultural change may indicate something of these "vast experiments," may possibly show the general direction the urban masses are tending. It is the purpose of this paper to sketch the outlines of such an examination.

The postulates of the examination are to be found in the concept of culture, as developed in recent social thought, especially by anthropologists and sociologists. According to their views, "a culture" is a socially organized and transmitted structure of behavior and thought. The structure is integrated functionally, that is, its elements provide more of a unity than of a conflict of services to life and have coherence psychologically in terms of a relatively clearly focused outlook on life. The basis of this integration is a process of social interaction, through which individual interests and needs are organized into collective forms or patterns. In the growth of culture, the social process impels individuals to new modes of action and thought—innovations, they are called—and these new modes, in turn, become organized as enduring patterns, through selection in the social process. The evolution of any structure of human behavior and thought, when viewed in historical perspective, is recognizable as the evolution of a cultural tradition which,

from time to time as new social conditions arise, assimilates new elements in what may be called a reorientation of the tradition. The newly assimilated elements, it may be believed, seldom outweigh those persisting from the past.

This conception of the evolution of behavior and thought also predicates that, although cultural development goes forward constantly both by the loss of old elements and by the assimilation of innovations, there may be far-reaching disturbances in a cultural tradition which, disorganizing a long-persisting integration, produces finally a new integration. At the base of such new integration, setting its pattern and tendency of growth, is the social process through which individual behavior and thought are originally organized and finally assimilated into transmitted materials. In the words of A. A. Goldenweiser,

> In its constituent elements culture is psychological and, in the last analysis, comes from the individual. But as an integral entity culture is cumulative, historical, extra-individual. It comes to the individual as part of his objective experience, just as do his experiences with nature, and, like these, it is absorbed by him, thus becoming part of his psychic content.[1]

It is from the point of view of these predications that the industrial city can be seen as having special significance for cultural development. Relative to the life that prevailed in the traditional countryside and the old market and port towns, is not difficult to understand that the industrial city tends to organize a new structure of behavior and thought. The original patterns of this structure, as they emerged in Manchester, England,

[1] A. A. Goldenweiser, *History, Psychology, and Culture* (New York, 1933), p. 59.

have been sketched in another essay in this volume;[2] here it is important to emphasize that the industrial city, as a focus of technological, economic, political, intellectual, and esthetic changes, organized cultural influences from many sources in a social process in which the constantly increasing populations participated. Whatever the influences of industrial cities, these influences move in the social interaction that arises in city populations, as individuals carry on their occupations, pursue their interests, and obtain their satisfactions. In terms of the concept of culture, the industrial city is, then, a milieu which everywhere has the same general elements and everywhere supports the development of a structure of behavior and thought from these elements. Because it is a predication of the concept of culture that both behavior and thought, although individually expressed, are socially organized, this milieu may be conceived as bringing about, through time, the transformation of the various organizations of behavior and thought carried in the traditional culture. Thus, for example, the organizations of behavior and thought characterizing the historic sociocultural types—the peasant, the noble, and the priest—are transformed into new structures of behavior and thought, which, however different for workers, technicians, and entrepreneurs, are nevertheless the common base of their lives.

Some of the aspects of this developing structure of behavior and thought may be briefly noted. Its primary elements are evident in the intricate division of labor, which, instead of standardizing and routinizing work as commonly supposed, gives it a manifold variety of forms which make the new urban workers not a "uniform mass" but a composite of diversified types. In contrast to the historic peasants, the members of the new industrial working class possess individuality in a great variety of forms. This developing structure of thought and behavior is also evident in new social services, in new amusements, in new intellectual and artistic pursuits, as well as in new technological and economic procedures. Also the new structure of behavior and thought is embodied in new standards of consumption, in new relationships of the sexes and the members of families, in new positions of the several age groups, in new circumstances affecting health, and in new causes of death. For individuals, these aspects are elements of a changing behavior and mentality; for the industrial city milieu, they are attributes fixed upon individuals coming under its influences.

From the point of view of cultural development, it is necessary to conceive of the beginnings of this structure of behavior and thought as appearing in the early industrial cities, of its elements spreading and maturing as industrial cities have grown, and, finally, of these elements becoming integrated through an intellectual outlook upon or a feeling for life shaped in terms of the frame of reference organized in experience as it goes on among the masses who now live in industrial cities. This matter may be stated in another way. If the industrial city, considered as the social milieu of a new structure of behavior and thought, is influencing ever larger parts of national populations, this influence is evident, on the one hand, in the dislocation of old forms of behavior and thought in the several national traditions and, on the other hand, in the appearance and spread of new forms. However, at the moment, because the dislocation of the old forms intensifies the emotional attachments

[2] See Chap. X.

to them, the new ones are not recognized. If at the moment such is the case, the prevailing confusion is understandable in the feeling that, although the old modes of behavior and thought no longer serve life, there is nothing to replace them. In truth, however, the modes of behavior and thought of a *new* culture may be implicit in the industrial city, requiring only recognition and acceptance to become the basis of conscious action. In the words of Robert H. Lowie, the anthropologist, "Culture, it seems, is a matter of exceedingly slow growth until a certain 'threshold' is passed, when it darts forward, gathering momentum at an unexpected rate."[3] The present disturbed situation in western culture, where the industrial city originated and has had its fullest development, may be only the approach to such a "threshold."

Before turning to a consideration of some of the aspects of industrial-city life which may be factors at the "threshold" of a cultural change, it is well to note that no one meant to create the industrial city or, as currently designated in the United States, the "metropolitan urban area." It arose as entrepreneurs pursued their interest —profits—and engineers served that interest by technological ingenuity. But once created, it became something other than a center of business and machine industry, that is, it became a milieu having the power to organize socially a structure of behavior and thought for those coming under its influence. For this reason the industrial city may ultimately react on business and industry, giving them new forms, in spite of the interests of entrepreneurs. It seems that commonly men do two things when they perform an act, first, what they intend to do and, second, what they do not intend

[3] Robert H. Lowie, *Culture and Ethnology* (New York, 1917), p. 78.

to do. And often the second thing is more important than the first. Certainly this seems to be the case with those persons who, while their intentional activities were chiefly concerned with making money, unknowingly created the industrial city, which, as a social milieu, is now the matrix of cultural change.

An examination of the development of industrial cities shows three classes of factors which may be considered as having significance for further cultural development. Although these factors may not have originated completely in the industrial city, their influence in contemporary life is focused in its milieu, so that they must be considered as elements of a complex of urban psychological influences. These three classes of factors may be designated: (1) the paradox of economic liberalism, (2) conditions having origin in machine technology, and (3) conditions of urban association. Each of these classes of psychological factors ramifies through contemporary society, having many manifestations and exciting many comments. However, only in the industrial city or the metropolitan urban milieu can they be viewed objectively.

By the paradox of economic liberalism, the central predications of which are too widely accepted to require statement here, is meant that entrepreneurial activity has created conditions which not only restrict the freedom of individuals but also reveal that the presumptions that universal competition promotes the automatic realization of a constantly advancing well-being are false. The restrictions on individual freedom of action have objective form in the hierarchies of employment which have appeared as technological developments have brought together ever larger units of capital. For individuals employed in these hierarchies, economic advancement is more a matter of rising from grade to grade than a shift from the status "employee" to the status "entrepreneur." Moreover, in these hierarchies economic power is exercised from the top downward. Through the "right to fire," the qualities of behavior that bring advancement become less and less those summed up in the phrase "individual initiative" and more and more those implied in the word "loyalty." Actually "conformity" rather than "initiative" is the quality desired in an ever-increasing body of individuals who occupy the status of employee. It is also important to note that economic power exerted from the top of these hierarchies upon individuals in the lower levels of employment does interfere upon occasions with the exercise of personal liberties in areas of life quite beyond that of the economic functioning of the hierarchies. The effect of this interference is to impose upon more and more individuals a regimentation in terms of private interests. Indeed, in many ways the current assertion of the doctrines of economic liberalism is merely a defense for economic power that functions as private regimentation.

Probably no more concise statement of the contradiction between the theory of economic liberalism and the fact of the private regimentation which prevails among the populations of industrial cities can be cited than the following words from Walter Lippmann's column, "How Liberty Is Lost":

To have economic independence a man must be in a position to leave one job and go to another; he must have enough savings of some kind to exist for a considerable time without accepting the first job offered. . . . the industrial worker who has a choice between working in one factory and not working at all, the white collar intellectuals who compete savagely for the relatively few private positions and for posts in the bureaucracy—these are the people who live too precariously to exercise their liberties or to defend them. They have no savings. They have only their labor to sell, and there are very few buyers of their labor. Therefore, they have only the choice of truckling to the powerful or of perishing heroically but miserably.[4]

Who are the great to whom these workers shall truckle? The private employers or the politicians who promise jobs? The economic and political crises which have already swept away some liberal regimes, and which now threaten the remainder, root in this social soil.

In this connection, it is worth observing that, from the cultural point of view, the mere criticism of a social order cannot be the basis of social reconstruction. Indeed, if a program of social reform or amelioration can be successfully based on a critique of a social order, progress away from the conditions giving rise to the paradox of economic liberalism should have been rapid, since the rise of the early industrial cities, for the eloquence of the writers of those times on these conditions has not been surpassed by writers of the present century. But to be able to point out social evils—even, in fact, to understand their origin—is not to become adequate to deal with them. For they cannot be dealt with in terms of themselves or even in terms of the institutions which give rise to them. In other words, the evils cannot be dealt with merely as problems of distress, unemployment, and the like, or as aspects of a social order retaining the essential characteristics described in the doctrines of economic

[4] *New York Herald Tribune*, July 16, 1938.

liberalism; they must be dealt with in terms of the potentialities of cultural change, implicit in the industrial city milieu. To know these potentialities involves not the emotional excitement raised by pointing to the evils, but a technique of analysis of the factors in cultural development. And to the development of this technique few social critics have made contributions.

In turning to a consideration of the two other classes of factors which are elements of the industrial city milieu, namely, conditions having their origin in machine technology and conditions of urban association, it is necessary to point out that the items listed under these headings have been arrived at in a certain way. This way has been an isolation of the repetitive, or recurring elements in industrial urban life, or, in other words, the finding of its continuously pervasive elements. This mode of analysis has been adopted on the ground that a culture, as an integrated and persisting structure of behavior and thought, is constructed psychologically upon a relatively stable order of stimuli, in terms of which patterns of reaction are developed. To such repetitive stimuli the great part of an industrial population react, and the recurring reactions become the determining tendencies of the development of the urban structure of life. Culture, it must be remembered, is both a psychological and a social phenomenon.

This way of analysis is not unfamiliar in American historiography. In fact, the classic essay, *The Significance of the Frontier in American History,* by Frederick Jackson Turner, which has received the lip, if not the mind service of a generation of students of American history, embodies it. The fundamental postulate of this essay is that a persisting underlying influence gave distinctive patterns to national life and furthermore created an intel-

lectual outlook which unified the national culture. Certainly the following excerpts can be so understood.

The existence of an area of free land, its continuous recession, and the advance of American settlement westward explain American development.

Behind institutions, behind constitutional forms and modifications, lie the vital forces that call these organs into life and shape them to meet changing conditions. . . .

The frontier individualism has from the beginning promoted democracy. . . .

The result is that to the frontier the American intellect owes its striking characteristics. That coarseness and strength combined with acuteness and inquisitiveness, that practical inventive turn of mind, quick to find expedients, that masterful grasp of material things, lacking in the artistic but powerful to effect great ends, that restless, nervous energy, that dominant individualism, working for good and for evil, and withal that buoyancy and exuberance which comes with freedom, these are traits of the frontier, or traits called out elsewhere because of the existence of the frontier.[5]

In terms of the concept of culture, the fact of "free land" may be understood as having established patterns which, as the frontier was pushed westward, were worked into the various phases of national life and, as individual experience and behavior were organized in these patterns, came to embody a pervasive psychological reaction which was the source of the subjective tradi-

[5] "The Significance of the Frontier in American History," *The Early Writings of Frederick Jackson Turner,* compiled by E. E' Edwards (Madison, 1938), pp. 185–229, at pp. 186, 220, 227–28.

tion of the national culture. In a sense, therefore, an analysis of current American developments in cultural terms is not greatly different from the mode of thinking which led Turner to his view of national development.

In every culture the integration of man with physical nature, in terms of technology, is significant in the life of the people who carry the culture. From this integration flows the wealth which supports the social order and certain basic judgments on life that have entered always into social attitudes, religious beliefs, and moral practices. There is no need here to discuss these phenomena, as they have long existed in cultures having an agrarian base. From contemporary technology come, it seems, at least three recognizable conditions that may contribute to the shaping of new cultural forms:

First: The sense of human control. Machine technology is operated by energy produced and controlled by man; in fact, it represents the fullest expression of his rationality. He creates power, orders its flow, governs its movement, and determines its resultant. In this circumstance exists ground for the assumption that what man achieves in one field of action, he may also do in another field. As a result of man's triumph in technology, it may be that he feels more able to command his fate socially. The emergence of the concept "planned economy" roots at least partly in this circumstance.

Second: The utility of objective knowledge. That knowledge is power is appreciated by the simplest mechanic; in terms of a special body of knowledge, every machine operator or machine fixer performs his task. This circumstance boldly insists that it is knowledge which functions to give success in every situation, that myth, tradition, and special interest must give way to knowledge—and the knowledge meant is worldly, factual,

and utilitarian. By implication, therefore, machine technology supports the view that social distress exists either because of lack of knowledge or because of the unwillingness to apply what is at hand.

Third: The increasing capacity to produce wealth. With the advent of machinery and applied science in agriculture and industry, man's capacity to produce wealth expanded enormously. For example, between 1920 and 1930 the agricultural population of the United States decreased by 4,000,000 persons, while agricutural production increased by 25 percent; now agricultural economists estimate that the agricultural population, not counting the back log of persons who would have migrated to cities if jobs had been available, could be decreased by at least 3,000,000 persons without seriously affecting the agricultural production necessary to maintain national consumption at present standards. It has been estimated that since about 1870 the capacity to produce in manufacturing industries has increased 3 per cent per year. Especially important is the fact that the increase of productivity has gone on steadily during the present depression decade. This fact is relevant to the present situation, which finds industrial production near the 1929 level without the employment of an equal number of workers.

These three conditions having their origin in contemporary technology— the sense of human control, the utility of objective knowledge, and the increasing capacity to produce wealth— point more and more directly to an economy in which human control, exercised with knowledge rather than with self-interest, may utilize the new capacity, to produce wealth for the support of a more secure life.

In closing this comment on the new conditions of life that have come with contemporary technology, it should be noted that one does not need to be a philosopher in order to know them, for they run constantly in the experience of all who actually work at the production of real goods. In other words, these conditions are part and parcel of the life of the masses of industrial cities.

The conditions of urban association are certainly no less significant for setting the direction of cultural change than those arising in contemporary technology. In fact, because they have existence in social interaction, they are primary to these influences which, after all, are reactions of men to physical nature and not of men to men. Culture, it may be noted, stands between man and nature, whereas man comes to culture through the social process.

From this point of view four conditions of industrial urban association are significant:

First: The disintegration of localism and tradition. Innumerable social stimuli flow through the contemporary urban population. Newspapers, movies, and radio pour the world into their eyes and ears; from these visual and aural images there is no escape. By the number and impact of these social stimuli, local prejudices and old traditions are disintegrated. By this wearing away, the urban masses are freed to take on views which harmonize with their social environment—the industrial city as a whole, not merely as a place where labor is sold and a profit is made. Indeed, the rise of propaganda, i.e., the organized control of mass opinion, has its origin in this circumstance, for as the masses are released from local and traditional opinions, they become free to move in new directions. Propaganda is organized by special interests in order to determine this direction. In the end, however, the movement of mass mentality will necessarily be in the direction set by the milieu which exists in the going experience of thousands of individuals.

Second: The cult of uniformity. As social stimuli flow continuously through the urban masses by way of machine-made commodities and routinized social services, manners, customs, and tastes are shaped into a wide conformity. This conformity is the necessary base of the organization of a complex social order among a large population; it makes for frictionless movement among large aggregates of individuals, who can, as a result, move together in actions not possible for them when they were embedded in local communities. Conformity serves the need for orderly coöperation in the intricate processes of urban society.

Third: The diversification of individual behavior. In communities antedating industrial cities, refinement, elegance, and taste were, in the main, attributes of small classes; to belong to these classes meant the possession of an explicit moral code, special forms of dress and manner, and particular intellectual affectations. In some respects these class attributes survive now, but among urban masses individual tastes find release from such controls. Thus there appear among urban populations innumerable groups pursuing self-selected interests, and individuals are permitted wide variations from all norms of conduct. The modern urban milieu is fostering a diversification of intellectual, artistic, and amusemental pursuits, unheard of in earlier types of communities. Individual energies are free to find expression in more ways than ever before. The industrial city well exemplifies the sociological principle that as social organization becomes more complex, individuals necessarily have more opportunity for development.

Fourth: The reorientation of the right of property. From the point of view of the concept of culture, the social rather than the economic factor is decisive in historical development. Thus it need cause no surprise that the social milieu of the industrial city is affecting the right of property—indeed, the whole relationship of men and wealth. The prevailing concept of property was derived from societies mainly agrarian in their economic and social organization. It is a concept developed mainly in terms of tangible goods, for it emphasizes possession on the ground that from possession flow the benefits of ownership. Now it appears that property in this sense has been becoming less and less important in the lives of all urban dwellers. Urban dwellers, even those having great wealth, can own very little of the property upon which their lives continually depend. The rich and the poor alike are dependent upon a continuity of services—water, food, light, heat, protection—which are maintained only through social coöperation. And they demand not ownership of these services, but their continuous functioning, regardless of ownership. Similarly, the owner of tangible property, whatever it may be, can produce little with the property that contributes to real satisfaction. His property probably functions to create any wealth that gives real satisfactions only through a minute division of labor, and such wealth is produced only through the maintenance of this division of labor. Finally, since the individual in the modern urban economy, no matter who he may be, can command few real goods through the possession of real property, he must possess some claim upon wealth which can be executed in diverse ways; for only by such execution can he acquire the diversity of real goods which supports urban modes of living. Thus it appears that in the modern industrial city the ownership of property is far less important to the

support of individual life than the maintenance of certain fundamental economic services and the establishment of some kind of claim on currently produced real goods. In fact, the elaboration of the modes of ownership through various kinds of legal claims—securities, trusts, insurance annuities, and social security claims—is an adjustment to this growing social orientation of the right of property.

However confused and clouded this exposition of the factors in the industrial urban milieu has been, it has made these factors far more clear than they are. Actually they exist today as part of the chaos previously noted. They are vaguely felt impulses, uncertain judgments, and befogged visions; they are neither defined nor oriented. However, they run in the experience of urban masses, as life goes on in terms of the labor market, machine technology, and urban association; and, as combined in a day-by-day routine, they form a frame of reference which for these masses, without conscious effort on their part, becomes the point of departure of feeling and thinking. Thus from this frame of reference issues, in the life of the masses, new attitudes toward their problems, new definitions of their interests, and new concepts of what life ought to be like. More important still in the day-by-day routine of behavior, as organized under the influence of this complex of urban forces, are the elements which may be combined in new patterns of behavior that will constitute the culture which is correlative with the modes of thinking and feeling set in this frame of reference. In other words, the frame of reference, as the subjective content of life shaped by the complex of urban forces, and the day-by-day routines of behavior, as the objective content of life shaped by this complex, together form the psychological basis for the integration of thought and behavior in a new culture.

In the concept of culture, it is postulated that at any time there are a limited number of possible modes of thinking and acting; therefore, as far as the contemporary world is concerned, if the old forms of thought and behavior are to be displaced (as, indeed, they are being displaced), the complex of urban forces which shapes this frame of reference and day-by-day routine of behavior of the urban masses fixes the possibilities for the future. It is pertinent to state here that because this frame of reference and this day-by-day routine of behavior are organized through social interaction, they affect, to some degree, the smaller specialized urban groups as well as the urban masses, for this reason contemporary cultural change is not merely an adjustment to the rise of a new social class. It is, in fact, far more fundamental, for it is touching all classes, compelling those which have been dominant to alter the forms of their control if they are to remain dominant. The twentieth century cannot have any kind of social order; it must have one oriented in terms of the contemporary industrial urban milieu.

If one seeks a general heading under which to sum up the most significant aspect of the cultural change under way in nations whose chief communities are industrial cities or metropolitan urban areas, it would seem to be the phrase "a reëducation of the masses." Before the rise of industrial cities, the overwhelming proportion of population in all lands consisted of peasants—socially isolated, superstitious, tenacious of the land, and illiterate. As industrial cities grew, the peasant element declined and the urban masses formed. It should be recognized that, as the masses shifted to the cities, they brought with them the mentality of peasants; this has been a primary condition in their reëducation which, even today, the contrivers of propaganda know how to use. But, once in the city, the new circumstances of life—the labor market, machine technology, and urban association—began to affect their behavior and thought. It is not contended that the urban masses have been or are now conscious of this process of reëducation; it is only argued that they necessarily act and think under its effects, and that such action and thought are the elements of the cultural change now under way.

5 The Impact of

Social conflict, cultural dislocation, economic deprivation, and political disorganization have all been part of the urban scene for the past two centuries. To what extent these conditions were caused by urbanization or by other great historical forces, including industrialization, technological innovation, population expansion, immigration, social and cultural change, is not entirely clear. Rural America in the nineteenth century and indeed many previous societies faced these same problems, and the observable urban changes arose from sources common to the city and the country alike. In turn, urbanization affected many historical events and forces. Inquiry into the causes and effects of urbanization and its relation to industrialization and other historical forces will be the task of future generations of scholars. What we do know is that for several centuries modern society has been undergoing a profound and rapid upheaval. The city was directly engaged in the accelerating commercial and industrial revolution that swept the country and, consequently, its inhabitants were especially affected. Moreover, the concentration of population made the disruption more noticeable.

Urbanization

In the turmoil of population growth the city had to countenance many problems encompassing the entire urban life style and environment. The rise of unfavorable circumstances and the inadequacy with which they were handled are evident in the presence of slums and general housing conditions, the lagging intra-urban transportation systems and traffic congestion, the danger of disease and the lack of city health and sanitation facilities, the danger of conflagration and the outdated fire facilities, the increase in violence and disorder and the antiquated police system, and the crowded conditions and the paucity of recreational facilities. The once simple urban social institutions became complex. Fundamental groups such as the family and the church were transformed. Even the concept of time, in terms of work and leisure, was significantly altered.

Economic relationships also underwent change as technology and specialization began to dominate the system of production. The work force at industrial plants lost the limited degree of intimate relations that had once existed between management and employees, and the laborer became less a skilled craftsman and more a factor of production. His status was further depressed by the rise of large-scale industry and monopolies, the growth of transportation resulting in national competition, and the availability of immigrants and child labor. These circumstances, leading to a decline in his economic position, were the genesis of much of the urban deprivation and of many of the conflicts that erupted between the new industrial worker and his boss. Quite visible in the last half of the nineteenth century was the blatant disparity of wealth between the social classes within the cities.

Underlying these transformations was the increase in urban population, which from 1860 to 1910 rose seven-fold. Much of this increase came about in the larger cities. Chicago, with approximately thirty thousand people in 1850, was a relatively uncomplicated community and was able to provide for its citizens the necessary urban services and opportunities for a livelihood. By 1890 the population had mushroomed to over a million and was deluged with a backlog of untouched demands. Interacting with these simple demographic changes was the impact of technology and of dynamic capitalistic institutions, which forced the urban worker to revise his image of himself.

The influx into the nation's cities of hundreds of thousands of immigrants and rural migrants posed a distinctive problem. Many of the immigrants had departed from intolerable conditions of economic and social crises and had arrived in the new world in an extremely low social position. Therefore, the impoverishment they experienced in the city could be seen as a product more of their Old World condition than of the urban process. But the urban-industrial environment certainly took its toll as well, for it threw up many obstacles for the immigrant to overcome. The experience of a transatlantic move was itself a highly disruptive process, and the cultural shock was aggravated by a sense of alienation effected partially through the hostile reaction of the native population. The foreigners, along with the native rural migrants, who likewise had experienced a formidable drastic cultural metamorphosis, formed an urban poor.

Some of the political problems of American cities emerged from their administrative structures, which had been designed originally to deal with smaller communities. These structures, while capable of performing the limited functions required in a pre-industrial age, were no longer adequate. The physical growth of the cities called for the expansion of services, such as water and sewage, and the building of facilities, including streets, schools, and civil buildings. Few city governments could meet these demands promptly or cheaply, and, as the civic needs were postponed and the debts, from what had already been done, mounted, businessmen allied with professional politicians sought the power to get things done, even if ignoring the law was necessary. The immigrants, too, had needs to be fulfilled, and when the old-line political leadership failed to respond, they turned to the new political boss within their various ethnic groups.

When both the businessman and the immigrants sought special privileges from these bosses the source of corruption and disruption of the political process dramatically appeared.

The readings in this section form a logical extension of the last essay, by Ralph E. Turner, since they continue the description of the impact of the urban-industrial society. The first selection, by Robert H. Bremner, describes and explains the impoverished conditions of the slums and the unsympathetic response of the fortunate classes toward the poor. Chicago slums typified the consequences of urban development in the late nineteenth century. The excerpt from Bessie Pierce's study describes these consequences, as well as the characteristics and the problems of the labor force. Robert Ernst's selection focuses on the slums of New York, which were largely made up of immigrants. It depicts their constant struggle for survival. The growth of immigrant ghettos along ethnic or religious lines was mainly a matter of economic circumstances or choice, but the rise of the black ghetto, as described by Allan H. Spear, was not. The black ghetto, a unique urban phenomenon, has its own economic, physical, and social ramifications.

Political problems were generated by the failure of social groups to communicate with each other, another result of the process of urbanization. This crisis led first to fragmentation and then to the flourishing of the political boss. Elmer E. Cornwell, Jr., describes the rise of the boss and his urban machine, with particular emphasis on the role of the immigrant.

The city, which in its inception presented rich opportunities attractive to many people, was becoming an impoverished environment. We know that the task of effectively dealing with these problems has not yet been accomplished. However, it was during the Progressive Era that the first step, awareness, slowly dawned on urban people, as will be seen in the next section.

The Discovery of Poverty

Robert H. Bremner*

Large numbers of Americans first awoke to the social problem of poverty at a time when the nation was pouring forth unprecedented quantities of wealth and promising even richer harvests for the future. During the first two centuries of the country's development most Americans took it for granted that the majority of men would always be poor. Poverty was the state from which thousands of emigrants fled when they embarked, in hope or despair, on the difficult journey to the New World; in the form of hardship, privation, and suffering it was the lot, not only of the first settlers on the alien coast, but of generations of pioneers on successive inland frontiers. An increase in wealth, with a consequent improvement in general living standards, was the condition precedent to an aroused interest in poverty, for only in an era of material advance could want seem incongruous; and only in the nineteenth century when, decade by decade, the output of farm, factory, and mine climbed to higher and higher totals, did Americans begin to question the age-old assumption that poverty was the normal condition of the masses.

Unfortunately, the very economic processes that promised ultimately to free mankind from want had the immediate effect of aggravating, rather than alleviating, the distress of the working class. Mechanization and the factory system, by minimizing the value of traditional crafts and skills, reduced the bargaining power of the

individual workman almost to the vanishing point; what little he had left was lost in contests with other men— and women and children, too—for jobs which one was as competent to fill as another. The prize in these races nearly always went to the cheapest. Despite the fiction of freedom of contract, all the advantages in the arrangement of terms of employment lay with the hirer. Employers, impelled not only by desire for profit but also by the necessity for meeting the competition of rivals, drove sharp bargains with their hands; they altered pay and hours as they saw fit and dismissed help whenever and for whatever reason they chose. These hard facts were made yet harsher by the prevailing theory of political economy which held that the welfare of individual laborers was a matter of small consequence either to employers or to the state.

Under the circumstances, especially in the hard times that followed the panics of 1819 and 1837, numbers of Americans sank into depths of degradation and dependency previously unknown in this country. At mid-century there was ample evidence that a poverty problem, novel in kind and alarming in size, was emerging in the United States. Many other issues clamored for attention, and then, as later, most Americans found admiration of wealth a more profitable occupation than contemplation of misery. Nevertheless a sizable body of men and women agreed that there was no valid excuse, moral or economic, for the presence of want in the midst of plenty; they condemned the bending of human lives to the will of the machine as inhumane and unwise; and they expressed regret

*Reprinted with permission from Robert H. Bremner, *From the Depths: The Discovery of Poverty in the United States,* New York: New York University Press, 1956, 3–15.

and concern at the signs of growing estrangement between social classes.

It was in the slums of the larger cities that Americans discovered the new poverty that was invading the nation in the wake of industrialization, urban growth, and immigration. Here were new worlds of wretchedness characterized by ways of life foreign to American experience and menacing to conventional standards of decency. "It is often said that 'one half of the world does not know how the other half lives,'" observed the pioneer sanitary reformer, Dr. John H. Griscom, in the 1840's. Almost half a century before the publication of Jacob Riis's *How the Other Half Lives,* and in language strikingly similar to that Riis was to employ, Griscom described "the mournful and disgusting condition" in which thousands of the "laboring population" of New York passed their lives.

In Boston, at almost the same time, William Ellery Channing was denouncing the practice of "letting cellars and rooms which cannot be ventilated, which want the benefits of light, free air, and pure water, and the means of removing filth!" The inhabitants of these rooms were constantly exposed to "putrid, damp, and noisome vapors" which, in Channing's opinion, worked sure destruction upon their characters and bodies. They had less access to the blessings of nature than the birds and the beasts, he said; and they were denied "those cheering influences of the elements" that even savages enjoyed.

When Griscom and Channing wrote, as for many years thereafter, the most notorious slum in the nation was the Five Points district of New York City. A popular novelist of the period compared the Five Points to a great basin made of brick and mortar collecting "all the nauseous drainage of the higher thoroughfare." That energetic sight-seer, Charles Dickens, visited the Five Points by night during his first tour of the United States. In *American Notes* (1842) he depicted the "leperous houses" of the district; they appeared to have been made prematurely old by debauchery, he thought, and their broken and patched windows seemed "to scowl dimly, like eyes that have been hurt in drunken frays." Investigating the attic of one battered structure (under the guard of two policemen), Dickens watched fascinated as half-awakened creatures crawled from their corners "as if the judgment hour were at hand and every obscene grave were giving up its dead."

The initial reaction of the fortunate classes to slum dwellers was one of repugnance rather than compassion. Dickens could not resist asking whether the scavenging hogs owned by the inhabitants of the Five Points did not occasionally wonder why their masters walked upright and talked instead of grunting. Robert M. Hartley, founder of the New York Association for Improving the Condition of the Poor, denied that the "debased poor" were deserving of sympathy. "They love to clan together in some out-of-the-way place," he reported, "are content to live in filth and disorder with a bare subsistence, provided they can drink, and smoke, and gossip, and enjoy their balls, and wakes, and frolics, without molestation." Another observer, a clergyman, stated that residents of cellar lodginghouses were devoid of moral feeling and sense of shame. "They are not as decent as brutes," he said, referring to the unfortunate inhabitants of a tenement which he described as "impregnated with a stench that would poison cattle." Josiah Strong, zealous advocate of home and foreign missions, characterized slum life as "a commingled mass of venomous filth and seething sin, of lust and drunkenness, of pauperism and crime of every sort." As late as 1894 a report of the United States Commissioner of Labor defined slums as "dirty back streets, especially such as are inhabited by a squalid and criminal population."

In the planless, rapidly growing cities extremes of fortune and misfortune often dwelt side by side. Poverty might be dismissed as a personal matter but the slums could not be brushed aside so easily. Regions of "squalid want and wicked woe" lay little more than a stone's throw from busy commercial streets and comfortable residential districts. Periodically, murderous and destructive riots beginning in the turbulent slums terrorized entire cities for days at a time. During the middle third of the century brawling regularly marked the observance of the Sabbath, the celebration of holidays, and the conduct of elections in the congested wards where the poor lived. It was not entirely without reason or in a spirit of pure snobbery that Charles Loring Brace, organizer of the Children's Aid Society, referred to the inhabitants of these blighted areas as "the dangerous classes."

Where casual observers saw the slum as the refuge of the already criminal and degenerate, philanthropists such as Brace and Hartley emphasized the importance of the slum environment in producing undesirable citizens. Brace was frankly fearful of "that vast and ignorant multitude, who, in prosperous times, just keep their heads above water . . . and who look with envy and greed at the signs of wealth all around them." For this very reason he counseled against indifference toward the poor. Hartley argued that bad housing was a prime factor in weakening the ability of laborers to support themselves, an almost insuperable obstacle to the economic, moral, or religious elevation of the poor, and, consequently, a major cause of the high taxes about which the well-to-do grumbled. Horace Greeley's *New York Tribune* summed up the reformers' case against the slums in 1864:

In those places garbage steams its poison in the sun; there thieves and prostitutes congregate and are made; there are besotted creatures who roll up blind masses of votes for the rulers who are a curse to us; there are the deaths that swell our mortality reports; from there come our enormous taxes in good part; there disease lurks, and there is the daily food of pestilence awaiting its coming.

Like many of his contemporaries, Greeley believed that the most serious menace held out by the slums was the constantly increasing threat to public health. "Public" being a vague term, the reformers sometimes expressed the idea in language better calculated to appeal to the self-interest of the prosperous classes. "It is a well-established fact that diseases are not confined to the localities where they originate, but widely diffuse their poisonous miasma," advised a sanitary report issued in 1853. "Hence, though the poor may fall in greater numbers because of their nearer proximity to the causes of disease, yet the rich, who inhabit the splendid squares and spacious streets . . . often become the victims of the same disorders which afflict their poorer brethren."

By the 1860's the connection between insanitary conditions in crowded tenements and recurring epidemics of typhoid, cholera, smallpox, and other diseases was fairly well recognized. Nevertheless, for many years thereafter both charity agents and public-health officials reported frequent instances of dangerous and offensive violations of the most elementary principles of hygiene. In 1884 an inspector employed by the Association for Improving the Condition of the Poor noted that in a house typical of hundreds of others the plumbing was "as much an inlet for sewer gas as an outlet for waste water." Close by the one hydrant serving all the occupants of a five-story tenement the inspector found the only toilet accommodations available to the tenants of the building: a row of privies whose floors were "slippery with urine" and whose seats, "foul with abominable matter," were arranged in long, undivided ranges. As long as such plague spots were tolerated, Greeley's prediction that the slums would someday exact a frightful revenge upon society was realized, not once, but repeatedly, in city after city across the nation.

The simplest and most frequently advanced explanation for the manifold problems created by the slums was immigration. In the earlier part of the century, at least in those sections where labor was in short supply, the newcomers were welcomed enthusiastically. The *Chicago American* rejoiced in 1835 because

the floodgates of enterprise seem to be let loose upon us and the multiudes are crowding on to this young land, as if the pestilence were behind, eager to find a better home, where they can build their fortunes and their hopes, and enjoy the plenty which our fat fields yield to the hand of industry. . . .

From an early date the seaboard cities regarded the matter in an entirely different light. In 1819, in its *Second Annual Report*, the New York Society for the Prevention of Pauperism listed immigration as the principal cause of pauperism. The Society bemoaned the likelihood that for years to come "winds and waves will still bring needy thousands to our seaports" and warned that New York was "liable to be devoured by swarms of people."

Samuel F. B. Morse, author of two widely circulated books whose contents are clearly suggested by their titles, *Foreign Conspiracy Against the Liberties of the United States* (1834) and *Imminent Dangers to the Free Institutions of the United States Through Foreign Immigration* (1835), was an unsuccessful candidate for mayor of New York in 1835. Two years later, however, the Whigs and Native Americans secured the election of their candidate to the office. In his first message to the council the new mayor complained that the hordes of foreigners were driving native workmen into exile, "where they must war again with the savages of the wilderness." He continued his attack on the immigrants with these observations:

It is apprehended they will bring disease among us; and if they have it not with them on arrival, they may generate a plague by collecting in crowds within small tenements and foul hovels. What is to become of them is a question of serious import. Our whole Alms House Department is so full that no more can be received there without manifest hazard to the health of every inmate. Petitions signed by hundreds, asking for work, are presented in vain; private associations for relief are almost wholly without funds. Thousands must therefore wander to and fro on the face of the earth, filling every part of our once happy land with squalid poverty and profligacy.

Similar expressions of opinion became more common as the depression of 1837 wore on; and they became even more familiar after the great influx of Irish and German emigrants in the late 1840's and early 1850's. Behind immigration nativists professed to see a sinister design on the part of Old World tyrannies to destroy the United States by inundating it in a flood of paupers and criminals. Certain European cities did, in fact, rid themselves of such paupers as could be induced to emigrate by paying their passage to America. Thus, in 1839, in the midst of the depression, a miserable company of immigrants, many still wearing the uniform of the Edinburgh almshouse, arrived in New York; their transportation had been arranged by the overseers of the poor of Edinburgh.

The necessity of caring for these and other immigrants who were unable to support themselves imposed a considerable burden on American taxpayers and philanthropists. In some cities uncontrolled immigration had the effect of doubling, or more than doubling, the cost of poor relief; not infrequently the foreign-born outnumbered native-born Americans three to one on the rolls of private charities. The harshness which nineteenth-century students thought appropriate to the administration of charity and relief stemmed in no small part from the settled conviction that numerous applicants for aid had brought disaster upon themselves, and inconvenience to the community, by their ill-advised and uninvited removal to the United States.

In the heat of their resentment against the European practice of shipping destitute persons to this country, Americans tended to overlook other and more important reasons why recent immigrants were so often compelled to ask for relief or charity. Most of them were poor to begin with, and some exhausted what meager resources they possessed in getting to America. Many were lured from home by false pictures of ease and abundance painted by high-pressure agents of shipping companies. The voyage was so difficult and steerage conditions so bad that not a few of the immigrants (one out of every six in some years) died on the way, sometimes leaving widows or orphans to make their way unaided by husbands or fathers. Those who survived arrived undernourished and in poor health; they were met by sharpers who preyed on their ignorance and bewilderment. When they found work they were paid so little that they could scarce build up reserves to tide them over sickness or unemployment. A recent student comments: "If the economic pattern of the time had involved a fair return for the great contribution of the immigrant, the number of foreign-born paupers would have been negligible."

In the latter half of the century population movements, like everything else, were conducted on a grander scale than ever before. Of the approximately twenty million persons who migrated to the United States in the nineteenth century, all but about four million, or roughly four out of five, came after 1860. Now the tendency to blame immigration for whatever was disreputable in American life became almost irresistible. Not only pauperism and crime, but hard times, political corruption, intemperance, and pestilence were laid at the door of the newcomers. A new prejudice against the allegedly inferior races of southern and eastern Europe reinforced the earlier Protestant bias against Catholic immigrants. Nativists in the 1850's, resenting the foreign-born voters' activity in politics, had sought not only to restrict the admission of foreigners but to limit the political rights of those already in the country. Later and more reputable reformers deplored the misuse of the suffrage by the "ignorant and vicious poor," especially the immigrants in the slums, who gave their fealty to saloonkeeping bosses in exchange for petty kindnesses and pauperizing gifts of money, food, and fuel. Thomas Bailey Aldrich called his poem "Unguarded Gates" (1892) a "protest against America becoming the cesspool of Europe," and declared that Kipling's description of the government of New York—"a despotism of the alien, by the alien, for the alien, tempered with occasional insurrections of decent folk"—applied to every American city.

As the century drew to a close there was suspicion at nearly all levels of society that the immigrants, if not actually bent on the destruction of American institutions, were nevertheless quite capable, either through illiteracy or political immaturity, of subverting the foundations of the republic. Conservatives, never very confident of the ability of their fellow citizens to withstand the temptations of foreign radicalism, protested that each ship bearing degraded and undesirable persons to American ports carried an invisible cargo of anarchism, communism, and other dangerous doctrines. Meanwhile, spokesmen for labor declared that industry's systematic policy of flooding the labor market with aliens was the major cause of unemployment and low wages. The most moderate view, and the most valid, was that uncontrolled immigration greatly complicated the poverty problem in the United States by yearly increasing the numbers of the very poor.

The immigration question kept the problem and, to a certain extent, the plight of the desperately poor before the nation. As already suggested, some observers attributed the hardships encountered by American labor in its struggle for decent standards of work and wages to the competition of "pauper labor" recruited overseas. But the furor over immigration also tended to obscure fundamental economic questions in a fog of religious and national prejudices. It provided such a convenient rationale of all the nation's ills that other industrial issues received less attention than they deserved. John R. Commons, writing in the mid-nineties, commented that the only labor problem that seemed to excite much interest among clergymen and church members was working on the Sabbath.

From time to time an occasional student such as Orestes Brownson, deeply stirred by the crosscurrents of political democracy and industrial servitude, described the relations between capital and labor as a class struggle. For the most part, however, through all the vicissitudes of the nineteenth century, most American writers clung to the belief that paternalism offered the proper solution to industrial problems. If only employers could be induced to deal kindly with employees, they reasoned, workmen would respond by rendering faithful and loyal service. Then labor strife would disappear; there would be no sweating, no unions, no strikes, and no black lists. Capital, as befitting its superior position, would act as the guardian of the interests of labor. Subordinate, but not exploited, labor would become the stanch support of capital.

That something like this relationship prevailed in certain establishments is beyond question. But there were many more instances in which neither capital nor labor was content to play the role assigned it by benevolent outsiders. One factory manager boasted: "I regard my workpeople just as I regard my machinery. So long as they can do my work for what I choose to pay them, I keep them, getting out of them all I can." Some employers, however, regarded their machinery with more tenderness than their work-people—at least the high toll of industrial accidents seemed to indicate an extravagance in regard to human costs in otherwise economically managed enterprises. A sympathetically portrayed businessman in a novel published in the 1880's summed up the whole problem when he remarked of certain industrialists, "They want to become rich in five years and how can they do that except by oppression?"

Whether justly or not, many workers were dissatisfied with both the conditions and the rewards of their labor. Whenever they were strong enough to do so they delivered their protest at the polls, through trade-unions, and by acts of violence. Strikes for the ten-hour day were plentiful in the boom years before the depression of 1837; fifty years later they were being waged for the eight-hour day. During the seventies, eighties, and nineties workingmen expressed their discontent with existing conditions in a series of strikes that outdid in number and virulence any yet known in American history. It is almost impossible for a later generation to conceive of the chaotic upheavals that periodically rocked whole communities at a time when industrial relations consisted of intimidation on one side and terrorism on the other, when spying was countered by sabotage, and when a "labor dispute" meant an armed skirmish between embattled strikers and entrenched employers.

As a rule public opinion condemned strikes; for the anarchy of labor was deemed more reprehensible than the despotism of capital. Many observers unhesitatingly put the blame for industrial strife on "socialistic agitators and communistic tramps." Nevertheless, these bitter conflicts brought to light shocking examples of exploitation, and their total effect was to com-

pel thoughtful men and women to give more serious study to labor problems. The novelist and essayist Charles Dudley Warner believed unionism "an extraordinary tyranny," but he was willing to admit its usefulness in focusing public attention upon "certain hideous wrongs, to which the world is likely to continue selfishly indifferent unless rudely shaken out of its sense of security."

Incessant industrial warfare convinced a number of students that something must be done to compel employers to treat their workers better. Remedial action, including the enactment of factory laws, seemed imperative both on humanitarian grounds and to remove a major cause of social tensions. Cardinal Gibbons chided employers for paying less heed to the welfare of the driver of the horsecar than to the well-being of the car horse. Josephine Shaw Lowell, a nationally known leader in scientific philanthropy, early announced her conviction that fair wages rather than doles of charity were the answer to industrial unrest. W. S. Rainsford, pastor of a leading institutional church in New York City, declared that a visit to Pittsburgh at the time of the Homestead strike had removed all doubt from his mind as to the need for unions. The lesson of Homestead, he said, was that workingmen must cooperate with one another if they were to secure the simplest of human rights.

Such expressions of opinion were deplored by conservatives, who denied that employers had neglected their responsibilities to employees, and maintained that any outside interference with industrial labor policies, whether by workers' organizations or by legislation, was an invasion of the prerogatives of management. Furthermore, they argued, there was no cause for complaint since everyone agreed that the average workingman in 1890 was better off in every way—except possibly in morality and respect for authority—than his grandfather in 1830. Throughout the century the conservative prescription for labor's discontent was not higher wages but harder work and stricter economy. Employers' spokesmen criticized the movement for a shorter workday on the grounds that ten hours instead of twelve, or eight instead of ten, would result only in increased idleness and dissipation. During the depression of 1819 distressed families were urged to take advantage of the saving offered by a recipe for a cheap and wholesome dish composed of rice and mutton suet. Philanthropists offered similar advice in later emergencies; toward the end of the century a New England insurance executive invented a cookstove called the Aladdin Oven, and drew up principles of food preparation which he estimated would save working-class families five cents a day per person—sufficient, he thought, to enable laborers to subsist adequately on prevailing wages.

Household economy was a singular panacea to press upon the working poor at a time when the idle rich were indulging themselves in riotous extravagance. The real weakness of the conservative argument, however, was that it failed to reckon with the tendency of men to compare themselves with their contemporaries rather than with their ancestors. As Josiah Strong pointed out, if material conditions had altered greatly in two generations, men had changed even more. They had more wants and more confidence in their ability to satisfy them, more education and more self-respect. The unrest which was so characteristic of the closing decades of the nineteenth century had its origin in the fact that a great many of the working people were unwilling to live out their days in the social steerage.

Few experiences were more unsettling to the average American's peace of mind than the depressions which, although always unexpected, recurred with almost monotonous regularity at intervals of from fifteen to twenty years after 1819. Long before the end of the century the nation had become familiar with soup lines, demonstrations by the unemployed, demands for the relief of debtors—rich as well as poor—lamentations over past errors, and dire predictions for the future. "Let every individual calculate for himself what he, personally, has lost, what chances have been sacrificed by him, what he might have done, and what he might have been, if the prosperity of the country had not been arrested," mused a writer in 1840. We cannot gauge the precise extent to which these calamitous events shook the common man's confidence in hard work and thrift as an unfailing recipe for security. There is no doubt, however, that loss of jobs, farms, and saving as a result of cyclic panics and price fluctuations led to widespread disillusionment and bitterness. Even men and women who were not directly affected by bank or business failures had reason to fear that their means of livelihood might be snatched from them by remote and impersonal forces. Thus early, threads of anxiety were being woven into the traditionally optimistic fabric of American character.

In normal times Americans were accustomed to think of unemployment as exclusively the problem of the inefficient and indolent. Conservatives stuck to this view even in depression years. They recommended that relief be dealt out sparingly lest the recipients be tempted into permanent dependency. Respectable folk looked upon "tramps," a numerous but ill-defined group, as pariahs deserving only "the toe of a boot by day and a cold stone floor by night." Under the impact of hard times, however, it was easier to grasp the distinction between voluntary and enforced idleness. From the 1840's onward, although in insignificant numbers until after the depression of 1893, some students were willing to admit that "nonemployment" was a constant problem, affecting the competent no less than the incompetent, the industrious as well as the slothful. In the late thirties and forties Greeley's sympathies went out to the respectable mechanic "whose cry was, not for the bread and fuel of charity, but for Work!" Almost fifty years later a *Tribune* writer, Helen Campbell, commented that the real issue was quite different from pauperism: it was the tragic, undeserved embarrassment of persons who wanted no charity and needed no correction.

Dearth of work had a psychological as well as economic significance in the United States because the entire American creed of individualism and self-help was based on the assumption that earnest seekers could always find honest employment. Unemployment was by no means a new phenomenon, but never before the closing decade of the nineteenth century had its shadow hung so heavily over so many men and women. The sons and daughters of farmers and village tradesmen who had migrated to the cities to obtain salaried positions in stores and offices were more vulnerable than their parents had been to business crises. The immigrants who had deserted ancestral villages in Europe to swell the ranks of the American industrial army had

nothing but their weekly wages to serve as bulwarks against want. At the end of the century urban Americans, in a real but novel sense, were living in a state of dependency. Even though, as individuals, they experienced unemployment only briefly and at rare intervals, they experienced unemployment only briefly and at rare intervals, if at all, the nagging fear of it was almost chronic with them.

This does not mean that the average citizen despaired of the future. Far from it. Despite misgivings about his present situation he believed that there lay ahead, and almost within reach, a more wholesome and commodious plane of life for all men. The expectation of reaching the promised land of security and plenty in the foreseeable future gave Americans confidence and hope. If doubts sometimes overtook men of small or moderate means, the reason was not so much that the climb was steep as that their footing was unsure.

Americans were immensely proud that in their land the long-despised common man had raised himself to a new level of material well-being. Yet they had not rid themselves of the chilling presence that Edward Bellamy called "the specter of uncertainty." Perhaps it was because they had risen so high that the possibility of plunging downward seemed so frightful. The insecurity of their position led them, by almost imperceptible degrees, to question and ultimately to alter their attitudes toward poverty.

Society and Labor in An Expanding City

Bessie L. Pierce[*]

Chicago's meteoric rise to an enviable position among the great cities of the United States in the last half of the nineteenth century was but the fulfillment of the dreams and boasts of her citizens. Louder than the voices of those who, viewing the devastation of the Great Fire of 1871, expressed the fear that Chicago would never rise again, were the voices of others, optimistic and daring, who prophesied that their city would outstrip her rivals and even challenge the great port of New York.

In the years that followed, there poured into a new city streams of newcomers to add to the approximately 298,000 residents already there, to invigorate and inspire an already aggressive and tireless people on the quick-stepping march toward economic hegemony. Within only ten years after the Fire the population rose to 503,185, and by 1890 it had passed the million mark to make Chicago second city of the continent.[1] Even in an era characterized by rapid urban expansion, a growth of nearly 268 per cent in the twenty years following 1870 was breath-taking.

An expansion in territory accompanied the city's amazing growth in population; between 1871 and 1893 the area included within the corporate limits increased from a little more than thirty-five square miles to slightly

more than 185 miles. The density of the annexed area was below that of the city proper, which in 1870 was 8,505.2 per square mile and by 1880 was 14,314.5. By 1890, as a result of the annexation, density had fallen to 6,343.4, the lowest of the great cities of the country.[2] This extension of territory, however, had not come without controversy. Along with better government, lower taxes, and more protection of public health and safety, the proponents of annexing outlying towns saw improved housing for a constantly growing number of people. Those who objected to becoming a part of the city feared not only the opposite of these benefits, but also the coming of the saloon, a rise in real estate prices, and generally less responsible government.[3]

[2] The relative standing of the large cities was as follows:

City	Population density per square mile	
	1880	1890
New York	29,932	37,563
Philadelphia	6,567	8,092
Chicago	14,314.5	6,343.4
Boston	9,806	12,358

City	No. persons per dwelling	
	1880	1890
New York	16.37	18.52
Philadelphia	5.79	5.6
Chicago	8.24	8.6
Boston	8.26	8.52

U.S., *Eleventh Census, 1890*, "Population," pt. I, cxci; Chicago Department of Public Works Bureau of Maps and Plats, *Map of Chicago Showing Growth of the City by Annexations and Accretions* (Chicago, 1933). To arrive at density, population figures were divided by area. Chicago area figures for 1890 were taken from the map cited. Computation is as of June 1, since 1890 census figures are of that date. The total Chicago annexation of June 29, 1889, alone was 125,363 square miles.

[3] The most spirited opposition to expansion arose in the town of Hyde Park. The number of wards, eighteen in 1875, became thirty-four in 1889. Chicago, *Council Proceedings, 1889–90*, pp. 336–37. See map.

[*]From *A History of Chicago*, Volume III, by Bessie L. Pierce. Copyright © 1957 by the University of Chicago. Reprinted by permission of Alfred A. Knopf, Inc.

[1] U.S., *Ninth Census, 1870*, I, "Population," 380–91, *Tenth Census, 1880*, [I], "Population," 536–41, *Eleventh Census, 1890*, [I], "Population," pt. I, lxvii 580–83, 670–73. In 1890 Chicago was a city of 1,099,850. Unless otherwise indicated, the United States census is the source for population figures in this chapter.

But the 150 square miles added to the city by 1893 did not solve the housing problem, which was already assuming formidable proportions. Despite the large decrease in the number of people per square mile, the number of persons per dwelling remained substantially the same in 1890 as ten years before. Nearly twice as many lived in the slums as in the city at large. Around the central business district stretched an arc of homes belonging to those on the lowest rung of the economic ladder, the latest arrivals. With enhanced economic status, they too moved farther away from the business section into modest abodes of wood and, occasionally, of brick, devoid of distinctive architectural beauty but less crowded and more comfortable. Still farther out, businessmen, among others, sought the Elysian remoteness of the outskirts of the city where they could, if desired, have horses, a cow, and chickens, and where spaciousness and light contrasted refreshingly with the circumscribed and grimy surroundings of the downtown district. As early as 1874 a contemporary observer declared that "ninety-nine Chicago families in every hundred will go an hour's ride into the country, or toward the country, rather than live under or over another family, as the average New Yorker or Parisian does."[4]

Railroads in alliance with real estate promoters encouraged and facilitated the migration to the suburbs by offering service to would-be commuters. As time passed, Southsiders in increasing numbers were furnished accommodations by the Illinois Central, the Chicago, Rock Island and Pacific, the Michigan Central, the Baltimore & Ohio, the Pittsburgh and Fort Wayne,

the Michigan Southern, the Chicago & Eastern Illinois, the Grand Trunk, and the Chicago and Western Indiana. By 1874 the Illinois Central, for example, had twelve trains daily at ten cents a trip for the residents of Hyde Park. The Rock Island attracted others to Washington Heights and Morgan Park. To the north and northwest the Chicago and North Western, the Chicago, Milwaukee and St. Paul, and the Chicago and Evanston served in similar manner. The Chicago, Burlington & Quincy, the Wisconsin Central, and the Chicago, Alton and St. Louis carried residents of the West Side to and from their work. By 1887 combined suburban trains transported about 27,000 persons daily. At their insistence the legal rate of speed within the city limits was increased in 1890 from ten to twenty miles per hour and to thirty in the outlying areas.[5]

But those who toiled long hours in the factories and served in unskilled occupations could neither spend time in commuting nor afford the luxury of suburban living. Their homes, perforce, must be near the place of work and remote from quiet and space. Within two years after the Fire, humble, wooden cottages reflecting in design and color the national idiosyncrasies of Germans, Swedes, and other laborers, rose outside the fire limits.

From the North Side at Fullerton Avenue west of Lincoln and southward to North Avenue and westward to the north branch of the river, workmen, particularly skilled mechanics, profiting by the prosperity induced by rebuilding the city, put up their own unpretentious homes. Investors followed this example. Similar construction proceeded to the west of Mil-

[4] In the slums the population in 1890 averaged 15.5 persons per dwelling. (U.S. Commissioner of Labor, *Seventh Special Report*, p. 19.) Chamberlin, *Chicago and Its Suburbs*, p. 188.

[5] *Ibid.*, pp. 353, 410, 420, 445; *Chicago Tribune*, Jan. 4, 1883, June 12, 1887, March 11, 14, 1890; Citizens' Association of Chicago, *Annual Report . . . , 1886* (Chicago, 1886), p. 9; Chicago, *Council Proceedings*, *1889-90*, pp. 1448-51.

waukee Avenue and south to Kinzie Street, and from Madison Avenue to Ogden Avenue east of Western to Twelfth Street. South of the Chicago, Burlington & Quincy tracks at Sixteenth Street still more workmen's houses dotted the level stretches of land, until they embraced territory near Blue Island, Brighton, Thirty-third and Western Avenue, the stockyards section, and the Rock Island carshops at Fifty-first and Wentworth Avenue.

Fringing these streets were the dwellings of others who, also affected by the necessity of an inexorable economy, had built small, inartistic cottages with little regard to sanitation. At Canalport, about six miles southwest of the downtown district, the reaper manufacturers, C. H. McCormick and Brother, constructed near their factory one-story cottages for their workmen and two-story houses for their mechanics, who, because of poor transportation facilities, could not reach their place of work by seven o'clock in the morning.[6]

Still farther away from the central business district was the company town of Pullman, after 1881 the much publicized social and industrial experiment of George M. Pullman and the Pullman's Palace Car Company. Here, by 1884, lived 8,203 people—clergymen, company officers, and operatives—in red-brick and terra-cotta cottages, usually of two stories, predominant among buildings of "advanced secular Gothic" and Queen Anne design. Monotonous in appearance, even the smallest of the houses nonetheless afforded physical comfort to the occupants, providing them with water, gas, and closets, and in the largest with the luxury of a bathroom.[7]

Different indeed were the ramshackle dwellings of the poor on the periphery of the business section. Workingmen whose daily pay made possible only the bare necessities of life dwelt in nearness to one another in one- and two-story houses. Rear-lot shacks without foundations or plumbing stood close by the house at the front of a lot 25 by 125 feet. One-family houses pocketed several swarming hives of children and adults. Within one room, entire families had a noisome abode, a place of women's work by day and sleep by night. Cooperative households, usually made up of men, divided the expenses of shelter and food in cramped, insanitary quarters. Dank, darkly shadowed cellars, pantries and clothes-closets converted into sleeping-rooms, housed the habitual lodger, who, at times, also shared the bed of a member of the family. In the slums, privacy was a luxury seldom enjoyed.

Because they could find no other place to live, newcomers of the lowest income bracket flocked into these run-down houses, shacks, and even barn lofts, places "unfit for habitation by a civilized people."[8] Overcrowding and

[6] Hoyt, *One Hundred Years of Land Values in Chicago*, pp. 104–7; *Chicago Tribune*, May 18, 1873; *Industrial Chicago*, I, *The Building Interests*, 66; William T. Hutchinson, *Cyrus Hall McCormick*, II, *Harvest 1876–1884* (New York, 1935), 513.

[7] Pierce, *As Others See Chicago*, pp. 245–49; Bogart and Thompson, *The Industrial State 1870–1893*, pp. 208–9; Charles Dudley Warner, "Studies of the Great West, IV Chicago," *Harper's New Monthly Magazine*, LXXVII (June, 1888), 126; Richard T. Ely, "Pullman: A Social Study," *ibid.*, LXX (Feb., 1885), 452–66. The paternalistic philosophy back of the Pullman experiment and the effect of such a plan on workers met occasional criticism. Ely, in his article, pointed out the meritorious features, but drew attention to what he considered defects.

[8] The words of William H. Genung of the Bureau of Tenement and Factory Inspection. Chicago Department of Health, *Report 1881 and 1882*, pp. 5, 30, 48; *The Sanitary News*, I (Nov. 1, 1882), 16; *Hull-House Maps and Papers*, pp. 3–6; Edith Abbott and Associates, *The Tenements of Chicago, 1908–1935* (Chicago, 1936), pp. 17–18. The reports of the Department of Health are an excellent source on housing conditions.

filthiness were their lot and custom. Under such conditions only the neighborhood saloon offered the comforts and congeniality coveted after a day's hard work; consequently expenditures for beer were disproportionate to those for nourishing food. The prevalence of rickets in children was sad and convincing evidence of the lack of a proper diet.[9]

Within three years after the Fire so unkempt and dirty had these houses become that the Board of Health urged municipal regulations to deal with the most odious and dangerous practices. But a lethargic city council and a passive public opinion proved unresponsive. Not until 1880 did a municipal ordinance give the Department of Health the right to inspect and regulate sanitary conditions even in places of employment. Only by permission of an owner could a domicile be entered, except in cases of smallpox and cholera. An active campaign of education by health officials and the press to overcome the opposition of those who insisted that a man should have complete jurisdiction of his home resulted in a statute enacted by the state legislature in 1881.[10] This law required plumbers and architects to submit building plans to the health commissioner before beginning construction. Thus strengthened, the Department of

Health proceeded to establish rules as to lights, drainage, plumbing, air shafts, and the ventilation of rooms and water closets.[11]

Upon the passage of the law, inspectors from the Health Department surveyed plans for new tenements and examined previously erected dwellings, directing many improvements and correcting some unsatisfactory conditions.[12] But the canons of decent living and the admonitions of the Department of Health continued to be disregarded. Privy vaults, even in sections where there was a public sewer, remained in common use. As late as 1886 it was estimated that more than one-third of the population had no other toilet accommodations, a situation which prompted the Department of Health to urge legislation "to stamp out this disgusting and unnecessary practice among a civilized community of this enlightened age, and to prevent a further pollution, of not alone the soil upon which we dwell, but also the very air we breathe."[13]

Pollution of water used in both cooking and drinking which came from "filthy tanks in water closet rooms," unhealthful arrangements of piping waste matter, and other revolting conditions also alarmed vigilant

---

[9] Chicago Department of Health, *Report 1881 and 1882*, p. 31; U.S. Commissioner of Labor, *Ninth Special Report*, pp. 44, 45; Joseph Kirkland, *loc. cit.*, p. 26.

[10] The ordinance of 1880 was for "the regulation and inspection of factories, workshops, stores, warehouses, yards, and all other places of employment." (Chicago, *Council Proceedings, 1880–81*, p. 157; Chicago Department of Health, *Report 1879 and 1880*, p. 14.) A similar ordinance passed in 1879 was defective and no appropriation was made for its operation. *Ibid.*, *1881 and 1882*, p. 25, *1879 and 1880*, p. 14; Chicago, *Council Proceedings, 1880–81*, p. 157; Chicago Department of Health, *Report 1886*, pp. 48–54. Tenement houses were defined as "houses sheltering three or more families keeping house independently." (*Ibid.*, *1881 and 1882*, p. 30.) Act of May 30, 1881. Illinois, *Laws, 1881*, p. 66.

[11] Chicago Department of Health, *Report 1883 and 1884*, pp. 46–47, *1881 and 1882*, p. 25. The Department of Health drew plans for a model tenement to guide future builders. *Ibid.*, pp. 28–29; Citizens' Association of Chicago, *Annual Report, 1880*, pp. 11–12.

[12] Chicago Department of Health, *Report 1886*, p. 54, *1883 and 1884*, pp. 14–16, *1881 and 1882*, p. 61, *1885*, pp. 65–66. *The Municipal Code* of 1881 listed in considerable detail rules of health and sanitation for the "owner, lessee or keeper of any tenement-house, lodging-house, boarding-house or manufactory . . ." City of Chicago, *The Municipal Code of Chicago* (Chicago, 1881), pp. 330–35.

[13] Chicago Department of Health, *Report 1886*, pp. 60–61. See also *ibid.*, 1892, pp. 64–65. It was not until 1894 that the Council outlawed the privy vault on premises "abutting upon or adjoining any street, alley, court or public place," in which was located a public sewer. Chicago, *Council Proceedings, 1894–95*, p. 809.

health officials, powerless to effect improvements as rapidly as cleanliness and the public health required. Reports on mortality in the various wards of the city showed a close correlation between sanitation and health. In 1882 fully half the children of Chicago died before reaching five years of age, and the next year the Department of Health pointed out the distressing fact that deaths in the tenement wards outnumbered those in the residence wards almost three to one. In the Fourteenth Ward, the most thickly settled of the city, with a large foreign population, the highest rate of child and zymotic mortality occurred.[14]

All these conditions of living existed in the several divisions of the city where dwelt the poor. But as the years advanced they were especially prevalent in the West, as factories multiplied in this section and the supply of housing proved unequal to the demand. Near Hull House, in a third of a square mile containing large undigested groups of foreigners, all the sorry and sinister aspects of such an existence could be found. From this section, as from all others of like character, the better-to-do inhabitants moved away at the first opportunity, leaving to newly arrived immigrants a legacy of dilapidation and filth.[15]

Before the 'nineties the slum and its accompanying sorrows reflected the transition of Chicago from village to city in far less time than the transition

had taken elsewhere. As early as 1881 in the Fourteenth Ward alone 1,107 buildings housed 18,976 persons, of whom 10,113 were adults and 8,863 less than fifteen years of age.[16] In this predominantly German section, Poles and Scandivanians pressed hard upon the earlier German arrivals and upon each other, until over 55,000 of its 65,000 people dwelt in houses caring for three or more families. At the same time in the southwest wards where the Bohemians resided, more than one thousand families averaged but two rooms to a family.[17] By the 'nineties, over 49 per cent of the people lived in dwellings housing more than ten occupants. By 1893, the slum population was estimated as 162,000, second largest in the country. Although not so tightly packed as those of New York, Chicago slums possessed all the planlessness of the urban development which typified late nineteenth-century America.[18]

[16] The Fourteenth Ward was in the West Division. It was bounded on the east by the north branch of the Chicago River. Its boundary ran south along Ashland to North Avenue, west on North Avenue to Crawford (city limits until 1889), south on Crawford to Chicago Avenue, east on Chicago to Ashland Avenue, south on Ashland to Ohio and east on Ohio to the river. Chicago, *Council Proceedings, 1874–76,* p. 578, *Municipal Code, 1881,* p. 129.
[17] Chicago Department of Health, *Report 1881 and 1882,* pp. 30–31, *1885,* p. 18. In 1882, W. H. Genung pointed out in his report of Tenement and Factory Inspection that "the whole number of occupants of tenement houses is about equal to the foreign population, not because of their nationality, but because it is the wage-workers of *all* [sic] nationalities who are compelled to occupy tenement houses . . . The tenement houses occupied by native Americans are well-furnished in flats and otherwise arranged for separate families, containing a small proportion of children. The tenements of Germans are usually comfortably built but having less of the so-called modern conveniences; but the other nationalities, as a rule, live in close quarters . . ." *Ibid., 1881 and 1882,* p. 47.
[18] U.S. Commissioner of Labor, *Seventh Special Report,* p. 19; Marcus T. Reynolds, "The Housing of the Poor in American Cities," American Economic Association, *Publications,* VIII (1893), 18–19.

[14] Chicago Department of Health, *Report 1881 and 1882,* pp. 52, 84, *1883 and 1884,* p. 16, *1885,* pp. 19, 43. The Fifth, Sixth, Seventh, Eighth, Fifteenth, Sixteenth, and Seventeenth wards had high mortality. It should be noted that the birth rate of native whites of foreign-born parents was higher than that of native whites of white parents. See Appendix table.
[15] The section was bounded by Halsted Street on the west, State Street on the east, Polk Street on the north, Twelfth Street on the south. *Hull-House Maps and Papers,* pp. 3–14; Jane Addams, *Forty Years at Hull-House* (New York, 1935), pp. 97–101; Abbott, *op. cit.,* p. 30.

As Chicago expanded her economic empire and took on the sophistication of a maturing economy, increasing opportunities lured laborers from far and near. Work bench and market counter, profession and craft, the house of business and the factory, all gave promise of employment and complete living. But the golden flow which issued from the city's humming activity seeped inequitably into the hands of those who toiled to produce it, and while some accumulated handsome rewards for their efforts, many found that fortune had passed them by. Even in the best of times, those at the bottom of the economic order subsisted on a narrow margin, and when depression struck they sank into want and wretchedness. The workers' lot was hard. Theirs was a life of struggle, a quest for an elusive industrial democracy. When hope was strong, they fought for a fair share of society's gains. When despair supplanted hope, they fought only to live, their insecurity breeding unrest and hatred.

The mounting importance of Chicago from 1870 to 1890 as a center of industry and commerce and the growth of the labor force operated reflexively. The total employed during the two decades rose over four times to reach 458,313. Although diverse nationalities contributed their brain and brawn, their indigenous skills and aptitudes, native workers more and more dominated the scene as the American-born children of immigrants were added to the early and original stock.[19] In every major occupational field they constituted by 1880 the largest national group, with the Germans, the chief foreign-born element, having outdistanced immigrants from the British Isles, principally Irish. Again in 1890 this ranking held, but the relative importance of these two foreign groups was diminished by an influx of workers from Sweden, Norway, and other countries.[20]

That the economy had attained maturity was evidenced conclusively by the distribution of workers among the various occupations. Manufacturing and mechanical work employed the greater number, commanding, by 1890, the services of nearly half the labor force.[21] The city's importance as a center of trading transactions was reflected in the large number of persons connected with them—the bankers and brokers, the merchants, hucksters, and peddlers—each in his own way indispensable to the hegemony Chicago came to enjoy. Despite the over-all dominance of Americans, some lines held a special attraction for certain nationals. Thus the Germans and the Irish, famed as dispensers of food and drink, composed about two-thirds of the foreign born classed in 1890 as bartenders, saloon-keepers, and restaurateurs.[22]

[19] For a statistical presentation of the number employed in various occupations and the distribution of national groups, see for 1870 Pierce, *A History of Chicago*, II, 150–55, 499–500; for 1880 and 1890 the Appendix tables of this volume. Unless otherwise noted, figures for *1880* are based on U.S., *Tenth Census, 1880*, [I], "Population," 703–11, 870, and those for 1890, on U.S. *Eleventh Census, 1890*, [I], "Population," pt. II, 628–29, 634–35, 638–39, 648–51, 704–5, 710–11.

[20] In the 1890 census the classification "colored" appears. It includes persons of Negro descent, Chinese, Japanese, and civilized Indian. No similar classification was made in 1880. Such variations are frequently encountered in the enumerations.

[21] In 1880 laborers, comprising about 26 per cent of the total, were the largest category engaged in manufacturing and mechanical occupations. Carpenters, painters, brick and stone masons, plumbers and pipe fitters accounted for about 15 per cent; coopers, sawmill operatives, and cabinet workers and upholsterers about 5 per cent; iron and steel workers about 3 per cent. In 1890 laborers still made up 26 per cent; the four building trades, 18 per cent; the three woodworking trades, 4 per cent; iron and steel workers, 4 per cent. There was one apprentice for each 83 workers in 1880 and one for each 54 in 1890.

[22] In 1890 merchants, dealers, and peddlers made up the largest employment group in trade, or about 38 per cent. Sales people

Approximately one-tenth of the labor force gained a living in domestic and personal service, a field in which the proportion of native workers decreased slightly between 1880 and 1890, as their places were filled by immigrants from the British Isles, Germany, Sweden, and Norway. Additional thousands of workers went into transportation and communication. The number in these occupations approximately doubled with the passing of each decade, and the increase from 1870 to 1890 exceeded twenty-five thousand. With the expansion of business and the extension of the city's territory, the number in steam railroading increased from 4,857 to 11,694, while employees of the street railways jumped 269 per cent. Alongside these, the gain of nearly ten thousand in drayage and hauling gave further satisfaction to those looking for such obvious signs of progress in a field closely linked with the major enterprises of manufacturing and distribution.

In most professions Americans predominated, representing in 1880 about 68 per cent and in 1890 about 72 per cent of the total. Next in numbers were the Germans, who in 1880 made up about 12 per cent of those in the professions, but whose relative strength declined during that decade to 9 per cent. Greater numbers in the professions sharply delineated the accelerated tempo of a cultural urbanization. In the decade of the 'eighties a gratifying gain particularly in the fields of medicine and the law occurred, but it failed to keep pace with the needs of the extraordinarily growing population. More men trained as architects and civil engineers mirrored a spreading realization of the values of beauty and accuracy of design and construction. An increasing number of musicians and teachers of music bore striking testimony to a gradual softening of the harsh outlines of living in a rapidly changing society. To this refinement more foreign born contributed by 1890 than did Americans, as they shared with others the trained talent of their homelands. Artists and teachers of art, not listed in the federal census of 1880, also attested by their strength of 376 in the next decennial enumeration to the deepening inroads which the arts were making.[23]

Symptomatic of the greater complexity of the occupational pattern was the relatively high increase in clerical employees. Although this branch trailed in 1870, it climbed to fourth place by 1890. Also symptomatic was the change in the number of accountants from only two just before the Fire to twenty-five in the next twenty years. The modernization of business management made necessary the hiring of typists and stenographers, among whom by 1890 were more women than the number of both sexes in clerical work only ten years before. Least numerous of all were those in the pub-

---

followed or were about 17 per cent, with agents and collectors about 13 per cent, and messengers, packers, and porters about 10 per cent. Revised occupational classifications based on those used in the census of 1930 have been adopted for 1880 and 1890 as they were for 1870 (Pierce, *A History of Chicago*, II, 151). This reclassification leaves some workers listed as "unclassified and unknown." Figures so adjusted have greater comparability from year to year and are more applicable to present-day conditions. All computations unless otherwise noted in the following pages are based on the itemized totals as shown in the Appendix tables.

[23] Nurses and midwives, not listed in the 1880 census, number 1,333 in 1890; physicians and surgeons, 918 in 1880, 1,794 in 1890; lawyers, 1,035 in 1880, 2,144 in 1890; musicians and teachers of music 817 in 1880, 2,179 in 1890; dentists 171 in 1880, not listed in federal census 1890. According to the city directory of 1893 there were 600 dentists. The city directories listed 23 civil engineers in 1883, in 1893 there were 110; 126 architects in 1883 and 600 in 1893. The lag of the professionally trained in relation to population growth is illustrated by one physician in 1880 to each 548 people and one to each 613 people in 1893.

lic service and in agriculture, the latter reflecting the rise of Chicago as the great center of the Midwest's industrialization, its smoking factories by 1890 overshadowing all else.

Not all enjoyed an equality of opportunity as they went about the city looking for work. It was always hard for the colored, especially the Negro, unless he joined the ranks of those in domestic and personal service, where, in 1890, there were approximately eleven times as many as in other forms of employment.[24] The colored worker had but token representation in the skilled trades and in the professions, aside from a fairly numerous representation in the latter as musicians and teachers of music. Even as common laborers they accounted for less than 2 per cent of all so employed.[25]

Women, too, faced on the one hand by relentless economic pressures and on the other by a willingness, if not desire, to work outside the home, numbered five times more in 1890 than in 1870 as members of the labor force. Within these twenty years their proportion to the total rose about 3 per cent, and of the 88,088 gainfully employed about 41 per cent went into domestic and personal service. They

contributed appreciably to the manufacturing and mechanical pursuits, less so to clerical work and to trade and the professions.[26] As factory hands they were attracted predominantly into the clothing industries, particularly men's, and in smaller numbers into printing and publishing, and the manufacture of boots and shoes, and hosiery and knit wear, which, despite hard working conditions, long hours, and low pay, many preferred to employment as domestic servants.[27] Even in the most appallingly unhealthful sweatshops the female labor force by 1892 was approximately three times that of men, their total having reached 13,000 in about 800 shops.[28]

[26] Of the number of women employed, about 31 per cent went into manufacturing and mechanical occupations, 10 per cent into clerical work, and 6 per cent into trade and the professions. (Based on adjusted census figures.) Data on women in factories and workshops are reported incompletely each year in the Report of the Tenement and Factory Inspectors to the Commissioner of Health, *Report of the Department of Health*, in *Annual Reports of the Various Departments of the City of Chicago, 1882–1892*. These figures cannot be compared with those from the federal census because different bases of tabulation are used.

[27] In the 'seventies the pay for domestics was $2.00 to $4.00 a week plus board and room (Chicago Board of Trade, *Eighteenth Annual Report 1875* p. 227). In the early 'seventies women received about 85 cents a day for sewing (*Mrs. George M. Pullman Papers*, Nov. 4, 1871, [*Mss.* courtesy of Mrs. Philip Miller]). Sales girls often made less than $4.00 a week (*Chicago Tribune*, Dec. 17, 1871.) Where women worked with men in the same trade or occupation their wages were from 25 to 50 per cent less than the wages of men employed in the same trade or occupation. Chicago Board of Health, *Report, 1881*, p. 80.

[28] Illinois Bureau of Labor Statistics, *Seventh Biennial Report, 1892*, pp. 357–443, XIV–XV. In a group of 4,576 women workers surveyed in 1892, who were employed in 90 different establishments in various types of occupations, about one-third of 1 per cent made $20 or more a week, 15 per cent made less than $4.00. The average wage was $6.22. For a survey of the type of occupations women engaged in and wages paid, see the first section of the above report, which had over 300 pages devoted to working women in Chicago. Another large section dealing with sweatshops has a great amount of information regarding women's employment in this type of work.

[24] About 57 per cent of the colored employed were in personal and domestic service in 1890. In that year there were 40,296 servants in Chicago, or one for each 27 inhabitants; Philadelphia had one for each 24, New York one for each 19, Boston one for each 18. About 11 per cent of all servants in Chicago, 24 per cent of those in Philadelphia, and 9 per cent each of those in New York and Boston were colored. In Atlanta, where there was one servant for every 14 people, 96 per cent were colored.

[25] According to the federal census of 1890 there were but 16 colored among the city's 7,847 machinists, 3 among 2,959 cabinetmakers, 2 among 3,679 plumbers and pipe fitters, and 37 among over 20,000 carpenters and joiners. As lawyers, they numbered 6; as physicians and surgeons, 11; as engineers and surveyors, 3; as professors and teachers, 18. For listings of the mid-'eighties see I[saac] C. Harris, comp., *The Colored Men's Professional and Business Directory of Chicago*, pp. 12, 22, *passim*.

The economic necessity which took women from the home and made wage earners of them was also responsible for the 5,673 boys and girls from ten to fifteen years of age listed in the 1880 federal census as engaged in some occupation. Within the sweatshops they toiled for ten or more hours a day alongside their elders. Most of these child laborers came from immigrant homes. Here, in ramshackle buildings, in basement, loft, or stable —mere firetraps with no fire escapes —little girls averaged fifty cents a week as pay in the coat shops for sewing on buttons or pulling basting threads. As time went on, they might become hand sewers and they then, perhaps, might get two to two and a half dollars a week. They shortly became twisted and bent in body, the stooped positions familiar in their elders to be theirs also in the years to come.

Less numerous than the little girls in the sweatshops were the boys under sixteen, generally employed as messengers or errand runners, their years, too, empty of play and schooling. Both sexes labored in the furniture factories, in the publishing and printing establishments, and in places where meat packing was carried on. Indeed, the greatest number of children who worked could be found in the numerous manufactories of the city, and the next highest number went into trade and transportation. In the retail dry goods stores thousands of cash boys and girls answered the clerk's call when transactions were completed, and many little boys added to the family income their small pay of a few cents a day earned in the retail grocery stores.[29] Bootblacks and news-

boys in increasing numbers appeared on the streets, especially in the advancing 'eighties, while street musicians and flower venders eagerly solicited a few pennies in exchange for what they had to offer.[30]

Probably no aspect of the increasingly complex problem of labor elicited so much comment as did that of the child worker. As time went on, the voices of those recommending the employment of children as the best way to prevent crime and to train them in thrift and industry grew feebler. In turn, the socially minded—publicists, reformers, and educators—all spoke with unequivocal opposition and earnestness as they comprehended the meaning of signs of physical debility and an uneducated citizenry. More and more the responsibility for a continuation of such deplorable conditions was placed upon those employers who engaged in them. "They are," said Henry Demarest Lloyd, "blood-guilty for every wrong they do to their neighbor's child, just as much as if done to their own. And society is guilty to the extent of the sum of individual guilt."[31]

If the struggle of women and children for daily bread was particularly relentless, it was a struggle shared by all workers. Years of depression beggared those who had not been far from want; even skilled craftsmen were willing to work for board alone in

---

[29] U.S., *Tenth Census, 1880,* [I], "Population," 870, "Report on the Social Statistics of Cities," pt. II, 511, *Eleventh Census, 1890,* "Population," pt. II, lxxxv; "Factory and Tenement Inspectors' Report," Chicago Board

of Health, *Reports, 1884–93, passim*; Illinois, Bureau of Labor Statistics, *Seventh Biennial Report, 1892,* pp. 364–70, 374–75; *Hull-House Maps and Papers,* pp. 37, 38, 51.

[30] *The Knights of Labor,* III (April 25, 1888), 4, V (June 1, 1889), 8, VII (Nov. 7, 1891), 1; *The Chicago Times,* July 10, Aug. 3, 1888; *Chicago Tribune,* Dec. 13, 1880, Aug. 14, 1887; *The Sanitary News,* I (Feb. 1, 1883), 75; *Chicagoer Arbeiter-Zeitung,* June 14, 1888; *L'Italia,* Dec. 17, 1892.

[31] *The Knights of Labor,* II (May 7, 1887), 1. It should be noted that child labor declined during the 1880's but was not eliminated even with the passage of laws.

order to eat.[32] But the general insecurity of the working class seemed especially evident and terrifying in the days of prosperity when wages lagged behind soaring prices, and the invisible hand of inflation clutched each man's dollar. Between 1879 and 1881 food prices leaped an estimated 50 to 100 per cent, while wages generally remained stationary, and over-all living costs increased another 15 to 40 per cent the next year. Only the grim alternatives "either to work harder and longer, or eat less food and wear less clothing" were open to the average worker. Even in good times, the Illinois Bureau of Labor Statistics concluded, half of the "more intelligent, industrious and prosperous" were unable to stay solvent through their own efforts, and had "to depend upon the labor of women and children to eke out their miserable existence."[33]

Despite such conditions, laborers nevertheless flocked to Chicago to participate in the prosperity which the expanding city seemed to offer. Di-

rectly after the Great Fire there was plenty to do. From as far away as the British Isles came "skilled artisans" hoping to share in a daily wage of five to seven dollars which, it was said, they could earn.[34] But the exhilaration over plentiful work was short-lived, for in another year the panic ravaged the country, and throughout Chicago, as elsewhere, spread unemployment and suffering. Appeals for assistance in finding jobs poured into the Woman's Aid Association Employment Bureau. Skilled and unskilled alike were thrown out of work, and where employees were retained, reductions in wages ensued. The growth of industry, which had been stimulated by the city's rebuilding, stopped dead in its tracks. Closing banks swept away the savings of thrifty thousands, and even the rich were touched by the palsying depression.[35]

[32] *The Inter Ocean*, May 11, 1873; *Chicago Tribune*, Sept. 1, 1873; B. W. Raymond to Louis Reardley, March 6, 1874, *Benjamin W. Raymond Letter Book*, 1874 (*Ms.* Chicago Historical Society), p. 93.

[33] That workmen benefited by fixed wages when prices fell was sometimes claimed. Higher wages than the "inexorable" laws of supply and demand justified, others held, were unattainable. During the long depression of the 'seventies average earnings of unskilled labor fell from $25 a week in 1873 to $9.00 a week in 1879. *Chicago Tribune*, Nov. 14, 1885; *Chicago Morning News*, April 21, 1881; Illinois, *Report of the Special Committee on Labor* . . . (Springfield, 1879), p. 37; Illinois Bureau of Labor Statistics, *Second Biennial Report, 1882*, pp. 288, 351, *Eight Biennial Report, 1894*, p. 6; *The Economist*, X (Dec. 16, 1893), 633.

[34] Over forty million dollars were reported spent for supplies and for labor by October, 1872. Maximum wages for bricklayers were $4.00 to $4.50 per day. Carpenters got $3.50 a day, said to have been less than the scale in Pittsburgh, Philadelphia, St. Louis, and other cities. Living costs were high, and carpenters struck in Sept., 1872, for $4.00 a day. The following month bricklayers struck for a $4.00 wage and an eight-hour day. *The Chicago Times*, Jan. 19, 1874; *Chicago Tribune*, Oct, 26, 28, 29, 1871, Sept. 17, 24, Oct. 10, 11, 12, 20, 1872; *The [London] Times*, March 22, 1872; *Illinois Staats-Zeitung*, Oct. 5, 8, 1872; *The Western Catholic*, Sept. 28, 1872.

[35] *Chicago Tribune*, Sept. 27, Nov. 26, 28, 1873; *Illinois Staats-Zeitung*, July 21, 1879; Andreas, *History of Chicago*, III, 714. Failures of savings banks in the later years of the depression, due in considerable measure to corruption and mismanagement which depression conditions exposed, afflicted especially the working class. James, *The Growth of Chicago Banks*, I, 501–9.

The Living Conditions of the Immigrant

Robert Ernst*

During the first few days after landing at New York, the immigrant felt lonely and bewildered. Having looked forward with curiosity and hope to his arrival, he now found himself in a land of strangers and strange customs. As one Scotchman put it, if he should die, there would be none to mourn him.

The first concerns of the newcomer were shelter and food. If he had no relatives or friends with whom he could live temporarily, he walked to one of the many boardinghouses in the vicinity of Greenwich Street or the dingy side streets near the East River docks. Despite the evil notoriety of some of these hostelries, most were honestly run. However, nearly all were old buildings with damp cellars and little ventilation, poor sanitary conveniences, and flies, bedbugs, and wharf rats as permanent guests. Frequently, the parlor was a beer cellar, saloon, or grocery and provision store, where the new boarder might see "two barrels of whiskey—one colored red with oak juice and sold for 'first-rate Cognac brandy,' and the other answering with the most limpid assurance to the various demands for gin, Monongahela, or schnapps." The landlord enjoyed greater profits from liquor sales than from room rents, which ranged from fifty cents to three dollars per week, nearly always payable in advance. German boardinghouses sometimes maintained forwarding agencies for their constantly shifting occupants, many of whom sought private lodgings elsewhere at the first opportunity.

The boardinghouse dwellers were predominantly male, but entire families of immigrants sometimes rented the small, single rooms for several weeks after landing. Immigrant families left the boardinghouses as soon as possible and settled in the old private residences which had been converted into tenements in anticipation of their coming. Not only families but single men found it cheaper to rent rooms in tenements, where they shared their quarters with fellow countrymen.

The location of the immigrant communities which grew up in New York was determined by three basic elements: employment, housing conditions, and group consciousness. To find work was one of the first objectives of the newcomer, and he tried to live within easy walking distance of his job. From the Battery north to the foot of Hubert Street on the Hudson, and east to Corlear's Hook on the East River, lay three miles of waterfront crowded with slips and warehouses. The nucleus of large-scale activity was South Street, the shipping merchants' mecca, where the wharves jutted out like rake prongs into the East River. Smaller vessels, chiefly schooners and sloops, tied up in the Hudson, but east of the Battery large ships landed their Western produce from Albany and their lumber, granite, lime, and fish from New England. At Old Slip and Coffee House Slip were vessels southward bound for Baltimore, Philadelphia, Richmond, and other cities where they picked up cargoes of coal, tobacco, cotton, lumber, and naval stores. A floating population of sailors and longshoremen congregated on the docks, and cartmen, porters, and casual laborers trudged with their heavy loads into the

*Reprinted with permission from Robert Ernst, *Immigrant Life in New York City, 1825–1863*, New York: Columbia University Press, 1949, 37–40, 48–60.

side streets. That there were so many laborers in the lower wards was a logical outcome of this employment, and likewise, ship carpenters, caulkers, riggers, ropemakers, sailmakers, and other skilled artisans were dependent upon the shipping trade.

A few blocks from the waterfront, merchants and importers gave employment to ambitious clerks and workmen, native and foreign. Pearl Street, winding along the East Side, was the early home of the wholesale dry goods dealers, who lived above their stores. Boarding with them were clerks, bookkeepers, or junior partners, mostly Americans but including a growing number of English, Scotch, Irish, and Germans. The retail dry goods trade was carried on mostly in William Street. By the middle of the century the dry goods jobbing and importing district had extended to William, Broad, Pine, Cedar, and Liberty streets. Businessmen of other trades established themselves at similar focal points. In 1830 the hatters, fur merchants, and stove dealers centered around Water Street, between Pearl and South; the silk dealers were clustered in Hanover Square, the wholesale druggists in Fletcher Street from Pearl to the East River, and the wholesale grocers in Front Street paralleling South. In the area of the old Beekman marsh known as "the swamp," leather dealers entrenched themselves in the vicinity of Beekman and Ferry streets. Thirty years later these business districts had expanded but remained in the same general areas, and Broadway had blossomed into a promenade of beauty and fashion, lined with bookshops, jewelry, upholstery, hat and cap, tailoring, millinery, and large retail dry goods stores. With the dispersion of trade throughout the lower tip of the metropolis, native and immigrant wine dealers, tavern keepers, confectioners, and grocers plied their trades and bargained with foreign-born importers offering exotic cargoes from Sicily, Madeira, Bordeaux, or the Caribbean.

Because of this ceaseless commercial activity, property values below City Hall rose to phenomenal heights. By 1840 the value of real estate in the First, Second, and Third wards was assessed at one third of the total for Manhattan Island. The speculative value of this land led owners to neglect the upkeep of residential properties which would be torn down and replaced by commercial buildings. Meanwhile, the dilapidated old structures served a purpose: they housed the in-pouring immigrant tide. Although the population of the first three wards was small, the proportion of aliens rose from one ninth of the total in 1835 to one fifth in 1845 and three fifths in 1855. During the famine years of the late forties the Irish crowded into the boardinghouses and tenements in the Greenwich Street area, and in the late fifties this vicinity was host to thousands of transient Irish, Germans, Scandinavians, Spanish-speaking peoples, and Italians.

To live in the lower wards required some money. The penniless stranger, wholly without means, could not afford the relative luxury of a boardinghouse. His search for shelter without cost led him to sparsely populated sections north of the settled part of town. In the twenties and thirties Irish immigrants clustered around the "Five Points," a depressed and unhealthy area on the site of the filled-in Collect swamp in the old Sixth Ward. Here, at little or no cost, the poorest of the Irish occupied dilapidated old dwellings and built flimsy shanties with whatever materials they could gather. In the heart of the Five Points was the Old Brewery, erected in 1792 on the banks of the Collect and long famous for its beer. Transformed into a dwelling in 1837, the Old Brewery came to house several hundred men, women, and children, almost equally divided between Irish and Negroes, including an assortment of "thieves, murderers, pickpockets, beggars, harlots, and degenerates of every type."

As early as 1830 the Sixth Ward, and the Five Points in particular, had become notorious as a center of crime, and the riots of 1834–1835 were supposed to have originated in their long-settled Irish neighborhood. The criminality of the area was usually overemphasized, but poverty was widespread, and thousands of law-abiding inhabitants led wretched lives in cellars and garrets. To the original Irish and native population, including Negroes, came new accretions: English, Germans (including Jews), Polish Jews, more Irish; and in the fifties, Italians and laborers and workers in near-by clothing factories, machine shops, and foundries. The ward remained predominantly Irish, however, 42 per cent of its inhabitants in 1855 being natives of the Emerald Isle. By this time an even larger proportion of Irish lived to the east in the built-up, commercial, and industrial Fourth Ward, where they accounted for nearly half the population. Spreading along Water, Cherry, and Monroe streets, they moved north and east. In the Second, Fourth, and Seventh wards facing the East River, the Irish comprised 38 per cent of the inhabitants. These wards served as a distributing point for thousands of refugees from the Emerald Isle, and the easy ferriage across the river brought to Brooklyn an Irish population which spread over an area less severely constricted by land speculation than Manhattan.

As stores, businesses, and dwellings were erected in southern Manhattan, homeless immigrants trudged farther to the limits of the built-up region. They occupied barren areas of rocks and hills, where, as squatters on the land, they erected flimsy one-room shanties and eked out a precarious semirural existence. Thus developed New York's "shanty town." With few exceptions, the shanty dwellers were Irish and German. "Dutch Hill," a steep precipice at First Avenue and Fortieth Street became in the sixties a well-known squatter colony, where the foreign-born inhabitants tended their cows, pigs, goats, and fowl, and worked in near-by quarries and manure heaps. Along the Hudson from Fortieth to Eightieth streets west of Sixth Avenue lived a shanty population of Irish and German ragpickers, cinder gatherers, and laborers. Many of them were employed in grading, paving, and sewering streets, removing rocks, or excavating for building purposes. Some worked in the stables of the city railroads and stage companies or labored in near-by Central Park, which was laid out in the latter fifties. In 1864 the New York *Times* estimated at twenty thousand the number of squatters, who paid neither rent nor taxes.

. . .

As New York's wharves became crowded with warehouses amid a scene of noisy and ceaseless activity, the wealthier inhabitants moved elsewhere, and their homes passed into the hands of boardinghouse keepers and of real estate agents. White-collar employees and workingmen, finding it necessary to live near the docks, warehouses, stores, and workshops, occupied these old dwellings and found them a blessing. However, as property values rose in the lower wards, rents were raised, and those tenants who could afford it followed their former proprietors into the upper wards. The rest sought cheaper quarters in the old neighborhood.

To meet the demand for rooms and apartments, owners and agents converted old homes into tenements by erecting partitions for the accommodation of three or more families. Unscrupulous owners made room for more by dividing their space into "the smallest proportions capable of containing human life within four walls." Beginning in the thirties, immigrant families poured into these reconstructed buildings, the Irish becoming their principal occupants, although in some houses Negroes crowded "from cellar to garret." Thus appeared the first stage in the development of the modern New York slum.

Housing facilities could not keep pace with the incoming tide of foreign workingmen and their families, and the insistent demand for shelter at low rentals resulted in the development of a second type of tenement. When owners discovered that converted dwellings yielded substantial profits in rents, they constructed new buildings designed especially as tenement houses. Usually such a building contained a narrow hall opening from a street or court; on each floor, including the cellar, two suites of rooms opened into the hall. Front and rear rooms of the building contained windows, but the bedrooms and closets in the middle were dark. In most cases there was another tenement in the back yard, frequently altogether enclosed and accessible only through an alley. Alongside these buildings and in the yards were many little, irregular frame structures, some in dilapidated condition, serving partly as sheds and partly as homes for the overflow of the tenements. Such haphazard combinations of front and rear buildings on the same lot created an intricate array of rear courts and alleys, notoriously dark, foul-smelling, and encumbered with accumulations of filth.

As immigration intensified the housing shortage, the insistent demand for rooms and apartments induced owners to rent basements, attics, and even lofts and stables to eager but poor homeseekers. In the seven wards below Canal Street, the gross density of population per acre climbed from 94.5 persons in 1820 to 163.5 in 1850, while the average block density increased from 157.5 to 272.5 in the same period. In the Seventh Ward, with a large Irish population, and the Tenth Ward, which included many Irish and Germans, the average block density rose from 54.5 persons per acre in 1820 to 170.9 in 1840.

A considerable number of immigrants moved into cellars, where rents were cheaper and where, consequently, diverse ages, sexes, races, and nationalities crowded together. In 1843, 7,196 persons were living in cellars. During the great waves of Irish and German immigration, the basement population expanded so that by the middle of the century about twenty-nine thousand persons were living underground. Thereafter, the number of cellar residences decreased as newer and larger tenements were built, and by 1863 it was estimated that only eighteen thousand persons lived in cellars. Typical of overcrowded cellars was a house in Pike Street which contained a cellar ten feet square and seven feet high, with one small window and an old-fashioned inclined cellar door; here lived two families consisting of ten persons of all ages. The occupants of these basements led miserable lives as troglodytes amid darkness, dampness, and poor ventilation. Rain water leaked through cracks in the walls and floors and frequently flooded the cellars; refuse filtered down from the upper stories and mingled with the seepage from outdoor privies. From such an abode emerged the "whitened and cadaverous countenance" of the cellar dweller.

Population could expand only northward on Manhattan Island. This limitation increased the competition for apartments in an area of already inflated property values and drove rentals upward. Immigrants who had lived in cities in the Old World resented the high rents which they were forced to pay and cried out bitterly against the rapacity of landlords. Disillusioned about the city's living conditions, an English workman grumbled that for a New York room with bare, whitewashed walls and no sanitary facilities, the rent was double that in London. As middleclass private dwellings disappeared, the clerical workers and artisans also relapsed into tenement lives.

Tenement houses were rented by the week or month. Many an owner was enriched by charging $3.00 to $13.00 per month for apartments, and seventy-five cents to $1.25 per week for single rooms twelve feet square. In this system of rent gouging, the chief figure was an agent, or sublandlord, who leased a house or group of houses for several years. The owner thereby was assured of an income and relieved of responsibility for direct supervision of tenants, while the agent collected the rents and sometimes saved enough money to purchase the property in a short time. Since the agent was a speculator whose interest was to make as large a profit as he could, he thought in terms of risk and reimbursement, not of tenant welfare. "He measures rooms, and estimates—not their capacities for accommodating human life in health and comfort—but their capability of containing human life to pay the rent."

Despite the fact that many poor tenants frequently moved about in response to changing employment conditions, they were conscientious about paying their rent. The reason was fear of eviction. This possibility placed the tenant at the mercy of the landlord and put rent before fuel and clothing. For those who had acquired a small amount of personal property, the consequences of eviction were disastrous. A wife's property could be seized as well as her husband's and sold on execution for his nonpayment of rent. Only such items as necessary food and clothing, cooking utensils and tableware, fuel for sixty days, a few pieces of furniture, the family pictures, and a few books, including the Bible, were exempt from levy or sale. To insure that rents would be paid, some landlords maintained blacklists of delinquent tenants; evicted persons thus found it difficult to rent new homes.

Newspapers, both native and foreign-language, were full of protests against evictions and high rents. They reported spontaneous meetings of lodgers to combat the inhumanity of the landlords and the raising of rents. At a mass meeting in 1848, tenants demanded that the legislature limit profit in rents to 7 per cent on assessed valuation and put a stop to the practice of ejecting one paying tenant in order to rent to another. They called for a city tax of 3 per cent on all unimproved lots. A proposition before the legislature to incorporate companies of capitalists to build tenements was condemned as tending to encourage the combination of capital for the supression of the poor. Finally, the formation of a lodgers' league was urged to protect the interests of the tenants against property owners and their agents.

The wide gulf between tenants and owners was emphasized by the unhealthy physical aspects of tenement life. To the immigrant who had been a city dweller in Europe it was no novelty to settle in apartments which lacked proper lighting and ventilation, but the peasant from rural Ireland or southern Germany was forced to make a difficult adjustment to living conditions in New York. Instead of the fresh country air, he breathed the foul miasma of cramped and insalubrious quarters; instead of the surrounding daylight of farm and field, there was little but gloom and darkness. Daylight rarely entered more than one of the two or three rooms in the apartments of the poor, and cross ventilation was usually an impossibility. Samuel Gompers, the immigrant cigar maker and future labor leader, wrote:

Our apartment in Sheriff Street was a typical three-room home. The largest, the front room, was a combined kitchen, dining-room, and sitting-room with two front windows. There were two small bedrooms back, which had windows opening into the hall. We got water from a common hydrant in the yard and carried it upstairs. The toilet was in the yard also.

When water for bathing and washing had to be fetched from street pumps or near-by wells, bodily cleanliness was more of an ideal than a reality. Not only was it impossible to bathe, but insufficient space and air hindered home laundering. To overcome this situation, private philanthropy erected a "People's Washing and Bathing Establishment" in Mott Street in the early fifties. A few years later a *Verein* was formed to crusade for free baths for the German working population. All such ventures failed, however; it is likely that most immigrants bathed in the Hudson, East, or Harlem rivers. One of the chief attractions of Sunday excursions was a swim in the ocean, in Long Island Sound, or in the Hudson above the city, where bathers were free of the polluted waters of lower Manhattan.

The deficiency of water in the tenement areas was largely responsible for the accumulation of filth. Nearly all the old buildings, and many of the newer ones, lacked toilet facilities. Back-yard, wooden privies were common, but they could not accommodate the large number of inhabitants they were intended to serve. Through overuse and improper care, the privies remained a constant menace to health, and their contents, instead of being drained or carried away, frequently overflowed to the surface and created breeding places of disease.

Had the city maintained adequate inspection and control of tenement sanitation, New York might have avoided its reputation for dirtiness. City ordinances provided for the regulation of privies, cesspools, sewers, gutters, and cemeteries, but these laws were poorly enforced, particularly in tenement localities, where complaints proved ineffective. The lack of official supervision was largely the result of maladministration, employment of incompetent health officers, and the fear of infringing upon the presumed rights of private property. Owing to the paucity of sewers, the question of sanitation was of city-wide concern. As late as 1857 only 138 miles of sewers had been constructed in nearly 500 miles of streets, leaving unsewered "nearly three fourths of the city, including some of the most densely populated and filthy portions." Waste water drained into yards and alleys, filled the sinks, and broke into cellars and foundations; some 24,000,000 gallons of sewage matter daily accumulated in such areas and in the gutters and streets of the city.

The streets were cleaned under a contract system which resulted in neglect and avoidance of responsibility. In the absence of a paid municipal street-cleaning force, contractors vied to receive "the highest compensation for the smallest discharge of duty." Imperfectly drawn contracts provided loopholes for evasion, and the spirit of the law was repeatedly violated. The contractors usually subcontracted for the cleaning of the several wards, the subcontractors often letting out further subcontracts; meanwhile, the low wages, uncertainty of pay, and harsh treatment of the laborers who did the actual cleaning contributed to the ineffectiveness of the system. The haphazard removal of garbage forced even cleanly inhabitants to violate the law. They dumped into the streets the contents of their unemptied refuse containers. Since poor women were the usual offenders, sympathetic policemen hesitated to tear them from their families by hauling them off to jail.

In New York, where it was asserted that overcrowding was greater and that there was less concern and expenditure for the welfare of the slum population than in any other large city, the lower wards became the scene of frequent accidents among workingmen and their families. The concentration of shipyards, docks, and manufacturing plants in lower Manhattan exposed the laborer to collisions in cluttered streets, falling timber and brick, and collapsing walls. This peril was likewise an ever present possibility in the tenements and boardinghouses wedged amid factories, slaughterhouses, stables, and lumber and coal yards. When inadequately inspected buildings crumbled on their foundations and antiquated firetraps suddenly were consumed in flame, the danger became real. Where front doors and windows were the only fire escapes, the inhabitants were compelled to "roast or break their necks." Typical of such catastrophes were the $600,000 fire in the Woolsey sugar factory at Clinton and South streets and a frightful explosion in Hague Street, both in the winter of 1849–1850.

Life in the slums was a continual struggle with illness and death. The high incidence of disease in New York was directly related to the sanitary condition of tenement dwellers, of whom a large number were the foreign born or their children. In the crowded immigrant quarters quarantine was an impossibility, and the communicable diseases suddenly erupted into epidemic proportions. The Sixth Ward was a center of contagion, typhoid breaking out among the Irish and Germans in 1837, typhus in 1842, and cholera in 1849. Respiratory diseases likewise took their toll. Tuberculosis, pneumonia, and bronchitis were common, and scrofula was called "the great scourge of the pauper population."

That immigrants suffered more heavily from disease than the native population was well known. During the ten years from 1849 to 1859, of all persons admitted to Bellevue Hospital, a public institution, 83.9 per cent were foreign-born. According to the unusually complete report of the city inspector for 1857, three of every five deaths from cancer in that year occurred among the immigrants; tuberculosis took the lives of 656 more immigrants than natives. Deaths from all causes were always proportionally higher among the foreign population than among the natives. More than half of the persons over ten years of age who died in 1840 were immigrants. In the latter fifties aliens accounted for 36.6 per cent of all deaths, but had the city statisticians considered parentage, the number of deaths in immigrant families would have produced a far higher percentage. The mortality of children of foreign parents showed a great excess over those of American parents, an eloquent proof of their poverty and lack of proper medical care. Nearly two thirds of New York City's total mortality in 1857 were children under the age of five, the majority undoubtedly of foreign parentage. A physician of Providence, Rhode Island, wrote:

> It is well known that the foreign population, as a class, in this city, and in other cities in this country, are under entirely different sanitary influences from the American population. The greater portion of the foreign population live in a miserable class of tenement houses, with

all the want of conveniences, and positively injurious influences of such houses; their social habits are not calculated to preserve health; and a knowledge of the laws of hygiene is entirely wanting among them. Of course, the children of foreign parents are subject to the same injurious influences upon health, and suffer from them more than the parents themselves.

Despite the hospital facilities of the port of New York, diseases were introduced by newly arriving immigrants, and their spread was inevitable in the densely populated tenement districts. The largest annual number of deaths from typhoid, typhus, dysentery and diarrhea occurred during the periods of the greatest influx of immigrants—from 1847 to 1855. Fleeing the famine in their native land, many starving and diseased Irish left the emigrant ships, spread their diseases, and died shortly afterward.

Among the immigrants, the Irish were the chief victims of disease, and Irish-born patients of city institutions were nearly always in the majority. Natives of Ireland comprised 53.9 per cent of New York City's foreign-born inhabitants in 1855, but at Bellevue Hospital, 85 per cent of all the foreign born admitted from 1849 to 1859 were born in Ireland. The comparatively good health of the Germans is in striking contrast with the Irish. While 29.4 per cent of the city's foreign-born population were natives of Germany, only 6.25 per cent of admissions to Bellevue were German-born. Thus the proportion of Germans admitted to the hospital was only one fifth of the proportion of Germans in the total immigrant population of New York. In explanation it was asserted that the Germans were more cleanly and orderly in their living habits, but it is more likely that their generally superior economic status enabled them

to live in comparatively comfortable surroundings. Moreover, the German immigrants, as a rule, were not so physically debilitated as were the poorer Irish, particularly those escaping famine in their native land and fortunate enough to survive the horrors of the voyage in tightly packed emigrant ships from Liverpool. The greater financial resources of the Germans were indicated by the statistics of the German Society relating to the annual immigration of Germans at the port of New York. Perhaps for similar reasons other nationalities sent proportionally few persons to Bellevue. The English comprised 6.9 per cent of the foreign born, yet only 4.56 per cent of admissions to the hospital were natives of England; the Scotch accounted for 2.6 per cent of the alien population, yet only 1.78 per cent of the Bellevue admissions were born in Scotland.

As in the case of other diseases, the insanity rate among the foreign born was considerably higher than that of the native Americans, and that of the Irish was by far the highest of the foreign born. Over three fourths of the admissions to the city lunatic asylum on Blackwell's Island from 1849 to 1859 were of alien birth; two thirds of these were natives of Ireland. The resident physician at the asylum admitted his inability to account satisfactorily for the high proportion of foreign insane. "Very few of the indigent insane of this city," he asserted, were

sent to the State Asylum at Utica, and none to Flushing, Hudson, or the Bloomingdale Asylum. Either the ratio of insane is very much less among the natives, or they are kept at their homes. Probably the first supposition is true, and this may arise in part from the shipment of the insane from Europe during a lucid interval.

Nevertheless, it is also likely that many natives had better means of taking care of their insane and at the same time were unwilling that their kin associate with the foreign-born insane at a public institution.

Insanity, apparently was common among newly arrived immigrants. This phenomenon was attributed to the "privations on shipboard," "the changes incident to arriving in a strange land," and to "want of sufficient nourishment." In 1854 thirty-five of the hundred patients admitted to the Lunatic Asylum and chargeable to the Commissioners of Emigration had been in New York City less than one year, although many were only temporarily deranged and soon recovered. Insanity was prevalent especially among young women, according to one physician, who ascribed it to "the combined moral and physical influences of their leaving the homes of their childhood, their coming almost destitute to a strange land, and often after great suffering.

If physical and mental illnesses could be traced to the conditions of immigration or to existence in New York's slums, ignorance, lack of cleanliness, and inadequate medical care also played their part. Attracted by cheap prices, many poor families bought impure food from hucksters and basement storekeepers. Medical advice was ignored by many, the Irish being the chief offenders. While the Irish exposed their children to inclement weather, the Germans went to the other extreme, confining their sick to overheated rooms and excluding fresh air. Superstition and home remedies were applied to all sorts of common ailments and disabilities. To her bald and toothless son in New York an English mother wrote, "You can have false teeth that is a very common thing and you must get some Castor Oil and rum and rub your head every morning."

Credulous persons were fair targets for the army of charlatans who offered a pill for every ill. Advertisements for patent medicines appeared in nearly every newspaper, particularly in the German papers. For twenty-five cents one could buy a box of Dr. Furbarsch's *Vegetabilische Lebenspillen* for the cure of fever, colds, scrofula, worms, hemmorhoids, and "all delicate female ailments." Van Pelt's Indian Vegetable Salve, costing fifty cents, was for the treatment of "breast ailments," burns, and carbuncles; *Pastilles de Paris* were good for colds and bronchitis; Tarrant's Cordial Elixir of Turkey Rhubarb for indigestion and dyspepsia; "innocent-pills," "bloodcleaning pills," "family pills," and "anti-diarrhea pills" vied with "syrup of naphtha," "lung balsam," and "marshmallow drops" as specifics or cure-alls. At one dollar a box, "Ladies Silver Pills" were "the rich man's friend and the poor man's need."

Despite insufficient medical care, poor immigrant families were not completely without the services of doctors. European physicians, surgeons, dentists, specialists, and midwives offered consultation and aid either free of charge or at nominal fees. Occasionally, these doctors co-operated with immigrant aid societies. In 1843, for instance, thirteen German physicians agreed to treat the poor gratis upon presentation of a certificate of need from the German Society. Besides employing doctors for the free treatment of needy Germans, the society also spent several hundred dollars annually for medicines and paid the bills of the dispensaries which leading Germans founded in the lower part of the city. Ultimately, a German hospital was established in 1866, but only after a long agitation by community-conscious German businessmen, physicians, and philanthropists. Likewise, the dream of a Jewish hospital was slow of realization, and it was not until

1855 that the Jews' Hospital was opened to patients. A Jewish clinic, however, was organized a few years earlier to meet the crying need for free medical service. The Irish failed to develop such a degree of medical co-operation. Overburdened with work among the poor, the relatively few Irish physicians faced an insuperable task of giving medical attention to the multitude of Irish immigrants who could not pay for it. When the Irish fell sick and home remedies did not avail, they sought admission to the city dispensaries and hospitals, where they were nearly always in the majority. The only organized medical aid among the Irish was through their benevolent and fraternal associations, a form of mutual aid common to all immigrant groups.

The helplessness of the immigrant poor was reflected in the large proportion of foreign-born paupers. City almshouse statistics prior to 1849 were unreliable, but during the next decade detailed figures revealed that fully three quarters of all persons admitted to the almshouse were born outside the United States. After the middle of the century, extensive immigration co-incided with rising living costs to aggravate the already precarious existence of the newcomer, and in 1852 more than half the needy in all the Atlantic seaboard cities were Irish and German immigrants, mostly day laborers. In the Empire City alone, half of the persons relieved by the Association for Improving the Condition of the Poor were Irish; three eighths, German and other nationalities; while only one eighth were born in the United States. Then depression struck. In 1854 and 1855, and again in 1857, the number of indigent poor mounted to unheard-of figures as unemployment stalked the city and mass meetings demanded public works to feed the starving. It was an ominous sign that in the year of Lincoln's election fully 86 per cent of the paupers in New York City were of foreign birth.

Huddled together in teeming tenements, in squalid alleys and court-yards, immigrants came into frequent conflict with the law, particularly in the extremely poor neighbor-hoods of the Fourth and Sixth wards. Panel thieves operated in the "Dutch" groceries of Duane, Thomas, and Anthony streets and in West Broadway, hardened murderers and harbor thieves congregated in Cherry and Water streets and on the wharves, and gangs of criminal hoodlums like the "Kerryonians" and the "Dead Rabbits" haunted the Five Points and the Bowery. Most immigrant lawbreakers, however, were individuals incapable of organized crime. In the vast majority of cases, they were arrested by the police on charges of petty thievery, drunkenness, or disorderly conduct. Family worries involving illnesses and deaths, the monotony and uncertainties of work in New York, and the isolation and friendlessness of the immigrant were relieved by frequent trips to the tippling shop. Love of liquor, fostered in Ireland by the hopeless outlook of the Irish peasantry, was further encouraged in New York by innumerable bartenders. Nor was hard drinking limited to the children of Erin, for the English and Scotch liked their whiskey too, and the French and Germans, traditionally wine and beer drinkers, included lovers of rum, brandy, and schnapps. Under the influence of drink, desperate and reckless individuals forgot their sufferings and their sorrows, committed assault or robbery, and wound up in jail. Of the total number of persons committed to the city prison during the nine years 1850–1858, seven eighths were recorded as "intemperate," most of them immigrants, unmarried, and between the ages of twenty and forty.

Immigrants were easy prey for policemen who, unwilling to risk their jobs by raiding gambling dens, brothels, and criminal hideouts, kept a sharp eye for slight misdemeanors committed by persons of no political influence. Because of alien habits or unfamiliarity with the English language, some foreigners unintentionally violated city ordinances; others, who happened to be present at brawls and riots, were subjected to arbitrary arrest. As common among the poor as the boisterous conduct of the intemperate was the addiction to petty stealing. The culprits apparently stole needed goods more often than money, and sometimes they were arrested merely on suspicion, as is evidenced by this press report:

ARRESTS—John McGorty and Michael Dowd were arrested for stealing a keg of white lead; John McKeeney on suspicion of having stolen $34; Jane Mullen for stealing a wash tub; Mary Donahan stole 34½ yards of calico from the premises of Mr. Taylor, 31 Catharine st.

After their apprehension, the guilty and innocent alike were herded into the overcrowded city prison. Petty offenders mingled with confirmed felons, the sane with the insane, and children with jaded adults reeking of alcohol. During 1859, 23 per cent of the persons arrested in New York City were native Americans, 55 per cent were born in Ireland, 10 per cent in Germany, 7 per cent in England and Scotland, and 5 per cent in other countries. These figures are less significant, however, than the rate of criminal convictions for each nationality. In the courts of special sessions, slightly less than one per cent of the native American population of New York City were convicted in 1859, while 5.5 per cent of the Irish, 3 per cent of the Scotch, 2.5 per cent of the English, 2 per cent of the Canadians, 1.5 per cent of the French, an 1.2 per cent of the Germans were convicted. The high proportions of foreign-born criminals are misleading, however, for the vast majority of crimes were committed by persons between the ages of twenty and forty, and it was this age group which was so largely filled with the foreign born. Among the immigrant groups, the Germans were known for their law-abiding qualities, and the Jews, most of whom were Germans, appear to have had the lowest incidence of criminality. "There are far less charges of crime alleged against the Jews as a class, than against any other equal portion of citizens in our city," reported the *National Police Gazette*. Yet when a Jew was arrested, the newspapers noted that he was a Jew, whereas the creed of others was rarely given.

Dens of gambling and vice dotted lower Manhattan. Despite the ban on lotteries passed by the state legislature in 1832, New York gamblers bought tickets for lotteries in other states, in Cuba, or in Europe, or they turned to the policy game. Negroes were the main victims of this numbers racket, but many immigrant women were also "daily won to its infatuation." There is no evidence, however, that the foreign born gambled more than the natives; Jonothan Green's curious "Report on Gambling" hardly mentioned foreigners.

Prostitution appears to have been almost as common among American women as among immigrants, but in either case poverty was the chief inducement to vice. In their failure to make ends meet, immigrant girls, devoid of family life, walked the streets in despair or drifted into dance halls and brothels, where in some instances they were exploited by women of their own nationality. Of 2,000 prostitutes examined in 1858 at the Penitentiary Hospital on Blackwell's Island—in effect, the city's venereal hospital—762 were natives of the United States and 1,238, or five eights of the total, were immigrants. The largest proportion was born in British territory: 706 in Ireland, 104 in England, 63 in British North America, 52 in Scotland, and one in Wales, while 257 were natives of the German states, 17 of Switzerland, and 13 of France. More than 45 per cent of these foreign-born prostitutes had lived in the United States less than five years, and of these, 21 per cent were residents of less than one year. Of the 2,000 women, native and immigrant, three eighths were between the ages of fifteen and twenty, and fully three quarters were younger than twenty-six.

Forced by circumstances to spend their formative years amid poverty, vice, and crime, children of the poorest immigrants grew up without family guidance and the restraining influences of church and school. Parents, who were subject to definite social controls in Europe, were unable to assert authority over children whose views of life were gained from experiences with " 'flash-men,' engine-runners, cockfighters, pugilists, and pickpockets . . . and . . . low theaters." For the boys of the streets, the Golden Rule was an altogether impossible precept, especially when they were "stuck and short" and "had to live." Girls, pitiable and deserted, sometimes the daughters of prostitutes, made a scant living as fruit, nut, and candy peddlers, by petty thievery, or "by more questionable means." Drifting loose upon society, the homeless, friendless, and lawless youth created serious problems of juvenile delinquency in New York as early as the 1820's. The vagrant and criminal children of foreign parentage admitted to the House of Refuge over a period of three decades were far more numerous than those of native parentage. Although specific offenses committed by children were not reported before 1863, nearly all the children sent to the House of Refuge during the four years 1863–1866 were charged with petty larceny and vagrancy; but some were accused of disorderly conduct, assault and battery, manslaughter, rape, arson, forgery, and other crimes.

Such were the living conditions of the foreign born. The New York tenement houses appeared in response to the needs of a growing population in congested lower Manhattan. Crowding into the hurriedly reconstructed dwelling or, later, into specially designed tenements, immigrant families occupied the poorest districts of the city, where life and limb were jeopardized by the failure to enforce housing regulations, the presence of factories and other industries in their midst, the uncleaned streets, the ineffective sewage system, the absence of bathing facilities, the futility of quarantining diseased persons, the widespread ignorance and lack of medical care, and the high incidence of pauperism, crime, vice, and juvenile delinquency. Persons of middle age or older, having little opportunity to rise to a comfortable living standard, eked out a bare existence in the forgotten streets of the lower wards. Younger men and women, more often their children, improved their status and moved to cleaner, safer neighborhoods, vacating their former rooms and flats for occupancy by more recent immigrants. As this process was repeated year by year, the foreign settlements acquired a fluidity made possible by the immigrants' occupational skills and their adjustment to the employment opportunities in New York.

The Making of the Black Ghetto

Allan H. Spear*

There were, then, many Chicagos by the end of the century. The reformers faced not merely the problem of an exploited working class, but of numerous worker enclaves, each clinging proudly to its own traditions. The newcomers' ignorance of American economic and political life made them particularly susceptible to the blandishments of unscrupulous employers and political bosses. A few of the reformers, such as Jane Addams and Graham Taylor, attempted to bring the immigrants into the mainstream of the city's life while at the same time respecting and even encouraging their cultural diversity. But many old-stock Chicagoans—and this included many of the sons and daughters of the earlier immigrants—were hostile, or at best patronizing, toward the ways of the newcomers.

Of Chicago's many ethnic groups, none had a longer local history than the Negroes. According to tradition, the first permanent settler on the site of Chicago was a black trader from Santo Domingo, Jean Baptiste Pointe de Saible, who built a cabin on the mouth of the Chicago River in about 1790. The beginning of Negro community life in the city can be traced to the late 1840's, when a small stream of fugitive slaves from the South and free Negroes from the East formed the core of a small Negro settlement. Soon there were enough Negroes in Chicago to organize an African Methodist Episcopal church, and within a decade several more churches and a

number of social and civic clubs were flourishing. By 1860, almost a thousand Negroes lived in Chicago. A small leadership group, headed by a well-to-do tailor, John Jones, participated in antislavery activities and articulated the grievances of a people who already found themselves the victims of segregation and discrimination.

Despite the presence of an active antislavery movement, Negroes in antebellum Chicago were severely circumscribed. Residents of downstate Illinois frequently characterized Chicago as a "sink-hole of abolition" and a "nigger-loving town"; yet the sympathy that many white Chicagoans expressed for the Southern slaves was not often extended to the local Negroes. To be sure, the anti-slavery press, on occasion, noted approvingly the orderliness and respectability of the city's Negro community, but little was done to improve the status of the group. Chicago's Negroes could not vote, nor could they testify in court against whites. State law forbade intermarriage between the races. Segregation was maintained in the schools, places of public accommodation, and transportation. Chicago's abolitionists regarded these conditions as side issues and manifested little interest in them.

Between 1870 and 1890, the Chicago Negro community grew from less than four thousand to almost fifteen thousand and developed a well delineated class structure and numerous religious and secular organizations. After the fire of 1871, the community became more concentrated geographically. Most Negroes lived on the South Side, but were still well interspersed with whites. Although a majority of

*Reprinted from *Black Chicago: The Making of a Negro Ghetto, 1890–1920* by Allan H. Spear by permission of the University of Chicago Press, © 1967 by the University of Chicago. All rights reserved. Published 1967.

the city's Negroes worked as domestic and personal servants, a small business and professional class provided community leadership. St. Clair Drake and Horace Cayton described the Chicago Negro community of this period as

a small, compact, but rapidly growing community divided into three broad social groups. The "respectables"—church-going, poor or moderately prosperous, and often unrestrained in their worship—were looked down upon somewhat by the "refined" people, who, because of their education and breeding, could not sanction the less decorous behavior of their racial brothers. Both of these groups were censorious of the "riffraff," the "sinners"—unchurched and undisciplined.

During the postwar years, the formal pattern of segregation that had characterized race relations in antebellum Chicago broke down. By 1870, Negroes could vote. In 1874, the school system was desegregated. A decade later, after the federal civil rights bill was nullified by the United States Supreme Court, the Illinois legislature enacted a law prohibiting discrimination in public places. Despite these advances, however, the status of Negroes in Chicago remained ambiguous. They continued to face discrimination in housing, employment, and, even in the face of the civil rights law, public accommodations. But they were not confined to a ghetto. Most Negroes, although concentrated in certain sections of the city, lived in mixed neighborhoods. Negro businessmen and professional men frequently catered to a white market and enjoyed social, as well as economic, contacts with the white community. And although Negro churches and social clubs proliferated, there were still few separate civic institutions. Local Negro leaders were firmly committed to

the ideal of an integrated community in which hospitals, social agencies, and public accommodations would be open to all without discrimination.

From the beginning, the experience of Chicago's Negroes had been, in significant ways, separate from the mainstream of the city's history. No other ethnic group had been legally circumscribed; no white minority had been forced to fight for legal recognition of citizenship rights. In 1890, despite the improvement in the Negroes' status since 1865, many of their problems were still unique. In a chiefly industrial city, they worked principally in domestic and service trades, almost untouched by labor organization and industrial strife. The political and economic turmoil of the late nineteenth century seemed to have little effect on the city's Negroes. No Jane Addams or Graham Taylor sought to bring them within the reform coalition that was attempting to change the life of the city. Generally ignored by white Chicagoans, Negroes were viewed neither as a threat to the city's well-being nor as an integral part of the city's social structure. Most responsible whites probably held the view quoted by Ray Stannard Baker: "We have helped the Negro to liberty; we have helped to educate him to stand on his own feet. Now let's see what he can do for himself. After all, he must survive or perish by his own efforts."

Still, the story of Chicago's Negroes in the late nineteenth and early twentieth centuries is interwoven with the general history of the city. As their numbers increased between 1890 and 1910, Negroes became ever more conspicuous, and the indifference with which they had been regarded in the nineteenth century changed to hostility. Labor strife, ethnic tension, political corruption, and inefficiency—the problems of greatest concern to white Chicagoans—all helped determine the status of the city's Negroes. So too did the rise of racist doctrines that many old-stock Chicagoans applied indiscriminately to Negroes and the "new" immigrants. The virulently anti-Negro works of Thomas Dixon, the Chautauqua addresses of South Carolina's Senator Benjamin Tillman, as well as the anti-immigration propaganda of Prescott Hall, Henry Pratt Fairchild, and Madison Grant epitomized an age of race chauvinism in which Anglo-Americans strove to preserve a mythical racial purity.

The profound changes that took place in the Chicago Negro community between the 1890's and 1920 had both internal and external dimensions. On the one hand, they were the result of the mounting hostility of white Chicagoans. Whites grew anxious as a growing Negro population sought more and better housing; they feared job competition in an era of industrial strife when employers frequently used Negroes as strikebreakers; and they viewed Negro voters as pawns of a corrupt political machine. All of these fears were accentuated by the rise of a racist ideology that reinforced traditional anti-Negro prejudices. On the other hand, Negroes were not passive objects in the developments of the early twentieth century. Their response to discrimination and segregation, the decisions their leaders made, and the community activities in which they engaged all helped to shape the emerging Negro ghetto. The rise of Chicago's black ghetto belongs to both urban history and Negro history; it was the result of the interplay between certain trends in the development of the city and major currents in Negro life and thought.

Between 1890 and 1915, the Negro population of Chicago grew from less than fifteen thousand to over fifty thousand. Although this growth was overshadowed by the massive influx of Negroes during and after World War I, this was nevertheless a significant increase. By the eve of World War I, although Negroes were still a minor element in the city's population, they were far more conspicuous than they had been a generation earlier. The population increase was accompanied by the concentration of Negroes into ever more constricted sections of the city. In the late nineteenth century, while most Negroes lived in certain sections of the South Side, they lived interspersed among whites; there were few all-Negro blocks. By 1915, on the other hand, the physical ghetto had taken shape; a large, almost all-Negro enclave on the South Side, with a similar offshoot on the West Side, housed most of Chicago's Negroes.

The increasing physical separation of Chicago's Negroes was but one reflection of a growing pattern of segregation and discrimination in early twentieth-century Chicago. As the Negro community grew and opportunities for interracial conflict increased, so a pattern of discrimination and segregation became ever more pervasive. And perhaps the most critical aspect of interracial conflict came as the result of Negro attempts to secure adequate housing.

The South Side black belt could expand in only two directions in the early twentieth century—south and east. To the north lay the business district, which was moving south; in fact, commercial and light industrial concerns were pushing Negroes out of the area between Twelfth and Twenty-second Streets. West of Wentworth Avenue was a district of low-income immigrant homes, interspersed with railroad yards and light industry; the lack of adequate housing made this area undesirable for Negro expansion. East of State Street, on the other hand, was a neighborhood suitable for Negro residential requirements. This area, bounded by Twelfth and Thirty-ninth Street, State Street and Lake Michigan, had, in the 1880's and early 1890's, included the most fashionable streets in the city—Prairie and Calumet Avenues. But by 1900, the wealthy residents were moving to the North Side, leaving behind them comfortable, if aging, homes. South of Thirty-ninth Street was an even more desirable residential area—Kenwood and Hyde Park—and across Washington Park from the southern extremity of the black belt were the new and attractive communities of Woodlawn and Englewood. In these areas, between 1900 and 1915, the lines were drawn in the struggle for housing that would subsequently lead to full-scale racial war. If no major battle was fought before 1915, there were at least several preliminary skirmishes that set the pattern for future, and more serious, confrontations.

Negro expansion did not always mean conflict, nor did it mean that a neighborhood would shortly become exclusively black. In 1910, not more than a dozen blocks on the South Side were entirely Negro, and in many mixed areas Negroes and whites lived together harmoniously. But as Negroes became more numerous east of State and south of Fifty-first, friction increased and white hostility grew. When a Negro family moved into a previously all-white neighborhood, the neighbors frequently protested, tried to buy the property, and then, if unsuccessful, resorted to violence to drive out the interlopers. In many cases, the residents organized to urge real estate agents and property owners to sell and rent to whites only. The whites often succeeded in keeping Negroes out, at least temporarily. When their efforts failed, they gradually moved out, leaving the neighborhood predominantly, although rarely exclusively, Negro.

Such incidents occurred with only minor variations throughout the prewar period. In 1900, three Negro families brought about "a nervous prostration epidemic" on Vernon Avenue. Five years later, an attempt to oust Negroes from a Forrestville Avenue building landed in court. In 1911, a committee of Champlain Avenue residents dealt with a Negro family in the neighborhood by the "judicious use of a wagon load of bricks"; the *Record-Herald* described the affair as "something as nearly approaching the operations of the Ku Klux Klan as Chicago has seen in many years." Englewood residents, two years later, did not have to go quite so far; the objectionable party, this time a white man with a Negro wife, agreed to sell his property to a hastily organized "neighborhood improvement association." A Negro who moved into a home on Forrestville Avenue in 1915, on the other hand, termed an offer of this type "blackmail," but after several days of intimidation, he too submitted and sold his property.

Perhaps the most serious incident, and the one which provides the most insight into the nature of the housing conflict, occurred in Hyde Park—Chicago's most persistent racial trouble spot—in 1909. A separate town until 1892, Hyde Park was still an area of pleasant, tree-shaded streets, large, comfortable homes, and a vigorous cultural life centered on the campus of the new but thriving University of Chicago. Negroes were no strangers to the community: for many years a few families, mostly house servants and hotel employees who worked in the neighborhood, had clustered on Lake Avenue near Fifty-fifth Street, on the eastern edge of Hyde Park. Now this community began to expand and Negroes occupied homes in nearby white blocks.

White Hyde Parkers responded to

the Negro "invasion" with a concerted drive to keep Negroes out of white areas. The Hyde Park Improvement Protective Club was organized in the autumn of 1908; headed by a prominent attorney, Francis Harper, it soon boasted 350 members, "including some of the wealthiest dwellers on the South Side." In the summer of 1909, the Club issued a manifesto: Negro residents of Hyde Park must confine themselves to the "so-called Districts," real estate agents must refuse to sell property in white blocks to Negroes, and landlords must hire only white janitors. To implement this policy, the Club appointed a committee to purchase property owned by Negroes in white blocks and to offer bonuses to Negro renters who would surrender their leases. Moreover, the Club threatened to blacklist any real estate firm that defied its edict. "The districts which are now white," said Harper, "must remain white. There will be no compromise."

Despite the efforts of the Negro residents of Hyde Park to counter the activities with indignation meetings and boycotts, the white campaign continued. The neighborhood newspaper supported the Improvement Club, and Harper maintained that he had "received hosts of letters commending the course of the organization." When the Club was unable to persuade a Negro family to move voluntarily, the neighbors used more direct tactics: vandals broke into a Negro home on Greenwood Avenue one night and broke all the windows; the family left the next day. In September, the Club announced a boycott of merchants who sold goods to Negroes living in white neighborhoods. It urged separate playgrounds and tennis courts for Negroes in Washington Park, and, in its annual report, advocated segregation of the public schools. "It is only a question of time," a Club spokesman predicted, "when there will be separate schools for Negroes throughout Illinois." The group operated more quietly after 1909, but it had achieved its major goal. The little Negro community on Lake Avenue dwindled in size and the rest of Hyde Park remained white for forty years.

The Hyde Park episode well illustrates the intensification of anti-Negro feeling in the early twentieth century. This feeling could even create strong sentiment among whites for a return to formalized segregation—separate schools and recreation facilities. Some white Chicagoans spoke of the necessity for a residential segregation ordinance. The incident also provided an early example of techniques that were to become increasingly important as whites continually tried to stem the tide of Negro residential "invasion": the neighborhood improvement association, the community newspaper, the boycott, and in the last resort, violence. Furthermore, the episode was significant because it occurred in a middle- and upper-class community, and its victims were middle- and upper-class Negroes attempting to find comfortable homes among people of their own economic status. The housing problem for Negroes was not restricted to the poor; even the affluent were blocked in their quest for a decent place to live.

The unwillingness of whites to tolerate Negroes as neighbors had far-reaching results. Because Negroes were so limited in their choice of housing, they were forced to pay higher rents in those buildings that were open to them. Real estate agents frequently converted buildings in marginal neighborhoods from white to Negro and demanded rents 10 to 15 per cent higher than they had previously received. Sophonisba Breckinridge of Hull House estimated that a Negro family "pays $12.50 for the same accommodations the Jew in the Ghetto received for $9 and the immigrant for $8." One realty company inserted two advertisements for the same apartment in a daily newspaper: one read, "seven rooms, $25"; the other, "seven rooms for colored people, $37.50." High rents often forced Negro families to take in lodgers. A 1912 survey of 1,775 South Side Negroes reported that 542, or 31 per cent, lived as lodgers in the homes of others.

Living conditions in much of the black belt closely resembled conditions in the West Side ghetto or in the Stockyards district. Although Negroes could find some decent homes on the fringes of the Negro section, the core of the black belt was a festering slum. Here was an area of one- and two-story frame houses (unlike the older Eastern cities Chicago had, as yet, few large tenements), usually dilapidated with boarded-up porches and rickety wooden walks. Most of the buildings contained two flats and, although less crowded than houses in the Jewish, Polish, and Bohemian slums, they were usually in worse repair. The 1912 survey revealed that in a four-block area in the black belt, only 26 per cent of the dwellings were in good repair —as compared to 71 per cent in a similar sampling in a Polish neighborhood, 57 per cent among Bohemians, and 54 per cent in the ethnically mixed Stockyards district. "Colored tenants," the survey reported, "found it impossible to persuade their landlords either to make the necessary repairs or to release them from their contracts; . . . it was so hard to find better places in which to live that they were forced to make the repairs themselves, which they could rarely afford to do, or to endure the conditions as best they might."

White real estate agents, insensitive to class differences among Negroes, made no attempt to uphold standards in middle-class Negro neighborhoods as they did in comparable white districts. They persistently rented flats in "respectable" Negro neighborhoods to members of the "sporting element," thus forcing middle-class Negroes to move continually in search of decent areas to live an rear families. As a result, neighborhood stability was at best temporary. The streets east of State, which had become the mecca of the Negro middle class in the late 1890's, began to decline by 1905. A few years later the district was characterized by "men and women half clothed hanging out of a window," "rag-time piano playing . . . far into the night," and "shooting and cutting scrapes."

Municipal policy regarding vice further complicated the situation. City authorities, holding that the suppression of prostitution was impossible, tried to confine it to certain well-defined areas where it could be closely watched. The police frequently moved the vice district so as to keep it away from commercial and white residential areas. Invariably they located it in or near the black belt, often in Negro residential neighborhoods. The chief of police declared that so long as prostitutes confined their activities to the district between Wentworth and Wabash, they would not be apprehended. Neighborhood stability, then, was threatened not only by the influx of Negro "shadies," but by the presence of an officially sanctioned vice district catering primarily to whites.

Periodic attempts to clean up the red-light district received little support from Negro leaders who believed that such campaigns would merely drive the undesirables deeper into Negro residential neighborhoods. When legal prostitution was finally abolished in 1912, these fears were fully realized; vice in Chicago continued to be centered in the black belt. Fannie Barrier

Williams, a prominent Negro civic leader, summed up the plight of the middle- and upper-class Negro: "The huddling together of the good and the bad, compelling the decent element of the colored people to witness the brazen display of vice of all kinds in front of their homes and in the faces of their children, are trying conditions under which to remain socially clean and respectable."

The pattern of Negro housing, then, was shaped by white hostility and indifference: limited in their choice of homes, Negroes were forced to pay higher rents for inferior dwellings and were frequently surrounded by prostitutes, panderers, and other undesirable elements. This, together with the poverty of the majority of Chicago Negroes, produced in the black belt the conditions of slum-living characteristic of American cities by the end of the nineteenth century.

The most striking feature of Negro housing, however, was not the existence of slum conditions, but the difficulty of escaping the slum. European immigrants needed only to prosper to be able to move to a more desirable neighborhood. Negroes, on the other hand, suffered from both economic deprivation and systematic racial discrimination. "The problem of the Chicago Negro," wrote Sophonisba Breckinridge,

is quite different from the white man and even that of the immigrants. With the Negro the housing dilemma was found to be an acute problem, not only among the poor, as in the case of the Polish, Jewish, or Italian immigrants, but also

among the well-to-do. . . . Thus, even in the North, where the city administration does not recognize a "Ghetto" or "pale", the real estate agents who register and commercialize what they suppose to be a universal race prejudice are able to enforce one in practice.

The development of a physical ghetto in Chicago, then, was not the result chiefly of poverty; nor did Negroes cluster out of choice. The ghetto was primarily the product of white hostility. Attempts on the part of Negroes to seek housing in predominantly white sections of the city met with resistance from the residents and from real estate dealers. Some Negroes, in fact, who had formerly lived in white neighborhoods, were pushed back into the black districts. As the Chicago Negro population grew, Negroes had no alternative but to settle in well-delineated Negro areas. And with increasing pressure for Negro housing, property owners in the black belt found it profitable to force out white tenants and convert previously mixed blocks into all-Negro blocks. The geographical dimensions of Black Chicago in the early twentieth century underwent no dramatic shift similar, for instance, to Negro New York, where the center of Negro life moved to previously all-white Harlem in less than a decade. Negroes in Chicago were not establishing new communities. But to meet the needs of a growing population, in the face of mounting white resistance, Negro neighborhoods were becoming more exclusively Negro as they slowly expanded their boundaries.

Bosses, Machines, and Ethnic Groups

Elmer E. Cornwell, Jr.*

Though the direction of the causal relationship may be difficult to establish, the classic urban machine and the century of immigration which ended in the 1920's were intimately intertwined phenomena. This fact is not always recognized as fully as it should be. Much of the literature on bosses and machines, beginning with the muckrakers, but not excluding more recent studies with less overt moralistic flavor, carries the implication that such factors as the dispersal of power in urban government—under weak mayor charters and through rivalries among state, county, city and special district authorities, all plowing the same field but none with full responsibility for its cultivation—invited the machine's extralegal reconcentration of power. It is also true that attitudes engendered by a business society whose prime movers characteristically had their eye on the "main chance"—and specifically on traction franchises and the like—also fostered the growth of the essentially entrepreneurial role and amoral attitude of the boss.

RELATION OF MACHINE TO IMMIGRATION

When all this has been said, however, the fact still remains that the classic machine would probably not have been possible, and certainly would not have been so prominent a feature of the American political land-

scape, without the immigrant. Essentially, any disciplined grass-roots political organization rests upon a docile mass base which has in some manner been rendered dependable, predictable, and manipulable. The rank and file of the Soviet Communist party is disciplined by a combination of ideological allegiance, fear, and hope of reward. The average party supporter in a liberal-democratic society cannot be so disciplined under ordinary circumstances, at least not for long. The newly arrived immigrant was a special case, however. He was characteristically insecure, culturally and often linguistically alien, confused, and often in actual want. Thus, even if he had valued the franchise thrust upon him by his new political mentors, its careful exercise would have taken a low priority in his daily struggle for existence. In most cases, he did not value or even understand the political role into which he was being pushed.

Thus, it was the succeeding waves of immigrants that gave the urban political organizations the manipulable mass bases without which they could not have functioned as they did. And, until immigration dried up to a trickle in the 1920's, as one generation of newcomers began to espouse traditional American values of political independence, there was always a new group, often from a different country of origin, to which the machine could turn. As long as this continued to be possible, machines persisted, and once the immigrant base finally began to disappear, so did most of the bosses of the classic model. In a very real sense, then, the one phenomenon was dependent on the other.

The argument can be made that

*Reprinted with permission from Lee S. Greene, ed., *City Bosses and Political Machines*, Vol. CCCLIII, *The Annals of the American Academy of Political and Social Science*, Philadelphia: The American Academy of Political and Social Science, 1964, 28–34.

there were other machines that clearly were not immigrant-based in this sense. All generalizations, especially those in the social sciences, are but proximate truths. At the same time, machines based on white, Protestant, "old stock" clienteles were not wholly unrelated in their motivation and operation to the factor of immigration. Platt's smooth-functioning organization in New York State[1] and Blind Boss Brayton's contemporary operation in Rhode Island[2] were both based, in the immediate sense, on what Lincoln Steffens called "the good old American stock out in the country."[3] And yet recall that both of these states were highly urbanized even in the 1890's and early 1900's when these two worthies flourished and had ingested disproportionate numbers of immigrants. As of 1920, when 38 per cent of the total United States population was foreign born or of foreign parentage, the corresponding percentages for New York and Rhode Island were 64 and 71.[4] These facts alone suggest what the political history of both makes clear: these rural "old stock" machines existed largely as means of political defense against the newcomers and doubtless would not have existed had there been no immigrants.

The point, then, is that, whereas in the cities the immigrants sold their political independence for the familiar currency of favors and aid, their rural native cousins were sometimes prompted to do the same, in part out of desire for cultural-religious as well as political, and perhaps at times economic, self-protection. Recollection of the Know-Nothing era of militant nativist activity a half-century earlier suggests that this kind of cultural-religious antagonism can be a very potent political force indeed. An analogous explanation could even be offered for the existence of machines in the South like that of Harry Byrd in Virginia, by simply substituting the perceived Negro threat for the danger of engulfment by foreigners in the North. And, curiously enough, the two examples of reasonably thoroughgoing machine-like organizations that flourished in the otherwise inhospitable English soil—Joseph Chamberlain's Birmingham caucus[5] and Archibald Salvidge's "machine" in Liverpool[6]—also were at least indirectly related to the problem of Irish home rule, and, in Liverpool, to actual rivalry with Irish immigrants over religion and jobs.

In short, whatever else may be said about the conditions and forces that spawned the classic machine, this kind of disciplined political entity must rest at bottom on a clientele which has felt it necessary to exchange political independence—its votes, in a word—for something seen as more essential to its well-being and security. In general, such a group will be the product of some kind of socioeconomic disequilibrium or cultural tension which finds its members in an insecure or seriously disadvantaged situation. Thus, the immigrant was willing to submit to the boss in exchange for aid—real or imagined—in gaining his foothold in the new environment, and the old-stock machine supporters, North or South, submitted in part for protection against swarming aliens or a potential Negro threat to white dominance.

[1] See Harold F. Gosnell, *Boss Platt and His New York Machine* (Chicago: University of Chicago Press, 1924).

[2] See Lincoln Steffens, "Rhode Island: A State for Sale," *McClure's Magazine*, Vol. 24 (February 1905), pp. 337–353.

[3] Lincoln Steffens, *Autobiography* (New York: Literary Guild, 1931), p. 367.

[4] E. P. Hutchinson, *Immigrants and their Children* (New York: John Wiley, 1956), p. 27.

[5] See J. L. Garvin, *The Life of Joseph Chamberlain* (3 vols.; London: Macmillan, 1932–34).

[6] Stanley Salvidge, *Salvidge of Liverpool* (London: Hodder and Stoughton, 1934).

THE CLASSIC MACHINE IN OPERATION

It cannot be assumed that the process of machine exploitation of succeeding groups of newcomers was a smooth and simple operation. Any formal organization, political or otherwise, must maintain a continuing balance among a series of often contradictory forces.[7] Its very existence rests on the success with which it achieves its objective—in the case of a political party, the winning of elections and, thus, power. In the long run, this success depends on the organization's continuing ability to tap fresh sources of support as time goes on and old reliances dwindle and may at times depend on keeping newly available resources away from its rival or rivals. For the machine, this has meant wooing each new ethnic contingent. Yet this process of growth and renewal will inevitably threaten the very position of many of the proprietors of the organization itself by recruiting rivals for their roles. Any organizational entity must not only achieve its corporate goals but, to survive, it must also satisfy the needs and desires of its members as individuals. If it fails in this, its supporters will vanish and its own objectives remain unattainable. Specifically, for the machine, this fact of organizational life often tempered missionary zeal and tempted its members to protect even an eroding *status quo*.

Usually the machine did yield in the long run to the political imperative that all groups of potential supporters must be wooed, if for no other reason than to keep them from the enemy. The short-term risk to the present leadership often must have

appeared minimal. The plight of the newcomers was so pitiful, their needs so elemental, and their prospects of achieving security and independence so problematical in the foreseeable future that they must have appeared like a windfall to the machine proprietors. Thus, after initial hesitancy, the Irish were taken into Tammany and found their way into the ranks of the clientele of other big city party organizations.

The ways in which immigrant political support was purchased are familiar and need no elaborate review here. They had at least three kinds of needs which the ward heeler could fill on behalf of the party leadership. Above all, they needed the means of physical existence: jobs, loans, rent money, contributions of food or fuel to tide them over, and the like. Secondly, they needed a buffer against an unfamiliar state and its legal minions: help when they or their offspring got in trouble with the police, help in dealing with inspectors, in seeking pushcart licenses, or in other relations with the public bureaucracy. Finally, they needed the intangibles of friendship, sympathy, and social intercourse. These were available, variously, through contact with the precinct captain, the hospitality of the political clubhouse, the attendance of the neighborhood boss at wakes and weddings, and the annual ward outing.[8]

As has often been noted, these kinds of services were not available, as they are today, at the hands of "United Fund" agencies, city welfare departments with their platoons of social workers, or through federal social security legislation. The sporadic and quite inadequate aid rendered by the boss and his lieutenants thus filled a

---

[7] For an elaboration of this approach to the internal dynamics of the machine, see James Q. Wilson, "The Economy of Patronage," *Journal of Political Economy*, Vol. 69, pp. 369–380.

[8] One of the most readable depictions of these machine functions is to be found in Edwin O'Connor's novel *The Last Hurrah* (Boston: Little, Brown, 1956).

vacuum. Their only rivals were the self-help associations which did spring up within each ethnic group as soon as available resources allowed a meager surplus to support burial societies and the like. The fact that the politicians acted from self-serving motives in distributing their largess, expecting and received a *quid pro quo,* is obvious but not wholly relevant. At least it was not relevant in judging the social importance of the services rendered. It was highly relevant, of course, in terms of the political power base thus acquired.

Some of the later arrivals following the pioneering Irish were in at least as great need of aid. The Irish did speak English and had had some experience with political action and representative institutions at home. This, plus the fact that they got here first, doubtless accounts for their rapid rise in their chosen party, the Democracy. The groups that followed, however, usually did not know English and bore the additional burden of a cultural heritage that had less in common with the American patterns they encountered than had been the case with the Irish. And, too, almost all groups, the Sons of Erin included, differed religiously from the basic Protestant consensus of their Anglo-Saxon predecessors.

As group followed group—not only into the country but into the rickety tenements and "river wards" reserved, as it were, for the latest arrivals—the processes of absorption became more complex. The Irish ward politicians doubtless had, if anything, more difficult bridging the cultural and language gap to meet the newcomers than the "Yankees" had had in dealing with themselves some decades earlier. Also, while it may well be that the Yankees gave up their party committee posts fairly willingly to the Irish, because politics was not essential to their well-being either economically or psycho-

logically, the Irish were in a rather different position when their turn came to move over and make room.[9] They had not fully outgrown their dependence on politics for financial and psychic security. Thus, the conflicting demands of the machine for new sources of support versus the reluctance of the incumbents to encourage rivalry for their own positions, produced tension. In the long run, however, most of the new ethnic groups found their place in the party system. In some cases, as with the Italians, the Republicans, generally less skillful in these arts, won support by default when the Irish were especially inhospitable.

THE MACHINE AS SOCIAL INTEGRATOR

There is another side to the coin of machine dependence on the continuing flow of immigrants. The "invisible hand"—to use an analogy with Adam Smith's economics—which operated to produce social benefits out of the *quid pro quo* which the ward heelers exchanged for votes was at work in other ways, too. Henry Jones Ford noted in the 1890's, while discussing the role of party:[10]

This nationalizing influence continues to produce results of the greatest social value, for in co-ordinating the various elements of the population for political purposes, party organization at the same time tends to fuse them into one mass of citizenship, pervaded by a common order of ideas and sentiments, and actuated by the same class of motives. This is prob-

[9] See the author's "Some Occupational Patterns in Party Committee Membership," *Rhode Island History,* Vol. 20 (July 1961), pp. 87–96.
[10] *The Rise and Growth of American Politics* (New York: Macmillan, 1911), p. 306.

ably the secret of the powerful solvent influence which American civilization exerts upon the enormous deposits of alien population thrown upon this country by the torrent of emigration.

Again, in other words, the selfish quest by the politician for electoral support and power was transmuted by the "invisible hand" into the major force integrating the immigrant into the community.

This process has had several facets. In the first place, the mere seeking out of the immigrants in quest of their support, the assistance rendered in getting them naturalized (when it was necessary to observe these legal niceties), and so forth were of considerable importance in laying the foundation for their more meaningful political participation later. In addition, the parties have progressively drawn into their own hierarchies and committee offices representatives of the various ethnic groups. The mechanics of this process were varied. In some cases, there doubtless emerged leaders of a particular group in one ward or neighborhood who, if given official party status, would automatically bring their followings along with them.[11] On other occasions, new ethnic enclaves may have sought or even demanded representation in exchange for support. Perhaps prior to either of these, the machine sought to co-opt individuals who could speak the language and act as a cultural bridge between the party and the newcomers. Depending on the situation, it probably was essential to do this and impossible for precinct captains of a different background to develop adequate rapport. It is at this point that ethnic group rivalry in the organization becomes difficult. Gratitude to the boss for ini-

tial admission into the lower ranks of the hierarchy would be bound to change in time into demands, of growing insistence, for further recognition of the individual and his group.

These general patterns can to some extent be documented, at least illustratively. The tendency for the urban machines to reap the Irish vote and later much of the vote of more recent arrivals is well known. The process of infiltration by group representatives into party structure is harder to identify precisely. With this in mind, the author did a study of the members of party ward committees in Providence, Rhode Island, the findings of which may reflect trends elsewhere.[12] Analysis of committee membership lists or their equivalent going back to the 1860's and 1870's showed initial overwhelming Anglo-Saxon majorities. For the Democrats, however, this majority gave way, between the 1880's and 1900, to a roughly 75 per cent Irish preponderance, while the Republican committees stayed "Yankee" until after the First World War. Then, in the 1920's, both parties simultaneously recruited Italian committeemen to replace some of the Irish and white Protestants, respectively. Today, both have varied, and roughly similar, proportions of all major groups in the city population. In other cities, the timing of shifts and the ethnic groups involved will have differed, but the general process and its relation to local patterns of immigration were doubtless similar.

It is incredible, viewed now with hindsight, how reckless the American republic was in its unpremeditated policy of the open door and the implied assumption that somehow, without any governmental or even organized private assistance, hundreds of

---

[11] *Ibid.*, p. 307.

[12] "Party Absorption of Ethnic Groups," *Social Forces*, Vol. 38 (March 1960), pp. 205–210.

thousands of immigrants from dozens of diverse cultures would fit themselves smoothly and automatically into a native culture which had its own share of ethnocentrism. The fact of the matter was that the process did not operate smoothly or particularly effectively. There were tensions and incidents which accentuated cultural differences and engendered bitterness. These ranged, chronologically, all the way from the abuses of the more militant Know-Nothings to the Ku Klux Klan activity of the 1920's.

Economically, most occupational doors that did not lead to manual labor jobs were closed to the Irish and later arrivals and were only gradually pried open after much time had passed and many lasting intergroup enmities had been engendered. Here again, the party organizations represented one of the few mechanisms, public or private, that lubricated a process of integration which, in its very nature, was bound to generate enormous amounts of friction. Besides drawing group representatives into its councils, party work also was one of the few career ladders available to the immigrant and his ambitious sons. Here, status could be achieved, as well as a comfortable income, one way or another, when few other routes were open. This became not just status for the individual but a measure of recognition and acceptance for the group as a whole through the individual's success. In fact, not only did the newcomer use this alternative career ladder, but he carried over into the political sphere some of the "Horatio Alger" quest for success and other aspects of an essentially pragmatic, materialistic American culture as well.

Politics for the machine politician never was an ideological enterprise or a matter of beliefs and principles. As someone once said, the boss had only seven principles, five loaves and two

fishes. Rather, politics was an entrepreneurial vocation like any other business. Banfield and Wilson have written: "A political machine is a business organization in a particular field of business—getting votes and winning elections. As a Chicago machine boss once said . . . it is 'just like any sales organization trying to sell its product.' "[13] The politician's aim was and is so to invest his supply of capital—jobs, favors, and the like— as to earn a profit, some of which he will take as "income" and the rest reinvest in quest of larger returns. In other words, the immigrant political leader took the one vocation open to him, politics, and made it into as close an approximation as he could of the more valued business callings in the society, from which he was effectively barred. He acted out the American success story in the only way open to him.

Obviously, the foregoing is not designed to portray the machine as a knight-errant rescuing American society from its willful folly. In the first place, the folly was not willful, and perhaps not folly. In the second, the boss's contribution toward making the melting pot melt should not be overrated. At the same time, many have testified—as does the record itself— to the almost unique ability of party as organization to bring people together across cultural and similar barriers. As Glazer and Moynihan have written of New York City:[14]

. . . political life itself emphasizes the ethnic character of the city, with its balanced tickets and its special appeals. . . . For those in

[13] Edward Banfield and James Q. Wilson, *City Politics* (Cambridge: Harvard and M.I.T. Presses, 1963), p. 115.
[14] Nathan Glazer and Daniel Patrick Moynihan, *Beyond the Melting Pot* (Cambridge: Harvard and M.I.T Presses, 1963), p. 20.

the field itself, there is more contact across the ethnic lines, and the ethnic lines themselves mean less, than in other areas of the city's life.

Ticket-balancing, or United Nations politics, as it is sometimes called, is perhaps symbolic of the ultimate step in the process of granting group recognition and confirming the fact that something approaching intergroup equality has been achieved. Either, as with the Manhattan Borough presidency and the Negro group, certain prescriptive rights become established to a particular office or to one place on a city-wide ticket or ethnic allocation is made using the background of the head of the ticket as point of departure.

In short, the classic urban machine rested upon the immigrants, while at the same time it fostered their integration into American life. It also made, in the process, a major contribution to the over-all American political style. It is true that politics as a pragmatic entrepreneurial vocation owes much in America to the contributions of Burr, Van Buren, Weed, Marcy (to the victor belong the spoils), and, in a sense, to Andrew Jackson himself. Thus, Richard Hofstadter's attribution of one of the two central systems of political ethics in America to the immigrants is only partially valid.[15] He is clearly correct, however, in suggesting that a political style which stressed "personal obligations, and placed strong personal loyalties above allegiance to abstract codes of law or morals"[16] was congenial to the machine politicians and their followers, and they made it their own, developing its full implications in the process. At the same time, the immigrant versus old stock cultural cleavage prompted the latter to espouse the more vigorously the typically middle-class, reformist style which stresses honesty, impartiality, and efficiency. These two styles or ethics, since the late nineteenth century, have, by their interaction, shaped both the evolution of urban politics and the machinery of urban government.

[15] Richard Hofstadter, *The Age of Reform* (New York: Knopf, 1955), pp. 8 ff.
[16] *Ibid.*, p. 9.

6 The Rising Concern

Excepting those directly affected, most people in the 1870's and 1880's were unaware of the deplorable conditions of urban life. Some malignancies, such as epidemics and civil disorder, forcibly thrust themselves into the public eye, and for the preservation of general health and property, the community quickly responded. However, most of the problems specifically relating to the quality of urban life were neglected. Only gradually did public awareness grow. Congress and state commissions conducted investigations about the slums, and writers like the novelist, Theodore Dreiser, and the journalist, Jacob Riis, vividly portrayed urban conditions. These exposures contributed greatly toward awakening Americans to the wretchedness around them.

Awareness, however, as we saw in the discussion of the growth and development of urban services in Section 3, was not enough to produce action. The community had to possess an adequate technology. By the late nineteenth century this requirement no longer presented insurmountable difficulties, because industrialism had developed new materials, machines, and techniques for rebuilding the city. The new difficulty was to obtain the necessary

for Urban Life

financial support. Rapid expansion, the expense of constantly improving technology, and the drain on the treasuries through political corruption meant that many cities were financially incapable of responding to everything necessary. Consequently, the areas directly affecting commerce and industry, such as extension of streets and the erection of public buildings, received priority. Little money was left for education, recreation, or ameliorating the social and physical condition of the urban poor.

Even more of a stumbling block was the reluctance of the community to accept either private or public responsibility for these urban needs. The late nineteenth century was an age influenced by Social Darwinist thinking, which held that one's social and economic condition was one's individual responsibility and that any substantial public action would encourage pauperism. Early minimal efforts to deal with urban problems had come from private sources. Charities established institutions which cared for the destitute or provided specific functions, such as medical care or educational and vocational opportunities. Some of these charities were formed along ethnic or religious lines. The concept of giving direct aid to the poor for their general needs was rejected by traditional charitable organizations, which believed that such programs would demoralize the respectable poor.

Churches, concerned more with the spiritual than the secular world supported the Social Darwinist position. Then in the 1880's, through the Social Gospel Movement, they became interested in the physical welfare of man and began to play a more positive role. Religious leaders were far from unanimous in their willingness to make a full social commitment, but several prominent leaders played a part in enlightening their contemporaries to the social conditions in cities and to the need for the church to help alleviate them. From this interest emerged the "institutional church," which established lodging houses, and educational, recreational, and other facilities.

All of these efforts had limited outright success. Probably their greatest influence was in providing information about urban poverty and stimulating greater public concern. The efforts of the church and of private and voluntary associations were supplemented by the flood of governmental reports, books, and articles which gradually shifted the public's attitude from viewing poverty as the result of personal shortcomings and vice to seeing it as an outgrowth of an unfavorable environment. Only with the acceptance of the idea that a healthy environment is a socially desirable goal could broader private and public action be expected. The isolated and alienated immigrant and rural migrant posed specific problems, which were germane to the establishment, late in the century, of the Settlement House Movement. This movement's efforts were broad in scope in that, rather than focusing on one issue, it sought to deal with the social, cultural, economic, and political problems of its constituency. Gradually public programs evolved in health care, child welfare, housing, adult education, recreation, municipal welfare, and in other areas. The reasons for this change in public attitude are complex and vary from group to group. Both the dissemination of information about urban conditions and the change in philosophical attitude were necessary. Some people were moved for humanitarian reasons, and others, concerned less with the *conditions* that led to social disruption, acted for purely prudential reasons. Both advocacy of and opposition to the tide of reform that was beginning to sweep the country were found at all levels of society.

Attempts to deal with urban problems were frequently thwarted by the inefficiencies and corruption of urban government. Turning to state governments for special commissions to handle such problems as water, sewage, or police protection was not the solution, since it led to the diffusion of authority, financial chaos, and the breakdown of civic morale. Reformers finally were provoked into trying to clean up municipal government. Integrity in government, in an age of efficiency, was an end in itself, but administrative and electoral reform were also advocated, since many reformers became convinced that the solutions to urban problems required a city government rendered more effective by the participation of a wide spectrum of the electorate. Urban reform in the Progressive Era involved the gradual growth of civic pride in a well-run and productive city government.

The selections that follow discuss the rising concern for urban life among a variety of groups and classes. Some of the questions that are raised are: Who were the reformers? What were their backgrounds and interests? Were they motivated by practical concerns or by ideology? Not all the views held by historians are presented, but enough is said to provide an understanding of the implications of the questions and a few of the arguments. The readings also are concerned with the substance of urban programs and to what extent they were successful. The various planning efforts during the progressive period were particularly important, since several of them institutionalized the desire to bring about rational control of the urban environment. Several of the groups interested in planning urban growth are discussed. One of the older institutions, the Protestant church, is seen as it was affected by urbanization and as it awoke to the realities of the city.

Urban reform during the Progressive Era reflected a growing community consciousness, but the efforts to deal with the problems were inadequate. Long range goals and consensus as to the best approaches in planning were conspicuously absent. As growth continued and expectations rose, so did the urban complexities and the rising demand for public action. A new form, the metropolis, the subject of the following section, presented a challenge for which the twentieth century was not yet prepared.

Reform in Municipal Government

Samuel P. Hays*

In order to achieve a more complete understanding of social change in the Progressive Era, historians must now undertake a deeper analysis of the practices of economic, political, and social groups. Political ideology alone is no longer satisfactory evidence to describe social patterns because generalizations based upon it, which tend to divide political groups into the moral and the immoral, the rational and the irrational, the efficient and the inefficient, do not square with political practice. Behind this contemporary rhetoric concerning the nature of reform lay patterns of political behavior which were at variance with it. Since an extensive gap separated ideology and practice, we can no longer take the former as an accurate description of the latter, but must reconstruct social behavior from other types of evidence.

Reform in urban government provides one of the most striking examples of this problem of analysis. The demand for change in municipal affairs, whether in terms of over-all reform, such as the commission and city-manager plans, or of more piecemeal modifications, such as the development of city-wide school boards, deeply involved reform ideology. Reformers loudly proclaimed a new structure of municipal government as more moral, more rational, and more efficient and, because it was so, self-evidently more desirable. But precisely because of this emphasis, there seemed to be no need to analyze the political

forces behind change. Because the goals of reform were good, its causes were obvious; rather than being the product of particular people and particular ideas in particular situations, they were deeply imbedded in the universal impulses and truths of "progress." Consequently, historians have rarely tried to determine precisely who the municipal reformers were or what they did, but instead have relied on reform ideology as an accurate description of reform practice.

The reform ideology which became the basis of historical analysis is well known. It appears in classic form in Lincoln Steffens' *Shame of the Cities*. The urban political struggle of the Progressive Era, so the argument goes, involved a conflict between public impulses for "good government" against a corrupt alliance of "machine politicians" and "special interests."

During the rapid urbanization of the late 19th century, the latter had been free to aggrandize themselves, especially through franchise grants, at the expense of the public. Their power lay primarily in their ability to manipulate the political process, by bribery and corruption, for their own ends. Against such arrangements there gradually arose a public protest, a demand by the public for honest government, for officials who would act for the public rather than for themselves. To accomplish their goals, reformers sought basic modifications in the political system, both in the structure of government and in the manner of selecting public officials. These changes, successful in city after city, enabled the "public interest" to triumph.[1]

*Reprinted with permission from Samuel P. Hays, "The Politics of Reform in Municipal Government in the Progressive Era," *Pacific Northwest Quarterly*, LV (October, 1964), 157–169.

[1] See, for example, Clifford W. Patton, *Battle for Municipal Reform* (Washington,

Recently, George Mowry, Alfred Chandler, Jr., and Richard Hofstadter have modified this analysis by emphasizing the fact that the impulse for reform did not come from the working class.[2] This might have been suspected from the rather strained efforts of National Municipal League writers in the "Era of Reform" to go out of their way to demonstrate working-class support for commission and city-manager governments.[3] We now know that they clutched at straws, and often erroneously, in order to prove to themselves as well as to the public that municipal reform was a mass movement.

The Mowry-Chandler-Hofstadter writings have further modified older views by asserting that reform in general and municipal reform in particular sprang from a distinctively middle-class movement. This has now become the prevailing view. Its popularity is surprising not only because it is based upon faulty logic and extremely limited evidence, but also because it, too, emphasizes the analysis of ideology rather than practice and fails to contribute much to the understanding of who distinctively were involved in reform and why.

Ostensibly, the "middle-class" theory of reform is based upon a new type of behavioral evidence, the collective biography, in studies by Mowry of California Progressive party leaders,

by Chandler of a nationwide group of that party's leading figures, and by Hofstadter of four professions—ministers, lawyers, teachers, editors. These studies demonstrate the middle-class nature of reform, but they fail to determine if reformers were distinctively middle class, specifically if they differed from their opponents. One study of 300 political leaders in the state of Iowa, for example, discovered that Progressive party, Old Guard, and Cummins Republicans were all substantially alike, the Progressives differing only in that they were slightly younger than the others and had less political experience.[4] If its opponents were also middle class, then one cannot describe Progressive reform as a phenomenon, the special nature of which can be explained in terms of middle-class characteristics. One cannot explain the distinctive behavior of people in terms of characteristics which are not distinctive to them.

Hofstadter's evidence concerning professional men fails in yet another way to determine the peculiar characteristics of reformers. For he describes ministers, lawyers, teachers, and editors without determining who within these professions became reformers and who did not. Two analytical distinctions might be made. Ministers involved in municipal reform, it appears, came not from all segments of religion, but peculiarly from upper-class churches. They enjoyed the highest prestige and salaries in the religious community and had no reason to feel a loss of "status," as Hofstadter argues. Their role in reform arose from the class character of their religious organizations rather than from the mere

D.C., 1940), and Frank Mann Stewart, *A Half-Century of Municipal Reform* (Berkeley, 1950).

[2] George E. Mowry, *The California Progressives* (Berkeley and Los Angeles, 1951), 86–104; Richard Hofstadter, *The Age of Reform* (New York, 1955), 131–269; Alfred D. Chandler, Jr., "The Origins of Progressive Leadership," in Elting Morrison *et al.*, ed., *Letters of Theodore Roosevelt* (Cambridge, 1951–54), VIII, Appendix III, 1462–64.

[3] Harry A. Toulmin, *The City Manager* (New York, 1915), 156–68; Clinton R. Woodruff, *City Government by Commission* (New York, 1911), 243–53.

[4] Eli Daniel Potts, "A Comparative Study of the Leadership of Republican Factions in Iowa, 1904–1914," M.A. thesis (State University of Iowa, 1956). Another satisfactory comparative analysis is contained in William T. Kerr, Jr., "The Progressives of Washington, 1910–12," *PNQ*, Vol. 55 (1964), 16–27.

fact of their occupation as ministers.[5] Professional men involved in reform (many of whom—engineers, architects, and doctors—Hofstadter did not examine at all) seem to have come especially from the more advanced segments of their professions, from those who sought to apply their specialized knowledge to a wider range of public affairs.[6] Their role in reform is related not to their attempt to defend earlier patterns of culture, but to the working out of the inner dynamics of professionalization in modern society.

The weakness of the "middle-class" theory of reform stems from the fact that it rests primarily upon ideological evidence, not on a thorough-going description of political practice. Although the studies of Mowry, Chandler, and Hofstadter ostensibly derive from behavioral evidence, they actually derive largely from the extensive expressions of middle-ground ideological position, of the reformers' own descriptions of their contemporary society, and of their expressed fears of both the lower and the upper classes, of the fright of being ground between the millstones of labor and capital.[7]

Such evidence, though it accurately portrays what people thought, does not accurately describe what they did. The great majority of Americans look upon themselves as "middle class" and subscribe to a middle-ground ideology, even though in practice they belong to a great variety of distinct social classes. Such ideologies are not rationalizations or deliberate attempts to deceive. They

are natural phenomena of human behavior. But the historian should be especially sensitive to their role so that he will not take evidence of political ideology as an accurate representation of political practice.

In the following account I will summarize evidence in both secondary and primary works concerning the political practices in which municipal reformers were involved. Such an analysis logically can be broken down into three parts, each one corresponding to a step in the traditional argument. First, what was the source of reform? Did it lie in the general public rather than in particular groups? Was it middle class, working class, or perhaps of other composition? Second, what was the reform target of attack? Were reformers primarily interested in ousting the corrupt individual, the political or business leader who made private arrangements at the expense of the public, or were they interested in something else? Third, what political innovations did reformers bring about? Did they seek to expand popular participation in the governmental process?

There is now sufficient evidence to determine the validity of these specific elements of the more general argument. Some of it has been available for several decades; some has appeared more recently; some is presented here for the first time. All of it adds up to the conclusion that reform in municipal government involved a political development far different from what we have assumed in the past.

---

[5] Based upon a study of eleven ministers involved in municipal reform in Pittsburgh, who represented exclusively the upper-class Presbyterian and Episcopal churches.

[6] Based upon a study of professional men involved in municipal reform in Pittsburgh, comprising eighty-three doctors, twelve architects, twenty-five educators, and thirteen engineers.

[7] See especially Mowry, *The California Progressives*.

Available evidence indicates that the source of support for reform in municipal government did not come from the lower or middle classes, but from the upper class. The leading business groups in each city and professional men closely allied with them initiated and dominated municipal movements. Leonard White, in his study of the city manager published in 1927, wrote:

> The opposition to bad government usually comes to a head in the local chamber of commerce. Business men finally acquire the conviction that the growth of their city is being seriously impaired by the failures of city officials to perform their duties efficiently. Looking about for a remedy, they are captivated by the resemblance of the city-manager plan to their corporate form of business organization.[8]

In the 1930's White directed a number of studies of the origin of city-manager government. The resulting reports invariably begin with such statements as, "the Chamber of Commerce spearheaded the movement," or commission government in this city was a "businessmen's government."[9] Of thirty-two cases of city-manager government in Oklahoma examined by Jewell C. Phillips, twenty-nine were initiated either by chambers of commerce or by community committees dominated by businessmen.[10] More recently James Weinstein has presented almost irrefutable evidence that the business community, represented largely by chambers of commerce, was

the overwhelming force behind both commission and city-manager movements.[11]

Dominant elements of the business community played a prominent role in another crucial aspect of municipal reform: the Municipal Research Bureau movement.[12] Especially in the larger cities, where they had less success in shaping the structure of government, reformers established centers to conduct research in municipal affairs as a springboard for influence.

The first such organization, the Bureau of Municipal Research of New York City, was founded in 1906; it was financed largely through the efforts of Andrew Carnegie and John D. Rockefeller. An investment banker provided the crucial support in Philadelphia, where a Bureau was founded in 1908. A group of wealthy Chicagoans in 1910 established the Bureau of Public Efficiency, a research agency. John H. Patterson of the National Cash Register Company, the leading figure in Dayton municipal reform, financed the Dayton Bureau, founded in 1912. And George Eastman was the driving force behind both the Bureau of Municipal Research and city-manager government in Rochester. In smaller cities data about city government was collected by interested individuals in a more informal way or by chambers of commerce, but in larger cities the task required special support, and prominent businessmen supplied it.

The character of municipal reform is demonstrated more precisely by a brief examination of the movements in Des Moines and Pittsburgh. The Des Moines Commercial Club inaugu-

---

[8] Leonard White, *The City Manager* (Chicago, 1927), ix–x.

[9] Harold A. Stone *et al.*, *City Manager Government in Nine Cities* (Chicago, 1940); Frederick C. Mosher *et al.*, *City Manager Government in Seven Cities* (Chicago, 1940); Harold A. Stone *et al.*, *City Manager Government in the United States* (Chicago, 1940). Cities covered by these studies include: Austin, Texas; Charlotte, North Carolina; Dallas, Texas; Dayton, Ohio; Fredericksburg, Virginia; Jackson, Michigan; Janesville, Wisconsin; Kingsport, Tennessee; Lynchburg, Virginia; Rochester, New York; San Diego, California.

[10] Jewell Cass Phillips, *Operation of the Council-Manager Plan of Government in Oklahoma Cities* (Philadelphia, 1935), 31–39.

[11] James Weinstein, "Organized Business and the City Commission and Manager Movements," *Journal of Southern History*, XXVIII (1962), 166–82.

[12] Norman N. Gill, *Municipal Research Bureaus* (Washington, 1944).

rated and carefully controlled the drive for the commission form of government.[13] In January, 1906, the Club held a so-called "mass meeting" of business and professional men to secure an enabling act from the state legislature. P. C. Kenyon, president of the Club, selected a Committee of 300, composed principally of business and professional men, to draw up a specific proposal. After the legislature approved their plan, the same committee managed the campaign which persuaded the electorate to accept the commission form of government by a narrow margin in June, 1907.

In this election the lower-income wards of the city opposed the change, the upper-income wards supported it strongly, and the middle-income wards were more evenly divided. In order to control the new government, the Committee of 300, now expanded to 530, sought to determine the nomination and election of the five new commissioners, and to this end they selected an avowedly businessman's slate. Their plans backfired when the voters swept into office a slate of anti-commission candidates who now controlled the new commission government.

Proponents of the commission form of government in Des Moines spoke frequently in the name of the "people." But their more explicit statements emphasized their intent that the new plan be a "business system" of government, run by businessmen. The slate of candidates for commissioner endorsed by advocates of the plan was known as the "businessman's ticket." J. W. Hill, president of the committees of 300 and 530, bluntly declared: "The professional politician must be ousted and in his place capable busi-

ness men chosen to conduct the affairs of the city." I. M. Earle, general counsel of the Bankers Life Association and a prominent figure in the movement, put the point more precisely: "When the plan was adopted it was the intention to get businessmen to run it."

Although reformers used the ideology of popular government, they in no sense meant that all segments of society should be involved equally in municipal decision-making. They meant that their concept of the city's welfare would be best achieved if the business community controlled city government. As one businessman told a labor audience, the businessman's slate represented labor "better than you do yourself."

The composition of the municipal reform movement in Pittsburgh demonstrates its upperclass and professional as well as its business sources.[14] Here the two principal reform organizations were the Civic Club and the Voters' League. The 745 members of these two organizations came primarily from the upper class. Sixty-five per cent appeared in upper-class directories which contained the names of only 2 per cent of the city's families. Furthermore, many who were not listed in these directories lived in upper-class areas. These reformers, it should be stressed, comprised not an old but a new upper class. Few came from earlier industrial and mercantile families. Most of them had risen to

---

[13] This account of the movement for commission government in Des Moines is derived from items in the Des Moines *Register* during the years from 1905 through 1908.

[14] Biographical data constitutes the main source of evidence for this study of Pittsburgh reform leaders. It was found in city directories, social registers, directories of corporate directors, biographical compilations, reports of boards of education, settlement houses, welfare organizations, and similar types of material. Especially valuable was the clipping file maintained at the Carnegie Library of Pittsburgh.

social position from wealth created after 1870 in the iron, steel, electrical equipment, and other industries, and they lived in the newer rather than the older fashionable areas.

Almost half (48 per cent) of the reformers were professional men: doctors, lawyers, ministers, directors of libraries and museums, engineers, architects, private and public school teachers, and college professors. Some of these belonged to the upper class as well, especially the lawyers, ministers, and private school teachers. But for the most part their interest in reform stemmed from the inherent dynamics of their professions rather than from their class connections. They came from the more advanced segments of their organizations, from those in the forefront of the acquisition and application of knowledge. They were not the older professional men, seeking to preserve the past against change; they were in the vanguard of professional life, actively seeking to apply expertise more widely to public affairs

Pittsburgh reformers included a large segment of businessmen; 52 per cent were bankers and corporation officials or their wives. Among them were the presidents of fourteen large banks and officials of Westinghouse, Pittsburgh Plate Glass, U.S. Steel and its component parts (such as Carnegie Steel, American Bridge, and National Tube), Jones and Laughlin, lesser steel companies (such as Crucible, Pittsburgh, Superior, Lockhart, and H. K. Porter), the H. J. Heinz Company, and the Pittsburgh Coal Company, as well as officials of the Pennsylvania Railroad and the Pittsburgh and Lake Erie. These men were not small businessmen; they directed the most powerful banking and industrial organizations of the city. They represented not the old business community, but industries which had developed and grown primarily within the past fifty years and which had come to dominate the city's economic life.

These business, professional, and upper-class groups who dominated municipal reform movements were all involved in the rationalization and systematization of modern life; they wished a form of government which would be more consistent with the objectives inherent in those developments. The most important single feature of their perspective was the rapid expansion of the geographical scope of affairs which they wished to influence and manipulate, a scope which was no longer limited and narrow, no longer within the confines of pedestrian communities, but was now broad and city-wide, covering the whole range of activities of the metropolitan area.

The migration of the upper class from central to outlying areas created a geographical distance between its residential communities and its economic institutions. To protect the latter required involvement both in local ward affairs and in the larger city government as well. Moreover, upper-class cultural institutions, such as museums, libraries, and symphony orchestras, required an active interest in the larger municipal context from which these institutions drew much of their clientele.

Professional groups, broadening the scope of affairs which they sought to study, measure, or manipulate, also sought to influence the public health, the educational system, or the physical arrangements of the entire city. Their concerns were limitless, not bounded by geography, but as expansive as the professional imagination. Finally, the new industrial community greatly broadened its perspective in governmental affairs because of its new recognition of the way in which factors throughout the city affected business growth. The increasing size and scope of industry, the greater stake in more varied and geographically dispersed facets of city life, the effect of floods on many business concerns, the need to promote traffic flows to and from work for both blue-collar and managerial employees—all contributed to this larger interest. The geographically larger private perspectives of upper-class, professional, and business groups gave rise to a geographically larger public perspective.

These reformers were dissatisfied with existing systems of municipal government. They did not oppose corruption per se—although there was plenty of that. They objected to the structure of government which enabled local and particularistic interests to dominate. Prior to the reforms of the Progressive Era, city government consisted primarily of confederations of local wards, each of which was represented on the city's legislative body. Each ward frequently had its own elementary schools and ward-elected school boards which administered them.

These particularistic interests were the focus of a decentralized political life. City councilmen were local leaders. They spoke for their local areas, the economic interests of their inhabitants, their residential concerns, their educational, recreational, and religious interests—i.e., for those aspects of community life which mattered most to those they represented. They rolled logs in the city council to provide streets, sewers, and other public works for their local areas. They defended the community's cultural practices, its distinctive languages or national customs, its liberal attitude towards liquor, and its saloons and dance halls which served as centers of community life. One observer de-

scribed this process of representation in Seattle:

> The residents of the hill-tops and the suburbs may not fully appreciate the faithfulness of certain downtown ward councilmen to the interests of their constituents. . . . The people of a state would rise in arms against a senator or representative in Congress who deliberately misrepresented their wishes and imperilled their interests, though he might plead a higher regard for national good. Yet people in other parts of the city seem to forget that under the old system the ward elected councilmen with the idea of procuring service of special benefit to that ward.[15]

In short, pre-reform officials spoke for their constituencies, inevitably their own wards which had elected them, rather than for other sections or groups of the city.

The ward system of government especially gave representation in city affairs to lower- and middle-class groups. Most elected ward officials were from these groups, and they, in turn, constituted the major opposition to reforms in municipal government. In Pittsburgh, for example, immediately prior to the changes in both the city council and the school board in 1911 in which city-wide representation replaced ward representation, only 24 per cent of the 387 members of those bodies represented the same managerial, professional, and banker occupations which dominated the membership of the Civic Club and the Voters' League. The great majority (67 per cent) were small businessmen—grocers, saloonkeepers, livery-stable proprietors, owners of small hotels, druggists—white-collar workers such as

---

[15] *Town Crier* (Seattle), Feb. 18, 1911, p. 13.

clerks and bookkeepers, and skilled and unskilled workmen.[16]

This decentralized system of urban growth and the institutions which arose from it reformers now opposed. Social, professional, and economic life had developed not only in the local wards in a small community context, but also on a larger scale had become highly integrated and organized, giving rise to a superstructure of social organization which lay far above that of ward life and which was sharply divorced from it in both personal contacts and perspective.

By the late 19th century, those involved in these larger institutions found that the decentralized system of political life limited their larger objectives. The movement for reform in municipal government, therefore, constituted an attempt by upper-class, advanced professional, and large business groups to take formal political power from the previously dominant lower- and middle-class elements so that they might advance their own conceptions of desirable public policy. These two groups came from entirely different urban worlds, and the political system fashioned by one was no longer acceptable to the other.

Lower- and middle-class groups not only dominated the pre-reform governments, but vigorously opposed reform. It is significant that none of the occupational groups among them, for example, small businessmen or white-collar workers, skilled or unskilled artisans, had important representation in reform organizations thus far examined. The case studies of city-manager government undertaken in the 1930's under the direction of Leonard White detailed in city after city the

particular opposition of labor. In their analysis of Jackson, Michigan, the authors of these studies wrote:

> The *Square Deal*, oldest Labor paper in the state, has been consistently against manager government, perhaps largely because labor has felt that with a decentralized government elected on a ward basis it was more likely to have some voice and to receive its share of privileges.[17]

In Janesville, Wisconsin, the small shopkeepers and workingmen on the west and south sides, heavily Catholic and often Irish, opposed the commission plan in 1911 and in 1912 and the city-manager plan when adopted in 1923.[18] "In Dallas there is hardly a trace of class consciousness in the Marxian sense," one investigator declared, "yet in city elections the division has been to a great extent along class lines."[19] The commission and city-manager elections were no exceptions. To these authors it seemed a logical reaction, rather than an embarrassing fact that had to be swept away, that workingmen should have opposed municipal reform.[20]

In Des Moines working-class representatives, who in previous years might have been council members, were conspicuously absent from the "businessman's slate." Workingmen acceptable to reformers could not be found. A workingman's slate of candidates, therefore, appeared to challenge the reform slate. Organized labor, and especially the mineworkers, took the lead; one of their number, Wesley Ash, a deputy sheriff and union member, made "an astonishing run" in the

[16] Information derived from same sources as cited in footnote 14.

[17] Stone *et al.*, *Nine Cities*, 212.
[18] *Ibid.*, 3–13.
[19] *Ibid.*, 329.
[20] Stone *et al.*, *City Manager Government*, 26, 237–41, for analysis of opposition to city-manager government.

primary, coming in second among a field of more than twenty candidates.[21] In fact, the strength of anticommission candidates in the primary so alarmed reformers that they frantically sought to appease labor.

The day before the final election they modified their platform to pledge both an eight-hour day and an "American standard of wages." They attempted to persuade the voters that their slate consisted of men who represented labor because they had "begun at the bottom of the ladder and made a good climb toward success by their own unaided efforts."[22] But their tactics failed. In the election on March 30, 1908, voters swept into office the entire "opposition" slate. The business and professional community had succeeded in changing the form of government, but not in securing its control. A cartoon in the leading reform newspaper illustrated their disappointment; John Q. Public sat dejectedly and muttered, "Aw, What's the Use?"

The most visible opposition to reform and the most readily available target of reform attack was the so-called "machine," for through the "machine" many different ward communities as well as lower- and middle-income groups joined effectively to influence the central city government. Their private occupational and social life did not naturally involve these groups in larger city-wide activities in the same way as the upper class was involved; hence they lacked access to privately organized economic and social power on which they could construct political power. The "machine" filled this organizational gap.

Yet it should never be forgotten that the social and economic institutions in the wards themselves provided the "machine's" sustaining support and gave it larger significance. When reformers attacked the "machine" as the most visible institutional element of the ward system, they attacked the entire ward form of political organization and the political power of lower- and middle-income groups which lay behind it.

Reformers often gave the impression that they opposed merely the corrupt politician and his "machine." But in a more fundamental way they looked upon the deficiencies of pre-reform political leaders in terms not of their personal shortcomings, but of the limitations inherent in their occupational, institutional, and class positions. In 1911 the Voters' League of Pittsburgh wrote in its pamphlet analyzing the qualifications of candidates that "a man's occupation ought to give a strong indication of his qualifications for membership on a school board."[23] Certain occupations inherently disqualified a man from serving:

> Employment as ordinary laborer and in the lowest class of mill work would naturally lead to the conclusion that such men did not have sufficient education or business training to act as school directors. . . . Objection might also be made to small shopkeepers, clerks, workmen at many trades, who by lack of educational advantages and business training, could not, no matter how honest, be expected to administer properly the affairs of an educational system, requiring special knowledge, and where millions are spent each year.

These, of course, were precisely the groups which did dominate Pittsburgh government prior to reform. The

[21] Des Moines *Register and Leader*, March 17, 1908.
[22] *Ibid.*, March 30, March 28, 1908.

[23] Voters' Civic League of Allegheny County, "Bulletin of the Voters' Civic League of Allegheny County Concerning the Public School System of Pittsburgh," Feb. 14, 1911, pp. 2–3.

League deplored the fact that school boards contained only a small number of "men prominent throughout the city in business life . . . in professional occupations . . . holding positions as managers, secretaries, auditors, superintendents and foremen" and exhorted these classes to participate more actively as candidates for office.

Reformers, therefore, wished not simply to replace bad men with good; they proposed to change the occupational and class origins of decision-makers. Toward this end they sought innovations in the formal machinery of government which would concentrate political power by sharply centralizing the processes of decision-making rather than distribute it through more popular participation in public affairs. According to the liberal view of the Progressive Era, the major political innovations of reform involved the equalization of political power through the primary, the direct election of public officials, and the initiative, referendum, and recall. These measures played a large role in the political ideology of the time and were frequently incorporated into new municipal charters. But they provided at best only an occasional and often incidental process of decision-making. Far more important in continuous, sustained, day-to-day processes of government were those innovations which centralized decision-making in the hands of fewer and fewer people.

The systematization of municipal government took place on both the executive and the legislative levels. The strong-mayor and city-manager types became the most widely used examples of the former. In the first decade of the 20th century, the commission plan had considerable appeal, but its distribution of administrative responsibility among five people gave rise to a demand for a form with more centralized executive power; consequently, the city-manager or the commission-manager variant often replaced it.[24]

A far more pervasive and significant change, however, lay in the centralization of the system of representation, the shift from ward to city-wide election of councils and school boards. Governing bodies so selected, reformers argued, would give less attention to local and particularistic matters and more to affairs of city-wide scope. This shift, an invariable feature of both commission and city-manager plans, was often adopted by itself. In Pittsburgh, for example, the new charter of 1911 provided as the major innovation that a council of twenty-seven, each member elected from a separate ward, be replaced by a council of nine, each elected by the city as a whole.

Cities displayed wide variations in this innovation. Some regrouped wards into larger units but kept the principle of areas of representation smaller than the entire city. Some combined a majority of councilmen elected by wards with additional ones elected at large. All such innovations, however, constituted steps toward the centralization of the system of representation.

Liberal historians have not appreciated the extent to which municipal reform in the Progressive Era involved a debate over the system of representation. The ward form of representation was universally condemned on the grounds that it gave too much influ-

[24] In the decade 1911 to 1920, 43 per cent of the municipal charters adopted in eleven home rule states involved the commission form and 35 per cent the city-manager form; in the following decade the figures stood at 6 per cent and 71 per cent respectively. The adoption of city-manager charters reached a peak in the years 1918 through 1923 and declined sharply after 1933. See Leonard D. White, "The Future of Public Administration, *Public Management,* XV (1933), 12.

ence to the separate units and not enough attention to the larger problems of the city. Harry A. Toulmin, whose book, *The City Manager,* was published by the National Municipal League, stated the case:

> The spirit of sectionalism had dominated the political life of every city. Ward pitted against ward, alderman against alderman, and legislation only effected by "log-rolling" extravagant measures into operation, mulcting the city, but gratifying the greed of constituents, has too long stung the conscience of decent citizenship. This constant treaty-making of factionalism has been no less than a curse. The city manager plan proposes the commendable thing of abolishing wards. The plan is not unique in this for it has been common to many forms of commission government. . . .[25]

Such a system should be supplanted, the argument usually went, with city-wide representation in which elected officials could consider the city "as a unit." "The new officers are elected," wrote Toulmin, "each to represent all the people. Their duties are so defined that they must administer the corporate business in its entirety, not as a hodge-podge of associated localities."

Behind the debate over the method of representation, however, lay a debate over who should be represented, over whose views of public policy should prevail. Many reform leaders often explicitly, if not implicitly expressed fear that lower- and middle-income groups had too much influence in decision-making. One Galveston leader, for example, complained about the movement for initiative, referendum, and recall:

> We have in our city a very large number of negroes employed on the docks; we also have a very large number of unskilled white laborers; this city also has more barrooms, according to its population, than any other city in Texas. Under these circumstances it would be extremely difficult to maintain a satisfactory city government where all ordinances must be submitted back to the voters of the city for their ratification and approval.[26]

At the National Municipal League convention of 1907, Rear Admiral F. E. Chadwick (USN Ret.), a leader in the Newport, Rhode Island, movement for municipal reform, spoke to this question even more directly:

> Our present system has excluded in large degree the representation of those who have the city's well-being most at heart. It has brought, in municipalities . . . a government established by the least educated, the least interested class of citizens.
>
> It stands to reason that a man paying $5,000 taxes in a town is more interested in the well-being and development of his town than the man who pays no taxes. . . . It equally stands to reason that the man of the $5,000 tax should be assured a representation in the committee which lays the tax and spends the money which he contributes. . . . Shall we be truly democratic and give the property owner a fair show or shall we develop a

[25] Toulmin, *The City Manager,* 42.

[26] Woodruff, *City Government,* 315. The Galveston commission plan did not contain provisions for the initiative, referendum, or recall and Galveston commercial groups which had fathered the commission plan opposed movements to include them. In 1911 Governor Colquitt of Texas vetoed a charter bill for Texarkana because it contained such provisions; he maintained that they were "undemocratic" and unnecessary to the success of commission government. *Ibid.,* 314–15.

tyranny of ignorance which shall crush him.[27]

Municipal reformers thus debated frequently the question of who should be represented as well as the question of what method of representation should be employed.

That these two questions were intimately connected was revealed in other reform proposals for representation, proposals which were rarely taken seriously. One suggestion was that a class system of representation be substituted for ward representation. For example, in 1908 one of the prominent candidates for commissioner in Des Moines proposed that the city council be composed of representatives of five classes: educational and ministerial organizations, manufacturers and jobbers, public utility corporations, retail merchants including liquor men, and the Des Moines Trades and Labor Assembly. Such a system would have greatly reduced the influence in the council of both middle- and lower-class groups. The proposal revealed the basic problem confronting business and professional leaders: how to reduce the influence in government of the majority of voters among middle- and lower-income groups.[28]

A growing imbalance between population and representation sharpened the desire of reformers to change from ward to city-wide elections. Despite shifts in population within most cities, neither ward district lines nor the apportionment of city council and school board seats changed frequently. Consequently, older areas of the city, with wards that were small in geographical size and held declining populations (usually lower and middle class in composition), continued to be over-represented, and newer upper-class areas, where population was growing, became increasingly underrepresented. This intensified the reformers' conviction that the structure of government must be changed to give them the voice they needed to make their views on public policy prevail.[29]

It is not insignificant that in some cities (by no means a majority) municipal reform came about outside of the urban electoral process. The original commission government in Galveston was appointed rather than elected. "The failure of previous attempts to secure an efficient city government through the local electorate made the business men of Galveston willing to put the conduct of the city's affairs in the hands of a commission dominated by state-appointed officials."[30] Only in 1903 did the courts force Galveston to elect the members of the commission, an innovation which one writer described as "an abandonment of the commission idea," and which led to the decline of the influence of the business community in the commission government.[31]

In 1911 Pittsburgh voters were not permitted to approve either the new city charter or the new school board plan, both of which provided for city-wide representation; they were a result of state legislative enactment. The governor appointed the first members of the new city council, but thereafter they were elected. The judges of the court of common pleas, however, and not the voters, selected members of the new school board.

The composition of the new city council and new school board in Pittsburgh, both of which were inaugurated

---

[27] *Ibid.*, 207–208.
[28] Des Moines *Register and Leader*, Jan. 15, 1908.

[29] Voters' Civic League of Allegheny County, "Report on the Voters' League in the Redistricting of the Wards of the City of Pittsburgh" (Pittsburgh, n.d.).
[30] Horace E. Deming, "The Government of American Cities," in Woodruff, *City Government*, 167.
[31] *Ibid.*, 168.

in 1911, revealed the degree to which the shift from ward to city-wide representation produced a change in group representation.[32] Members of the upper class, the advanced professional men, and the large business groups dominated both. Of the fifteen members of the Pittsburgh Board of Education appointed in 1911 and the nine members of the new city council, none were small businessmen or white-collar workers. Each body contained only one person who could remotely be classified as a blue-collar worker; each of these men filled a position specifically but unofficially designed as reserved for a "representative of labor," and each was an official of the Amalgamated Association of Iron, Steel, and Tin Workers. Six of the nine members of the new city council were prominent businessmen, and all six were listed in upper-class directories. Two others were doctors closely associated with the upper class in both professional and social life. The fifteen members of the Board of Education included ten businessmen with city-wide interests, one doctor associated with the upper class, and three women previously active in upper-class public welfare.

Lower- and middle-class elements felt that the new city governments did not represent them.[33] The studies carried out under the direction of Leonard White contain numerous expressions of the way in which the change in the structure of government pro-

duced not only a change in the geographical scope of representation, but also in the groups represented. "It is not the policies of the manager or the council they oppose," one researcher declared, "as much as the lack of representation for their economic level and social groups."[34] And another wrote:

There had been nothing unapproachable about the old ward aldermen. Every voter had a neighbor on the common council who was interested in serving him. The new councilmen, however, made an unfavorable impression on the less well-to-do voters. . . . Election at large made a change that, however desirable in other ways, left the voters in the poorer wards with a feeling that they had been deprived of their share of political importance.[35]

The success of the drive for centralization of administration and representation varied with the size of the city. In the smaller cities, business, professional, and elite groups could easily exercise a dominant influence. Their close ties readily enabled them to shape informal political power which they could transform into formal political power. After the mid-1890's the widespread organization of chambers of commerce provided a base for political action to reform municipal government, resulting in a host of small-city commission and city-manager innovations. In the larger, more heterogeneous cities, whose sub-communities were more dispersed, such community-wide action was extremely difficult. Few commission or city-manager proposals materialized here. Mayors became stronger, and steps were taken toward centralization of representation, but the ward system

[32] Information derived from same sources as cited in footnote 14.

[33] W. R. Hopkins, city manager of Cleveland, indicated the degree to which the new type of government was more responsive to the business community: "It is undoubtedly easier for a city manager to insist upon acting in accordance with the business interests of the city than it is for a mayor to do the same thing." Quoted in White, *The City Manager*, 13.

[34] Stone *et al.*, *Nine Cities*, 20.
[35] *Ibid.*, 225.

or some modified version usually persisted. Reformers in large cities often had to rest content with their Municipal Research Bureaus through which they could exert political influence from outside the municipal government.

A central element in the analysis of municipal reform in the Progressive Era is governmental corruption. Should it be understood in moral or political terms? Was it a product of evil men or of particular socio-political circumstances? Reform historians have adopted the former view. Selfish and evil men arose to take advantage of a political arrangement whereby unsystematic government offered many opportunities for personal gain at public expense. The system thrived until the "better elements," "men of intelligence and civic responsibility," or "right-thinking people" ousted the culprits and fashioned a political force which produced decisions in the "public interest." In this scheme of things, corruption in public affairs grew out of individual personal failings and a deficient governmental structure which could not hold those predispositions in check, rather than from the peculiar nature of social forces. The contestants involved were morally defined: evil men who must be driven from power, and good men who must be activated politically to secure control of municipal affairs.

Public corruption, however, involves political even more than moral considerations. It arises more out of the particular distribution of political power than of personal morality. For corruption is a device to exercise control and influence outside the legal channels of decision-making when those channels are not readily responsive. Most generally, corruption stems from an inconsistency between control of the instruments of formal governmental power and the exercise of informal influence in the community. If powerful groups are denied access to formal power in legitimate ways, they seek access through procedures which the community considers illegitimate. Corrupt government, therefore, does not reflect the genius of evil men, but rather the lack of acceptable means for those who exercise power in the private community to wield the same influence in governmental affairs. It can be understood in the Progressive Era not simply by the preponderance of evil men over good, but by the peculiar nature of the distribution of political power.

The political corruption of the "Era of Reform" arose from the inaccessibility of municipal government to those who were rising in power and influence. Municipal government in the United States developed in the 19th century within a context of universal manhood suffrage which decentralized political control. Because all men, whatever their economic, social, or cultural conditions, could vote, leaders who reflected a wide variety of community interests and who represented the views of people of every circumstance arose to guide and direct municipal affairs. Since the majority of urban voters were workingmen or immigrants, the views of those groups carried great and often decisive weight in governmental affairs. Thus, as Herbert Gutman has shown, during strikes in the 1870's city officials were usually friendly to workingmen and refused to use police power to protect strikebreakers.[36]

Ward representation on city councils was an integral part of grass-roots influence, for it enabled diverse urban communities, invariably identified with

[36] Herbert Gutman, "An Iron Workers' Strike in the Ohio Valley, 1873–74," *Ohio Historical Quarterly*, LXVIII (1959), 353–70; "Trouble on the Railroads, 1873–1874: Prelude to the 1877 Crisis," *Labor History*, II (Spring, 1961), 215–36.

particular geographical areas of the city, to express their views more clearly through councilmen peculiarly receptive to their concerns. There was a direct, reciprocal flow of power between wards and the center of city affairs in which voters felt a relatively close connection with public matters and city leaders gave special attention to their needs.

Within this political system the community's business leaders grew in influence and power as industrialism advanced, only to find that their economic position did not readily admit them to the formal machinery of government. Thus, during strikes, they had to rely on either their own private police, Pinkertons, or the state militia to enforce their use of strikebreakers. They frequently found that city officials did not accept their views of what was best for the city and what direction municipal policies should take. They had developed a common outlook, closely related to their economic activities, that the city's economic expansion should become the prime concern of municipal government, and yet they found that this view had to compete with even more influential views of public policy. They found that political tendencies which arose from universal manhood suffrage and ward representation were not always friendly to their political conceptions and goals and had produced a political system over which they had little control, despite the fact that their economic ventures were the core of the city's prosperity and the hope for future urban growth.

Under such circumstances, businessmen sought other methods of influencing municipal affairs. They did not restrict themselves to the channels of popular election and representation, but frequently applied direct influence —if not verbal persuasion, then bribery and corruption. Thereby arose the graft which Lincoln Steffens recounted in his *Shame of the Cities.* Utilities were only the largest of those business groups and individuals who requested special favors, and the franchises they sought were only the most sensational of the prizes which included such items as favorable tax assessments and rates, the vacating of streets wanted for factory expansion, or permission to operate amid antiliquor and other laws regulating personal behavior. The relationships between business and formal government became a maze of accommodations, a set of political arrangements which grew up because effective power had few legitimate means of accomplishing its ends.

Steffens and subsequent liberal historians, however, misread the significance of these arrangements, emphasizing their personal rather than their more fundamental institutional elements. To them corruption involved personal arrangements between powerful business leaders and powerful "machine" politicians. Just as they did not fully appreciate the significance of the search for political influence by the rising business community as a whole, so they did not see fully the argument that the political leader manipulated voters to his own personal ends, that he used constituents rather than reflected their views.

A different approach is now taking root, namely, that the urban political organization was an integral part of community life, expressing its needs and its goals. As Oscar Handlin has said, for example, the "machine" not only fulfilled specific wants, but provided one of the few avenue to success and public recognition available to the immigrant.[37] The political leader's arrangements with businessmen,

[37] Oscar Handlin, *The Uprooted* (Boston, 1951), 209–17.

therefore, were not simply personal agreements between conniving individuals; they were far-reaching accommodations between powerful sets of institutions in industrial America.

These accommodations, however, proved to be burdensome and unsatisfactory to the business community and to the upper third of socio-economic groups in general. They were expensive; they were wasteful; they were uncertain. Toward the end of the 19th century, therefore, business and professional men sought more direct control over municipal government in order to exercise political influence more effectively. They realized their goals in the early 20th century in the new commission and city-manager forms of government and in the shift from ward to city-wide representation.

These innovations did not always accomplish the objectives that the business community desired because other forces could and often did adjust to the change in governmental structure and reëstablish their influence. But businessmen hoped that reform would enable them to increase their political power, and most frequently it did. In most cases the innovations which were introduced between 1901, when Galveston adopted a commission form of government, and the Great Depression, and especially the city-manager form which reached a height of popularity in the mid-1920's, served as vehicles whereby business and professional leaders moved directly into the inner circles of government, brought into one political system their own power and the formal machinery of government, and dominated municipal affairs for two decades.

Municipal reform in the early 20th century involves a paradox: the ideology of an extension of political control and the practice of its concentra-

tion. While reformers maintained that their movement rested on a wave of popular demands, called their gatherings of business and professional leaders "mass meetings," described their reforms as "part of a world-wide trend toward popular government," and proclaimed an ideology of a popular upheaval against a selfish few, they were in practice shaping the structure of municipal government so that political power would no longer be broadly distributed, but would in fact be more centralized in the hands of a relatively small segment of the population. The paradox became even sharper when new city charters included provisions for the initiative, referendum, and recall. How does the historian cope with this paradox? Does it represent deliberate deception or simply political strategy? Or does it reflect a phenomenon which should be understood rather than explained away?

The expansion of popular involvement in decision-making was frequently a political tactic, not a political system to be established permanently, but a device to secure immediate political victory. The prohibitionist advocacy of the referendum, one of the most extensive sources of support for such a measure, came from the belief that the referendum would provide the opportunity to outlaw liquor more rapidly. The Anti-Saloon League, therefore, urged local option. But the League was not consistent. Towns which were wet, when faced with a country-wide local-option decision to outlaw liquor, demanded town or township local option to reinstate it. The League objected to this as not the proper application of the referendum idea.

Again, "Progressive" reformers often espoused the direct primary when fighting for nominations for their candidates within the party, but once in control they often became cool to it because it might result in their own defeat. By the same token, many municipal reformers attached the initiative, referendum, and recall to municipal charters often as a device to appease voters who opposed the centralization of representation and executive authority. But, by requiring a high percentage of voters to sign petitions—often 25 to 30 per cent—these innovations could be and were rendered relatively harmless.

More fundamentally, however, the distinction between ideology and practice in municipal reform arose from the different roles which each played. The ideology of democratization of decision-making was negative rather than positive; it served as an instrument of attack against the existing political system rather than as a guide to alternative action. Those who wished to destroy the "machine" and to eliminate party competition in local government widely utilized the theory that these political instruments thwarted public impulses, and thereby shaped the tone of their attack.

But there is little evidence that the ideology represented a faith in a purely democratic system of decision-making or that reformers actually wished, in practice, to substitute direct democracy as a continuing system of sustained decision-making in place of the old. It was used to destroy the political institutions of the lower and middle classes and the political power which those institutions gave rise to, rather than to provide a clear-cut guide for alternative action.[38]

The guide to alternative action lay in the model of the business enterprise. In describing new conditions which they wished to create, reformers drew on the analogy of the "efficient business enterprise," criticizing current practices with the argument that "no business could conduct its affairs that way and remain in business," and calling upon business practices as the guides to improvement. As one student remarked:

The folklore of the business elite came by gradual transition to be the symbols of governmental reformers. Efficiency, system, orderliness, budgets, economy, saving, were all injected into the efforts of reformers who sought to remodel municipal government in terms of the great impersonality of corporate enterprise.[39]

Clinton Rodgers Woodruff of the National Municipal League explained that the commission form was "a simple, direct, businesslike way of administering the business affairs of the city . . . an application to city administration of that type of business organization which has been so common and so successful in the field of commerce and industry."[40] The centralization of decision-making which developed in the business corporation was now applied in municipal reform.

The model of the efficient business enterprise, then, rather than the New England town meeting, provided the positive inspiration for the municipal reformer. In giving concrete shape to this model in the strong-mayor, commission, and city-manager plans, reformers engaged in the elaboration of

[38] Clinton Rodgers Woodruff of the National Municipal League even argued that the initiative, referendum, and recall were rarely used. "Their value lies in their existence rather than in their use." Woodruff, *City Government*, 314. It seems apparent that the most widely used of these devices, the referendum, was popularized by legislative bodies when they could not agree or did not want to take responsibility for a decision and sought to pass that responsibility to the general public,

rather than because of a faith in the wisdom of popular will.

[39] J. B. Shannon, "County Consolidation," *Annals of the American Academy of Political and Social Science*, Vol. 207 (January, 1940), 168.

[40] Woodruff, *City Government*, 29–30.

the processes of rationalization and systematization inherent in modern science and technology. For in many areas of society, industrialization brought a gradual shift upward in the location of decision-making and the geographical extension of the scope of the area affected by decisions.

Experts in business, in government, and in the professions measured, studied, analyzed, and manipulated ever wider realms of human life, and devices which they used to control such affairs constituted the most fundamental and far-reaching innovations in decision-making in modern America, whether in formal government or in the informal exercise of power in private life. Reformers in the Progressive Era played a major role in shaping this new system. While they expressed an ideology of restoring a previous order, they in fact helped to bring forth a system drastically new.[41]

The drama of reform lay in the competition for supremacy between two systems of decision-making. One system, based upon ward representation and growing out of the practices and ideas of representative government, involved wide latitude for the expression of grass-roots impulses and their involvement in the political process. The other grew out of the rationalization of life which came with science and technology, in which decisions arose from expert analysis and flowed from fewer and smaller centers outward to the rest of society. Those who espoused the former looked with fear upon the loss of influence which the latter involved, and those who espoused the latter looked only with

[41] Several recent studies emphasize various aspects of this movement. See, for example, Loren Baritz, *Servants of Power* (Middletown, 1960); Raymond E. Callahan, *Education and the Cult of Efficiency* (Chicago, 1962); Samuel P. Hays, *Conservation and the Gospel of Efficiency* (Cambridge, 1959); Dwight Waldo, *The Administrative State* (New York, 1948), 3–61.

disdain upon the wastefulness and inefficiency of the former.

The Progressive Era witnessed rapid strides toward a more centralized system and a relative decline for a more decentralized system. This development constituted an accommodation of forces outside the business community to the political trends within business and professional life rather than vice versa. It involved a tendency for the decision-making processes inherent in science and technology to prevail over those inherent in representative government.

Reformers in the Progressive Era and liberal historians since then misread the nature of the movement to change municipal government because they concentrated upon dramatic and sensational episodes and ignored the analysis of more fundamental political structure, of the persistent relationships of influence and power which grew out of the community's social, ideological, economic, and cultural activities. The reconstruction of these patterns of human relationships and of the changes in them is the historian's most crucial task, for they constitute the central context of historical development. History consists not of erratic and spasmodic fluctuations, of a series of random thoughts and actions, but of patterns of activity and change in which people hold thoughts and actions in common and in which there are close connections between sequences of events. These contexts give rise to a structure of human relationships which pervade all areas of life; for the political historian the most important of these is the structure of the distribution of power and influence.

The structure of political relationships, however, cannot be adequately understood if we concentrate on evidence concerning ideology rather than practice. For it is becoming increasingly clear that ideological evidence is no safe guide to the understanding of practice, that what people thought and said about their society is not necessarily an accurate representation of what they did. The current task of the historian of the Progressive Era is to quit taking the reformers' own description of political practice at its face value and to utilize a wide variety of new types of evidence to reconstruct political practice in its own terms. This is not to argue that ideology is either important or unimportant. It is merely to state that ideological evidence is not appropriate to the discovery of the nature of political practice.

Only by maintaining this clear distinction can the historian successfully investigate the structure of political life in the Progressive Era. And only then can he begin to cope with the most fundamental problem of all: the relationship between political ideology and political practice. For each of these facets of political life must be understood in its own terms, through its own historical record. Each involves a distinct set of historical phenomena. The relationship between them for the Progressive Era is not now clear; it has not been investigated. But it cannot be explored until the conceptual distinction is made clear and evidence tapped which is pertinent to each. Because the nature of political practice has so long been distorted by the use of ideological evidence, the most pressing task is for its investigation through new types of evidence appropriate to it. The reconstruction of the movement for municipal reform can constitute a major step forward toward that goal.

Urban Liberalism in the Age of Reform

J. Joseph Huthmacher*

Most historians of twentieth-century America would agree that the effective beginnings of the present-day "people's capitalism"—the present-day liberalism—can be traced back to the Progressive Era. And most of them would agree that the essential ingredient which made possible the practical achievement of reforms at that time was the support by city dwellers who, at the turn of the century, swung behind reform movements in large numbers for the first time since America's rush into industrialism following the Civil War. True, the Populists and other agrarian radicals had done spadework on behalf of various proposals in the late nineteenth century, such as trust regulation, the income tax, and direct election of senators. But their efforts had gone unrewarded, or had been frustrated by enactment of half-way measures. Not until the reform spirit had seized large numbers of urbanites could there be hope of achieving meaningful political, economic, and social adjustments to the demands of the new industrial civilization.

Between 1900 and 1920 American statute books became studded with the results of urban-oriented reform drives. The direct primary, the initiative, the Seventeenth Amendment; the Clayton Act, a revived Interstate Commerce Commission, and the Federal Trade Commission; workmen's compensation, child labor laws, and Prohibition—these and many other achievements testified to the intensity of Progressivism. It is admitted, of course, that not everything done in the name of reform was desirable. Some measures, notably Prohibition, are counted today as being wrongheaded, while some political panaceas like the direct primary elicited an undue degree of optimism on the part of their exponents. Nevertheless, the Progressive Era did witness America's first modern reform upsurge, and much of substantial worth was accomplished. Moreover, it established patterns and precedents for the further evolution of American liberalism, an evolution whose later milestones would bear the markings "New Deal" and "New Frontier."

In accounting for the genesis and success of urban liberalism in the Progressive Era, however, the historians who have dominated its study thus far have concentrated on one population element, the urban middle class, and its Yankee-Protestant system of values. "The great majority of the reformers came from the 'solid middle class,'" Professor George E. Mowry tells us. "If names mean anything, an overwhelming proportion of this reform group came from old American stock with British origins consistently indicated." Professor Richard Hofstadter adds that "the key words of Progressivism were terms like *patriotism, citizen, democracy, law, character, conscience* . . . terms redolent of the sturdy Protestant Anglo-Saxon moral and intellectual roots of the Progressive uprising."[1] The component parts of this amorphous middle class, and the reasons for their new

*Reprinted with permission from J. Joseph Huthmacher, "Urban Liberalism and the Age of Reform," *Journal of American History*, XLIX (September, 1962), 231–241.

[1] George E. Mowry, *The Era of Theodore Roosevelt, 1900–1912* (New York, 1958), 86; Richard Hofstadter, *The Age of Reform* (New York, 1955), 318.

interest in reform at the turn of the century, have been described by various scholars.[2] We have been told about the "white collar" group which saw, in the increasing bureaucratization of big business, the blotting out of its traditional belief in the American "rags to riches" legend. Some writers have dwelt upon the middle-class intellectuals—writers, publicists, ministers, college women, professors—who, in response to changing patterns of social thought represented by the rise of "realism" in literature, religion, and the social sciences, determined to uplift the living conditions of their less fortunate brothers. Others have examined the "Old Aristocracy" threatened by a "status revolution," and fighting to maintain the degree of deference that had been theirs before the rise of the newly rich moguls of business and finance.

Imbued with this mixture of selfish and altruistic motives, reinforced by the pocketbook-pinching price inflation that got under way in 1897, the urban middle-class reformers set out to right the wrongs of their society. They introduced a variety of new democratic techniques into our political mechanics, in an attempt to break the grip of the corrupt bosses who manipulated irresponsible immigrant voters and unscrupulous businessmen in ways that subverted good government. They augmented the government's role as watchdog over the economy, either to maintain the traditional "small business" regime of competitive free enterprise, or at least to make sure that oligopolists passed on to consumers the benefits of large-scale operation. Through the activities of their philanthropic organizations, coupled

with support of paternalistic labor and social welfare legislation, the middle-class reformers also sought to uplift the standards of the alien, slum-dwelling, urban working class to something more closely approximating the Yankee-Protestant ideal. So runs the "middle-class" interpretation of Progressivism, an interpretation which has set the fashion, by and large, for scholarly work on the subject.

There is no doubt, of course, that discontented elements among the urban middle class contributed much to Progressivism, or that the historians who have explored their contributions and their motives deserve the plaudits of the profession. Nevertheless, it may be pertinent to ask whether these historians have not overstressed the role of middle-class reformers, to the neglect or exclusion of other elements— such as organized labor—who have had something to do with the course of modern American liberalism.[3] More particularly, a number of circumstances call into question the assertion that "In politics . . . the immigrant was usually at odds with the reform aspirations of the American Progressive."[4] If such were the case, how does one explain the drive and success of Progressive Era reform movements in places like New York and Massachusetts—states that were heavily populated with non-Protestant, non-Anglo-Saxon immigrants and sons of immigrants? How could reformers suc-

[2] Mowry, *Era of Theodore Roosevelt*; Hofstadter, *Age of Reform*; C. Wright Mills, *White Collar* (New York, 1951); Eric Goldman, *Rendezvous with Destiny* (New York, 1952); Samuel P. Hays, *The Response to Industrialism*, 1885–1914 (Chicago, 1957).

[3] The suggestions made in this and the following paragraphs stem primarily from the author's research for *Massachusetts People and Politics, 1919–1933* (Cambridge, Mass., 1959), and for a projected biography of Senator Robert F. Wagner of New York. Senator Wagner's papers are deposited at Georgetown University, Washington, D.C.

[4] Hofstadter, *Age of Reform*, 180–81. It is clear, of course, that Professor Hofstadter is referring not only to the first-generation immigrants themselves, but to the whole society which they, their offspring, and their culture were creating within our industrial, urban maze.

ceed at the polls or in the legislatures in such states if, "Together with the native conservative and the politically indifferent, the immigrants formed a potent mass that limited the range and the achievements of Progressivism"?[5] Moreover, how does one explain the support which individuals like Al Smith, Robert F. Wagner, James A. Foley, James Michael Curley, and David I. Walsh gave to a large variety of so-called Progressive measures in their respective office-holding capacities?[6] Surely these men do not conform to the middle-class, Yankee-Protestant "Progressive Profile" as etched by Professor Mowry.[7]

If the Progressive Era is to be considered a manifestation of the Yankee-Protestant ethos almost exclusively, how does one explain the fact that in the legislatures of New York and Massachusetts many reform bills received more uniform and consistent support from representatives of the urban lower class than they received from the urban middle-class or rural representatives? Some of the most ef-

fective middle-class reformers, such as social worker Frances Perkins, realized this fact at the time and charted their legislative strategy accordingly.[8] It may be pointed out also that, even when submitted to popular referendums, typically Progressive measures sometimes received more overwhelming support in the melting-pot wards than they received in the middle-class or rural constituencies. This was the case, for example, in Massachusetts when, in 1918, the voters passed upon a proposed initiative and referendum amendment to the state constitution. Such circumstances become especially compelling when we remember that reform measures, no matter how well formulated and publicized by intellectuals, cannot become effective in a democracy without skillful political generalship and—even more important—votes.

Marshaled together, then, the foregoing evidence suggests that the triumphs of modern liberalism in the Progressive Era, and in subsequent reform eras, were owed to something more than a strictly middle-class dynamism. It indicates that the urban lower class provided an active, numerically strong, and politically necessary force for reform—and that this class was perhaps as important in determining the course of American liberalism as the urban middle class, about which so much has been written.

Today's liberals look to the "northern" Democrats and the "eastern" Republicans—those whose elections are due largely to the votes of the urban working class—for support of their proposals. If, as is contended, this phenomenon of urban lower-class liberalism can be traced back beyond the election of 1960, beyond the New Deal, and to the Progressive Era, then the probing of its chronological origins

---

[5] *Ibid.*, 181.

[6] Oscar Handlin, *Al Smith and His America* (Boston, 1958); Joseph F. Dinneen, *The Purple Shamrock: The Honorable James Michael Curley of Boston* (New York, 1949); Dorothy G. Wayman, *David I. Walsh: Citizen Patriot* (Milwaukee, 1952). See also Arthur Mann, *La Guardia: A Fighter against His Times* (Philadelphia, 1959). Among the measures which Robert F. Wagner introduced as a New York state senator between 1909 and 1918 were the following: a bill to provide for direct election of United States senators; a bill to authorize a twenty million dollar bond issue for conservation and public development of state water power; a direct primary bill; a short-ballot bill; a resolution to ratify the federal income tax amendment; a bill establishing the Factory Investigating Commission; a civil rights bill; a woman suffrage amendment to the state constitution; numerous bills for child labor regulation; a bill to extend home rule to municipalities; a bill to establish a minimum wage commission for women; a bill limiting the issuance of labor injunctions; a bill to authorize municipal ownership of power; and a corrupt practices bill.

[7] Mowry, *Era of Theodore Roosevelt*, chap. 5.

[8] Frances Perkins, *The Roosevelt I Knew* (New York, 1946), 12–26.

and the operational details of its emergence present wide fields for fruitful research. In the process of such studies, many other questions will present themselves to the investigator. What were the sources of lower-class interest in reform? How did its sources affect its nature, specific content, and practical effects? How, if at all, did urban lower-class liberalism differ in these respects from urban middle-class liberalism? At the risk of premature generalization, tentative suggestions, indicated by research thus far conducted, may be set forth regarding these matters.

The great source of urban working-class liberalism was experience. Unlike the middle-class reformers, who generally relied on muckrackers, Social Gospelers, and social scientists to delineate the ills of society, the urban working class knew at first hand the conditions of life on "the other side of the tracks." Its members and spokesmen grew to manhood "in the midst of alternately shivering and sweltering humanity in ancient rat-infested rookeries in the swarming, anonymous, polyglot East Side, an international center before the U.N. was dreamed of," where "souls and bodies were saved by the parish priest, the family doctor, and the local political saloonkeeper and boss who knew everyone and was the link between the exploited immigrant and the incomprehensible, distant law."[9] Such people were less imbued than the middle class with the "old American creed" which expounded individualism, competition, and laissez-faire free enterprise as the means of advance from "rags to riches." Their felt needs, largely of the bread and butter type, were of the here and now, and not of the middle-class variety which fastened

upon further advancement to a higher station from one already fairly comfortable. Moreover, their constant immersion in the depths of human misery and frailty, and the semi-pessimistic nature of their religious psychology, limited their hopes for environmental improvement within the bounds of reasonable expectation. Their outlook tended to be more practical and "possibilistic" than that of some middle-class Progressives who allowed their reform aspirations to soar to Utopian heights, envisaging a "Kingdom of God on Earth" or a perfect society to be achieved by means of sociological test tubes. Finally, the previous political experience of the immigrant workers, centering about their security-oriented relations with a paternalistic ward boss, conditioned them to transfer the same functioned conception to the city, state, and national governments as they became progressively aware of their ability, through their voting power, to make those governing bodies serve their needs. Consequently, their view of government was much less permeated with fears of paternalism and centralization than that of traditionally individualistic middle-class reformers, many of whom abated their attachment to the laissez-faire principle with only the greater trepidation.[10]

The influence of these conditioning factors seems clearly discernible in the specific types of reform programs to which the urban lower class and its spokesmen lent greatest support. It is commonplace to say, for example, that the immigrants were not interested in political machinery reforms simply as reforms. Unlike the remaining middle-class "genteel reformers," they did not look upon political tinkering as the be-all and end-all of reform. Yet it is an injustice to imply that the

[9] Robert Moses, "Salute to an East Side Boy Named Smith," *New York Times Magazine* (October 8, 1961), 113.

[10] See Hofstadter, *Age of Reform*, chap. 6.

immigrants' attitude on this matter was due to an inherent inability to comprehend the Yankee-Protestant concept of political behavior, and that they were therefore immune to all proposals for political reform. These lower-class voters seemed willing enough to support specific proposals which would enable them to secure the voice necessary to satisfy their economic and social needs, recognizing, quite properly, that the latter were the real sources of society's maladjustment. Since the rural areas of Massachusetts generally controlled the Bay State legislature, the urban working class supported the initiative and referendum amendment which might enable them to by-pass tight-fisted rural solons. Since the same situation prevailed in the New York legislature, the New York City delegation was glad to secure popular election of United States senators. In brief, it would seem that the line-up on such questions depended more upon local conditions of practical politics than upon the workings of a Yankee-Protestant ethos.

In the realm of economic reform, pertaining particularly to the problem of "big business," indications are that the urban lower class tended—unwittingly, of course—to favor the "New Nationalism" approach of Herbert Croly and Theodore Roosevelt over the "New Freedom" of Wilson and the trust-busters. Its members had seldom experienced the white collar group's "office boy to bank president" phenomenon themselves. They had never been part of the "Old Aristocracy," and hence had not suffered a downward revision in status at the hands of big business moguls. They shared few of the aspirations of the industrial "small businessman" and, indeed, recognized that the latter was all too frequently identified with sweatshop conditions. Consequently, the urban lower class was little stirred by Wil-

sonian cries to give the "pygmies" a chance. To workers the relative size of the employer's establishment was quite immaterial so long as he provided job security and adequate wages and working conditions, and passed some of the benefits of large-scale production on to consumers in the form of lower prices. Governmental stabilization of the economy and regulation of big business might well prove more successful in guaranteeing these conditions than would government anti-trust drives. As a result, we find urban lower-class representatives introducing a large variety of business regulatory measures on the local and state levels during the Progressive Era. And it is symbolic, perhaps, to find Senator Robert F. Wagner introducing the National Industrial Recovery Act in 1933, while Senator David I. Walsh of Massachusetts had sponsored somewhat similar, forerunner, measures in Congress during the 1920's.

What has been said above indicates the basis for urban lower-class interest in the many types of social welfare and labor measures which became novelties, and then commonplace enactments, during the Progressive Era. If the middle class faced the fear of insecurity of status, then the working class faced an equally compelling fear of insecurity of livelihood and living conditions. The precarious condition of the lower class had now become known even to those on the better side of the tracks and, partly for humanitarian reasons and partly to defend their own civilization against a "revolution from below," middle-class reformers had become interested in social justice movements—which involved "doing things for others." But the recipients of this benevolence might surely be expected to show at least an equal interest in such movements—which involved doing something for themselves. That such was the case is clearly indicated by study of the legislative history of measures like workmen's compensation, widows' pensions, wages and hours legislation, factory safety legislation, and tenement laws in the legislatures of New York and Massachusetts during the Progressive years. The representatives of lower-class constituencies were the most active legislative sponsors and backers of such bills and, in collaboration with middle-class propagandists and lobbyists, they achieved a record of enactments which embraced much of the best and most enduring part of the Progressive Era's heritage.

The operations of the New York State Factory Investigating Commission are a case in point. Established by the legislature following the tragic Triangle Shirtwaist Company fire in 1911, the Commission recommended and secured passage of over fifty labor laws during the next four years, providing a model factory code that was widely copied in other states. The Commission's most active legislative members were State Senator Robert F. Wagner and Assemblyman Alfred E. Smith, two products of the East Side, while its most effective investigator and lobbyist was Miss Frances Perkins, a middle-class, college trained social worker. (It should be noted also that the Commission received notable assistance from Samuel Gompers and other leaders of organized labor.) Again it is rather striking to observe that the Social Security Act of 1935, which began the transfer of industrial security matters from the state to the national level, was introduced by Senator Wagner, to be administered by a federal Department of Labor headed by Miss Perkins.

Effective social reform during the Progresive Era, and in later periods, seems thus to have depended upon constructive collaboration, on specific issues, between reformers from both the urban lower class and the urban middle class (with the further co-operation, at times, of organized labor). Of course, such co-operation could not be attained on all proposals that went under the name of social "reform." When, during the Progressive Era, certain old-stock, Protestant, middle-class reformers decided that the cure for social evils lay not only in environmental reforms, but necessitated also a forcible "uplifting" of the lower-class immigrants' cultural and behavior standards to "100 per cent American" levels, the parting of the ways came. Lower-class reform spokesmen had no use for compulsory "Americanization" through Prohibition, the closing of parochial schools, or the enforcement of puritanical "blue laws." Nor had they any use for immigration restriction laws which were based upon invidious, quasi-racist distinctions between allegedly "superior" and "inferior" nationality stocks.[11] To them reform, in so far as the use of government compulsion was concerned, was a matter of environment. The fundamentals of a man's cultural luggage—his religion, his emotional attachment to his "old country" and its customs, his habits and personal behavior—were of concern to himself and his God, and to them alone. The lower-class reformers were products of the melting pot, and most of them took seriously the inscription on the base of the famous

[11] "If the literacy test was not applied to the Irish and the German, why should it now be applied to the Jew, the Italian or the Slav of the new immigration? Like our ancestors, they are now flying from persecution, from ignorance, from inequality; like our ancestors they expect to find here freedom and equal opportunity. Are we going to deny them an equal opportunity? Are we going to withhold from them the equality and opportunities which our fathers enjoyed?" (Excerpt from a speech by Robert F. Wagner in the New York State Senate, on a resolution which he introduced in 1917 petitioning Congress not to pass the literacy test bill. Wagner Papers).

statue in New York harbor. True, there were many religious and ethnic differences among the component elements of the lower class, which often resulted in prejudice and violence. But each of these elements resented the Old Stock's contention that all of them were equally inferior to the "real Americans" of Yankee-Protestant heritage, and they resisted the attempts, which grew as the Progressive Era wore on, to enforce conformity to a single cultural norm.

In so far as conformity-seeking "cultural" reforms were enacted in the Progressive years, then, the responsibility must be assigned to urban middle-class reformers, joined in this instance by their rural "bible belt" brethren. The lower class can share no part of the "credit" for reforms like Prohibition. But in resisting such movements, were they not waging an early fight on behalf of what we today call "cultural pluralism"—acceptance of which has become a cardinal tenet in the standard definition of "liberalism" in the modern world? Indeed, it may not be too much to say that in all three fields of reform—the political and economic, as well as the social— indications are that the urban lower-class approach was more uniformly "advanced" than that of the middle class, in the sense of being more in line with what has become the predominant liberal faith in modern America. After all, does not the lower-class reform impulse, as outlined above, resemble the "hard-headed," "realistic, and pluralistic liberalism for which spokesmen like Reinhold Niebuhr and Arthur Schlesinger, Jr., plead today, so that the "Children of Light" might not fall easy prey to the "Children of Darkness"?[12]

[12] See, for example, Reinhold Niebuhr, *The Children of Light and the Children of Darkness* (New York, 1945); Arthur M. Schlesinger, Jr., *The Vital Center* (Boston, 1949).

It is not contended, of course, that all members of the urban working class became interested in reform during the Progressive Era, any more than it can be contended that all members of the urban middle class did so. The same "sidewalks of New York" that produced Al Smith and Robert Wagner continued to produce their share of "unreconstructed" machine politicians, whose vision never rose above their own pockets. Nor is it argued that the nature and zeal of lower-class attachment to liberalism remained constant throughout the twentieth century, or that the degree of co-operation attained with other reform minded elements remained unchanging. In the 1920's, for example, mutual suspicion and distrust, based largely on ethnic or "cultural" differences, seem to have displaced the former mood of limited collaboration between lower- and middle-class spokesmen, and in these changed circumstances Progressive-type measures found little chance of enactment. It is also possible that the high level of general prosperity prevailing since 1941 has vitiated urban working-class devotion to economic reform, and that the increasing degree of acceptance enjoyed by ethnic elements formerly discriminated against is causing their members to forget the lessons of cultural pluralism. All of these matters deserve further study.

The last-mentioned problems, dealing with the contemporary scene, may lie more properly within the realm of the political scientist and sociologist. But surely the evolution of America's twentieth-century liberal society, from the Progressive Era through the New Deal, is a province for historical inquiry. It is suggested that the historians who enter it might do better if they modify the "middle-class" emphasis which has come to dominate the field and devote more attention to exploring hitherto neglected elements of the American social structure. Such exploration necessitates tedious research, focusing at first on the local and state levels, in unalluring source materials such as local and foreign-language newspapers, out-of-the-way manuscript collections, and the correlations between the make-up and voting records of small-scale election districts. In the course of this research, however, our conception of the Progressive Era, and of recent American history as a whole, may undergo change. In fact, it may even begin to appear that "old fashioned" political historians, if they inform their work with up-to-date statistical and social science skills, still have as much to contribute to our knowledge of ourselves as do the intellectual and social historians, who are, perhaps, sometimes prone to over-generalize on the basis of historical psychoanalysis.

The Roots of Urban Planning

Roy Lubove*

During the late nineteenth and early twentieth centuries, the American city entered a new phase of its history. The long-term demographic revolution, which concentrated a majority of the population in urban areas, was completed by 1920. Americans of the progressive era were thus the first to confront the reality of urban dominance. Many reform efforts of the period—labor legislation, Americanization, prohibition, housing, public health, and good government—were related to problems of city life. More generally, urbanization was synonymous with industrialization and its challenge to traditional institutions. The fact that the progressive era witnessed the definitive transition from a rural to an urban civilization has important implications for the historiography of the period. Potentially, urbanization might serve as a fruitful conceptual framework for interpreting political, economic, and social change.

A substantial body of historical literature on progressivism deals with political events, particularly on the national level. Business developments, including the rise of the corporation, have received considerable attention. In recent years, a number of historians have examined social reform ideologies, welfare organization, and related social issues such as immigration and prohibition. Necessarily, the city often provides the setting for these studies, but a more systematic analysis of the relationship between urbanization and institutional change is needed. Any such analysis will require that

historians devote greater attention to the shaping of the urban physical environment. The city, after all, is basically an artifact, a physical container within which complex human interactions occur; social organization and relationships are greatly influenced by land-use and housing patterns. Prior to the late nineteenth century, urban land and housing were viewed as commodities, subject to the laws of supply and demand. As in the broader economic system, competitive market disciplines presumably guaranteed order and progress. By the late nineteenth century, however, Americans had become less confident that market disciplines would suffice. Planners, housing reformers, and others launched a search for norms of public intervention. They aspired to enlarge the scope of public decision-making. These efforts to institute public controls over land-use and to improve the quality of the housing environment are central to a historiography which adopts urbanization as a conceptual tool. Conservation, housing codes, zoning, city planning, park development, the City Beautiful movement, and the Garden City idea differed in origin, but shared a common objective —an enhanced role for the architect, planner, and welfare expert at the expense of the business interests which had traditionally determined urban land-use policy. The remainder of this essay will be devoted to these movements.

Conservation experts made profound, if indirect, contributions to urban planning. They introduced the concept of scientific, efficient resource

*Roy Lubove, *The Urban Community: Housing and Planning in the Progressive Era,* © 1967. Reprinted by permission of Prentice-Hall, Inc., Englewood Cliffs, New Jersey.

utilization. Urban lands could be interpreted as one such resource; and urban social reformers frequently adopted the rhetoric of conservation to justify their efforts to improve living and working conditions. They spoke in terms of the need to "conserve" human resources often wasted or exploited in a complex industrial society. Conservation leaders such as John Wesley Powell, Elwood Mead, and Benton MacKay moved beyond resource policy into the realm of social and community theory. Linking up with the "country life" and "back-to-the-land" movements, these men sought to coordinate new land use and rural community organization principles. Critical of American pioneer tradition which acquiesced in rapid, speculative disposition of the national domain, conservation leaders proposed a policy of administered land use combined with group settlement and the introduction of cooperative institutions.

The settlement of the Plains and Rocky Mountain Region after the Civil War had dramatized the need for radical changes in the national land system. The familiar rectilinear survey and the Homestead principle of dispersed settlement proved increasingly inappropriate as the frontier reached the 100th meridian, where rainfall averaged less than twenty inches a year. John Wesley Powell, geologist in charge of the United States Geographical and Geological Survey of the Rocky Mountain Region, was among the first to formulate an alternative policy. He emphasized that scientific land classification was imperative in a region containing a limited amount of arable land, dependent upon irrigation. These same circumstances demanded a more flexible formula than the rectangular, 160-acre Homestead allotment. Powell suggested that farms of 80 acres and ranches of 2,560 acres were better suited to the region. To insure equitable and efficient water-use, he proposed the establishment of irrigation and pasturage districts. Each would be controlled by nine or more individuals who would be guaranteed access and title to water. These districts might form the nucleus of rural communities; if settlers grouped their homes "to the greatest possible extent," they would benefit more than in the case of the dispersed homestead from the "local social organizations of civilization."[1]

Powell's emphasis upon the advantages of cooperative institutions and group settlement and his interest in the social implications of contrasting land-use systems represented a major contribution to the American planning tradition. He anticipated subsequent programs of scientific land-use, rural cooperation, and rural community planning. The basic principle of administered land-use, coordinated with social objectives, was as applicable to an urban setting as to a rural setting.

Landscape architects served to some degree as the urban counterpart of Powell and his successors in the conservation field. They exerted a major influence in establishing new criteria for urban form and social welfare. Post-Civil War landscape architects such as Frederick Law Olmsted, H. W. S. Cleveland, and Charles Eliot were genuine radicals who espoused the ideal of an urban-rural continuum, or continuous city-park garden. In their haste to conquer the wilderness, Americans had come to view the city as a man-made environment which subdued nature, if it did not obliterate

[1] John Wesley Powell, *Report on the Lands of the Arid Region of the United States, with a More Detailed Account of the Lands of Utah*, ed. Wallace Stegner (Cambridge, Mass.: Harvard University Press, 1962), p. 34. Originally published March, 1879.

it. Landscape architects, heirs to the romantic Gothic revival and the "picturesque" estate planning of Andrew Jackson Downing, evolved a new conception of urban form the long-range significance of which cannot be exaggerated. Their ideal was the community which "would combine the advantages of both town and country" and would "so alternate open spaces with areas occupied by dwellings that it would practically occupy one vast garden."[2]

This community norm resulted in a number of distinctive planning objectives. A naturalized urban environment or urban-rural continuum implied, first of all, a democratization of the country estate and suburb, with their attributes of spaciousness and beauty. Landscape architects sought to bring the country into the city, providing environmental amenities hitherto reserved for those who possessed mobility and wealth. In large measure, this achievement depended upon the development of a comprehensive park-boulevard system which would include not only large rural reservations, but also small neighborhood parks or squares.

Comprehensive park development necessitated long-range, systematic planning. If a city failed to reserve land for future park use according to a definite plan, it would become increasingly difficult to acquire suitable sites at reasonable prices. The ideal of a comprehensive park system directed the attention of landscape architects beyond city limits. They were among the first to emphasize the functional interdependence of city and regional hinterland and to urge the establishment of regional planning agencies. The Boston Metropolitan Park Commission pioneered in American regional planning. As early as the 1890's

it voiced the need for cooperative effort among park, water, and sewerage authorities.

In seeking a satisfactory relationship between man, space, and nature in the urban community, landscape architects not only popularized the notion of public planning, but undermined the tyranny of the gridiron subdivision. They stressed, first, the desirability of a differentiated street system. Inspired by the great boulevards of Europe, particularly those of Haussmann's Paris, they advocated their use in American cities to expedite travel, to link the units of the city-regional park system, and to serve as a kind of linear park. Basically, the standardized gridiron plan was incompatible with the urban-rural continuum principle. Often the gridiron was a form of pseudo-planning. It brilliantly served the purposes of rapid, speculative subdivision and transfer, but sacrificed existing advantages of site and topography. Landscape architects maintained that the principles of picturesque planning were as valid for the ordinary residential subdivision as for the great rural park or country estate.

The romantic suburb became the most extreme, exotic example of the naturalistic residential subdivision. Llewellyn Park (New Jersey), the first, was begun in the ante-bellum period. The romantic suburb was subsequently popularized by Olmsted and Vaux's Riverside (Illinois), where a picturesque informality contrasted sharply with the "constantly repeated right angles, straight lines, and flat surfaces which characterize our large modern town."[3] In its spaciousness, elimination of the corridor street, and

---

[2] *Report of the Board of Metropolitan Park Commissioners* (Boston, January, 1893), p. 72.

[3] "Riverside, Illinois: A Residential Neighborhood Designed over Sixty Years Ago," in *Preliminary Report upon the Proposed Suburban Village at Riverside, Near Chicago, by Olmsted, Vaux and Co.*, ed. Theodora Kimball Hubbard, *Landscape Architecture*, 21 (July, 1931), 274.

integration of human and natural environment, the romantic suburb suggested an entirely new approach to residential design.

The urban-rural continuum principle contributed to one of the great social achievements of the so-called Gilded Age. Between the 1860's and 1890's many American cities established the foundations for their modern park system. New York and Philadelphia had begun in the 1850's with Central Park and Fairmount Park, respectively. Park commissions were later established in Brooklyn, Boston, Detroit, Chicago, Indianapolis, Kansas City, Milwaukee, Minneapolis, St. Paul, and other cities. The significance of these commissions transcended that of the parks they created. They were among the first municipal planning agencies, and marked a major step in the expansion of municipal welfare functions.

In their crusade for parks and open space, landscape architects did not respond solely to esthetic imperatives. They interpreted parks as a means to the creation of an urban environment compatible with health and social stability. Parks and boulevards acted as buffers against the spread of fires. They provided a salubrious relief from the "artificial" stimuli of urban life, and in tenement districts they offered amenities "which the rich win by travel or by living in luxurious country seats." Extensive, embellished open spaces filled a void in the existence of the urban masses, setting in motion the "purest and most ennobling of external influences." They provided alternatives to "unwholesome, vicious, and destructive methods of seeking recreation."[4] Though they may have exaggerated the social advantages of parks, landscape architects pioneered in efforts to coordinate environmental and social planning in the urban community.

In certain respects, landscape architects and housing reformers pursued similar ends. Both sought to achieve social objectives through environmental melioration. Both favored a greater measure of public decision-making at the expense of private interests. They viewed the tenement park, or playground as an oasis in a concrete jungle, offering sunlight, fresh air, and opportunities to satisfy gregarious instincts in a socially permissible fashion. The park thus served as an instrument of social control.

For housing reformers, however, open space was supplementary to the main objective—enactment of legislation which imposed minimum structural and sanitary standards. In pursuit of restrictive legislation, the housing movement developed close ties with public health officials. Enforcement of housing codes was frequently assigned to health departments. Public health experts were, for obvious reasons, equally concerned with problems of overcrowding, impure water, and faulty sewerage. The accomplishments of housing reformers after 1900 were attributable, in good measure, to their association with the broader public health movement. Confirmation of the germ theory of disease had opened a new era in public health; the claims of housing reformers that substandard housing generated disease were established on a scientific, rather than empirical, basis. The struggle against tuberculosis, rampant in over-

[4] Charles Eliot, *A Report upon the Opportunities for Public Open Spaces in the Metropolitan District of Boston, Massachusetts, Made to the Metropolitan Park Commission, 1892* (Boston, 1893), p. 10; "Report of Egbert L. Viele,"

First Annual Report of the Commissioners of Prospect Park, Brooklyn (January 28, 1861), p. 28; and Frederick L. Olmsted, *The Park for Detroit* (December, 1882), p. 18.

crowded, low-income neighborhoods, cemented the alliance between the health and housing movements. Finally, as strongly as any group, health officials endorsed the principle of public environmental control, and in the process greatly enlarged the scope of municipal welfare functions.

Housing and health reformers looked upon restrictive legislation as the key to housing betterment. They also hoped that widespread investment in semi-philanthropic "model" tenements would increase the supply of good, low-cost housing. The Octavia Hill method of housing management represented a third approach. Originating in England, the Octavia Hill method implied resident supervision, high maintenance standards, and some control over the tenants' personal lives. Both the model housing and Octavia Hill schemes were designed, in effect, to withdraw low-income housing from the speculative market. Public service, rather than maximum profit, constituted the rationale for investment. Restrictive legislation, on the other hand, did not substitute for speculative development. It insured, presumably, that housing standards did not drop below statutory minimums. Otherwise, competitive market mechanisms were free to operate.

The Octavia Hill method, of course, did not produce houses. Model tenement schemes never attracted enough investors to seriouesly challenge the speculative builder. Surplus capital in an expanding economy found more profitable outlets. For all practical purposes, housing remained the province of the petty entrepreneur, tempered by community standards embodied in restrictive legislation. Despite European precedents, few proposals for direct or indirect government subsidy appeared before World War I. Beginning around 1917 a number of architects and housing economists—Edith Elmer Wood, Robert D. Kohn, Frederick L. Ackerman, and Charles H. Whitaker—launched a drive to discredit the "negative" approach to housing in favor of "constructive" European-type legislation. They looked enviously to England, Germany, and Belgium, where public housing, tax exemption, and low-interest loans to cooperatives, limited-dividend companies, or building and loan associations were used to increase the supply of low-cost housing.

Constructive housing legislation in this country was consistently opposed by Lawrence Veiller, the leading apostle of restrictive codes, founder of the National Housing Association, and author of the influential New York State Tenement House Law of 1901. Most city and state housing codes after 1901 were based upon the New York law or the model laws prepared by Veiller and published by the Russel Sage Foundation. Veiller condemned constructive legislation as socialistic and self-defeating in the long run. A limited program of government financial assistance would not supply the need; a massive program would drive out private enterprise entirely and place an enormous burden upon taxpayers.

Under Veiller's leadership the housing movement progressed in organization and effectiveness. Yet restrictive legislation possessed severe limitations. At best it could prevent the worst housing, but could not insure a sufficient supply of good housing at costs or rentals appropriate to the lowest income groups. The same objections raised against government subsidy could apply to restrictive legislation. High standards, rigidly enforced, might discourage private enterprise by cutting profit margins. Restrictive legislation, finally, did not provide adequate guidance for improvements in residential site-planning and design.

In view of the objections to constructive housing legislation in America, the only alternative way to improve housing standards while reducing costs was through progress in construction and design. Few American architects, however, applied their talents to problems of low-cost housing. I. N. Phelps Stokes of New York represented a notable exception. Stokes diverged from the mainstream of American housing reform in stressing design innovation rather than restrictive legislation. The latter, Stokes complained, not only raised costs but also discouraged experimentation and architectural creativity. Stokes linked his proposals for design innovation with an ingenious plan for urban renewal. He proposed to the New York State Tenement House Commission of 1901 that the municipality acquire and raze tenement blocks. The two perimeter strips, about 40 feet wide and running lengthwise along each block, would then be sold to limited-dividend companies, who would build tenements two rooms in depth. The central portion of the blocks would be used for parks and courts.

Nothing came of Stokes' proposals, which implied an expansion of the building unit from the single lot to the block. Working with limited capital and one or a few lots at a time, the builder had no opportunity, let alone desire, to experiment with new designs or groupings of mass and space. Decentralized and technologically primitive, the building industry could not benefit from the economies of scale. It was confronted by a challenge of mass production for which it was unequipped by modern standards of technology and management.

Implicit in the movements discussed was the belief that men could consciously control the physical and social environment of their communities. Competitive market disciplines, the "invisible hand," had not sufficed as a source of order and progress. Landscape architects and conservation leaders sought not only an enlargement of public administrative and welfare functions, but also major reconstructions in community form. The same was true of the City Beautiful movement, which flourished from approximately 1893 to 1910.

The City Beautiful, although important in the evolution of the comprehensive city planning idea in America, has frequently been described as a catastrophe. It allegedly stimulated a neo-classicism which stifled functionalist expression in architecture. An exaggerated emphasis upon municipal ornamentation and embellishment presumably diverted attention from utilitarian concerns in the formative years of American city planning. Despite its limitations, which included a failure to deal with the urban housing problem, the City Beautiful did make several useful contributions to American urban life. It helped incorporate the park movement of the nineteenth century into twentieth-century city planning. Landscape architects such as Charles M. Robinson and George E. Kessler were conspicuous among the leaders of the City Beautiful. Few of their plans lacked provision for extensive park-boulevard development. Through their work, in part, the urban-rural continuum principle entered the mainstream of twentieth-century planning. The almost universal interest in park improvement suggests, furthermore, that the City Beautiful was not entirely devoid of utilitarian or social significance. Similarly, though City Beautiful contributions to housing betterment were minimal, the movement encouraged municipal regulation of eyesores or nuisances: bill-board displays, poles, noise, and overhead wires.

In the Brunner-Carrère plan for Grand Rapids, Michigan (1909), one even finds early proposals for comprehensive zoning.

Probably the most distinctive legacy of the City Beautiful was the ideal it embodied of the city as a deliberate work of art. It aspired to universalize the beauty and planned unity which Americans had perceived in the Chicago World's Fair of 1893. The dream city which had risen along Chicago's lake front struck with the force of revelation: "The fair! The fair! Never had the name such significance before. Fairest of all the world's present sights it is. A city of palaces set in spaces of emerald, reflected in shining lengths of water which stretch in undulating lines under flat arches of marble bridges, and along banks planted with consummate skill." The Fair's vital lesson was the supreme "need of design and plan for whole cities," now that "everyone saw plainly that, though a pond be beautiful, a grassy lawn or bank beautiful, a building beautiful, all of these elements wrought into a harmonious design attain another and greater beauty, and that the beauty of the whole is superior to that of each of the several parts of the composition exploited separately."[5] The ephemeral White City stimulated a mood of dissatisfaction with the "awful monotony of ugliness" which reigned in the real cities where people lived and worked. This mood the City Beautiful translated into a quest for communities planned as works of art.

The ideal of the city as a work of art invigorated the tradition of civic design which extended back to colonial Williamsburg, Annapolis, and, not least, L'Enfant's Washington. It was necessary, however, to divest this tradition of its aristocratic connotations. Prophets of the City Beautiful thus assured Americans that the proposed civic centers, grand boulevards, and sculptural and artistic embellishments were truly democratic in contrast to the "work of art in its secluded gallery."[6] Such amenities expressed the pride of a democratic people in their communities and, like public parks, insured equal access to advantages once reserved for the affluent. The City Beautiful elevated public standards of taste and inspired a civic loyalty which transcended ethnic and class fragmentation.

The City Beautiful led to the preparation of plans for numerous American communities. These schemes usually ignored housing and other social problems, but the City Beautiful nonetheless performed a valuable service in introducing new environmental ideals. It popularized the notion that the city was more than an economic machine and that planning was necessary to prevent further visual deterioration. The City Beautiful aspired, through planning, to reconcile industrialization with the great Renaissance-Baroque and indigenous traditions of urban beautification.

A challenge to contemporary urban form, more profound in its social implications than the City Beautiful, came from the Garden City movement. First proposed by Ebenezer Howard of England in 1898, the Garden City was conceived as an alternative to the Victorian industrial city. The scheme appealed to planners disillusioned with the visual and social fruits of speculative capitalism in the urban setting; and to others who had lost confidence in market disciplines as

[5] Candace Wheeler, "A Dream City," *Harper's Magazine*, 86 (May, 1893), 833; and Daniel H. Burnham, "White City and Capital City," *Century Magazine*, 63 (February, 1902), 619.

[6] Frederick S. Lamb, "Municipal Art," *Municipal Affairs*, 1 (December, 1897), 682.

a source of urban order. It interested land and tax reformers who viewed slum housing as an inevitable consequence of high land values fostered by speculation and overcrowding. The opportunities for large-scale planning attracted socially oriented architects who believed that the maximum effectiveness of their profession depended upon the design of total environments rather than fragments.

Howard and his collaborators attempted to demonstrate at Letchworth, England the viability of Garden City principles: (1) urban decentralization; (2) the establishment of cities limited in size, but possessing a balanced agricultural-industrial economy; (3) use of a surrounding greenbelt to help limit size, and to serve as an agricultural-recreational area; (4) cooperative landholding to insure that the community rather than private individuals benefited from appreciation of land values; and (5) the economic and social advantages of large-scale planning. In the questions it raised about the form and structure of cities, and in the solutions proposed, the Garden City was perhaps the most radical of the twentieth-century urban reform movements. Letchworth, followed by Welwyn Garden City (and the New Towns after World War II), demonstrated that the Garden City represented a practical radicalism.

The Garden City, a formidable undertaking, made little progress in the United States. Americans tended to emphasize the more limited "garden suburb" as better suited to immediate, widespread application. They frequently cited England's Bournville and Port Sunlight as examples of the planned industrial garden suburb. Hampstead Garden Suburb served as a demonstration of good residential design. In their zeal to promote low-density model communities which would relieve population pressures in older cities, Americans performed something of a disservice to the Garden City. They tended to identify it with almost any variety of low-density suburban subdivision whether or not it satisfied Howard's criteria. The Garden City idea in the early American planning movement served primarily as a stimulus for more limited schemes of residential or industrial decentralization.

In seeking to convince businessmen, philanthropists, and commercial developers of the desirability of model garden communities, American reformers cited German as well as English experience. They pointed to the Krupp towns of Alfredshof and Altenhof, near Essen, and Hellerau, outside Dresden, as examples of planned worker colonies. These German and English garden communities demonstrated to their satisfaction that a practical alternative to further metropolitan centralization existed. The advantages of garden suburb-development included efficient land-use, low density, provision for recreational needs, and prevalence of the private home rather than the multi-family tenement.

American precedents for model community planning, residential or otherwise, were sparse. The romantic suburb such as Riverside, Illinois, had only limited applicability. More practical as models were the few "essentially commercial developments, usually of high-grade property, as exemplified at Garden City, L.I., and Roland Park, in the suburbs of Baltimore." A few additional semi-philanthropic and commercial subdivisions of a model variety appeared after 1910. Sponsored by the Russell Sage Foundation as a residential suburb for persons of "modest means," Forest Hills Garden (Long Island) was meant to demonstrate the application of "scientific, aesthetic, and economic principles and methods to the problem of housing civilization."[7] Even though attractive commercial subdivisions such as Forest Hills Gardens, the J. C. Nichols Country Club District (Kansas City), and Shaker Heights (Cleveland) were pale reflections of the Garden City, they served a useful purpose. They displayed the advantages of large-scale development in which streets and lots were related to "topography, building site, strategic lines of communication, uses or needs."[8]

Much interest in planned garden communities in the early twentieth century focused upon model industrial towns. Presumably, businessmen possessed not only the necessary capital, but also concrete incentives such as lower rents, more space, and significantly, a stable labor force. Nonetheless, the outstanding example of a planned industrial community in the nineteenth century may have served ultimately to discourage business firms from assuming responsibility for town development. Despite its superior physical environment, Pullman, Illinois, had not averted labor strife in the 1890's. If anything, workers resented the Pullman Company's benevolent feudalism. Employers could cite the Pullman experience in answer to the reformer's argument that housing was a legitimate concern of industry. Community planning always remained incidental to production. It was seen as a necessary evil rather than an opportunity to discharge social obligations or to pioneer in residential design.

A few companies did hire prominent architects to design new industrial towns. John Nolen was particularly prominent in this work. He prepared the plan for the garden village of the Mount Union Refractories Company at Kistler, Pennsylvania, and was also the planner for Kingsport, Tennessee. The outstanding opportunity for advanced industrial town planning was lost, however, in the founding of Gary, Indiana, by the United States Steel Corporation. By the 1920's there were only a few garden spots in the dreary desert of American industrial towns, and a handful of experiments in residential subdivision (which rarely benefited low-income groups). This limited achievement demonstrated the inadequacies of a reform program dependent upon the vision or altruism of philanthropists, employers, and commercial developers.

The concept of planned urban growth was firmly established in America by the close of the first decade of the twentieth century. In the context of the broader social reform crusade of the Progressive era, the various movements discussed helped undermine faith in competitive market disciplines as the primary source of urban progress. Profession city planning, an institutional expression of the desire for conscious, rational control of the urban environment, emerged after 1909. That year witnessed the founding of the National Conference on City Planning, followed by the American City Planning Institute in 1917. A number of universities included planning courses in their curricula. Many cities created planning commissions, usually in the form of an independent citizens body.

Following New York City's comprehensive zoning resolution of 1916, hundreds of communities enacted similar legislation. It became the planner's key technical tool, necessary for control of urban land use, but one whose limitations were not clearly recognized

[7] Grosvenor Atterbury, "Model Towns in America," *Scribner's Magazine*, 52 (July, 1912), 21, 25.
[8] J. C. Nichols, "Financial Effect of Good Planning in Land Subdivision," National Conference on City Planning, *Proceedings* (1916), p. 97.

in the early years. Zoning statutes could be manipulated for purposes of racial or class segregation. Equally important, zoning was negative in character, like restrictive housing legislation. It could prevent the worst consequences of indiscriminate land-use, perhaps, but it could not insure good site-planning and residential design. Like housing codes based upon specification rather than performance standards, zoning could thwart creativity and experimentation.

The era of professional planning, particularly by the 1920's, was marked by a gradual transformation of the planners' role from reformer to technician. Prior to World War I, the planner was necessarily a social reformer: he sought to impose land-use and other public controls over the urban environment, where none had existed previously. He had to justify planning as a necessary administrative function in the modern urban community. In the early years professional planning was affiliated with the parks, City Beautiful, Garden City, housing and other municipal reform movements which espoused normative goals and broadened the planner's perception of his function. Increasingly, however, the professional planner evolved into a technician who minimized normative goals—structural or institutional innovation—and became the prophet of the "City Scientific" or "City Efficient." Technical matters relating to zoning, law, finance, capital expenditure, and transportation became his province. He did not seek fundamental changes in urban form and structure, but projected existing demographic and institutional trends into the future as a basis for planning.

The emergence of planning as a profession coincided with a municipal efficiency crusade. Bureaus of Municipal Research were established in numerous cities in the early twentieth century.

Commission and city manager plans of government were instituted with the somewhat contradictory goals of regenerating municipal democracy and enlarging the role of the expert. These developments evolved from and nurtured the belief that the "proper administration of cities is as much of a scientific procedure as is that of directing the affairs of a large business institution, for a city is just as much of a unit as is a business concern."[9] The planner evolved as a kind of municipal efficiency expert, in charge of the physical plant.

The planner's identification with the municipal efficiency movement, the "City Scientific," helps explain his conservative viewpoint. Professionalization served as another constraint. Prior to the 1920's, planning consisted of a loose agglomeration of architects, engineers, and civic reformers who varied in background and preparation. For all practical purposes, the planner defined his own function. With the development of professional training and association came efforts to define skills, create a group identity, channel career opportunities, and determine the appropriate administrative setting for planning in the municipal hierarchy. Such rationalization, in turn, served to discourage broad reform objectives in favor of more limited goals appropriate to professional technical skills and career opportunities.

Significant in explaining the planner's role transformation by the 1920's was his increasing preoccupation with transportation problems. Planning emerged as a profession at the same time that the automobile came into widespread use. Improvements in street and circulation patterns took high priority. The transportation challenge enabled planners to exercise their technical skills and demonstrate their

[9] The City Plan Commission, *City Planning for Newark* (Newark, N.J., 1913), p. 3.

usefulness without challenging the institutional status quo. The problem of moving the urban population absorbed the planner's attention, resulting in an epidemic of proposals for street widening, traffic control, and rerouting of vehicles. Narrow streets of the pre-automobile age had become obsolete; relief from traffic congestion was the "need in cities which is attracting the most attention."[10]

As the planning profession's concern for housing and related social issues diminished towards the 1920's, the housing movement itself floundered. World War I sharply inflated housing costs, producing severe shortages throughout the nation. The speculative developer withdrew from the low-income market. In a period of scarcity and rising costs, restrictive legislation became not only ineffectual, but also irrelevant. It was not surprising that the vigorous housing reform movement of the Progressive era declined. It had reached a cul-de-sac. Restrictive legislation could not build houses, but Americans were not yet prepared to concede the necessity for government financial participation. The demonstrable inadequacies of restrictive legislation in the early 1920's did, however, lead to serious consideration of proposals for "constructive" legislation and a couple of significant experiments.

Proposals for government involvement in housing finance were scarce prior to World War I. President Roosevelt's Homes Commission, appointed in 1908, attempted to deal with the District of Columbia's notorious alley slums. But it could not acquire Congressional approval for the low-interest loans to limited-dividend companies which it recommended. Neither did Congress approve bills introduced into the House in 1913 and 1915 authorizing the use of postal savings deposits for housing loans. One minor achievement was a 1915 Oklahoma law authorizing home loans of up to $2000 by the Commissioners of the Land Office.

The most significant pre-war experiment in constructive legislation took place in Massachusetts, where a Homestead Commission had been established in 1911. Influenced by the state-assisted "back-to-the-land" movement in Australia and New Zealand, the Commission urged that Massachusetts finance a suburban demonstration project. It hoped to prove that good homes and garden plots could be erected for workers at a "reasonable profit." A successful demonstration would assist in achieving the Commission's chief goal—reversal of the trend toward urban concentration, with its many environmental and social evils. The Commission succeeded in winning a $50,000 appropriation which it used to build twelve homes in Lowell. Abolished shortly thereafter, the Massachusetts Homestead Commission transcended in significance the few homes it produced. It not only pioneered in constructive housing legislation, but also invariably related housing to broader regional considerations such as the urban-rural balance of population. The Commission stressed the economic and social advantages of careful site-planning, and in 1913 it sponsored a mandatory planning law for Massachusetts cities.

Begun after the United States entered World War I, the Commission's Lowell project was quickly overshadowed by the federal housing program of 1918–19. A serious housing shortage, particularly in armaments and ship-building centers, had forced the federal government to act in the interests of war production efficiency. Op-

[10] John Nolen, *Lancaster, Pennsylvania, Comprehensive City Plan* (Lancaster, Pa.: City Planning Commission of Lancaster, 1929), p. 30.

erating through the U.S. Housing Corporation and the Emergency Fleet Corporation of the U.S. Shipping Board, the government built homes for several thousand families. Despite the pressures of war-time haste, and shortages of labor and materials, the federal program marked a turning point in American housing. For the first time it enabled architects such as Robert D. Kohn, Frederick L. Ackerman, and Henry Wright to experiment extensively with the large-scale community planning identified with the Garden City and suburbs of England. It established a precedent for federal aid to housing, and demonstrated that government financial assistance combined with large-scale residential planning might radically improve housing conditions in American cities.

The acute housing shortage which followed the war reached its peak between 1919 and 1921, stimulating numerous proposals for government assistance. Only California, however, responded in a direct, constructive manner. The Veterans' Farm and Home Purchase Act of 1921 authorized state purchase or construction of homes and farms for sale to veterans on liberal credit terms. California invested $24 million in nearly 5,000 homes and 250 farms within seven years. Ambitious by the standards of the time, the program lacked the communitarian features of California's earlier venture in constructive housing legislation. A Land Settlement Act of 1917, based upon the recommendations of a Commission on Land Colonization and Rural Credits, had established a Land Settlement Board which sponsored the two farm villages of Durham and Delhi.

In New York State the immediate response to the post-war housing crisis consisted of a series of rent control measures and a tax exemption law which failed to limit profits or rentals.

It proved to be a speculative bonanza which increased the housing supply in New York City but did not benefit low-income groups. A continued shortage of low-cost housing, particularly in the Metropolis, and the efforts of the New York State Commission of Housing and Regional Planning, led finally to the Limited-Dividend Housing Act of 1926. This measure authorized tax exemptions for companies approved by a State Board of Housing. The legislature, unfortunately had eliminated provision for a state housing bank to supply low-cost capital. Tax exemption alone produced only a handful of apartment projects, all in New York City. The New York State Housing Law of 1926 was nonetheless significant. It combined government financial assistance with efforts through the State Board of Housing to encourage good site-planning of multi-family dwellings.

The Regional Planning Association of America (RPAA), organized in 1923, had been closely identified with the struggle to launch a constructive housing program in New York State. Throughout its ten-year existence, the RPAA remained a small, informal group, the inner circle of which consisted of three architects (Clarence S. Stein, Henry Wright, and Frederick L. Ackerman), Benton MacKaye, a forester and conservationist, and Lewis Mumford. The RPAA marked both the end and beginning of an era in housing and planning. Its program was rooted, in part, in the reform movements of the late nineteenth century and Progressive period: conservation, landscape architecture and park planning, the Garden City, housing betterment. An ideological continuity existed in the RPAA's revolt against speculative capitalism. It voiced, in an extreme way, earlier aspirations to substitute the disciplines of the expert —architectural, planning, and welfare —for those of the market.

Out of these earlier traditions, blended with a number of European influences, the RPAA forged a unique, creative synthesis. Best described as "community planning," this synthesis consisted of a unified approach to three variables which profoundly influenced the form and growth of cities: residential site-planning practices, housing costs, and the regional distribution of population, resources, and institutions. In the area of residential planning, the RPAA stressed the economic and social advantages of large-scale or "quanta" development. The group aspired, second, to combine new residential planning techniques with painstaking cost analysis. It became clear, in this connection, that the supply and cost of capital was critical; consequently, the RPAA became identified with efforts to acquire through government an ample supply of low-cost capital for home-building. Finally, the RPAA urged a regional reconstruction which encompassed the establishment of Garden Cities or New Towns, the renewal of existing cities (made economically feasible through decentralization), and preservation of the countryside.

In the case of large-scale or quanta development, the primary influence was the Garden City. It suggested to members of the RPAA the desirability of a new orientation to urban growth. They went beyond Howard's critique of metropolitan agglomeration, however, to propose not only New Towns but also a generalized process of cellular, organic city-building—by "superblock" and neighborhood units as well as entire communities. The work of Raymond Unwin and Barry Parker at Letchworth Garden City, the suburbs of Hampstead and Earswick, and the British war-housing communi-

ties provided them with concrete demonstrations in quanta planning. It was only through enlargement of the development unit, the RPAA maintained, that the architect or planner could exploit existing advantages of site and topography; benefit from the economies of scale, including street and utility expenditures; efficiently group open space; and provide in advance for the necessary complement of social and recreational facilities.

Community planning precedents in America which influenced the RPAA included the federal housing program of World War I and superior examples of industrial town development: Kingsport, Tennessee; Kistler, Pennsylvania; Neponset Garden Village, East Walpole, Massachusetts; Tyrone, New Mexico; and Indian Hill Village, Worcester, Massachusetts. Of great importance was the tradition of the romantic and garden suburb. Here the corridor street was eliminated, the subdivision scale enlarged, and the human residence integrated into its naturalistic setting. The superblock design, used by Wright and Stein at Radburn (New Jersey) and Chatham Village (Pittsburgh), incorporated all these principles. In these communities, the architects combined the quanta planning tradition and the urban-rural continuum ideal as a basis for residential subdivision.

The RPAA insisted that unified, large-scale development produced a residential environment biologically and visually superior to that of the small speculative builder, whose narrow-lot flats spanned monotonous gridiron streets. Equally important, in the eyes of the RPAA, the cellular principle of planned urban growth was better suited to the ordinary family needs of the modern urban population. If the population of residential units was known in advance, and development was unified, it was easier to plan for necessary social and commercial facilities. A distinct advantage in the use of the superblock, differentiated street system and cul-de-sac (as at Radburn and Chatham Village) was the separation of pedestrian and vehicular traffic. The efficient grouping of open space in the form of extensive recreational facilities and the superblock interior park represented another advantage of quanta planning. Members of the RPAA believed that these amenities, incorporated into the texture of the residential design, were a necessary response to the changing ratio between work and leisure time in the twentieth century. Finally, the RPAA hoped that urban growth along cellular lines would stimulate civic association. Spatially defined, visually attractive residential environments might counteract, to some extent, the centrifugal pressures of modern urban life. Such environments might reduce the vast abstraction of the city to the more comprehensible scale of the block and neighborhood. These efforts to coordinate physical and social planning were central to the RPAA's synthesis. In this respect, it diverged from the mainstream of professional planning.

Always concerned with practical matters of cost, members of the RPAA came to view the scarcity of low-interest capital as a major obstacle to housing betterment. Indeed, urban development by quanta units required great concentrations of capital in contrast to that needed by the small, speculative builder, who worked on a shoe-string equity. As mentioned earlier, the RPAA worked to establish permanent programs of government financial assistance. If limited-dividend or cooperative housing companies could be supplied with sufficient capital, the low- and even middle-income housing market might be withdrawn from the speculative sphere altogether. In es-

sence, the RPAA aspired to transform urban land and housing into public utilities rather than commodities fluctuating in a competitive market system.

The RPAA's community planning synthesis hinged, ultimately, upon its ideals of regional reconstruction. Identified particularly with Lewis Mumford and Benton MacKaye, the regional program drew from a variety of European and American sources. Mumford was greatly influenced by the Scottish biologist and planner, Patrick Geddes, who emphasized the interdependence of city and country and aspired to a regional unity of "place, work, and folk—environment, function, and organism."[11] Mumford was influenced also by the French regionalist tradition, extending from the Provençal romantics of the mid-nineteenth century through efforts to establish the region as an administrative, economic and cultural unit in the early twentieth century. French regional geographers such as Vidal de la Blanche directed Mumford's attention to the ecology of regions and the manner in which human institutions affected the balance of nature. In this country the colonial New England farm-village provided him with clues to regional development. The early New Englanders had adopted a pattern of nucleated settlement. Communities, loosely federated in a regional Congregational polity, were limited is size, but were economically balanced and inclusive in terms of necessary religious-civic institutions. From America Mumford also drew liberally upon the work of George Perkins Marsh, the nineteenth-century geographer who protested against the wanton exploitation of America's natural resources and warned of the consequences resulting

[11] Patrick Geddes, *Cities in Evolution: An Introduction to the Town Planning Movement and to the Study of Civics* (London, 1915), p. 198.

from thoughtless disruption of nature's equilibrium.

A forester by profession, a New Englander by adoption, Benton Mac-Kaye personified the indigenous regional tradition. His regional theory, expressed in the *New Exploration* (1928), combined the communitarian values of the New England farm-village, the romantic naturalism of Thoreau, and the conservationist emphasis upon scientific resource development. MacKaye was the originator of the famed Appalachian Trail and an advocate of rural electrification.

The RPAA claimed that the gasoline engine and electric power provided a technological basis for regional reconstruction. The question, essentially, was whether the residential and industrialization decentralization already in progress would be controlled, or whether it would result in a formless, low-density suburban diffusion which devoured land and produced community fragments lacking a sound economic base. The RPAA believed that this kind of decentralization was no suitable alternative to the metropolitan centralization of the nineteenth century. "Dinosaur" cities, as Stein described great agglomerations such as New York and Chicago, were neither necessary nor efficient in light of modern technology. In order to survive, they required vast overheads in the form of expenditures for transit and utility systems. Congestion of population forced intensive land utilization, creating additional overheads through inflated property values. This led to further congestion, and more intensive land use, in an endless cycle.

The process of speculative appreciation made it difficult to produce low-cost, low-density housing and discouraged liberal acquisition of land for recreational or civic purposes.

As an alternative to metropolitan centralization and suburban diffusion, the RPAA proposed the "regional city." By regional city the RPAA meant not some ideal form, but rather a new orientation to city-building in the regional context. The term suggested a regional grouping of community types of all kinds, large and small, based upon a planned regional balance of population, resources, and institutions. In the regional city pattern, size would be a function of explicit social objectives.

The RPAA marked the beginning and end of an era. It climaxed the efforts, launched in the late nineteenth century, to establish public controls over urban form and land-use. This implied a greater decision-making role for government agencies and social technicians at the expense of private business interests. In effect, the RPAA embodied the ideal of administered, planned urban growth which emerged during the Progressive period. On the other hand, the community planning synthesis of the RPAA represented a wholly new approach to urban form and social organization. Progressive era reformers aspired to ameliorate the environmental and social pathologies of existing cities; the RPAA maintained that this could not be accomplished without fundamental innovations in residential design and housing finance in a context of regional planning.

The Church and the City

Henry F. May*

Labor conflicts provided the drastic, sudden shocks that were necessary to shatter Protestant complacency. An almost equally powerful, though more gradual influence on church opinion was the rapid growth of great cities.

Industrial and commercial centers of a new scale, drawing their millions not only from Europe and Asia but also from America's rural population, were changing the nature of American society in countless ways during the last two decades of the century. As the cities became the centers of progress in the arts, sciences, business, industry and philanthropy, they developed also as breeding grounds of poverty, misery, vice and crime. In the contrast between Fifth Avenue and the disease-ridden Lower East Side, class gulfs were dramatized as never before in America. In the prewar and early postwar periods, only a small minority of the clergy had realized the menace of city conditions. Now more and more found them impossible to ignore.

In the eighties and nineties a series of religious writers, themselves overwhelmed by city realities, set themselves to the task of awakening their brethren. Charles Loring Brace, the Congregationalist reformer who devoted his life to the welfare of city children, had already published one of the first of the city exposés. In his next book Brace ventured further into analysis and increased his demand for action, charging that the church was neglecting a humanitarian tradition that

*Reprinted with permission from Henry F. May, *Protestant Churches and Industrial America*, New York, Harper & Row, 1949, 112–124. The selection here does not constitute Professor May's entire explanation of the rise of the Social Gospel (see especially his preface to the recent paperback edition, 196.

had belonged to it throughout the ages.

Besides appealing for an expansion of charitable work, Brace, shocked by the evidence of extreme inequality, called for a more just distribution of wealth. Pursuing this topic, he found much in common between Christianity and socialism, citing the early communism of the Disciples, the agrarianism of Jewish land laws, and even "a certain tone throughout the gospels, if not of 'communism,' at least in favor of greater distribution of wealth than would suit modern ideas."

By no means a radical, Brace rejected socialism on many counts. Since he was absorbed in the direct, immediate needs of the city poor for relief, he had little to say about the labor movement, though it is interesting to note the moderation of his reaction to 1877: "I believe myself that, in general, the laboring classes do not receive their fair share. Strikes are one of their means of getting more."

For some audiences, social criticism incidentally contained in such humanitarian appeals was particularly effective. Stated in terms of concrete experience and coupled with a plea for church action along comparatively familiar lines, Brace's opinions were comparatively well-received even in a period when Christians were still overwhelmingly conservative.

In the middle eighties, perhaps because of the effects of depression and labor struggle, Protestant concern with urban problems rapidly increased. The conservative *Churchman* commented favorably on W. C. Preston's *The Bitter Cry of Outcast London*, insisting, however, that reform must be "slow and patient," since if every poor family in New York were now given a good dwelling, they would be as wretched as ever in six months.

With less insistence on traditional dogma, William W. Adams described a New England factory town in the *Andover Review*. His description makes the reader see clearly the dirty brick buildings, the rows of little gray-white ramshackle houses, the swarm of hungry children, the pale, dull faces, the crowd around the saloon on payday. The only remedy he suggested, however, was a recognition by the employer of his moral responsibility.

The most stirring of all books on the problem of the city were those by Josiah Strong, a Congregationalist minister who developed strong social-Christian views. Like many of his fellows, Strong had in his youth forsaken the stern old theology, after an exhausting mental struggle, for Bushnell's more optimistic doctrines. Yet it is clear that theology alone did not determine the direction of his thought. Strong himself, discussing the end-of-the-century development of a belief in the salvation of society as well as the individual, attributed this tendency to two main causes. These were, first, "the change in civilization, during the past century, from an individual to a social type," and "the progress of science, which has revealed the interdependence of body and mind, and the influence of physical conditions on spiritual life." It is this appreciation of the importance of the environment, drawn largely from his knowledge of the new urban conditions, that gave his works their striking power.

Strong's message was conveyed in two powerful and early studies of the effects of the city. In *Our Country,* especially, Strong created a sense of momentous and immediate crisis. This crisis was important partly because it was taking place in America; Strong was full of a jingoism surpassing even Beecher's, and prophetic of imperial expansion:

> Then this race of unequaled energy, with all the majesty of numbers and the might of wealth behind it—the representative, let us hope, of the largest liberty, the purest Christianity, the highest civilization —having developed peculiarly aggressive traits calculated to impress its institutions upon mankind, will spread itself over the earth. If I read not amiss, this powerful race will move down upon Mexico, down upon Central and South-America, out upon the islands of the sea, over upon Africa and beyond. And can any one doubt that the result of this competition of races will be the "survival of the fittest"?

Despite this magnificent destiny, America's present state as described by Strong was by no means rosy. Like his contemporaries he deeply feared mass immigration, especially of Catholics. The most serious danger of all was the development in America of deep class distinctions, expressed in declining real wages and in the "feudal" brutality of some capitalists. All these dangers were at their worst in cities, where renegade Catholics, beset by poverty, made the best recruits to socialism and revolution.

In vigorous terms Strong insisted that palliative measures were not enough:

> The slums are the "putrefying sores" of the city. They may be mollified with the ointment of missions and altogether closed at one point, but it will be only to break out at another until there is a constitutional treatment which shall purge the poison of the social system.

Modern capitalists, with their power to control prices and employment, were as powerful and more irresponsible than feudal lords; their rule was "a despotism vastly more oppressive and more exasperating than that against which the thirteen colonies rebelled." The industrious laborer, not getting his share of the wealth he helped to produce, "ought not to be satisfied until justice is done him."

Strong prophesied an immediate, climactic crisis which would test our institutions gravely. This supreme peril would come when free land was exhausted. Industries and cities would be greater, class differences deeper, and eventually a terrible depression would throw millions out of work.

> . . . then, with the opportunity, the means, the fit agents, the motive, the temptation to destroy, all brought into evil conjunction, THEN will come the real test of our institutions, then will appear whether we are capable of self-government.

Despite these apocalyptic predictions Strong was essentially neither radical nor pessimistic. Socialism and individualism, social responsibility and property rights could be reconciled if the church took up her proper mission and became "the controlling conscience of the social organism." If this came about, all problems would be solved—socialism would disappear, Christian principles of private property would be reaffirmed, the struggle of capital and labor would be ended by co-operation and commercial dishonesty would disappear.

This was the alternative which Strong continually presented, catastrophe or regeneration. And, for all his dire warnings, Strong was enough of an American optimist to be confident that the nation would choose the road of salvation. His fervent, evangelistic appeal, pointing to fearful perils and offering bright hopes, was

cut in a pattern calculated to appeal to thousands of Christians. *Our Country* was, appropriately, published by the American Home Missionary Society, a fact regretted by the *Christian Union* only because "Its circulation ought not to be confined to Congregationalists, nor to the clergy, nor even to church people." A repeated best seller, *Our Country* was the *Uncle Tom's Cabin* of city reform.

Two years later it was followed by a similar city exposé, S. L. Loomis' *Modern Cities*. Loomis shared to the full Strong's virulent suspicion of the foreign-born and especially the Catholic workingman:

> With some important exceptions those who come from foreign lands, both Catholics and Protestants, bring with them most crude and imperfect notions of religious truth. No Christian culture lies behind them. They have never breathed a Christian atmosphere. Ideas with which all Americans, whether of pious parentage or not, have been familiar from childhood, are strange to them. . . . The whole method of our services, adapted to the cultured, Christianized elements of our society, is so far above them that it fails to secure their interest and attention. When one of them strays into a church, the chances are that he finds nothing there for him.

As an aspect of his discussion of evangelistic difficulties, Loomis pointed out that the industrial worker often received low wages, worked long hours, and was subject to recurrent unemployment. The breach between employer and employee was widened by trade-unions, for which Loomis had little use. Partly because of the class feeling developed by unions, immigrant laborers avoided Protestant city churches. Because these institutions were "usually attended and sustained by persons of means and intelligence," the misguided workingmen considered them "the churches of the capitalists." It was this separation from good influences that, to Loomis, explained the serious growth of corruption, drink, crime, pauperism and anarchism, all of which *Modern Cities* described in frightening terms.

Like Strong, Loomis confined his proposals for a solution to an increase in Christian evangelism, especially for the lower classes. To be effective, city evangelists must, he urged, know the conditions of the urban poor and give a respectful hearing to their complaints and proposed remedies, no matter how misguided these might be.

Loomis' book, more conventional in its approach than Strong's and somewhat less startling in its language, was also well received by the church press. The drastic impact of Strong and Loomis on contemporary Protestant opinion was further demonstrated by one of their few adversaries, a southern Methodist minister named John B. Robins. Robins, admitting that the two books had been "generally read and universally commended," attacked them for presenting too gloomy a prospect. Great wealth, he said, was not a curse but a blessing, the natural result of Christian progress; immigrants and even their church would be altered for the better by the spirit of the time.

As for socialism, Robins pointed out, correctly, that Strong had given a disproportionate emphasis to the doctrine of small anarchist groups, disregarding moderate and gradualist socialist schools. Less conservative than his opponents, Robins believed that the existing order, with its inequality and oppression, was intolerable, and approved the discontent that had produced socialism. In time, he predicted, socialism's "selfish" elements would

vanish under the beneficent influences of Christian American institutions and "This movement, with its obnoxious qualities eliminated, exalted by human sympathy, and glorified by human compassion, will yet reform, bless and crown our industrial and social systems.

Full of the spirit of the new theology, Robins rested his confidence in the future on God's guidance of the world through the Immanent Christ. Though he was more receptive than his opponents to new social ideas, his mystical optimism made the total effect of his book almost quietistic. For the public of the eighties, Strong's mixture of vivid exaggeration and strenuous evangelism was undoubtedly more effective.

At the end of the decade a number of books on city conditions made some impression on clerical readers. In 1889 Helen Campbell's striking *Prisoners of Poverty* attacked hardhearted clergymen who ascribed poverty to vice and confined their preaching to "thou shalt nots": "To souls that sit at ease and leave to 'the power that works for righteousness' the evolution of humanity from its prison of poverty and ignorance and pain, it is quite useless to speak." Jacob Riis' stirring and widely-read *How the Other Half Lives* appeared in condensed form in the *Christian Union,* immediately following a condensation of Booth's *In Darkest England.*

In 1891 Louis A. Banks, a Boston Methodist minister, described to his congregation the disgusting conditions prevalent in the city's sweat-shops. Banks' concrete details were so shocking and his indignation so telling that the sermons aroused something of a storm. A sample letter from a member of his congregation cited standard economic doctrine to prove that the sweaters were doing a favor to the women and children they employed and warned Banks against arousing class hatred.

W. T. Stead, a British journalist of strong Protestant beliefs and reformist social convictions, published in 1894 a plea for city reform that had almost as great an impact on religious circles as *Our Country*. In language even more sensational than Strong's, Stead described Chicago's miserable present and exalted future. Agreeing with many of its citizens, Stead believed that the Windy City was the future world's capital. This gave increased point to his vivid descriptions of police brutality and venality, protected vice, corrupt politicians, inadequate charities, taxes that fleeced the poor and other present evils.

Stead's proposed remedy was typical of the evangelist approach. The city was to be regenerated through a new "Church Catholic and Civic." Since existing Protestant churches were rich men's clubs, the new civic church would arise out of the city government which, whatever its shortcomings, at least recognized the principle of human brotherhood by its inclusion of all citizens. Administrative reforms would be made, the "Devils" of Plutocracy, Intolerance, and Intemperance would be cast out, and close relations would be established between the church and labor unions, to the benefit of both.

Stead wound up his book with a prophetic description of twentieth-century Chicago that might stand as a monument to the hopes of the nineteenth-century reformer. In his picture of the future the Church of Chicago, with the Catholic archbishop as president and Jenkin Lloyd Jones, a liberal Unitarian minister, as vice-president, rules the city by the golden rule. "On the word of a patrolman" has become the standard phrase to express complete honesty. Marshall Field and Siegel, Cooper and Co. have both been given to the city with their complete stocks. The churches in the working-class districts are surrounded at the dinner hour by "grimy" workmen listening to organ recitals over their dinner pails. In a rousing climax, the book describes a civic reception to the German Emperor, who has crossed the ocean to see for himself Chicago, the ideal city of the twentieth-century world.

Stead's book did not bring all Chicago immediately to the mourner's bench, and the most loyal Chicagoan must admit that twentieth-century realities have fallen short of his dream. Yet the book was not entirely without concrete results. Its message was first delivered to a huge mass meeting, theoretically representing all classes. From this meeting stemmed the Civic Federation of Chicago, a powerful reform pressure group. Some slight temporary success was achieved by efforts for church-labor co-operation, and the city's ministers federated for district social work. An organization arising out of labor unions and calling itself "The Modern Church" preached a crusade for humanity once a fortnight in the Labor Temple. The book was roundly damned by the city's secular newspapers, while local religious journals remained half impressed and half indignant. Perhaps the greatest single tribute to its effectiveness was the sudden disappearance of the stocks of the first edition, evidently bought up by "the interests." Stead helped to open the eyes of religious and social-minded people to urban evils and played some part in the development of the semi-religious reform spirit that was rife in the Chicago of Jane Addams and Florence Kelley.

Like *Uncle Tom's Cabin* or *The Jungle,* these dramatic exposures of city evils were effective, not because of any originality, but because they described conditions which many people knew something about. Thousands of ministers were experiencing at first-hand the conditions described by Strong or Stead.

To many Christians the most shocking fact was that which was simplest and most easily realized; that city wage earners were staying away from church. Even in the early seventies, realistic Protestants had pointed to this gloomy fact. Now the problem of the "unchurched masses," usually linked to the threats of drink, Romanism and radicalism, dominated the discussions of many denominational and interdenominational groups and was widely argued in the religious press.

Some Protestant writers still refused to admit the reality of the menace, denying that the church was losing ground with a touchy indignation that seemed to make the failure all the more obvious. In 1881 Daniel Dorchester published a volume designed to refute any idea that all was not well, concluding from his interpretation of census figures that the churches were increasing three times as fast as the population. These conclusions were gleefully attacked by the always somewhat anticlerical *Nation,* which pointed out that Dorchester and other optimistic clerics were guilty of such statistical lapses as counting children among church members, and then multiplying members by four to account for "children and other adherents." The argument was widely taken up by optimists and pessimists alike.

Other church comment, admitting the fact of the lack of working-class attendance, tended still to accept the loss complacently. In 1883, for instance, a Protestant spokesman answering a critic turned the argument around:

It does not need proof that the classes which are eminently non-intelligent or non-respectable, are . . . like our friend, almost to a man, non-church-goers. . . . Church members average much more moral, intelligent, and wealthy that non-church-members. This is the natural result of their church-training.

The *Andover Review* also considered it

. . . by no means a result altogether of evil that the churches stand for what is respectable and even refined, nor within proper limits, that certain lines of social cleavage appear in the group of people in denominations and in the several churches. . . . Let the fact be recognized, then that as the church includes the better classes of society, it will be disliked by the worse classes who are yet outside. . . .

Most clerical opinion, however, by now both admitted and deplored the fact of working-class alienation and sought for diagnosis and remedy. By the middle eighties only a few Protestants were suggesting an explanation that later seemed obvious: that workingmen stayed away from church because the churches were indifferent or hostile to labor's most pressing demands. This sweeping answer was suggested in 1884 by a letter to the *Homiletic Review* from John Swinton, a radical but Christian labor journalist. It is not surprising that the editors felt obliged to apologize for printing Swinton's "severe, and, as we think, undeserved, censure upon the clergy as a body." The letter, one of the first of many similar attacks from labor spokesmen, indicted ministers for indifference to suffering and injustice, claiming that in a long career of fighting the battles of the poor the author had never encountered a clergyman on the side of reform. Church philanthropy he dismissed as an emphasis on superficial at the expense of basic evils. The first thing for the churches to do, Swinton bitterly concluded, was to learn something of the conditions of the poor. "Whether they would reach the masses then seems a vain question; for I do not think that one-tenth of the wage-earning classes in New York believe in Christianity at all: but let them try."

The *Homiletic Review's* reply demonstrated complete unfamiliarity with the point of view which prompted this attack. In answer to Swinton's charge that church philanthropic enterprise was either futile or of secondary importance from *labor's point of view,* the editors cited instance after instance of charity, evangelism, and even work for the causes of anti-obscenity and antidivorce.

Yet some more social-minded ministers were wondering whether there might not be a grain of truth in such charges as Swinton's. Undoubtedly the realization of working-class alienation caused many Protestant leaders to re-examine their social attitudes.

The most immediate and concrete result of the challenging disclosures was, however, a tremendous expansion of the evangelical and welfare work already under way. Snobbish congregations were urged to be more hospitable to ill-dressed worshipers; churches that had moved to new residential neighborhoods established missions in the slums; revival meetings were directed specifically at city workers. More important, the social settlement movement, started in America in the eighties and flourishing by the nineties, brought knowledge of the lives of city populations to young ministers. Institutional churches with their clubrooms and gymnasiums, co-operative city missions, young people's organizations, brotherhood and deaconess societies and all the familiar paraphernalia of American Protestant welfare work grew and flourished during these years. The Salvation Army, imported in 1880, brought city poverty to the attention of many by its spectacular methods.

The whole movement of institutional expansion arose from the evangelical and humanitarian problems of the city. Essentially untheoretical in itself, it nevertheless exerted an important indirect influence on church social theory. In the long run, welfare work was bound to bring into question the traditional dogmas on the nature of poverty and wealth.

These dogmas did not give in without a fight. Some opponents of the new institutions still pointed out the peculiar blessings of poverty or its indispensability to progress and civilization; others continued to insist that misery was always a punishment for vice. Still others, like a writer in the *Independent,* insisted

> Let one half the money now given to temporal aid be expended in spiritual work in preaching the Gospel, and the poor will be better provided for and suffer less than they would, if ten times that amount were bestowed upon them in charity.

Even some of those who accepted the new movements reconciled them with the old doctrines. Urban ills and institutional methods could be seen as new versions of poverty and charity, both of which might still be considered as part of God's plan rather than as manifestations of social failure. New methods of social work were seen by some as new means for the traditional Christian duty of giving alms; almsgiving promoted religion and prevented unrest. Conservatively interpreted, church philanthropy could serve as an antidote to social criticism rather than as a cause of it.

Inevitably, however, some of the

sensitive young ministers and laymen who spent grim years in city missions, trying to relieve poverty that seemed to increase, learning to know as individuals people whom the last generation had labeled "the vicious poor," found themselves unable to accept the conventional complacent explanations of poverty.

Charles L. White, describing the work of the American Baptist Home Missionary Society among urban immigrants in the nineties, stated that the missionaries usually "have taken the part of labor, contending for its rights," although they have maintained a firm stand against "violence." Graham Taylor, one of the leading exponents of settlement training for ministers, explained his own early and doubtless typical reaction to this kind of experience:

As men came up from the pitfalls dug by themselves and others, they taught me, on the one hand, that the fallen could rise, and, on the other hand, that the conditions under which they fell could and should be changed, so as to make it easier to live right and harder to go wrong in every community.

In 1896 the College Settlement Association sent to the residents in its settlements a questionnaire which asked, among other things, whether the recipients' "attitude toward social and industrial questions" had undergone any changes during settlement residence. Some answered that they had become more conservative, "convinced that spiritual evils were far worse than temporal," or that "the social question will in no degree be solved by sympathy toward one class to the exclusion of another." Others were perplexed, stirred without having reached conclusions. A third group became definitely more sympathetic to the efforts of working people to bet-ter their own condition, convinced even "that the only weapon of the poor against the oppression of competition was in organization to maintain their rights." These three groups probably represented adequately the reactions of church settlement workers. Which was the largest group cannot be determined.

A by-product of church experience in cities was a changed attitude toward immigration. Despite widespread clerical hostility to some immigrant groups, church writers up to the early eighties usually opposed restriction, particularly when it was demanded by organized labor. Church papers continued especially to defend the Chinese, praising their thrift and docility, contrasting them unfavorably with their union opponents. The *Congregationalist* in 1884 still represented prevailing church opinion when it opposed restriction except for Mormon converts and socialist-anarchists.

Gradually, however, fear of the effects of immigration became more powerful than the traditional reasons for opposing restriction. The Irish had never been as hospitably received as the Chinese. In 1881 the *Watchman* complained of their radical influence on the American working class. Southern and eastern Europeans, often painted as free-thinkers and socialists, were no more popular among Protestant spokesmen. As writers like Strong depicted urban centers of radicalism and irreligion swarming with immigrants, church attitudes toward immigration altered. By the end of the decade even conservative Protestants were beginning to agree with labor's demand for restriction, though different grounds were urged.

In many ways, both tacit and expressed, American Protestants in the eighties and nineties were stirred and shaken by the great changes in American life which cities made manifest.

Washington Gladden, describing the effect of his early experience in Brooklyn, spoke for a generation:

One could not help wondering whether in liberating the force which gathers men into cities, and equipping it with steam and electricity, a power had not been created which was stronger than the intelligence which seeks to control it; whether such aggregations of humanity, with wills no better socialized than those of the average nineteenth-century American, are not by their own action self-destructive. I do not mean that I reasoned out this query, at that time; but some sense of the appalling nature of the municipal problem was certainly present with me.

7 Metropolitanization

The appearance and growth of the metropolis and its eventual dominance of the national landscape is the principal theme of American urban history in the twentieth century. Nineteenth-century urbanization has been treated by historians as the development of separate communities. Rarely, however, were the larger communities self-contained; they served instead as centers for a hinterland. The regional centers had emerged in consequence of geographic conditions, economic and technological factors, and the drive for power. As Julius Rubin pointed out in Section 2, regional centers quite early had some of the characteristics of a metropolis, albeit not the name. In time, the distinction between urban and rural within a fluid geographic area disappeared, and the modern metropolis, as we define it now, came into being. By 1910 the federal census recognized the emergence of this phenomenon and designated twenty-five metropolitan districts, each encompassing a central city of at least 200,000 people and adjacent integrated areas. By 1940 a majority of Americans lived in areas thus defined. Americans had become metropolitan even before they had become aware that they were members of a

society that was no longer rural but urban. It is the rapidity of the process of metropolitanization and the lack of sufficient awareness of what was happening that partially explains the urban crisis of the 1960's.

Emigrants from the farm and immigrants from abroad provided the increase in population which contributed to urban growth. The newcomers filled the center city, while the older inhabitants began moving to the suburbs. The reasons for this pattern of movement may be seen in the economic and technological changes that took place during the industrial revolution. A division of labor evolved in which the central city provided personal services and specialized economic, social, cultural, and educational functions for a larger population. Improvements in building techniques, communication, and transportation, particularly the automobile, permitted increased density, while at the same time encouraged the exodus to the suburbs. As people on the periphery of cities, through their work or need for city services, began to interact with people in the core, they contributed to the metropolitanization process. The new close relationship between city and suburb was fostered by the lure of the city on the one hand, the traditional American anti-urban attitude on the other, and government policies favoring home ownership and low-density development. Support for highway construction, zoning regulations and home financing funds, particularly through the G. I. Bill of Rights after World War II, encouraged the dispersion of the population. Indeed, the same forces which earlier had made possible classical urbanization were now, in the twentieth century, making possible metropolitan dispersion.

The concept of a metropolitan region involves more than simply the political boundaries of the central city and a broader area of high-density population. In defining a metropolis, one must consider the multiple relationships that develop between the core and its hinterland. People who live outside city limits but who work, seek services, purchase goods, and use the cultural and leisure-time facilities in the central city, are very much a part of the metropolis. Old communities, once self-contained, and new suburbs carved out of farmland develop over time economic, social, and cultural linkages with the region's urban center. Through the growth of this interdependent complex the metropolis emerges. Some scholars interpret the end result of this process as a new socio-economic entity. The historian must describe not only the phenomenon but also the process and its implications for human and institutional development.

In the selections that follow, the authors argue that metropolitanization represents a new form of human settlement. The readings treat the historical processes that molded it, the nature of its structure, and the advantages and problems that characterize it. In the 1920's, faced with old problems compounded and grown more complex, people developed what one author terms a "metropolitan consciousness." Furthermore, among the newer directions that urban patterns took was decentralization into suburbia, as exemplified specifically by Los Angeles. Finally, such areas began to cluster together, and by mid-century the movement had gone from metropolis to megalopolis.

This section suggests only implicitly the many problems of twentieth-century America. A more explicit discussion is left for the following section.

The Outburst of the Metropolis

Blake McKelvey*

Americans, curious about the growing diversity and complexity of their society, found much to ponder in the 1920 Census. Not only did they now for the first time exceed 100 million in number, but a clear majority of them were urbanites, and more than two-thirds of these were residents of one or another of the fifty-eight metropolises that had absorbed over half the decade's population gains. Few observers could view the tabulation of that growth without projecting it forward to 1930 and beyond. Even *The New York Times* looked ahead with forebodings to 1950, when a predicted population of 194,208,566, most of it crowded into cities, would, its experts warned, face a diminishing food supply. In contrast, urban spokesmen throughout the country happily saw their towns soaring to new heights, both numerically and physically.

A surge of vitality did in fact enliven most of the great cities. Thronging with newcomers from many sources, they progressively absorbed an ever-larger share of the nation's productive energies and brought it a new burst of prosperity. Although the status they achieved as statistical units in the census tables had no substance in administrative law, most of the fifty-odd metropolises developed a very real sense of their identity as communities. Citizen leaders in many places hastened in the early twenties to tackle the new problems that appeared on every hand. Undaunted by the mounting burdens, they strove to check the fragmentation of local government and to lay the foundations for metropolitan action.

ACCELERATED METROPOLITAN GROWTH

Everybody knew, long before the preliminary census data appeared in November 1920, that the big cities were bursting their seams. A widespread housing shortage, advancing rents, overcrowded schools, and mounting congestion in the streets, all reflected the rapid population growth of the leading metropolitan centers. Yet these and other inadequacies failed to check the flood of newcomers from rural areas, North and South, as well as many again from abroad. Instead, the overcrowded central cities proceeded to disgorge and scatter an increasing number of their former inhabitants over the adjoining territory and into satellite towns. Thus the rapidity of their growth helped to determine the structural character as well as the problems of the emerging metropolises.

Accelerated indirectly by the war, the metropolitan movement acquired a new momentum. Servicemen, the majority of whom had hailed from rural districts, flocked by the thousands to the great cities, both adding to their problems and contributing to their vitality. Immigrants from abroad, reduced to a trickle during the war, bounded from a low of 110,000 in 1918 to 430,000 in 1920 and to 805,-000 the next year, and most of these newcomers crowded into the big cities where their relatives and ethnic fellows could help them find shelter and jobs. War workers, recruited in great

*Reprinted with permission from Blake McKelvey, *The Emergence of Metropolitan America, 1915–1966*, New Bruswick, N.J.: Rutgers University Press, 1968, © 1968 by Rutgers, the State University.

numbers from rural areas, many from the South, had acquired new urban tastes and skills and seemed more inclined to bring their younger brothers and sisters to the cities, even when jobs were scarce, than to return themselves to the farms.

The old questions as to which came first, jobs or people, was tentatively dodged by the metropolis as it drew newcomers from many sources and for a great variety of reasons, only one of which was the employment at higher wages that they hoped to find. Most newcomers had no specific jobs in view, and often weeks passed before they found any. All that the majority knew was that employment was depressed on the farms and the wages even more so. Fortunately the inrush of people itself created jobs and stimulated enterprising men to launch new ventures.

Los Angeles was the prime example of such a town. Profiting from the high repute of its southern California climate, from the glamour of its film studios, and from the recent discovery of oil in its soil, the mushrooming city ranked third in rate of growth by 1920, and second by 1930. In a few short decades it had become the fourth metropolis in size without developing a specialized industrial base or even a definable business center.

In contrast, Akron and Detroit, first and second in rate of growth among the metropolises of 1920, were building on a plentiful supply of factory jobs. As the leading producers, respectively, of tires and cars, they prospered from the expanding demand for automobiles. Houston, Oklahoma City, and Tulsa, among other oil producers, benefited in another way from that industry. As Southern towns with vast hinterlands, they had the additional advantage of growing up with newly awakened regions; as a result they managed by diversification to maintain high growth rates for a longer period than, for example, more specialized and more constricted Akron.

The cities that really captured the lead in the twenties, however, were the resort towns. Recreation centers, such as Atlantic City and St. Petersburg, had drawn crowds of visitors in earlier years and in sufficient numbers to maintain growing staffs of permanent residents. But it was in the twenties that retirees and other citizens began to settle in large colonies at these and other resorts, boosting them into the front rank in urban growth. Miami, with a 234.4 per cent increase in the twenties, outdistanced even Los Angeles, whose 133 per cent growth, partly due to the same factors, assured it second place. At least five of the top ten in metropolitan growth were resort cities or drew newcomers because of the attractions they offered as residential centers.

Yet more important statistically to urban growth than either recreation or industry were the commercial and service functions that characterized the emerging metropolis. For the first time since the start of the industrial revolution in America almost a century earlier, the steady rise of that portion of the nation's employed who were factory workers was checked; after reaching a peak of 30.8 per cent in 1920, they dropped in the course of the decade to 28.9 per cent. Even in such predominantly industrial metropolises as Detroit and Pittsburgh, Milwaukee and Rochester, the largest gains were recorded in the trade, clerical, or professional categories. Of the seven metropolises with 50 per cent or more employed in industry in 1920, only Akron retained that ratio a decade later, and its growth was now the second slowest in the group.

This diversity reflected a highly significant trend of the twenties—the increased productivity of industrial man-hours. Thus, while the number of persons engaged in manufacturing dropped between 1923 and 1928 from 96.3 to 90.0 per cent of the 1919 total, the volume of production increased from 122 to 136 per cent of the former level. Moreover, the output per person mounted in these years from 126.7 to 149.5 per cent of the 1919 rate despite a drop in the average number of hours per week. The increased output of the cities, accompanied by the increased leisure, created new jobs in distribution, in service, and in recreation. And since the real wages of all employed workers likewise rose in these years from 119 to 132 per cent of the 1919 base, the cities, especially the great metropolises, were better able to sustain the commercial, civic, and cultural functions that characterized the great central cities. These activities included the huge department stores and specialty shops, the banks and hotels and restaurants, the towering office blocks and civic administrative clusters, the theatres and museums and galleries, all of which competed for downtown space, as well as the parks and zoos and public and private sport arenas and other resorts that clustered around the outskirts of the affluent cities.

Of course the importance of those functions most characteristic of the metropolis was more apparent in large centers already securely established than in cities still striving to gain admittance to that category. Among the latter, except for the half dozen resort cities and another half dozen state capitals whose administrative functions were increasing rapidly, an expanding industrial base was of prime importance. What was essential, in any case, was an activity that produced a surplus beyond the local need (the "export-base construct," as later economists would name it) either for export or to attract visitors or traders or new industries into town. A regional source of fuel for power could provide the means for a "takeoff," but in the densely urbanized Northeast, a basic industry serving outside markets generally supplied the chief ingredient of growth.

The increased output per industrial man-hour, by boosting the return on capital, speeded technological developments that brought new industries and expanded old ones. Moreover, labor organizations, or the mounting fear that low wages would promote them, induced management, following Henry Ford's lead, to share the returns of the larger output with the workers in sufficient measure to create an expanding market for the consumer goods now in more plentiful supply. With the additional aid of new forms of consumer credit, the public not only absorbed the flood of cars and earlier products but also bought up the new radios and other items that helped to create new industrial opportunities.

Many of the older metropolises benefited as the new industries swelled their local exports; several of the fourteen cities first included in the metropolitan tables in 1920 also demonstrated their industrial vitality. Some of the newcomers would thrive as regional centers, San Antonio and Salt Lake City, for example, but others, such as Akron and Youngstown, won a secure place among the leading industrial cities. Most of the thirty-five included in that group contributed to the increased output that added 26 per cent to the value of the nation's manufactured products during the twenties. And at the close of the decade, when a new census definition lowered the population requirement, most of the thirty-nine cities added to the metropolitan category had strong industrial specialties. Some like Canton, Ohio, Chattanooga, Tennessee, Flint, Michigan, and South Bend, Indiana, would have made it under the old definition.

The optimism that mounting numbers engendered among a town's inhabitants often disappeared when the same citizens considered the threat that overpopulation posed to the nation. This concern, which overshadowed the opposing fear that cities, because of their low birth rates, would deplete the nation's population, was aggravated in the early postwar years by sensational predictions of food shortages to come, as well as by the inadequate supply of housing and the unemployment that spread from city to city in 1920 and 1921. News reports of a rising flood of immigrants added to the alarm and helped to replace the Americanization movement of the war period with an exclusionist campaign.

Many forces contributed to the change in policy. Old and predominantly rural hostilities toward foreigners, especially those of the Catholic or the Jewish faith, were fanned into intense hatred by extremist groups such as the Ku Klux Klan and by nativist spokesmen such as Lathrop Stoddard and Henry Ford. The formerly strong opposition of some industrial leaders to a policy of immigrant exclusion had been shaken by the Red scare that swept the country after the Bolshevik revolution. Organized labor, alarmed in its turn by the wide extent of unemployment, moved for a temporary suspension of immigration. But neither these representatives of urban economic interests nor the progressive friends of the immigrants in many cities could support the extreme measures proposed by the exclusionists in 1920. After long debate a temporary quota system, advanced as a compromise, finally won adoption in 1921.

Boston and New York quickly became aware of the hardships imposed by the new law. A crisis developed as the steamship lines, frantic to deliver their immigrant passengers before the quotas were filled, brought thousands of eager migrants to these principal ports. Soon the accommodations on Ellis Island were jammed to capacity, and several boatloads of disappointed immigrants had to be returned to Italy and Poland, whose quotas were most seriously overtaxed. Industrialists, ready late in 1922 to employ additional workers, joined many disinterested friends of the immigrants, as well as their ethnic societies, in protesting this inhuman policy. As recovery dispelled the fear of unemployment, labor leaders too became less opposed to immigration; in fact their success in forming laborers' unions in several cities in 1923 kindled a new interest in these unskilled newcomers.

But if the major urban groups were ready to permit the 1921 law to expire, the nativists both rural and urban were girding to replace it with a stronger measure. Not only were they determined to cut the annual quota from 3 to 2 per cent, but they proposed to shift the census base from 1910 to 1890 in order both to reduce the size of the total and to alter its ethnic character. The earlier count, which antedated the great wave of immigrants from Southern and Eastern Europe, promised a selection of newcomers more in keeping, they declared, with the traditional American stock. This prospect attracted support from the South and the West and also from rural districts in the Northeast. In an effort to make it more palatable to representatives of the industrial states, Pennsylvania Senator David A. Reed introduced an amendment providing that a rationing system based on the national origins of the current population be substituted after two years for the 1890 base. That stipulation was accordingly adopted in the new Immigration Restriction Act of 1924.

The new law sharply reduced the flow of immigrants, but it did not seriously check the growth of cities. When the migrants from abroad declined from 706,000 in 1924 to an average of 300,000 annually for the rest of the decade, the cities responded by drawing increased numbers from rural America. For the first time the farming population, despite its high rate of births, dropped almost a million in number as some 6 million left for near and distant cities. Migrants from the South to the North increased in number, both Negro and white, and again most of them headed for the great metropolises. Generally, as in the previous decade, they followed the principal rail lines into the North, overshadowing in the process the old east-west migration. But while the South sent over a million to Northern cities, its rural districts contributed more than twice as many to the cities and towns of the South.

In some Northern cities such as Buffalo, not on a direct north-south route, the in-migrants hailed from widely scattered cities and towns, rather than from a restricted local or distant hinterland. Most Northern cities continued to attract immigrants from abroad, and in the twenties these newcomers still equaled natives of the state moving from the farms and outnumbered migrants from the South by approximately 4 to 1. Only the heavy-industry metropolises and a few others that had drawn a large influx from that region during the war years continued to pull strongly from that direction. As a result most cities, in the South as well as the North, received a more diversified mix of newcomers than ever before.

In Chicago, Detroit, Pittsburgh and St. Louis, however, and a half dozen more, including New York, the migration from the South was accelerated. Indeed their dependence on it was strengthened after 1924 when the new immigration quotas drastically reduced the number admitted from Southern and Eastern Europe, which had for three decades supplied the unskilled labor their heavy industries required. In some, notably Detroit, new colonies of Southern whites also appeared; in others the already congested Negro districts overflowed their boundaries, occupying especially those tracts whose ethnic quotas were most drastically curtailed. In West Philadelphia, for example, they acquired homes sold by Jews moving up the ladder. In Chicago the black belt extended southward, and two new colonies of Negroes developed in former Jewish and Italian districts. In New York City, which attracted 170,000 additional Negroes, more than doubling its total, Harlem presented an ideal location. Not only were its accommodations relatively modern and its prospects in 1920 bright, but the Italian and Jewish colonies there, lacking sufficient replacement, offered little resistance to the mounting wave of newcomers. These included Spanish-speaking Negroes from the West Indies, over 50,000 in number, and other thousands from the cotton fields of the Deep South; by 1930 the nonwhite population of Harlem had reached 164,566, making it the largest community of Negroes in the land.

Together the Northern cities absorbed during the twenties over 600,-000 Negro migrants from the South. While some of these came from Southern cities, the urban centers of the South more than recouped their losses by attracting other Negro migrants from their hinterlands. Altogether the rural districts of the South sent some

1.5 million Negroes to Northern and Southern cities, and despite their high birth rates the rural Negroes dropped slightly in number. For the first time Negroes resident in urban centers exceeded those on the farms by at least a half million. With another two million resident in villages, chiefly in the South, the 5.2 million urban Negroes did not quite match the whites whose urban percentage was now 57.7, yet the Negro's urban gains during the twenties were more striking, and in fact they were most dramatic in the rapidly growing metropolises, which by 1930 numbered 96 places and included 54,753,645 residents.

EXPANDING METROPOLITAN PATTERNS

Whatever the sources of their growth, the big cities drew more newcomers than they could accommodate in traditional ways, and many for the first time disgorged more inhabitants than they attracted. The changing character of the in-migrants spurred the outward movement of former residents in some places, but changes in urban transportation, in industrial technology, and in housing standards were equally if not more responsible for the new suburban expansion that converted a score of growing cities into budding metropolises and spread the outer limits of several of the older ones to more than double their former size. This expansion, which was in some respects a flight from the city, helped to transform the prototype of the central city and gave shape to the largest community that surrounded it.

Of course the suburban migration dated back many decades in most cities, but it began in the twenties to acquire a new character. The streetcar suburbs and steam-train satellites of an earlier date had had an independent, small-town quality that gratified the nostalgic yearnings of many urbanites who romanticized the village community. Harlan Douglass described one as seen from an outlying hilltop in Union City, New Jersey, in 1925: "In the immediate foreground lies the Village. Its three spires lift their points, and one who knows can pick out the school, the Woman's Club building, the cluster of stores, and the plaza of the railway station. Its inhabitants, half-buried in foliage, are uncrowded."

With the advent of the automobile as a commuting agent, the aspects of suburbia changed radically. Every side road drew its venturesome settlers, some of whom laid out spacious estates and erected villas to match, while others built their own houses in the long evenings and newly acquired weekends that stretched out over a period of years and often saw the open spaces, which had drawn them there, gradually fill up with other escaping urbanites. As the number of auto registrations mounted from 8 to 17 million in the early twenties, and to 23,060,421 by the close of the decade, the number of families migrating to the suburbs also multiplied. The open spaces between the old villages and the satellite cities attracted a third of these migrants and grew more rapidly than any other urban category.

Many of the older suburbs enjoyed an impressive growth, too. Around Atlanta, Cleveland, Milwaukee, and Buffalo, among other rapidly growing metropolises, the incorporated suburbs increased 100 per cent or more. Some of these were or now became industrial suburbs, and in the early twenties, during the heyday of the interurban trolleys, their prosperity seemed assured and their growth helped to boost the average for small cities above that of the large-city category. They were, however, integral and dependent

parts of metropolitan districts, as became evident toward the close of the
decade when collapsing interurbans
seriously blighted their growth.

Yet the central cities were still absorbing the largest share of the urban
gains. Although their percentage of the
increase dropped from 70.7 to 54.8
during the twenties, numerically their
growth exceeded by a half million that
of the same cities in the previous decade. In many places these newcomers
occupied formerly vacant tracts or, in
the South and West, newly annexed
districts, but in some older cities a
shift to high-density multiple dwellings
was required to provide accommodations. Few of the apartment houses
that began to appear in New York,
Chicago, and other congested metropolises exceeded seven stories, for the
great majority of the new "cliff dwellers," as they were sometimes called,
still climbed to their floors. In the
central business cores of these and
many other cities, however, hotel and
business blocks were soaring to twenty
and more stories, with the result that
problems of congestion, for both daytime and nighttime residents, were
commanding attention.

The human congestion was less
acute, of course, than that of traffic
in the streets. In the early postwar
years the increased number of private
cars and motor trucks had cleared the
streets of their accustomed clutter of
wagons, speeding the movement of
trolleys as well as of other traffic. The
relief was of brief duration, however,
as the cars multiplied. Accidents also
mounted alarmingly, prompting the
organization of a new technology for
traffic control.

"Traffic has increased several times
faster than the population in all our
principal cities," declared Robert H.
Whitter, a planning consultant at
Cleveland in 1920. The problem was

more critical in some cities than in
others, and the response varied accordingly. In Rochester, after an appalling year during which 164 fatal
accidents were recorded, 24 caused by
automobiles in the streets, various
groups joined to launch a safety campaign in 1918, the first in the land,
which was repeated for five successive
years, checking the mounting toll despite a twofold increase in the number
of cars. This program inspired similar
efforts under the direction of the newly
formed National Safety Council, in
St. Louis, Kansas City, and elsewhere.

Efforts to improve the flow of traffic were widespread. Control towers
and "wooden policemen" appeared at
a few busy intersections in several
cities in the early twenties. In 1922
New York intsalled a series of signal
lamps at twenty-six street crossings
along Fifth Avenue rigged to be
changed simultaneously by one officer.
Two years later the General Electric
Company perfected a simplified stop-
go signal light that could be operated
by a time clock, and Cleveland introduced a system that permitted traffic
to flow without a break along its principal arteries. In order to clear the
roadway for more efficient use, New
York and Philadelphia banned parking along their major streets in 1922,
and lesser cities began to limit the
blocks available for standing cars.
Boston in 1926 moved to require fees
for such parking. Many cities felt the
need for new and broader arteries, and
several projected one or more, but
Detroit, the automobile capital, was
the first in 1924 to propose a system
of divided highways and loops.

Rapid growth encouraged innovation and spurred urban leaders to seek
technical solutions for their problems.
Thus George H. Herrold, the street
superintendent in St. Paul, devised a
traffic-density map in 1923 that at-

tracted wide use as a planning tool. Housing reformers too were perfecting new methods of measuring the need for additional dwellings; in 1920 they related housing demands for the first time to specific income levels. Few denied the urgency of the problems, but agreement often ended there as rival groups of experts promoted conflicting solutions.

Such conflict was especially intense in the housing field. The aging Lawrence Veiller favored a reliance on regulatory measures that now seemed inadequate to the younger reformers who urged more forthright state action or, failing that, an appeal to the federal government to resume its housing program.

Nowhere was the housing crisis more acute than in New York State. To cope with it, Governor Alfred E. Smith had created a Reconstruction Commission in 1919 and named Clarence Stein as chairman of its housing committee. Stein, a young architect well acquainted, as a settlement volunteer, with the problems of poor slum dwellers, had highlighted their needs in his report. Governor Smith strongly endorsed Stein's proposals for a state housing agency and for local city housing boards empowered to acquire land and, if necessary, to construct houses with the aid of state housing credits. These measures required an amendment of the state constitution, and Governor Smith called a special session for that purpose in 1920. But the legislature, having previously adopted a rent-control measure supported by Veiller, was content to supplement that law with another granting tax exemption to stimulate new private construction.

Civic leaders tackled the housing shortage in various ways in different cities. Hard-pressed New York and Washington maintained wartime rent controls longer than most other towns,

and several followed New York's lead in granting tax exemptions on new construction. As director of the National Housing Association, Veiller promoted these and other regulatory measures through its monthly journal, *Housing Betterment,* in which he also publicized the activities of private and philanthrophic housing companies. In a review of fifteen such projects in 1922 he hailed Mariemont, a Cincinnati suburb designed by John Nolan, as America's outstanding garden city. Other projects in Louisville, New Orleans, and Detroit attracted his favor, and Milwaukee received special praise for the cooperation achieved between city, county, and private developers. Veiller, who was also critical of the public-housing program in Britain, attacked successive proposals for subsidized housing in New York, Boston, Chicago, and Los Angeles. Private investors, if given proper encouragement, could, he maintained, meet the nation's housing needs.

Home building did revive at a rapid rate in 1922 and succeeding years, not only in New York City but widely throughout the country. Mounting costs, however, priced the new houses far above the reach of the average urban workers and created a new differential between the suburbs, where most of the new construction occurred, and the central cities, where many old houses were remodeled as multiple dwellings for the poor. The new construction failed to relieve the pressure on the inner city slums, as several investigations revealed. Edith Abbott compiled a detailed survey of the wretched housing in a 33-acre slum district in Chicago; Bleeker Marquette, uncovering similar conditions in Philadelphia, spurred its Housing Association to debate the need for public assistance as well as for more diligent regulations. These and other surveys in Detroit and Cleveland, St. Louis and

Boston, and a half dozen other metropolises, raised new questions as to the proper location for new housing and the difficulty of relocating the slum dwellers.

Charles D. Norton, chairman of an Advisory Committee on a City Plan for New York (he had formerly been active in the planning movement of Chicago), became convinced in 1915 that the only hope for a solution of Manhattan's dilemmas lay in the adoption of a master plan for the entire metropolitan region. When the city officials refused to take the lead, he persuaded the Russell Sage Foundation to set up a research and planning staff to prepare a regional plan for Greater New York. With Frederick A. Delano, Robert W. De Forest, and John M. Glenn among its directors, it commanded wide respect and was able to engage as its director of research and planning Thomas Adams, a distinguished regional planner currently working in Canada who had formerly been president of the Town Planning Institute of Great Britain.

The New York Regional Plan achieved unprecedented scope. It studied not only highway and housing needs but also economic and population trends, the effects of proposed highway and rapid-transit improvements on land values, and the proper placement and density of residential and industrial developments. A former associate and staunch admirer of Ebenezer Howard in England, Thomas Adams sought to avoid the dangers of overcrowding that were inherent in the combination of rapid-transit with highrise apartments. But he was also determined to make his plans so realistic and feasible that they would win acceptance by civic authorities concerned with assessment rates and municipal costs. He boldly attacked the overdevelopment of residential skyscrapers and joined with others in bringing

Howard to New York in 1928 to help launch a drive for the construction of garden cities in America.

The close relation between rapid transit and skyscrapers was widely debated in those years. Boston had to abandon the 5-cent fare in order to restore the solvency of its mixed system of elevateds, subways, and streetcars which fanned out to all points of the compass. Many cities abandoned the 5-cent fare on their transit lines, but New York battled fiercely to retain that fare throughout its vast system in order to assure the builders of the new towers that increasingly covered central and lower Manhattan a sufficient flow of daytime inhabitants. Philadelphia extended its rapid-transit lines to serve its skyscraper district. But Detroit, with 19 buildings of twenty or more stories and 100 of ten or more, rejected a proposed subway in 1929; as the automobile capital, it turned, with Los Angeles, to planning for the development of a superhighway system and a widespread suburban pattern.

If the 5-cent fare seemed essential in New York City, so was economical housing. When private builders failed to supply new housing within the range of the average resident, Governor Smith appointed a State Commission on Housing and Regional Planning to seek a solution. Its reports, starting in 1924, documented the need and revealed the widening gap between the sale or rental price of new dwellings and the workingman's wage. Homeownership, though mounting in the suburbs, was declining in the inner city, where landlords were escaping rent controls by remodeling old houses into apartments. Governor Smith proposed the creation of a housing bank to spur construction by nonprofit corporations; the legislature, however, while ready in 1926 to create a State Housing Board to regulate limited-dividend corporations, refused to extend public credit for such ventures.

Yet the reports did have some constructive results. Clarence Stein, chairman and most active member of the commission, took the lead in forming the City Housing Corporation in 1924 in which he joined with Henry Wright, a fellow architect, in a plan to build a housing project of high standards at minimum costs. Stein had helped the year before to organize an informal group sometimes called the Regional Planning Association of America, which drew into its circle such men as Lewis Mumford, Charles H. Whitaker, Clarence Perry, all writers and critics, as well as Alexander Bing, a realtor whose wealth and idealism made him an enthusiastic backer of Stein's model-housing projects. Stein and Wright journeyed to England in 1924 to see its famous garden cities and to confer with Ebenezer Howard and Raymond Unwin, their principal founders. Unwin's oft-quoted precept, "Nothing gained by overcrowding," became the keystone of their plans as developed at Sunnyside in 1926 and at Radburn three years later.

Sunnyside and Radburn represented a great advance over previous housing projects, both in America and abroad. They embodied many garden-city concepts brought from England as well as those of the American community-center movement now championed by Clarence Perry. They were the first large housing projects designed for occupancy by families with automobiles, but they carefully restricted the channels of this traffic in order to preserve a park-like dwelling space throughout the community. The favorable publicity they received may have influenced the plans of some limited-dividend companies in other cities and provided a significant model for future housing developments.

Planned at the start as low-cost housing, both Sunnyside and Radburn proved when completed to be much too costly for low-rental occupancy. Housing companies, seeking to reach low-income groups, turned instead to another architect whose higher density apartment groups nevertheless retained a park-like arrangement that traced its origin, too, to Howard and the British new towns. Andrew J. Thomas achieved recognition through his design of the Metropolitan Life Insurance Apartments, opened in 1924, and of various projects sponsored by John D. Rockefeller, Jr., and by the Amalgamated Clothing Workers of America. The spacious courts and sunny gardens included in these high-density projects won praise from many planners, including Thomas Adams, who, however, favored the lower density of Sunnyside and Radburn for suburban developments. A survey by the Michigan Housing Association in Detroit in 1928 first devised an index of congestion to determine when and under what conditions housing was objectionable.

Many critics, not least the editors of the *American City,* deplored the congestion created by the skyscraper, but in 1929, when that magazine published a survey of cities and their skyscrapers, it was the few it overlooked that protested, not those weighted down with tall buildings. Its first tabulation showed 4,778 buildings of ten stories or more, and 377 that soared twenty or more stories. Approximately half the total were located in New York City, but each of thirty other metropolises had 20 or more skyscrapers of ten or more stories. Washington with 20 still had a moderately unbroken skyline, but Chicago, with 384 over ten and 65 over twenty stories, was beginning to rival New York for mass congestion. San Francisco with 105 over ten stories, Atlanta with 31, Buffalo with 26, and Birmingham with 22 protested the article's inadequate recognition of their density; only Kansas City, with 37, modestly asked that its reported total of 60 be scaled down.

INNER CITY CONCERNS AND PLANNING

The skyscraper rivaled the automobile as the symbol of success in the twenties. One was the sign of a prosperous community, the other of an affluent family. Few even among the planners realized how opposed these two symbols were and how sharp their rivalry would become. Yet the tension they developed was evident in every city as the needs of the central district vied with the drawing power of the suburbs for the town's limited resources. Private citizens and groups, enterprising companies, and municipal authorities championed first one and then the other side of this contest between urban centralization and diffusion, between the core and the periphery of the metropolis.

Inner-city concerns predominated in the early postwar years. The large numbers of the unemployed, both ex-service men and discharged war workers, prompted many cities to launch public-work programs in 1919. These included port improvements at St. Louis, an extension of the waterworks at Denver and of the sewers at Louisville, a vast program of street pavement at Boston, and the construction of numerous public buildings, including more than a score of community halls erected as war memorials, notably one at Bridgeport and a larger one at Baltimore. Herbert Hoover presided over a conference called by President Harding to promote local efforts to supply jobs. When a poorly timed cut in federal appropriations resulted in the closing of many employment offices, local city councils or chambers of commerce rallied to reopen most of them. Houston and its suburbs joined forces to launch the construction of inland docking facilities of such dimensions that the federal government was finally impelled to send its dredges to deepen a shipping canal from the Gulf.

As industrial recovery eased the unemployment crisis, many cities experienced a construction boom. New urban-dwelling starts doubled in 1921 and doubled again in the next two years. A Committee of One Hundred in Cleveland laid the cornerstone in 1921 of an auditorium said to be the largest in the nation. Designed to seat 13,000 and to accommodate big conventions and exhibitions, it occupied one side of the civic center and spurred similar efforts in Denver, Memphis, and other cities. In like fashion, Houston's ship canal stimulated inner-harbor navigation improvements at New Orleans, and other harbor improvements at San Francisco, Los Angeles, Seattle, and Portland that cost in the twenties over $100 million. Philadelphia pressed forward with the demolition of structures blocking the route of its projected Fairmont Parkway on which it expected to spend $17 million. The completion in 1925 of the Holland Tunnel, linking Manhattan with New Jersey's highways and permitting 2,000 cars to pass through each tube every hour, was hailed as the decade's $48 million engineering masterpiece; two years later a second tunnel, a mile in length, linked Detroit with Canada.

The mounting flood of cars, rushing in and out of the cities every day, required new facilities at both ends of the drive. As one town after another limited parking on the streets, the conversion of empty lots in the central district for parking purposes introduced a new cause of inner-city blight. Nearby merchants nevertheless profited from the trade these lots brought, and several cities—Cleveland, Chicago, and Los Angeles among them—provided public parking courts in 1924. Sensing the commercial value of parking space, a Kansas City developer organized a Stop and Shop Company that autumn and constructed on the city's outskirts a retail shopping project which provided free and adequate parking space and supplied a model for suburban shopping centers in St. Louis the next year, and soon throughout the country. In 1928 Detroit opened the first large ramp garage, capable of holding 1200 cars.

At the same time city folk out for a drive needed places to stop, too. Many towns, eager to attract visitors from afar, leased vacant fields on the outskirts and opened them as tourist camps. A few provided shelters with cookstoves and minimal sanitary facilities for the tourists who erected their own tents, built their own fires, and enjoyed a brief return to nature. Plagued by the problems these camps created, most cities quickly abandoned them to private operators, one of whom, in charge of a large "Camp Ground" near El Paso, Texas, in 1926, erected a number of wooden "bungalettes" for rent at $1.50 a night, and soon had a steady stream of tourists. Minneapolis established the first Gateway Tourist Bureau in 1928 with impressive headquarters on a major highway entering the city, where it supplied literature and answered questions for 54,900 tourists in its first eight-month season.

The trolley companies still carried the major burden of resident travel in most of the large metropolises, but their passenger loads were dropping in the late twenties. The 5-cent fare so jealously guarded before the war had largely disappeared, and even the service-at-cost contracts so confidently promoted in the early twenties began to lose their charm by the end of the decade. John Bauer, the *National Municipal Review*'s expert on public-

utility rates and services, urged city officials to restore a measure of competition in the transit field by chartering independent bus companies; by the late twenties, however, when the transit companies had bought up all such franchises in Buffalo and several other cities, the hope of developing competitive service dwindled. Only the competition of the private automobile was proving effective, and the result was not better but less frequent and more costly service. A proposal in 1929 that cities provide public parking lots at the suburban ends of their transit lines failed to attract wide application.

The central cities continued to enjoy an advantage in most aspects of municipal engineering. Their water and sewer systems were more adequate and their police and fire departments more thoroughly organized. Most of the fire horses were retired in the early twenties, and the police horses soon after, as the two services turned rapidly to motor-driven equipment. The fire departments perfected electric signaling devices and experimented with the use of chemicals, but they made no breakthrough comparable to that of the police with the introduction of radio, first at Berkeley, California, in 1929. Within a few months Detroit had thirty-five police cars equipped with radio receivers, and ten other cities hastily introduced similar equipment.

In addition to the traditional public-safety functions, some cities were assuming new responsibilities. Pittsburgh and Chicago were among the first to recognize the need for forthright action to reduce the smoke nuisance. "Atmospheric sanitation" was the euphemistic phrase coined by a group of engineers at the University of Illinois in an endeavor to tackle this growing problem without stirring too much opposition from local boosters. Soon several cities, determined to protect their reputation for clear skies, such as

Salt Lake City, New Orleans, and Kansas City, created municipal bureaus to promote the improvement of furnaces and the use of anthracite rather than soft coal. A dozen other cities joined the movement before the end of the decade—Cincinnati, Cleveland, and Akron in Ohio, St. Louis and Denver in the West, Rochester and New York in the East; nevertheless, in 1929 only Cleveland was adjudged adequately staffed for the job.

The age of the automobile also made it imperative that cities in the snow belt clear their streets of snow in the winter. Rochester and Buffalo, generally the hardest hit, had annually tackled their drifts for a decade before the great blizzards of 1914 and 1920 alerted other cities to the problem. Straight-blade snowplows attached to dump trucks replaced the early horse-drawn V-plows by the twenties, when mechanical snow loaders also made their appearance, the first at Chicago in December 1920. Caterpillar tractors, equipped with plow blades, joined the battle in New York the next February when a record 12½-inch snowfall threatened a $10 million loss in business. Since one freak storm could tie up and inflict serious damage on a city like Philadelphia or Washington, far from the snow belt, most of the leading metropolises of the North and Midwest had to equip themselves with snowplows and enroll emergency crews to man them. The city engineer in Duluth proposed the use of salt on the streets, but it did not win favor in this decade except as an aid in clearing downtown crosswalks.

Improved snowplows arrived just in time to help keep the newly established airways open throughout the year. In 1919, when the federal government announced plans for an air-mail service, it designated thirty-two cities as suitable stops if landing fields were provided. When service was inaugu-

rated a year later, twenty-one cities had fields ready for use or in the course of preparation, most of them as private promotions. Within another three years Chicago, Philadelphia, Detroit, Boston, and Kansas City had opened municipal air terminals, and other large cities soon followed. Cleveland, which almost lost its air-mail service in 1924 because of the poor condition of the two private landing fields, dedicated a 2000-acre municipal port the next July, the largest in the country, and recorded 4,000 landings during the first year. As the number of airfields multiplied, approaching 5,000 by 1928, the urgent need to bring this land use under the control of responsible city planners focused new interest on that municipal function.

Local airports made another contribution to city planning by supplying planes to take aerial photographs, which Nelson P. Lewis, a leading city planner, hailed in 1922 as a significant new tool for the profession. That latter term was becoming more truly appropriate as twenty-five colleges offered courses in city planning in 1925; Harvard, where James Sturgis Pray had delivered the first series of lectures in 1909, established a Graduate School of City Planning in 1930. Of the 150 cities with planning officials in 1923, twenty-five issued published reports. Every metropolis of 300,000 or more inhabitants had accepted planning as a municipal function by that date. Two years later the National Conference on City Planning launched its new quarterly, *City Planning*.

Some of the early zoning laws were losing their force because of the numerous exceptions granted by the appeal boards. Conflicting political factions in New York City made the twenties a period of frustration for its zoning reformers. In Los Angeles the local Municipal League suspected the presence of graft. The courts, however, consistently upheld these laws, and 261 cities, including all the major metropolises, had zoned themselves by the close of 1924 when Boston finally adopted its law.

If the major task of the early planners was, as Lewis put it, to correct "earlier mistakes" in the city's development, some real accomplishments were achieved in these years. The Chicago plan, launched with much fanfare in 1909, was now fulfilling its promise as the new Illinois Central terminal, a sports stadium, and the Field Museum approached completion on the lakefront, while the Wacker Drive, a two-level highway bordering the south bank of the Chicago River, built at a cost of $22 million, eased congestion in the central business district. Camden's plan for a circular boulevard and a civic center, like the equally imaginative river development and civic center planned for Columbus, Ohio, was still in the paper stage, but DesMoines and Cleveland were now reaping the rewards of similar planning before the war.

Cleveland's accomplishments rivaled those of any other city in the land. Malcolm B. Vilas, president for many years of the Citizens' League of Cleveland, had made it an effective proponent of practical planning. A civic-center plan, adopted in 1900, was now almost completed and adjoined the Union Terminal, a transit and transport focus. A cultural and educational campus, projected in 1919 five miles from the center, had by 1930 attracted a cluster of fourteen institutions including the Cleveland Art Gallery. The city had won its battle for a Metropolitan Park Board in 1918; it now had over 9,000 acres under development and secured the cooperation of Cuyahoga and neighboring counties and towns in the formation of the Cuyahoga Planning Congress, which supervised an extensive development

of major highways throughout the metropolitan region. The League's success in these endeavors spurred Vilas and his associates to press for the establishment of a metropolitan government in 1929; when defeated in the legislature, they prepared to launch a new attempt the next year.

Of the many civic-center plans submitted by citizen committees and other groups before the war, few had been developed. Arnold Brunner, who had helped to draft several of these plans, deplored the failure of American cities to carry them forward. The problem was in large part a fiscal one, for while some states were assisting their capital cities to develop civic centers, as at Denver, Harrisburg, and Des Moines, and others helped to bear the cost of their central parks, as at Boston, elsewhere the planners and their sometimes grandiose proposals had to compete with the traditional municipal services for the limited funds available. The mounting costs of local government had prompted most states to place a top limit, generally of 2 per cent of the assessments, on the taxing powers, with another 2 per cent on the bonding powers of municipalities. When in 1927 the Detroit Bureau of Government Research made a thorough study of Detroit's expenditures over a period of years, it discovered that, contrary to the general belief, the city's per capita costs had in fact shown a drop that justified new expenditures for improvements. Detroit was encouraged to press forward with its loops and parkways; Dayton and St. Louis launched vast riverfront developments in the next year or two.

In many places the desired improvements extended beyond the city limits and required negotiation with other municipalities. Baltimore established a metropolitan water district in 1925 in order to avoid competition for limited resources, and Washington organized a Suburban Sanitary Commission to plot and develop sewers and other facilities throughout the area. The successful performance of several earlier special-function metropolitan districts at Boston, New York, and Philadelphia, where water, sewer, or park authorities had linked otherwise independent municipalities in joint operations, encouraged the creation in 1923 of the New York Port Authority, the organization in 1926 of the National Capital Park and Planning Commission for Washington, and two years later the formation of a Metropolitan Water District that allied eleven neighbors of Los Angeles in a unified project.

Thus in the twenties scattered cities, eagerly seizing their opportunities, sometimes evolved original programs that quickly won adoption elsewhere. Enterprising industrialists similarly developed technological innovations to meet urban needs, and their promotional efforts and advertisements helped to support such journals as the *American City,* which in its turn eagerly publicized each new advance. A stimulating diversity resulted, giving vitality to the material aspects of America's urban development in the twenties, and calling for an equally imaginative effort to devise administrative and governmental agencies capable of directing and supporting still larger metropolitan ventures.

THE SEARCH FOR METROPOLITAN GOVERNMENT

Forced to stop at the city line, city planning seemed increasingly impotent in the twenties as the interdependence of the broader metropolitan community became apparent. Many civic clubs and research bureaus, long advocates of planning, urged the merits of metropolitan planning, even of metropolitan government. When the suburban passion for autonomy and the hostility of rural-dominated legislatures blocked these developments, the cities tried various compromises, but the difficulties inherent in fractured communities complicated many facets of urban government. As one reform after another met cool reception at the state capitals, leaders of the hard-pressed metropolises began to appeal through their national organizations for broader public support and, in a few instances, for federal assistance.

Richard S. Childs, the embattled reformer who had struggled valiantly to keep the *National Municipal Review* afloat with the support of the League's 3,000 members, had a thrilling experience in April 1921. Invited to address the first convention of the newly formed League of Women Voters, he was astonished to find the hall crowded with 1,000 delegates and to learn that they represented local chapters that claimed over 2 million members. The confidence with which they approved an $80,000 budget convinced him that here was "a new civic army" whose leader, Mrs. Carrie Chapman Catt, sounded very much like a municipal reformer, and most of whose planks and resolutions had a very familiar ring.

Despite the economic recession and the wave of intolerance, there was cause for optimism in the early twenties. Such obstacles actually strengthened the municipal reformers by providing new and challenging issues. As unemployment called forth some of the municipal improvements noted above, fears of ethnic radicals placed a renewed emphasis on nonpartisan elections and professional administration. As the recession and the Red scare faded, urban expansion acquired the boom proportions necessary to implement reforms; and civic leaders began again to express a friendly welcome toward newcomers. In Elizabeth, New Jersey, for example, a League of

Neighbors conducted annual festivals for several years patterned after a Festival of Nations and Homelands Exhibit staged in 1920 by the Rochester Chamber of Commerce. Indeed in some cities, when the reformers finally awoke to the possibility of enrolling the revived ethnic associations in their civic leagues, they found the practical politicians already seated respectfully on their platform.

If, on the national level, progressivism receded in the 1920's, on the urban level it enjoyed a new burst of vitality. Old established City Clubs in New York, Chicago, Cleveland, Milwaukee, and Portland, Oregon, took the lead in varied endeavors, and new clubs and municipal leagues appeared in numerous other cities. Even New Orleans, still basking in its Old South traditions, saw the formation in 1922 of a civic Council which rallied thirty-five local organizations behind a concerted drive to clean up and improve the streets.

The National Association of Civic Secretaries, soon renamed the Government Research Council, drew the leaders of these varied groups together for mutual stimulation at the annual meetings of the National Municipal League. Of the fifty-five organizations represented at the League's thirteenth meeting in Philadelphia in 1923, eighteen were men's City Clubs, seven were Women's City Clubs, and fifteen of the others were research bureaus. A list of active research bureaus, compiled that year by the Detroit Bureau, reported the employment of almost a hundred professional staff members by civic organizations of this type in twenty-nine cities. Some of the City Clubs assigned research projects to volunteer citizen committees, and most of these, plus the Women's City Clubs and the local municipal associations, actively promoted the reforms their committees and staffs recommended.

Few, however, matched the activity of the New York City Club under the leadership for many years of Raymond V. Ingersoll.

Several of these bodies maintained or prompted their cities to establish municipal reference libraries. Efforts to persuade the federal government to create a national municipal bureau to collect and coordinate information on all cities, though frequently renewed in these years, failed to achieve success. The New York Bureau, reorganized in 1925 as the Institute of Public Administration, undertook many research projects in other cities and helped to launch independent bureaus in a dozen more places scattered from Newark in 1923 to Los Angeles five years later. After Dr. Frederick A. Cleveland, who directed much of this field work, resigned to enter industrial research, the broader activity of the New York Bureau dwindled, and in 1927 the Government Research Council cooperated with the National Municipal League in establishing a clearinghouse for information on cities. Russell Forbes, secretary of the Council, became director of the Municipal Administrative Service, which opened an office that February on Broadway.

Most of the clubs and bureaus, having themselves accepted a nonpartisan approach to civic problems, sought to exclude politics from city government. Both the commission and city-manager plans had nonpartisan predilections, and the newly popular scheme for proportional representation, although it called for party nominations, sought to free the Council from partisan control. Most of the cities captured by the city-manager forces in this decade inserted nonpartisan provisions in their charters and several included proportional representation as well. Outstanding among the new city-manager cities were Cincinnati and Cleveland, Kansas City and Rochester, all larger than previous city-manager cities; the success of their campaigns encouraged advocates of city-manager charters in still larger metropolises, Philadelphia and New York among them, to hope briefly for similar victories. Yet the victories were not in every case lasting, as Cleveland discovered after five years and Akron after three, when, with several others, they repealed their city-manager charters.

Generally the city-manager failures, relatively few in number, were political rather than administrative in character. Restrained from political activity themselves, the managers depended on their backers to supply such leadership, and when the latter failed to produce it, an opposing political faction sometimes seized control. In Cleveland they restored the strong-mayor system, which Boston had devised some years before. Both Detroit and Milwaukee clung to that system, and Buffalo, abandoning its commission form, was one of several metropolises that now elected a "strong" mayor.

Cincinnati successfully combined the merits of the two systems. Possessing an abundance of leadership from the start, the Cincinnatus Association continued to supply political backing to successive city managers, enabling them to devote their full talents to administration. The Association, formed originally as a Sunday evening dinner club and forum, assumed an active role in local politics in 1921 when young Charles Taft, son of the former President, returned from Yale to practice law in the city. Taft, however, was only one of several in the Association who became indignant at the policies of the Republican boss. In order to break the boss's hold on the city, the Association drafted a city-manager charter and waged a triumphant campaign for its adoption; in the process it elected Murray Seasongood, one of

its members as mayor, and brought Colonel C. O. Sherrill from Washington to serve as city manager. Sherrill's administrative reforms, continued by his successor, Clarence A. Dykstra, won Cincinnati the reputation of best-governed city. The unique feature of its government was not the provision for proportional representation that some other cities shared but the continued leadership supplied by the Cincinnatus Association, which regularly ran a slate of candidates and, by an effective use of the radio and other campaign methods, won a majority in successive councilmanic contests. After four years, when Seasongood stepped down as mayor, Russell Wilson, assistant editor of the *Times-Star* and president of the Association, succeeded him and continued to provide vigorous leadership in the political arena.

Of course Cleveland, Cincinnati's rival to the north, also had a group of dedicated reformers in the powerful Citizen's League and found an able administrator in its first city manager, William R. Hopkins. But Cleveland's more rapid growth raised problems that prompted its leaders to seek a merger of city and county functions. In the battle for consolidation they had to go to the state legislature, where the Republican boss in the Cincinnati region, fearful of a similar move by that city, rallied suburban and rural forces throughout the state to block the measure. Disillusioned with non-partisanship and weakened by numerous resignations because of the city's constricted budgets, the city-manager candidates, despite a determined campaign in their behalf by the League of Women Voters, lost control of the council in 1929.

Many city managers made their peace with the politicians, as Walter Lippmann advised at the Pittsburgh meeting in 1925, before the decade closed. As a result they were able to carry through important improvements and to introduce new technical advances. Improved water pumps and pipes, for example, increased the efficiency and reduced the cost of waterworks extensions; motorized equipment improved and speeded the collecting of garbage, the cleaning of the streets, and the mixing and spreading of cement and other road surfaces. All could work together on these and other engineering reforms, reviewed in a special edition of the *American City* in 1930. But when a municipality had to reach beyond its borders to find a new water source, an outlet for its sewers, or some other regional objective, even a mayor with firm political ties could not always secure the necessary approval of the legislature, as New York's Mayor James J. Walker, among others, discovered. Thus Daniel W. Hoan, Socialist mayor of Milwaukee, though a favorite of many Wisconsin Progressives, saw his plans for city-county consolidation defeated in the rural-dominated legislature.

The desire for consolidation or for some other form of city-county integration was beginning in the late twenties to dominate the thinking of many metropolitan leaders. In some states in the South and the West a city's power to annex adjoining territory that was not separately incorporated offered a workable solution, as Baltimore, Houston, and Los Angeles demonstrated. Although most attempts to consolidate the city and county governments failed in this decade (at Seattle in 1923, at St. Louis in 1926 and again in 1930, as well as at Cleveland in its two attempts), a few cities, notably Denver and Los Angeles, secured the passage of compromise measures. For the larger metropolises this was no longer a major consideration, for the city limits in the case of New York and greater Philadelphia as well as greater Chicago encompassed more than one

county. The persistence of separate county functions proved wasteful in their cases, but the real problem in these and other metropolises was to develop procedures for integrating the governmental activities of their expanding districts.

Progress reports on the work of the New York Regional Plan Association prompted similar efforts in other major metropolises. The Chicago City Club submitted a proposal in 1923 for integrated planning by the 340 local governmental authorities active in the Chicago metropolitan district, but action was deferred. A Regional Planning Federation of the Philadelphia Tri-State District, organized in 1926 by its planners and supported by their corporate and other friends, raised $60,000 and engaged a staff to make a preliminary survey of the mutual problems affecting the residents of the 2000-square-mile tract within a 30-mile radius of Philadelphia. Boston and San Francisco soon had similar federations and engaged such able planners as John Nolan and Harlan Bartholomew to conduct their metropolitan surveys. Following the Cleveland pattern, Chicago finally got a Regional Planning Association, which brought officials of three states and two counties together for conferences on highways, airways, zoning, and other mutual concerns.

Planners in a dozen other metropolises were soon holding conferences and projecting surveys. Two in particular made new forward steps. A New York State Conference on Regional and City Planning held at Buffalo in 1924 spurred the organization of a Niagara Frontier Planning Board, which was appointed by the officials of six cities, twenty-two villages, and two counties, with Chauncey J. Hamilton of Buffalo as its chairman. As the first official body engaged in regional planning, its successive reports attracted wide interest. Even the federal government, alerted at least to Washington's limited powers, authorized the creation of a National Capital Parks and Planning Commission to which President Coolidge named five members in April 1926 with Frederick Law Olmstead as chairman.

Clarence Stein supplied the rationale of this movement when he declared, at the regional planning conference in Buffalo, that "No city is master of its own destiny." That wider planning was necessary, many agreed, but Professor Thomas H. Reed of the University of Michigan, after a study of metropolitan regions in Europe, concluded that regional planning commissions were only a temporary makeshift and that strong metropolitan governments were indispensable. However, when Pittsburgh endeavored in protracted negotiations to bring its near neighbors together in a federated metropolitan government, its successive charter proposals met first a legislative block, then a legislative revision, and finally a defeat in 1929 when voters in several of the 120 polled cities and towns rejected it, although the total vote was 2 to 1 in favor. Professor Reed, who as director of the research staff had drafted the charter, urged that it be redrafted and resubmitted, but the onset of the depression diverted attention.

The Pittsburgh experience raised again the problem of legislative reapportionment. While the charter's final defeat was at the local level, a stringent requirement of a two-thirds vote in two-thirds of the constituencies, irrespective of their size, had been inserted by a rural-dominated legislature. Similar frustrations in Chicago, which had almost half the population but less than a third of the legislators, and in Detroit, with a third of the population and less than a sixth of the legislators, prompted talk of secession and the formation of separate city-states. Baltimore got several additional representatives through a constitutional amendment it initiated and passed, but it had modestly asked for only a third of its numerical proportion. In Connecticut forty-one cities large and small, with five-sixths of the populations, had only one-third of the representatives in the legislature. Several state constitutions required a reapportionment after each decennial census, but in states such as New York, Illinois, Ohio, Michigan, and California, where entrenched rural representatives feared the dominance of rising metropolises, the legislatures repeatedly disregarded the constitutional provision. Only the governors, who represented the majority of the voters, spoke out for the cities, and their traditional stand in behalf of home rule was now proving a handicap to expanding metropolises.

Frustrated by their repeated rebuffs from the state legislatures, municipal leaders made frequent appeals to public opinion. In articles and surveys they sought either to allay or to override the hostility of the rural representatives. Occasionally they took their cases to the courts, only to find them unwilling to infringe on the prerogatives of the legislatures, as in the *Fergus* v. *Marks* decision in Illinois in 1926, when the judge refused to order that body to fulfill its constitutional duty to reapportion the state. Appeals to the federal courts or to other federal authorities were infrequent, yet increasingly, throughout the twenties, this possibility was gaining attention.

Federal aid to cities received occasional mention at National Municipal League conventions. Professor William Anderson of the University of Minnesota, who spoke on that subject in 1924, was not concerned with monetary assistance, of which the cities received very little and only indirectly through the states, but with the administrative services that benefited cities. Among these he included harbor improvements, postal services, weather reports, and many potential services under the commerce and general-welfare clauses. Secretary Herbert Hoover was more specific when he responded in 1927 to a request from the *American City* for a list of Commerce Department activities affecting cities. In addition to the recently established Division of Building and Housing, he cited the work of the Bureau of Standards in upgrading urban purchasing departments and utilities, the surveys of the Coast and Geodetic Offices, and the valuable information supplied by the Census Bureau to urban planners as well as to urban promoters and citizens generally. The Secretary's list, particularly that last point, was of keen interest and prompted editor Buttenheim to recall his repeated efforts since 1912 to persuade successive Presidents to establish a Federal Bureau of Municipalities; perhaps, he suggested, the Secretary, who had recently been elected President, will finally provide this essential source of information.

Metropolitan Growth and Decentralization

Leo F. Schnore*

A great deal of effort has been devoted to research in metropolitan growth and decentralization in recent years. In particular, the detailed statistical studies by Thompson, Bogue, and Hawley have provided a clear image of the main demographic facts. However, a search of the literature reveals two important omissions: nowhere is there available a succinct historical recapitulation that provides a summary description of metropolitan development from its beginning to the present time; and, as a probable consequence, the literature contains very few explicitly developmental hypotheses regarding metropolitan growth and decentralization. This paper is addressed to these two broad problems. First, a brief narrative account of metropolitan growth and development is offered. Second, a number of implications derived from the review are set out in the form of concrete problems for research. In each problem the focus is upon process, in a frank effort to offset the static orientation of the available literature. Moreover, a number of the hypotheses refer specifically to the influence of transportation, a factor frequently mentioned but rarely studied in the metropolitan context. The historical treatment is deliberately phrased in very general terms. Most of the statements are well established, although diverse in origin; others rest upon more limited evidence; and a few, while frankly speculative, are phrased as questions for empirical research and not as final answers.[1]

A HALF-CENTURY OF METROPOLITAN GROWTH

Metropolitan development can best be conceived as a new form of urban growth especially characteristic of twentieth-century America.[2] It must be recognized, of course, that a large increase in urban population antedated this century. Cities have grown faster than rural areas since 1820. The first decade of this century, however, marked the end of one important phase of urban development, being the last decade in which migration from other countries contributed large numbers to the growth of American cities. The decade from 1910 to 1920, including as it did World War I, witnessed the stemming of the great streams of migrants from overseas, and over-all urban growth was slowed as a result.[3]

[1] Both the historical narrative and the derived outline of research problems are based on the premise that the general pattern of metropolitan development should be established before individual variations are examined in detail. This is not to derogate case studies of individual areas, an extremely valuable source of hypotheses. However, an excessive concern with apparent exceptions appears to be premature at this point; a more fruitful approach is the documentation of major trends. Once the broad set of relationships has been firmly established, the exceptions become variations around these central tendencies, which are themselves subject to explanation.

[2] See N. S. B. Gras, *An Introduction to Economic History* (New York: Harper & Bros., 1922); and R. D. McKenzie, *The Metropolitan Community* (New York: McGraw-Hill Book Co., 1933).

[3] Natural increase was apparently not a compensating factor of any consequence during this period, for city dwellers failed to reproduce at replacement levels. There is

*Reprinted from *The American Journal of Sociology*, Leo F. Schnore, "Metropolitan Growth and Decentralization," LXIII(September, 1957), 171–180, by permission of the University of Chicago Press. Copyright 1958 by the University of Chicago.

Restrictive legislation in the 1920's, including a rigid system of quotas, prevented the resumption of international migration on a prewar scale, but the national population continued to increase, and cities grew rapidly, but now, however, largely by internal migration. The attenuated growth of cities in the 1939–40 decade was also the result of a decline in migration, but in this instance it consisted of a lessened flow of internal (i.e., rural-to-urban) migrants. Job opportunities in urban areas, drastically reduced during the depression, multiplied during the early 1940's, largely due to wartime demands. Urban employment was maintained at fairly high levels in the years immediately following World War II as the nation returned to a peacetime economy, and it was further stimulated by the outbreak of hostilities in Korea.

What have been the metropolitan concomitants of twentieth-century urban growth? Part A of Table 1 shows inter-decade rates of increase within the entire continental United States. In this table the total land area of the nation is represented according to metropolitan status. The first distinction is that between metropolitan and non-metropolitan parts. The next subdivision in the table distinguishes between the metropolitan central cities and their surrounding "rings." Growth rates for urban and rural parts of the ring are then shown separately. Finally, within the "rural" portion of the ring, separate growth rates are given for incorporated and unincorporated areas. Part B expresses all these rates as ratios of the national increase, providing a control over variation in over-all growth between decades.[4]

Table 1 shows that the presently defined metropolitan areas have captured a disproportionately large share of the total national increase in population throughout the entire fifty-year period. Within metropolitan areas, however, central growth has become progressively slower, while the ring has tended to grow more and more rapidly. It is this over-all pattern of differential growth in favor of the peripheral area that is usually labeled "decentralization," although these rates reflect only *net* changes arising from a variety of sources.

A part of the slowed city growth is the result of the cities' failure or inability to annex the surrounding densely settled areas. Probably more significant, however, are two complementary trends in migration and residential mobility: a tendency for residents of the central city to move in increasing numbers to various parts of the adjacent ring area and a tendency for migrants from outside the metropolitan area to move directly to the ring rather than to the city itself. The total effect is a *relative* decentralization or net peripheral growth in excess of that of the center. As far as migration and mobility are concerned, de-

evidence, however, that this long-established fact did not hold during the most recent intercensal decade (see Donald J. Brogue and Emerson Seim, "Components of Population Change in Suburban and Central City Populations of Standard Metropolitan Areas, 1940 to 1950," *Rural Sociology*, XXI [September–December, 1956], 265–75).

[4] Official definitions of the 168 Standard Metropolitan Areas, recognized by the Census Bureau, have been retrojected to 1900, so that area is held constant. The "old" (1940) census definition of "urban" is used throughout. Because of differences in areal definition, these rates differ in minor detail from those given in Donald J. Bogue, *Population Growth in Standard Metropolitan Areas, 1900–1950* (Washington: Government Printing Office, 1953), Table 1. Bogue's data refer to 162 metropolitan areas with "county-equivalent" areas used in New England in place of the town-based areas defined by the Census Bureau. Because the official definitions of the Standard Metropolitan Areas are used here, the data are not directly comparable with those reported in Warren S. Thompson, *The Growth of Metropolitan Districts in the United States, 1900–1940* (Washington: Government Printing Office, 1947).

TABLE I

RATES OF INCREASE IN POPULATION, BY METROPOLITAN STATUS, 1900–1950

METROPOLITAN STATUS	1940–50	1930–40	1920–30	1910–20	1900–1910
A. Interdecade Rates of Population Increase					
Total United States	14.5	7.2	16.1	14.9	21.0
Non-metropolitan	6.1	8.5	6.0	6.7	13.6
Metropolitan	22.0	8.4	27.5	25.9	32.5
Central cities	13.8	5.5	24.2	27.9	37.1
Rings	34.2	13.4	33.2	22.4	25.6
Urban	26.0	8.0	42.6	35.9	49.2
Rural	45.2	21.3	22.0	9.4	8.4
Incorporated	34.1	13.2	28.6	24.1	45.0
Unincorporated	46.5	22.3	21.2	7.8	5.6
B. Ratios of Total National Increase					
Non-metropolitan	0.43	1.18	0.37	0.45	0.65
Metropolitan	1.52	1.17	1.71	1.74	1.55
Central cities	0.95	0.76	1.50	1.87	1.77
Rings	2.36	1.86	2.06	1.50	1.22
Urban	1.79	1.11	2.65	2.41	2.34
Rural	3.12	2.96	1.37	0.63	0.40
Incorporated	2.35	1.83	1.78	1.62	2.14
Unincorporated	3.21	3.10	1.32	0.52	0.27

Source: Leo F. Schnore, "Patterns of Decentralization" (unpublished doctoral dissertation, University of Michigan, 1955), Table 101, p. 214.

centralization has two sources—outward *relocation* from the center and growth via *accretion* at the periphery. As yet, however, the relative contributions of these two distinct types of movement have not been firmly established.[5]

Despite our inadequate answers to these basic questions, however, recent studies have established some important relationships between the extent of decentralization and certain struc-

[5] The relative importance of these two migrant streams are known for only a few areas and for a limited and probably atypical time period. Migration data from the 1940 Census can be examined in terms of the 1935 places of residence of migrants living in metropolitan central cities and rings in 1940 (see Warren S. Thompson, *Migration within Ohio, 1935–1940* [Oxford, Ohio: Scripps Foundation for Research in Population Problems, 1951], and Amos H. Hawley, *Intrastate Migration in Michigan, 1935–1940* [Ann Arbor: University of Michigan Institute of Public Administration, 1953]).

tural and functional characteristics of metropolitan areas. One way to present these is to take a deliberately oversimplified view of metropolitan development as a more or less continuous process and to introduce the findings of recent research in historical sequence.

At the turn of the century most urban centers were still rather compact and self-contained entities. Most of the larger cities were at deep-water sites, although a few had begun to develop inland at railway intersections. The residents were concentrated near the principal workplaces, living in tenements and row houses, and most of them walked to work or rode on public vehicles. The horsecar was still very much in evidence on the city streets, although it was being replaced by the electric streetcar. However, the automobile was still a novelty, and its price was beyond the means of all but the wealthy. Some of the latter who could afford the time and the cost of the trip had already begun to live outside the congested city and to travel to their places of business by automobile or by interurban railway.[6]

These railways—powered by steam or electricity—spread out from the largest cities in radial strings, and along their lines began to appear clusters of dwellings. In the interstices lay wide areas of open country, much of it in farms. Small villages scattered throughout this open country served the immediate needs of the farm population. These subcenters lay at intersections of rural roads and near the railway lines, and through them were distributed the processed goods required by the agricultural population. They also served as the primary collection points for the produce of the agricultural hinterland.

Larger urban subcenters within the orbit of the central city provided the hinterland with less frequently needed goods. In addition to serving as collection and distribution points, these larger places were frequently engaged in the processing of goods, particularly if water power was immediately available. Most industry, however, was still concentrated in the large city, where the economies of steam power could be best realized.[7] As a rule the larger subcenters had direct railway service to the central city; over these lines flowed the overwhelming bulk of interurban freight. At any rate, the whole arrangement of urban and village agglomerations came to resemble a planet and its satellites.

The larger cities were still growing more rapidly than the smaller places, chiefly through migration, and the rural population was suffering continued losses as more and more efficient methods of farming were put into use and as smaller subsistence farms were consolidated into larger holdings. The surplus agricultural population flowed toward the city, probably in a series of intermediate moves, to be joined there by migrants from foreign countries.[8]

Metropolitan areas during the early years of the century were thus characterized by an axiate or star-shaped form of settlement. Most urban places beyond 10 or 15 miles remained largely independent of the center. Within that zone, however, interurban railways were gradually able to provide more regular service; as time passed, more and more people working in the city found it possible to live outside its formal boundaries. These early suburbanites lived in new residential developments within walking distance of the railway commuter stations. In Hoyt's words, "as these communities gradually coalesced in solid bands, the settled area maps of the New York and Chicago metropolitan areas showed long finger-like appendages extending out, with large vacant areas lying in between. This was the result of the faster travel time on the suburban railroads than on other means of transportation."[9]

An appreciation of the importance of the railroad during the early part of this century can be gained from a

---

[6] Adna F. Weber, *The Growth of Cities in the Nineteenth Century* (New York: Columbia University Press, 1899).

[7] National Resources Committee, *Our Cities: Their Role in the National Economy* (Washington: Government Printing Office, 1937), pp. 29–30.

[8] Early urban research, of course, concentrated on the clusters of ethnic settlements within large cities. However, comparative data on segregation are notably deficient for more recent periods.

[9] Homer Hoyt, "The Influence of Highways and Transportation in the Structure and Growth of Cities and Urban Land Values," in Jean Labatut and Wheaton J. Lane (eds.), *Highways in Our National Life* (Princeton: Princeton University Press, 1950), p. 202.

review of historical statistics (Table 2). At the turn of the century, there were more than four times as many railway locomotives as motor vehicles in operation. As late as 1910, there were more miles of railroad track than miles of surfaced highways in use. After 1920, however, the number of motor vehicles increased significantly, while the number of locomotives began to decline. Similar trends can be discerned when the two types of route are compared.

World War I brought two particularly significant developments. First, migration from abroad, which had provided a large share of the city's manpower needs, was practically cut off. The demands of war, however, compelled urban manufacturing centers to increase their output. To staff the mills and plants, they had to depend on attracting people from other parts of the nation, and for the first time the migrant streams began to include large numbers of Negroes, particularly from the South.[10]

[10] Thus began a South-to-North movement that continues unabated. Most Negro migrants continue to move directly to the central city rather than to the metropolitan ring. Racial differentials in the various migrant streams involved in decentralization have yet to be fully reported.

The second crucial development occasioned by the war was the rapid increase in the number of motor vehicles. Burdened to their capacity, the railroads were simply unable to carry all the freight that had to be shipped. Motor trucks, which had been used primarily for local hauling within the city, were pressed into service to move less bulky goods between urban areas. An extensive program of highway improvement on all levels of government was put into effect, and hard-surfaced roads began to crisscross the areas surrounding the largest centers.

In effect, truck transportation was subsidized by governmental funds, for highways were publicly financed. In addition, some of the methods learned under the pressure of the wartime demand for motor transport were applied to the production of private automobiles. Many of the techniques of modern mass production—later adopted in almost every sector of the economy—were first developed in the automobile industry.

The years immediately following World War I, although marked by a few minor fluctuations, ushered in a period of expansion. Enormous strides were made in industrial productivity, and, as national production increased,

TABLE II

RAILROAD AND MOTOR VEHICLE ROUTES AND CARRIERS, 1900–1950

Year	Railroad Trackage (Miles)	Surfaced Highways (Miles)	Railroad Locomotives (No.)	Motor Vehicles (No.)
1950	223,779	1,714,000	42,951	48,566,984
1940	223,670	1,367,000	44,333	32,035,424
1930	249,052	694,000	60,189	26,531,999
1920	252,845	369,000	68,942	9,239,161
1910	240,293	204,000	60,019	468,500
1900	193,348	128,500	37,663	8,000

Source: U.S. Bureau of the Census, *Historical Statistics of the United States, 1789–1945* (Washington: Government Printing Office, 1949), Tables K-29, K-34, K-175, K-182, and K-229, and *Continuation to 1952 of Historical Statistics of the United States, 1789–1945* (Washington: Government Printing Office, 1954), same tables.

significant advances occurred in real wages. The techniques of mass production and increased mechanization reduced the manpower required in industry. Since a similar trend was continuing in agriculture as an effect of the introduction of power machinery, the surplus population from both agriculture and industry gradually shifted into occupations providing for the distribution of goods and services.[11]

Spatial changes followed from these technological innovations. At the same time that these fundamental transitions were taking place in the national economy, the physical pattern of the large city and its surrounding area began to undergo crucial alterations. Decentralization, which had occurred first in only the largest centers, became a significant aspect of the growth of many smaller cities in the 1920's; both industry and population were scattering as a response to the development of the motor vehicle. The hard-surfaced route, of course, was adaptable to the movement of people as well as to the carrying of goods. The elaborate networks of main arteries and feeder routes around large and middle-sized cities permitted a number of the functional components of the community to break away from the center. Most of them located at intersections in the highway network. Urban subcenters appeared in increasing numbers and grew at rates in excess of that of the center. New construction was started in volume in the periphery of both large and middle-sized cities. As residential population gathered in sufficient densities, retail and service establishments arose to provide the suburbanites with urban conveniences.

With the increased ease of travel, however, some of the larger subcenters underwent a significant transition. They lost their high degree of independence and fell under the dominating influence of the metropolis. For example, many establishments devoted to the provision of luxury goods abandoned operations in the subcenters, being unable to compete with the metropolis, which was now easily accessible to a wide market. At the same time, the principles of mass production were increasingly adapted to distribution, and chains of retail outlets began to appear, particularly in the convenience-goods lines. Such units, under a single ownership and directed from a site in the central city, could take advantage of the economies of mass buying and standardization. During the same period, significant changes in communication came about with the development of the radio and the telephone. Instantaneous contact with a broad area became possible, and the independence of subcenters was diminished accordingly.

At the same time, industry became increasingly free to locate away from the city itself, as cheap electrical power replaced steam.[12] The telephone permitted peripheral location of production facilities while the functions of management and control could remain in the center. In addition, the widespread ownership of the automobile meant a more mobile labor force. Heavy industry, which tends to operate more efficiently in one-story buildings occupying large areas, apparently was particularly attracted by the lower costs of land in the ring, where the competition of alternative uses was less intense.

However, not all elements of the community were equally free to participate in this outward movement: during the early phase of decentraliza-

---

[11] For the original distinction between "primary," "secondary," and "tertiary" industries and occupations see Colin Clark, *The Conditions of Economic Progress* (2d ed.; London: Macmillan Co., 1951).

[12] National Resources Committee, *op. cit.*

tion, many activities were bound to the center as securely as in previous years. The retailing of luxury goods and the provision of infrequently needed services were particularly obliged to remain in central locations, in order to maintain maximum access to a large potential market. The functions of management and direction also appeared to cling to the central location, perhaps in order to facilitate contact with other units engaged in communication, finance, and marketing.

At any rate, the depression of the 1930's appears to have accentuated the trends of differential growth incipient in many areas in previous years. With decreased job opportunities to offer, central city growth dropped to a low level, with many cities sustaining net losses. The growth of the residential population of the metropolitan ring, although reduced from the levels of the previous decade in many instances, tended to remain above that of the center and of the nation as a whole. Although there is little evidence of a genuine "back-to-the-farm" movement during this decade, it appears that there was considerable piling-up of potential migrants in the outlying areas.

It is clear, however, that, within metropolitan rings, "rural" growth exceeded urban during the depression decade, and the growth of unincorporated rural areas was in excess of that of small incorporated places.[13] The threat of war and the subsequent armament drive in the last years of the decade probably pushed the interdecade growth rates of many central cities to higher levels than would otherwise have been realized. In spite of the probable resumption of heavy cityward migration toward the end of the thirties, ring growth tended to exceed the growth of even the smaller metropolitan cities. A distinct majority of the cities of 50,000 and over were now exhibiting the pattern of relative decentralization formerly seen around only the larger cities.[14]

Finally, the most recent intercensal decade (1940–50) has witnessed a progressive diffusion of the patterns that had begun years earlier in the largest centers. Not only metropolitan centers but the larger satellites within the metropolitan orbit are decentralizing. The growth of "rural" and unincorporated area continues to outstrip that of the urban and incorporated places. The physical form of the metropolitan area, which had been axiate in pattern, is filling in, and the area resembles a great amorphous mass, although outlines of the older star-shaped pattern can still be discerned. More important, the functional boundaries of the metropolitan area, as indicated by the outward shift of high growth rates, appear to have shifted from a ring of approximately 10 miles to one of 20–25 miles in diameter.[15]

Throughout these fifty years of transition, a number of structural and functional circumstances appear to have been related to centrifugal growth, the most important of which is sheer size of population. In fact, most of the other factors associated with centrifugal growth are themselves associated with metropolitan size. Regional location also appears to be a factor of real significance. Other variables associated with size and regional location, however, show associations with decentralization that remain when these two variables are controlled.

[13] The old (1940) definitions of "urban" and "rural" used here tend seriously to overstate the rural component; many people classified as rural are actually urbanites by any reasonable functional definition.

[14] Donald J. Bogue, *Metropolitan Decentralization: A Study of Differential Growth* (Oxford, Ohio: Scripps Foundation for Research in Population Problems, 1950).

[15] Amos H. Hawley, *The Changing Shape of Metropolitan America: Deconcentration since 1920* (Glencoe: Free Press, 1956).

In addition to the primary variables, recent research has indicated that the areas in which decentralization occurred first and proceeded furthest tend to have densely populated central cities, in which growth has been slow during the last fifty years. They are most frequently older coastal cities. Manufacturing activity within the area has been decentralizing throughout most of the period.[16] All these findings, when taken together, suggest the importance of what might be termed the "maturity" of metropolitan areas. Those areas which have exhibited the earliest and most extreme evidence of decentralization appear to have reached an advanced stage of maturity that is merely reflected in the structural and functional characteristics enumerated here. In a rough sense, in fact, decentralization is an index of the maturity of metropolitan areas.

SOME RESEARCH IMPLICATIONS

In addition to the research needs touched upon previously, a number of other problems, present themselves for empirical scrutiny. A whole category of research problems can be subsumed under the rubric of the sources of differential growth within metropolitan areas. In addition to the relative contributions of natural increase and net migration, we need to know the origins of migrants by areal and functional types. Another whole range of empirical questions emerges when we consider the demographic and functional composition of the various parts of the metropolitan area and the migrant

streams that flow between them. Imposing as these problems are, however, they relate only to the residential population of metropolitan areas.[17]

In addition to a concern with the redistribution of residential population, of course, a full description of the changing organization of the metropolitan area must treat the other sociological units that constitute the total community. It appears that all the typically urban activities—the so-called "secondary" and "tertiary" functions of fabrication, distribution, and control[18]—have been subjected in some degree to the same forces of decentralization that have so dramatically altered the residential settlement pattern within local areas. The reduction of the friction imposed by distance has had noticeable effects in almost every sphere of life.

With respect to secondary (manufacturing) activities, there is obviously increasing freedom to locate at the margins of the community. As Bogue points out, "economists and industrialists have discovered that under modern conditions of transport it is no longer necessary for great industries to be located within the limits of the central city. There is a broad zone of indifference, probably several miles in diameter, which is locationally suitable."[19] Tertiary activities (trade, services, etc.) are probably affected similarly by changes in locational tolerance, but they have been less

---

[16] *Ibid.* In each instance the direction of association between a given variable and centrifugal growth tends to be the same as that found between the variable in question and metropolitan size. The direction of these relationships remains the same, although reduced in extent, within size classes. Although no single area can be found to possess every one of the characteristics, they tend to be associated with one another.

[17] Albert J. Reiss, Jr., has recently suggested a number of excellent topics for research in this area (see "Research Problems in Metropolitan Population Redistribution," *American Sociological Review,* XXI [October, 1956], 571–77). A number of his topics, however, are static in orientation. Another valuable discussion is contained in Henry S. Shryock, Jr., "Population Redistribution within Metropolitan Areas: Evaluation of Research," *Social Forces,* XXXV (December, 1956), 154–59.

[18] Clark, *op. cit.*

[19] Donald J. Bogue (ed.), *Needed Urban and Metropolitan Research* (Oxford, Ohio: Scripps Foundation for Research in Population Problems, 1953) p. 40.

carefully studied. The decentralization of functions such as wholesaling, storage, and distribution deserves more research. These activities have been traditionally viewed as centrally oriented, but recent developments in metropolitan organization warrant a reconsideration of this assumption. Faster and more frequent transportation, for example, may have decreased the need for central warehouse facilities. The handling of freight since the development of the motor truck has become a much more flexible operation, and a great deal of storage is apparently affected en route, without the necessity for maintaining large stockpiles and inventories immediately at hand.

Many administrative functions may also be increasingly free to leave the center and locate at the periphery of the metropolitan community. For example, the central offices of large insurance companies, whose chief contacts are with agents scattered throughout the nation, may represent a type of administration that can be as efficiently managed in the ring as in the center. The control and direction of other industries, however, which require frequent contact with lawyers, brokers, news media, advertising agencies, and out-of-town buyers may continue to require central location. Further research should identify the other units with which a given function is in most frequent contact—via both transportation and communication facilities—in addition to its requirements for space, in both amount and kind. These facts would provide valuable clues to the amount of decentralization to be anticipated among various functions.

Functional differences between suburban and satellite places still remain to be explored, and detailed knowledge of them is necessary for a full description of the social and economic organization of the expanded community.[20] In addition, more should be learned of the growth tendencies of different types of subnuclei in the metropolitan ring. Employing satellites, for example, show patterns of growth notably different from those of exclusively residential suburbs.[21] The growth of more specialized areas, including educational and recreational centers, may show divergent patterns in keeping with their narrowly specialized roles in the whole metropolitan area.

Trends in population growth within the central city itself are worthy of further exploration. Physical congestion in the center has frequently been advanced as a cause of decentralization. Most large cities have high proportions of habitable land that remains vacant,[22] but a substantial portion of it is in small parcels held for speculation, forcing prices beyond the limits possible for residential development.

At the same time, a more accurate description of the role of congestion can probably be gained by turning attention to traffic, itself a product of the separation of land uses seen in residential decentralization.[23] Traffic densities probably exert a greater influence than the more frequently measured densities of residential population. The daily massing of great volumes of people and vehicles in central areas may inhibit movement to such an ex-

[20] See Sanford M. Dornbusch, *A Typology of Suburban Communities: Chicago Metropolitan District 1940* ("Urban Analysis Reports," No. 10 [Chicago: Chicago Community Inventory, May, 1952]), and Leo F. Schnore, "The Functions of Metropolitan Suburbs," *American Journal of Sociology*, LXI (March, 1956), 453–58.

[21] Leo F. Schnore, "The Growth of Metropolitan Suburbs," *American Sociological Review*, XXII (April, 1957), 165–73.

[22] Harland Bartholomew, *Land Uses in American Cities* (Cambridge: Harvard University Press, 1955).

[23] Donald L. Foley, "Urban Day-Time Population: A Field for Demographic-ecological Analysis," *Social Forces*, XXXII (May, 1954), 323–30.

tent that the center loses its traditionally favored position as the point of maximum accessibility to the entire metropolitan area.

A closely related area of metropolitan research offers great promise for cross-cultural comparisons. A number of studies of the daily journey to work have been conducted in both Europe and the United States.[24] The studies in this country have been based primarily upon by-product data from traffic research, and being limited to areas with particularly serious traffic problems, the American investigations probably represent a biased sample of all urban areas. Many of the European studies, however, have been based upon census materials, for the census schedules of most European nations include at least one question regarding the place of work of members of the employed labor force.[25] This is one of the rare instances in which the United States census lags behind data-collection in other nations of the world. Information on place of work in future censuses in this country would permit a much more complete description of the functional organization of the entire metropolitan area; the daily circulations and exchanges—centrifugal, centripetal, and lateral—between the various subparts of the area could then be accurately determined.[26]

Previous remarks imply that long-distance commuting is restricted to upper-income groups. However, the rapid increase in automobile ownership in all social strata in our society has made suburbs and satellites, as well as the unincorporated places in the ring, accessible to those with moderate incomes and even to some with lower incomes. Wherever zoning regulations are not in effect, cheap housing can be built on cheap land. Scattered research has suggested that the European pattern on part-time farming by urban workers may become established in the vicinity of many American industrial cities, particularly near those in which factory work is seasonal.[27] Ride-sharing arrangements between urban workers who live in the ring are still another device permitting peripheral residential location of families which otherwise could not afford the high cost of transportation to the center.[28] More generally, trends in housing have had an important place in this entire development, but here research is seriously deficient. With the passage of the years, the techniques of mass production have been adapted to the construction of dwellings. We need to know the dynamic causal factors operating to bring about areal differentials in construction of various types within the metropolitan community. Such knowledge would throw light upon the problem of the

[27] Nathan L. Whetten and R. F. Field, *Studies of Suburbanization in Connecticut*, No. 2: *Norwich: An Industrial Part-time Farming Area* (Storrs: Connecticut State College Agricultural Experiment Station Bull. 226 [1938]); W. R. Gordon, *Satellite Acres* (Kingston: Rhode Island State College Agricultural Experiment Station Bull. 282 [1942]); Walter Firey, *Social Aspects of Land Use Planning in the Country-City Fringe* (East Lansing: Michigan State College Agricultural Experiment Station Bull. 339 [1946]); Glenn H. Beyer, *Housing and Journey to Work* (Ithaca: Cornell University Agricultural Experiment Station Bull. 877 [1951]).

[28] Leo F. Schnore, "The Separation of Home and Work: A Problem for Human Ecology," *Social Forces*, XXXII (May, 1954), 336–43. The so-called "marginal labor force" appears to be physically marginal to industrial cities. This suggests that the "rural-urban fringe" is amenable to identification in functional (occupational) as well as areal terms. The latter conception, in fact, may be extremely misleading in many instances.

[24] *Ibid.*; and Kate K. Liepmann, *The Journey to Work* (New York: Oxford University Press, 1944).

[25] Foley, *op. cit.*

[26] The rapid advances made in sampling techniques should permit this valuable addition to the 1960 Census. Technical problems can be solved by experimentation with alternative methods in the Current Population Survey and in special state and local censuses prior to adoption in the federal decennial census.

redistribution of residential population, as well as other functional components, such as industrial and commercial establishments.[29]

In this connection, some research should be directed toward delineating more carefully some of the differences in socioeconomic level between suburban and satellite places within the metropolitan ring. Rental and income data are now available for at least the larger incorporated places in the ring, and these can be easily supplemented by statistics on education and occupational and ethnic composition. Many observers have suggested the emergence of rigid segregation in the suburbs along social and economic lines. Indeed, it is said that the mass production of suburban housing attracts persons of similar status,[30] an economic compulsion toward segregated living which seems to be further implemented by zoning. Whether these trends are any more coercive, however, than the forces that have long made for segregation *within* the city is a matter for future research.

This discussion has made use of the newly developed census concept of the Standard Metropolitan Area. Every use in research of such a statistical reporting unit, of course, constitutes something of a test of its validity. There is some evidence that the Standard Metropolitan Area encompasses only the zone of most rapid growth in recent years, but both Bogue and Hawley have shown that the influence of the metropolis is reflected in the growth rates of areas many miles beyond the commuting zone. Beyond this zone of primary interchange, of course, lies a much broader hinterland in which integration with the center is expressed through indirect contacts. Thus research cannot be confined to the Standard Metropolitan Area alone. The area of direct contact with the center, however, appears to be well delineated by the definition. At any rate, the utility of these areas as reporting units is enhanced by the vast amount of data assembled on a county basis by other governmental and private agencies. Fuller use of the data will permit at least tentative answers to many current questions.

Many problems of administration and planning arise out of our ignorance of the details of change in the form of the community. The provision of accurate descriptions of community structure is the responsibility of sociological research, but the task is far from complete. If we are ever to solve the host of practical problems so rapidly developing in the wake of decentralization, we shall have to assemble more and more facts. But, even more important, we shall have to provide conceptual schemes with which to interpret these facts.

The problems raised in this paper point to the fact that we need a complete theory, subsuming both structural and functional aspects of all the constituent units of the community. Moreover, such a theory should be capable of generating testable hypotheses referring to both static and dynamic relationships between variables. Technological innovation, land-use conversion, segregation, population growth and redistribution—all these are terms referring to *processes*. Any sound conceptual approach must be

---

[29] Dorothy K. Newman, "Metropolitan Area Structure and Growth as Shown by Building-Permit Statistics," *Business Topics*, IV (November, 1956), 1–7. Within metropolitan areas, new housing construction is especially rapid in the ring. Although Newman presents data for only a small number of areas, all but 8 of the 168 currently recognized Standard Metropolitan Areas have higher proportions of newly constructed dwelling units in the ring than in the central city.

[30] Leslie Kish, "Differentiation in Metropolitan Areas," *American Sociological Review*, XIX (August, 1954), 388–98.

phrased in dynamic terms such as these, if for no other reason than that the modern metropolitan community is constantly changing.

The construction of such a theory will be no mere intellectual exercise. As one demographer has recently asserted:

> One of the reasons for such strong disagreements and conflicting recommendations about so-called "decentralization" is that specialists in the field of urban population and human ecology have failed to produce a theory of urban growth that is valid for the mid-20th century.

Perhaps we have been overly concerned with perfecting a static theory of city structure. . . . Our study of structure needs to be accompanied by a rigorous program of research into growth and change. Research in urbanism and metropolitanism should have dynamic as well as static aspects.[31]

One can only agree with these ambitious goals and hope that the discussion contained in this paper will contribute to their ultimate achievement.

[31] Bogue, *Needed Urban and Metropolitan Research*, p. 38.

Los Angeles, The Fragmented Metropolis

Robert M. Fogelson*

Urbanization had an overwhelming impact on the landscape of greater Los Angeles. Before 1885 the region was predominantly rural. Flocks of sheep foraged on the Santa Ana plain, and thousands of acres went uncultivated in western Los Angeles. Immense wheat fields covered the San Fernando Valley ranches, and corn stalks grew tall on the El Monte farms. Vineyards were planted symmetrically in eastern Los Angeles, and orchards were tended in clusters in the San Gabriel Valley. These flourishing valleys and the nearby mountains overwhelmed small settlements such as Anaheim and Pasadena. Even in Los Angeles, then the section's first and the state's third city, more than 90 per cent of its thirty-six square miles were rustic. Everywhere bountiful gardens relieved the severe earth, fragrant fruits diluted the pungent mesquite, and agriculture imposed its quiet on the region. Nowhere did the population, facilities, and businesses of the region's urban centers intrude much upon the sights, smells, and sounds of the agrarian environment.

Immigration and enterprise, of course, created a market for residential and commercial property after 1850; but the transformation of rural land into urban property was the responsibility of private enterprise not municipal authority. Corporate utilities provided service only when convinced that anticipated revenues justified initial expenditures; they made commitments cautiously even under

*Reprinted by permission of the publishers from Robert M. Fogelson, *The Fragmented Metropolis: Los Angeles, 1850–1930*, Cambridge, Mass.: Harvard University Press, Copyright, 1967, by the President and Fellows of Harvard College.

favorable circumstances. Individual developers undertook improvements only when confident that current demand exceeded existing supply; thus their activities were limited to the minor booms of the early 1870's and 1880's. For these reasons the transformed portion of Los Angeles did not extend more than two miles from the town's center before 1885. And since many landholders found agriculture sufficiently profitable and conversion prohibitively expensive, subdivision proceeded sporadically and erratically even in central Los Angeles.

The separation of homes from stores and shops accompanied the expansion of Los Angeles. Unsuccessful Americans, unassimilated Chinese, and unadjusted Mexicans still rented rooms in dilapidated and overcrowded adobes and shacks amid rundown hotels, gambling dens, and houses of prostitution near the old plaza. But prosperous and respectable native Americans and European immigrants who refused to live there purchased lots and erected houses on outlying tracts in the southern and western flats and the northern and eastern hills. At the same time many businessmen moved from central to southern Los Angeles. While retailers followed the residential subdivisions, wholesalers pressed towards the railroad station; while professionals concentrated in the Temple Street vicinity, craftsmen spread all over the south-central section. These enterprises extended over only a few blocks, but, dominating the town's economy, they formed its principal commercial center in 1885.

Incipient industrialists who considered this district too congested and costly sought larger and cheaper parcels elsewhere. Some attempted to exploit local water power and obviate high-priced coal by constructing plants close to the Los Angeles River. Others followed their lead when the Southern Pacific routed its main line alongside the river. By 1885 a small but active manufacturing complex—made up of a gas plant, flour mills, rail yards, and slaughterhouses—had emerged there. Land-use segregation did not encompass the agricultural (and thus the largest) portion of Los Angeles, however. Nor was it complete, extensive, and irreversible elsewhere. The poor and the minorities still lived in the old business center, the residential, commercial, and manufacturing areas were not yet far apart, and the inclinations of the town's entrepreneurs alone sanctioned this arrangement. From the perspective of the people of Los Angeles, however, land-use segregation was desirable and deserved encouragement.

The developers shaped the town's layout as well as its land-use. They favored the traditional American gridiron—an arrangement of perpendicularly interesting streets—which simplified subdivision and, they believed, reduced expenses and facilitated marketing. "I have planned for straight lines and not for curved ones in the street alignments," a civil engineer reported to a San Gabriel Valley subdivider. "The advantages gained are economy of survey and platting and probably better sale for the property than if it were cut up on curves." The developers divided the rest of the land into suburban lots, from 5,000 to 7,000 square feet in size and twice as deep as wide, which fronted on narrow thoroughfares and supplied space for modest houses surrounded by front lawns, small gardens, and rear yards. The developers covered the tracts with streets and lots, reserving little or no property for community purposes, and disposed of their holdings as rapidly as possible, permanently relinquishing responsibility for the subdivision's future.

The purchasers or contractors who designed the buildings faithfully reproduced the picturesque patterns then prevailing in the United States. Distinguished by wide verandas, wooden shingles, bay windows, and mansard roofs, their Victorian homes looked like country cottages fashionable in both the Pacific Northwest and northern California. Replete with Corinthian columns, iron façades, Renaissance cornices, and ornamental towers, their business blocks closely resembled commercial edifices familiar in Seattle and Sacramento alike. While southern Californians boasted of their unique climate, history, and resources, nothing in the setting, structure, and materials of their architecture evoked these features—except, ironically, the deteriorating Mexican adobes. With its rustic landscape, limited dispersal, segregated land-use, gridiron layout, and picturesque aesthetic, Los Angeles differed little in appearance from the typical town of the late nineteenth-century American West.

After 1885 Los Angeles became increasingly urban. As a result of the prodigious growth of the population, the widespread demand for property, and the marked advance of industry, herds were moved out of the region, crops were harvested for the last time, and orchards were relentlessly destroyed. Henceforth the landscape of greater Los Angeles was dominated by homes, offices, stores, and factories; streets, sidewalks, and railways; and water mains, gas pipes, electric lines, and sewers. The cities covered the countryside; Anaheim spread over the southeastern plain, Pasadena extended to the Sierra Madre Mountains, and the amount of land subdivided in Los Angeles proper increased more than one hundredfold. Even in the distant eastern San Gabriel and western San Fernando valleys, which were still cultivated, and the steep Hollywood and Baldwin Hills, which were yet wasteland, the services and facilities requisite for development were available by 1930.

Although Los Angeles had to expand into a vast urban center—after all, two million new inhabitants and a billion dollars of additional business had to be provided with adequate transportation, water, utilities, property, and buildings—it did not have to emerge as the dispersed metropolis par excellence. Yet with far fewer people and much less manufacturing than metropolitan Chicago and Philadelphia, greater Los Angeles, as Table I reveals, encompassed many more square miles. Also, with slightly more persons and much less industry than metropolitan Detroit and Boston, it numbered far fewer residents per square mile. Moreover, whereas the population ratio of central city to outlying suburbs exceeded sixteen to one in Pittsburgh and reached twenty-three to one in St. Louis, it came to fewer than three to one in Los Angeles. In 1930, therefore, the structure of greater Los Angeles differed radically from that of the typical American metropolis—a divergence not wholly attributable to the material progress of southern California.

Los Angeles' chronology contributed to this incongruity. The metropolis grew slowly in the era of the horse car, rapidly during the period of the electric railway, and even faster in the age of the private automobile. But so did Detroit and Minneapolis which, as Table I indicates, were less extensively and less evenly dispersed. Los Angeles' geography also expedited dispersal. The southern and western plains extended to the ocean and the northern and eastern valleys to the mountains; so no natural barriers con-

TABLE I

AREA AND DENSITY OF SELECTED METROPOLITAN DISTRICTS, 1930

Metropolitan district	Population (in thousands)	Area in sq. miles	Population per sq. mile	Population per sq. mile in central city	Population per sq. mile outside central city
New York	10,901	2,514	4,336	23,179	1,001
Chicago	4,365	1,119	3,890	16,723	1,077
Cleveland	1,195	310	3,852	12,725	1,230
Milwaukee	743	242	3,076	14,056	824
Philadelphia	2,847	994	2,865	15,242	1,035
Detroit	2,105	747	2,819	11,375	881
Boston	2,308	1,023	2,257	17,795	1,560
Minneapolis-St. Paul	832	525	1,584	8,384	231[a]
St. Louis	1,294	822	1,574	13,475	573[b]
Los Angeles	2,319	1,474	1,572	2,812	1,045
San Francisco-Oakland	1,290	828	1,563	15,105	509[c]
Pittsburgh	1,954	1,602	1,201	13,057	815

Source: U.S. Bureau of the Census, *Fifteenth Census of the United States: 1930. Metropolitan Districts* (Washington, 1932), pp. 35, 49, 57, 73, 115, 129, 131, 140, 159, 165, 171, 193, 203, 215.
  [a] Excluding St. Paul.
  [b] Excluding East St. Louis.
  [c] Excluding Oakland.

centrated settlement. But, except for Lakes Michigan and Erie, respectively, greater Milwaukee and Cleveland were likewise unobstructed, and they too far exceeded Los Angeles in overall and differential densities. Hence neither timing nor nature fully accounted for the physical uniqueness of the Los Angeles landscape.

Changes in the operation, management, scope, and regulation of transportation and utilities also removed restraints on expansion in Los Angeles. The connection between electric railways and real estate subdivision and the subsequent monopolization of the street and interurban lines by Huntington and Harriman spurred the creation of an extensive radial transit network. Municipalization of the waterworks supplanted a private company, responsible to its stockholders and devoted to profits, with a public department, responsive to the community and committed to expansion. The highway authorities and Metropolitan Water District supplemented the corporations and the city by providing motor thoroughfares and domestic water to places off the railroads and outside Los Angeles. And both local and state commissions compelled the gas, electric, and telephone utilities to serve customers whenever they deposited funds to construct additions to the distributing systems. These improvements were permissive not compulsory, however; they encouraged but did not compel subdivision.

Differences in kind among the developers fostered dispersal in Los Angeles too. There were still operators who relied upon persuasion instead of capital, amateurs who converted property in their spare time, and promoters who marketed small and cheap subdivisions. But now there were also investors such as Henry E. Huntington who possessed funds to undertake almost any project, professionals such

as H. J. Whitley who made development their life's work, and entrepreneurs such as Robert C. Gillis who transformed whole sections of Los Angeles into exclusive suburbs. Wealthier, more capable, and more imaginative than their predecessors, they gave an entirely new dimension to subdivision. Nevertheless, like the companies and agencies that extended facilities under pressure from consumers and voters, the Huntingtons, Whitleys, and Gillises transformed real estate according to the preferences of their prospective purchasers.

Hence the unique dispersal of Los Angeles reflected not so much its chronology, geography, or technology as the exceptional character of its population. It was not like Chicago—a typical concentrated metropolis—inhabited largely by impoverished and insecure European immigrants, who, in their attempt to find work and fellowship, were confined to the city's teeming tenements and crowded ghettos. The model of the dispersed metropolis, Los Angeles was populated principally by native Americans with adequate resources and marketable skills, who faced the problems of adjustment confidently because of a common language and similar background. Relatively affluent and secure, the native Americans had a much wider choice than the European immigrants of housing and communities—to both of which, as newcomers in quest of a well-rounded life more than a remunerative occupation, they gave an extremely high priority.

Moreover, the native Americans came to Los Angeles with a conception of the good community which was embodied in single-family houses, located on large lots, surrounded by landscaped lawns, and isolated from business activities. Not for them multifamily dwellings, confined to narrow plots, separated by cluttered streets, and interspersed with commerce and industry. Their vision was epitomized by the residential suburb—spacious, affluent, clean, decent, permanent, predictable, and homogeneous—and violated by the great city—congested, impoverished, filthy, immoral, transient, uncertain, and heterogeneous. The late nineteenth- and early twentieth-century metropolis, as the newcomers in Los Angeles perceived it, was the receptacle for all European evils and the source of all American sins. It contradicted their long-cherished notions about the proper environment and compelled them to retreat to outskirts uncontaminated by urban vices and conducive to rural virtues. And though native Americans everywhere shared these sentiments, they formed a larger portion of the populace in Los Angeles than in other great metropolises. Here then was the basis for the extraordinary dispersal of Los Angeles.

The developers, who were predominantly native Americans, responded sympathetically. "I can't understand why anyone should oppose the expansion of the city," one remarked. "If people did not go into the outside

tracts that are being opened up they would be forced into apartments." Even more important, they knew that these preferences generated profitable opportunities in subdivision, particularly in the outlying sections where real estate was still inexpensive. For these reasons they transformed southern California's vast countryside into Los Angeles' sprawling suburbs. The purchasers subsequently constructed houses there, and by 1930 Los Angeles, as Table II shows, had more single-family and fewer multi-family dwellings than any comparable American metropolis—except to some extent Philadelphia. Since most newcomers preferred to rent accommodations until they decided where in the metropolis to settle, however, only slightly more than one-third of them owned their homes.

The developers realized that a homogeneous population and compatible land-use were no less essential than a proper layout to the suburban vision. To this end they devised appropriate deed restrictions. These not only prohibited occupancy by Negroes and Orientals in most tracts and, in the more exclusive ones, fixed mini-

TABLE II
FAMILIES AND DWELLINGS IN SELECTED CITIES, 1930

City	Number of families (in thousands)	Number of dwellings (in thousands)	Per cent of total dwellings		
			1-family	2-family	3-or-more-family
Los Angeles	*369*	*301*	*93.9*	*3.8*	*2.4*
Philadelphia	458	398	91.6	6.1	2.3
San Francisco	179	119	88.3	5.9	5.9
Washington	126	85	87.9	8.0	4.1
Baltimore	194	163	86.7	10.8	2.5
Detroit	370	263	79.7	15.5	4.8
Pittsburgh	155	117	77.4	18.0	4.5
Cleveland	222	146	69.2	23.2	7.6
St. Louis	215	141	64.1	29.1	6.8
New York	1,723	557	52.8	24.5	22.7
Chicago	843	403	52.0	28.9	19.1
Boston	179	89	49.5	25.5	25.0

Source: U.S. Bureau of the Census, *Fifteenth Census of the United States: 1930. Population. Volume VI. Families* (Washington, 1933), p. 72.

mum costs for houses so as—in one developer's words—"to group the people of more or less like income together." They also forbade commercial and industrial activities in most subdivisions, and, again in the more fashionable ones, outlawed all but the single-family houses deemed—by most Los Angeles residents—"the foundation of this country's security." (Whereas the restrictions on use, though not on race, normally expired after one or two decades in ordinary developments, they usually extended in perpetuity in more pretentious ones. In short, deed restrictions were employed by the subdividers to ensure that most of greater Los Angeles' suburbs would stay strictly homogeneous and purely residential.

Los Angeles' extraordinary dispersal was thereafter accelerated by its populace's extreme mobility. At first most newcomers found the entire region as enchanting as one woman who confided in her diary that "[southern] California seems so pretty all over that it is hard to say which is the best part." But, guided by tangible considerations such as climate, topography, accessibility, and price, they eventually selected a subdivision, purchased a lot, and built a house. They rarely remained there long, however. It was not just that the influx of Mexicans, Japanese, and Negroes and the expansion of commerce and industry threatened the homogeneity and rusticity of many subdivisions. It was also that the native Americans felt little attachment to neighborhoods which, like themselves, were so new as to be devoid of any meaningful institutional ties. Thus, so long as the real estate market remained active, these people moved time and again to more prestigious, though no less homogeneous and rustic, suburbs elsewhere in Los Angeles.

The aspirations of the Mexicans,

Japanese, and Negroes who initially settled in the central Los Angeles ghetto also fostered residential dispersal in outlying parts of the metropolis. Although the colored minorities there lived in houses and not tenements, they, no less than the white majority, preferred modern homes in suburban settings. But developers only subdivided tracts for them which, as a result of inferior drainage or other disadvantages, were not otherwise marketable. Hence colored people with funds and determination had no alternative save to attempt to enter the few subdivisions where deed restrictions had never been applied or had already expired. But there they often encountered the opposition of white landowners who explained that, though they had—as they put it—no objection to colored people "in their place," "they must not crowd us out and lower the value of our property." Still, they sometimes secured houses outside central Los Angeles, and, as their white neighbors fled in panic, other colored people succeeded them, forming suburban enclaves and furthering residential dispersal in greater Los Angeles.

Los Angeles' unmatched residential dispersal was only one manifestation of the community's antiurban ethos. Its unprecedented business decentralization was another, though it was barely evident as late as 1920. By then suburbanization had brought about a thorough, extensive, and permanent land-use segregation in the metropolis. For the thousands of Mexicans, Japanese, and Negroes who lived amidst commerce and industry in the small ghettos of central Los Angeles and San Pedro there were a million white Americans who resided in the suburbs sprawling north to Hollywood, east to Pasadena, south to Long Beach, and west to Santa Monica. Moreover, greater Los Angeles extended so far into the countryside that only electric trains and motor cars connected its homes, stores, and factories—a pattern not only preferred by the populace and imposed by the developers, but also sanctioned by city and county authorities. Land-use segregation was characteristic of other American metropolises, however, and so the uniqueness of Los Angeles' landscape had not yet extended by 1920 beyond its residential dispersal.

Here as elsewhere, the downtown district dominated the region's business. It was clearly the locus of employment; according to a traffic survey conducted in January 1924, 1.2 million persons a day, or more than the entire population of the city, traveled to and from the section bounded by Temple, Figueroa, Pico, and Los Angeles Streets. It was also the center of commerce. "It is a common sight on the highways," a utility company executive observed in 1915, "to see large trucks . . . headed for some town outside Los Angeles crowded, filled to the brim, but returning empty." As the focus of Los Angeles' economy, moreover, downtown expanded from a few small shops and offices covering several blocks in 1885 to many large mercantile and professional buildings spread over a square mile in 1920— the most concentrated section in southern California. And though most people took more pride in the outlying residential suburbs than the central business district, they believed that it had achieved a position in Los Angeles comparable to the Loop in Chicago and Lower Manhattan in New York.

Downtown also steadily shifted south and west, and its center moved from Spring and Third in 1885 to Sixth and Hill in 1920. New buildings there gained the retail trade, a banker noted in 1909, because shoppers encountered congestion further north and east. The extreme fluctuations in

values that accompanied this movement sorely distressed property owners, and they called on private enterprise and public authority to anchor the central business district. The construction of financial houses on Spring, utility headquarters on Fifth, department stores on Broadway, and (incipiently) a civic center at Temple permanently fixed downtown Los Angeles' location in the 1920's. In the meantime, however, its function changed. Between 1885 and 1920, as Chart 1 reveals, office buildings and department stores increased their share of downtown space at the expense of hotels and stores. These changes notwithstanding, the central business district still held more than three-quarters of Los Angeles' commercial and professional enterprise in 1920.

Industry, by contrast, was not concentrated downtown. This was not because the small manufacturers who operated lofts found land there too expensive. Although some who did moved to the depressed district north of Temple Street and the rundown section south of Pico Street, over half of the city's lofts were still located in the central business district in 1920. It was rather because the large industrialists, who, unlike merchants, lawyers, and small manufacturers, derived few advantages from a central location, required more space than was available downtown at any price. They preferred to locate in the vicinity of the original industrial district in southeastern Los Angeles which was served by the Southern Pacific, Santa Fe, and Pacific Electric and consisted of large undeveloped tracts. When the Goodyear Tire and Rubber Company decided to establish its Pacific coast branch facilities in Los Angeles, for example, it transformed an immense parcel south of downtown and west of the railroad tracts into a massive manufacturing center.

For other heavy industries, the waterfront district was the choice location. It had not only immediate access to the harbor and direct contact with the transcontinental lines, but also abundant water and power, adequate rail and truck connections, and inexpensive acreage, factors that strongly attracted industrialists. When the Ford Motor Company decided to abandon its downtown automobile factory, for instance, it bought property at Long Beach large enough to house its sprawling assembly plant and close enough to the water to receive parts by ship. Manufacturers were able to exploit inexpensive acreage here by virtue of the existing rail transportation and public utilities, but they were unable to build plants elsewhere in the metropolis because of the absence of these facilities. Just as commerce was concentrated in the central business district until 1920, industry, while somewhat decentralized, was confined to the downtown, southeastern, and waterfront vicinities.

Business centralization was thus far compatible with residential dispersal in Los Angeles—as in other American metropolises—because of its land-use patterns, transport facilities, and utility services. The scattered suburban population did not form a large enough market for outlying retail enterprises, and the radial electric railways, which did not supply cross-town service, provided swift and inexpensive transit in and out of downtown. Hence the metropolis' merchants felt little incentive to relocate stores and found little difficulty in attracting customers. Moreover, the transcontinental railroads (and, less important, the Pacific Electric) did not operate freight trains everywhere in Los Angeles. Nor did the private companies and public agencies distribute utilities throughout the entire metropolis. Thus, as the existing industrial districts contained enough acreage at reasonable prices,

the manufacturers, like the merchants, found centralization profitable as well as obligatory.

These conditions changed soon after 1920. The retail market grew prodigiously in the suburbs, reflecting not so much the increase of immigration—which was accompanied by the expansion of territory—as the changes in the character of the populace. First, in response to the influx of single persons, entrepreneurs erected outlying apartment houses. Their proportion of new construction advanced, as Chart 2 shows, from 8 per cent in 1920 to 53 per cent in 1928. An extremely small fraction of all housing in Los Angeles, apartment houses were so concentrated as to raise densities in communities such as Hollywood and on thoroughfares such as Wilshire Boulevard. Second, in response to the wealth of many residents, developers created very exclusive subdivisions such as Beverly Hills and San Marino which had enormous purchasing power. Although the subdividers restricted business there, they reserved lots along major arteries for commerce. Nonetheless, these changes were essentially permissive. They generated opportunities for mercantile enterprise in the suburbs, but they did not compel established businesses to desert downtown.

The failure of the electric railways, however, did just that. The street and interurban lines were heavily congested as early as 1910: "There are times in the rush hours," the Los Angeles *Examiner* reported "when every foot of trackage in the business district is covered with trolley cars." Subsequently, the electric railways had to share the surface with private automobiles, the number of which in Los Angeles County soared from under 200,000 in 1920 to over 500,000 in 1924. By then 262,000 motorcars traveled in and out of downtown everyday and, with the trains, so tightly jammed the streets that, as distraught witnesses complained to the California Railroad Commission, it was very hard to reach the central business district. The municipal authorities attempted to alleviate this congestion, but to little avail. And in time the electric railways, plagued by automobile competition that increased their expenditures and reduced their revenues, so curtailed service and raised fares that the car supplanted the train as the principal means of transportation in Los Angeles.

The central business district profoundly felt the repercussions. Since at least twenty autos were required to convey as many people as one train, traffic became heavier, travel took longer, and parking space became scarcer. The optimists predicted that these troubles, delays, and expenses would discourage drivers and compel them to ride the railways again. Others disagreed, arguing that the residents, faced with these alternatives, would avoid downtown before they returned to the trains. The pessimists proved more perceptive. Between 1923 and 1931, while the population within ten miles of the central business district expanded 50 per cent, the number of people entering downtown Los Angeles increased only 15 per cent. "The automobile has brought a distinct change in the city building," a visitor who observed these trends predicted. "The day is not far distant when vehicular congestion will be so great down town that enterprising merchants will be establishing great department stores in outlying business centers where shoppers can be conveniently served."

The triumph of motor transport facilitated the decentralization of industry too. The extensive county highway and city street systems enabled manufacturers—long dependent on the railroads—to move freight throughout the region by trucks. Widespread automobile ownership, combined with sprawling suburban subdivisions, also rendered hitherto remote and still cheap residential locations accessible to the working force. The expansion of utility facilities undermined another basis for industrial concentration. The municipal authorities provided inexpensive water and power throughout the city, and regional districts and private companies supplied service at slightly higher rates elsewhere. Hence, when rapid industrial development in the 1920's made land in the still desirable downtown, southeastern, and waterfront sections extremely expensive, the industrialists had a far greater choice of sites.

The decentralization of commerce and industry followed. In response to the expansion of suburban retail markets and the inaccessibility of central Los Angeles, prominent mercantile concerns relocated old stores and opened new ones along Wilshire, Hollywood, and other fashionable boulevards. Downtown, which now consisted of even fewer shops, hotels, and lofts and more office buildings, governmental structures, and garages, had only about half of the metropolis' commercial and professional enterprise and was only one, and by no means the most stylish, of its business districts. Meanwhile, in conjunction with local realtors, mammoth manufacturing firms established segregated industrial complexes throughout Los Angeles. Steelmakers constructed furnaces at Torrance, oil producers erected refineries at El Segundo, aviation companies built hangars near Santa Monica, and motion picture magnates spread studios over the San Fernando Valley. Hence business decentralization, combined with residential dispersal, created an urban form in greater Los Angeles consistent with its growth and yet unique in the United States in 1930.

The Governmental Dilemma of the Metropolis

Scott Greer*

Late in the last century a distinguished commentator on American life noted that municipal government was the one conspicuous failure of our society. Coming from Britain, where local government is administered by the middle class in terms of its understanding of the general welfare, Lord Bryce was shocked.[1] American cities, with elaborate machinery for enforcing democracy, were run by gangs. Tammany Hall shamelessly bribed, corrupted, and sold out the policy of New York City to the highest bidder. The men who ran our governments operated by a moral code whose chief distinction was that between "honest graft" and "dishonest graft." (The immortal phrase is from Plunkitt of Tammany Hall, whose self-designed epitaph was "He seen his opportunities and he took them.")[2] Enormous contracts were sold for private income; criminals bought hunting licenses from the police; ordinary enterprise paid tribute to the *condottieri* of City Hall.

There is more to this picture, however. Seth Low, Mayor of Brooklyn at the time of Lord Bryce's visit, appends a rebuttal to the last edition of the Englishman's book. Eloquently, he makes a major point. At whatever cost in plunder and crime, the cities of America in the last half of the nineteenth century grew tenfold. Urban population increased from less than

four million to more than thirty million. A rapidly growing nation which was 15 per cent urban in 1850 was 40 per cent urban by the turn of the century. It was a true population explosion. And as Low points out, these floods of people were housed, order was maintained, streets were built, transport was established, water was brought in, and wastes were carried away. What wonder that many mistakes were made? More impressive is the over-all achievement. The fantastic expansion of the urban plant in nineteenth century America is one of the most striking examples of collective achievement.

Lord Bryce, however, might still retort, "Yes, but at what a cost." And most of the unnecessary cost of that development was due to governmental structure inadequate to the burdens of explosive urbanization. To understand this we must look at American definitions of municipal government. These were the rules, inherited from the past, codified in law and the state constitutions, which set the limits within which our urban governments could develop. They were quite inadequate to the floods of history.

THE NORMS OF LOCAL GOVERNMENT IN THE UNITED STATES

American cities ceased to be administered by appointed delegates of the state after the Revolutionary War. Instead, an effort was made to combine dominance by the state legislatures with Jacksonian democracy. At the price of considerable simplification, let us say that Jacksonian ideology was translated into these norms. (1) The city was responsible to the ordinary

*Reprinted with permission from Scott Greer, *Governing the Metropolis*, New York: John Wiley & Sons, 1962, 45–57.

[1] James Bryce, *The American Commonwealth*, London and New York: Macmillan and Company, 1889.

[2] George Washington Plunkitt, *Plunkitt of Tammany Hall* (as recorded by William Riordan), New York: McClure-Philips and Company, 1905.

citizen through universal manhood suffrage; (2) office was open to all and could be managed successfully by any citizen; (3) the citizens had a sacred right to local self-rule. The results were chiefly visible in the incompetence and peculation common to urban government. With massive public works, a flood of culturally illiterate new citizens, and the exposure of all key offices to the electorate, government became a key form of private enterprise to its practitioners. And, because of their interdependence within the urban area, many nonpolitical persons were drawn willy-nilly into the "ring" that ran the city. The basic ambivalence between local self-rule and the doctrine that the legal city was merely a creature of the State led to frequent special and discriminatory acts at the state capitol. The big, wicked city was deemed incapable of governing itself. State legislatures responded with "ripper legislation" aimed at destroying powers of the city. Some major cities, such as Memphis and Mobile, were actually abolished. The police force of St. Louis is still partially controlled from Jefferson City, the little capitol city of Missouri.[3]

At the same time, the state constitutions provided easy means of incorporating new municipalities. Under the "right to local self-rule," state constitutions also specified extremely difficult processes for annexation or amalgamation of existing cities. Furthermore, translation of this right into political form meant that the city was required to gain the consent of the citizens for any major change in police power and fiscal capacity. Thus tax rates, bond issues, structural changes, annexations and mergers, were submitted to the voters. *Vox populi* was indeed interpreted as *vox Dei*—the voice of the people was considered to be the only legitimate voice where major change was concerned. Wherever a group of residents saw their common interest demanding it, a municipality could be created. It was extremely difficult to destroy the legal entity once it was created without the consent of the citizens, while formal change was almost impossible except by referendum.

This governmental response to social change was one typical of social organizations. Every effort was made to persist in the earlier patterns of behavior, for such patterns represented commitments for many persons. In the face of the astronomical increase in population, in social functions, in the scale of the total society, every effort was made to carry on local government business as usual. For upon the existing scheme of things rested the plans and hopes of political bosses, ward heelers, contractors, private businessmen, ethnic enclaves—all those concerned with the city government as a major factor in their lives and business.

The emphasis during the period of rapid urbanization was upon getting the job done. If the city needed a streetcar grid, or a rapid transit, and the unwieldy city council objected, bribe the council. If the electoral machinery with its laundry list of elected officers made rational voting impossible, accept the organized machinery of the parties. If a hundred thousand new citizens did not understand Anglo-Saxon traditions of self rule let the "pols" teach them the ropes. It was a strategy of opportunism and expediency. In the process, the polity of the city was degraded; it became a necessary tool for the achievement of ends by private enterprise. The great capital investments of the period were largely the creation of private capital, working

[3] For an extensive discussion of the underlying political norms and their translation into governmental rules, see Charles R. Adrian, *Governing Urban America*, Second Edition, New York: McGraw-Hill Book Company, 1961.

with franchises, contracts, and permits bought, stolen, or forced from the elected officials of local governments. When, in short, the burdens upon government became too much for the legitimate system of government, ways were found to circumvent the system.

HOW THE CITIES GREW UP

Needless to say, there was little concern for long-range planning in such a system. Government followed private enterprise: the labor force surged into a booming city, bringing its families and problems and social costs with it. Willy-nilly, government accepted the consequences—in the maintenance of public safety, the provision of charity, the extension of the city's physical plant, the policing of labor-management relations, the struggle to control organized criminal rings. Rather than planning for the future, urban government was continually struggling with its debts to the past, and it was always in arrears.

There was, after all, little to guide a planner. The forecasting of urban growth is still a primitive science, and in the earlier days of urbanization when there was no precedent for such growth, nobody really understood what was happening. Thus the framework of local government was not radically reexamined in the light of the vast social transformation described earlier. Instead, reformers concentrated on the most obvious abuses in the existing system. They struggled to take the policy away from the political machines (those organizations interested primarily in the monetary rewards of politics) through the institution of nonpartisan government, civil service systems, and eventually the city manager form of government. The reformers were, in short, chiefly concerned with civilizing a governmental jungle where politics was simply a form of private enterprise.

However, the city was already changing under their feet, and with its change new problems emerged. The commuter trains, and later the electric railways, opened many new sites for settlement, some of them far beyond the city limits. Those with the resources in money and time began to move outward from the central city. The suburban dispersal had begun. As they moved outside city boundaries, the resources of the central city were no longer at their disposal. The suburban enclaves were faced with the housekeeping problems of the spatial community; under the permissive constitutional provisions, they solved them through incorporating their residential neighborhoods as villages or towns. Thus the central cities began to be surrounded by a series of satellites, incorporated and protected by governmental walls.

For a time the satellites did not constitute a problem. When the boundaries of the central city nudged those of the suburb, the suburb was annexed with little difficulty. However, such annexation came to a halt in the 1920's. Since that period most metropolitan areas have presented the same picture: a "land-locked" central city, increasingly aged and obsolete, surrounded by a growing patchwork of suburban municipalities. The key question is this: why did the boundaries of the central city cease to expand, following its dispersed population? We cannot answer with certainty; however, a comparison of central city and suburban population may be helpful.

CENTRAL CITY VERSUS SUBURBS

It was in the 1920's that the automobile revolution began to make vast areas on the outskirts of the cities available for residential sites. Country towns became nuclei for white-collar commuter settlements: empty pastures and cornfields became the sites for large scale housing development. But the people who left the central city for the suburbs were not a random assortment. As we have seen they were distinguished from those who remained behind by social rank, ethnicity, and life-style.

The automobile was at first used mostly by the upper social ranks. Its costs were substantial. Those who could bear these costs were also persons likely to want new residences, and new construction was largely on the periphery of the city. The older central city, with its structures dating back to the Age of Steam, had little space to offer those in search of new sites, but on the outskirts the supply was greater than the demand. There were, thus, powerful economic arguments for the location of new middle-class neighborhoods in the suburbs. With their construction, however, the physical difference between the two parts of the metropolis was augmented. The suburbs were new, middle-class, residential neighborhoods: the inner city was a mixture of workplace, markets and homes, surrounded by mile upon mile of older neighborhoods.

The new suburbs were also apt to be "exclusive." That is, they exercised formal and informal controls to prevent the "wrong kind of people" from moving in. Ethnic minorities, the foreign-born, Jewish, Catholic, or non-white citizens of the metropolis found the governmental walls of the suburbs impossible to scale. They perforce remained behind in the central city. Thus, with continuing in-migration of Negroes, Puerto Ricans, and Mexicans, the central city became ever darker in complexion, while the suburbs looked ever more "lily white" in contrast. The suburbs are, today, overwhelmingly populated by the white (or as Kipling called them, the "pinko grey") urbanites, usually a generation or more removed from the original immigrants. Most identifiable minority groups still live in the older central city.

We have noted earlier the increasing choice in life-style available to urban Americans. That kind of life which we have called familism, dedicated to children, home, and neighborhood, is best carried on in areas populated by similar people. In America, those who choose familism have a strong prejudice for the single-family dwelling unit secure in the middle of its fifty foot lot. Neighborhoods made up of such dwellings demand a great deal of horizontal space, space not to be found in the old central city without expensive demolition and rebuilding. With the automobile revolution, however, enormous new spaces became available on the outskirts. The suburbs attracted a population emphatically biased towards the familistic life-style, rather than the more unbane existence of the apartment houses in the densely developed center.

DIFFERENCE IN PEOPLE AND
DIFFERENCE IN GOVERNMENT

Suburban folk tend to be of higher social rank, of white "old American" heritage, and committed to a familistic way of life. Though much of the city population is similar, much of it is different indeed. The older dwellings house a working-class population. The ethnic minorities, particularly the non-white enclaves, populate broad expanses of the city's housing grid. Those with a more urbane lifestyle remain in the city (and sneer at suburbia), while those committed to familism live in the outer wards of the city, or wait for the day when they can afford a suburban ranch house.

Such variation produces a lurid ideology—"the city is old and overrun by Negroes; the suburbs are shallow, jerry-built, cheap." This is reinforced by the governmental variation between the areas—"central city government is crooked; suburban government is trivial." The central city is one massive governmental unit, while the suburbs contain hundreds of little municipalities, with over 1,400 local units in the New York metropolitan area alone. Government in the city is big government. It represents a great deal of power, money, and technology, and it seems far away and hard to understand. It is also partisan government. In the suburbs the small municipalities are usually nonpartisan, and the white middle class feels that it has solved the problem of local government by taking politics out of government. In short, there are weighty differences between suburbs and central city with respect to physical plant, population types, governmental structure, and the political process. We will discuss the latter items in more detail; it is sufficient for the moment to indicate the very real differences between the two halves of the metropolitan complex.

The suburban municipalities are going concerns. Though they are small and weak, compared to the colossus at the center, most of them provide basic governmental services, collect taxes, and exercise the police power. Most important of all, they exercise a monopoly on the powers of municipal government as defined by the constitutional government of the states. While they hold such powers no other government can do so. And this is not unrelated to their reason for being.

THE ORIGINS OF SUBURBAN MUNICIPALITIES

Many of the early suburbs were collective responses to the problems created by interdependence. Small residential enclaves built their own power plants, sewers, water systems, because they could not share those of the central city and could not interest private enterprise in the job. Many of them were also incorporated to allow for a tighter control over land-use development and population than was possible for unincorporated neighborhoods. But recently, many suburban municipalities have one major purpose for their citizens: incorporation protects the residential community from annexation and governmental control by a larger unit. They are, in effect, governmental game preserves whose citizens are relatively immune to municipal law. Some suburban municipalities are simply industrial sites, freed from municipal smoke control and other nuisances; some are tax-free preserves for industry; some protect their citizens from adequate taxes and from housing codes, allowing them to build shanty towns, to keep chickens and cows, or to carry on home crafts and the like on rutty lanes without fire protection; some are governmental shelters where gambling, prostitution and other generally illicit activities are permitted.

In short, the Jacksonian ideology, appropriate enough to an agrarian society, produces a paradoxical governmental structure in the metropolis. It is free enterprise in the founding of governments, and every municipality for itself. The ease of incorporation allows for a multiplicity of municipalities, created for the most diverse purposes. (Many towns in Dade County, Florida, were incorporated for the sole purpose of securing liquor licenses; a state law allowed only two to a municipality.) All of these municipalities, once in being, constitute the *only* legitimate delegates of municipal powers. With respect to any larger problem or purpose, they are "dog in the manger" governments; they will not act, nor allow other governments to do so.

Any governmental entity, once in being, is difficult to disband. This is particularly true of the suburban municipality. The Jacksonian ideology supports rule by friends and neighbors, nurturing suspicion of the Big City. Whatever the truth, it flatters the citizens with an image of their community as a semi-rural small town, a repository of the rustic virtues.[4] And, translated into the constitution of the state, the Jacksonian ideology requires popular consent for the extermination of any municipality. When campaigns occur to abolish, annex, or amalgamate such governments, however, all who think they benefit from the *status quo* are vocally opposed. Any existing structure builds up some differentially distributed advantages—somebody prefers it to alternatives. When this is combined with the poetry of rusticity, the staying power of the municipality is clear. Thus the Dade County suburb, originally incorporated for the purpose of securing two liquor licenses, today stands for home, mother, democracy, and virtue. The imaginary boundary lines and the place name become symbols, made to contain the diverse values of the residential neighborhoods.

THE GOVERNMENTAL DICHOTOMY AND SOME CONSEQUENCES

Today, a bird's eye view of the metropolitan governmental structure would typically encompass the great circle of the central city and the dozens or hundreds of small units clustered side by side on the outskirts. More literally, the central city would be marked by higher, denser structures, shelving downwards rapidly to the peripheries; the suburbs would be horizontal, dispersed, with perhaps one-fifth the population of the inner central city per square mile. From a bird's eye view we would also note that the air over suburbia is often filled with fumes

[4] For a lively picture of the changing American picture of the city, see Anselm Strauss, *Images of the American City*, New York: The Free Press of Glencoe, Inc., 1961.

and smoke from the center. The whole urban complex lies across one or two great watersheds, and streams flow across governmental boundaries, bearing effluvia from here to there. The flow of traffic also moves momentarily throughout the area, without regard to municipal boundaries, knitting together the scattered sites for human activity in a larger system of action. In short, one would see the governmental division as arbitrary with respect to many of the collective systems of human action which constitute the being of the city.

Indeed, the entire urban complex is in many ways a unity. The scattered thousands are interdependent in each of the ways we have detailed; they man the complex, exclusive work organization we have discussed earlier. The wealthy suburbanites depend upon the unskilled ethnic laborers and machine operatives of the central city for the social product that feeds them. The central city banks depend upon the suburban investors; the suburban department stores depend on the central city banks. All of the residents together are subject to the age-old kinds of interdependence detailed earlier: they require order in inter-group relations, protection of person and property, and the maintenance of a transport system, water and sewage systems, fire protection and public health. In short, there is a sense in which we can call the metropolitan area a unity.

This unity, however, is not reflected in government. The problems created by contiguity and mutual dependence are not allocated to any government which includes all of those affected and affecting others. The central city government does not work in close cooperation with those of suburbia; how could it? Suburban governments are themselves uncoordinated, with no center of power and information. Yet the cooperation of suburbia is frequently crucial to the programs in the central city: traffic on a freeway system which ends abruptly in the main street of a country town is apt to back up halfway to City Hall, and smoke abatement will be less than complete until the suburban industrial park complies. There is, however, no normative prescription in Jacksonian philosophy for the forced integration of local government. Nor is there a constitutional formula that frees the governmental structure from the heavy hand of the referendum voter. Thus many important problems generated in the metropolitan complex are insoluble within the existing governmental structures. Our political culture lags far behind the emerging problems of the metropolitan world in which we live. It is embedded in the folk thought of the citizen and the phrases of the law.

SOME AUGURIES AND A QUESTION

Meanwhile, massive changes continue. In two decades our cities will grow by more than fifty million people. Most of the net growth will be in suburbia.[5] Even today, 49 per cent of our total metropolitan population lives in the suburban fringe. Thus the one large-scale government in the metrop-

[5] See Philip Hauser, *Population Perspectives*, New Brunswick, N.J.: Rutgers University Press, 1960, Chapter 4, p. 101.

olis, that of the central city, will encompass a dwindling proportion of the land in use and the people in residence. There is little indication that the manufacture of small municipalities in suburbia will cease. While the scale of organization in the United States progressively increases, while work, play, religion, and other major activities are carried out through very large-scale organizational networks, local government moves doggedly in the opposite direction. Our ability to plan and provide for the entire metropolitan complex within the inherited framework of local self-government is declining relative to our ability to exercise over-all control in other segments of our lives.

Yet certain problems are inescapable. We refer, once again, to the minimal needs of human collectives living in cities. These problems are so basic that, should they not be solved, the city would perish. But our cities do not appear to be in such mortal danger, so we must ask: how is the polity maintained so that the resources and order requisite for these millions may indeed be predictably there when they need them? In answering this question, we shall consider first the government of the old central cities. Then we shall turn to the congeries of municipalities on the fringe, that dark and unknown governmental realm called suburbia.

The Outcome of Metropolitan Growth

Jean Gottmann*

The Northeastern seaboard of the United States is today the site of a remarkable development—an almost continuous stretch of urban and suburban areas from southern New Hampshire to northern Virginia and from the Atlantic shore to the Appalachian foothills. The processes of urbanization, rooted deep in the American past, have worked steadily here, endowing the region with unique ways of life and of land use. No other section of the United States has such a large concentration of population, with such a high average density, spread over such a large area. And no other section has a comparable role within the nation or a comparable importance in the world. Here has been developed a kind of supremacy, in politics, in economics, and possibly even in cultural activities, seldom before attained by an area of this size.

A VERY SPECIAL REGION: MEGALOPOLIS

This region has indeed a "personality" of its own, which for some three centuries past has been changing and evolving, constantly creating new problems for its inhabitants and exerting a deep influence on the general organization of society. The modern trends in its development and its present degree of crowding provide both examples and warnings for other less urbanized areas in America and abroad and call for a profound revision of many old concepts, such as the usually accepted distinctions between city and

country. As a result new meanings must be given to some old terms, and some new terms must be created.

Great, then, is the importance and significance of this section of the United States and of the processes now at work within it. And yet it is difficult to single this area out from surrounding areas, for its limits cut across established historical divisions, such as New England and the Middle Atlantic states, and across political entities, since it includes some states entirely and others only partially. A special name is needed, therefore, to identify this special geographical area.

This particular type of region is new, but it is the result of age-old processes, such as the growth of cities, the division of labor within a civilized society, the development of world resources. The name applied to it should, therefore, be new as a place name but old as a symbol of the long tradition of human aspirations and endeavor underlying the situations and problems now found here. Hence the choice of the term *Megalopolis,* used in this study.

Some two thousand years before the first European settlers landed on the shores of the James River, Massachusetts Bay, and Manhattan Island, a group of ancient people, planning a new city-state in the Peloponnesus in Greece, called it *Megalopolis,* for they dreamed of a great future for it and hoped it would become the largest of the Greek cities. Their hopes did not materialize. Megalopolis still appears on modern maps of the Peloponnesus but it is just a small town nestling in a small river basin. Through the centuries the word *Megalopolis* has been used in many senses by various people,

*Reprinted with permission from Jean Gottmann, *Megalopolis: The Urbanized Northeastern Seaboard of the United States,* Twentieth Century Fund, New York, 1961, 3–16.

and it has even found its way into Webster's dictionary, which defines it as "a very large city." Its use, however, has not become so common that it could not be applied in a new sense, as a geographical place name for the unique cluster of metropolitan areas of the Northeastern seaboard of the United States. There, if anywhere in our times, the dream of those ancient Greeks has come true.

AN URBANIZED AREA WITH A NEBULOUS STRUCTURE

As one follows the main highways or railroads between Boston and Washington, D.C., one hardly loses sight of built-up areas, tightly woven residential communities, or powerful concentrations of manufacturing plants. Flying this same route one discovers, on the other hand, that behind the ribbons of densely occupied land along the principal arteries of traffic, and in between the clusters of suburbs around the old urban centers, there still remain large areas covered with woods and brush alternating with some carefully cultivated patches of farmland. These green spaces, however, when inspected at closer range, appear stuffed with a loose but immense scattering of buildings, most of them residential but some of industrial character. That is, many of these sections that look rural actually function largely as suburbs in the orbit of some city's downtown. Even the farms, which occupy the larger tilled patches, are seldom worked by people whose only occupation and income are properly agricultural. And yet these farm areas produce large quantities of farm goods!

Thus the old distinctions between rural and urban do not apply here any more. Even a quick look at the vast area of Megalopolis reveals a revolution in land use. Most of the people living in the so-called rural areas, and still classified as "rural population" by recent censuses, have very little, if anything, to do with agriculture. In terms of their interests and work they are what used to be classified as "city folks," but their way of life and the landscapes around their residences do not fit the old meaning of urban.

In this area, then, we must abandon the idea of the city as a tightly settled and organized unit in which people, activities, and riches are crowded into a very small area clearly separated from its nonurban surroundings. Every city in this region spreads out far and wide around its original nucleus; it grows amidst an irregularly colloidal mixture of rural and suburban landscapes; it melts on broad fronts with other mixtures, of somewhat similar though different texture, belonging to the suburban neighborhoods of other cities. Such coalescence can be observed, for example, along the main lines of traffic that link New York City and Philadelphia. Here there are many communities that might be classified as belonging to more than one orbit. It is hard to say whether they are suburbs, or "satellites," of Philadelphia or New York, Newark, New Brunswick, or Trenton. The latter three cities themselves have been reduced to the role of suburbs of Uew York City in many respects, although Trenton belongs also to the orbit of Philadelphia. (See Fig. I, the distribution of population density.)

The "standard metropolitan areas,"[1] first used by the U.S. Bureau of the Census in 1950, have clarified this confused situation somewhat but not

[1] The U. S. Bureau of the Census defined a standard metropolitan area as "a county or group of contiguous counties which contains at least one city of 50,000 inhabitants or more. In addition to the county, or counties, containing such a city, or cities, contiguous counties are included in a standard metropolitan area if according to certain criteria they are essentially metropolitan in character and socially and economically integrated with the central city." In New England, "towns and cities, rather than counties, are the units used in defining standard metropolitan areas."

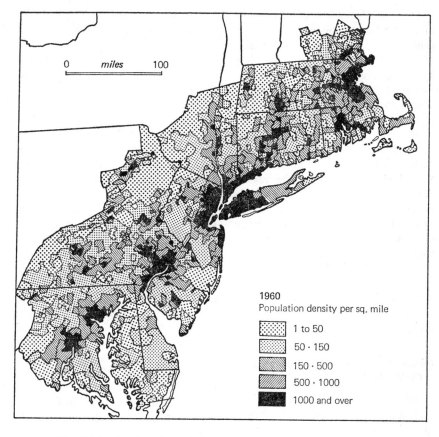

Fig. I. The density of population according to the 1960 Census, by minor civil divisions.

entirely. For example, the New York–Northeastern New Jersey standard metropolitan area cuts across political boundaries to reveal the relationships of this vast region to the core city of New York. And yet the mechanical application of the term "standard metropolitan area" has resulted in the establishment of separate areas for Trenton, which is closely tied to both Philadelphia and New York, and for Bridgeport, which is for many practical purposes part of the New York area. Similar problems can be found in other parts of Megalopolis.[2]

[2] For the 1960 Census the term "standard metropolitan area" was changed to "standard metropolitan statistical area." The definition was modified and a somewhat different set of

criteria used which resulted in breaking down several of the formerly recognized larger metropolitan areas into smaller such units. The results thus achieved may be more precise in some respects but in the case of Megalopolis they may cause some confusion. The New York–Northeastern New Jersey standard metropolitan statistical areas: one for New York in New York State and three in New Jersey, those of Paterson-Clifton-Passaic, Jersey City, and Newark. The stricter definition of metropolitan integration of adjoining counties now excludes Somerset and Middlesex counties, formerly classified as metropolitan. As a result the percentage of the population of New Jersey residing in metropolitan areas fell from 89.9 in 1950 to 78.9 in 1960—a statistical trend surprising to those who know how much more metropolitan—or should we say Megalopolitan—the whole of New Jersey grew through the 1950's. To compensate for such an impression and for the separation between New York City and Northeastern New Jersey, a new term has been created and defined: "Standard Consolidated Areas," of

Thus an almost continuous system of deeply interwoven urban and suburban areas, with a total population of about 37 million people in 1960, has been erected along the Northeastern Atlantic seaboard. It straddles state boundaries, stretches across wide estuaries and bays, and encompasses many regional differences. In fact, the landscapes of Megalopolis offer such variety that the average observer may well doubt the unity of the region. And it may seem to him that the main urban nuclei of the seaboard are little related to one another. Six of its great cities would be great individual metropolises in their own right if they were located elsewhere. This region indeed reminds one of Aristotle's saying that cities such as Babylon had "the compass of a nation rather than a city."

MEGALOPOLIS—MAIN STREET AND CROSSROADS OF THE NATION

There are many other large metropolitan areas and even clusters of them in various parts of the United States, but none of them is yet comparable to Megalopolis in size of population, density of population, or density of activities, be these expressed in terms of transportation, communications, banking operations, or political conferences. Megalopolis provides the whole of America with so many essential services, of the sort a community used to obtain in its "downtown" section, that

---

which there were two (recognized for 1960) in the country: the New York–Northeastern New Jersey area (which included Somerset and Middlesex counties in New Jersey), and the Chicago–Northwestern Indiana area. The recognition of these broader areas was intended to stress "the special importance of even more inclusive metropolitan statistics" (see Executive Office of the President, Bureau of the Budget, *Standard Metropolitan Statistical Areas*, U. S. Government Printing Office, Washington, D.C., 1961). The metropolitan area of Philadelphia remained unchanged in both its Pennsylvania and New Jersey parts.

it may well deserve the nickname of "Main Street of the nation." And for three centuries it has performed this role, though the transcontinental march of settlement has developed along east-west axes perpendicular to this section of the Atlantic seaboard.

In recent times Megalopolis has had concentrated within it more of the Main Street type of functions than ever, and it does not yet seem prepared to relinquish any of them. Witness, for example, the impact of the Federal government in Washington, D.C., as it tightens up over many aspects of national life; the continued crowding of financial and managerial operations into Manhattan; New York's dominance of the national market for mass communication media, which resists all attempts at erosion; and the pre-eminent influence of the universities and cultural centers of Megalopolis on American thinking and policy-making. Megalopolis is also the country's chief façade toward the rest of the world. From it, as from the Main Street of a city, local people leave for distant travel, and to it arriving strangers come. For immigrants it has always served as the chief debarkation wharf. And just as passing visitors often see little of a city except a few blocks of its Main Street, so most foreign visitors see only a part of Megalopolis on their sojourns in the United States.

Just as a Main Street lives for and prospers because of the functions of the whole city, rather than because of any purely local advantages of its own, so is Megalopolis related to the whole United States and its resources. In general, Megalopolis itself was blessed only moderately by nature. It has no vast expanse of rich soils (there are some good soils but more poor ones), no special climatic advantages (its cyclonic climate is far from ideal), and no great mineral deposits (though there are some). In these respects it cannot compare with the generous natural potential of the Middle West or Texas or California. But it does excel in locational advantages—deep harbors of a drowned shoreline, on which its principal cities were early established, and a connecting-link relationship between the rich heart of the continent and the rest of the world. By hard work man has made the most of these locational resources, the most outstanding ones in an otherwise average natural endowment. As a result, early in its history Megalopolis became a dynamic hub of international relations, and it has maintained and constantly expanded that role to the present day. It is now the most active crossroads on earth, for people, ideas, and goods, extending its influence far beyond the national borders, and only as such a crossroads could it have achieved its present economic preeminence.

MEGALOPOLIS AS A LABORATORY OF URBAN GROWTH

Modern technology and social evolution provide increasing opportunity in urban pursuits on the one hand, and on the other steadily improving means of producing more agricultural goods with less manpower. The forces at work in our time, coupled with the growth in population, are, therefore, bound to channel a rising flow of people toward urban-type occupations and ways of life. As this tide reaches more and more cities they will burst out of old bounds to expand and scatter all over the landscape, taking new forms like those already observable throughout Megalopolis. This region serves thus as a laboratory in which we may study the new evolution reshaping both the meaning of our traditional vocabulary and the whole material structure of our way of life.

Tomorrow's society will be different from that in which we grew up, largely because it will be more urbanized. Nonagricultural ways of life will be followed by more and more people and will occupy much more space than they ever did, and such changes cannot develop without also deeply modifying agricultural life and production. So great are the consequences of the general evolution heralded by the present rise and complexity of Megalopolis that an analysis of this region's problems often gives one the feeling of looking at the dawn of a new stage in human civilization. The author has visited and studied various other regions of the world but has not experienced such a feeling anywhere else. Indeed, the area may be considered the cradle of a new order in the organization of inhabited space. This new order, however, is still far from orderly; here in its cradle it is all in flux and trouble, which does not facilitate the analyst's work. Nevertheless, a study of Megalopolis may shed some light on processes that are of great importance and interest.

A STUDY IN ENTANGLED RELATIONSHIPS

As the work of data-gathering and analysis progressed it became evident that the key to most of the questions involved in this study of Megalopolis lies in the interrelationships between the forces and processes at work within the area rather than in the trends of growth or the development of techniques. Thus the trend of population increase, easy to measure and perhaps to forecast approximately, provides less insight into the nature of the area than do the interrelations existing between the processes that caused the local population to grow, those that attracted certain kinds of people to Megalopolis, and those that supplied the swelling crowds with the means to live and work together there. Many of these processes are statistically measurable and some of them can be mapped, but the degree to which each of them stems from the others or determines them is a much more subtle matter, and is more basic to an understanding of what is going on and what can be done about it.

Most regional studies stay on the safer and more superficial grounds of statistical description and functional classifications. Had this report followed that pattern it would have been devoted mainly to summing up the abundant data available from the Censuses and other sources of general information about the various characteristics of Megalopolis. A description of natural conditions, such as topography, climate, hydrography, and vegetation, would have introduced a historical sketch to be followed by chapters on population, industries, trade, transportation and communications, the real estate market, other occupations, and descriptions of the main cities and of the general features of "rural areas." Such a report would have concluded with a description of present problems and forecasts of the future presented by means of graphs, based on the assumption that the trends of the past twenty to fifty years will continue for the next twenty years.

A mere compilation of such data would probably be of service to some people but it could hardly help those who need further insight into and understanding of the basic problems of the area. By attempting to find out more about the deeper processes and their entanglements, one may hope to achieve a more fundamental kind of knowledge, which can be applied to another area or projected into the future more safely, though not always more easily. This is why the present report is organized along a somewhat less classical outline, its goal being a more reasoned discussion and an objective analysis. For such complicated phenomena as the social and economic processes at work in Megalopolis there are, of course, numerous and interlocking determining factors. The author has endeavored to search for *all* these factors, keeping in mind their multiplicity and entanglements and avoiding any arbitrary choices among them.

OUTLINE OF THIS REPORT

Part One presents a sketch of the *dynamics of urbanization* and attempts to show, in terms of the region's history, why things have come to be as they are and where they are. Although this section is largely descriptive it cannot avoid raising some new questions.

Part Two takes up what may be called the *"modern revolution in land use."* The new mixture of urban and rural must be dissected and each part related to the others in the newly developing system. Separation between place of work and place of residence creates within the area the system of daily "tidal" movements involved in commuting. Over these are superimposed other currents, some seasonal and some irregularly recurrent. These reflect relations between different parts of Megalopolis that stem from more complicated needs than the simple journey from home to work. These other needs grow more complicated and more general as average family income rises and both goods and activities that were once considered dispensable come to be regarded as necessary by large numbers of Megalopolitans. As Montesquieu observed two centuries ago, on the eve of the Industrial Revolution, "It is the nature of commerce to make the superfluous useful and the useful necessary." Perhaps it is not commerce but just human nature that produces this sequence. At any rate it has certainly been proven true of the consumption of goods, and now it seems to apply to the consumption of activities and space. The modern urban revolution, so apparent already in the affluent society of Megalopolis, devours time and space as well as food and industrial goods, and the fulfilling of these needs requires many types of movements.

These various tidal movements involve a reshaping of land use. Much agricultural land has been taken over by residential and industrial development. On the remaining farms a new specialized type of agriculture is developing, which requires less space than did the old system of farming. Woods have spread over much of the land abandoned by the farms, and this expansion of forests calls for new methods and concepts of forestry management, to provide for recreational and other suburban needs and for a better conservation of the landscape and of wildlife. Simultaneously the old city cores or "downtowns" are evolving toward decline or renewal, while uptowns, suburbs, and outer suburbia are becoming interlocked in a new and still constantly changing web of relationships. Regional integration is taking on forms unknown a generation or two ago, and the old system of local, state, and national authorities and jurisdictions, which has changed little, is poorly suited to present needs.

New *patterns of intense living* that have become normal in Megalopolis affect not only land use. They also exert a strong influence on the economic and social foundations of society, and Part Three endeavors to describe the problems thus created. The density of activities and of movement of all kinds is certainly the most extraordinary feature of Megalopolis, more characteristic even than the density of population and of skyscrap-

ers. It has become a means of maintaining economic growth and stabilizing society; but how far can it go without destroying itself? For example, the growth of Megalopolis owes much to the automobile, but highway traffic jams are beginning to strangle city activities and to take the pleasure and efficiency out of driving a car. At the same time cars contribute to the ruination of other means of transportation, made more necessary than ever by the massive tidal currents of people and goods. The self-defeating effect of dense concentrations may be observed also in other fields than transportation. Many industries, for example, are now aiming at decentralization. The intense living of Megalopolis makes a great deal of waste inescapable, waste of space and time as well as of materials. For a long time such waste may have seemed justifiable, for, paradoxically, the crowding that caused it brought higher economic yields. Now this crowding seems at times to defeat its own aims. Why and how does such intense living grow and threaten itself? Answers to these queries build up a general picture of a dynamic and properous society, obviously responsible for maintaining the growth of large-scale urbanization but responsible also for the problems the process creates and for finding the badly needed solutions.

It is easier to accept responsibility for solutions than to provide them. The many millions of people who find themselves *neighbors in Megalopolis,* even though they live in different states and hundreds of miles from one another, are barely becoming aware of the imperatives of such a "neighborhood." Part Four attempts to point them out. Responsible public opinion is becoming conscious of the problems involved, and the struggle to find solutions has started. It is especially difficult because no one problem can be tackled without affecting the others. Transportation, land use, water supply, cultural activities, use and development of resources, government and politics—all are interrelated.

Today it is essential that solutions be found to save this area from decay and to reassure the nation and the world about the kind of life modern urbanization trends presage for the future. Megalopolis has been built and often reshaped by its people. These people are now wealthier, better educated, and better endowed with technological means than ever. They ought to be able to find ways of avoiding decline of the area.

FOR THE BETTER OR FOR THE WORSE?

The preceding paragraph may seem to imply an unwarranted optimism about society's ability to control itself. True, history records a long list of brilliant civilizations that have sunk under the pressure of internal decay and external jealousy. We remember their names: Babylon, Corinth, Sparta, Athens, Rome, and many others. In the shadowy vistas of ancient times they vanished into the distance like shipwrecked ships loaded with ambition and precious cargo. Can such a fate be looming in the offing for Megalopolis? Modern urban sprawl is viewed by many as a threat to progress and general welfare. What is happening in Megalopolis today has been described as a pathological phenomenon, a sickness, a cancer. Such views are held by distinguished and respectable citizens of the area. One may well be alarmed by their invectives, all the more so as one does not have to go far away from Megalopolis to hear expressions of distrust and jealousy inspired by the amazing concentration of wealth and power in the great seaboard cities. Are people both in and

out of this extraordinary region united in condemning it?

Urban growth in general has been discussed and condemned on moral grounds for a long time. Such debate is expectable and desirable, but on the whole history has shown the condemnation to be unjust, as can be seen by a brief review of some of the consequences of crowding.

Contrasts between rich and poor, for example, are especially striking in the crowded communities of cities. These may exist in rural areas too, but there they are diluted by scattering and veiled in greenery. The growth of urban pursuits (industries, trade, services) sharpens the contrasts by condensing them into a smaller area. Rich and poor live within short distances of one another and mix together in the streets in a way that often arouses righteous indignation. It seems brutally amoral to witness destitution neighboring on elegant sophistication, poverty mixing with prosperity. And yet, alas, a growing city's environment can hardly escape offering such sights. For many centuries there was an enormous difference between the advancement possible in trade and industry on the one hand and in farming on the other (though modern farm mechanization and subsidies to agriculture have substantially increased the profit possibilities of farming), and so to rise economically within the span of one lifetime has traditionally been easier in cities than in rural areas. The affluence of those who have so risen draws to the city large groups of humbler people, who come there to profit by the local abundance of money and the volume of spending and to serve the wealthier. In contrast to the more conservative "open" country, the "closed-in" city offers a more dynamic environment, socially and economically.

In cities, too, other vicious aspects

of economic growth and social life have always been more evident than in the country. As urban development was accelerated by the Industrial Revolution, some of these vicious aspects became increasingly obvious. Slums and mobs grew worse than ever, making the urban landscape ethically and aesthetically shocking to those who cared about the people. From his sojourns in an industrializing western Europe, and especially from Paris during the French Revolution, Thomas Jefferson brought back impressions that reinforced his normal Virginian opposition to great cities and the development of manufactures or large-scale commerce. As slums and mobs became more general in European cities in the first half of the nineteenth century there arose more awareness about the classes of society and social injustice. There was more discussion of these matters, and the early Socialist doctrines were largely inspired by them. Then came the teachings of such philosophers as Fourier and Proudhon in France and Engels and Karl Marx in Germany, opposing great urban concentration as much as great concentration of capital. Engels' writings on the slums and working conditions in the then fast-developing British cities, such as Manchester, are well known. Because urban conditions of living and working were largely at the root of nineteenth-century Socialist doctrines, Karl Marx stressed that his theories applied much more to the industrialized countries of western Europe, which had accumulated large amounts of capital, than to the rural, little-urbanized countries to the east. Twentieth-century events have proved him wrong on this score, however, for communism has conquered the mainly rural countries, and the forms of socialism that developed in the more urban and capitalistic countries of the West have turned away from Marxism.

Crowding of population within a small area creates shortages of various resources, and most of the crowded people are bound to suffer in some ways because of the shortages. To alleviate them, to make crowding more bearable and the population happier, ways and means of constantly better distribution must be found. Otherwise no lasting growth can develop, and the whole enterprise will soon be doomed. From the struggle against such shortages have come some of mankind's most important advances. In the arid areas of the Middle East, for example, early civilization arose when people first congregated around the main springs and permanent rivers. As the settlement grew, the supply of both water and irrigable land became scarce. To insure survival of the people a proper distribution system had to be achieved, and rules and regulations had to be set up and accepted. Thus organized society, ruled by law, was born. Because authorities were needed to enforce law, political power arose, and people organized themselves to avoid more oppression than was necessary. Everywhere, the more crowded people have become in cities the more they have craved both security and freedom. Modern political life and its concepts of liberty, self-government, and democracy are the products of urban growth, the inheritance of cities in process of growth and development—places such as Jerusalem, Athens, Rome, Bruges, Florence, Paris, London, to mention only those that have been most studied by historians. And the same places, or similar urban centers, have contributed most of our scientific and technological developments, either because people there were struggling to solve pressing problems or because urban societies make possible a leisurely enough elite, some of whose members can devote themselves to disinterested research and a search for a better understanding of the universe.

Thus urban crowding and the slums and mobs characteristic of it may be considered growing pains in the endless process of civilization.

In the same way, the picture of Megalopolis is not as dark as the outspoken pessimists and frequent protests would seem to paint it. Crowded within its limits is an extremely distinguished population. It is, *on the average,* the richest, best educated, best housed, and best serviced group of similar size (i.e., in the 25-to-40-million-people range) in the world. The area is still a focus of attraction for successful or adventurous people from all over America and beyond. It is true that many of its sections have seen pretty rural landscapes replaced by ugly industrial agglomerations or drab and monstrous residential developments; it is true that in many parts of Megalopolis the air is not clean any more, the noise is disturbing day and night, the water is not as pure as one would wish, and transportation at times becomes a nightmare. Many of these problems reflect the revolutionary change that has taken place as cities have burst out of their narrow bounds to scatter over the "open" countryside. In some ways this suburban sprawl may have alleviated a crowding that had threatened to become unbearable, for residential densities of population per square mile have decreased. But new problems have arisen because of the new densities of activities and of traffic in the central cities and because the formerly rural areas or small towns have been unprepared to cope with the new demands made upon their resources. New programs are needed to conserve the natural beauty of the landscape and to assure the health, prosperity, and freedom of the people. In spite of these problems, however, available statistics demonstrate that in Megalopolis the population is on the average healthier, the consumption of goods higher, and the opportunity for advancement greater than in any other region of comparable extent.

Thus the type of urban growth experienced here generates many contrasts, paradoxes, and apparently contradictory trends. It calls for debate and naturally excites passionate opinions for and against it. Are its results for the better or for the worse? It is not for our generation to moralize on the matter, but to strive to make the outcome be for the better, whatever obstacles may be in the way. Megalopolis stands indeed at the threshold of a new way of life, and upon solution of its problems will rest civilization's ability to survive. In the search for such solutions there will be found no easy keys to success, no "gimmicks" or "open-sesames." Solutions must be thought out, ironed out, and constantly revised in the light of all the knowledge that can be acquired by all concerned. It is the author's hope that this report, a systematic and sometimes critical analysis of the past and present of Megalopolis, will contribute to the gathering of such knowledge and to its distribution. At the same time, it will tell the story of an extraordinary region as its people have made it.

8 Contemporary

The problems facing contemporary urban America are not new. The readings in the preceding sections expose their long-term presence. Deprivation, social tensions, poor housing, waste problems, violence, inefficient government, high taxes, and transportation difficulties are bemoaned by succeeding generations. Sometimes these problems take distinctive forms in different periods. Horse-drawn carriages, hubs deep in mud, were as much a problem to the eighteenth-century community as trolley congestion in the central business district was to the late nineteenth, or the traffic jam on the freeway is to the twentieth. The rapid concentration of population during the nineteenth century continued to demand from the community more foresight, interest, and activism than the community could supply. Economic change and the process of urbanization itself, in the face of a slowly evolving positive social attitude, aggravated old problems and created new ones for each generation. The attempt to keep pace with these needs always presented an acknowledged challenge. There never seemed to be time to permit the pause essential for concerted action.

Urban Problems

Progress has been made in solving some difficulties, particularly those which threaten the entire population or in which the more powerful interest groups have a sizable stake. Members of the upper class dealt with problems initially through private action or subscription. When they realized that dangers such as disease and fire in any section of the city could adversely affect them, they supported broad community action. Only minimal progress has been made in dealing with most of the long-standing problems, and often the improvement has been counteracted by an increase in the complexity of urban life. For example, governments have become more efficient, but metropolitanization, as we saw in Section 7, has led to their fragmentation. Concomitantly with social progress, the public has come to expect more from collective action and government programs and agencies. The educational system has improved significantly over that of the nineteenth century, but the need for greater sensitivity and knowledge to cope with society's demands, the rising expectations of larger numbers of people, and the broadening of the concept of equal opportunity have placed increased burdens on education, and the school situation notoriously continues to spawn major crises.

It appears that the post-World War II era is more aware of urban problems and that the ability and resources to deal with them exist. Financial difficulties remain pressing as demands increase for use of limited revenue, and the large cities decline in ability to pay their own way. Since the state and federal government possess greater taxing powers, the cities must rely on them more and more for aid. A growing awareness that the United States is an urban nation and that the well-being of its cities is essential for national health has gradually led to more federal interest and action directly in the cities. This attention does not mean that the battle over responsibility for the full range of urban problems has been resolved; opposition to new social legislation continues. Often the struggle is over the question of priorities. With resources always limited, a decision such as whether to rebuild the business district or residential areas leads to conflict. Although old issues have been replaced by new ones, the debate echoing that of the nineteenth century—whether programs should be conducted through private or public efforts—shows no signs of waning.

Gradually another difficulty in urban policy is receiving recognition, that of ensuring proper and meaningful direction. The thrust of the urban effort in the twentieth century has been to render efficient the operation of urban affairs. Efficiency has been emphasized in specific functions of the city: that government should be run smoothly and productively, that streets and highways should be built at low cost and should reflect traffic patterns accurately, and that the various services should be transferred from political to professional control. But if the city manager, in providing good government, has not reflected the desires of the majority, or if the highway, in serving automobiles, has disrupted people's lives, or if the police department, in establishing an efficient organization, has lost communication with the neighborhood, few people have shown concern for the consequences. The emphasis on professionalism or on a more orderly way of dealing with the city has not been accompanied by an equal concern for the social or humanitarian implications of programs. What will become the classic example of this neglect is the manner in which cities in the 1950's tackled urban renewal. In order to build sterile high-rise dwellings or new business or commercial facilities, neighborhoods were bulldozed and the lives of thousands of people were disrupted. Professional planners, primarily interested in physical needs, have ignored the social and human needs of the community.

A fundamental weakness in the contemporary perspective on urban problems has been the assumption that if the general community is in a sound economic condition, everyone will benefit. Some have believed that urban renewal would guarantee benefits to all. Their reasoning has been that the rebuilding of the central business district and the construction of new homes would be reflected in a flourishing economy and prosperity for everyone

in the community. Unfortunately, the direct impact of the
programs brought hardship to some, but more importantly,
everyone did not prosper. Slums continued, welfare payments rose,
and people remained unemployed. The larger community is made
up of separate groups, each with its special needs. In a less
sociological but more humanistic view, the city is composed of
individuals, and people have a wide spectrum of needs, not only
economic, but also political, social, cultural, and intellectual.
Satisfying merely economic or physical needs, in the form of
providing simple subsistence or living space, or ensuring an
efficiently run city, is not enough. If the social condition of an
urban people has serious deficiencies or if the people feel
politically alienated, problems will remain as intractable as ever.

The readings in this section are by no means exhaustive, but
they represent some of the kinds of urban problems identified by
scholars in a variety of fields, such as history, economics, political
science, and philosophy, and by practitioners in federal, state, and
local government. The first selection, by Sam Bass Warner, Jr.
indicates why American cities have failed to cope with the
challenge of urban problems in the twentieth century. Using
Philadelphia in the 1920's as a case study, he suggests that the
unwillingness of its citizens to act is reflective of all large American
cities. Wilfred Owen discusses the crisis in transportation that
has plagued American cities and some of the alternatives that are
feasible in this area. Suburbia, created primarily by the new modes
of transportation, has in turn created new problems for the old
cities. Robert C. Wood's selection describes the values and
implications of the suburban political ideology. Charles Abrams
reverts to the core city and the problems of slums and housing
and the failure of urban renewal. The selection from the Kerner
Commission Report deals with the most conspicuous failure of
America, race relations. It describes the racial disorders that shook
American cities in the summer of 1967 and summarizes its findings
as to the basic causes. Lawrence Haworth analyzes the other
major failure of prosperous America, poverty. Rejecting a simple
definition, he provides a broad humanistic approach to the
problem. The last reading, by Jack Meltzer, discusses the weaknesses
and dangers of current programs to "save our cities" and offers a
framework for a complete rethinking of governmental programs.

The problems of urban America defy accurate and
comprehensive categorization, and yet, certain heuristic
distinctions can be employed in any general analysis of the city.
Man, who makes up cities, has political, economic, social, cultural,
and philosophical dimensions. Urban problems can be considered
from the point of view of each one of these dimensions, either
autonomously or in various combinations. A different tack is to

think in terms of rather specific aspects of the city—finance, utilities, transportation, communications, housing, schools, industry, employment, consumption, protection, recreation, physical environment, esthetics, government, social services, values, and social and racial attitudes—while remembering that the single aspect is part of a larger environmental context. In order to begin to understand these problems fully, an interdisciplinary approach is necessary. The efforts in this direction will be considerably aided by a greater knowledge of urban history, which will provide not only a perspective in time, but also, through its concern with the entire range of human behavior, a more humanistic orientation

Public Need and Political Failure

Sam Bass Warner, Jr.*

To an historian, twentieth-century urban America presents a picture of endlessly repeated failures. The problems of the American city have been known for a very long time; yet they persist. Novelists, social critics, settlement workers, and reporters in the early 1900's painted a reasonably complete portrait of urban America.

In 1910 the poor lacked steady, well-paid work, adequate housing, and decent medical care. They were segregated into one-quarter of the city, ill protected from crime, their children without good schools or adequate recreation. The vast majority of city dwellers, the working class and middle class, though living in adequate but ugly shelters were over-regimented by the conditions of work and the constraints of their urban environment. Despite the protection of unions for some and despite affluence for others, the mass of city dwellers lacked any effective means to humanize their lives. The physical environment of unbroken rows of housing and social environment of diurnal tides of workers destroyed any possibility of effective small-community life for most American city dwellers. Rigid, low-cost education trained their children for lives of future regimentation. When possible, by saloon, by ballpark, by theatre, by train, by excursion boat, working-class and middle-class Americans sought momentary escape from their urban world. The rich, using their wealth to create insulated enclaves within the city or beyond it, escaped the constraints of commonplace urban life. Their innovations for escape, outdoor sports, the weekend, the country club, and the summer place set the fashions for later mass imitation.

Since 1910 enormous changes have taken place. American cities have so radically altered their form and structure that observers describe the present as a wholly new era.[1] Yet despite half a century of private building, of municipal, state, and federal effort, the cities of America still lack full employment, racial integration, decent housing for the poor, safe streets, good schools, good clinics and hospitals, adequate recreation facilities, an abundance of small-community urban life, and a government structure which could begin to achieve these long-missing goals. Escape from the city, as the habits of affluent Americans show, is still the best buy for those who can afford it.

Why this lack of progress? Why, inasmuch as Americans have built new, or vastly enlarged, over one hundred big cities since 1910 and have almost completely reworked old giants like New York?[2] Why, indeed, when in this same period England and Sweden and Holland, and many other European countries to a lesser degree,

---

[1] There were in 1910 seventy metropolises with central cities of 50,000 inhabitants and urbanized metropolitan areas of at least 100,000. By 1960 the number of such metropolises had grown to 176.

[2] Jean Gottmann, *Megalopolis: The Urbanized Northeastern Seaboard of the United States* (New York, 1961); John W. Dyckman, "The Public and Private Rationale for a National Urban Policy," *Planning for a Nation of Cities* (Sam Bass Warner, Jr., ed., Cambridge, 1966), 23–42.

*Reprinted with permission from Sam Bass Warner, Jr., *The Private City: Philadelphia in Three Periods of Its Growth*, Philadelphia: University of Pennsylvania Press, 1968, ix–xi, 214–223. Copyright © 1968 by the Trustees of the University of Pennsylvania.

have developed the programs and institutions needed to meet the very urban problems that we in America seem unable to confront?

There are many reasons for the twentieth-century American urban failure, but an important one is historical. Long before the great World Wars, long before the settling of the immigrant and Negro slums, and long before the balkanization of metropolitan politics, Americans had fixed upon a tradition whose habits and goals bore especially hard upon big cities. Big cities require habits of community life, an attention to sharing scarce resources, and a willingness to care for all men, not just all successful men, that the American tradition could not fulfill once cities became large and industrialized.

Under the American tradition, the first purpose of the citizen is the private search for wealth; the goal of a city is to be a community of private money makers. Once the scope of many city dwellers' search for wealth exceeded the bounds of their municipality, the American city ceased to be an effective community. Ever afterwards it lacked the desire, the power, the wealth, and the talent necessary to create a humane environment for all its citizens. From that first moment of bigness, from about the mid-nineteenth century onward, the successes and failures of American cities have depended upon the unplanned outcomes of the private market. The private market's demand for workers, its capacities for dividing land, building houses, stores and factories, and its needs for public services have determined the shape and quality of America's big cities. What the private market could do well American cities have done well; what the private market did badly, or neglected, our cities have been unable to overcome.

The twentieth-century failure of urban America to create a humane environment is thus the story of an enduring tradition of privatism in a changing world. The story is a complicated one. It doesn't separate itself nicely into good and evil, times of victory and times of defeat; rather it is the story of ordinary men and commonplace events that have accumulated over time to produce the great wealth and great failure of twentieth-century American cities. Moreover, the story is a long one, reaching back to the eighteenth-century, when our tradition first was set in its modern form.

PRIVATISM AND POLITICAL FAILURE

In the end the failure of the industrial metropolis was political. Although much of urban life is inescapably public the genius of Philadelphia in the 1920's lay not in its public institutions but in its containment of masses of people in thousands of private settings. The single-generation family, the private company's work group, and the income-segregated neighborhood were the metropolis' basic units, and they were the secret of its productivity and social peace. These same units, however, when they confronted the traditional forms of American municipal politics did not produce a creative competition.

By the twentieth century Philadelphia politics had become highly stylized. Three groups of leaders competed for control of public offices: reformers, locally oriented professionals, and state and nationally oriented professionals.

Since the middle of the nineteenth century Philadelphia's wealthy lawyers and businessmen took only an occasional interest in local politics unless they had an immediate interest in downtown business or real estate. When most business leaders did take an interest they were cast in that peculiar modern role of "reformer." The peculiarity of this role consisted in its turning participation in government into a philanthropic activity. These wealthy lawyers and businessmen carefully defined themselves as amateurs, helping out for a brief time, as if the municipal corporation were ordinarily someone else's affair, the governing institution of someone else's city.[3]

Others did indeed regard the municipal corporations and local government as their own affair, worthy of full-time attention. These were the professional politicians, men whose interests and actions had set the terms of political competition since the Civil War. The professional politicians can be divided into two groups—the locally oriented, and the state and federally oriented. The former sought to create power in organizing the wards and districts of Philadelphia in order to control Philadelphia city and county offices and to benefit from the private business done with these governments; the latter, working from a base outside the city, sought to control the blocks of Philadelphia votes in order to gain power in state and federal political competition. The most conscientious research would be required to arrive at a judicious estimate of which of these two groups of professional political leaders did the most damage to the city of Philadelphia.

Since the early nineteenth century the presence of neighborhood militia and firehouse gangs had made it possible for local politicians to maintain a continuous ward organization rather than having to assemble their followers afresh at each election. The professional politician, however, paid for the use of these gangs. The price was in-

tensive work serving the needs and prejudices of his low-income wards. In the twentieth century the south Philadelphia machine of Congressman William S. Vare and his brothers continued this demanding tradition. Their machine was the core of the Republican organization of Philadelphia, and in alliance with leaders from other inner wards of the city it could deliver the largest single block of votes at any election for any candidate.

Three brothers, Edwin, George, and William, had built the machine. It had been slow and arduous work. Their power had come slowly, earned with years of petty services to south Philadelphians and encouraged by the support of shifting coalitions with Republican factions outside the city. In 1922 only William, the youngest, still lived.

William had been born December 4, 1867, the son of a south Philadelphia truck farmer. His was a Methodist family of English and old Massachusetts immigration. William's career advanced much less rapidly than would have been the normal pace for a contemporary college graduate. He quit school and the farm chores at twelve to go to work as a cash boy in Wanamaker's store. Then in 1883, when he was sixteen years old, his political career began. In that year he went out to work for one of his brothers who peddled stove oil through the streets of south Philadelphia. On this job, and subsequent jobs as a produce peddler, William learned the streets and neighborhoods of his political base. Parades were William's special delight throughout his lifetime, and he began this pleasure when he was eighteen by organizing a mummer's club for the New Year's Day parades.

In the mid-eighties his brothers successfully seized control of south Philadelphia's Ward One Republican Organization. In 1886, when he turned twenty-one, William's district elected

---

[3] The pattern of reform politics in the twenties is nicely characterized in a contemporary novel by Francis Biddle *The Llanfear Pattern* (New York, 1927), Ch. 18.

him representative to the Ward One Republican Committee.[4]

From 1890 to 1926 the Vare brothers held a succession of city, county, and state elective offices. Edwin and William both served terms in Congress as representatives of south Philadelphia. In addition, for many years the Vares obtained lucrative building contracts from the city and ran the municipal trash and garbage routes in their southern and central wards.

This machine linked several interest groupings: those seeking the non-civil-service jobs in the city and county government, and those seeking recommendations to civil service positions; those who wished favorable representation before municipal officials, and the city's magistrate courts; and those with private business with the municipal and county government or whose business depended on local custom. William Vare's leading backers were a coal dealer and an owner of a fleet of taxis.[5]

A decayed version of Philadelphia's old equal-opportunity tradition covered this cluster of interests with an umbrella of familiar rhetoric. "Service" was William Vare's personal slogan. To show the machine's readiness to better the common citizen's lot, its candidates promised anything and everything that had popular appeal, whether it was a high school stadium, the return of the five-cent fare, better traffic conditions, more efficient government, and of course, lower taxes. Vare candidates tended to promise everything, but they also had the locally oriented organization's bias for making these promises on a ward-by-ward basis. One rule, however, could not be breached. The root of the

Vare's power grew in the south Philadelphia ethnic ghettos, and like Boss Martin Lomasney in Boston, the Vares maintained a crude ethnic peace in their districts. One candidate for mayor had to be repudiated when he compared south Philadelphia to the slums of Moscow.[6]

The peak of William's career came in 1926 when he was elected to the United States Senate from Pennsylvania. The Senate, however, refused to seat him. The Vares had a very unpleasant reputation for dishonest election practices, false voter registration, illegal accompaniment of voters into the voting booths, purchase of votes from poor citizens, the use of paid repeat voters, ballot-box stuffing, and false counting. None of the brothers had ever been convicted of such crimes, but Philadelphia elections were conducted amidst charges of such practices, and an occasional offender was arrested and convicted. After three years of investigation and delay Vare was denied his seat in the U.S. Senate on the ground that he had spent too lavishly in the Republican primary. The conclusion was an im-

[4] William S. Vare, *My Forty Years in Politics* (Philadelphia, 1933), 37–43, 47–55.

[5] Sixty-ninth Congress, First Session, *Report of the Special Committee Investigating Expenditures in Senatorial and General Elections*, Pt. I (Washington, 1926), 451–452, 493.

[6] The Vare Machine, William F. Vare, *Forty Years*, espec. 29–30, 118–119. The county offices were the most numerous non-civil service positions since the major departments of the city all had civil service since 1905. In 1920, exclusive of the school department, there were 15,372 city and county positions. Of these 12,817 were civil service posts, 2,555 were non-civil service. The largest city departments were Public Safety 6,754 employees, Public Works 3,239 employees, Public Health 1,890 employees. Mayor of Philadelphia, *First Annual Message of J. Hampton Moore* (Philadelphia, 1921), 873–876. Court and criminal service groups, Spencer Ervin, *The Magistrates Courts of Philadelphia* (Philadelphia, 1931), 105–107; Law Association of Philadelphia, *Report on the Crimes Survey Committee* (Philadelphia, 1926), 450–453 Fred D. Baldwin, "Smedley D. Butler and Prohibition Enforcement in Philadelphia 1924–1925," *Pennsylvania Magazine*, LXXXIV (July, 1960), 352–368; election promises *Philadelphia Evening Bulletin*, August 18, 1923, September 12, 1927; ward-by-ward promises, September 8, 1923.

proper one since his rivals, Senator George W. Pepper and Governor Gifford Pinchot, had each declared larger expenditures, and Pepper had surely spent the most. Partisan pressure and the Vares' unsavory reputation can only account for William's failure to be seated.[7]

In any case, after almost forty years of power and effort the Vares could boast of very little constructive results for Philadelphia or Philadelphians. As congressmen the brothers had, of course, supported the south Philadelphia Navy Yard, and as city councilors they had encouraged all sorts of public works measures for south Philadelphia wards. William, although by no means a leader in these movements, had been instrumental in guiding the final bills through the Pennsylvania legislature for workmen's compensation, child labor, hours of labor for women, Mother's Assistance welfare payments, and the constitutional amendment giving women the vote. Also he had unsuccessfully sponsored old-age pension measures.[8]

Finally, in 1905 William Vare had responded favorably to requests of school reformers to help pass a new state school law as a Republican organization measure. The event was an interesting one since it showed that the machine separated school from county and city issues. In this case the Vares supported for the educational system the very kinds of reforms they often fought against in municipal and county government. This incident also showed the irresistible power in the American urban tradition of any reform which united the business community with a strong equalitarian campaign.

The 1905 school law created for the cities and towns of Pennsylvania a modern, centralized, bureaucratic management of schools. In Philadelphia power was taken from the forty-two sectional school boards out in the wards and placed in the hands of a small Board of Education and a strong superintendent of schools. The Board of Education continued, as in the past, to be appointed by the judges of the Courts of Common Pleas, so presumably the Board remained as amenable to political organization pressure as did the judges the Republican organization nominated. An orderly eligible list for teacher appointments was to be established.

Altogether the school reform of 1905 resembled the attempts to get identifiable responsibility and expert, executive management that were later embodied in a series of anti-machine programs: in Mayor Blankenburg's reforms of 1912–1916, the new Philadelphia charter of 1919, and the Pennsylvania Administrative Code of 1923. The Vares however, did not object to the changes. Apparently their machine did not depend upon school jobs and school business for its power. Also the 1905 school reform was linked in the public mind with the drive to make high school education easily available to all Philadelphia children who wanted it. Uniform, centralized, professional management had become tied with the proposals for industrial and commercial high schools for the non-college bound student. The big district high school, serving all classes and talents of children, resulted, and in the process of achieving this equalitarian uniformity the old elite college preparatory Central High School was destroyed. As always with American municipal institutions, the possibility of serving all the publics of the city,

---

[7] Common newspaper voting fraud charges, *Philadelphia Evening Bulletin*, October 29, 1919, August 30, 1923, August 31, 1923, September 21, 1927, November 9, 1927. The hearing on the primary centered on corrupt practices in Pittsburgh, Sixty-ninth Congress, First Session, *Report of the Special Committee . . .* , 35–36, 91–136, 268, 451–458, 492–508.

[8] Vare, *Forty Years*, 22, 131.

rich and poor, with a variety of institutions, instead of restricting the system to a few dreary uniform ones, proved to be beyond the capabilities of the Board of Education and the citizens of Philadelphia.[9]

The state and federally based professional politicians proved no more useful to the city than the Vares, who were, after all, to some extent their product. The line of descent of leadership in Pennsylvania Republican politics ran from the Camerons, the father Simon, (1867–1877) and the son Donald (1877–1887) to Matthew S. Quay (1887–1911), to Boise Penrose (1911–1921). In the 1920's Joseph R. Grundy of the Pennsylvania Manufacturers Association and the Mellons of the Gulf Oil Corporation of Pittsburgh disputed control of the state party with William Vare. The entire list of Republican state leaders had been an able, unscrupulous group whose power rested on uniting party service to business with business financial support of the party. In the years since the Civil War they had succeeded in driving the Democratic Party into an ever narrower compass so that from 1895 to 1935 Pennsylvania politics were Republican politics.

The power and success of the state Republican rule proved a great misfortune to Philadelphia since it sharply narrowed the issues of political competition. The state party's goals and methods became the focus of all Pennsylvania politics. The party was the subject of campaigns, not the problems of Pennsylvania's economy and institutions. In the twentieth century two issues overshadowed all the rest: honesty in government, and big-busi-

[9] Vare, *Forty Years*, 63–64; Public Education Association of Philadelphia, *Twenty-fourth Annual Report* (Philadelphia, 1905), 5, 31–34; William H. Cornog, *School of the Republic, 1893–1943* (Philadelphia, 1952), 224–232; Donald W. Disbrow, "Reform in Philadelphia under Mayor Blankenburg, 1912–1916," *Pennsylvania History*, XXVII (October, 1960), 379–396.

ness domination of government. The first issue should not have been a major concern in a well-led democratic society. The second issue prevented the state from dealing with the difficult and important matters of social welfare and economic development, which became more and more serious as the twentieth century advanced.

The polarities of state politics repeated themselves in Philadelphia. In Pennsylvania in the 1920's political conflict paired coal companies with their unions, electric utilities with the Public Service Commission, and the traditions of politicians' patchwork office practice with the state administrative code. In Philadelphia similar pairs appeared between textile manufacturers and their unions, the Philadelphia Transit Company and the municipal corporation; regular city employees and the experts. Although splits in Republican machine leadership twice allowed the independent Republican Gifford Pinchot to be elected governor (1923–1927, 1931–1935) these dualities consumed most of his energies. The state and federal Republican leadership was so conservative that it could not see the important economic development issues in Pinchot's power studies, although his program could have aided Pennsylvania's growth as well as keeping the utilities prosperous. No more did Governor Pinchot, or other Republican leaders, see the enormous state expenditure on roads over the years from the Sproul Bill of 1911 to the Great Depression as an extraordinary public effort to be allocated with as much care as electric power. Nor did the state Republican leaders sponsor the economic and social legislation necessary to alleviate the disorders of poverty which affected Philadelphia and large sections of Pennsylvania. Rather, after a decade of opposition they blocked state relief measures in the early 1930's when one-quarter of Pennsylvania's workers were unemployed. Finally, the whole negative attitude toward government which characterized the Republican state and federal leadership encouraged a least-cost, low-quality orientation toward all public institutions and programs whether they were police departments or schools, hospitals or highways.[10]

Lacking a state or local Republican Organization leadership which could define contemporary problems in terms which led to public action, and given the issues of honesty and business domination which the leaders did create, Philadelphia's politics became a highly stylized activity. The elections of the 1920's repeated a contest between Republican organization coalitions and loosely joined opposition groups. The opposition might be styled modernizers.

The nature of this contest between the organization and the modernizers can be observed in the primary elections for Republican candidate for Mayor of Philadelphia. The organization's coalitions began with the Vares' south Philadelphia machine and its allies in the inner, poor, wards of the city. Ward leaders in west Philadelphia and in the northeast and northwest joined after considerable bargaining among local and state Republican leaders. These coalitions did not always come together easily. In 1911 a conflict between the Vares faction and Boise Penrose, the state leader, allowed an independent mayor, Rudolph Blankenburg, to be elected for a term (1912–1916). A similar conflict gave Congressman J. Hampton Moore the mayoralty in 1919. Throughout the early

twentieth century the Republican organization candidates won or failed for mayor on the popular appeal and strength of a politically and economically conservative, locally based, local-serving, personal party organization.

Aligned against this organization stood a vague grouping of people who have been variously styled as reformers, progressives, and cosmopolitans. At the time they called themselves independent Republicans. They seemed to have been, in large measure, a new group of middle and upper-income voters who knew something of the world beyond their neighborhood and city, who responded to appeals for business-like, but not expensive, performance of municipal services, reduction of the municipal debt, civil service, use of experts honesty in voting and administration, and the prosecution of some new projects like transit, high schools, or a municipal convention hall. In short, the opposition to the organization were modernizers, people who voted to make the city more like the Philadelphia they knew; it should conduct its business like a downtown office or a modern factory or store and it should offer its services at a level of quality which matched that of the new sections of the city.[11]

A tabulation of the votes for Republican organization candidate for mayor in the primaries of 1919, 1923 and 1927 clearly shows the distribution of the organization and modernizing

[10] Sylvester K. Stevens, *Pennsylvania, Birthplace of a Nation* (New York, 1964), 264–282; Wayland S. Dunaway, *A History of Pennsylvania* (Englewood, 1948), 456, 479; Gifford Pinchot, "Giant Power," *The Survey*, LI (March, 1924), 561–562 and balance of this month's issue on power.

[11] Samuel P. Hays, "The Social Analysis of American Political History 1880–1920," *Political Science Quarterly*, LXXX (September, 1965), 373–394; Vare, *Forty Years*, 117–119. Voting participation, measured by the number of votes cast in the Republican primaries for mayor as a percentage of the estimated ward population did not show any strong differences between the core wards where the less well-to-do lived and the ring wards of the suburbanites. The core percentage of voters to population was 16.1 percent (1919), 19.1 percent (1923), 20.6 percent (1927); the ring 17.5 percent (1919), 16.0 percent (1923), 20.3 percent (1927). These variations can be explained by the attractiveness of the candidates to the core or ring voters. [See Table I.]

voters. Each of the four major districts of Philadelphia can be divided into core and ring, the core wards being those of least new construction in the twenties, the ring wards being the growing edge of the city. This core-and-ring division is thus a division between those districts which the middle and upper-working class were leaving in the twenties and those districts which they sought out. In all elections and in all districts of the city, save south Philadelphia in 1923, the old core wards voted most heavily for the organization candidate for mayor, the new ring wards voted most heavily for the independent candidates. Moreover, the difference in voting proportions between the core and ring increased steadily from 1919 to 1927, indicating that the cleavage between organization and modernizers was growing sharper, as indeed, were the physical and social conditions of their two worlds. [See Table I.]

This polarity of voters, expressed in Philadelphia in the twenties as the conflict between the organization and the modernizers, perpetrated the city's long political tradition. Like the American Revolutionary conflict between the radicals and the merchants, or the early industrial debate between the Democrats and the nativists, it reflected the private structure and orientation of the city, not its public problems. The unwillingness and inability of Philadelphia's citizens in all periods to conceive of democratic regulation of their private economic affairs prevented the political conflicts from defining the problems of the city in a way suitable for public action.

During the Revolution the radicals had not understood the regional and international basis of Philadelphia's economy; its merchants, in turn, failed to appreciate a democratic society's need to guarantee its citizens a fair distribution of a limited food supply.

In the early industrial era the highly charged equalitarian conflicts for worker and ethnic representation in government obscured the very changes of industrialization which unsettled the city's everyday life.

In the twentieth century the economically and politically conservative debate between Republican organization followers and the modernizers mirrored the growing class segregation of the city, but it utterly avoided dealing with the mounting social welfare and economic and physical development issues which constituted both the disorders and the potential of the metropolis.

From first to last, the structure of Philadelphia had been such that, with the exception of the brief and creative union of equalitarian goals and business leadership in the early nineteenth century, no powerful group had been created in the city which understood the city as a whole and who wanted to deal with it as a public environment of a democratic society. In 1930 Philadelphia, like all large American cities, stood as a monument to the tradition of the private city.

TABLE I

REPUBLICAN PRIMARY ELECTIONS FOR MAYOR 1919–1927 VOTE FOR THE "ORGANIZATION'S" CANDIDATE BY RING AND CORE

Percentage of District's Total Vote

Ring Wards of	1919	1923	1927
Northeast	46.7	76.7	37.9
South	43.5	91.3	66.2
West	42.1	71.6	51.4
Northwest	38.5	66.2	36.5
Ring	41.8	71.1	42.9
Core	53.7	84.2	68.0
All City	49.8	80.1	58.1

Source: Calculated from election returns published in the *Philadelphia Evening Bulletin*, October 10, 1919, September 19, 1923, September 22, 1927.

Problems of a Motor Age

Wilfred Owen*

American cities have become increasingly difficult to live in and to work in largely because they are difficult to move around in. Inability to overcome congestion and to remove obstacles to mobility threaten to make the big city an economic liability rather than an asset.

The crisis in transportation is largely the result of the growing concentration of population and economic activity. In 1960 more than 125 million people were living in the cities and suburbs of the United States. Each year urban America is spreading at the rate of a million acres—an area as large as the state of Rhode Island. In the past decade and a half, the growth of urbanization has been equivalent to duplicating the populations of metropolitan New York, Detroit, Los Angeles, Chicago, and Philadelphia.

This concentration of people and resources in urban areas would have been impossible without the mobility and supply lines afforded by transportation. The capacity of the transport system and the low cost and dependability of transport services have enabled an increasing number of people to seek the economic, social, and cultural opportunities that urban living ideally provides. But paradoxically, metropolitan cities have now grown to the point where they threaten to strangle the transportation that made them possible.

The paradox is particularly striking because the past several decades have seen more revolutionary changes in

transportation than all previous history. With the technical ability to solve its transportation problems well in hand, the modern city is confronted by a transportation problem more complex than ever before. Despite all the methods of movement, the problem in cities is how to move.

One reason for this dilemma is the fact that urban areas have been unable to adjust to the changing conditions brought about so rapidly by the technological revolution in transportation. The older urban centers, with physical characteristics that were fixed in less mobile times, have been staggered by the impacts of recent innovation. And the newer suburbs have compounded the transportation problem by duplicating the errors of downtown and by creating problems of public administration and finance that traditional governmental organization was not designed to meet.

THE PROBLEM AND ITS IMPACT

Every metropolitan area in the United States is confronted by a transportation problem that seems destined to become more aggravated in the years ahead. Growth of population and expansion of the urban area, combined with rising national product and higher incomes, are continually increasing the volume of passenger and freight movement. At the same time, shifts from rail to road and from public to private transportation have added tremendous burdens to highway and street facilities. They have created what appear to be insuperable terminal and parking problems. Continuing economic growth and the certainty of further transport innovation threaten

*From Wilfred Owen, *The Metropolitan Transportation Problem*, rev. ed. (Washington, D.C.: The Brookings Institution, 1966), pp. 1–25. Copyright 1966. Reprinted with permission.

to widen the gap between present systems of transportation and satisfactory standards of service.

Manifestations of the transportation problem in urban areas include the mass movement between work and home and the cost that it represents in money, time, and wasted energy. The transit industry is experiencing rising costs and financial difficulties, while the rider is the victim of antiquated equipment and poor service. Obsolescence and inadequate capacity have become characteristic of the highway network, and terminal problems mean high costs and delays for all forms of transportation. The speed of traffic in central business districts during so-called "rush hours" is frequently as low as six to ten miles an hour, and the problem is finding not only the room to move but a place to stop. The scattered location and obsolete design of freight terminals and the absence of satisfactory physical relationship among the several methods of transportation create a heavy volume of unnecessary traffic as well as delays and high costs that penalize business, the consumer, and the community.

For a nation with 85 million motor vehicles, relatively little has been accomplished toward adapting the city to the automotive age. A limited mileage of urban highways has been built to adequate standards, but for the most part traffic still moves on an antiquated gridiron of streets laid out long before the needs of the automobile were known. These streets were designed principally for convenient real estate platting and access to property rather than for mechanized transportation. Despite the congestion of city thoroughfares, the automobile and truck have been left to park haphazardly along the curb and to load and unload in the street where space is so badly needed for movement.

Highway standards are generally in inverse relation to the needs of traffic. The modern highway in open rural areas often degenerates in urbanized areas to an obsolete right-of-way crowded on both sides with commercial activities strung out in unsightly array to create what has been aptly called America's longest slums. In the city, the concentration of traffic on narrow streets with their numerous crossings means that the speed and service potentials of the motor vehicle cannot be realized. The accident toll is outrageous. Since the turn of the century, half a million people have been killed in motor vehicle accidents on city streets and millions of pedestrians have been injured.

The greatest transportation difficulties are experienced while commuting between home and work. The separation of housing facilities from employment centers together with the rapid expansion of the urban area have created a pendulum movement from home to work that accounts for a larger volume of passenger traffic than any other type of weekday travel. This movement is frequently accomplished with the most antiquated facilities and under the most frustrating conditions. The trip to work often cancels the gain from shorter hours on the job, and the daily battle with congestion is in sharp contrast to other improvements in modern working conditions.

Half a century of neglect has meant a long-term deterioration of transit service and failure to keep pace with technological change. Rising costs and declining patronage have led to a succession of fare increases and further reductions in service. In many cases, it has been impossible to set aside necessary allowances for depreciation of equipment, and the industry as a whole has been unable to attract sufficient capital to renew, modernize, or extend its services for the nearly eight billion riders per year who depend on public carriers.[1]

The cost of providing the physical facilities required to meet urban traffic requirements has reached astronomical levels. High costs of land and damage incident to construction and the tremendous capacity and complicated design of the facilities required in built-up urban areas have thus far combined to make a full-scale attack impossible. Fifty-two billion dollars spent for urban streets during the past four decades has been grossly inadequate to achieve a reasonable quality of transportation service. The cost and complexity of highway construction is indicated by the fact that some expressways cost from $10 million to $30 million per mile.

The contrast between these needs and the financial possibilities of meeting them is not indicative of easy solution. Many metropolitan cities in the United States are suffering from a chronic shortage of funds. Today nine tenths of the mounting expenses of city governments are for services that did not exist at the turn of the century —traffic engineering, airports, parking facilities, health clinics, and a long list of others. At the same time, every city is being overwhelmed with demands for better schools, housing, recreation facilities and other public services along with improved transportation.

City governments burdened by the heavy outlays required to accommodate ever-growing volumes of city traffic frequently find that attempts to relieve congestion serve only to move

[1] The terms "transit" or "mass transportation" are synonymous and include surface street car, bus, or trolley bus in local urban service as well as rail rapid transit operating on exclusive rights-of-way, generally subway or elevated. The term "public transportation" includes transit or mass transportation plus rail commuter services and taxis.

the critical point somewhere else. Expressways or parking facilities established to meet the demand attract further use and magnify the need. Moreover, new facilities mean not only heavy capital outlays but the loss of large areas of land from the tax rolls, reducing receipts at the same time that added revenues are being sought.

HISTORICAL NATURE OF URBAN CONGESTION

The urban transportation problem, although often thought of as relatively new and associated with the automobile and the United States, is both global and historic. All over the world the trend from agricultural economies to urban industrialization continues, and cities in every part of the globe are struggling with similar problems of achieving acceptable standards of urban mobility. Even where automobiles are few, the bus and truck and bicycle combine with less modern methods of movement to create a degree of chaos comparable to the least penetrable crosstown streets of New York.

The big city and its transportation problems were confounding the experts over a century ago, long before the complications of internal combustion. When the population of London increased from approximately one million in 1831 to over four million 60 years later, the poorer inhabitants of the city were forced to abandon the high-rent districts to commercial uses and the city was practically abandoned at night. Out of the resulting tide of traffic that ebbed and flowed from home to work came the commuter, or as he was more appropriately called in earlier times, the journeyman. One hundred years ago his oppression was experienced on foot, and a daily spectacle was "the streams of walkers two, three and four miles long, converging on the city."[2] But with the continued spread of the suburbs, the possibility of so solving the home-to-work problem became impractical and an ambitious program of railroad construction and bus operation was undertaken to cope with it. By the early 1890's a thousand London horse buses were carrying over 100 million passengers per year, and 400,000 daily commuters were carried into the city by rail.

Meanwhile American cities sought to relieve traffic congestion by constructing elevated and subway facilities. Surface transit vehicles were usurping so much street space in Boston more than 60 years ago that a subway was constructed to clear the way for other vehicles using the streets.[3] In 1905 congested traffic at rush hours was described as the number one problem of large cities in the United States, and pictures of urban traffic jams in the days of horse-drawn vehicles and electric cars attest to the fact that congestion was bad long before the motor vehicle made it worse. As early as 1902, the question was whether better results could be obtained "by starting on a bold plan on comparatively virgin soil than by attempting to adapt our old cities to our newer and higher needs."[4]

Although the urban transportation problem is both long-standing and world-wide, its characteristics are not everywhere alike. The problem varies widely among cities of different sizes, types, ages and locations. Problems of a large metropolitan city are very different from those of a smaller town, and large cities themselves differ widely

according to their history, topography, wealth, and function. But the long-standing nature of urban traffic congestion and its world-wide scope suggest, despite a variety of forms, that underlying factors may be universal and only partially related to modern methods of transport. Basic causes appear to be excessive crowding of population and economic activity into small areas of land and the disorderly arrangement of land uses that has maximized transport requirements. The great bulk and density of urban buildings and the concentration of employment in the downtown area have created a volume of passenger and freight movement that has become increasingly difficult to accommodate effectively regardless of transportation method. The congestion of people, horses, and street cars before the appearance of motorized transport, the rush-hour madness of the New York subways, and the lines of automobiles inching their way through the traffic circles of Washington are all manifestations of a continuing imbalance between transportation demand and available transport capacity.

TRANSPORTATION AND URBAN GROWTH

Transportation has played a leading role in the congestion of cities. At an earlier time, heavy densities of population developed because the urban radius was limited to distances that could be covered on foot, or at best by horse. As lines of intercity communication were developed to serve the urban cores of the industrial age, they solved the problems of long-distance transportation that made it possible for great centers of production and employment to supply and support themselves.

But within the urban area, transport innovations were less successful in pro-

[2] C. H. Holden, *The City of London, A Record of Destruction and Survival* (1951), p. 166.

[3] Edward Dana, "Reflections on Urban Transit," An address before the Canadian Club, Montreal, April 21, 1947.

[4] Ebenezer Howard, *Garden Cities of Tomorrow* (1902), p. 134.

viding a better distribution of population and economic activity. Innovation itself could not assure the mobility that economic interdependence in an urban complex requires. Transportation facilities were designed primarily to carry people and goods into the center of the city where there were already too many people and an over-concentration of economic activity. Lack of transportation in the early stages of urban growth combined with the recent development of mechanical transport have created an urban environment in which "each great capital sits like a spider in the midst of its transportation web."[5]

The proportion of the population of the United States in urban places of all sizes has increased from 6 per cent in 1800 to 70 per cent in 1960. During the past decade, the spectacular growth of urban population has placed tremendous additional burdens on transportation in a short period of time.

From 1950 to 1960, when the population increased by 28 millions, 84 per cent of this growth took place in the nation's 212 metropolitan areas. The population of these areas increased by 26 per cent. The largest growth took place in suburban areas, which registered an increase of 49 per cent compared to the 11 per cent increase in central cities.[6] (See Chart I.)

From 1960 to 1963, when there was a gain of 7.4 millions in the total population, 80 per cent of this took place in metropolitan areas. Population in these areas rose to 119 millions in 1963, and the growth rate of the suburbs was more than three times that of the central cities.[7]

The result of these trends has been to concentrate transportation problems in a relatively small number of metropolitan areas. From 1950 to 1960, the population of metropolitan areas increased 53 per cent in Los Angeles and Houston, 45 per cent in Dallas, 35 per cent in Washington, D.C., 30 per cent in Seattle, 28 per cent in Minneapolis–St. Paul, and 25 per cent in Detroit.[8] In 1960 five metropolitan cities had more than three million people, 19 had between one million and three million, and 29 had between 500,000 and a million. The 24 most populous urban areas contained more than 60 million people.

The intensity of the transportation requirements in these urban places and the importance of urban transportation systems are indicated by relating the magnitude of city population to the postage-stamp areas that they encompass. Sixty per cent of the nation's people are located in 1 per cent of the nation's land. Thirty-three per cent of the population is concentrated in one-tenth of 1 per cent of the area of the country. The metropolitan area of New York City contains more people than the combined populations of Arizona, Delaware, Idaho, Maine, Montana, Nevada, New Hampshire, New Mexico, North and South Dakota, Rhode Island, Utah, Vermont, and Wyoming.

The high proportion of the population in the urban category and the small amount of land devoted to urban uses mean that the density of urban population is very high and conse-

[5] Lewis Mumford, *The Culture of Cities* (1938), p. 323.

[6] The rate of population growth for the United States from 1950 to 1960 was 1.7 per cent per year for the country as a whole, less than 1 per cent outside metropolitan areas, and 2.3 per cent within these areas. Growth of the metropolitan areas themselves was 1 per cent in central cities and 4 per cent in the outlying areas U. S. Bureau of the Census, "Growth of Metropolitan Areas in the United States: 1960 to 1963," *Population Characteristics*, Series P-20, No. 131, September 4, 1964, Table A.

[7] Estimates for 1963 from U. S. Bureau of the Census, "Growth of Metropolitan Areas in the United States: 1960 to 1963," *Population Characteristics*, Series P-20, No. 131, September 4, 1964, Table 1.

[8] U. S. Bureau of the Census, *Census of Population: 1950* and *Census of Population: 1960*.

CHART I
POPULATION INCREASE, 1950–60

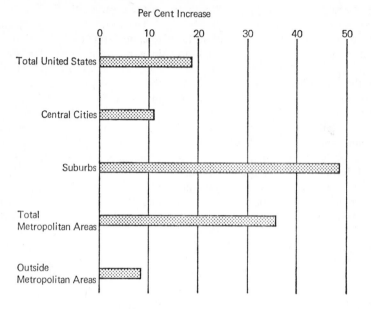

quently that the load on transportation facilities is very heavy. In 1960, there were 24,697 persons per square mile in New York City, and in Manhattan the figure was 77,000 per square mile. This compares with about 50 people per square mile for the country as a whole. In Chicago there were 12,959 persons per square mile, and in Philadelphia 15,743. There were 11 cities in the United States that had a population density of more than 11,000 per square mile.

Population figures do not measure the full magnitude of the transportation problem, for in addition to those who live in the city a large number of people come into the city during the daytime to work. This problem is indicated in the chart on page 11, which shows the resident and daytime populations in major cities in 1950. In 57 cities the daily flow of workers added another ten million people to the congestion at the center.[9] The daytime

population of Boston, for example, was 34 per cent above the census figures of resident population, Pittsburgh had to accommodate 49 per cent more people during the day than at night, and in Newark, New Jersey, the population doubled during daylight hours.

The intensification of urban crowding that results from the daily influx of commuters is measured by the fact that whereas in 1950 only 4 per cent of the population in the five largest cities of the United States resided within a radius of one mile from the central business district, the estimated daytime population within a mile of the center amounted to 30 per cent of the total population in each city. Less than 15 per cent of the residents of these largest cities lived within a two-mile radius from the centers, but estimated daytime population in that area amounted to half the resident population of each city.

To accommodate the heavy concentrations of people in urban centers, and to supply the factories and stores of the city with materials and goods

[9] Associated Universities, Inc., *Reduction of Urban Vulnerability, Report of Project East River,* Pt. V (July 1952), p. 14.

CHART II
INCREASE OF DAYTIME OVER RESIDENT POPULATION

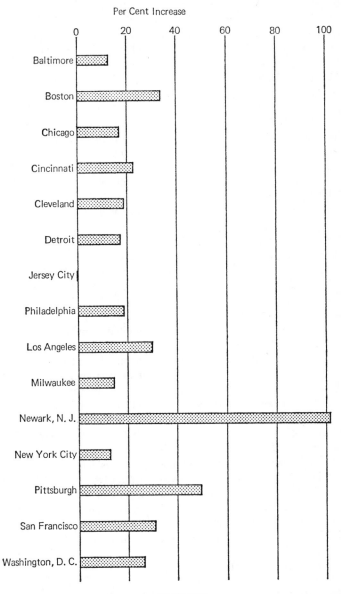

requires a tremendous volume of movement under the most difficult space limitations. Supplying 100 million urban residents calls for the transportation of 2,000 million tons of materials per year. For every urban dweller an average of some 18 tons of materials is consumed annually.[10]

[10] The President's Materials Policy Com-

mission, *Resources for Freedom*, Summary of Vol. I (June 1952), p. 7. The task of feeding the city is illustrated by the collective appetite of New York City, whose daily diet consists of 2.5 million loaves of bread, 5 million quarts of milk, 15 million pounds of fresh fruits and vegetables, 4 million pounds of meat, and close to 30,000 gallons of wine. Every day 36,000 tons of refuse must be trucked away. Gilbert Millstein, "Statistics: Most of Them Superlatives," *New York Times Magazine* (February 1, 1953), p. 29.

How much the final consumer must pay to have the essential channels of mobility and supply kept open is not known, but the marvel is that the biggest cities are rarely inconvenienced by any visible break in the life lines on which they depend. The principal problems of which the average urban resident is aware are the inconveniences, discomforts, and exasperation of coping with the mounting obstacles to personal mobility.

CITY VS. SUBURB

Relatively low-cost, reliable, and high-capacity transportation services have made possible these heavy concentrations of population and economic activity in the big city. The railroad lines to downtown, the subways, and the radial highways have supported congestion by creating the center and leading to it, and by making possible the furnishing of supplies, the marketing of urban products, and the maintenance of minimum standards of mobility.

But more recently transportation has become an agent of dispersal as well, making possible the avoidance of concentration and promoting a diffused pattern of industrial and residential development. Symbolic of the new role of transport are the two-car family, the truck and bus, and the circumferential highway. The trend will continue with the impetus of vertical take-off aircraft, the heliport, and private travel by air. The problems of overcoming transportation difficulties are giving way to the possibilities of exploiting the advantages of transportation. The relative force of these two opposite aspects of transportation development will continue to play an important part in determining the character of urbanization in the future.

Currently, the most notable charac-

teristic of urban change is the rapid growth of the fringes and the loss of population in central core areas. But there has been little evidence that declines in population or economic activity will be sufficient to diminish transport problems in the heart of the city in the near future. In New York City, for example, the population of Manhattan reached its peak in 1910 and declined thereafter until 1930. By 1950, there was an increase of 100,-000 above the 1930 figure but between 1950 and 1960 population gradually declined by one quarter million. However, during this period Manhattan's loss was offset by an equal population increase in Queens.[11] The effect has not been to diminish the intensity of development close in but only to reduce the relative importance of New York City in the metropolitan area. Thus the fringe counties that contained only 8 per cent of the metropolitan population in 1910 accounted for 38 per cent in 1960, while the population of Manhattan declined in relative importance from 31 per cent of the metropolitan total in 1910 to 11 per cent in 1960.[12]

Similar trends in Chicago indicate that the high-density areas of the city are losing population very gradually. The resident population of Chicago within two miles of the center reached a peak in 1910, after which it declined sharply until 1940, then rose again.[13] The same pattern of change took place in the zone two to four miles from the center. Beyond the four-mile zone pop-

[11] The Port of New York Authority, *Metropolitan Transportation — 1980*, New York, 1963, p. 347.

[12] The same, p. 348. Most of this shift had already taken place by 1930, however, when the figure was down to 16 per cent.

[13] It may be assumed, however, that the growth recorded by the close-in areas during the decade of the 1940's was not a reversal of the long-run trend but was occasioned by the wartime shortage of housing, which resulted in doubling up as well as the use of previously vacant dwellings.

ulation has been increasing over a long period of time. The maximum rate of growth is taking place in the areas eight miles out and beyond. (See Chart III.)[14]

In Philadelphia a century of population movement has not greatly reduced the high density of population within the city itself. In 1950, the number of people in the one- to two-mile zone was still 175 times greater than in the 18–25 mile zone. Within three miles of the city center there were almost a million people in 1950, the same as in 1900. The only difference was that with the spreading of the metropolitan area, total population within two miles of the center was a much smaller percentage of the metropolitan total compared to sixty years ago.[15] Urban redevelopment may be expected to result in further reduc-

CHART III
DISTRIBUTION OF CHICAGO POPULATION
(DISTANCE FROM CENTER OF CITY)

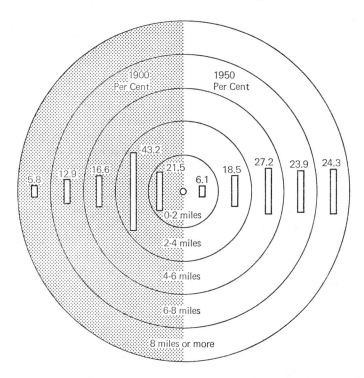

[14] As a result of these trends, the proportion of the population of Chicago living within two miles of the center declined from 17 per cent in 1910 to 6 per cent in 1950; and the proportion living eight miles out or beyond rose from 9 per cent to 24 per cent. Actually the number of people in the close-in zone was the same in 1930 and 1950, and the only substantial change from 1930 to 1950 was in the outer zone. *Growth and Redistribution of the Resident Population in the Chicago Standard Metropolitan Area*, A Report by the Chicago Community Inventory to the Office of the Housing and Redevelopment Coordinator and the Chicago Plan Commission (1954), p. 18.

[15] In 1950, 11 per cent of the total metropolitan population lived within two miles of the center compared to 24 per cent in 1900. Hans Blumenfeld, "The Tidal Wave of Metropolitan Expansion," *Journal of the American Institute of Planners,* Vol. 20 (Winter 1954), p. 13.

tions in population density. The close-in areas of Philadelphia three to five miles from City Hall are expected to lose one fifth of their population by 1980.[16] Yet even with substantial losses there will still be a heavy concentration of people and economic activity.

For the majority of American cities, there will continue to be density reductions close in. These reductions plus the growth of the suburbs will further reduce the relative importance of the city itself, but substantial loosening up of the older congested areas will still leave heavy concentrations of urban population. Thus the urban area as a whole faces continuing problems of traffic congestion near the center along with the additional demands for suburban mobility and commutation service between suburb and center.

Employment trends parallel population trends. In New York City, for example, it is estimated that the decrease in the total number of jobs will be 64,000 in 1965 compared to the 1956 figure, while in the metropolitan area as a whole there will be an increase of 457,000 jobs. The proportion of total regional employment accounted for by New York City declined from 66 per cent in 1946 to 56 per cent in 1965, and thousands of people are now commuting from the city outward to get to work.[17] But there has been no visible decline in the magnitude of daily movement to the center.

Despite the spreading industrial growth in the suburbs, the city proper still retains a major share of the manufacturing activity in metropolitan areas. From the standpoint of the transportation problem of the city, growth trends have not diminished the factors contributing to traffic congestion. The kinds of industrial establishments moving out of the city are those with a relatively low number of employees per unit of area, whereas office work centering in the downtown area involves a high density of employment and the type of employment that creates the greatest peak-hour traffic.

As population and industry have grown in the suburbs, retail business has expanded rapidly outside the city limits, and the percentage of metropolitan area sales being transacted in the city has declined. Again, however, the new stores have been necessary to accommodate the growth of population and income, and for the most part retail trade in the central city still flourishes.

Building permits for the year 1954 showed that half of the nation's construction took place in the suburbs of metropolitan areas and 31 per cent in central cities. The remainder was accounted for by nonmetropolitan areas.[18] These figures indicate that suburban growth has not destroyed the economic vitality in the central city. The tremendous suburban expansion has not appreciably altered the concentration of urban activity nor diminished the underlying causes of traffic congestion. What looked like dispersion a short while ago has been largely new growth, and this growth has of necessity taken place in the outer fringes where room for expansion is still available.

---

[16] Information from the Philadelphia Urban Traffic and Transportation Board.

[17] Regional Plan Association, Inc., *Population 1954–1975 in the New Jersey–New York–Connecticut Metropolitan Region*, Bulletin 85, p. 25. Also, Port of New York Authority, *Metropolitan Transportation — 1980*, 1963, pp. 349–50.

THE OUTLOOK FOR URBANIZATION

Despite the patterns of urban growth to date, and the presumption that cen-

[18] *Washington Post and Times Herald* (June 29, 1955).

trifugal forces will gain rather than lose strength in the future, there is still no clear indication of the extent to which present trends in urban growth will continue. We do not know to what degree economic changes and developments in technology will alter the process of urbanization. Future growth may mean that existing densities in central cities will be substantially maintained or again increased; that conversely the downtown area and much of the central city will continue to give way before the onrush to the suburbs. Changes are also being introduced through planned cities of very different design that are making their appearance in many parts of the country.

Congestion and blight have multiplied the difficulties and frustrations of urban life, and in many places the growth of concentrated living seems to have passed the point of diminishing returns. Further vertical growth and urban sprawl both promise to compound the difficulties of providing transportation and other community facilities in the second half of the century. The threat of greater congestion has raised the question whether a nation born of farms is destined to die of cities.[19]

The belief that this could in fact be the case has been reinforced by a growing realization that until world peace can be guaranteed, the closely-packed city is particularly vulnerable to nuclear destruction. "A nation which keeps its wealth, its productive capacity, its population, and its administration huddled together in a few metropolitan areas, invites blackmail and courts disaster."[20] We are told on the one hand that "all the long-range dangers and disadvantages of our sit-uation can be mitigated—even if none of them can be entirely eliminated—by judicious dispersal of our basic industries and productive population."[21] On the other hand, it is contended that the dangers of fall-out threaten to devastate so wide an area that to flee has become futile.

According to Frank Lloyd Wright, the deadline for decentralization has been so shortened by the threat of nuclear warfare that the urbanite must either be willing to get out of the city or be resigned to blowing up with it. Protection against enemy attack is no longer to be found in banding together in cities, and the possibilities of arriving at a more even distribution of the population over the unused areas of the country have been vastly increased by recent innovations. This is especially true of developments in transportation. In the light of these considerations alone, it may be that "further centralizations of any American city are only postponements of the city's end."[22]

Many of the economic advantages of urban living have in any event already been neutralized. The city has become the victim of diseconomies that are reflected in high costs of living, including high costs of moving. Distribution costs and the difficulties of personal mobility often cancel other attractions of urban life. The theoretical benefits of urban location are frequently submerged in the rising discomforts and declining satisfactions of much that the city has to offer. The growing distances that must be covered from home to work, from one place of business to another, and from one friend to another tend to overcome the advantages of propinquity that the city is supposed to afford.

[19] Elmer T. Peterson, ed., *Cities Are Abnormal* (1946), p. v.
[20] "Must Millions March?", *Bulletin of the Atomic Scientists*, Editorial (June 1954), p. 194.
[21] The same, p. 195.
[22] Frank Lloyd Wright, "The Future of the City," *Saturday Review of Literature* (May 21, 1955), p. 12.

But more serious charges can be leveled at the urban area today. Blight and slums render large sections of the big city unfit for living. Although the wealth of the United States can be expressed in glowing statistics, about 20 per cent of the residential areas of its cities are slums. These slum areas contain one third of the urban population. To support them takes 45 per cent of the costs of municipal government, yet the same areas contribute only 6 per cent of total property tax revenues.[23] In New York City a quarter of a million dwellings lack toilet or bath, recreation facilities and open space are grossly inadequate, and even sunlight and air are at a premium.

Can we, then, provide a more satisfactory urban environment in new locations as transport technology enables us to move out and begin anew? The assumption that we can is often shaken by the newer suburbs. They have taken on many of the most objectionable aspects of the older blighted sections.[24] In attempting to flee from the undesirable conditions of the downtown area, frequently we have succeeded only in taking our mistakes with us.[25]

The idea of moving out to seek the health and enjoyment of air and sunlight has been a natural reaction to the noise and dirt of the city, but the endless spreading of cities has resulted in pushing the country farther and farther away. As a result, those who

seek the restfulness or beauty of the countryside must constantly move outward to avoid the progressive waves of those who continue the escape from older blighted districts. This unplanned suburban development has resulted in the sprawl of large cities, the lengthening journey to work, and the growing difficulty of moving around.

Transportation has contributed in other ways to the diminishing desirability of urban living. The hazards and congestion of the highways, the noise and fumes of the motor vehicle, and the unsightliness of the gas station and used car lot have all added to the run-down character of the urban region. Transportation has created many of the conditions that people strive to escape, but it has also provided the means of escaping them and therefore the means of avoiding solutions. And it has transported slums to the suburbs.

The solution is not to abandon the city, therefore, but to assure that the inadequacies of the close-in urban area are corrected and that new suburban developments avoid the mistakes of the past. In some cities the congestion of the central city seems to have reached the saturation point, but we may also be arriving at an economic limit to the outward spread of the metropolis made possible by improved methods of transportation. As the increasing radius of travel resulting from modern transport permits us to move farther from the center, the cost of community facilities of all kinds increases. The higher densities of more compact urban areas of lesser size may offer a more economical alternative.

It can hardly be contended, however, that the degree of metropolitan concentration reached today is necessary for the success of either business or the arts and sciences. Many of the activities that were necessarily located in the center of the city before the

[23] National Association of Home Builders, *A New Face for America* (1953), p. 6. Data from Federal Works Agency, Public Buildings Administration.

[24] For a view of what is happening to "prosperous" suburbs see "Blight — Suburban Style," *Urban Land* (May 1955).

[25] "The far-flung metropolitan city of the motor age contains suburban slums and blighted commercial areas which are as appalling in their way as the old tight-packed city slums of the railway age." C. McKim Norton, "Metropolitan Transportation," *An Approach to Urban Planning*, Gerald Breese and Dorothy E. Whitman, eds. (1953), p. 82.

development of better means of transport and communications now could be decentralized and dispersed. The fact that some degree of concentration is an economic advantage does not lead to the conclusion that maximum concentration is the ultimate goal.

On the other hand, the big city can be defended on economic, social, and cultural grounds. The phenomenon of the metropolitan city derives from the fact that co-operative action makes possible greater productivity and higher standards of living, and it permits public services and amenities to be supplied more effectively and often at lower cost. A large labor force makes feasible the specialization required by large-scale industry and provides the skills needed for today's highly technical production processes. Even the availability of sufficient numbers of consumers to enjoy the fruits of modern production is predicated on the profitable markets afforded by concentrations of population. Advantages likewise stem from the variety of contacts and educational opportunities afforded by a larger population.

In any event, those who like the country have thus far been outnumbered by those who prefer a crowd, and the view that the city is bound to disappear has not as yet been borne out by events. More people are being attracted to cities and their urbanized surroundings than desire to remain rural, and at the center there continues to be a struggle between horizontal and vertical growth that has seen both sides claiming victory.

ALTERNATIVE TRANSPORTATION SOLUTIONS

What the future of the city will be or what the city of tomorrow ought to be like are questions closely related to the provision of transportation. Transport innovation will to a large degree dictate what is possible, and the extent to which transport policy is directed to achieving urban goals will help determine what is feasible. Many observers believe that a continuing downward trend in mass transportation is inevitable as car ownership expands and as highway and parking facilities are further developed to cope with traffic congestion. This would presumably hasten the decline of the center. Others take the view that in the relatively dense areas of the central city the attempt to accommodate the continuing trend toward private automobile transportation is a costly mistake that can end only in the ruination of downtown and the frustration of urban dwellers. The greater efficiency of mass transportation must be exploited, it is contended, by devoting more attention and money to the modernization and expansion of public conveyance, which in turn will preserve the downtown area.

One of the basic questions, then, concerns the relative emphasis to be placed on expressways and parking facilities to accommodate automobile use as compared to the modernization of mass transportation facilities aimed at restoring lost patronage and reducing the number of vehicles entering the city. If the latter course were followed, would it be possible to promote greater use of transit or would the urban resident either insist on using his private car or go elsewhere to work or shop or to do business? The correct decision is of basic importance to the future of the city and its people. The costs of transport modernization will be very high regardless where the emphasis is placed. But the cost of doing the wrong things or of simply doing nothing could be higher. For the ability to provide a circulatory system of acceptable standards will be an important factor in the economic survival of the urban economy.

The view that better mass transportation is the way out of the current situation is based on the contention that attempts to use the motor vehicle in an environment established before motoring needs were known are bound to be unsuccessful. Failure will be in the form of either downtown congestion or desertion. Mass transportation is capable of moving many times more people than automobiles can move, and under restricted space conditions should provide a more effective method of transportation. The problem of urban congestion has become so great that many communities are coming to the conclusion that there could never be sufficient highway and parking capacity to permit the movement of all people in private cars.

The opinion is frequently expressed that cities are suffering from "automobile blight"; that if the automobile were banned from downtown areas and satisfactory mass transportation provided instead, congestion would be relieved and greater freedom of movement would assure economic survival for the city. "The cities just cannot resign themselves to automobiles and let mass transportation slide to ruin and extinction. They must preserve mass transportation or stagnate."[26] Downtown is doomed to die, it is contended, unless cities stress movement of people rather than movement of vehicles. With this sentiment there appears to be widespread agreement. "Eventually cities will be places few people will want to live in, work in, or even visit unless they act to restrict private transportation."[27]

The mass transportation solution does not stimulate universal admiration, however. According to Mumford, while congestion originally provided the excuse for the subway, the subway has now become the further excuse for congestion. Small cities where people walked and rode bicycles were in a better position to take advantage of motor transport than cities that invested heavily in trolleys and rapid transit.[28]

If mass transportation is not the answer, what of the possibilities of modern highways to relieve the city of the congestion that inadequate transportation once made necessary? Critics insist that elaborate urban expressways are futile because of the tremendous reservoir of traffic waiting to absorb any new street capacity. According to this view, expressways and parking facilities not only will not solve the problem of congestion but will actually make it worse. The traffic engineer who tries to accommodate the private automobile "is doomed to inevitable failure . . . the better he does his job the greater will be his failure."[29]

But the position is also taken that the automobile, far from being a cause of urban congestion, has in fact made possible a necessary deconcentration of population through the decentralization of urban living and working. The endless streams of traffic that choke today's downtown streets make it natural to suppose that the private car has been responsible for the congestion of our cities, but it can be argued that the opposite is actually the case. "The only relief from congestion has been possible because of the motor vehicle."[30]

[26] John Bauer, "The Crisis in Urban Transit," *Public Management* (August 1952), p. 176.

[27] W. H. Spears, quoting Joseph W. Lund in "Transit Is Dynamic," *Mass Transportation* (September 1954), p. 40.

[28] Mumford, *The Culture of Cities*, pp. 243, 441.

[29] Walter Blucher, "Moving People — Planning Aspects of Urban Traffic Problems," *Virginia Law Review*, Vol. 36 (November 1950), p. 849.

[30] Arthur B. Gallion and Simon Eisner, *The Urban Pattern* (1950), p. 193.

Still another view is that neither automobiles nor mass transportation nor any other mechanical contrivance can solve the problems of urban congestion. "As a solution of the traffic problem these devices are pure deception."[31] Putting the emphasis on supplying transportation facilities rather than controlling the demand, it is maintained, serves only to aggravate congestion. "As long as nothing is done fundamentally to rehabilitate the cities themselves, the quicker will people forsake them" and the greater the problems for those left behind to cope with.[32]

We have the assurance, therefore, that the problem of congestion in urban areas has been precipitated by the automobile; that the automobile, on the contrary, has been our escape from congestion; that the automobile and mass transportation are both guilty of promoting congestion; and finally that neither is the primary culprit, but rather a host of other factors that have resulted, thanks to modern technology, in the successful attempt to crowd too many people and too much economic activity into too little space. And of the city itself we are told that preservation of the vast investment in urban America will assure both economic salvation and nuclear annihilation.

Metropolitan areas thus face the difficult task of arriving at decisions that will determine to a major degree the physical and financial future of tomorrow's city. Should they emphasize expressways and parking facilities to accommodate automobile use, or modernize mass transportation facilities in the hope of restoring lost patronage and reducing the number of vehicles entering the city? Or will solutions depend instead on the extensive replanning and rebuilding of the American city? The next two chapters will explore the transportation problems of metropolitan areas and what is being done about them. This will set the stage for later exploration of a more comprehensive approach to urban mobility and its relation to urban finance, administration, and renewal.

[31] Mumford, *The Culture of Cities*, p. 296.
[32] Charles M. Nelson, "Expressways and the Planning of Tomorrow's Cities," in *Proceedings* of the Annual National Planning Conference, American Society of Planning Officials, Los Angeles, August 13–16, 1950 (1951), p. 121.

The Challenge of Suburbia

Robert C. Wood*

Suburbia, defined as an ideology, a faith in communities of limited size and a belief in the conditions of intimacy, is quite real. The dominance of the old values explains more about the people and the politics of the suburbs than any other interpretation. Fundamentally, it explains the nature of the American metropolis. It indicates why our large urban complexes are built as they are, why their inhabitants live the way they do, and why public programs are carried out the way they are. If these values were not dominant it would be quite possible to conceive of a single gigantic metropolitan region under one government and socially conscious of itself as one community. The new social ethic, the rise of the large organization, would lead us to expect this development as a natural one. The automobile, the subway, the telephone, the power line certainly make it technically possible; they even push us in this direction.

But the American metropolis is not constructed in such a way; it sets its face directly against modernity. Those who wish to rebuild the American city, who protest the shapeless urban sprawl, who find some value in the organizational skills of modern society must recognize the potency of the ideology. Until these beliefs have been accommodated reform will not come in the metropolitan areas nor will men buckle down to the task of directing, in a manner consonant with freedom, the great political and social organizations on which the nation's strength depends. A theory of community and a theory of local government are at odds with the prerequisites of contemporary life and, so far, theory has been the crucial force that preserves the suburb. There is no economic reason for its existence and there is no technological basis for its support. There is only the stubborn conviction of the majority of suburbanites that it ought to exist, even though it plays havoc with both the life and government of our urban age.

THE AMERICAN MINIATURE

If a belief in small government and small society helps explain why the modern suburb exists in an age of bigness, the suburban renaissance should not be surprising. The conviction that provincial life is best has been with us for a long time and it has endured in the face of greater attacks than the ones contemporary America presents. We show our instinctive commitment to the ideology by the fact that we rarely examine its assumptions critically. We show our conscious allegiance by the oratorical homage we pay to the ideal of small neighborhoods, single homes, and political jurisdictions of limited size.

It is difficult to overestimate the vigor and pervasiveness of the belief. Three centuries stand behind the heritage—a full two hundred years of spectacular success and one hundred years of abject failure. The first period endowed the American cult of localism with its basic articles of faith: an assertion that local communities should maintain their own identity and manage their own affairs, and justification for that assertion by the claim that the small society is the natural

*Reprinted with permission from Robert C. Wood, *Suburbia: Its People and Their Politics*, Boston: Houghton Mifflin Company, 1959, 18–21, 66–69, 74–75, 83–87.

home of democracy. The last hundred years added endurance and stubbornness to the ideal by the very adversity which the reality of the urban world inflicted upon it. But whether made confident by success or contentious by disaster, the creed has remained to shape the American metropolis and make it what it is today.

. . .

CRISIS IN AUTONOMY

The nostalgic image found a new frame then, in suburbia, and its popularity justified suburban independence. Faith in the ideology discouraged the creation of new political institutions to serve the entire metropolitan area and provided an appealing rationale for the preservation of local town halls and county court houses. It served to crystallize the new region into hundreds of small communities, each more or less conscious of its own identity.

But was suburbia a legitimate recipient of the legacy? Did it offer a genuine renaissance or only a pale counterfeit of the real article? The suburb, after all, was not an early New England town, a southern market center, or a western trading village. The United States was no longer rural, but urban and industrial, and destined to become more so. The pattern of large-scale organization, the values of togetherness, the political philosophy of positive government, all penetrated suburbia, made it something more and less than a replica of earlier times. There was an economic interdependence of the region as a whole, a new pattern of social intercourse throughout the area, and these developments had both direct and subtle influences on the reinvigorated jurisdictions. In the short run at least, the immediate answer to the question as to whether or not the suburb was the carrier of the grassroots faith depended upon

the success of the local governments in maintaining their autonomy. If they went under and were absorbed by the metropolis, then no amount of imagery could re-establish the small community in its essential form.

In the beginning, this issue of genuineness and the critical role of suburban independence was scarcely recognized. The new environment was overlooked, and men took at face value the revival of the small-scale jurisdictions surrounding the large cities and the apparent renaissance of independent, healthy community life after one hundred years of somnolence. The issue in municipal reform throughout the last half of the nineteenth century had been so much the question of size—how to reduce urban congestion or manage it in accordance with historic values—and the solutions had been so tentative that its seemingly automatic resolution was accepted with delight, and with little critical examination.

For those who had emphasized the necessity of breaking up the mammoth city to guarantee a satisfactory local government, the suburb was an intimation of dreams about to come true. More pleasing still, their aspirations were turning into reality quite naturally, without the tremendous political and educational efforts that Geddes and Howard thought necessary. Writing at the turn of the century, Adna Weber could view the development of suburban towns even then as "the most encouraging feature of the whole situation." "The rise of the suburbs," he wrote, "is what furnishes the solid basis of a hope that the evils of city life, so far as they result from overcrowding, may be in large part removed . . . It will realize the wish and prediction of Kingsley, 'a complete interpenetration of city and country, a complete fusion of their different modes of life and a combination of the advantages of both, such as no country in the world has ever seen.'" And twenty-five years later, Harlan Douglass could speak of the suburban evangel, and after a biting indictment of the city, look to a new motivation for life in the satellite town of open land and cottage home. He could confidently predict, "A crowded world must be either suburban or savage." For the first planners, the trend was nothing awesome, but a movement devoutly prayed for and constantly encouraged.

Even the more pragmatic municipal reformers, those who believed they had solved the problem of size by political and administrative adjustments, never claimed that their program of reform was superior to the genuine article. Proportional representation, nonpartisanship, the short ballot, the small council had been offered as substitutes in a large city for the direct self-government possible in smaller places. Certainly these experts felt that the suburbs could profit by employing a city manager and business methods of organization and administration, but they did not believe that the suburban trend was contradicting their own efforts. Instead it appeared to reduce the size of their job, for now they could concentrate on the central cities of the metropolitan areas, secure in the knowledge that the surrounding towns could take care of themselves.

Of course, a nagging doubt as to what was happening to the metropolitan region as a whole tugged at the National Municipal League's conscience, and metropolitan problems were discussed spasmodically at annual meetings from 1917 to 1925. But the League did not publish its first report on the government of metropolitan areas until 1930, and although the study was hailed as "the first comprehensive survey of its kind," it arrived at no specific recommendations. In-

deed, its conclusions were regarded as "so general in their scope that it is virtually impossible to disagree with them—a sure sign that they have little value." The perfection of the structural and procedural mechanisms of reform continued to hold the center of the stage, and though there were hints that suburbia might cause trouble, they received low priority on the agenda.

So the trend intensified, and far from vanishing, the number of governmental units within each metropolitan area multiplied at an astonishing rate. In 1900, the New York region had 127 minor civil divisions, by 1920, 204; in Cook County (Chicago) there were 55 in 1890 and 109 in 1920; around Pittsburgh, 107 units existed in 1920 where thirty years earlier only 91 were formally incorporated. For the seventeen largest cities, incorporations of new governments around the fringe of the city went on and on—most rapidly at the turn of the century, but steadily for the next fifty years. Between 1952 and 1957 alone, 170 new municipalities came into being in metropolitan areas and 519 new special districts were created. By 1957, there were over 3000 governments that could be said to possess more or less general municipal powers, and there was, of course, that awesome figure of 15,658 legally distinguishable local units. Village, hamlet, school district, city, county, town, they were each one equipped with the legal prerogatives of government, each claiming to speak for a separate constituency. They jostled one another in the crowded confines of the metropolitan backyard, jealous of their authority and suspicious of their neighbors.

· · ·

From the organizational as well as the financial point of view then, the failure of the city to expand concurrently with the growing urban area seemed disastrous. The "crazy quilt hodge podge of local governmental agencies" could appear to H. G. Wells as far back as 1910, "like fifteenth century houses which have been continuously occupied by a succession of enterprising but short-sighted and close-fisted owners, and which have now been, with the very slightest use of lath and plaster partitions and geyser hot-water apparatus, converted into modern residential flats." To Victor Jones, thirty years later, the problem of metropolitan government remained much the same: "The need for servicing a large population scattered under the jurisdiction of many units of local government, most of which are crippled by limited powers over a restricted area, by inadequate tax resources and by such consequences of premature subdivision as heavy indebtedness and extensive tax areas." And Betty Tableman, writing in 1951, insisted indignantly that "no governmental unit is an island. Sins of omission and commission of any one municipality affect not only its own citizens but all persons living in the metropolitan area." Criminals were escaping because no police jurisdiction had effective control; fires raged while unused equipment lay idle across artificial boundaries; sewage dumped in a river by one government contaminated the neighboring jurisdiction's lake; master highway plans could not be completed on an area-wide basis. The urban center was no longer, in Luther Gulick's words, "floating around in a great and green rural hinterland." Rather, "it is now elbow to elbow with other paved urban centers."

Suburbia was not, then, to slip smoothly into the modern world, as its first supporters had fondly imagined. It was causing trouble, real trouble, for the metropolis of which it was a part. The first tenet of its political ideology—independence for each locality—no longer had an eco-nomic or social base, and the justification for autonomy apparently collapsed. A collection of small governments, without financial self-sufficiency and some spatial isolation from each other, made for ineffective political structures, and the principle of autonomy no longer went hand in hand with its companion doctrine—democracy—to justify these small-scale reconstructions of an earlier culture. The two doctrines were turned against each other, and the close democracy a suburb promised almost guaranteed ineffective government for the region as a whole. The threat to American localism was not from Washington or the state capitals; the creed was doing itself in and its greatest virtue had been subverted into its greatest vice.

. . .

SUBURBIA TRIUMPHANT

Annexation, consolidation, merger, country-city separation—suburbia considered all of them and concluded usually that it wanted none of them. It preferred legal autonomy and small town politics above all, and it continued to expand. The New York region by 1954 boasted 1071 separate jurisdictions; Chicago, 960; Philadelphia, 702; St. Louis, 420; until, all in all, 14 per cent of all local governments in the United States were in the metropolitan areas. Against all appeals that this multiplicity fostered political irresponsibility and defeated "both the theory of popular control and the government's ability to provide services," the suburbs were adamant. They knew that what reform actually entailed was a reunion, at least in part, with the central city and its corrupt politics, its slums, immigrants, criminals, and the vicious elements from which they had only recently escaped. The reformers had demonstrated the expense of maintaining this isolation, but to most suburbanites, the figures merely proved that the price of liberty was always high.

In only one way did the suburbs adjust to modernity. When obvious breakdowns appeared in basic public utilities, metropolitan-wide institutions were permitted, so long as they were not governments. Public corporations, authorities, special districts were popular with suburbanites; they were self-supporting and businesslike in form. They were allowed to assume the money-making activities of local government—the building and operation of bridges, tunnels, terminals, and airports—and because they were run by state-appointed commissioners, aloof from the undignified ordeal of vote-getting, they were acceptable. By that curious *non sequitur* so appealing to Americans—that the authorities had "taken government out of politics"—the suburbs reasoned they had nothing to fear. These institutions could not be threats because they were not governments.

Thus the only way in which big organizations entered local government was by masquerade. The metropolitan agencies now at work are in the form of *ad hoc* special districts, in highways, sanitation, airports, mosquito control, water, garbage collection, hospitals, almost every conceivable local activity. The New York Port Authority, the Boston Metropolitan District Commission, the transit authorities, the Golden Gate Bridge and Highway District, these have been the novelties permitted. No period in American history saw more inventions in forms of pseudo government than the decades between 1920 and 1950, when the baffling array of "nonpolitical" boards, commissions, and agencies sprang up across the country.

They were, of course, pseudo governments. Victor Jones was quite right when he wrote that their lack of direct accountability and numerical addition to the local governments already in existence "confuses the citizens and voters and makes it difficult to secure responsible local government in large urban communities." But the suburbs were satisfied; if the small town could not carry out a local function, then it was better to remove the program from government entirely. Grassroots democracy or big business—no other vehicle is trustworthy in the United States.

There was stubborn resistance, however, to all proposals for genuine government. The answer could be found in the words of Arthur E. Morgan about Great Neck, Long Island, in the twenties: "All the people in that area moved in about the same time. They were young married couples with one or two children . . . the men have a volunteer fire department and have recently built a beautiful fire house which is equipped for recreational purposes as well . . . The women very often do the shopping cooperatively. If anyone is ill, everyone will do her bit to help . . . The church is a community church. The minister is young and has done much for all ages. A social is held once a month for the married couples. There are frequent dances for the young people. It seems that something is going on every week." Or it could come in the forthright declaration of the resident of Tarrytown that "I would feel that I had surrendered some of my manhood if I gave to the politicians in White Plains the legal right to control in the slightest degree the education of my children."

However presented, the suburban choice in the twentieth century had been to retain the form of government most closely resembling Jefferson's legacy—a choice, moreover, made in defiance of the compelling values of the modern world: large-scale organization, efficiency, economy and rationalization. Fortuitously supported by two decades of prosperity, the suburbanite has been able to brush aside the specter of municipal bankruptcy, ignore the obviously illusory nature of his legal autonomy, and retain his independent community. The nation's wealth for the moment supports his idol, and the Great Society, at least in the political sense, is excluded from his hearth and home.

This overwhelming victory implies, of course, some serious weaknesses in the doctrines of metropolitan reform. One tactical error seems clear immediately: for all their energy and ingenuity, for all their battle cries of annexation, merger and federation, the reformers have mounted only a limited offensive. They have challenged the feasibility of small government and small communities in the twentieth century, but they have never seriously questioned the desirability of small government whenever it can possibly be sustained. In the end, the reformers have offered only an alternative program for better metropolitan financial and administrative management; they have never promised a better brand of politics.

This reluctance to launch a full-scale attack on the ideology as well as the practicality of small government diminishes the prospects for reform's success. It allows the suburb the heroic role of defender of democracy, even though it remains the villain in the melodrama of metropolitan development. Thus the suburb possesses an almost impenetrable line of defense, for what citizen, faced with a choice of an ineffective government democratically controlled or an effective government less democratically controlled, will not wrap himself in high moral principle and choose the first?

By refusing to challenge the grassroots faith itself, reformers are forced back to a single argument: that the suburban claim to the status of a small community is necessarily counterfeit. Yet, even here, taking their stand as hard-bitten realists, they are on weak ground. They assume that the loss of financial self-sufficiency among the suburban governments and the end of social isolation means inevitably the collapse of small town life and consciousness. On this assumption reformers conclude that the suburban commitment to the colonial legacy must be, of necessity, illusionary. And, on this assumption, they have constructed the best alternative structure they can devise in the belief that some day suburbanites will realize that their allegiance is nostalgia, a commitment to a shadow world which existed only in the past.

But it is a serious mistake to believe that an ideology simply reflects the social and political organization in a particular period of history, lingering for a while, but ultimately giving way to an expression of a new reality. When they are powerful enough, ideologies may shape—as well as mirror —the world about them. This fact metropolitan reformers are discovering today, for it is not the simple memory of the heritage which thwarts their efforts. It is the power of that heritage as a very real expression of the aspirations and values of the present generation which blocks the progress of reform.

In the final analysis, Wells and Mumford, as the early discoverers of the organization man, never challenged the suburban evangel to any real effect for a good reason: the more closely suburbs are studied, the more genuine their claim to provinciality appears. In many essential qualities many suburbs seem like the American small towns of the past, much more impervious to modern life than is commonly supposed.

Slums, Housing, and Urban Renewal

Charles Abrams*

The slum, which has been called the shame of the cities, is also the sperm of the public housing and urban renewal concepts. It is as distasteful a four-letter word as any in the dictionary. The word is a piece of cant of uncertain origin, little more than a century old.[1] The *Encyclopedia of Social Reform*[2] suggested that it was a corruption of "slump," meaning swamp, but there are indications that it is cousin to slime, which in turn is derived from "lime," meaning mud. It links both slop[3] and scum and also has the cadence of slush, slovenly, slut, slump, slug, slubber, slob, slub, sludge, slummock, slutch, and slutterly. Slum gives its meaning the moment it is uttered.

Since a word can be repellent as well as a persuader, and since slum is both, it has spurred emotions on the hustings, the pulpit, and the bench. Unlike words such as substandard, tenement, and insanitary housing, it is short, electric, and suited to newspaper headlines. From the day slum entered the language of social reform, its mere mention was enough to revolt the good citizen, win the support of the crusading press, and dedicate official action to its extinction.

The slum, however, is easier to revile than to remedy. During England's industrializing period some of its luminaries implied that the slum dweller was to blame. They defined slums as the dirty back streets or alleys shared by the poor and criminal classes. If the all too fertile slumdwellers could be exhorted to be more chaste (chastity would hold down their numbers), shun whiskey (giving up drink would make them more frugal), and fear God (piety would keep them honest, peaceful, and clean), slums would disappear. The filthy habits of the slum dweller himself were also held to be the cause of slums in America.[4]

Other reformers blamed the landlord.[5] His rents were seen as swallowing up all profit and unless something was done to check him, it was feared he would soon rule the world.

A whole series of laws were enacted both in England and America aimed at compelling landlords to improve their dwellings. But the slum dweller never fully escaped reproach and, in fact, association of the criminal classes with slums still colored the slum definition in the 1934 edition of *Webster's New International Dictionary*.

In the 1920s, writers like Edith Elmer Wood,[6] taking their cue from the more recent and more enlightened programs of England and the continent, began to highlight the disparity

---

*From pp. 19–22, 40–53, 78–82, 84–85, 287–289 in *The City is the Frontier* by Charles Abrams. Copyright © 1965 by Charles Abrams. Reprinted by permission of Harper & Row, Publishers.

[1] Thus the *Oxford Dictionary* cites an 1828 usage from the History of Gaming (p. 28): "Regaling in the back-parlour (vulgo *slum*) of an extremely low-bred Irish widow."

[2] Funk and Wagnalls, 1897, p. 1260.

[3] It was Middle English *cousloppe* that gave us slop and sloppy. A cowslip is a flower that grows in cowslop.

[4] *Health Department* v. *Dassori*, 21 App. Div. 348, 47 N.Y.S. 641 (October 15, 1897).

[5] The landlord in the United States was accused as far back as 1817 when Gerrit Forbes, New York City Inspector of Health, wrote: "And we have serious cause to regret that there are in our city so many mercenary landlords who only contrive in what manner they can stow the greatest number of human beings in the smallest space" (Robert W. DeForest and Lawrence Veiller, *The Tenement House Problem*, Macmillan, 1903, II, p. 69).

[6] *The Housing of the Unskilled Wage-Earner*, Macmillan, 1919.

between income and shelter cost as a main factor responsible for slum life. The building industry, it was contended, was not producing houses at costs the slum people could afford. At first, nonprofit housing built by government was advocated,[7] but it was soon concluded that only if the housing were subsidized would rents be low enough for the poor to afford them.

The argument made no impression until the depression period, when three circumstances conspired to make subsidized housing politically palatable. When many among the 13 million unemployed in the 1930s found themselves homeless or crowded into slum flats, it seemed illogical as well as impolitic to assert that all these people could be criminal, filthy, and inebriated. The second factor was the stagnant state of the building industry, which, it was felt, was holding back an economic recovery. Tearing down slums and building new housing would employ workers. The third factor was the experimental mood of the New Dealers who were willing to try anything as a pilot effort that would stimulate purchasing power. Public housing seemed to offer the dual prospects of economic and social amelioration in a single package.

After a number of pilot housing operations, the federal government in 1937 officially redefined the slum to encompass the physical condition of the buildings, the absence of amenities, and the overcrowding of the land. This new emphasis on structure made society partly to blame and imposed upon government the obligation to eradicate slums. They would be demolished by local housing authorities set up by the cities, which would build good housing on the sites and let it to the slum dwellers at rents within

their means. The federal government would provide the necessary annual subsidies. Fortunately, there was a slum surplus in those days, and as slum dwellers were ordered out of their homes to make way for their own social progress, a few moved into the new public housing built for them, while the rest drifted into other available slums or emigrated to farms or to other cities.

As economic conditions improved, however, slum vacancies began to fill up. A number of cities began to experience a shortage of both higher-priced dwellings as well as slums.[8] When, for example, a few slum blocks were razed to make way for the Triborough Bridge approach in New York City, slum rents in the area went up by 25 per cent. Overcrowding within dwellings and ransom rents—not the physical condition of buildings —became the more painful aspects of slum life. Slum demolition should have stopped, and vacant or under-occupied land should have been selected for low-rent projects so as to increase the housing supply for the less privileged.[9] But slum clearance had already gained a political momentum which could not be stayed. Politicians eager for a headline were busily competing for a place on the steam shovels. Social workers and reformers were highlighting the crime, disease, and delinquency in slums, while courts were incorporating their statistics into eloquent opinions that made the evils of slum life *res adjudi-*

---

[7] *Ibid.*, p. 259.

[8] From March to October 1936, vacancies were cut in half in New York City, while the median vacancy rate in all types of residential structures in cities showed a decline of vacancies from 7.3 per cent in 1933 to 2 per cent in 1936 (*Report on Living and Housing Conditions to Mayor Fiorello H. LaGuardia*, New York City Housing Authority, January 25, 1937, p. 16).

[9] See Charles Abrams, *Shelter* (1939), reprinted in M. B. Schnapper, *Public Housing in America*, H. W. Wilson, 1939, p. 88.

cata. Slum clearance was now not only a lawful undertaking by government but a moral obligation as well.

Under the federal public housing program, nearly 200,000 substandard dwellings were eliminated by June 30, 1953; and of all the housing units built under the Housing Act of 1937, 89 per cent were on slum sites, only 11 per cent on vacant land. As other slums went down due to private demolitions, code enforcement, and highways, the slum supply shrank further. The net housing supply available to the low-income family was thus steadily diminished as one slum after another was consigned to the wrecking crew.

. . .

The housing problem is more than the slum and more than the predicament of the low-income family. It spurs migrations from cities and deters movements into them. It is the source of many discontents among the millions of mishoused or dishoused families yearning to be rehoused. It affects family budgets, security, happiness, and stability. It is tied into the issues of segregation and neighborhood decay. Though the federal government looks upon housing shortage and other imperfections of the housing market as factors in national employment and economic activity, few other problems have more serious impacts on the economic well-being of cities and the social well-being of their citizens.

THE PATHOLOGY OF HOUSING

The diseases of housing rival those in pathology. They include irritations over spatial, physical, and financial limitations. They are involved with neighborhood tensions, the shortcomings of neighborhood schools, transportation, and police protection; lack of proper playgrounds, parks, and open spaces; noise, smoke, smells, smog, drafts, dirt, insects, and vermin. The personal vexations of the housing problem are not only multiple and complex but they defy categorization.

Over a period of twenty-five years of teaching in both graduate and adult education classes, I have asked some 2,500 people to list their housing complaints. The answers have been a variety of cravings and disaffections which go far beyond anything revealed by the Census and beyond anything that has been resolved by the Federal Housing Administration, Veterans Administration, or the wrecking-crew prescriptions of the housing acts. Complaints have survived the recent spurt in repairs and the increase in the number of homeowners. They would survive even if we knocked down every hovel, built a bold surplus of public housing, and stepped up FHA-aided projects to validate the most optimistic home-building predictions.

The trials of central city life bring out a diversity of protests, which include troubles with landlords and rent hikes, influxes of minority groups and school problems, air pollution, odors, neighborhood deterioration and disrepair, the long journey to work and up the stairs.

The first wail announcing the baby's presence accents the house's intractability, and each year of the baby's growth points up some unanticipated failing in structure or surroundings. Lack of space comes first, followed by a myriad of agitations—overexertion, the pressure of rent, the complaints of a neighbor, the annoyances of the stairs, or of a knocking radiator once taken in stride. With each year that passes, house and neighborhood become more distressingly interlinked, emphasizing inadequacies or disappointments—in school, play space, or street. The drive is then for a more suitable house in a more suitable neighborhood (usually suburban), but it may distort the budget, stretch the distance to the job, impose the added burden of an automobile or two, and make the father's presence in the household more like that of a visiting relative.

Other special problems include a landlord's prohibition of pets which brings heartbreak, particularly to the very old and the very young. Since the automobile, contact with animals has all but disappeared from urban life, and the popularity of Westerns on television may be ascribed at least partly to the nostalgia for the horse. When the Cambridge (Massachusetts) Housing Authority tried to enforce a regulation against dogs or cats, tenant protests made front-page news for days and finally forced a concession. A *New York Times* copyreader, sued by his landlord for keeping two Siamese cats alleged to be a nuisance, made a test case and won. But usually the landlord triumphs in the encounter. The pet must go.

Spatial shortage is one of the more frequent complaints. To get the space they need, families may pay rents beyond their means, live too far from school or work, or in neighborhoods and homes unsuited to their requirements. Yet in 212 metropolitan areas, more than 2.8 million households or 20 per cent of all renters paid 35 per cent or more of their income for shelter. Almost all of these families paying such rentals earned less than $4,000 a year. Twenty or at most 25 per cent for shelter is regarded as the maximum, but this proportion is a hardship for poorer families who would have barely enough for life's necessities even if they paid nothing for rent.

The distribution of families by their total money income in 1962 as reported by the Bureau of the Census is given in Table I.

TABLE I

Total Money Income of Families	Number of Families (Thousands)	Per Cent
Under $1,000	1,950	4.2
$1,000 to $1,999	3,469	7.4
$2,000 to $2,999	3,901	8.3
$3,000 to $3,999	4,325	9.2
$4,000 to $4,999	4,669	9.9
$5,000 to $5,999	5,424	11.5
$6,000 to $6,999	5,100	10.9
$7,000 to $7,999	4,023	8.6
$8,000 to $9,999	5,804	12.3
$10,000 to $14,999	6,019	12.8
$15,000 and over	2,314	4.9
Total	46,998	100.0

In other words, more than half the American families earned less than $6,000 and a fifth had less than $3,000. The cost of new private single-family homes in 1963 averaged $18,-000, a figure far beyond the reach of lower-income families.

THE DISPLACED AND EVICTED

Involuntary removals, including those necessitated by job changes and evictions, have shown a marked increase in recent years. The causes include not only public projects but industrial movements, or an order by the Defense Department to close military installations. A decision by the Reynolds Metals Company to leave Louisville, Kentucky, put six hundred houses on the market all at once and depressed values. The poor labor relations of a large firm in Stamford, Connecticut, led to its removal from the area with a similar impact on the housing market. A few companies, upon withdrawing from an area, have generously taken over their employee's houses and offered them for resale, but they have found that too much capital was tied up for too long. Most companies are not generous, except to those whose talents are indispensable.

Eviction because of public works, code enforcement, or urban renewal (not to mention private developments) are among the other aggravations. Before 1934, evictions to make way for public improvements were confined to traditional needs such as school sites, roads, and public buildings. The road program was much smaller, code enforcement was minimal, and urban renewal nonexistent. The demolition of a city's workshops and stores or the eviction of 8,000 families from a single site, as in New York's West Side renewal area, would have been unthinkable.

Following 1934, major land operations covering 10 to 30 acres per project arrived with public housing and expanded with public works programs and urban renewal. The more extensive public operations such as freeways, renewal operations, toll roads, parking lots, airports, and other enterprises, played an important part in the increase of demolition. The net losses from the housing inventory during the 1950–1956 period was more than 200,000 units a year. During the 1957–1959 period it had leaped to 475,000 a year.

In California, with its newer stock of houses, no less than 359,000 units —10 per cent of the 1950 inventory —had been erased by 1960 through private action, highway programs, code enforcement, urban renewal, or the elements.[10]

The emphasis on demolition and evictions has made life for many families an unending trek from one slum or furnished room to another. Building a stable life within a context of rootless living is virtually impossible. Children are uprooted from schools, parents separated from friends, and rootlessness ultimately gives way to hopelessness.

THE AGED

The aged are the most numerous among those neglected by the housing industry. The passage of two decades has seen the aged grow both in numbers and in the severity of their housing problems. From 1950 to 1960, the general population increased by only 19 per cent, but the older population grew by 35 per cent.[11] People 62 years of age or over number 21 million, and by 1980 they are expected to number 30 million. Older people are more prone to have special problems—8 out of 10 have chronic illnesses; they spend twice as many hours in hospitals as those under 65. Proximity to doctors and institutional facilities is therefore essential.

They also have rent and income problems, for their median income is about half of those under 65. Half have less than $3,000 annually, a third less than $2,000 annually, while half the single persons have less than $1,050 a year.[12] About half are in another special group—they are either widowed, divorced, separated, or single. There are 8 million of these elderly people living alone.

The housing problem of the older person is both unique and difficult. Some are sensitive to the harder climates, are more exposed to the dangers of home and street accidents, and are less poised to grapple with the demands of the 5–7 room house. Two-thirds live in their own homes, gen-

[10] In California, the proportion of families scheduled to be displaced by urban renewal in the two years from July 1962 was 44 per cent for urban renewal and 56 per cent for code enforcement, highways, and other causes. In programs awaiting certification, the proportions were 31 per cent for urban renewal, 14 per cent for highways, 48 per cent for code enforcement, and 7 per cent for other causes.

[11] The age group 85 and over grew by more than 61 per cent.

[12] *Report on Housing for Senior Citizens,* Subcommittee on Housing, Senate Committee on Banking and Currency, 87th Cong., 2nd. Sess., June 15, 1962, p. VII.

erally bought in earlier years, and many of these are now ill-suited to their needs.

A study by the Cornell University Center for Housing and Enrivonmental Studies showed that the poorest in health tended to occupy the poorest housing. About 45 per cent of all aged households were classified as in need of better accommodations.[13]

A California study in 1961[14] concluded that living with relatives was a distasteful alternative for most elderly people. Most want housekeeping arrangements, most would like to own their homes (but rooming house life is more acceptable to men than women). Though public housing offers the cheapest accommodations (average rent is $32 and median income $1,500) it provides for only a tiny fraction of the elderly. If, for example, only 10 per cent of California's aged who were living in 1962 with relatives or in rooming houses were to apply for public housing, their number would exceed the total of the state's public housing units for families of all ages. FHA-insured loans (under Section 231 of the Housing Act) resulted in median monthly rents in 1963 of $118. Federal direct loans below market interest rates accommodate those with incomes well above $3,500 per year, and in any event as of December 1964, the number of projects in process was small, and funds were reserved for less than 19,000 units. Federal aid to nonprofit groups has produced dwellings mostly for the higher-income families among the elderly—median monthly rent of completed units in 1963 was about $87. The nursing home program is also for those with higher incomes.

In short, no federal program is serving any substantial number of the low-income elderly. Because many of these people live in old housing, they are also among the first victims of demolition through urban renewal, public works, or code enforcement. What should be the cocktail hour of life becomes their bitter evening.

THE MISFITS

A contributing factor to the housing troubles of families is the inability of the building market to meet their real needs. The housing industry is geared to meeting effective demand, not need, and the most effective market is for the "average family." This average family is composed of a husband, a wife, one to three children, and an occasional relative. In the 1940s such families made up less than half of all families occupying dwelling units; and, except for some token programs, the housing produced today is still unsuited to the needs of most American households. Occasionally, housing is built to suit the well-to-do husband and wife with no children but little is produced to suit the needs of the atypical families, particularly those with low or moderate incomes as well as the person living alone, two males or females living together (including the elderly), large families or seven or more persons, widowers with children, the physically limited, and other groups. These groups must pay the penalty for their antistatistical behavior.

There are also the families with atypical occupational patterns, a large group of which comprises those with both husband and wife working. Neither the home nor the neighborhood is set up to lighten the chores of the working females, particularly the mothers, many of whom prefer to go on relief or collect unemployment insurance instead of paying a nursemaid

[13] *Ibid.*, p. VIII.
[14] Wallace F. Smith, *Housing for the Elderly*, Institute of Business and Economic Research, University of California, 1961.

two-thirds of their earnings. By contrast, Sweden's school children are called for during the mother's working hours at no cost. Some of the Swedish projects have cooperative kitchens and cooperative cleaning services especially designed for working mothers. But this sort of thinking has not yet entered into the calculations of officialdom.

Other neglected housing problems are those of professional persons who work at home, families whose shop is in the home, married graduate and undergraduate students, and migrant laborers and seamen.

SKID ROW

Perhaps the most dramatic of those among the housing misfits is the skid-rower, whose "home" is found in every big city from Boston to San Francisco. Cities look upon him as dispensable if not undesirable. Because skid rows are mostly in or near the city centers, they have become a main target of the bulldozer.

Skidrowers occupy old flop houses in which finding a bed is a daily gamble. Some sleep on the streets or in hallways or pile up on the floors of a city shelter—if there is one.

The skidrowers are a miscellaneous lot—semisettled or settled panhandlers, homeless workingmen, chronic alcoholics and criminals, the elderly, the disabled, and the unemployed.[15]

Many pensioners and ordinary workers find in skid row the cheapest and often the only accommodations available. Though skid rows are generally looked upon as the most sterile and extinguishable parts of town, they are often labor centers for agricultural, unskilled, and semi-skilled workers who can be recruited for work away from their "homes." (Automation,

however, is cutting down on their work opportunities.) In skid row, the sensitive poor can spend least for clothing and care without social embarrassment. Welfare and social agencies can send older or disabled clients to skid row because lodgings are cheaper. They are cheaper because they are cramped, deteriorated, and often vermin-infested; many are fire-traps.[16]

The sidewalks of New York City's Bowery and the vestibules of nearby stores are the beds of many who shun the city-owned flop-house on East Third Street. Behind its grim façade are hundreds of old, handicapped men, some legless, with ill-fitting artificial limbs—most of them a premature step from the grave.

On one rainy day I visited the boiler room of the flophouse, thirteen feet below street level. Thirty infirm or crippled men, mostly elderly, were sitting on wooden backless benches; and in the adjacent storeroom were ninety others, many leaning on crutches. The room stank of sweat and disinfectant. A large sign on the cellar wall read, "Check All Your Valuables. The City of New York is Not Responsible . . ."

The situation was hardly better for the homeless younger men. About 40 per cent in New York's Bowery flophouse might have become useful citizens if they had a home or were given a chance. But New York is a big, busy city in which most people do not look, do not know, or do not care.

No big city has even ventured a solution for its skidrow problem or for the homeless, though one or two are playing with the idea. Most cities do not even have a flophouse for their skidrowers; they either look to urban renewal as the way of "solving" the problem or press the skidrower to

[15] *The Homeless Man on Skid Row*, Chicago Relocation Bureau, September 1961.

[16] *Ibid.*, p. 13.

move to some other city. If the skid rows are destroyed, some occupants will drift to those in the other cities; many others will remain—deprived of the only shelters they had, miserable as they were.

THE OVERMORTGAGED SOCIETY

That the housing situation is thorny for the city dweller does not mean that the quarter-acre is clover for the suburbanite. The growth of the suburb has widened the choices for the middle- and upper-income family. It provides the breadwinner with more open space, a touch of the green instead of the grey, an escape from the city's afflictions, an opportunity to do some weekend tinkering, and the feeling, right or wrong, that the downpayment now guarantees him a home he can call his own. The suburb, in short, does provide a new housing alternative.[17] But many choose the alternative, less because it is the answer to the family's prayer than because it is their only escape from an environment that has become ill-suited or unbearable for them. Others move because of the city's poorer schools. The choice of the suburb carries with it the commuting problem and the installment payments on the automobile. If the job is in the city and the commutation is long, the father is unable to see his children or aging parents as often as he should.

Not the least of the problems confronting the suburban home owner is that buying a home and furnishing it raises the proportion of income he should normally pay for shelter, and while the long-term FHA mortgage makes the monthly payments smaller, it also prolongs the duration of the

[17] For an interesting study of the virtues and problems of the move to suburbia see Herbert J. Gans in *The Urban Condition*, ed. Leonard J. Duhl, Basic Books, 1963, p. 184.

personal obligation and the risk. The average breadwinner buying a home under the 90 per cent mortgage generally commits himself to the maximum he can afford, and if he loses his job, suffers a salary cut, or binds himself to an extra car, he may find his mortgage jeopardizing his tenure. For the first dozen years or so, amortization of the mortgage just about parallels the depreciation rate. As long as the price level continued pointing upward, the home buyer was lucky. The price level on homes bought from the time of the deep depression up to 1957 has been accommodating for most buyers and helped many to build up substantial equities.

At the close of 1960, however, the total outstanding residential mortgage debt had soared to $160 billion. About 88 per cent of the total was on one- to four-family houses, and this was steadily on the increase. With the 80–100 per cent mortgage, we have become a nation of debtors; the value of our homes has been fluctuating with the value of the dollar. When values fall or depression hits a particular area, foreclosures mount. An owner in a depressed area might tighten his belt or turn back his television set, but the mortgage lender is unyielding —particularly since the FHA arrangement allows him the option of foreclosing or demanding government bonds for his defaulted mortgage. No mechanism exists to insure the owner against loss of his home for a default due to temporary embarrassment. Failure to make a single payment during the mortgage term brings foreclosure and sometimes a judgment against the owner to boot.

In the 1960s, foreclosures hit their highest point since the deep depression. Defaults on home mortgages increased fivefold—from about 10,000 in 1957 to 52,000 as of December 1963. According to FHA, the "weakest link" has been the poor credit characteristics of the individual borrower.[18]

Nor does today's family enjoy that old feeling of warmth that comes with the burning of the mortgage. Modern mortgages are fireproof for the mortgagee (thanks to fire insurance) but not foreclosure-proof for the owner. To tap a larger market, Congress, instead of lowering mortgage interest, periodically authorized smaller downpayments and longer mortgage periods. These liberalizations resulted in higher outstanding balances throughout the life of the mortgage. As long as property values were rising, the home owner stayed ahead in the race for home security, and if he found it hard to maintain his mortgage he could sell. But after 1957 supply and demand came more nearly into balance, and easy sales became tougher. As the FHA Administrator conceded, it is important to keep in mind ". . . that from 1934 until recent years . . . FHA insuring operations have been carried on under most favorable market conditions. It is almost axiomatic that no serious error in mortgage finance can come to light in periods of rising prices."[19] But the error does come to light when the element of speculative increase no longer functions to vindicate misjudgments.

HOUSING INFLEXIBILITY

Neither family composition nor housing needs are constants. They vary with the life cycle, the birth and growth of children, the health, age, changing fortunes, and death of people. They vary also with the decisions of industry, job locations, building costs, and land availability. About 40 per cent

of all housing is more than forty years old. As the needs of families change, they must look not only to the new, mostly on the fringes, but also to the old, mostly in the cities.

Some 58.3 million dwelling units, good and bad, are available to 53 million American households. The older housing in the inventory includes both the dispensable and the salvageable. The salvageable is also more adaptable to change. The newer stock is generally less alterable either because zoning forbids substantial changes or because it does not lend itself to major alteration. It has been built to meet the requirements of the average family and none other. The median size of new homes financed with FHA-insured Section 203 loans was 1,182 square feet, representing a 22 per cent increase over the comparable FHA figure fifteen years earlier. Most had three bedrooms and 75 per cent were bought by people in the upper 50 per cent income group. A hundred thousand houses are sold annually as incomplete or "shell houses" to be finished when the owner can afford it. (The South is one of the best customers.) In 1963, another 151,000 living spaces were sold as mobile units, some of which are placed on permanent foundations.

Despite its age or obsolescence, a fair proportion of the city's older stock, though worn and seedy, has more space and height than those built after zoning was known, before building standards were elevated, and before power tools, paint spray guns, and pneumatic hammers came on the scene. They can also be altered, enlarged, or reduced in size to fit special needs or changing requirements of the life cycle. However one might scoff at the city's Baroque revivals or Kensington classics with their high stoops and ceilings, many can meet changing needs better than the latest split-level or economy

---

[18] Neal J. Hardy, FHA Administrator, in *Progress Report on Federal Housing Programs,* Subcommittee on Housing, Senate Committee on Banking and Currency, 87th Cong., 2nd Sess., August 29, 1962, p. 6.

[19] Hardy, p. 7.

house. Even New York's excoriated old-law tenements, built for the European immigrant at the lowest standards possible often had five rooms; and some are being turned into two-room efficiency units and studios for the intelligentsia of Greenwich Village and the Lower East Side. An air-conditioner makes even its windowless room serviceable.

The new suburban houses, however, will continue to exercise a tyranny that will not bend easily to the changing requirements of America's metamorphic families. These families can look ahead not only to a housing plant of less flexible units, but to a diminution of the older supply in the cities through slum clearance, highways, fire, obsolescence, or structural decay. Thus, the new houses in the city or suburb may suit the present but not the future. The old houses that might still serve the future are gradually disappearing.

Congress has belatedly acknowledged the importance of preserving as well as destroying the old crop. Age of a building is no longer disparaged, and terms for rehabilitation have been liberalized. But diversification of housing types is infrequent and the preservation of what exists has hardly gotten off the ground. The good alterable stock is being steadily reduced in the cities, while the suburb continues to be headed toward a rigid, tedious uniformity and an early obsolescence.

If, thanks to rising incomes, housing conditions have improved for some in recent years, the central city has reaped few of the dividends. Since much of its housing is frayed and therefore cheaper, it has become host to the poor as well as heir to their social problems. Much of what was sound and salvageable is being cut up or crowded with poorer people to conform to their meager budgets. Because the city is not poised to assume the increased costs of policing and servicing the deteriorating areas properly, or financing the improvement of its housing and neighborhoods, the exodus to suburbia continues to accelerate.

Slum properties were once considered good investments because they were always sure to be filled by immigrants from Europe and because they called for minimum maintenance charges—almost all the gross rent, after taxes, insurance, and loan charges, was net profit.

As the cities advanced toward stricter law enforcement, the old crop of landlords, facing the prospects of fines and even jail sentences, sold out. Simultaneously institutional mortgage lenders ceased lending on the properties. (In New York City these institutions had liquidated such holdings as far back as 1937.)

Many of the slum properties have been sold in recent years at liquidation prices to a new type of slum specialist. Simultaneously, a new crop of speculative mortgage lenders appeared who have been willing to take the risks of default in return for discounts ranging from 30 per cent of the face amount of first mortgages to as high as 50 per cent for the seconds.

Contrary to general belief, the new specialists are not tycoons but mostly small-scale operators looking for large profits with small stakes. The profits compensate them for troublesome management and for the collection of weekly rents from people, many of whom are unemployed, and for the growing risks of ownership. The values of these properties fluctuate not only with the imposition of more rigid standards and penalties but with the prospect of acquisition by the cities. Thus a sharp drop in prices occurred in New York City when a Brooklyn landlady was convicted of manslaughter after a fire consumed her tenants, and they rose with each prospect that the area might be designated for urban renewal or a housing project.

As the poorer people move to other parts of cities vacated by the middle class, repairs and improvements decline and more buildings become candidates for ultimate demolition.

The housing problem of the central cities will be solved only by expanding the supply and varieties of decent housing for all families at prices they can afford. This might help make the city more competitive with the suburb. Simultaneously the suburb must share the responsibility for housing those who require subsidies. Only with such a policy will the housing problem besetting American families approach solution and the cities have better than an even chance to survive.

. . .

THE AMERICAN CONCEPT OF URBAN RENEWAL

While renewing cities was long accepted as a national prerogative in the Old World, the assumption of national responsibility in America was a revolutionary concept, for under the doctrine of state sovereignty, the condition of the nation's cities was not a federal concern. This concept held fast even after the nation had become 70 per cent urbanized. That the state was never *concerned* about renewing its cities did not unbind the constitutional straitjacket.

It was apparent from the nature of the legislation that the main motivation that prompted the new national involvement was not the creation of the city beautiful, the city efficient, or the city solvent. It simply sought to expand slum clearance—already a national purpose—but it would now become another vehicle for private investment supported by new forms of federal assistance.

There was at least one questionable aspect of the new formula. The "serious housing shortage" which Congress's goal had promised to remedy was most serious for those city folk who occupied the slums marked for destruction. These slums may have been eyesores to the city officials, but they were shelters for the families who could afford nothing better. And so they occupied the several million homes that were ramshackle or dilapidated, and the millions of houses lacking toilets, baths, and running water or needing major repairs to make them livable.

It was indeed hard to see how removing the urban slum dwellers' houses, bad as they might be, could either cure the serious housing shortage to which the 1949 act dedicated itself or provide these people with homes they could afford. Congress's answer, however, seemed simple: (1) Some public housing moneys would continue to be earmarked for the cities under the original slum clearance formula to rehouse the families displaced, and (2) the evicted families could be moved into other quarters in the existing urban stock. The act authorized payment of the families' moving expenses to speed their departure.

There was another complication. As the economy expanded and as FHA aid and savings and loan mortgages were speeding the move of white families to the suburbs, millions of Negroes, Puerto Ricans, and Mexicans poured into the cities. These people moved into the slums vacated by many of those who were now buying suburban homes under the easier terms. Of the minority families moving into the cities, the Negroes were the most numerous. The faster the Negro family filled the vacancies in the cities, the faster was the white exodus from the sections he entered. Urban renewal's steam shovel functioned mainly in the areas where the minorities had secured their footholds. About 70 per cent of those scheduled for urban renewal evictions were nonwhite, and a substantial number of the rest were poorer folk, including elderly families. Since the Negro's income was only about half that of the whites, FHA-aided homes and those financed by the savings and loan associations were beyond his means; even if he could afford them, the new white suburbs would not allow him to come in.

The most home-hungry portion of the population now scurried about from one slum to another in search of more enduring footholds. Although the Housing Act of 1949 had authorized 135,000 public housing units annually, Congress after 1954 cut the authorization to 35,000—45,000 annually. The frittered public housing program became more a pretext than a refuge, for the program was hardly big enough to accommodate its own displacees, much less those displaced by road programs, code enforcement, and urban renewal as well. Surprisingly, not many of the displaced were either eligible, able, or anxious to move into the public housing projects. This was particularly true of the white displacees, many of whom looked upon them as institutionalized havens for the impoverished.

Despite its subventions, the renewal program for some reason could not get off the ground from 1949 to 1954. One reason was that it was new and untried. Regulations had to be framed, sites selected, land assembled and appraised, and builders found who were willing to invest in drawing plans and making estimates in the hope they would land the jobs. In areas with housing shortages, tenant resistance to eviction slowed the city's hand. Elsewhere private redevelopers seemed not too keen to bid for projects that would not bring the high rents required to pay the going charges. It seemed simpler to build in the suburbs than to brave the tedious routines. Besides, the federal financing terms for mortgages were not as lush as they were in the city's outskirts where the "Section 608" formula, which will be discussed later, was providing bonanza opportunities.

URBAN RENEWAL AND THE HOUSING PROBLEM

By 1954, it appeared clear that urban renewal needed modification to make it work. But one of the troubles was that some of the senators who had laboriously shaped and launched it, and who were now being asked to extend it, had unfaltering memories. They had offered urban renewal as a housing measure. Its catchwords (housing shortage, slums, and a suitable living environment for every American family) had tethered it firmly to housing reform. The act had defined an eligible area as one "which is predominantly residential in character" before acquisition, or which after acquisition is to be redeveloped "for predominantly residential purposes."

The slums to be torn down were what was meant by "residential in character." What was to be built on the site was to be better, if more expensive, housing. Through slum clearance and better housing would come better environments. Simultaneously, through public housing, the evicted slum dwellers would get better shelter at costs they could afford. It had all seemed simple and logical to the Senate sponsors.

Senator Robert Taft, who had been the measure's most forceful advocate, would not allow himself to be distracted by those who had pressed for an enlargement of purpose beyond housing, for the good senator was a Christian at heart to whom "no room at the inn" was a gnawing deficiency in a great and progressive society.

"I do not believe that public housing is socialism," Senator Taft told me in an interview, "if it is confined to the furnishing of decent housing only to that group unable to provide housing by its own means. We have long recognized the duty of the state to give relief and free medical care for those unable to pay for it, and I think shelter is just as important as relief and medical care."[20]

"Perhaps we do not care about them [the slum dwellers] so much," he said on another occasion, "but most of them have families and we do have an interest, I think, in providing equal opportunity for all the children of the families who are brought into being in the United States . . . particularly food, clothing, shelter, medical care and education. . . . All of us acknowledge the duty of the community to take care of those who are unable to take care of themselves."[21]

It was Taft's underlying liberalism which made him a champion of the less privileged and his circumspect conservatism that impelled him to keep the federal power from going "beyond housing and beyond the elimination of slums." The plight of the cities or the need for better cities was not to be confused with the need for housing. In holding to the "predominantly residential requirement," the Taft subcommittee had said it "is not convinced that the federal government should embark upon a general program of aid to cities looking to their rebuilding in more attractive and economical patterns."

Under the Taft formula, the principal devices were to be destruction and construction—destruction of slums, construction of housing for

"every American family." Higher-priced housing would accommodate those who could pay the redeveloper's market rents. (Under other programs FHA would take care of part of the middle-income group also.) Some "relocation" was seen as inevitable, but relocation was to be no substitute for public housing, which together with slum clearance and private rebuilding was an indispensable part of the Taft triad.

PERVERSION OF THE URBAN RENEWAL FORMULA

It was not long, however, before the renewal-public housing program (under which urban renewal displaced the public housing rehoused) lost contact with its public housing partner. Public housing, like the Moor in *Othello,* had done its reverence in justifying urban renewal and could now go.

. . .

The perversion was not entirely the fault of the officials. The formula had been faulty from the beginning. It was not devised to pull cities out of their troubles. There had been no independent investigation into the financial aspects of slum developments, the ramified nature of the housing problem, or the predicaments of central cities and the temptations they would enforce. It could have been foreseen that the slum dwellers would not be rehoused on the cleared sites and that little if any public housing would be built for them on vacant sites.[22] The economic motivation had been the dominant ingredient in federal housing recipes from the inception and the stated ideal of better housing for everybody had simply supplied the sweetening, the coloring, and some of

---

[20] *New York Post*, January 28, 1948.
[21] *New York Post*, April 27, 1949.

[22] For an exchange of views on this matter between Senator Douglas and the writer, see Charles Abrams, *Forbidden Neighbors*, Harper & Row, 1955, pp. 250, 251.

the political palatability. Since the welfare of the building industry had won equal place with the people's welfare in the 1949 act, it seemed inevitable that sooner or later the interests of the lower-income families would be forgotten. When the entrepreneurial and the general welfare are bracketed in the same legislation, it should not be surprising that the social purpose will be subordinated. It was.

. . .

Since urban environment in the United States is now influenced or created by government, it is clear that there should be objectives to guide official policies.[23] But except for a sweeping and undefined generalization in the 1949 Housing Act, promising a suitable living environment for every American family, there is not even the semblance of any environmental objectives for federal policy; nor, despite frequent references to community renewal programs and master plans, have any objectives been framed by states or cities.

One reason for the lack of objectives is that, if they are to be realistic, objectives, like master plans, must deal with the difficult problems of population location and distribution. In the past, public land policy was a main device for influencing population shifts. Today, there are also national housing programs carrying housing subsidies, federal policies on race discrimination, and a huge subsidy program for road expansion. But though federal policy can influence local, state, and regional policies, the attitudes of the old freewheeling business society have survived to induce a freewheeling pattern in officialdom. *Laissez faire* is operating between the federal government and the states, the states and their smaller

[23] For a more complete definition of objectives as distinguished from goals, programs, projects, and schemes, see Charles Abrams, *Man's Struggle for Shelter*, M.I.T. Press, 1964, pp. 214, 215.

jurisdictions, and between each local jurisdiction and its neighbors. To state objectives would mean resolving jurisdictional conflicts, passing laws, and making policies to carry them into effect—it is easier to let things happen in a universe of purposelessness, causelessness, and aimlessness. It is easier also to commit billions of dollars to roads and other improvements without openly identifying their implications and impacts. It is simpler to promise a "Great Society" or proffer a few pilot programs whose pilots never set full sail into the wind. The result is that, while federal programs accelerate the move to suburbia, slum clearance and urban renewal policies for cities effect population redistribution only within the borders of the cities themselves, e.g., from one slum to another but not from a city slum to a suburban location.

If the population flow is to be freer, not only must the suburb be made accessible to the poor family by proper federal aids, but the city must be made a better and more attractive place to come to and live in. No city, however, is complete master of its own destiny. Human poverty is a nationwide problem; minority concentrations and racial conflict stem from nationwide causes of long standing and should be national as well as local concerns; lack of adequate educational and training facilities, teachers, and classrooms, and the ignorance and sense of futility which lie at the root of much of the poverty problem can no longer be remedied by the cities out of their shrinking revenues; slums and slum life are no longer accepted as simply the products of a landlord's greed or a city's poor building code. Framing objectives on a local level only, while useful, will be incomplete unless set within the larger framework of federal objectives and federal policies affecting cities.

Yet the city and its citizens should not sit idly by, lamenting the city's fate or looking primarily to the urban renewal program for its salvation. There are some aspects of physical environment that are within their own power and are outside the scope of the renewal or public housing programs. A city also grows on the ideas and contributions of its citizens and on their will to build their city into something better. When the cities and their citizens know what they want, they will be better poised to press for the assistance they need from the state and federal governments. If, for example, every city had a "Goals Commission," which would draw on the views of its citizens for fresh ideas, there would be a better chance of winning the more appropriate federal and state programs.

Racial Problems and Civil Disorder

Kerner Commission Report*

The summer of 1967 again brought racial disorders to American cities, and with them shock, fear and bewilderment to the nation.

The worst came during a two-week period in July, first in Newark and then in Detroit. Each set off a chain reaction in neighboring communities.

On July 28, 1967, the President of the United States established this Commission and directed us to answer three basic questions:

What happened?

Why did it happen?

What can be done to prevent it from happening again?

To respond to these questions, we have undertaken a broad range of studies and investigations. We have visited the riot cities; we have heard many witnesses; we have sought the counsel of experts across the country.

This is our basic conclusion: Our nation is moving toward two societies, one black, one white—separate and unequal.

Reaction to last summer's disorders has quickened the movement and deepened the division. Discrimination and segregation have long permeated much of American life; they now threaten the future of every American.

This deepening racial division is not inevitable. The movement apart can be reversed. Choice is still possible. Our principal task is to define that choice and to press for a national resolution.

To pursue our present course will involve the continuing polarization of the American community and, ultimately, the destruction of basic democratic values.

The alternative is not blind repression or capitulation to lawlessness. It is the realization of common opportunities for all within a single society.

This alternative will require a commitment to national action—compassionate, massive and sustained, backed by the resources of the most powerful and the richest nation on this earth. From every American it will require new attitudes, new understanding, and, above all, new will.

The vital needs of the nation must be met; hard choices must be made, and, if necessary, new taxes enacted.

Violence cannot build a better society. Disruption and disorder nourish repression, not justice. They strike at the freedom of every citizen. The community cannot—it will not—tolerate coercion and mob rule.

Violence and destruction must be ended—in the streets of the ghetto and in the lives of people.

Segregation and poverty have created in the racial ghetto a destructive environment totally unknown to most white Americans.

What white Americans have never fully understood—but what the Negro can never forget—is that white society is deeply implicated in the ghetto. White institutions created it, white institutions maintain it, and white society condones it.

It is time now to turn with all the purpose at our command to the major unfinished business of this nation. It is time to adopt strategies for action that will produce quick and visible progress. It is time to make good the promises of American democracy to

*From the *Report of the National Advisory Commission on Civil Disorders* (Kerner Commission), 1–9, 203–206, 11–16, © 1968 by the New York Times Company. Reprinted by permission.

all citizens—urban and rural, white and black, Spanish-surname, American Indian, and every minority group.

Our recommendations embrace three basic principles:

To mount programs on a scale equal to the dimension of the problems:

To aim these programs for high impact in the immediate future in order to close the gap between promise and performance;

To undertake new initiatives and experiments that can change the system of failure and frustration that now dominates the ghetto and weakens our society.

These programs will require unprecedented levels of funding and performance, but they neither probe deeper nor demand more than the problems which called them forth. There can be no higher priority for national action and no higher claim on the nation's conscience.

We issue this Report now, four months before the date called for by the President. Much remains that can be learned. Continued study is essential.

As Commissioners we have worked together with a sense of the greatest urgency and have sought to compose whatever differences exist among us. Some differences remain. But the gravity of the problem and the pressing need for action are too clear to allow further delay in the issuance of this Report.

CHAPTER 1—PROFILES OF DISORDER

The report contains profiles of a selection of the disorders that took place during the summer of 1967. These profiles are designed to indicate how the disorders happened, who participated in them, and how local officials, police forces, and the National Guard responded. Illustrative excerpts follow:

NEWARK

. . . It was decided to attempt to channel the energies of the people into a nonviolent protest. While Lofton promised the crowd that a full investigation would be made of the Smith incident, the other Negro leaders began urging those on the scene to form a line of march toward the city hall.

Some persons joined the line of march. Others milled about in the narrow street. From the dark grounds of the housing project came a barrage of rocks. Some of them fell among the crowd. Others hit persons in the line of march. Many smashed the windows of the police station. The rock throwing, it was believed, was the work of youngsters; approximately 2,500 children lived in the housing project.

Almost at the same time, an old car was set afire in a parking lot. The line of march began to disintegrate. The police, their heads protected by World War I-type helmets, sallied forth to disperse the crowd. A fire engine, arriving on the scene, was pelted with rocks. As police drove people away from the station, they scattered in all directions.

A few minutes later a nearby liquor store was broken into. Some persons, seeing a caravan of cabs appear at city hall to protest Smith's arrest, interpreted this as evidence that the disturbance had been organized, and generated rumors to that effect.

However, only a few stores were looted. Within a short period of time, the disorder appeared to have run its course.

. . . On Saturday, July 15, [Director of Police Dominick] Spina received a report of snipers in a housing project. When he arrived he saw approximately 100 National Guardsmen and police officers crouching behind vehicles, hiding in corners and lying on the ground around the edge of the courtyard.

Since everything appeared quiet and it was broad daylight, Spina walked directly down the middle of the street. Nothing happened. As he came to the last building of the complex, he heard a shot. All around him the troopers jumped, believing themselves to be under sniper fire. A moment later a young Guardsman ran from behind a building.

The Director of Police went over and asked him if he had fired the shot. The soldier said yes, he had fired to scare a man away from a window; that his orders were to keep everyone away from windows.

Spina said he told the soldier: "Do you know what you just did? You have now created a state of hysteria. Every Guardsman up and down this street and every state policeman and every city policeman that is present thinks that somebody just fired a shot and that it is probably a sniper."

A short time later more "gunshots" were heard. Investigating, Spina came upon a Peurto Rican sitting on a wall. In reply to a question as to whether he knew "where the firing is coming from?" the man said:

"That's no firing. That's fireworks. If you look up to the fourth floor, you will see the people who are throwing down these cherry bombs."

By this time four truckloads of National Guardsmen had arrived and troopers and policemen were again crouched everywhere looking for a sniper. The Director of Police remained at the scene for three hours, and the only shot fired was the one by the Guardsman.

Nevertheless, at six o'clock that evening two columns of National Guardsmen and state troopers were directing mass fire at the Hayes Housing Project in response to what they believed were snipers. . . .

DETROIT

. . . A spirit of carefree nihilism was taking hold. To riot and destroy appeared more and more to become ends in themselves. Late Sunday afternoon it appeared to one observer that the young people were "dancing amidst the flames."

A Negro plainclothes officer was standing at an intersection when a man threw a Molotov cocktail into a business establishment at the corner. In the heat of the afternoon, fanned by the 20 to 25 m.p.h. winds of both Sunday and Monday, the fire reached the home next door within minutes. As residents uselessly sprayed the flames with garden hoses, the fire jumped from roof to roof of adjacent two- and three-story buildings. Within the hour the entire block was in flames. The ninth house in the burning row belonged to the arsonist who had thrown the Molotov cocktail. . . .

. . . Employed as a private guard, 55-year-old Julius L. Dorsey, a Negro, was standing in front of a market when accosted by two Negro men and a woman. They demanded he permit them to loot the market. He ignored their demands. They began to berate him. He asked a neighbor to call the police. As the argument grew more heated, Dorsey fired three shots from his pistol into the air.

The police radio reported: "Looters, they have rifles." A patrol car driven by a police officer and carrying three National Guardsmen arrived. As the looters fled, the law enforcement personnel opened fire. When the firing ceased, one person lay dead.

He was Julius L. Dorsey . . .

. . . As the riot alternately waxed and waned, one area of the ghetto remained insulated. On the northeast side the residents of some 150 square blocks inhabited by 21,000 persons had, in 1966, banded together in the Positive Neighborhood Action Committee (PNAC). With professional help from the Institute of Urban Dynamics, they had organized block clubs and made plans for the improvement of the neighborhood. . . .

When the riot broke out, the residents, through the block clubs, were able to organize quickly. Youngsters, agreeing to stay in the neighborhood, participated in detouring traffic. While many persons reportedly sympathized with the idea of a rebellion against the "system," only two small fires were set—one in an empty building.

. . . According to Lt. Gen. Throckmorton and Col. Bolling, the city, at this time, was saturated with fear. The National Guardsmen were afraid, the residents were afraid, and the police were afraid. Numerous persons, the majority of them Negroes, were being injured by gunshots of undetermined origin. The general and his staff felt that the major task of the troops was to reduce the fear and restore an air of normalcy.

In order to accomplish this, every effort was made to establish contact and rapport between the troops and the residents. The soldiers—20 per cent of whom were Negro—began helping to clean up the streets, collect garbage, and trace persons who had disappeared in the confusion. Residents in the neighborhoods responded with soup and sandwiches for the troops. In areas where the National Guard tried to establish rapport with the citizens, there was a smaller response.

NEW BRUNSWICK

. . . A short time later, elements of the crowd—an older and rougher one than the night before—appeared in front of the police station. The participants wanted to see the mayor.

Mayor [Patricia] Sheehan went out onto the steps of the station. Using a bullhorn, she talked to the people and asked that she be given an opportunity to correct conditions. The crowd was boisterous. Some persons challenged the mayor. But, finally, the opinion, "She's new! Give her a chance!" prevailed.

A demand was issued by people in the crowd that all persons arrested the previous night be released. Told that this already had been done, the people were suspicious. They asked to be allowed to inspect the jail cells.

It was agreed to permit representatives of the people to look in the cells to satisfy themselves that everyone had been released.

The crowd dispersed. The New Brunswick riot had failed to materialize.

CHAPTER 2—PATTERNS OF DISORDER

The "typical" riot did not take place. The disorders of 1967 were unusual, irregular, complex and unpredictable social processes. Like most human events, they did not unfold in an orderly sequence. However, an analysis of our survey information leads to some conclusions about the riot process.

In general:

The civil disorders of 1967 involved Negroes acting against local symbols of white American society, authority and property in Negro neighborhoods —rather than against white persons.

Of 164 disorders reported during the first nine months of 1967, eight (5 per cent) were major in terms of violence and damage; 33 (20 per cent) were serious but not major; 123 (75 per cent) were minor and undoubtedly would not have received national attention as "riots" had the nation not been sensitized by the more serious outbreaks.

In the 75 disorders studied by a Senate subcommittee, 83 deaths were reported. Eight-two per cent of the deaths and more than half the injuries occurred in Newark and Detroit. About 10 per cent of the dead and 38 per cent of the injured were public employees, primarily law officers and firemen. The overwhelming majority of the persons killed or injured in all the disorders were Negro civilians.

Initial damage estimates were greatly exaggerated. In Detroit, newspaper damage estimates at first ranged from $200 million to $500 million; the highest recent estimate is $45 million. In Newark, early estimates ranged from $15 to $25 million. A month later damage was estimated at $10.2 million, over 80 per cent in inventory losses.

In the 24 disorders in 23 cities which we surveyed:

The final incident before the outbreak of disorder, and the initial violence itself, generally took place in the evening or at night at a place in which it was normal for many people to be on the streets.

Violence usually occurred almost immediately following the occurrence of the final precipitating incident, and then escalated rapidly. With but few exceptions, violence subsided during the day, and flared rapidly again at night. The night-day cycles continued through the early period of the major disorders.

Disorder generally began with rock and bottle throwing and window breaking. Once store windows were broken, looting usually followed.

Disorder did not erupt as a result of a single "triggering" or "precipitating" incident. Instead, it was generated out of an increasingly disturbed social atmosphere, in which typically a series of tension-heightening incidents over a period of weeks or months became linked in the minds of many in the Negro community with a reservoir of underlying grievances. At some point in the mounting tension, a further incident—in itself often routine or trivial—became the breaking point and the tension spilled over into violence.

"Prior" incidents, which increased tensions and ultimately led to violence, were police actions in almost half the cases; police actions were "final" incidents before the outbreak of violence in 12 of the 24 surveyed disorders.

No particular control tactic was successful in every situation. The varied effectiveness of control techniques emphasizes the need for advance training, planning, adequate intelligence systems, and knowledge of the ghetto community.

Negotiations between Negroes—including your militants as well as older Negro leaders—and white officials concerning "terms of peace" occurred during virtually all the disorders surveyed. In many cases, these negotiations involved discussion of underlying grievances as well as the handling of the disorder by control authorities.

The typical rioter was a teenager or young adult, a lifelong resident of the city in which he rioted, a high school dropout; he was, nevertheless, somewhat better educated than his nonrioting Negro neighbor, and was usually underemployed or employed in a menial job. He was proud of his race, extremely hostile to both whites and middle-class Negroes and, although informed about politics, highly distrustful of the political system.

A Detroit survey revealed that approximately 11 per cent of the total residents of two riot areas admitted participation in the rioting, 20 to 25 per cent identified themselves as "bystanders," over 16 per cent identified themselves as "counter-rioters" who urged rioters to "cool it," and the remaining 48 to 53 per cent said they were at home or elsewhere and did not participate. In a survey of Negro males between the ages of 15 and 35 residing in the disturbance area in Newark, about 45 per cent identified themselves as rioters, and about 55 per cent as "noninvolved."

Most rioters were young Negro males. Nearly 53 per cent of arrestees were between 15 and 24 years of age; nearly 81 per cent between 15 and 35.

In Detroit and Newark about 74 per cent of the rioters were brought up in the North. In contrast, of the noninvolved, 36 per cent in Detroit and 52 per cent in Newark were brought up in the North.

What the rioters appeared to be seeking was fuller participation in the social order and the material benefits enjoyed by the majority of American citizens. Rather than rejecting the American system, they were anxious to obtain a place for themselves in it.

Numerous Negro counter-rioters walked the streets urging rioters to "cool it." The typical counter-rioter was better educated and had higher income than either the rioter or the noninvolved.

The proportion of Negroes in local government was substantially smaller than the Negro proportion of population. Only three of the 20 cities studied had more than one Negro legislator; none had ever had a Negro mayor or city manager. In only four cities did Negroes hold other important policy-making positions or serve as heads of municipal departments.

Although almost all cities had some sort of formal grievance mechanism for handling citizen complaints, this typically was regarded by Negroes as ineffective and was generally ignored.

Although specific grievances varied from city to city, at least 12 deeply held grievances can be identified and ranked into three levels of relative intensity:

First Level of Intensity

1. Police practices
2. Unemployment and underemployment
3. Inadequate housing

Second Level of Intensity

4. Inadequate education
5. Poor recreation facilities and programs
6. Ineffectiveness of the political structure and grievance mechanisms

Third Level of Intensity

7. Disrespectful white attitudes
8. Discriminatory administration of justice
9. Inadequacy of federal programs
10. Inadequacy of municipal services
11. Discriminatory consumer and credit practices
12. Inadequate welfare programs

The results of a three-city survey of various federal programs—manpower, education, housing, welfare and community action— indicate that, despite substantial expenditures, the number of persons assisted constituted only a fraction of those in need.

The background of disorder is often as complex and difficult to analyze as the disorder itself. But we find that certain general conclusions can be drawn:

Social and economic conditions in the riot cities constituted a clear pattern of severe disadvantage for Negroes compared with whites, whether the Negroes lived in the area where the riot took place or outside it. Negroes had completed fewer years of education and fewer had attended high school. Negroes were twice as likely to be unemployed and three times as likely to be in unskilled and service jobs. Negroes averaged 70 per cent of the income earned by whites and were more than twice as likely to be living in poverty. Although housing cost Negroes relatively more, they had worse housing—three times as likely to be overcrowded and substandard. When compared to white suburbs, the relative disadvantage is even more pronounced.

A study of the aftermath of disorder leads to disturbing conclusions. We find that, despite the institution of some post-riot programs:

Little basic change in the conditions underlying the outbreak of disorder has taken place. Actions to ameliorate Negro grievances have been limited and sporadic; with but few exceptions, they have not significantly reduced tensions.

In several cities, the principal official response has been to train and equip the police with more sophisticated weapons.

In several cities, increasing polarization is evident, with continuing breakdown of inter-racial communication, and growth of white segregationist or black separatist groups.

CHAPTER 3—ORGANIZED ACTIVITY

The President directed the Commission to investigate "to what extent, if any, there has been planning or organization in any of the riots."

To carry out this part of the Presi-

dent's charge, the Commission established a special investigative staff supplementing the field teams that made the general examination of the riots in 23 cities. The unit examined data collected by federal agencies and congressional committees, including thousands of documents supplied by the Federal Bureau of Investigation, gathered and evaluated information from local and state law enforcement agencies and officials, and conducted its own field investigation in selected cities.

On the basis of all the information collected, the Commission concludes that:

The urban disorders of the summer of 1967 were not caused by, nor were they the consequence of, any organized plan or "conspiracy."

Specifically, the Commission has found no evidence that all or any of the disorders or the incidents that led to them were planned or directed by any organization or group, international, national or local.

Militant organizations, local and national, and individual agitators, who repeatedly forecast and called for violence, were active in the spring and summer of 1967. We believe that they sought to encourage violence, and that they helped to create an atmosphere that contributed to the outbreak of disorder.

We recognize that the continuation of disorders and the polarization of the races would provide fertile ground for organized exploitation in the future.

Investigations of organized activity are continuing at all levels of government, including committees of Congress. These investigations relate not only to the disorders of 1967 but also to the actions of groups and individuals, particularly in schools and colleges, during this last fall and winter. The Commission has cooperated in these investigations. They should continue.

We have seen what happened. Why did it happen?

In addressing this question we shift our focus from the local to the national scene, from the particular events of the summer of 1967 to the factors within the society at large which have brought about the sudden violent mood of so many urban Negroes.

The record before this Commission reveals that the causes of recent racial disorders are imbedded in a massive tangle of issues and circumstances— social, economic, political, and psychological—which arise out of the historical pattern of Negro-white relations in America.

These factors are both complex and interacting; they vary significantly in their effect from city to city and from year to year; and the consequences of one disorder, generating new grievances and new demands, become the causes of the next. It is this which creates the "thicket of tension, conflicting evidence and extreme opinions" cited by the President.

Despite these complexities, certain fundamental matters are clear. Of these, the most fundamental is the racial attitude and behavior of white Americans toward black Americans. Race prejudice has shaped our history decisively in the past; it now threatens to do so again. White racism is essentially responsible for the explosive mixture which has been accumulating in our cities since the end of World War II. At the base of this mixture are three of the most bitter fruits of white racial attitudes:

Pervasive discrimination and segregation. The first is surely the continuing exclusion of great numberse of Negroes from the benefits of economic progress through discrimination in employment and education, and their enforced confinement in segregated hous-

ing and schools. The corrosive and degrading effects of this condition and the attitudes that underlie it are the source of the deepest bitterness and at the center of the problem of racial disorder.

Black migration and white exodus. The second is the massive and growing concentration of impoverished Negroes in our major cities resulting from Negro migration from the rural South, rapid population growth and the continuing movement of the white middle-class to the suburbs. The consequence is a greatly increased burden on the already depleted resources of cities, creating a growing crisis of deteriorating facilities and services and unmet human needs.

Black ghettos. Third, in the teeming racial ghettos, segregation and poverty have intersected to destroy opportunity and hope and to enforce failure. The ghettos too often mean men and women without jobs, families without men, and schools where children are processed instead of educated, until they return to the street—to crime, to narcotics, to dependency on welfare, and to bitterness and resentment against society in general and white society in particular.

These three forces have converged on the inner city in recent years and on the people who inhabit it. At the same time, most whites and many Negroes outside the ghetto have prospered to a degree unparalleled in the history of civilization. Through television—the universal appliance in the ghetto— and the other media of mass communications, this affluence has been endlessly flaunted before the eyes of the Negro poor and the jobless ghetto youth.

As Americans, most Negro citizens carry within themselves two basic aspirations of our society. They seek to share in both the material resources of our system and its intangible benefits—dignity, respect and acceptance. Outside the ghetto many have succeeded in achieving a decent standard of life, and in developing the inner resources which gave life meaning and direction. Within the ghetto, however, it is rare that either aspiration is achieved.

Yet these facts alone—fundamental as they are—cannot be said to have caused the disorders. Other and more immediate factors help explain why these events happened now.

Recently, three powerful ingredients have begun to catalyze the mixture.

Frustrated hopes. The expectations aroused by the great judicial and legislative victories of the civil rights movement have led to frustration, hostility and cynicism in the face of the persistent gap between promise and fulfillment. The dramatic struggle for equal rights in the South has sensitized Northern Negroes to the economic inequalities reflected in the deprivations of ghetto life.

Legitimation of violence. A climate that tends toward the approval and encouragement of violence as a form of protest has been created by white terrorism directed against nonviolent protest, including instances of abuse and even murder of some civil rights workers in the South; by the open defiance of law and federal authority by state and local officials resisting desegregation; and by some protest groups engaging in civil disobedience who turn their backs on nonviolence, go beyond the Constitutionally protected rights of petition and free assembly, and resort to violence to attempt to compel alteration of laws and policies with which they disagree. This condition has been reinforced by a general erosion of respect for authority in American society and reduced effectiveness of social standards and community restraints on violence and crime. This in turn has largely resulted

from rapid urbanization and the dramatic reduction in the average age of the total population.

Powerlessness. Finally, many Negroes have come to believe that they are being exploited politically and economically by the white "power structure." Negroes, like people in poverty everywhere, in fact lack the channels of communication, influence and appeal that traditionally have been available to ethnic minorities within the city and which enabled them—unburdened by color—to scale the walls of the white ghettos in an earlier era. The frustrations of powerlessness have led some to the conviction that there is no effective alternative to violence as a means of expression and redress, as a way of moving the system." More generally, the result is alienation and hostility toward the institutions of law and government and the white society which controls them. This is reflected in the reach toward racial consciousness and solidarity reflected in the slogan "Black Power."

These facts have combined to inspire a new mood among Negroes, particularly the young. Self-esteem and enhanced racial pride are replacing apathy and submission to "the system." Moreover, Negro youth, who make up over half of the ghetto population, share the growing sense of alienation felt by many white youth in our country. Thus, their role in recent civil disorders reflects not only a shared sense of deprivation and victimization by white society but also the rising incidence of disruptive conduct by a segment of American youth throughout the society.

Incitement and encouragement of violence. These conditions have created a volatile mixture of attitudes and beliefs which needs only a spark to ignite mass violence. Strident appeals to violence, first heard from white racists, were echoed and reinforced last summer in the inflammatory rhetoric of black racists and militants. Throughout the year, extremists crisscrossed the country preaching a doctrine of black power and violence. Their rhetoric was widely reported in the mass media; it was echoed by local "militants" and organizations; it became the ugly background noise of the violent summer.

We cannot measure with any precision the influence of these organizations and individuals in the ghetto, but we think it clear that the intolerable and unconscionable encouragement of violence heightened tensions, created a mood of acceptance and an expectation of violence, and thus contributed to the eruption of the disorders last summer.

The Police. It is the convergence of all these factors that makes the role of the police so difficult and so significant. Almost invariably the incident that ignites disorder arises from police action. Harlem, Watts, Newark and Detroit—all the major outbursts of recent years—were precipitated by routine arrests of Negroes for minor offenses by white police.

But the police are not merely the spark. In discharge of their obligation to maintain order and insure public safety in the disruptive conditions of ghetto life, they are inevitably involved in sharper and more frequent conflicts with ghetto residents than with the residents of other areas. Thus, to many Negroes police have come to symbolize white power, white racism and white repression. And the fact is that many police do reflect and express these white attitudes. The atmosphere of hostility and cynicism is reinforced by a widespread perception among Negroes of the existence of police brtuality and corruption, and of a "double standard" of justice and protection—one for Negroes and one for whites.

To this point, we have attempted only to identify the prime components of the "explosive mixture." In the chapters that follow we seek to analyze them in the perspective of history. Their meaning, however, is already clear:

In the summer of 1967, we have seen in our cities a chain reaction of racial violence. If we are heedless, we shall none of us escape the consequences.

CHAPTER 5—REJECTION AND PROTEST: AN HISTORICAL SKETCH

The causes of recent racial disorders are embedded in a tangle of issues and circumstances—social, economic, political and psychological—which arise out of the historic pattern of Negro-white relations in America.

In this chapter we trace the pattern, identify the recurrent themes of Negro protest and, most importantly provide a perspective on the protest activities of the present era.

We describe the Negro's experience in America and the development of slavery as an institution. We show his persistent striving for equality in the face of rigidly maintained social, economic and educational barriers, and repeated mob violence. We portray the ebb and flow of the doctrinal tides—accommodation, separatism, and self-help—and their relationship to the current theme of Black Power. We conclude:

The Black Power advocates of today consciously feel that they are the most militant group in the Negro protest movement. Yet they have retreated from a direct confrontation with American society on the issue of integration and, by preaching separatism, unconsciously function as an accommodation to white racism. Much of their economic program, as well as their interest in Negro history, self-help, racial solidarity and separation, is reminiscent of Booker T. Washington. The rhetoric is different, but the ideas are remarkably similar.

CHAPTER 6—THE FORMATION OF THE RACIAL GHETTOS[1]

Throughout the 20th century the Negro population of the United States has been moving steadily from rural areas to urban and from South to North and West. In 1910, 91 per cent of the nation's 9.8 million Negroes lived in the South and only 27 per cent of American Negroes lived in cities of 2,500 persons or more. Between 1910 and 1966 the total Negro population more than doubled, reaching 21.5 million, and the number living in metropolitan areas rose more than five-fold (from 2.6 million to 14.8 million). The number outside the South rose eleven-fold (from 880,000 to 9.7 million).

Negro migration from the South has resulted from the expectation of thousands of new and highly paid jobs for unskilled workers in the North and the shift to mechanized farming in the South. However, the Negro migration is small when compared to earlier waves of European immigrants. Even between 1960 and 1966, there were 1.8 million immigrants from abroad compared to the 613,000 Negroes who arrived in the North and West from the South.

As a result of the growing number of Negroes in urban areas, natural increase has replaced migration as the primary source of Negro population increase in the cities. Nevertheless, Negro migration from the South will continue unless economic conditions there change dramatically.

Basic data concerning Negro urbanization trends indicate that:
Almost all Negro population growth (98 per cent from 1950 to 1966) is occurring within metropolitan areas, primarily within central cities.[2]

The vast majority of white population growth (78 per cent from 1960 to 1966) is occurring in suburban portions of metropolitan areas. Since 1960, white central-city population has declined by 1.3 million.

As a result, central cities are becoming more heavily Negro while the suburban fringes around them remain almost entirely white.

The twelve largest central cities now contain over two-thirds of the Negro population outside the South, and one-third of the Negro total in the United States.

Within the cities, Negroes have been excluded from white residential areas through discriminatory practices. Just as significant is the withdrawal of white families from, or their refusal to enter, neighborhoods where Negroes are moving or already residing. About 20 per cent of the urban population of the United States changes residence every year. The refusal of whites to move into "changing" areas when vacancies occur means that most vacancies eventually are occupied by Negroes.

The result, according to a recent study, is that in 1960 the average segregation index for 207 of the largest United States cities was 86.2. In other words, to create an unsegregated population distribution, an average of over

[1] The term "ghetto" as used in this report refers to an area within a city characterized by poverty and acute social disorganization, and inhabited by members of a racial or ethnic group under conditions of involuntary segregation.

[2] A "central city" is the largest city of a standard metropolitan statistical area, that is, a metropolitan area containing at least one city of 50,000 or more inhabitants.

86 per cent of all Negroes would have to change their place of residence within the city.

CHAPTER 7—UNEMPLOYMENT, FAMILY STRUCTURE, AND SOCIAL DISORGANIZATION

Although there have been gains in Negro income nationally, and a decline in the number of Negroes below the "poverty level," the condition of Negroes in the central city remains in a state of crisis. Between 2 and 2.5 million Negroes—16 to 20 per cent of the total Negro population of all central cities—live in squalor and deprivation in ghetto neighborhoods.

Employment is a key problem. It not only controls the present for the Negro American but, in a most profound way, it is creating the future as well. Yet, despite continuing economic growth and declining national unemployment rates, the unemployment rate for Negroes in 1967 was more than double that for whites.

Equally important is the undesirable nature of many jobs open to Negroes and other minorities. Negro men are more than three times as likely as white men to be in low-paying, unskilled or service jobs. This concentration of male Negro employment at the lowest end of the occupational scale is the single most important cause of poverty among Negroes.

In one study of low-income neighborhoods, the "subemployment rate," including both unemployment and underemployment, was about 33 per cent, or 8.8 times greater than the overall unemployment rate for all United States workers.

Employment problems, aggravated by the constant arrival of new unemployed migrants, many of them from depressed rural areas, create persistent poverty in the ghetto. In 1966, about 11.9 per cent of the nation's whites and 40.6 per cent of its nonwhites were below the "poverty level" defined by the Social Security Administration (currently $3,335 per year for an urban family of four). Over 40 per cent of the nonwhites below the poverty level live in the central cities.

Employment problems have drastic social impact in the ghetto. Men who are chronically unemployed or employed in the lowest status jobs are often unable or unwilling to remain with their families. The handicap imposed on children growing up without fathers in an atmosphere of poverty and deprivation is increased as mothers are forced to work to provide support.

The culture of poverty that results from unemployment and family breakup generates a system of ruthless, exploitative relationships within the ghetto. Prostitution, dope addiction, and crime create an environmental "jungle" characterized by personal insecurity and tension. Children growing up under such conditions are likely participants in civil disorder.

CHAPTER 8—CONDITIONS OF LIFE IN THE RACIAL GHETTO

A striking difference in environment from that of white, middle-class Americans profoundly influences the lives of residents of the ghetto.

Crime rates, consistently higher than in other areas, create a pronounced sense of insecurity. For example, in one city one low-income Negro district had 35 times as many serious crimes against persons as a high-income white district. Unless drastic steps are taken, the crime problems in poverty areas are likely to continue to multiply as the growing youth and rapid urbanization of the population outstrip police resources.

Poor health and sanitation conditions in the ghetto result in higher mortality rates, a higher incidence of major diseases, and lower availability and utilization of medical services. The infant mortality rate for nonwhite babies under the age of one month is 58 per cent higher than for whites; for one to 12 months it is almost three times as high. The level of sanitation in the ghetto is far below that in high income areas. Garbage collection is often inadequate. Of an estimated 14,-000 cases of rat bite in the United States in 1965, most were in ghetto neighborhoods.

Ghetto residents believe they are "exploited" by local merchants; and evidence substantiates some of these beliefs. A study conducted in one city by the Federal Trade Commission showed that distinctly higher prices were charged for goods sold in ghetto stores than in other areas.

Lack of knowledge regarding credit purchasing creates special pitfalls for the disadvantaged. In many states garnishment practices compound these difficulties by allowing creditors to deprive individuals of their wages without hearing or trial.

CHAPTER 9—COMPARING THE IMMIGRANT AND NEGRO EXPERIENCE

In this chapter, we address ourselves to a fundamental question that many white Americans are asking: why have so many Negroes, unlike the European immigrants, been unable to escape from the ghetto and from poverty. We believe the following factors play a part:

The Maturing Economy: When the European immigrants arrived, they gained an economic foothold by providing the unskilled labor needed by industry. Unlike the immigrant, the Negro migrant found little opportunity in the city. The economy, by then ma-

tured, had little use for the unskilled labor he had to offer.

The Disability of Race: The structure of discrimination has stringently narrowed opportunities for the Negro and restricted his prospects. European immigrants suffered from discrimination, but never so pervasively.

Entry into the Political System: The immigrants usually settled in rapidly growing cities with powerful and expanding political machines, which traded economic advantages for political support. Ward-level grievance machinery, as well as personal representation, enabled the immigrant to make his voice heard and his power felt.

By the time the Negro arrived, these political machines were no longer so powerful or so well equipped to provide jobs or other favors, and in many cases were unwilling to share their influence with Negroes.

Cultural Factors: Coming from societies with a low standard of living and at a time when job aspirations were low, the immigrants sensed little deprivation in being forced to take the less desirable and poorer-paying jobs. Their large and cohesive families contributed to total income. Their vision of the future—one that led to a life outside of the ghetto—provided the incentive necessary to endure the present.

Although Negro men worked as hard as the immigrants, they were unable to support their families. The entrepreneurial opportunities had vanished. As a result of slavery and long periods of unemployment, the Negro family structure had become matriarchal; the males played a secondary and marginal family role—one which offered little compensation for their hard and unrewarding labor. Above all, segregation denied Negroes access to good jobs and the opportunity to leave the ghetto. For them, the future seemed to lead only to a dead man.

Today, whites tend to exaggerate how well and quickly they escaped from poverty. The fact is that immigrants who came from rural backgrounds, as many Negroes do, are only now, after three generations, finally beginning to move into the middle class.

By contrast, Negroes began concentrating in the city less than two generations ago, and under much less favorable conditions. Although some Negroes have escaped poverty, few have been able to escape the urban ghetto.

Deprivation and the Good City

Lawrence Haworth*

Like most wars, the imperative that we should fight poverty is more obvious than the reasons why we should. Typically, the question, "Why?" comes up after a war has begun. Yet, asking why we are fighting may seem an indulgence, practiced by those who can contribute little to the course of the battle. Few imagine that what is decided on as the reason for fighting has implications for the way we should fight. In wars our object is to win, and we identify winning with the surrender of the other side. No serious philosophical or moral questions arise. The end is clear, and one will know when it has been reached.

A war on poverty is different. Since not everyone agrees about what overcoming poverty would consist in, we lack a consensus regarding how the fight is going, and we cannot be sure we will know when the battle is won. It is not clear what winning would consist in because it is not clear to us what poverty is. And, paradoxically, we cannot decide what poverty is without having first decided why we should be fighting it.

It follows, then, that the essentially philosophical and moral question, "Why fight poverty?" is also a practical one. The answer has implications for the manner in which the war should be fought: differing views regarding what winning would consist in give rise to corresponding differences regarding what should be done in the interest of winning.

*"Deprivation and the Good City" by Lawrence Haworth is reprinted from *Power, Poverty, and Urban Policy*, Volume II, Urban Affairs Annual Reviews (1968), pages 27–47, edited by Warner Bloomberg, Jr. and Henry J. Schmandt, by permission of the Publisher, Sage Publications, Inc.

DEFINITION OF POVERTY

The air of paradox which surrounds these initial remarks may be dispelled by considering the implications of the most widely accepted definition of poverty for our attitude toward the effort to eliminate poverty. Commonly, poverty is defined in terms of annual income. This permits identification of a poverty-line. A family of four is said to be, in the relevant sense, "poor" if its annual income falls below the line; $3,000 is the figure currently mentioned. Now, one who accepts the definition should identify victory in the war on poverty with a condition in which no family of the appropriate size has an annual income that falls below the line. Strangely enough, however, by no means all who profess to be satisfied with the definition accept this implication. Not all agree that were no one to fall below the line, there would be no reason for concern about deprivation. Conversely, some envisage the possibility of this reason for concern being dissipated even though many families continue to fall below the line.

One may well wonder how these doubts could arise. If poverty consists in some particular condition, it could not persist after the condition is eliminated; nor could it fail to persist while the condition obtains. Necessarily, then, one who has such doubts is calling into question the aptness of the poverty-line definition. He is putting it to a test of relevance by confronting it with his intuitive sense of why poverty is objectionable and ought to be eliminated. Unless this confrontation occurs, there is danger that we will expend our energy on the wrong enemy.

And the confrontation cannot be successful unless we achieve clarity concerning why poverty ought to be eliminated. Our intuitive sense forms a good point of departure, but only that. In the end what we require is an account that formulates in clear language the reasons why we should be concerned enough about poverty to invest a noticeable percentage of our gross national product in the effort to eradicate or at least ameliorate it.

A definition of poverty must perform two major functions. First, it must be usable in the sense of facilitating identification of those who are to be beneficiaries of poverty programs. Were the definition couched in such terms as to lead different investigators to identify different persons or families as forming the relevant group, poverty programs would be marked by chaos. This is a methodological requirement and leads to the demand for an "instrumental" and quantitative definition. The second function of the definition is to identify the relevant group in the relevant way. That is, it should lead us to the group we ought to be concerned about, and it should identify the condition that ought to be corrected.

The poverty-line definition performs the first function admirably. This is understandable, since it was a ruling consideration in its formulation that it should do so. Indeed, the fact that there are census data which enable researchers to determine readily how many individuals fall below the line, where they live, and a variety of other facts about them, is largely responsible for the widespread acceptance of the poverty-line definition.

But this motive—to secure a definition that takes advantage of existing arrangements for gathering data—would lead to ludicrous results if the second function of a definition of poverty were ignored. In any case, we will derive our notions about how to fight poverty and what overcoming it consists in from our understanding of what poverty is. But it is inappropriate, even dangerous, to decide what poverty is by concentrating altogether on the methodological question, "What definition will be useful for purposes of empirical research?" while ignoring the moral question, "Why ought we to be concerned?" The definition should be so drawn that if we allow it to direct the fight against poverty, and use it to help us to decide how to fight is going, we are well served. And being well served in this connection means more than getting answers. It means that the answers are to the point in the sense that they bear on the real issues. To illustrate, present enthusiasm for a negative income tax is probably tied in some way to the poverty-line definition. The argument is disarmingly simple. If poverty consists in falling below the line, the object of a war on poverty must be to raise everyone up to the line. This goal can be accomplished with one stroke by passing a law that provides for supplementing the income of everyone who falls below the line by the required amount.

There are three ways in which a definition of poverty may fail. It may identify what it means to be poor— the condition in which poverty exists— but do this in a way that precludes our discovering who *are* poor. Or, it may provide a ready way of identifying the group who are poor without identifying the condition referred to in calling them poor. Finally, the definition may fail on both counts. It may identify the wrong group and the wrong condition.

We may ignore the third possibility. The distinction between the first and second parallels that between the intension and extension of a term. One may know the symptoms of a disease without knowing what the disease is, and by looking for symptoms may be able to identify every occurrence of it. This would be to know the extension of the term that refers to the disease, but not to know its intension. The analogy with disease makes clear the danger of adopting a definition of poverty that does not tell us what poverty *is* (its intension), and only shows us how to pick out the group who are poor (its extension). It also indicates, indirectly, the danger of taking up the question of what poverty is in isolation from the question, "Why fight poverty?" If one does not notice that the definition of a disease only tells how to find cases of it by identifying its symptoms, one may be led to fight the disease by fighting its symptoms. Cosmetics will hide the signs of measles. In the same way, if our definition of poverty does not tell us what poverty is, but by identifying its symptoms only shows us how to find the group who are "poor," we may be led to adopt poverty programs that, like cosmetics, cover up symptoms without getting to the real problem. For example, some hold that the real problem is inequality. For them, the fact that a portion of incomes falls below the line is only incidentally relevant. If all were above the line, but wide discrepancies remained, they would be as concerned about the problem of poverty as they are now. They might accept the poverty-line definition, but not because it identifies what it means to be poor. For them, poverty consists in having much less than others have, and is independent of how much any one has. But they might accept the poverty-line definition because it directs one to the group who are poor in the relevant sense. If inequality is the heart of the problem—if we ought to be concerned about the poor because they receive much less than others do and not because they receive so little—then a program aimed at raising the level of those who have least would promise to solve the problem of poverty only if it did not eventuate also in higher incomes for those who have most. A negative income tax might or might not be well-advised, depending on its long-range impact on the latter group.

THE GOOD CITY

The reasons people have for fighting urban poverty—and this is the only kind of poverty that shall concern us here—fall under three headings. These correspond with the three basic moral categories: goodness, justice, and prudence. Poverty is sometimes seen as a public problem, a defect in the city itself. So far as there is poverty in a city, it fails of being a good city. Second, poverty is often seen as a form of social injustice, a liability predicated of the people who are poor, not of the city they inhabit. Third, poverty is often objected to by those who are not themselves poor, as a threat to their own well-being. All three present good reasons for combatting poverty. The point of the discussion which follows is to clarify each, and to exhibit the implications it has for a war on poverty. Clarification of these reasons for fighting poverty leads to the conviction that none of the current definitions of poverty identifies the condition we ought to be focusing on in our struggle against it. That condition, it will appear, is not inequality, not low income, not lack of goods and services. It is instead a structural condition of the city, considered as an environment. And, in the last analysis, the object of the fight should be to mold that structure so that it meets the genuine needs of the city's inhabitants. Raising incomes, eliminating gross inequality, and increasing access to goods and services are relevant only insofar as they have impact on that structure.

All cities are beset by numerous problems, each of which forms a particular respect in which they are less than ideal and demand improvement. The object in attacking these problems may be simply to bring into being a good city, one that is on all sides and in all respects satisfactory. When poverty is seen as one such problem, it is viewed as a blemish on a city as a whole. This leads one to regard attempts to eliminate poverty as undertaken not for the benefit of any group within a city, not even the poor themselves, but simply for the good of the city.

Some find this point of view strange. They are accustomed to thinking of traffic and parking problems, congestion, air and water pollution, and urban sprawl and blight as essentially civic problems. Although they realize that it is people who are inconvenienced by such conditions, they have no difficulty in attributing the conditions to the city, so that it is seen as burdened by them and efforts to eliminate them are seen as efforts to improve it. Poverty, by contrast, is thought to involve only people; the city's involvement is thought to be restricted to the fact that the impoverished people reside in a city, though some might extend this to include the possibility that the city contains institutions that contribute to their poverty. But one does not ordinarily suppose that our interest in having a good city, which forms a motive for various efforts on the side of physical planning, might also reasonably constitute a motive for our efforts to eliminate poverty. Only unfamiliarity with the idea stands in the way of its general acceptance. If a person genuinely identifies with the city he inhabits, so that he associates his well-being with it and feels a spontaneous enthusiasm for any activity he perceives as likely to improve it, he is bound to apprehend urban poverty as a civic failing, no different than the failure to provide clean air and water and sufficient space for children to play, pedestrians to walk, motorists to park.

But if our reason for fighting poverty is that we see it as a blemish on the city, forming a particular respect in which the city fails of being a good city, then we shall require an understanding of what a good city would be like. Without clarity concerning our ideal for the city, we lack clarity concerning the objective that poverty programs should focus on, insofar as those programs are undertaken in order to improve the city itself. This result may seem unfortunate. We are asked to decide what a thoroughly good city would be like so that by referring to the conception of such an environment we can be assured that our efforts to eliminate poverty are relevant to the problem at hand. If those efforts have no tendency to make the city more nearly like the ideal, then the time, energy, and money they use up are wasted. There is a natural temptation to reject points of view which complicate matters, but here the complication introduced by the idea that the discussion of poverty must take off from a wide-ranging discussion of social ideals cannot be side-stepped. The situation resembles that which conscientious city planners face. They cannot intelligently decide how to attack any particular problem that falls within their orbit unless they have some conception of the form to be taken by the solution to all their problems. They require, in other words, a plan for the whole before they can plan intelligently for its parts.

I shall only summarize the conclusions to which I have been led in trying to clarify the conception of a good city. The beginning of wisdom in this connection is discovery of the sense in which a city is more than people and artifacts. From many points of view what is more important is that a city is or encompasses a life style or design for living laid down by the complex of urban institutions. In the largest view of the matter, poverty is a condition of the urban life style. Urban poverty consists, in the first instance, in the fact that the urban life style is impoverished; and people are deprived to the extent that their lives are settled by an impoverished life style. By a life style I mean the objective counterpart to the actual patterns of action an individual's life exhibits. In calling a life style objective I mean to underscore the idea that it is something solidly present, confronting the individual as a milieu that decisively shapes his patterns of action. It is a serious mistake to view a person's life as having been shaped by his own will, considered as an internal faculty that reaches decisions prompted by internal drives and needs, as if the context of action—the world one immediately confronts—were a vacuum open to any manner of entry that the person decides upon. Instead, this world forms a structured environment composed of determinate instrumentalities for action. These are the particular ways in which one's world allows one to act and to live—the institutional opportunities or roles available to him. In detail, this refers to positions in offices and factories, modes of participation in family life, recreational and educational opportunities, one's manner of worshipping God and of functioning as a consumer, and the character of one's involvement in local and national politics.

When these instrumentalities are considered as institutional opportunities, stress is placed on their character of laying out channels within which are located the whole of an individual's chances for developing and expressing himself, and therefore his chances for

living what he can regard as a decent life. When they are considered as roles, an additional feature is introduced, namely, that they constrain the individual's activity in the sense of laying down limits beyond which, for all practical purposes, he may not go in taking advantage of the opportunity. The constraints and opportunities are two sides of the same fact. We could not have one without the other. Were our world not an order of institutional constraints, neither would it present us with extensive opportunities for significant action.

The life style an individual confronts is the totality of roles or opportunities open to him, regarded not pluralistically but rather as a unified *way* of living, a design for living. His life style is not his in the sense that he makes it up, but in the same sense that a particular fate is his. So far as his life in society is concerned, indeed, it *is* his fate. To say this, however, is not to assert a deterministic or fatalistic view, if this means that people have no control over their destiny, no purchase for exercise of spontaneity. But the opportunity one has for such control and for exercise of spontaneity is itself settled by his life style. He may or may not be "fated to be free." The serf in a manorial village had less opportunity to control the ground conditions of his life than does the denizen of a small New England town. This did not arise from his lack of initiative or decisiveness, but was an unavoidable consequence of the life style ordered by manorial villages. Similarly, the relative freedom enjoyed by a Yankee is no credit to himself—he meets it. It may be a credit to his predecessors who, one might suppose, had something to do with the fact that those little places settle the life that they do.

It is important not to conceive the elements of a life style—roles or opportunities—in purely mechanical terms.

The limits of a role and the breadth of an opportunity are fixed in part, by bare technological conditions, in part by legal arrangements, and, not least, in part by ideas. These are all components of the role. Technological and legal factors set constraints but the ideas people hold about what is proper and improper are often more decisive in determining what they do. The ideas that define roles, however, are not in the first instance the ideas of those who assume the roles. The person does not bring them to the role, but meets them there as elements of his involvement, definite fixed features of the world in which he acts. These ideas are, in an extended sense, a society's moral code. Instead of thinking of this code as a body of moral rules designed to limit the person's "conduct," it is more realistic to think of it as a class name for the set of ideas that define the acceptable and unacceptable manners of functioning in the various institutional positions that give form to a society.

An implication of the view expressed here is that the idea of a good city is a conception concerning the character urban life styles should have. This conception in turn is a view about desirable traits of urban institutions. In asking what a good city would be like, one is asking what life styles are implied by the idea of city dwellers living in a way they would find as satisfactory as the human condition permits. The value of focusing on life styles, or on institutional traits which compose life styles, is that the resulting conception of a good city will be structural. In this way one may gain clues regarding what to do in the interest of reaching the ideal. If instead our thought stopped at the level of the individual by merely delineating a preferred way of acting without translating this into an account of the kind of environment that must exist if this way of acting is to be possible, the ideal would have no *use*.

What traits of institutions are implied by the idea of people living a life they would find on all sides satisfactory? If we are to answer the question by abstracting from all particular cities, so that the answer becomes applicable to any city, then the response must be quite formal and abstract. But it will not for that reason be without use, since by referring to it one who has a particular city in mind will be able to decide what it would take to improve that city by considering ways in which it may incorporate the formal and abstract traits that form the ideal.

The leading idea in pursuing an answer to such a question is that of self-development, self-realization, self-fulfillment. Whatever goals a person holds for himself, satisfaction for him (hence what he can call a good life) appears to consist in his fulfilling these ideals and thereby realizing himself in the sense of developing the potentialities that uniquely define him. These ideals do not ordinarily arise in a vacuum, but are representations in the individual of purposes that do or might characterize the overt institutional order. Everything depends on whether this order institutes opportunities for people to live in the way they must if they are to develop their natures to the fullest. Institutional opportunity—recreational, educational, vocational, artistic, religious, political, and familial—is strictly correlative to personal self-fulfillment. That is, there is nothing more a society can do for a person, from the standpoint of contributing to his chances of living a satisfactory life, than open to him maximal institutional opportunity along the lines suggested. Without this opportunity he has no chance of reaching a notable level of self-realization.

Analysis of the idea of self-realization makes it possible to give content to the correlative notion of institutional opportunity. Self-realization is partly a personal and partly a social affair. On one hand, the individual has a variety of personal capacities, the development and expression of which are indispensable to his own well-being. I have indicated that he must depend on the life style that his city confronts him with for whatever real chance he has to realize those capacities. On the other hand, he is a social creature and hence will not perceive himself to have made very much of his life if the sharpening of his unique capacities occurs in a way that isolates him from affective relations with others. From this second point of view, what the individual requires is a setting in which he is led to find common cause with his neighbors. As a characteristic of the overt, institutional order, this indicates the need for community, a condition in which the fragmentation and divisiveness of present urban life are replaced by a setting made cohesive by the presence of shared purposes. The idea is that each should confront a life style that permits him to come to terms with himself in activity that at the same time brings him into meaningful relations with others. These latter relationships are necessary to an individual's own development as a person.

A good city—considered as a place where the kinds of institutional opportunities that permit people to develop themselves to the fullest are found—must be a community or a group of communities. It is not important whether the basis for these communities is spatial or functional, that is, whether people find the larger social wholes with which they affectively identify to be geographically delimitable areas within which they establish their places of residence (neighbor-hoods), or functionally defined joint activities (their office, factory, church, or clan).

The other side of the coin is that within an overarching community the individual should find opportunities for his own development as a person. We may analyze this requirement into two parts. Personal growth requires a social environment in which are found extensive opportunities for significant action, a condition that I shall call moral power. It also requires that these opportunities impinge on the person in such a way that in following them out he is active, in short, self-determining or free. These two requirements—that the urban institutions which constitute life styles should ground moral power and freedom—are in turn analyzable into a set of institutional traits, or objective conditions that must obtain if life styles are to have the required impact on the persons who confront them. In the first place, moral power is a function of three institutional traits: richness, openness, and person-centeredness. First, a city's institutions should offer extensive opportunities for significant action, and in this sense should not be barren from a human point of view. This is the requirement of institutional richness. Second, the opportunities should be open to all, not merely in the legal and formal sense that all are allowed access, but in the more profound if informal sense of all being genuinely capable of enjoying this access should they choose to do so. The fact an employer does not discriminate among job applicants on the basis of race makes the job no more accessible or open to Negroes whose family and neighborhood environments have prevented them from developing competence to perform the job than it would be if there were a rule of law that excluded them. Third, moral power involves the ordering of institutional opportunities into a life style that is person-centered in the sense that it contemplates a total way of living consonant with the idea of personal integrity.

Freedom, to the extent that it is grounded in urban life styles, may also be analyzed into three institutional traits. The point of departure here is awareness that a person's capability of living as a free or self-determining agent is conditioned by the manner in which institutional opportunities are ordered. In the first place, it is obviously important whether these opportunities are discretionary or imposed. We may identify the requirement suggested by this fact as voluntariness, the requirement that roles should be so defined that participation in them is discretionary. Second, it is also important that the roles should be flexible. Inflexibility in this connection means a condition in which roles are narrowly defined in the sense that no one who takes them up is bound to act in one and only one way, so that in the act he is virtually reduced to the level of a machine. Flexibility, by contrast, is a condition that requires a person who takes up the role to make individual decisions regarding the manner in which it is to be carried out. The role thus leaves scope for alternative interpretations and room for maneuvering. Finally, the freedom encompassed in a way of life is affected by the extent to which the roles defining it are shaped by the persons who take them up. However inflexible and non-discretionary the institutional opportunities one confronts may be, if one has had a real voice in determining their form they are not constraints but they are tools by which one is enabled to shape his social destiny. This introduces the idea of social democracy, which in the present context is the requirement that people should have effective control over the institutional roles they confront, and thereby control over the life styles formed by the interrelationships of these roles.

This account of the good city is unfortunately highly sketchy and abstract. It may be summarized in the proposition that a good city is a community in which the participants are enabled to develop themselves as human beings in consequence of its richness, openness, person-centeredness, voluntariness, flexibility, and controllability.

POVERTY AND THE GOOD CITY

The relevance of the foregoing account to the topic of urban poverty may be seen by considering its bearing on the idea of a decent standard of living. The root idea behind the poverty-line definition is that poverty consists in incapacity to live up to a decent standard. The error in the definition (if it is intended to accomplish anything more significant than provide a ready way of identifying those who are poor) is its assumption that a standard of living consists solely or mainly in some degree of access to goods and services. It is very natural to make such a mistake in a consumption-oriented society. The alternative to defining a standard of living in terms of access to goods and services (the amount one is able to *consume*) is to define it in terms of opportunity to *act*. And the justification for adopting the second alternative—which forms the point of departure for the conception of a good city—is simply this: whatever positive sense one may gain of having lived a good life results not from the number and kinds of goods one has consumed but from the quality of the action one has been enabled to carry out, and from the impact of that action on oneself, in the sense of its effect of developing one's powers and of forming an integral person.

Taking seriously the idea that not consumption but action is the critical element in a standard of living leads one to identify poverty as severe deprivation with respect to capability to act in humanly relevant ways. Since this capability is grounded in urban life styles, the measure of poverty in a city is the extent to which it fails to satisfy the ideal of a good city.

It is possible for an entire city to be deprived, despite the monetary affluence of some of its denizens. This is the case when urban life styles are so constrained that not even the most affluent find opportunities to act in meaningful ways. When all of a city's institutional opportunities are inflexible, trivial, or compulsory, the community itself is poorer than it would be if no one who lived in the place had an annual income above $3,000.

It is obvious that the poverty of a city is unevenly distributed among its inhabitants. Some are poor in the profound sense of confronting a life style that does not offer extensive opportunities for significant action, while in the same sense others are rich indeed. The differences are partly tied to differences in income, a circumstance that gives a poverty-line definition whatever relevance to poverty it has. But there is a hidden danger associated with responding to this fact simply by undertaking to raise incomes. If the life style of the most deprived is one of the major causes of their low incomes, as Oscar Lewis has suggested, the result of raising incomes without altering the life style may well be that instead of eliminating poverty one merely changes the group upon whom it impinges. There are forces that maintain slums and assure full occupancy.

When these forces are not tampered with, but through job-retraining and other means we make it possible for present slum-dwellers to vacate the tenements, a vacuum is created in the slums that the outside forces will cause to be filled. The life style is there; others will enter and take it up. Not the amount but only the incidence of poverty will have been changed. This is the logical outcome of treating symptoms rather than causes.

The chief bearing of money on poverty is that it determines access to institutional opportunities and thereby contributes to the openness of institutions and of life styles. One is poor not because he has no money, but because, possibly owing to lack of money, he lacks also access to the social instrumentalities that make humanly significant action possible. In part, it is a simple matter of not having the price of admission—to a theater, university, or recreation area. But in larger part it is a matter of not having the character or competence (e.g. lack of verbal facility, lack of motivation, destructive orientation(that establishes one's capability of taking up an opportunity that is formally open. Often, lack of money is a prime reason why one has failed to form the requisite character or to develop the requisite competence.

The intention of these remarks is to place the financial aspects of the problem of poverty in a perspective that permits us to acknowledge the relevance of money to poverty, and at the same time enables us to avoid the mistake of supposing that being poor *consists in* lacking money or the consumer goods that money can buy. This perspective forces rejection of the view that raising incomes, minimizing inequalities of income, or providing commodities and services in lieu of incomes is the complete solution to the problem. Any strategy calculated to improve the quality of urban life is relevant to a war on poverty. The role of speaking specifically of such a war —and of a unique problem of "poverty"—rather than of the need and effort simply to shape actual cities so that they more nearly measure up to the ideal of a good city, is that it establishes an order of priority. It indicates that in the effort to improve the quality of urban life it would be humane to begin by altering those conditions that have differential impact on the least affluent, meaning by least affluent, again, those who have least access to whatever opportunities the city offers for people living decent lives.

THE JUST CITY

When we consider poverty as a form of social injustice, however, we cannot so easily assimilate the problem to that of improving the quality of urban life, nor can we so easily assimilate the war on poverty to the general attempt to solve the city's difficulties. This results from the peculiar force of the notion of injustice. The preceding discussion was based on the assumption that the principal beneficiary of a war on poverty is the city as a whole. But the view that recognizes poverty as a form of social injustice leads to the idea that the beneficiaries are the poor themselves, and that the war is being fought in order to improve their condition. Moreover, if we are fighting injustice, then the poor are not merely beneficiaries but they are a group who, as a group, are *wronged,* and in attempting to improve their condition we are undertaking to right the wrong. This circumstance makes the term "beneficiary" somewhat misleading. In any strict sense, if injustice is at issue, a poverty program is not something we do "for" the poor—as if morally we could enact it or not as we chose and as if it were morally indifferent

whether we do so or not—but the poor *exact* the program, they demand it as a matter of right. There is no charity in it, anymore so than there is charity in repaying a debt or paying properly exacted damages. Rather, as in repaying a debt or in making restitution (if the view that poverty is a form of social injustice has merit), we are bound to the poor themselves to enact programs aimed at alleviating poverty and to replace presently inadequate programs with more ambitious ones.

Before one can assess the claim that poverty is a form of injustice he must understand it. And for this purpose one must have an understanding of the concept of justice. The idea of justice is intimately allied with those of desert and equality. We tend to identify just treatment with getting what is deserved, so that paradigm cases of injustice are those of one who has much merit being badly treated, and one who has no merit being well treated. But we also regard markedly unequal treatment as unjust. These two notions of desert and equality are not entirely compatible. Desert is a differentiating concept; by referring to it we justify differential treatment. Since some have more merit than others, justice demands that people be differentially, therefore unequally, treated in a way that reflects their differing degrees of merit. The basis for one's desert is an open question, and fortunately one that need not be decided here. Some suppose that ancestry is the principal desert-basis, others place the emphasis on a person's past conduct, and still others stress competence as the proper measure of desert.

It is possible to associate the ideas of desert and equality by arguing, as Aristotle did, that proportioning rewards to desert involves maintaining equality in the proportions. If one who deserves little receives little, while another who deserves much receives much, then the justice manifested in this differential treatment of the two lies in the fact that the proportion of reward to desert is the same in both cases. But there seems little basis for the view that the idea of justice requires people to be treated equally in an absolute sense, so that it is always unjust for one person to have more of some value, such as money, than others have.

Many, however, hold that the idea of equality introduces a theme not present when justice is associated with desert. Equality suggests the conception of individual *worth*. This refers to a person's value as a person, independently of the differential merit he may possess in consequence of personal characteristics that distinguish him from others. Individual worth is thought of as an intrinsic characteristic. Perhaps it is not wise to ask whether people in this sense *have* worth. Instead, we should ask whether our common life is founded on the practice of ascribing such worth to people. Do we, and is it sensible that we should, treat people in a way that suggests we regard them as having equal worth, despite their differing degrees of merit? Most would say that we do and that we should. Every Western legal system is founded on this idea. Nor is it easy to conceive what our life would be like if it were not ordered around the notions that each person has worth or dignity as a person, and that despite differences in merit, all people have equal worth or dignity, and equally deserve to be treated as ends-in-themselves. One may even say that our capability of identifying human beings as "persons," and distinguishing them in this way from "things," depends on our ascribing to them intrinsic worth, and that the idea of their equality as persons presupposes their equal worth. For, by a "thing" we mean that which may legitimately be used wholly for our own

purposes and need not be regarded as itself having ends to which we ought to defer. By a "person," we mean instead that which has ends of its own to which some consideration should be given, so that we do not entirely use it as a means to our own ends. In fact, there seems no difference between treating a person as if he had ends of his own to which we ought to defer, and ascribing to him intrinsic worth.

At this point the fundamental sanity of the legal use of "person," in terms of which persons are regarded as "right and duty bearing units," may be seen. For, we would not attribute rights to an individual without also attributing duties, and to regard him as having rights is the same as to attribute to him ends to which we ought to defer, that is, to refuse to treat him merely as a means to our own purposes.

When the idea of personal worth, and the closely allied ideas of the dignity of the person—a dignity he is supposed to have entirely apart from his merit or ill-desert—is stressed, the very principle of justice demands that people be treated in a way that acknowledges their worth and dignity as persons. The idea of equality is, therefore, relevant to justice because of the supposition that all persons are, in respect to worth or dignity, equal. The fundamental right is that one's dignity or worth as a person should be acknowledged. All injustices are forms of violation of this right. And this right is an equal right—all share in it, and equally—in consequence of the fact that none has less worth or dignity than another.

What is involved in acknowledging a person's dignity or worth? It has been argued by Gregory Vlastos ("Justice and Equality," in Richard Brandt [ed.], *Justice,* Englewood Cliffs, N.J.: Prentice-Hall, 1962) whose account I am following rather closely here, that what mainly is at stake are well-being and freedom. Both are caught up in the idea of opportunity to act—opportunity to express oneself and to develop one's nature. One's worth as a person is acknowledged insofar as he enjoys an opportunity to develop his nature and to express that which has been developed. The fundamental right, then, is to enjoy such an opportunity; and social injustice consists in withholding that opportunity from some or all of the members of a society.

That all have an equal right to see their dignity or worth acknowledged means that all ought to enjoy equal opportunity to develop and express themselves. But in this connection the sense of the term "opportunity" must be carefully specified. In a rather superficial way, whether two people enjoy equal opportunity is a matter of whether they possess equal resources. If one is richer than the other, his opportunity to have the things money can buy is greater. But we would not say that this implies injustice.

In a more fundamental sense, the measure of one's opportunity is the extent to which what he is or has achieved can be chalked up to luck or his own initiative. The critical issue is whether discrepancies in the degree of well-being and freedom enjoyed by people are the outcome of remediable conditions which are or were beyond control of the disadvantaged persons. Slavery is a paradigm case. The inequality of opportunity between the slave and his master is not merely the trivial inequality consisting in the fact that the master enjoys greater freedom now, and is now better able to satisfy his needs and desires. The inequality is none of the slave's doing; it is not owing to bad luck, as when one loses a good bet, nor is it a result of the slave's failure to assert himself. The difference in their positions is the outcome of remediable conditions that are and were

beyond control of the slave himself. Or, more succinctly, he never had a chance. This is the basic reason why the institution of slavery is unjust.

An injustice is a case of a stacked deck, and unjust institutions are unfair in much the same sense that cheating at cards is. If the deck is not stacked and the deal is honest, then there is no unfairness in one person being dealt a "jack high" and another a full house. The inequality of their hands is important to the players, but morally irrelevant. But if the deck is stacked, or the deal dishonest, a slight discrepancy in the strength of the hands means considerable unfairness in the game.

The analogy suggests the two elements that form inequalities of opportunity in this more profound sense. The inequality may result from an initial condition that jeopardized a person's chances of *subsequently* enjoying as much freedom and well-being as others enjoy. Or, it may result from a continuing penalty imposed on him by discriminatory institutions. The first element is analogous to a stacked deck, arrangements that prejudice one's chances from the start, so that however fair the situation he subsequently confronts may be in itself, he is not able to take full advantage of it owing to the initial incapacitating conditions to which he was subjected. The most obvious way in which this occurs is by a person being born and growing up in a milieu that either causes him not to develop skills and habits necessary for subsequent participation in the life of the city, or causes him to develop habits or ideals that channel his energies in other directions. The second element is analogous to a dishonest deal. The person may have had an equal chance at the start, but may find that he is constantly discriminated against when he seeks to make the contacts in the surrounding urban world that would enable him to live in the way his developed faculties contemplate. The obvious example is job discrimination.

Urban institutions are unjust, then, to the extent they systematically deny to some an equal chance to enjoy the opportunities for personal growth that the city contains. This denial may occur when the society either erects discriminatory bars to participation or tolerates conditions that create extreme liabilities in persons which effectively disqualify them for participation, even in cases where there is no formal prohibition. The injustice of these arrangements stems from their bearing on the worth or dignity of the affected persons. Attributing to them equal worth as persons leads to the idea that they have a right to an equal chance to develop and express themselves. The arrangements referred to withhold such a right, and are for this reason and in this sense unjust.

The discussion has a clear bearing on the claim that urban poverty is a form of social injustice. Deprivation in one's standard of living is not as such unjust; consequently, neither is poverty, as such, unjust. But poverty is unjust when it is remediable and results from discriminatory institutions in either of the two ways mentioned above: when it results indirectly from discriminatory institutions that withhold from a person competence to participate in the genuine opportunities for significant action offered by the city, or when it directly results from discriminatory institutions that simply deny a group admission to the places where these opportunities are located.

One implication here is that it is inappropriate to become overly concerned about inequalities between the affluent and the deprived when the energy behind an assault on urban poverty is the sense of poverty as unjust. Mainly, inequality shows that a city possesses sufficient resources to remedy the condition of the deprived.

Similarly, one who is responding to the sense that poverty is unjust ought not to be overly concerned about the number of families whose income falls below a poverty-line. Even if their incomes were well above the line, the deprivation they experience might be unjust. And, in any case, where they stand relative to any such line has no bearing on the justice or injustice of their condition. What matters is why they are deprived, not the level of deprivation. Deprivation is unjust only when it results from discriminatory institutions.

There can be no question, then, that the bulk of urban poverty in the United States is unjust. For, as most now agree, the problem of poverty in the American city is largely indistinguishable from the race problem, and more particularly, the problem of the American Negro. And that problem is unquestionably one of institutionalized bias. Those who try to minimize the problem by calling attention to the wretched condition of the majority of people in Asia and by arguing that in the sense in which those people are poor the American Negro is affluent, wholly miss the point. The problem is not that the American Negro has relatively few of the things money can buy; it is, rather, that he has less opportunity to live a decent life than others have in a society which could improve his condition but which imposes this condition on him by maintaining discriminatory institutions. The fact that for the most part the discrimination is informal rather than legal, that it does not occur in violation of law but exists in the interstices of legal rules, neither diminishes nor magnifies its unjust character.

The relation between the conception of poverty one is led to by following out the idea that poverty is a form of social injustice, and the conception that results from regarding poverty as a defect of the city, is close indeed. Poverty-as-injustice is a more restricted condition. Of the six traits identified as constitutive of a good city, only one is relevant to justice. Any defect with respect to the six traits is a mark of deprivation, but what makes the deprivation unjust is lack of openness in a city's institutions. This trait, then, has a peculiar prominence in the conception of a good city. For, on one hand it is, along with the others, essential to the quality of urban life. But also, its absence transforms any defect with respect to the other five from a merely unfortunate situation, which in general ought to be corrected, to an unjust situation that anyone who can is *bound* to correct, in the same way as he is bound to repay his debts and honor his promises. To deny this obligation, as the preceding discussion establishes, is to reject the view that all human beings have equal dignity and worth. Or, more pointedly, it is to take the view that some human beings are not persons at all but things, tools that may be used but need not be respected.

PRUDENCE

The third good and sufficient reason for fighting poverty is prudential. While the second reason indicates much the same strategy in fighting poverty as the first and only implies a difference in emphasis, the prudential reason threatens to be idiosyncratic. If one's only reason for objecting to urban poverty is that it is a threat to oneself, then any way of fighting it

which minimizes the threat will do. Then gas chambers will do. But clearly a prudential argument is a good argument only in case the self-protection one is aiming at is compatible with the legitimate well-being of those against whom one would protect oneself. Otherwise arguing for one's own interest would be nothing but a way of insisting on a bias, and bias, as such, cannot be justified.

The real problem, then, is whether those who are not themselves poor *can* find a strategy that responds to the first two reasons for fighting poverty, and at the same time contributes in readily discernible ways to their own well-being. Unless such strategy is found, we may expect a hardening of the lines in riot-torn cities. It is not difficult for a middle-class white who lives in the vicinity of a race-riot to perceive that the poverty of the Negro is a major cause: people who devote the daylight hours to work they regard as worth doing do not devote the evening to looting stores. But whether the middle-class white responds in a constructive way to his perception depends on whether he feels there is a constructive response that will improve his own situation. And I cannot believe that any strategy will succeed that does not have the felt approval of middle-class whites, since in large measure their attitudes constitute the problem. We have, then, an additional reason for broadening our view of the war on poverty so that it is seen as an aspect of the effort to create a good city. For that effort is in everyone's interest.

Contemporary Urban Conflict

Jack Meltzer*

Cities have traditionally served as the setting for the in-migrant and the disadvantaged, and have been the place where these people have sought to fulfill their ambitions and realize their hopes. With metropolitanization, increased affluence (which has sharpened the gulf of social and economic disparity), and a hardening of the core group of disadvantaged who are embittered by the fruits of prejudice and discrimination, cities have found themselves confronted by population dispersion, their municipal plants in disrepair, with accompanying problems of inadequate tax resources and an increasing percentage of their populations disadvantaged for reasons largely national or regional rather than local.

A series of policies and programs have evolved which have substantially contributed to the current conflict. The need to add appreciably to the housing stock (in the face of a simultaneous increase in population and family formation, and a deterioration of the existing housing supply) and the concurrent individual and family desire and accompanying financial capacity to achieve substantial improvements in housing and environmental quality, have culminated in a vast program of federal financing of home construction. The rate of suburbanization attests to the impressive quantitative success of the undertaking. But the by-product has been an outflow of residents and industrial plants from the central city, further deterioration of its housing

stock, and an undermining of the central city's tax resources.

THE IRONY OF PROGRAMS DESIGNED TO "SAVE OUR CITIES"

The response of the cities (and the federal government) has been a series of programs and activities to "save our cities." The irony is that these very programs, by sharpening the conflict and dilemma, have altered the city's role as facilitator of urban change and reduced the city's capacity to manipulate among diverse groups and, therefore, to govern.

The irony is dramatized by the large number of white Americans, especially those of Northern second-generation immigrant families and low-income Southern white families, who are consumed by fear. Persuaded that Negroes are bestial and animal-like, the inflamed white does not see himself as barbaric, but rather as the courageous defender of home and family against rape and pillage. Negroes, to them, mean the Chicago West Side riots, Watts, broken families, illegitimate children, and teen-age gangs.

They make no distinction between riotous gangs and the Reverend Martin Luther King and his followers. It is to them a package of conspiracy. They see no relationship between the lack of Negro opportunity, which their own behavior confirms for the Negroes, and the acts of despair in the Negro ghettos, which they fear and condemn. They do not understand that the despair of the Negro is compounded by the bankruptcy of our educational and other programs. To the Negro, it appears that the only recourse available to salvage some shred of self-respect is

*"The Urban Conflict" by Jack Meltzer is reprinted from *Urban Affairs Quarterly*, Volume III, Number 3 (March, 1968) pages 3–20, by permission of the Publisher, Sage Publications, Inc.

a resort to either violence or the slogans of "black power." The result is a further deepening of the bitterness and hostility which divides Negro and white Americans.

The traditional reliance of the local political system on negotiated settlements, involving the selective distribution of public funds and the activation of multiple and diverse programs, has depended on either the existence of a general consensus as to social and economic values or sufficient flexibility in the total community's social and economic structure to permit accommodation without a confrontation among competing power groups. The abrasiveness of local issues is proof that neither alternative exists any longer.

The programs designed to save the central city have almost dealt it a death blow. Each central city program created to stem the tidal flow has tended to further weaken rather than strengthen the city's structure. Expressways perform the functions of railroads in an earlier era, by acting as stimulants to population dispersion and magnets of attraction. Increases in the property tax, the principal source of local revenue, have further strained the weakest and most vulnerable spot in the central city structure. The compulsion to stimulate development has frequently permitted toleration of the grossest forms of construction, including building activity at the expense of the city's assets, such as visual amenities, parks, and open land, which provided and continue to provide the city's distinctive quality. The city has, in other words, been quite willing to eat into the capital reserves which constitute its basic quality, to satisfy the drive to "save our central cities."

The programs to "save our cities" were predicted on three base points: the reinforcement of commercial, industrial, and institutional property commitments for tax and allied purposes; the retention and attraction of middle- and high-income individuals and families; and community stability. The expressway, urban renewal, and public housing programs were all created and administered to achieve these ends. Commercial areas have been modernized, and their sales and employment opportunities have been expanded. Markets have been restored in juxtaposition to commercial concentration, development, and expressways. Middle-income integrated areas have been achieved (frequently the only such achievement in the city). Institutions have secured space for growth in more amenable surroundings; and communities have been provided assurances and assistance which have promised to safeguard their inviolate character. Paradoxically, the successes for these programs (although hardly universal) are striking. Yet they account for the difficulty faced by cities in terminating or significantly altering their continued undertaking, because the achievements have reshaped the traditional character of the city. Whereas the city had been a fluid place where the restless could aspire, these programs have rigidified its institutional forms and have reduced the opportunities for social mobility. Stability and mobility challenge reconciliation.

The principal thrust has become the "spirit of city renewal." The major ingredient in this nurtured spirit is *stability*: save your neighborhood, avoid panic. Mobility and community fluidity are considered almost treasonable acts against place and city. Stability, in turn, is in large part associated with ethnicity, single-family home ownership, and social and economic homogeneity. The attitude is almost agricultural and rural in conception. The idea, however, has great appeal, particularly to those who have only recently achieved a modicum of economic security and, therefore, have only limited choices, and for whom investment in home and local institutions represent dominant values. The drive to save our cities, by modernizing the municipal plant and improving facilities and housing conditions in order to root people in the central city, has come to characterize nearly all of a central city's renewing activities.

CONTROVERSY AND CONFLICT

The ingredients for a direct confrontation and value conflicts have in consequence been self-created. Because, accompanying this drive to save the central city, there is the concurrent need to deal with our disadvantaged populations. Since the city is the place of residence of the largest concentrations of such disadvantaged populations, this national reality becomes a city reality. The push for "open occupancy" and the "open city," the inclusion of nondiscrimination clauses in a vast number of federal programs, the scattering of public housing projects, and the rent supplement program all tend to sharpen the weapons of controversy by directly confronting the value system built into the city's current programmatic responses.

The controversy and conflict is unavoidably compounded by the fact that the neighborhoods and communities in which the slogans of stability are most firmly entrenched are the neighborhoods and communities which provide the most realistic opportunities—geographically and financially—for the disadvantaged to bridge the wall of their containment. Thus, to the small number of advantaged among the minority population, "open occupancy" is the means whereby housing choices consistent with their financial achievements can be significantly opened to them in outlying and suburban areas. To the overwhelming number of disadvantaged among the minority popu-

lation, on the other hand, "open occupancy" may simply symbolize an avenue of escape into communities with sufficiently modest economic characteristics to accommodate their equally modest financial capabilities. From this vantage point, integration is not necessarily the product of "open occupancy." Rather, its effect is to extend the areas of minority occupancy as a consequence of expanded choice. Interestingly enough, the resistive communities most threatened by the geographic expansion of the minority and by "open occupancy" legislation have found new allies which they have not yet come to recognize. The drive for "black nationalism," "black power," and similar slogans is motivated by many of the same purposes which characterize the residents of the resistive "stable" communities which are now threatened; the minority reaction symbolized by the slogan "black power" seeks community self-determination and power over their patch of ground. It therefore constitutes more of an accommodation and less of an assault than the attempts to achieve "open occupancy" and an open city.

The minority reaction manifested in new slogans, violence, and universal discontent is the result, in major part, of the frustration born of conflict in the value structure. Bloodletting in the area of containment is cited as evidence of a lack of character, ambition, aspiration, and the American spirit of self-reliance. Yet a large number of public programs undermine the achievement of these very values: the poverty oath requirements associated with many of the welfare programs; the income restrictions in public housing; the punitive requirements attached to training activities; the visible stamps of difference which result from many public programs; the failure of ghetto schools to serve as an instrument of self-improvement on a scale matching either expectation or parallel achievement in other segments of the population; and a lack of housing provision at a rate and in a form which achieves desired levels of environmental quality. Self-reliance directed toward constructive purpose can neither be created nor survive in an atmosphere which discourages it and where opportunity does not exist to externalize emotional attitudes, exercise a degree of choice with respect to the course of one's life pattern, and exert influence on the decision-making process through existing or newly created institutional forms.

This conflict of values is a natural consequence of a city structure whose major asset and historical strength is a free-wheeling style, characterized by bustling, abrasive interaction. Reconciliation among the values in conflict is beyond achievement as long as the satisfaction demanded by a discontented portion of the population is dependent on the modification or alteration in the values of unyielding segments of the population. The result will be either a tense power standoff, violent confrontation, or a re-examination of the structure and style of the city political construction and response.

THE CITY'S RESPONSE

Governmental and private responses have been misdirected in fundamental ways. It may be more important, for example, to break the *walls of resistance* to the achievement by the disadvantaged of the expectations which our alleged public policy and recent legislative enactments have created, than to motivate the disadvantaged to break the *walls of their containment* and degradation. This analysis requires a reassessment of the value structure which gives stability and homogeneity more weight than access and opportunity. It also calls to question the

value structure in which the retention of property values in a community warrants more governmental safeguards than the achievement of a measure of acceptance for all segments of society. Positive encouragement should be given to those disadvantaged who seek to give evidence of their aspiration. But educational and other public programs, including incentives, directed toward the resisting communities which comprise armed fortifications are of no less priority. A "Headstart" program to prepare disadvantaged children for school is not one iota more important than a "Headstart" program to prepare advantaged children to welcome them. If we are sincere in our intentions, then every single activity of government which is directed toward the disadvantaged, such as the Office of Economic Opportunity, the Primary and Secondary Educational Act, the Economic Development Act, the Housing and Renewal Acts, etc., requires a parallel effort directed toward the advantaged.

The mere provision of planning, education, welfare, or other social services is, however, not enough. Service-oriented activities, albeit they are important, are generally detached and external. Cities respond to social need all too frequently by reciting an inventory of the services that are being or will be provided: day care centers, family counseling centers, health clinics, and a host of other services that are associated with city-wide specialized agencies and institutions that have developed over time.

In contrast, a reference to economic need does not elicit a recitation of the banking and other loan and credit services that are available. Instead, it elicits a discussion of the character, structure, and interplay among the economic forces that are operative, and culminates in a series of proposals flowing from the structural analysis.

Problems of the disadvantaged and urban change must also be viewed within the context of the entire social and economic structure. A social structure orientation is internally motivated and can stimulate a chain of activities which subsume services reflecting the rhythm and tempo of the people being assisted. Social need somehow fails to be dealt with in these terms, and is diminished by its *reductio ad absurdum* in a superficial discussion of needed public and private social services.

The peaceful protest demonstrations and the not-so-peaceful ghetto riots and teen-age ghetto gangs' disturbances provide evidence of restlessness and discontent stemming from the desire for an improved existence and the right to exercise choice. The challenge, therefore, is to convert riot and disturbance to constructive purpose and to build on the discernible evidence of pride and desire to be self-sufficient. These are assets on which Americans pride themselves, as portraying our national character. Discrimination and race hatred cannot go so deep that we would resist the cultivation of personal strength of character, for we resent the absence of these characteristics with equal fervor. We like to think that we rely on the consumer to establish private and public expenditure benefits by his behavior in the marketplace, and we have only reluctantly created elaborate devices to protect and be protected against the poor because of our patronizing assumption that they cannot perform effectively as consumers. In turn, we then resist attempts to either let the poor demonstrate or develop self-reliance and independence.

City welfare, planning, and education services need to readapt their premises and practices to reflect and reinforce the process of upward population mobility. An aspiring population, whether disadvantaged or in the stream of active self-improvement, is dependent on public programs that accept and encourage the existence of diverse communities and that regard communities as stages of advancement reflecting rising individual and family financial capacity. Public programs which are undertaken in relation to presumed yardsticks of absolute achievement obstruct the orderly process of urban change. The central theme of the urban system is fluidity, in which change is only achieved over time and public programs provide both direct and indirect assistance in accelerating the process of change and accommodating it in both personal and impersonal terms.

SCHOOL SYSTEMS

Take the school activity system as another example of our paralytic condition. Education is one of the last major public activities for which it is presumed that only professionals trained in that field have claims to leadership. Police departments are directed by non-police career individuals, planning agencies by people trained in other fields, and hospitals by non-medically trained administrators.

To put school systems in the charge of individuals who have not been identified throughout their professional careers with education, and who have not risen through the teaching and administrative school establishment, would lend encouragement to the innovation and creativity required to meet this most urgent urban problem. Leaders drawn from other fields would tend to break the rigid constraints on the educational system imposed by tradition and conventional practice. The desire for educational independence, free from political interference, has created burdens on any prospect for a completely successful educational breakthrough. The point may well have been reached where the penalties of independence thereby associated may warrant reassessment, in order to open windows on the educational activity system, to permit the entry of fresh air and new ideas.

Accompanying such a recommendation is the need to require that school superintendents be directly responsible to chief executives of the appropriate layer of government, and to transform boards of education into advisory citizen education committees. The chief executive is responsible for meeting and solving major urban social and economic issues within the orbit of his jurisdiction. Since schools are a critical ingredient in this process, how can one justify the current separation and division of policy, power and performance?

The sacrosanct protections, which have been sought by educators and rationalized by them as providing a defense against alleged societal corruption of the educational establishment, are simply no longer workable or acceptable. The freedom which is sought in education is for the teacher in the classroom and in research, not for the administrator who establishes policies and pursues programs which may be more profound in impact than all other local public activities combined. Yet it is the administrators' freedom which is safeguarded by asserting an independence from the electorate and the political and social structure of society. Such arrogance can no longer be tolerated, unless we are prepared to continue to accept the abysmal failure of urban education.

ADMINISTRATIVE REORGANIZATIONS

Take yet another example, the recent major New York City reorganization. In the fall of 1966, the Mayor recommended the creation of ten super-departments, generally reflecting the principal activity systems which have overtaken all of government, the professions, and society. The Mayor's proposal was advanced ostensibly as the means whereby efficiency would be increased and costs reduced. The recommendation represented the bringing together of existing departments grouped into ten massive enterprises: Housing and Development Administration, Economic Development Administration, Transportation Administration, Human Resources Administration, Financial Management Administration, Recreation and the Arts Administration, Health Services Administration, General Services Administration, Environmental Protection Administration, and Correction Administration. The Mayor of New York City has by this action formalized, institutionalized, and legalized governmental domination by the professional cadres. He has by this action asserted that government by proliferated function takes precedence over government pursuant to unified programs as determined by elected officials and in accordance with publicly stated policies. The fuel propelling the total transformation is presumed efficiency and economy. Less expensive and more hygienic administration may be achieved and, consequently, demonstrate the proposal's success, if the goals are an orderly table of organization, a modernized version of the Marquis of Queensbury rules to regulate departmental in-fighting, and a simplified system of budget accounting. If the purpose of the reorganization is an enhanced capacity to meet and resolve New York's urban problems, not only is the proposal likely to fail, but it will probably also compound and obstruct problem solutions. Gargantuas will have been created, with power which will most certainly grow over time. Each super-department will garner additional functions and activities which are duplicative and overlapping, but protected by their colossal, legally sanctioned power base. The net effect of all this, it may be predicted, will be to completely immobilize the executive capacity to plan and program in response to problem-solving requirements, and, in the process, to completely obscure the legislative function. The reorganization will defer or destroy the prospect for the effective development of a total city strategy, by surrendering executive leadership. Instead, professional identity and bias (the characteristic which differentiates the super-departments—i.e., each of the major activity areas) has been substituted to accommodate each group of professionals and their allies: the economic syndrome, the social welfare and social service syndrome, the resource syndrome, the housing and planning syndrome, the transportation syndrome, etc.

The reorganization proceeds on the thesis that there is merit in the strengthening, deepening, and intensification of the vertical response to governmental operation, keyed to functional differentiations. The executive will inevitably be confronted with a fragmented problem-solving capacity, since his ability to respond to problems uninhibited by entrepreneurial loyalty and administrative rigidities will have been severely diminished. In consequence, the reorganization constitutes a victory for functional professional self-determination, rather than a courageous demonstration of municipal commitment to problem solution free of administrative and professional constraint. It is not a break with bureaucracy, but a surrender to it.

The Mayor of New York City and, similarly, mayors of all other major cities should isolate those obstacles which deter citizens from achieving levels of satisfaction and from realizing their full potential, and coura-geously apply programs in such combinations as are demanded to eliminate the social and economic obstructions, without regard to professional and administrative sensitivities. To respond by assuaging the professional, by adding to his power and rigidifying administration, reduces the probability of achieving needed complex program combinations and reinforces bureaucratic resistance. It is pointless to increase the program mix between welfare, social service, and related activities all within a super-department, when what is needed is a free-wheeling program mix in complex proportions among the super-activity systems. The former is like building *thicker* walls between *enlarged* separate bedrooms for husband and wife, on the premise that this will increase conception.

The New York and similar proposals are a product of the "new breed" of politician with guaranteed, no-risk palliatives for every problem. The 1960's seem to be the age of the "clean-cut" politicians, generally drawn from business, who comprise an infusion into politics of the organization man and ostensibly represent the means by which the technological and management dilemma can be resolved. (These "clean-cut" politicians are often people who promise efficiency and economy, and little else.) They alternately appear liberal or conservative, since in fact they represent no point of view. They reflect, at any given moment, the prevalent currents of public opinion, and their actions result from inherent personal talents to respond and manage, rather than from deep convictions. They promise appointment of technicians, rather than policymakers or politicians, to high places of departmental responsibility. As individuals, they rely on a capacity to project their personalities and are characterized by middle-class values and higher-class tastes.

Although this group of politicians generally identifies with one or another of the major political parties (usually Republican, since this is likely to be the pattern of their personal associations), they advance their campaigns and themselves as above political party, and attempt to duplicate existing political organizational structures as an extension of self, in which links are sought directly with the public. Politically, they are amoral. They guide their behavior by public-relations dictates, in which the question of image is paramount. Issues are viewed principally in terms of the public's barometric reactions, and positions are assumed after "the flag is unfurled to see who salutes." They rely on the manipulations of the communications media to make them what they are not, or to make them appear what they believe the public would like them to be. They are interested and generally excel in making tactical decisions, since this reflects their training and experience, and show little awareness of or concern with strategy or long-term effects of their decisions. The increasing number of successes in the elections of the 1960's of this "new breed" of politicians represents the apparent culmination of a take-over of politics by a wedding between management and technology. The application of "clean-cut," businesslike solutions to the problems of our cities and government is essentially a surrender, couched in the language of the organization man, to professional and bureaucratic interests and domination.

RETHINKING URBAN GOVERNMENTAL PROGRAMS

Local programs consequently need substantial refashioning, so that each is measured, not by the degree to which it achieves stability or reinforces the status quo, but by the degree to which it reinforces aspiration and extends the range of choice and opportunity. This framework suggests an entire rethinking of governmental programs; it may mean additional movement of population out of the city to the suburbs, further losses of central city tax resources, and increased demands on the government to undertake projects which have less demonstrable and immediate financial feasibility than some other programs might have. However, the scale of federal, state, and local expenditures required to meet urban problems must inevitably increase, even under current circumstances—and most importantly, challenging programs that are predicated on human investments may create far more satisfactory payoffs than existing, institutionally devised activities which very often reinforce disparities. There is a whole spectrum of untapped opportunity to refashion and redirect existing programs and activities.

In the long run, the problems of the city relate to its jurisdiction, purposes, policies, and structure.

POLITICAL JURISDICTION

The fact that the central city contains the oldest housing and most outmoded facilities is primarily a fact of the chronology of development, and in consequence provides the most accessible and readily available shelter for the disadvantaged. However, the fact that such residence exists only within the confines of an historically determined political jurisdiction, which no longer encompasses the total continuous, concentrated, and contiguous population identified with the jurisdiction, can certainly not be justified except as a means of assuring the containment of those people viewed as undesirable.

This act of hostility reaches tragic proportions when the host of problems associated with the city is examined, and it becomes evident that their resolution depends on a scale of attention which coincides with the scale of the universe which was largely responsible for these same problems' creation. The need inevitably to deal with city and suburban problems on a metropolitan basis has been widely recognized, and its enunciation approaches a cliché. Various efforts in this direction are already evident, and further efforts can be expected.

The protagonists of metropolitan government have tended to depreciate the protests of suburban communities and others who have resisted these trends and have obscured the validity of much of the opposition. While the need for creating metropolitan instruments on a scale capable of dealing with a wide-ranging set of problems is clear, the simultaneous need exists to find the means whereby individuals can influence large and complex issues and those activities and life styles wholly within more modest geographic universes. Consequently, any discussion of metropolitan governmental structures should concurrently address this latter issue, by seeking to reconcile these purposes and exploring, at the same time, the dual questions involved. Such an examination should not be limited to the role of suburban communities juxtaposed to the central city; for, if the concept has merit, it should also be extended to the central city. Means should be found to subdivide the central city into units that permit the population within each new unit to influence both the character of their environment and the larger metropolitan decisions, in much the same manner as is sought by the suburbs.

This would suggest that there is an inherent value in having jurisdictional units of a small enough size that individuals can feel they have a direct voice in governing their local affairs, without sacrificing the larger scales required for the solving of many social, economic, and environmental problems. The values associated with small governmental jurisdictions (both corporate and special purpose, including education, parks, and recreation) should not be obscured. They can be preserved by the continued retention of the smaller units of government, which could vary prevalent practices and the form and character of their provision without dilution or diminution of the more uniformly applied urban system requirements and standards. The smaller units could, thereby, expand and extend the provision of facilities by a willingness to expend additional locally derived funds for these purposes. More importantly, these small jurisdictions could come to be administrative and special units within a larger "urban system" jurisdiction.

The central city could similarly be redivided into more manageable administrative sub-units, to stimulate responsiveness between the citizen and the administrative activities of government and to encourage diversity and broaden choice by expanding opportunities to do things differently. This approach would replace current practices which restrict choice in its own right and limit the numbers who are allowed to avail themselves of the restricted choices.

Small-unit jurisdiction is essentially managerial in scale. The principal functions successfully performed at the local level pivot on housekeeping and public works activities. The record of the city manager movement in this country, in cities generally of 250,000 population or less, and the public acceptance of its performance, demonstrate the opportunity which is thus provided to delimit areas of small jurisdictions and retain levels of government which maintain more intimate public and citizen relationships.

In a sense, new metropolitan forms provide the means for refashioning central city government and simultaneously creating, preserving, or strengthening local participation in government in the suburbs and the city. The result is a redefined "city metropolis" jurisdiction, whose powers are confined to those activities requiring large-scale attention and in which small-unit jurisdictions are retained to achieve variations in desired life styles.

THE "URBAN SYSTEM" AND POPULATION REDISTRIBUTION: POLICY IMPLICATIONS

The achievement of formal metropolitan arrangements which would constitute a new "city metropolis" jurisdiction may be a long and cumbersome process. However, counties, villages, towns, and communities within our cities can begin to give affirmative expression to these goals by positive efforts to attract residents of diverse condition and background. Precedents exist. We have been willing to take such affirmative action in a variety of refugee programs which placed the public squarely in the business of resettlement. Efforts to attract diverse groups to existing housing should be augmented by the initiation of private housing construction at a broad range of prices within community areas small enough to make up a single school district. Existing federal housing aids, such as public housing, 221d(3) privately financed low-income housing, and the rent supplement program, can be used to finance much of this construction. Such housing should be geared for and used to accommodate a range of families, including those displaced by public activity in the central city. Federal Housing Administration mortgage insurance, Veterans Administration mortgage insurance, housing loans from banks and savings and loan associations with federal insurance on deposit, and public works advances and loans for sewer, water, and other utilities should be conditional to (1) the provision of housing for diverse population groups or (2) the sufficient existence of such housing in close proximity and at a commensurate scale.

To encourage these developments, federal incentives need to be provided that would give local municipalities and local school districts funds to meet these added responsibilities. We accept this principle with respect to federal aid for schools impacted by federal activity, and are generous in its interpretation. No less is required for those who are impacted by our federal economy and are the victims of the national political system which has institutionalized discrimination. School districts can develop consortium arrangements with adjacent districts and experiment with campus high school complexes, which would transcend and serve more than one school jurisdiction. Junior colleges and community colleges, which are currently in planning and programming stages in many states and smaller geographic jurisdictions, should be located on the same basis as campus high schools. In this way, they would encompass and serve diverse community groups, with a variety of programs not exclusively directed toward the university-bound student.

Special programs are required also for the bulk of the disadvantaged population, who would either be incapable of availing themselves of these opportunities or, in the larger number of cases, would be unwilling to move to alien settings. The probabilities of their success, however, would be greatly enhanced by a consciously created climate of receptivity and commitment. The artificially bounded political jurisdiction of the city has become too tightly defined a universe for the city to be able to serve simultaneously as an incubator of aspiration and a dynamic competitor capable of using measures which may dilute or diminish its role as incubator. The fluidity of movement and the pattern of population settlement in the metropolitan areas, in contrast to earlier periods when the boundaries of the central city generally encompassed most concentrations of population, has now shifted the conditions in which the forces of change and the alternating tides of stability and mobility can be reconciled and accommodated. Ironically, the demand for a political form which more accurately reflects the scale and scope of the urban system may come at the very moment that the prospect of domination of the central city by the disadvantaged shakes the advantaged and is resisted by the disadvantaged for the same reasons.

Inherent in the "urban system" response is the opportunity to establish consistent policies without restricting individual choice, and, therefore, to make a total commitment of resources. The overcrowded and overbuilt slum areas, and the absolute increases in population, necessitate urbanization and population redistribution on an area-wide basis and a redefined density policy. The resistance of stable communities to minority in-migration hinders a policy which seeks to accommodate mobility as a means of satisfying individual and family aspirations for self-improvement. But this policy could be achieved, without the current penalties to the city, if the political, financial, and housing universe were the larger urban system. This would permit more rational programming, which would reflect the relationship between the changing and hopefully improving financial needs of individuals and families and the ability of recipient communities to meet their requirements. Concurrently, the total urban system response makes possible the affirmative undertaking of activities which are now inhibited by the threat they pose within the more limited and artificial central city jurisdiction. The opportunity would exist in education and housing, for example, to utilize programs as instruments of social policy which would begin to provide demonstrable evidence to the disadvantaged of public intention. In the process, this new programming approach would begin to restore the emotional equilibrium which is being destroyed by the increasing civil turmoil.

Population movement and redistribution and a system which reinforces and facilitates the process of continuous upward mobility are essential to a free society seeking to expand individual and family choice. Essential in the creation of such a system is a removal of the fictional conflicts of city versus suburb and the artificial—legally constituted—accompanying evasions, and a disposal of the claims of community self-determination as possessing an inherent validity which takes precedence over individual and family rights and aspirations. Place and patch are not inalienable: they are conditioned and qualified by the peaceful acceptance of the legally acquired claim of another to his place and patch. The inalienability resides in the right of movement and in the opportunity of choice in such movement. Moreover, not *less* population distribution, but an *acceleration* of population distribution, may be among the indicated solutions.

Bibliography

BIBLIOGRAPHICAL WORKS

Davis, Allen F. "The American Historian vs. the City," *Social Studies,* Parts 1 and 2, 61 (1965), 91–96, 127–35.

Dawson, Philip and Sam B. Warner, Jr. "Selection of Works Relating to the History of Cities," *The Historian and the City,* ed. Oscar Handlin and John Burchard. Cambridge, 1963, 270–90.

Glaab, Charles N. "The Historian and the American City: A Bibliographic Survey," *The Study of Urbanization,* ed. Philip M. Hauser and Leo F. Schnore. New York, 1965, 53–80.

McKelvey, Blake. "American Urban History Today," *American Historical Review* 57 (1952), 919–29.

DOCUMENT COLLECTIONS

Glaab, Charles N., ed. *The American City: A Documentary History.* Homewood, Ill., 1963.

Pierce, Bessie L., ed. *As Others See Chicago.* Chicago, 1933.

Smith, Wilson, ed. *Cities of Our Past and Present: A Descriptive Reader.* New York, 1964.

Speizman, Milton D., ed. *Urban America in the Twentieth Century.* New York, 1965.

Still, Bayrd, ed. *Mirror for Gotham.* New York, 1956.

Weiner, David, ed. *City and Country in America.* New York, 1962.

GENERAL WORKS

Glaab, Charles N. and A. Theodore Brown. *A History of Urban America.* New York, 1967.

Green, Constance McLaughlin. *The Rise of Urban America.* New York, 1965.

———. *American Cities in the Growth of the Nation.* New York, 1957.

Mumford, Lewis. *The City in History.* New York, 1961.

Weber, Adna F. *The Growth of Cities in the Nineteenth Century.* New York, 1899; Ithaca, 1963.

URBAN BIOGRAPHIES

Brown, A. Theodore. *The History of Kansas City.* 1 vol. Columbia, Mo., 1963, in progress.

Capers, Gerald M. *The Biography of a River Town: Memphis, Its Heroic Age.* Chapel Hill, 1939.

Green, Constance McLaughlin. *History of Naugatuck, Connecticut.* New Haven, 1948.

———. *Holyoke, Massachusetts.* New Haven, 1939.

———. *Washington.* 2 vols. Princeton, 1962 and 1963.

Lorant, Stephan. *Pittsburgh, The Story of an American City.* New York, 1965.

McKelvey, Blake. *Rochester*. 4 vols. Cambridge and Rochester, 1945–1961.

Osterweis, Rollin G. *Three Centuries of New Haven, 1638–1939*. New Haven, 1953.

Pierce, Bessie L. *A History of Chicago*. 3 vols. New York, 1937–1959, in progress.

Shlakman, Vera. *Economic History of a Factory Town: A Study of Chicoppee, Massachusetts*. Northampton, 1935.

Sibley, Marilyn M. *The Port of Houston: A History*. Austin, 1968.

Still, Bayrd. *Milwuakee*. Madison, 1948 and rev. ed. 1965.

Wertenbaker, Thomas J. *Norfolk*. 2d rev. ed. Marvin W. Schlegel. Durham, 1962.

PERIOD AND REGIONAL STUDIES

Coleman, Kenneth. *Confederate Athens*. Athens, Georgia, 1967.

Hirschfield, Charles. *Baltimore, 1870–1900*. Baltimore, 1941.

Lubove, Roy. *Twentieth Century Pittsburgh: Government, Business, and Environmental Change*. New York, 1969.

McKelvey, Blake. *The Urbanization of America, 1860–1915*. New Brunswick, N.J., 1963.

———. *The Emergence of Metropolitan America, 1915–1966*. New Brunswick, N.J., 1966.

Miller, William D. *Memphis During the Progressive Era, 1900–1917*. Memphis, 1957.

Pomerantz, Sidney I. *New York: An American City, 1783–1803*. New York, 1938.

Pomeroy, Earl. *The Pacific Slope*. New York, 1965.

Schlesinger, Arthur Meier. *The Rise of the City, 1878–1898*. New York, 1933.

Still, Bayrd. "Patterns of Mid-Nineteenth Century Urbanization in the Middlewest," *Mississippi Valley Historical Review* 28 (1941), 187–206.

Syrett, Harold C. *The City of Brooklyn, 1865–1898*. New York, 1944.

Vance, Rupert B. and Nicholas J. Demeratu, eds. *The Urban South*. Chapel Hill, 1954.

Weld, Ralph. *Brooklyn Village, 1816–1834*. New York, 1938.

Woodward, C. Vann. *The Origins of the New South*. New Orleans, 1951.

Young, James Sterling. *The Washington Community, 1800–1829*. New York, 1966.

TOPICAL AND SPECIAL STUDIES

Bridenbaugh, Carl. *Cities in Revolt*. New York, 1955.

Conkin, Paul F. *Tomorrow a New World: The New Deal Community Program*. Ithaca, 1959.

Coolidge, John. *Mill and Mansion: A Study of Architecture and Society in Lowell, Massachusetts, 1820–1865*. New York, 1942.

Curti, Merle. *The Making of an American Community: A Case Study of Democracy in a Frontier County*. Palo Alto, 1959.

Degler, Carl. "American Political Parties and the Rise of the City: An Interpretation," *Journal of American History* 51 (1964), 41–59.

Dunlap, George A. *The City in the American Novel, 1789–1900*. Philadelphia, 1934.

Dykstra, Robert R. *The Cattle Towns.* New York, 1968.

Elazar, Daniel J. "Urban Problems and the Federal Government: A Historical Inquiry," *Political Science Quarterly* 82 (1967), 505–25.

Faught, Millard C. *Falmouth, Massachusetts: Problems of a Resort Community.* New York, 1945.

Firey, Walter. *Land Use in Central Boston.* Cambridge, 1947.

Gelfant, Blanche H. *The American City Novel, 1900–1940.* Norman, Okla., 1954.

Haller, William, Jr. *The Puritan Frontier: Town Planning in New England Colonial Development, 1630–1660.* New York, 1951.

Hamming, Edward. *The Port of Milwaukee.* Rock Island, 1953.

Hoyt, Homer. *One Hundred Years of Land Values in Chicago.* Chicago, 1933.

Jackson, Kenneth T. *The Ku Klux Klan in the City, 1914–1930.* New York, 1967.

Lynd, Robert S. and Helen M. *Middletown.* New York, 1929.

————. *Middletown in Transition.* New York, 1937.

Miller, Zane L. *Boss Cox's Cincinnati: Urban Politics in the Progressive Era.* New York, 1968.

Nadeau, Remi A. *The City Makers: The Story of Southern California's First Boom.* Los Angeles, 1965.

Reps, John W. *The Making of Urban America: A History of City Planning in the United States.* Princeton, 1965.

Sellers, Leila. *Charlestown Business on the Eve of the American Revolution.* Chapel Hill, 1934.

Strauss, Anselm. *Images of the American City.* New York, 1961.

Tunnard, Christopher and Henry Hope Read. *American Skyline.* Boston, 1955.

Wade, Richard C. *Slavery in the Cities: The South, 1820–1860.* New York, 1964.

Walker, Robert H. "The Poet and the Rise of the City," *Mississippi Valley Historical Review* 49 (1962), 85–89.

Wertenbaker, Thomas. *The Golden Age of Colonial Culture.* Ithaca, 1942.

White, Morton and Lucia. *The Intellectual Versus the City: From Thomas Jefferson to Frank Lloyd Wright.* Cambridge, 1962.

Whitehill, Walter M. *Boston: A Topographical History.* 2d rev. ed. Cambridge, 1968.

THEORETICAL AND CONCEPTUAL STUDIES

Collected Works:

Handlin, Oscar and John Burchard, eds. *The Historian and the City.* Cambridge, 1963.

Hauser, Philip M. and Leo F. Schnore, eds. *The Study of Urbanization.* New York, 1965.

Hirsch, Werner Z., ed. *Urban Life and Forms.* New York, 1963.

Ware, Caroline F., ed. *The Cultural Approach to History.* New York, 1940.

Single Contributions:

Diamond, William. "On the Dangers of an Urban Interpretation of History," *Historiography and Urbanization: Essays in American History in Honor of W. Stull Holt,* ed. Eric F. Goldman. Baltimore, 1941, 67–108.

Glaab, Charles N. "The Historian and the American Urban Tradition," *Wisconsin Magazine of History* 47 (Autumn 1963), 12–25.

Haworth, Lawrence. *The Good City*. Bloomington, 1963.

Holt, W. Stull. "Some Consequences of the Urban Movement," *Pacific Historical Review* 22 (1953), 337–52.

Isard, Walter. *Location and Space-Economy: A General Theory Relating to Industrial Location, Market Areas, Land Use, Trade, and Urban Structure.* Cambridge, 1956.

Lampard, Eric E. "American Historians and the Study of Urbanization," *American Historical Review* 67 (1961), 49–62.

Lubove, Roy. "The Urbanization Process: An Approach to Historical Research," *Journal of the American Institute of Planners* 33 (1967), 33–39.

Madden, Carl H. "Some Temporal Aspects of the Growth of Cities in the United States," *Economic Development and Cultural Change* 6 (1958), 143–70.

———. "On Some Indications of Stability in the Growth of Cities in the United States," *Economic Development and Cultural Change* 4 (1956), 236–52.

Schlesinger, Arthur M. "The City in American Civilization," *Paths to the Present*. New York, 1949, 210–33.

Schnore, Leo F. "The City as a Social Organism," *Urban Affairs* 1 (1966), 58–69.

Smolensky, Eugene and Donald Ratajczak. "The Conception of Cities," *Explorations in Entrepreneurial History*, 2d ser. 2, (1965), 90–131.

Tisdale, Hope. "The Process of Urbanization," *Social Forces* 20, (1942), 311–16.

Wade, Richard C. "Urbanization," *The Comparative Approach To American History*, ed. C. Van Woodward. New York, 1968, 187–205.

Wirth, Lewis. "Urbanism as a Way of Life," *American Journal of Sociology* 44 (1938), 1–24.

Wohl, R. Richard. "Urbanism, Urbanity, and the Historian," *University of Kansas City Review* 20 (1953), 53–61.

——— and A. Theodore Brown. "The Usable Past: A Study of Historical Traditions in Kansas City," *Huntington Library Quarterly* 23 (1960), 237–59.

THE ESTABLISHMENT AND GROWTH OF URBAN CENTERS

Albion, Robert G. *The Rise of the New York Port, 1815–1860*. New York, 1939.

Belcher, Wyatt W. *The Economic Rivalry Between St. Louis and Chicago*. New York, 1947.

Gates, Paul W. *The Illinois Central Railroad and Its Colonization Work*. Cambridge, 1934.

Gilchrist, David T., ed. *The Growth of Seaport Cities, 1790–1825*. Charlottesville, 1967.

Goodrich, Carter. *Government Promotion of Canals and Railroads, 1800–1890*. New York, 1960.

Livingood, James W. *The Philadelphia-Baltimore Trade Rivalry, 1780–1860*. Harrisburg 1947.

Powell, Sumner Chilton. *Puritan Village: The Formation of a New England Town*. Middletown, 1963.

Rubin, Julius. *Canal or Railroad? Imitation and Innovation in the Response to the Erie Canal in Philadelphia, Baltimore, and Boston.* Philadelphia, 1961.

Scheiber, Harry. "Urban Rivalry and Internal Improvements in the Old Northwest, 1820–1860," *Ohio History* 71 (1962), 227–239.

Smith, Page. *As a City Upon a Hill.* New York, 1966.

Taylor, George R. "American Urban Growth Preceding the Railroad Age," *Journal of Economic History* 27 (1967), 309–39.

Wheeler, Kenneth. *To Wear a City's Crown: The Beginnings of Urban Growth in Texas, 1836–1865.* Cambridge, 1968.

Williamson, Jeffrey G. "Anti-Bellum Urbanization in the American Northeast," *Journal of Economic History* 25 (1965), 592–608.

THE GROWTH AND DEVELOPMENT OF URBAN SERVICES

Blake, John B. *Public Health in the Town of Boston, 1630–1822.* Cambridge, 1959.

Cassedy, James H. *Charles V. Chapin and the Public Health Movement.* Cambridge, 1962.

Conant, Ralph W., ed. *The Public Library and the City.* Cambridge, 1965.

Green, Samuel S. *The Public Library Movement in the United States, 1835–1893.* Boston, 1913.

Kramer, Howard D. "The Beginnings of the Public Health Movement in the United States," *Bulletin of the History of Medicine* 21 (1947), 352–376.

————. "Early Municipal and State Boards of Health," *Bulletin of the History of Medicine* 24 (1950), 503–529.

Lampe, A. B. "St Louis Volunteer Fire Department, 1820–1850," *Missouri Historical Review* 62 (1968), 235–259.

Rosen, George. *A History of Public Health.* New York, 1958.

Rosenberg, Charles E. *The Cholera Years.* Chicago, 1962.

Smerk, George M. "The Streetcar: Shaper of American Cities," *Traffic Quarterly* 21 (1967), 569–84.

Warner, Sam B., Jr. *Streetcar Suburbs: The Process of Growth in Boston, 1870–1900.* Cambridge, 1962.

Wilson, William H. *The City Beautiful Movement in Kansas City.* Columbia, Mo., 1964.

URBANIZATION AND INDUSTRIALIZATION

Alexandersson, Gunnar. *The Industrial Structure of American Cities: A Geographic Study of Urban Economy in the United States.* Lincoln, Neb., 1956.

Gras, N. S. B. *An Introduction to Economic History.* New York, 1922.

Hoselity, Bert F. "The City, the Factory, and Economic Growth," *American Economic Review* 45 (1955), 166–184.

Jaher, Frederick C., ed. *The Age of Industrialism in America.* New York, 1968.

Lampard, Eric E. "The History of Cities in the Economically Advanced Areas," *Economic Development and Cultural Change* 3 (1958), 81–136.

Marshall, Leon S. "The English and American Industrial City of the Nineteenth Century," *Western Pennsylvania Historical Magazine* 20 (1937), 169–80.

McLaughlin, Glen E. *The Growth of American Manufacturing Areas.* Pittsburgh, 1938.

Pred, Allan. *The Spatial Dynamics of U.S. Urban-Industrial Growth, 1800–1914: Interpretive and Theoretical Essays.* Cambridge, 1966.

THE IMPACT OF URBANIZATION

Atkins, Gordon. *Health, Housing and Poverty in New York City, 1865–1898.* Ann Arbor, 1947.

Cole, Donald B. *Immigrant City: Lawrence, Massachusetts, 1845–1921.* Chapel Hill, 1963.

Coll, Blanche D. "The Baltimore Society for the Prevention of Pauperism," *American Historical Review* 61 (1955), 77–87.

Dorsett, Lyle W. *The Pendergast Machine.* New York, 1968.

Drake, S. Clair and Horace R. Cayton. *Black Metropolis: A Study of Negro Life in a Northern City.* 2 vols. New York, 1962.

Farley, Reynolds. "The Urbanization of Negroes in the United States," *Journal of Social History* 1 (1968), 241–258.

Ginger, Ray. *Altgeld's America.* New York, 1958.

Green, Constance McLaughlin. *The Secret City: A History of Race Relations in the Nation's Capital.* Princeton, 1967.

Handlin, Oscar. *Boston's Immigrants, 1790–1865.* Cambridge, 1941.

Mandlebaum, Seymour. *Boss Tweed's New York.* New York, 1965.

Osofsky, Gilbert. "The Enduring Ghetto," *Journal of American History* 55 (1968), 243–55.

————. *Harlem: The Making of a Ghetto, Negro New York, 1890–1930.* New York, 1963.

Riis, Jacob A. *How the Other Half Lives: Studies Among the Tenements of New York.* New York, 1919.

Rischin, Moses. *The Promised City: New York's Jews, 1870–1914.* Cambridge, 1962.

Thernstrom, Stephen. *Poverty and Progress: Social Mobility in a Nineteenth Century City.* Cambridge, 1964.

THE RISING CONCERN FOR URBAN LIFE

Abell, Aaron. *American Catholicism and Social Action: A Search for Social Justice, 1865–1950.* Garden City, N.J., 1960.

————. *The Urban Impact on American Protestantism, 1865–1900.* Cambridge, 1943.

Buder, Stanley. *Pullman, An Experiment in Industrial Order and Community Planning, 1880–1930.* New York, 1967.

Crooks, James B. *Politics and Progress: The Rise of Urban Progressivism in Baltimore, 1895–1911.* Baton Rouge, 1968.

Davis, Allen F. *Spearheads for Reform: The Social Settlements and the Progressive Movement, 1890–1914.* New York, 1967.

Hancock, John. "Planners in the Changing American City, 1900–1940,"*Journal of American Institute for Planning* 33 (1967), 290–304.

Hirsch, Mark D. "Reflections on Urban History and Urban Reform, 1865–1915," *Essays in American Historiography: Papers Presented in Honor of*

Allan Nevins, ed. Donald Sheehan and Harold C. Syrett. New York, 1960, 109–37.

Hofstadter, Richard. *The Age of Reform: From Bryan to F. D. R.* New York, 1955.

Korman, Gerd. *Industrialism, Immigrants, and Americanizers: The View From Milwaukee.* Madison, 1967.

Lubove, Roy. *Community Planning in the 1920's: The Contributions of the Regional Planning Association of America.* Pittsburgh, 1965.

————. *The Progressive and the Slums: Tenement House Reform in New York City, 1890–1917.* Pittsburgh, 1963.

————. "The Twentieth Century City: The Progressive as Municipal Reformer," *Mid-America* 31 (1959), 195–209.

Mann, Arthur. *Yankee Reformers in the Urban Age.* Cambridge, 1954.

McKitrick, Eric L. "The Study of Corruption," *Political Science Quarterly* 72 (1957), 502–514.

Tager, Jack. *The Intellectual As Urban Reformer: Brand Whitlock and the Progressive Movement.* Cleveland, 1968.

Wade, Louise C. *Graham Taylor: Pioneer for Social Justice, 1851–1938.* Chicago, 1964.

METROPOLITANIZATION

Blumenfeld, Hans. *The Modern Metropolis: Its Origins, Growth, Characteristics, and Planning,* ed. Paul D. Spreiregen. Cambridge, 1967.

Bogue, Donald J. *Population Growth in Standard Metropolitan Areas, 1900–1950.* Washington, 1953.

Chapman, Edmund H. *Cleveland: Village to Metropolis.* Cleveland, 1965.

Glaab, Charles N. "Metropolis and Suburb: The Changing American City," *Change and Continuity in Twentieth Century America: The 1920's,* ed. John Braeman, *et al.* Columbus, 1968.

Hawley, Amos H. *The Changing Shape of Metropolitan America: Deconcentration Since 1920.* Glencoe, 1956.

Hoyt, Homer. *The Structure and Growth of Residential Neighborhoods in American Cities.* Washington, 1939.

Martin, Roscoe C. *The Cities and the Federal System.* New York, 1965.

McKenzie, Roderick D. *The Metropolitan Community.* New York, 1933.

Mowry, George E. *The Urban Nation, 1920–1960.* New York, 1965.

Schnore, Leo F. "The Growth of Metropolitan Suburbs," *American Sociological Review* 22 (1957), 165–73.

Thompson, Warren S. *The Growth of Metropolitan Districts in the United States, 1900–1940.* Washington, 1947.

Vernon, Raymond, *et al. New York Metropolitan Region Study.* 9 vols. Cambridge, 1959–1961.

United States Bureau of the Census. *The Growth of Metropolitan Districts in the United States, 1789–1945.* Washington, 1947.

CONTEMPORARY URBAN PROBLEMS

Anderson, Martin. *The Federal Bulldozer: A Critical Analysis of Urban Renewal, 1949–1962.* Cambridge, 1964.

Chinitz, Benjamin, ed. *City and Suburb: The Economics of Metropolitan Growth.* Englewood Cliffs, N.J., 1964.

Connery, Robert H., ed. *Urban Riots: Violence and Social Change.* New York, 1968.

Dahl, Robert A. *Who Governs? Democracy and Power in an American City.* New Haven, 1961.

Dobriner, William M., ed. *The Suburban Community.* New York, 1958.

Gans, Herbert J. *People and Plans: Essays on Urban Problems and Solutions.* New York, 1968.

Glazer, Nathan and Daniel Patrick Moynihan. *Beyond the Melting Pot.* Cambridge, 1959.

Gordon, Mitchell. *Sick Cities: Psychology and Pathology of American Urban Life.* New York, 1965.

Gottmann, Jean and Robert A. Harper, eds. *Metropolis on the Move: Geographers Look at Urban Sprawl.* New York, 1967.

Greer, Scott. *Metropolitics: A Study of Political Culture.* New York, 1963.

———. *Urban Renewal and American Cities: The Dilemma of Democratic Intervention.* Indianapolis, 1965.

Grodzins, Morton. *The Metropolitan Area as a Racial Problem.* Pittsburgh, 1959.

Hunter, David R. *The Slums: Challenge and Response.* New York, 1964.

Jacobs, Jane. *The Death and Life of Great American Cities.* New York, 1961.

Meyer, J. R., J. F. Kain, and M. Wohl. *The Urban Transportation Problem.* Cambridge, 1965.

Meyerson, Martin and Edward C. Banfield. *Politics, Planning, and the Public Interest: The Case of Public Housing in Chicago.* Glencoe, 1955.

Parsons, Talcott and Kenneth B. Clark, eds. *The Negro American.* Boston, 1966.

Rodwin, Lloyd, ed. *The Future Metropolis.* New York, 1961.

Shrag, Peter. *The Village School Downtown.* Boston, 1966.

Taeuber, Karl E. and Alma F. *Negroes in Cities.* Chicago, 1965.

Vernon, Raymond. *The Myth and Reality of Our Urban Problems.* Cambridge, 1962, 1966.

Warner, Sam B., Jr., ed. *Planning for a Nation of Cities.* Cambridge, 1966.

Weaver, Robert. *The Urban Complex: Human Values in Urban Life.* New York, 1964.

THE STUDY OF THE CITY IN THE SOCIAL SCIENCES

Altshuler, Alan A. *The City Planning Process: A Political Analysis.* Ithaca, 1965.

Banfield, Edward C. and James Q. Wilson. *City Politics.* Cambridge, 1963.

Bogue, Donald J. *The Structure of the Metropolitan Community.* Ann Arbor, 1950.

Burgess, Ernest W. and Donald J. Bogue, eds. *Contributions to Urban Sociology.* Chicago, 1964.

Daland, R. T. "Political Science and the Study of Urbanism: A Bibliographical Essay," *American Political Science Review* 51 (1957), 491–509.

Doxiadis, Constantine A. *Ekistics: An Introduction to the Science of Human Settlements.* London, 1968.

Hadden, Jeffrey K. and Edgar F. Borgatta. *American Cities: Their Social Characteristics*. Chicago, 1965.

Hauser, Philip M., ed. *Handbook for Social Research in Urban Areas*. Paris, 1964.

———— and Leo F. Schnore, eds. *The Study of Urbanization*. New York, 1965.

Hawley, Amos H. *Human Ecology: A Theory of Community Structure*. New York, 1950.

Isard, Walter. *Methods of Regional Analysis: An Introduction to Regional Science*. Cambridge, 1960.

Lynch, Kevin. *The Image of the City*. Cambridge, 1960.

Mayer, Harold M. and Clyde F. Kohn, eds. *Readings in Urban Geography*. Chicago, 1959.

Meier, Richard L. *A Communications Theory of Urban Growth*. Cambridge, 1962.

Reissman, Leonard. *The Urban Process: Cities in Industrial Societies*. Glencoe, 1964.

Schnore, Leo F. *The Urban Scene: Human Ecology and Demography*. Glencoe, 1959.

———— and Henry Fagin, eds. *Urban Research and Policy Planning*. Beverly Hills, 1967.

Stein, Maurice R. *The Eclipse of Community*. Princeton, 1960.

Thompson, Wilber R. *A Preface to Urban Economics*. Baltimore, 1965.

The Authors

CHARLES ABRAMS, who died in early 1970, was an urban sociologist whose special interest was city planning and housing. He was on the faculties of the City College of New York, Massachusetts Institute of Technology, the New School of Social Research, Columbia University, and Harvard University.

NELSON M. BLAKE is Professor of History at Syracuse University. Professor Blake's interests include American cultural and social history.

ASA BRIGGS is Professor of History and Vice-Chancellor at the University of Sussex. He has taught at the University of Oxford and the University of Leeds, and has been a member of the Institute for Advanced Studies (Princeton).

ROBERT H. BREMNER is Professor of History at Ohio State University.

CARL BRIDENBAUGH is University Professor and Professor of History at Brown University. He has served as the president of the American Historical Association, and his interest in early American history is primarily in the social and intellectual dimensions.

ELMER E. CORNWELL, JR. is Professor of Political Science and Chairman of his department at Brown University.

ROBERT ERNST is Professor of History at Adelphi University. Dr. Ernst is primarily interested in the early national period of the United States and the history of immigration and ethnic groups.

ROBERT M. FOGELSON is Associate Professor of History and City Planning at the Massachusetts Institute of Technology. He is also a member of the Harvard-M. I. T. Joint Center for Urban Studies.

CHARLES N. GLAAB is Professor of History at the University of Toledo and co-editor of the Urban History Group *Newsletter*.

CONSTANCE MCLAUGHLIN GREEN is an American historian who has served as chief historian for the Ordinance Department (U.S. Army), historian for the military research and development project office of the Secretary of Defense, and the head of the Washington D.C. history project.

SCOTT GREER is Professor of Sociology and Political Science and a member of the Center for Metropolitan Studies at Northwestern University. In addition to his interest in urbanization he has concentrated on social organization and stratification.

JEAN GOTTMAN is Professor of Geography at the University of Oxford. He has specialized in economic and political geography.

OSCAR HANDLIN is Charles Warren Professor of American History and Director of the Charles Warren Center at Harvard University. His primary interest is in American social and economic history.

LAWRENCE HAWORTH is Professor of Philosophy and Chairman of the Department of Philosophy at the University of Waterloo, Canada, and is engaged in research at the University's Planning and Resources Institute.

SAMUEL P. HAYS is Professor of History and Chairman of his department at the University of Pittsburgh. He has concentrated on the social analysis of American politics.

DWIGHT W. HOOVER is Professor of History at Ball State University. His primary interest is American intellectual history and recent historiography.

J. JOSEPH HUTHMACHER is Professor of History and the Director of the Graduate Program at Rutgers University. His major interest is in ethnic groups in American history and twentieth century social and political history.

EDWARD C. KIRKLAND is Emeritus Professor of History at Bowdoin College. His primary interest is in American economic history and New England history.

ROGER LANE is Associate Professor of History at Haverford College. He has concentrated on the study of nineteenth-century police forces.

ROY LUBOVE is Professor of History at the University of Pittsburgh. His primary interest is American social history and the history of social legislation.

BLAKE MCKELVEY is the City Historian for Rochester, New York and has been writing a comprehensive study of that city.

HENRY F. MAY is Margaret Byrne Professor of History at the University of California (Berkeley). His major interest is American intellectual history.

JACK MELTZER, a city planner, is Director of the Center for Urban Studies at the University of Chicago.

WILFRED OWEN is an economist and a member of the senior staff of the Brookings Institute.

BESSIE L. PIERCE is Emeritus Professor of History at the University of Chicago. She is noted for her work on the history of Chicago.

JULIUS RUBIN is Associate Professor of History and Economics at the University of Pittsburgh. He has specialized in economic history and development.

LEO F. SCHNORE is Professor of Sociology and Adjunct Professor of Urban and Regional Planning at the University of Wisconsin.

ALLAN H. SPEAR is Associate Professor of History at the University of Minnesota. His major interest is in black history and race-relations history.

BAYRD STILL is Professor of History and Head of the Department at New York University. In addition to his interest in urban history he has concentrated on immigration and the frontier.

GEORGE ROGERS TAYLOR is an economic historian who is currently Senior Resident Scholar, Eleutherian Mills-Hanley Foundation. He has been engaged in work on economic and transportation history.

RALPH E. TURNER, who died in 1964, was an intellectual and cultural historian and Durfee Professor of History at Yale University. Professor Turner was a founder of the United Nations Educational, Scientific, and Cultural Organization.

RICHARD C. WADE is Professor of History and member of the Center for Urban Studies at the University of Chicago.

ALLEN M. WAKSTEIN (A.B., University of Massachusetts, Ph. D., University of Illinois), the editor of this volume, is an Associate Professor of History at Boston College and an Associate of the Boston College Institute of Human Sciences.

SAM BASS WARNER, JR. is Professor of History at the University of Michigan. His interests are urban history and American social history.

ROBERT C. WOOD is Professor of Political Science at the Massachusetts Institute of Technology and Director of the Harvard-M.I.T. Joint Center for Urban Studies. He has served as chairman of the President's Task Force on Metropolitan and Urban Problems and as Under Secretary, Department of Housing and Urban Development.

CDEFGHIJ—VB—67543